Conflict, Political Accountability and Aid

Paul Collier's contributions to development economics, and in regard to Africa in particular, have marked him out as one of the most influential commentators of recent times. His research has centred upon the causes and consequences of civil war, the effects of aid, and the problems of democracy in low-income and natural-resource-rich societies. His work has also enjoyed substantial policy impact, having seen him sit as a senior adviser to Tony Blair's Commission on Africa and having addressed the General Assembly of the United Nations.

This collection of Collier's major writings, with assistance from Anke Hoeffler and Jan Gunning, and accompanied by a new introduction, provides the definitive account of a wide range of macroeconomic, micro-economic and political economy topics concerned with Africa. Within macroeconomics, there is a focus on external shocks, exchange rate and trade policies, while microeconomic topics focus on labour and financial markets, as well as rural development. Collier's book *The Bottom Billion* (Oxford University Press, 2007) has become a landmark book and this summation of the research underpinning it will be a superb guide for all those concerned with African development.

Paul Collier is Professor of Economics at Oxford University. He is the author of *The Bottom Billion* and winner of the Arthur Ross Book Award, the Lionel Gelber Prize, the Estoril Prize and the Corinne Prize.

Conflict, Political Accountability and Aid

Paul Collier

Routledge
Taylor & Francis Group

LONDON AND NEW YORK

First published 2011
by Routledge
2 Park Square, Milton Park, Abingdon, Oxon, OX14 4RN

Simultaneously published in the USA and Canada
by Routledge
270 Madison Avenue, New York, NY 10016

*Routledge is an imprint of the Taylor & Francis Group,
an informa business*

Typeset in Times New Roman by
RefineCatch Limited, Bungay, Suffolk

Printed and bound in Great Britain by CPI Antony Rowe,
Chippenham, Wiltshire

British Library Cataloguing in Publication Data
A catalogue record for this book is available from the British Library

Library of Congress Cataloging in Publication Data
Collier, Paul.
  Conflict, political accountability, and aid / Paul Collier.
    p. cm.
  Includes bibliographical references.
  1. Development economics. 2. Economic assistance—Developing
  countries. 3. Civil War—Economic aspects—Developing countries.
  4. Democracy—Developing countries. I. Title.
  HD75.C647 2010
  338.9109172′4—dc22
  2010012690

ISBN 13: 978-0-415-58727-3 (hbk)
ISBN 13: 978-0-415-58731-0 (pbk)

Contents

Figures

Tables

Introduction

This volume brings together a selection of my research papers published over the course of a decade. Over such a long period my thinking has, of course, evolved and sometimes changed quite radically. For example, *Aid Allocation and Poverty Reduction* reflected my views on aid around the Millennium. Five years later, when I wrote *The Bottom Billion*, I had already revised my ideas; *The Complementarities of Poverty Reduction, Equity, and Growth* better represents my current thinking.

My subjects have generally reflected the prevailing problems of those societies that were not yet developing successfully. Over time those problems have changed. Whereas in the 1980s the key issues had been macroeconomic, by the late 1990s the economic damage wrought by violent internal political conflict was too evident to ignore. I wondered whether the methods commonly deployed in economics might be useful in understanding the phenomenon, supplementing conventional political science analysis. Once started, an agenda of research opened up that took the next decade to complete. The nine papers on violent conflict included in this volume span this agenda.

The study of violent conflict introduced me to the larger terrain of political economy. The wave of democratization in low-income countries that followed the fall of the Soviet Union initially looked likely to have momentous economic consequences. With government newly accountable to citizens, the patronage elites that had ruled and ruined these societies looked set to be swept aside. The full beneficial effects of democracy may take decades to be realized and so even now any analysis can only be provisional. But as I researched the effects of elections on the level of political violence, on the management of natural resource bonanzas, and on economic policies, I came to regard my initial unqualified enthusiasm for them as naïve. The three papers on political economy included in this collection each set out evidence for concern.

Discourse on how international actors can best help the poorest countries is dominated by aid. As a student I was first taught development economics by Keith Griffin, a distinguished American who pioneered the critique of aid from the perspective of the political left. Currently, the critique of aid is being led from the political right by my distinguished Zambian former student,

Dambisa Moyo. As I noted, my views on aid have changed markedly over the decade. However, my rethinking cannot be plotted as a trajectory from support for aid to opposition, let alone across the political spectrum. Aid is complicated: unfortunately, the countries that need it most are usually those that are least able to use it. The answer is neither to flood them with aid nor to cut them off. Rather, the modalities by which aid is managed and administered need to vary according to the capacity of governments to use it well on behalf of their citizens. This would enable the volume of aid to be determined by need rather than by the capacity of governments to use it well. Beyond this rethinking of aid allocation, I have come to regard aid as something of a sideshow which attracts exaggerated media attention relative to other policies that the governments of developed countries have at their disposal and which could be more potent. Among the most potent, yet neglected, policies have been those concerned with international trade. Hence, the final group of articles covers a selection of my papers on aid and trade.

Violent conflict

Civil war afflicts many of the poorest countries. It is a human tragedy, but as a development economist my own concern has been that it impedes economic development. The papers on conflict in this volume span more than a decade and form the research base for my book *Wars, Guns and Votes*. They are presented here not according to when they were published, but in the sequence in which they are best understood. The first step in the sequence investigates what causes the onset of a civil war. Once a war has begun, logically the next step in the sequence is surely to pose the question how long it might last. I think that it is important to keep this question distinct from that of the initial cause: the factors that keep a civil war going need not be the same as those that expose the society to the initial risk. However, much of the statistical work on civil war conflates these two issues by posing the question as one of 'incidence': countries at war are compared and contrasted with those not at war. The third step in the sequence is to look at post-conflict situations: recovery and relapse. The fourth step is to assess the costs of civil war, including the lost income during the post-conflict phase until the society returns to its pre-conflict development path. Potentially, there is a fifth step in which the costs of civil war are compared with the costs of policy interventions designed to reduce the risk of war. The costs of civil wars that are averted then become the benefits of these interventions, permitting a cost-benefit analysis of policy options. This final step is, in effect, the Holy Grail of the quantitative study of conflict since it would set policies concerning conflict on the same intellectual basis as more conventional areas of public policy. In my work for the 'Copenhagen Consensus' I have attempted a few such estimates, though they should be understood as little more than illustrative of an approach and I do not include them here. Over the past decade the quantitative analysis of conflict has advanced remarkably attracting some brilliant researchers, and perhaps in another decade researchers will have moved the subject forward to this key stage.

'Greed and Grievance in Civil War' explores the statistical associations between the onset of conflict and prior socio-economic characteristics using global data for the period 1965–2000 averaged into five-year periods. There are limits to what such a global macro analysis can investigate. It does not address the short term events that might have led to the war: civil wars sometimes build up very gradually, but often they appear to be triggered by some key incident. To investigate such trigger events would require a different methodology. However, while proximate incidents such as the murder of a political leader might trigger conflict in some societies, in others with different preconditions the same incidents might not escalate into organized violence. Our study attempted to investigate these preconditions. A key finding of the paper was that three prior economic characteristics – low per capita income, slow growth, and dependence upon primary commodities – all appeared to be risk factors, whereas more obviously 'grievance'-related characteristics, such as inequality and the lack of democratic rights, did not. Two eminent political scientists, James Fearon and David Laitin, found similar results used broadly the same approach at around the same time, and I recommend their study for comparison.

'Beyond Greed and Grievance' revisits the same question. It puts forward the 'feasibility hypothesis': namely that in the relatively rare conditions in which rebellion is materially feasible, it will occur, though the ostensible rebel agenda is indeterminate. This more recent paper benefits from a large increase in the data available. It also makes more serious efforts to establish causality as opposed to correlation between past characteristics and subsequent conflict. While inferences can sometimes reasonably be made from correlations, it is obviously better to have stronger evidence for a causal connection. Where we attempted this in the new paper our core results were unaffected. The main change was that the effect of ethnic diversity appeared to be more straightforwardly adverse than we had previously found. The three central propositions of 'Greed and Grievance' have each subsequently been supported by the results of research by other scholars. That slow economic growth increases the risk of conflict was the key result of an ingenious study by Miguel *et al.* (2004). Similarly, Besley and Persson (2009) have found strong evidence that both revenues from the extraction of natural resources, and low per capita income are risk factors. Our more recent paper also generated some new results, such as the particularly good record of Francophone Africa. We interpreted the substantially lower risk of civil war in this sub-region as reflecting the distinctive security guarantees of the French government during the period, a strategy which was gradually phased out during the 1990s.

My own judgement is that there are likely to be diminishing returns to further macroeconomic analysis of the causes of conflict. More is likely to be learnt from spatial analysis within countries – why is violence located in particular places? – and detailed studies of rebel organizations – how are they funded, how do they get their arms, and how do they recruit?

The second step in the analysis is the study of the duration of conflict. Civil wars last more than ten times longer than international wars, and so understanding why this is the case is clearly important. However, statistically the question is much more demanding than understanding the onset of conflict. Whereas the study of onset depends upon finding systematic differences between peaceful and violent societies, the study of duration depends upon finding differences between societies where wars are short and those where they are long. Necessarily, this involves a drastic reduction in the size of the sample. We investigated whether there was a ripe time for peace efforts: does the chance of peace get higher or lower as the war continues? As far as we could see, the chance of peace in any particular year did not vary systematically with the duration. The low and fairly constant chance of peace is consistent with an explanation of the longevity of civil war based on the distinctive lack of commitment technologies which might enable the government to lock in to the terms of a settlement. Despite the apparent potential for a mutually beneficial return to peace, rebels cannot trust proffered terms. It is also consistent with an account of rebellion that discounts post-conflict goals relative to the benefits inherent in continued warfare.

The third step in the analysis is the study of the post-conflict period. Two issues seemed to be particularly pertinent: the risk of relapse into violence, and the recovery of the economy. Overall, around half of all civil wars are post-conflict relapses, so making post-conflict situations more secure would contribute substantially to global peace. 'Post-conflict Risks' [2009] applied the same statistical technique – hazard functions – to the question of post-conflict relapse into violence as 'On the Duration of Civil War' had used for the question of the chance of restoring peace. As with the chance of peace, one important issue is whether the risk varies systematically with time – technically this is shown by the shape of the hazard function. For post-conflict situations it is particularly pertinent: if there is a period of maximum danger then security interventions and other peace-promoting policies can be targeted on this period. We found that while there is a weak tendency for risks to fall with time, the restoration of security is very gradual. Essentially, the entire post-conflict decade is dangerous. We then investigated an array of political, economic and security policies to see whether they looked to be effective in reducing risks of relapse. Given the small sample size and the nature of the question, answers cannot aspire to being conclusive. A significant statistical correlation could potentially arise through a variety of complex and indirect routes. Nevertheless, given the paucity of knowledge about these issues, correlations can help to guide our understanding when combined with contextual knowledge. For example, one of the issues which we investigated was the effect of post-conflict elections. Such elections have been a central part of international strategies for securing the peace: the theory is that an election is instrumental in bringing about an accountable and legitimate government and thereby reduces the grounds for violent opposition. We found that post-conflict elections did not seem to have this effect: whereas in the year before the election the risk of relapse into violence indeed fell significantly, in the year following the election the risk rose by more than it had fallen. While it may conceivably be that this statistical pattern is not causal – for example, the timing of elections might be chosen so as to take advantage of a temporary lull in violence – our result was no surprise to practitioners and has a plausible explanation. In the period before an election groups that contest power have some incentive to put their efforts into winning votes rather than into violence, but once the result is declared there is a winner and a loser. An election outcome can undermine the willingness to share power and thereby increase the risks of violence. Another of our results was that peacekeeping appeared to be effective in reducing the risk of relapse into violence. Again this statistical association could conceivably come about through an indirect route: more peacekeepers might be sent to contexts that were inherently safer than those which are dangerous. Hopefully, as more data becomes available such remaining areas of uncertainty can gradually be resolved. However, a panel of Nobel Laureate economists who assessed the work as part of the 'Copenhagen Consensus' project concluded that the evidence for the effectiveness of peacekeeping was reasonable. Finally, as with the more general onset of conflict, we found some evidence that in post-conflict situations the economy mattered. A higher level of income and a faster rate of economic growth were both associated with a lower risk of relapse into conflict. There are obvious dangers that this particular result might not be causal: for example, good prospects for continued peace presumably help economic growth. However, the result is consistent with more robust evidence on the importance of growth for peace, and it is also inherently plausible.

The short paper on military spending post-conflict sets out a simple game-theoretic idea and tests it on post-conflict data. The idea is that whereas international peacekeeping might be stabilizing, military spending by the post-conflict government might be counterproductive. Inadvertently, high military spending might signal to the political opposition that the government means to use force to insist on its own priorities rather than share power. As peace continues the military position of the political opposition graduation deteriorates: it is unable to maintain its own military forces except in times of conflict. Hence, the more fearful is the opposition that the government intends to renege on any power-sharing deal, the stronger is its incentive to revert pre-emptively to violence before its military forces decay. If such effects of post-conflict military spending are important, then the government could reassure opponents by deep cuts in military spending, thereby signalling its intention not to renege on sharing the benefits of peace. An example of such deep cuts in the early stages of post-conflict is Mozambique, where the peace proved to be much more secure than in Angola where high military spending was maintained. We found that the statistical evidence is consistent with this theory: military spending in post-conflict situations has distinctively adverse effects.

If the economy matters then how best can economic recovery be promoted? 'Aid, Policy and Growth in Post-Conflict Societies' was an early attempt to investigate the economic recovery. In view of the small sample size that was then available, our results were preliminary and the topic needs to be revisited. We found that typically post-conflict economies catch up the ground lost during conflict. However, the rate of catch up varies enormously around the average of around one percentage point of growth per year over-and-above normal growth. The wide variation suggests that policy choices may be particularly important during the post-conflict period. If so, post-conflict priorities may need to be rethought. Typically, economic policy reform is crowded out by political disputes over constitutional design. Aid was invented for post-conflict recovery: the name for the World Bank was originally going to be the International Bank for Reconstruction. Hence, the size and timing of aid is potentially an important aspect of the recovery that international actors control. Our tentative conclusion was that aid was particularly conducive to growth in post-conflict situations but that it was more effective in the middle of the decade than in the early years. The timing of aid is an important issue because most donors have confined post-conflict aid to the first few years after the end of a conflict. Possibly, aid needs to be extended for a longer period. 'Post-Conflict Monetary Reconstruction' was a more narrowly focused investigation of inflation during and after conflict. Inflation is a form of hidden taxation and, unsurprisingly, during conflict governments resort to it. However, an increase in inflation during conflict tends to be persistent: once caught out by inflation that is higher than they expected, people revise upwards their expectations for subsequent inflation and reduce the real value of their money holdings. Hence, one costly legacy of conflict is reduced confidence in money as a store of value. We show that post-conflict aid helps to restore confidence in the currency by reducing the need to resort to deficit financing.

The final step in my work on conflict has been to investigate the costs of conflict. 'On Economic Causes of Civil War' estimated the reduction in growth during civil war at a little over two percentage points per year. Since the typical conflict lasts for around seven years, by the end of the conflict *per capita* income is around 15 per cent lower that it would have been in the absence of the war. Since the recovery rate during the post-conflict period is around one per cent, it takes around fifteen years to get back to the long term growth path. The cost of the civil war, simply in terms of lost output, is then the sum of the output lost over the 22 years between the onset of the war and the return to the growth path. The undiscounted present value of these losses is equal to around one-and-two-thirds years of the nation's income. This is, of course, an underestimate of the cost of a civil war: people die, others are made refugees, and there is an increase in disease which is highly persistent. So, the true costs of civil war are enormous.

One final adverse legacy of civil war is an increase in military spending. 'Unintended Consequences' investigated what drives such spending. It found evidence for both security-motivated spending, such as threats from neighbours, and interest-group motivated spending: military dictatorships spent more on the military than civilian regimes. We were particularly interested in the effect of spending by neighbours. This turned military spending into a form of regional public bad: the same spending that enhanced security for one nation reduced the perceived security of its neighbours and triggered a neighbourhood arms race. This work was subsequently used in support of a regional reduction in military spending by Nobel Peace Laureate President Arias of Costa Rica. His country is almost unique in having abolished its army.

The political economy of democracy

Until the fall of the Soviet Union most low-income countries were autocracies. The example of the democratization of Eastern Europe had a far-reaching influence and by the mid-1990s most low-income countries were holding contested elections and were at least nominally democracies. During the era of autocracy the lack of democracy was blamed for many of the problems experienced in low-income countries, and so I have become increasingly interested in whether democracy has delivered socio-economic progress.

In 'Democracy, Development and Conflict' we posed what I had expected to be a well-researched question: does democracy promote peace? We were surprised to find a virtual absence of published papers on the topic. Given the many potential routes by which democracy can be correlated with both conflict and economic development, econometric purists will be dismissive of any particular interpretation of statistical associations. However, the combination of strong statistical associations with plausible analytic interpretation is as near to robust knowledge as we are likely to get on this important question: in my view it is foolish to deny ourselves the evidence from statistical associations just because on their own they cannot be decisive. Our key finding was that whether democracies were at less or more risk of violence than autocracies depended upon the level of *per capita* income. Above a threshold of $2,700 democracies were safer than autocracies. They became increasingly safe as income rose whereas autocracies actually became more prone to violence as income rose. Below $2,700 relative safety was reversed, with autocracies less prone to violence than democracies, the difference being larger the lower was income. These results are, of course, disturbing for low-income democracies: the threshold of $2,700 is far above the income levels of poor countries. What they suggest is that for the low income countries, democracy should not be relied upon as the key strategy for social peace. Democracy may, of course, be highly desirable for other reasons. But defence against organized violence is likely to require other strategies. To strengthen the evidence we investigated not just civil war but as many other forms of political violence as we could find. Our results were consistent across nearly all of them.

Much of my recent work has been concerned with the management of natural resources, leading to my book *The Plundered Planet* (Oxford

University Press/Penguin, 2010). Natural resources constitute a large part of the little wealth that the poorest countries possess: they are potentially the lifeline to prosperity. Yet to date they have usually not been harnessed for development. In 'Testing the Neocon Agenda' we investigated whether democracy was the political transformation which would enable resource-rich countries to use their natural resources more effectively. The title is, of course, partly tongue-in-cheek, but the underlying idea is that the neoconservative rationale for the invasion of Iraq was that the resource-rich Middle East needed to democratize in order to unleash its development potential. Stated as such, the hypothesis is not unreasonable and it is straightforward to build a political-economy model which is consistent with it. However, as we showed in the paper, it is also possible to construct political-economy models in which resource rents distort political competition by reducing the need to tax citizens. The lighter is taxation the weaker are the demands for representation and accountability. Potentially, instead of democracy disciplining the use of resource rents, the resource rents undermine the normal functioning of democracy. When we turned to the empirical results the evidence supported this latter interpretation. In the absence of resource rents democracies out-performed autocracies measured in terms of economic growth, whereas with large resource rents autocracies outperformed democracies. We then distinguished between two distinct aspects of democracy, electoral competition and checks and balances. We found that all the damage of resource rents came through electoral competition, whereas with sufficiently strong checks and balances democracies could still outperform autocracies. An implication was that resource-rich countries needed a distinctive form of democracy with particular emphasis upon checks and balances. Finally, we investigated whether resource-rich countries got such distinctive polities. We found that on the contrary, over a period of decades checks and balances appeared to be undermined by the presence of resource rents.

Both 'Testing the Neocon Agenda' and 'Post-conflict Risks' had pointed to problems associated with electoral competition. One strand of my recent research has therefore focused on elections, both their conduct and their effects. 'Elections and Economic Policy in Developing Countries' investigates whether elections discipline governments into improvements in economic policy. Teasing out the effects of elections on policy is not easy. However, by using differences in the frequency of elections, and the fact that in many countries election dates are set by the constitution, we were able to address some of the obvious concerns about endogeneity. We found that elections had both cyclical and structural effects. The cyclical effects are unsurprising – as an election approaches economic policy deteriorates. Economic theory has some very fancy explanations for why such deterioration might occur. However, to my mind the most plausible is simply that the time horizon of governments shortens and they resort to populist policies which yield quick benefits at the expense of longer term costs. The more important results concerned the structural effects: allowing for the cycle, elections do succeed in disciplining governments into improvements in economic policy. Potentially our most important result is that this benign effect depends upon the conduct of elections. We were able to distinguish between well-conducted and badly conducted elections and found that only well-conducted elections worked. As might be expected, badly conducted elections failed to discipline governments. Following on from these disturbing results, my current research, which is still working its way through the publication process, is about what determines whether elections are properly conducted, and what can be done to improve conduct in the many elections where the wishes of voters are not adequately respected.

The final block of papers concerns aid and trade which has been a long-standing focus of my work. My ideas on aid have moved on since 'Aid Allocation and Poverty Reduction', but it was an influential paper which crystallized much of the thinking among policy-makers and academics around the Millennium. It was the first paper to provide a quantitative answer to the question of how to allocate aid between countries in such a way as to have the biggest impact upon poverty. It produced an answer by combining information on the depth of poverty, country-by-country, with information on the quality of economic policies and institutions. The idea was that aid could be most effective in countries which had both severe poverty and good policies and institutions. Since writing the paper I have become much more concerned with the special problems of the 'bottom billion'. I now think that aid, along with other policies, needs to be focused on the minority of developing countries that have been diverging from the rest of mankind. Often this means countries where policies and institutions are weak: the challenge is to devise ways of assisting that recognize these weaknesses and, at a minimum, do not compound them. The extent of my rethinking is reflected in 'The Complementarities of Poverty Reduction, Equity, and Growth', which is a critique of the World Bank's World Development Report on poverty, and of the approach taken by the international community in the Millennium Development Goals which underlay it. Complementing that overarching critique of development objectives, 'Does Aid Mitigate External Shocks?' investigates one of the distinctive problems of the poorest countries. Some of the countries of the bottom billion remain highly dependent for revenues upon the export of a few commodities the prices of which are highly volatile. The crash in global commodity prices that was triggered by the global financial crisis of 2008 plunged some of these countries into crisis. Fortuitously, I had been working on precisely the question of how such adverse shocks might be cushioned. The management of aid programs is not sufficiently responsive for it to be realistic to hope that aid could be increased during such shocks. Recognizing this limitation of aid allocation, we posed the simpler question of whether a high underlying level of aid provided a cushion. We found that it did: over-and-above any other effects that aid might have, it reduces the knock-on effects of a crash in commodity exports for GDP. An implication is that, other things equal, countries which are particularly vulnerable to such shocks should receive a higher inflow of aid.

However, in these difficult environments the role of aid, both for good and for bad, tends to be exaggerated: other policies are often more important, including the security policies that were the subject of the first block of papers in this volume. But security policies can be complemented by trade policies. 'Rethinking Trade Preferences: How Africa can diversify its Exports', sets out the case for using temporary trade preferences to pump-prime Africa into the global market for light manufactures, most notably garments. Diversification would be an effective way of protecting countries from commodity shocks and so a trade policy that promotes it can complement the cushioning effects of aid. As with most aspects of trade policy, the devil is in the detail of design. We show that the specification of 'rules-of-origin', seemingly a point of arcane detail, has been decisive in explaining why America's preference scheme, the Africa Growth and Opportunity Act, has had a much bigger impact than Europe's scheme, Everything but Arms.

The aftermath of the global economic crisis has widened the range of uncertainty as to how Africa will develop. The resurgence in commodity prices leaves many countries in a strong position to resume rapid growth. However, the extraordinary volatility of both prices and export volumes poses acute problems of economic management. The consequences of burst commodity booms were where my applied research of African economies began in the 1970s. I am encouraged that the present shocks appear to have been managed rather better. People learn from history, and perhaps even from research.

Part I
Violent conflict

1   Greed and grievance in civil war

With Anke Hoeffler

1.1 Introduction

Civil war is now far more common than international conflict: all of the 15 major armed conflicts listed by the Stockholm International Peace Research Institute for 2001 were internal (SIPRI, 2002).

In this chapter we develop an econometric model which predicts the outbreak of civil conflict. Analogous to the classic principles of murder detection, rebellion needs both motive and opportunity. The political science literature explains conflict in terms of motive: the circumstances in which people want to rebel are viewed as sufficiently rare to constitute the explanation. In Section 1.2 we contrast this with economic accounts which explain rebellion in terms of opportunity: it is the circumstances in which people are able to rebel that are rare. We discuss measurable variables which might enable us to test between the two accounts and present descriptive data on the 79 large civil conflicts that occurred between 1960 and 1999. In Section 1.3 we use econometric tests to discriminate between rival explanations and develop an integrated model which provides a synthesis. Section 1.4 presents a range of robustness checks and Section 1.5 discusses the results.

This analysis considerably extends and revises our earlier work (Collier and Hoeffler, 1998). In our previous theory, we assumed that rebel movements incurred net costs during conflict, so that post-conflict pay-offs would be decisive. The core of the paper was the derivation and testing of the implication that high post-conflict payoffs would tend to justify long civil wars. We now recognize that this assumption is untenable: rebel groups often more than cover their costs during the conflict. Here we propose a more general theory which juxtaposes the opportunities for rebellion against the constraints. Our previous empirical analysis conflated the initiation and the duration of rebellion. We now treat this separately. This paper focuses on the initiation of rebellion.[1] Our sample is expanded from a cross-section analysis of 98 countries during the period 1960–92, to a comprehensive coverage of 750 five-year episodes over the period 1960–99, enabling us to analyse double the number of war starts. Further, we expand from four explanatory variables to a more extensive coverage of potential determinants, testing for robustness to select a preferred specification.

1.2 Rebellion: approaches and measures

1.2.1 Preferences, perceptions, and opportunities

Political science offers an account of conflict in terms of motive: rebellion occurs when grievances are sufficiently acute that people want to engage in violent protest. In marked contrast, a small economic theory literature, typified by Grossman (1991, 1999), models rebellion as an industry that generates profits from looting, so that 'the insurgents are indistinguishable from bandits or pirates' (Grossman, 1999, p. 269). Such rebellions are motivated by greed, which is presumably sufficiently common that profitable opportunities for rebellion will not be passed up.[2] Hence, the incidence of rebellion is not explained by motive, but by the atypical circumstances that generate profitable opportunities. Thus, the political science and economic approaches to rebellion have assumed both different rebel motivation—grievance versus greed—and different explanations—atypical grievances versus atypical opportunities.

Hirshleifer (1995, 2001) provides an important refinement on the motive-opportunity dichotomy. He classifies the possible causes of conflict into preferences, opportunities, and perceptions. The introduction of perceptions allows for the possibility that both opportunities and grievances might be wrongly perceived. If the perceived opportunity for rebellion is illusory—analogous to the 'winners' curse'—unprofitability will cause collapse, perhaps before reaching our threshold for civil war. By contrast, when exaggerated grievances trigger rebellion, fighting does not dispel the misperception and indeed may generate genuine grievances.

Misperceptions of grievances may be very common: all societies may have groups with exaggerated grievances. In this case, as with greed-rebellion, motive would not explain the incidence of rebellion. Societies that experienced civil war would be distinguished by the atypical viability of rebellion. In such societies rebellions would be conducted by viable not-for-profit organizations, pursuing misperceived agendas by violent means.

Greed and misperceived grievance have important similarities as accounts of rebellion. They provide a common explanation—'opportunity' and 'viability' describe the common conditions sufficient for profit-seeking, or not-for-profit, rebel organizations to exist. On our evidence they are observationally equivalent since we cannot observe motives. They can jointly be contrasted with the political account of conflict in which the grievances that both motivate and explain rebellion are assumed to be well-grounded in objective circumstances such as unusually high inequality, or unusually weak political rights. We now turn to the proxies for opportunities and objective grievances.

1.2.2 Proxies for opportunity

The first step in an empirical investigation of conflict is a clear and workable definition of the phenomenon. We define civil war as an internal conflict with at least 1,000 combat-related deaths per year. In order to distinguish wars from massacres, both government forces and an identifiable rebel organization must suffer at least 5 per cent of these fatalities. This definition has become standard following the seminal data collection of Small and Singer (1982) and Singer and Small (1994). We use an expanded and updated version of their data set that covers 161 countries over the period 1960–99 and identifies 79 civil wars, listed in Table 1.1. Our task is to explain the initiation of civil war using these data.[3]

Table 1.1 Outbreaks of war

Country	Start of the war	End of the war	Previous war	GDP sample	Secondary schooling sample
Afghanistan	04/78	02/92			
Afghanistan	05/92	ongoing	*		
Algeria	07/62	12/62	*		
Algeria	05/91	ongoing	*	*	*
Angola	02/61	11/75			
Angola	11/75	05/91	*	*	*
Angola	09/92	ongoing	*	*	*
Azerbaijan	04/91	10/94			
Bosnia	03/92	11/95			
Burma/Myanmar	68	10/80	*	*	*
Burma/Myanmar	02/83	07/95	*	*	*
Burundi	04/72	12/73		*	*
Burundi	08/88	08/88	*	*	*
Burundi	11/91	ongoing	*	*	*
Cambodia	03/70	10/91	*		
Chad	03/80	08/88		*	
China	01/67	09/68	*	*	
Columbia	04/84	ongoing	*	*	*
Congo	97	10/97		*	*
Cyprus	07/74	08/74		*	
Dominican Rep.	04/65	09/65		*	*
El Salvador	10/79	01/92		*	*
Ethiopia	07/74	05/91		*	*
Georgia	06/91	12/93			
Guatemala	07/66	07/72	*	*	*
Guatemala	03/78	03/84	*	*	*
Guinea-Bissau	12/62	12/74			
India	08/65	08/65	*	*	*
India	84	94	*	*	*
Indonesia	06/75	09/82	*	*	*
Iran	03/74	03/75		*	*
Iran	09/78	12/79	*	*	*
Iran	06/81	05/82	*	*	*
Iraq	09/61	11/63	*		
Iraq	07/74	03/75	*	*	*

(continued overleaf)

Table 1.1 continued

Country	Start of the war	End of the war	Previous war	Gdp sample	Secondary schooling sample
Iraq	01/85	12/92	*	*	*
Jordan	09/70	09/70		*	
Laos	07/60	02/73	*		
Lebanon	05/75	09/92	*		
Liberia	12/89	11/91		*	
Liberia	10/92	11/96	*		
Morocco	10/75	11/89	*	*	*
Mozambique	10/64	11/75			
Mozambique	07/76	10/92	*	*	*
Nicaragua	10/78	07/79		*	*
Nicaragua	03/82	04/90			
Nigeria	01/66	01/70		*	*
Nigeria	12/80	08/84	*	*	*
Pakistan	03/71	12/71		*	*
Pakistan	01/73	07/77			
Peru	03/82	12/96		*	*
Philippines	09/72	12/96	*	*	*
Romania	12/89	12/89		*	*
Russia	12/94	08/96			
Russia	09/99	ongoing	*		
Rwanda	11/63	02/64			
Rwanda	10/90	07/94	*	*	*
Sierra Leone	03/91	11/96		*	*
Sierra Leone	05/97	07/99	*	*	
Somalia	04/82	05/88		*	*
Somalia	05/88	12/92	*	*	*
Sri Lanka	04/71	05/71		*	*
Sri Lanka	07/83	ongoing	*	*	*
Sudan	10/63	02/72			
Sudan	07/83	ongoing	*	*	*
Tajikistan	04/92	12/94			
Turkey	07/91	ongoing		*	*
Uganda	05/66	06/66		*	*
Uganda	10/80	04/88	*	*	*
Vietnam	01/60	04/75	*		
Yemen	05/90	10/94			
Yemen, Arab Rep.	11/62	09/69	*		
Yemen, People's Rep.	01/86	01/86	*		
Yugoslavia	04/90	01/92			
Yugoslavia	10/98	04/99	*		
Zaïre/Dem. Rep. of Congo	07/60	09/65			
Zaïre/Dem. Rep. of Congo	09/91	12/96	*	*	*
Zaïre/Dem. Rep. of Congo	09/97	09/99	*	*	*
Zimbabwe	12/72	12/79		*	*

Note: Previous wars include war starts 1945–94.

We now consider quantitative indicators of opportunity, starting with opportunities for financing rebellion. We consider three common sources: extortion of natural resources, donations from diasporas, and subventions from hostile governments.[4]

Klare (2001) provides a good discussion of natural resource extortion, such as diamonds in West Africa, timber in Cambodia, and cocaine in Colombia. In Table 1.2, we proxy natural resources by the ratio of primary commodity exports to GDP for each of the 161 countries. As with our other variables, we measure at intervals of five years, starting in 1960 and ending in

Table 1.2 Descriptive statistics

	Sample (n = 1167)	*No civil war* (n = 1089)	*Civil war* (n = 78)
War starts	0.067	0	1
Primary commodity exports/GDP	0.168	0.169	0.149
GDP *per capita* (const. US$)	4061	4219	1645
Diaspora (relative to population of country of origin)	0.017	0.018	0.004
Male secondary schooling (% in school)	43.42	44.39	30.3
GDP *per capita* growth (average for previous 5 years)	1.62	1.74	−0.23
Previous war (% with war since 1945)	20.8	18.5	53.8
Peace duration (months since last conflict)	327	334	221
Forest cover (%)	31.11	31.33	27.81
Mountainous terrain (%)	15.82	15.17	24.93
Geographic concentration of the population (Gini)	0.571	0.569	0.603
Population density (inhabitants per square km)	150	156	62
Population in urban areas (%)	45.11	46.00	32.7
Ethnic fractionalization (index, 0–100)	39.57	38.64	52.63
Religious fractionalization (index, 0–100)	36.09	35.98	37.70
Polarization $\alpha = 1.6$ (index, 0–0.165)	0.077	0.077	0.076
Democracy (index, 0–10)	3.91	4.07	1.821
Ethnic dominance (% with main ethnic group 45–90%)	0.465	0.465	0.452
Income inequality (Gini)	0.406	0.406	0.410
Land inequality (Gini)	0.641	0.641	0.631

Note: We examine 78—rather than the 79—war starts as listed in Table 2.1 because Pakistan experienced two outbreaks of war during 1970–74. We only include one of these war starts to avoid double counting.

1995. We then consider the subsequent five years as an 'episode' and compare those in which a civil war broke out ('conflict episodes') with those that were conflict-free ('peace episodes'). The descriptive statistics give little support to the opportunity thesis: the conflict episodes were on average slightly less dependent upon primary commodity exports than the peace episodes. However, there is a substantial difference in the dispersion. The peace episodes tended to have either markedly below-average or markedly above-average dependence, while the conflict episodes were grouped around the mean.[5] Possibly if natural resources are sufficiently abundant, as in Saudi Arabia, the government may be so well-financed that rebellion is militarily infeasible. This offsetting effect may make the net effect of natural resources non-monotonic.[6] The observed pattern may also reflect differences between primary commodities (which we defer to Section 1.3). Further, primary commodities are associated with other characteristics that may cause civil war, such as poor public service provision, corruption and economic mismanagement (Sachs and Warner, 2000). Potentially, any increase in conflict risk may be due to rebel responses to such poor governance rather than to financial opportunities.

A second source of rebel finance is from diasporas. Angoustures and Pascal (1996) review the evidence, an example being finance for the Tamil Tigers from Tamils in north America. We proxy the size of a country's diaspora by its emigrants living in the US, as given in US Census data. Although this neglects diasporas living in other countries, it ensures uniformity in the aggregate: all diasporas are in the same legal, organizational, and economic environment. We then take this emigrant population as a proportion of the population in the country of origin. In the formal analysis we decompose the diaspora into that part induced by conflict and that which is exogenous to conflict, but here we simply consider the crude numbers. These do not support the opportunity thesis: diasporas are substantially smaller in the conflict episodes.

A third source of rebel finance is from hostile governments. For example, the government of Southern Rhodesia pump-primed the Renamo rebellion in Mozambique. Our proxy for the willingness of foreign governments to finance military opposition to the incumbent government is the Cold War. During the Cold War each great power supported rebellions in countries allied to the opposing power. There is some support for the opportunity thesis: only eleven of the 79 wars broke out during the 1990s.

We next consider opportunities arising from atypically low cost. Recruits must be paid, and their cost may be related to the income forgone by enlisting as a rebel. Rebellions may occur when foregone income is unusually low. Since non-economists regard this as fanciful we give the example of the Russian civil war. Reds and Whites, both rebel armies, had four million desertions (the obverse of the recruitment problem). The desertion rate was ten times higher in summer than in winter: the recruits being peasants, income foregone were much higher at harvest time (Figes, 1996). We try three proxies for foregone income: mean income per capita, male secondary schooling, and the growth rate of the economy. As shown in Table 1.2, the conflict episodes started from less than half the mean income of the peace episodes. However, so many characteristics are correlated with per capita income that, depending upon what other variables are included, the proxy is open to other interpretations. Our second proxy, male secondary school enrolment, has the advantage of being focused on young males—the group from whom rebels are recruited. The conflict episodes indeed started from lower school enrolment, but this is again open to alternative interpretation: education may affect the risk of conflict through changing attitudes. Our third measure, the growth rate of the economy in the preceding period, is intended to proxy new income opportunities. Conflict episodes were preceded by lower growth rates. This is consistent with evidence that the lower is the rate of growth, the higher is the probability of unconstitutional political change (Alesina *et al.*, 1996).[7] Although the three proxies are all consistent with atypically low forgone income as an opportunity, low income could also be interpreted as an objective economic grievance.

The opportunity for rebellion may be that conflict-specific capital (such as military equipment) is unusually cheap. We proxy the cost of such capital by the time since the most recent previous conflict: the legacy of weapon stocks, skills, and organizational capital will gradually depreciate. Empirically, peace episodes are preceded by far longer periods of peace than conflict episodes (Table 1.2). While this supports the opportunity thesis, it could also be interpreted as reflecting the gradual decay of conflict-induced grievances.

Another dimension of opportunity is an atypically weak government military capability. An unambiguous indicator is if the terrain is favourable to rebels: forests and mountains provide rebels with a safe haven. We measure the proportion of a country's terrain that is forested, using FAO data. We could find no equivalent data on mountainous terrain: proxies such as altitude tend to misclassify both plateaus and rugged uplands. We therefore commissioned a new index from a specialist, John Gerrard. The descriptive statistics (Table 1.2) suggest that terrain may matter: in conflict episodes 25 per cent of the terrain is mountainous, versus only 15 per cent in peace episodes, although there is no difference in forest cover. Geographic dispersion of the population may also inhibit government capability: Herbst (2000) suggests that Zaire is prone to rebellion because its population lives around the edges of the country. We measure dispersion by calculating a Gini coefficient of population dispersion.[8] In fact, the concentration of the population is slightly lower prior to peace episodes (0.57) than prior to war episodes (0.6). Similarly, low population density and low urbanization may inhibit government capability. Empirically, prior to war episodes both population density and urbanization are low (Table 1.2).

A final source of rebel military opportunity may be social cohesion. Ethnic and religious diversity within organizations tends to reduce their ability to function (Easterly and Levine, 1997; Alesina *et al.*, 1999; Collier, 2001). A newly formed rebel army may be in particular need of social cohesion, constraining recruitment to a single ethnic or religious group. A diverse society might in this case reduce the opportunity for rebellion by limiting the recruitment pool. The most widely used measure of ethnic diversity is the index of ethno-linguistic fractionalization. This measures the probability that two randomly drawn people will be from different ethnic groups. We could find no measure of religious fractionalization, but we constructed one equivalent to that of ethnic fractionalization using data from Barrett (1982). If ethnic and religious divisions are cross-cutting, social fractionalization is multiplicative rather than additive. We could find no data relating religious and ethnic divisions and so we construct a proxy that measures the maximum potential social fractionalization.[9] The thesis that social cohesion enhances opportunity is not supported by the descriptive statistics: conflict episodes have atypically high fractionalization. This seems more consistent with a grievance interpretation, to which we now turn.

1.2.3 Proxying objective grievances

We consider four objective measures of grievance: ethnic or religious hatred, political repression, political exclusion, and economic inequality.

Ethnic and religious hatreds are widely perceived as a cause of civil conflict. Although such hatreds cannot be quantified, they can evidently only occur in societies that are multi-ethnic or multi-religious and so our proxies measure various dimensions of diversity. Our previously discussed measures of fractionalization are pertinent: inter-group hatreds must be greater in societies that are fractionalized than in those which are homogenous. However, arguably the source of inter-group tension is not diversity but polarization.[10] Fortunately, the allowable class of measures of polarization is quite limited. We adopt a general measure due to Esteban and Ray (1994)

$$P = K \sum_{i=1}^{n} \sum_{j=1}^{n} \pi_i^{1+\alpha} \pi_j d \tag{1}$$

where π_i denotes the percentage of people that belong to group i in the total population, $i = 1, \ldots, n$. This measure of polarization depends on the parameters K and α. K does not change the order, but is used for population normalization. Esteban and Ray show that α is bounded between zero and 1.6. We calculate the polarization measure for three different values of α, 0, 0.8 and 1.6, using primary data on ethnic composition.[11] In addition we investigate the variant of the Esteban-Ray measure proposed by Reynal-Querol. These measures indeed distinguish polarization from fractionalization: their correlation coefficient ranges between 0.39 ($\alpha = 1.6$) and 1.0 ($\alpha = 0$).[12] The descriptive data does not suggest that polarization is important: conflict and peace episodes have very similar mean values (Table 1.2).

We measure political repression using the Polity III data set (see Jaggers and Gurr, 1995). This measure of political rights ranges 0–10 on an ascending ordinal scale. Political rights differ considerably between conflict and peace episodes. We also investigate the Polity III measure of autocracy, and a measure of political openness published by Freedom House (the 'Gastil Index'). The quantitative political science literature has already applied these measures to conflict risk. Hegre *et al.* (2001) find that repression increases conflict except when it is severe.

Even in democracies a small group may fear permanent exclusion. A potentially important instance is if political allegiance is based on ethnicity and one ethnic group has a majority. The incentive to exploit the minority increases the larger is the minority, since there is more to extract (Collier, 2001). Hence, a minority may be most vulnerable if the largest ethnic group constitutes a small majority. We term this ethnic dominance. In Table 1.2 we define it as occurring if the largest ethnic group constitutes 45–90 per cent of the population. On this definition it does not appear important: it is as common in peace episodes as in conflict episodes.

The opening page of Sen's *On Economic Inequality* (Sen, 1973) asserts that 'the relation between inequality and rebellion is indeed a close one'. The poor may rebel to induce redistribution, and rich regions may mount secessionist rebellions to preempt redistribution.[13] We measure income inequality by the Gini coefficient and by the ratio of the top-to-bottom quintiles of income. We measure asset inequality by the Gini coefficient of land ownership. The data are from Deininger and Squire (1996, 1998). Inequality is slightly higher prior to the conflict episodes.

1.2.4 Scale effects

Our measures of opportunity, such as primary commodity exports, income, and school enrolment, are scaled by measures of country size. For given values of these variables, opportunities should be approximately proportional to size. Grievance might also increase with size: public choices diverge more from the preferences of the average individual as heterogeneity increases.[14] We are, however, able to control for three aspects of heterogeneity: ethnic, religious and income diversity. Empirically, the conflict episodes had markedly larger populations than the peace episodes.

1.3 Regression analysis

As set out above, the proxies for opportunity and objective grievances are largely distinct and so can be compared as two non-nested econometric models. There is, however, no reason for the accounts to be exclusive and the aim of our econometric tests is to arrive at an integrated model which gives an account of conflict risk in terms of all those opportunities and grievances that are significant.

We now attempt to predict the risk that a civil war will start during a five-year episode, through a logit regression. Our dependent variable, civil war start, takes a value of one if a civil war started during a five year episode (1965–69, ..., 1994–99). Episodes that were peaceful from the beginning until the end are coded zero. Ongoing wars are coded as missing observations as to not conflate the analysis of civil war initiation and duration.[15] If a war ended and another one started in the same period we coded these events as one. Some of our explanatory variables are time invariant. Those that are not are measured either for the first year of the period (e.g. 1965) or during the preceding five years (e.g. growth during 1960–64) in order to avoid endogeneity problems. Our results rest on how societies that experienced an outbreak of war differed from those that sustained peace.

We start with the opportunity model (see Table 1.3). The first regression (column 1) excludes per capita income and diasporas. Because per capita income and enrollment in secondary schooling are highly correlated, they cannot be used in the same regression ($\rho = 0.8$). Our diaspora measure is available only for 29 war episodes and so we explore it as an addendum. The variables included in the first regression permit a sample of 688 episodes (from 123 countries), including 46 wars.

Primary commodity exports are highly significant. Although their effect is non-linear, the risk of conflict peaks when they constitute around 33 per cent of GDP,[16] which is a high level of dependence. The other proxy for finance, the end of the Cold War, has the expected sign but is insignificant. The foregone earnings proxies are also both significant with the expected sign: secondary schooling and growth both reduce conflict risk. Our proxy for the cost of conflict-specific capital is the number of months since any previous conflict (back to 1945). To distinguish between this interpretation and the danger that the proxy might be picking up fixed effects, we add a dummy variable that is unity if there was a previous conflict post-1945. Our proxy has the expected sign and is on the borderline of significance, while the dummy variable is completely insignificant. When the dummy variable is dropped (column 2) the proxy becomes highly significant and no other results are changed. The proxies for military advantage also have the expected sign and are marginally significant: mountainous terrain, population dispersion and social fractionalization. Finally, the coefficient on population is positive and highly significant.

The third column replaces secondary schooling with per capita income. This permits a larger sample—750 episodes (from 125 countries) including 52 wars. Per capita income is highly significant with the expected negative sign. However, the change of variable and the expansion of sample have little effect on the other results—social fractionalization becomes significant and population dispersion loses significance. There is little to chose between these two variants of the model—secondary schooling gives a slightly better fit, but per capita income permits a slightly larger sample.

In the last two columns of Table 1.3 we introduce our diaspora variable. Since many observations are missing, the number of war episodes with complete data is radically reduced. In order to preserve sample size we therefore retreat to a more parsimonious version of the model. We drop four sample-constraining peripheral explanatory variables: social fractionalization,

Table 1.3 Opportunity model

	1	2	3	4	5
Primary commodity exports/GDP	18.149	18.900	16.476	17.567	17.404
	(6.006)***	(5.948)***	(5.207)***	(6.744)***	(6.750)***
(Primary commodity exports/GDP)^2	−27.445	−29.123	−23.017	−28.815	−28.456
	(11.996)***	(11.905)***	(9.972)**	(15.351)*	(15.366)*
Post-coldwar	−0.326	−0.207	−0.454		
	(0.469)	(0.450)	(0.416)		
Male secondary schooling	−0.025	−0.024			
	(0.010)**	(0.010)**			
Ln GDP per capita			−0.837	−1.237	−1.243
			(0.253)***	(0.283)***	(0.284)***
GDP growth	−0.117	−0.118	−0.105		
	(0.044)***	(0.044)***	(0.042)***		
Peace duration	−0.003	−0.004***	−0.004	−0.002	−0.002
	(0.002)	(0.001)	(0.001)***	(0.001)	(0.001)
	$p = 0.128$				
Previous war	0.464				
	(0.547)				
	$p = 0.396$				
Mountainous terrain	0.013	0.014	0.008		
	(0.009)	(0.009)	(0.008)		
	$p = 0.164$				
Geographic dispersion	−2.211	−2.129	−0.865		
	(1.038)**	(1.032)**	(0.948)		
Social fractionalization	−0.0002	−0.0002	−0.0002		
	(0.0001)	(0.0001)	(0.0001)**		
	$p = 0.109$	$p = 0.122$			
Ln population	0.669	0.686	0.493	0.295	0.296
	(0.163)***	(0.162)***	(0.129)***	(0.141)**	(0.141)**
Diaspora/peace				700.931	
				(363.29)**	
Diaspora corrected/peace					741.155
					(387.636)*
(Diaspora-diaspora corrected)/peace					823.941
					(556.024)
N	688	688	750	595	595
No of wars	46	46	52	29	29
Pseudo R^2	0.24	0.24	0.22	0.25	0.25
Log likelihood	−128.49	−128.85	−146.86	−93.27	−93.23

Notes: All regressions include a constant. Standard errors in parentheses, ***, **, * indicate significance at the 1, 5, and 10% level, respectively.

population dispersion, mountainous terrain, and the rate of growth in the previous episode. The remaining explanatory variables are thus per capita GDP, primary commodity exports, population, and the number of months since the previous conflict. Even with these data-restoring deletions, the sample size is reduced to 29 war episodes (and 595 observations). However, all the included explanatory variables remain significant. The size of the diaspora is not directly significant in the initiation of conflict (column 4). However, it is significant when interacted with the number of months since the previous conflict. 'Diaspora/peace' divides the size of the diaspora by the time since a previous conflict. The variable is positive and significant: a large diaspora considerably increases the risk of repeat conflict.

While this result may indicate that diasporas increase the risk of conflict through their finance of rebel organizations, it is also open to a more anodyne interpretation. Diasporas are endogenous to the intensity of conflict: when civil war occurs, people emigrate to the USA. Hence, the size of the diaspora might be proxying the intensity of conflict. The result may therefore be spurious: intense conflicts may have a higher risk of repetition. To test for this we decomposed observed diasporas into a component which is exogenous to the intensity of conflict and a residual endogenous component. For this decomposition we estimated a migration model, reported in Appendix 1.1. The size of the diaspora in a census year is predicted to be a function of its size in the previous census, time, per capita income in the country of origin, and whether there was a war in the intervening period. This model predicts the size of the diaspora with reasonable accuracy. For years subsequent to a conflict we replace the actual data on the size of the diaspora with an estimate from this regression. Thus, all post-conflict observations of diasporas are estimates which are purged of any effect of the intensity of conflict. The difference between actual and estimated figures is then used as an additional variable, measuring that part of the diaspora which is potentially endogenous to the intensity of conflict. Both of these measures are then introduced into the regression in place of the previous single measure of the diaspora. The results are reported in the final column of Table 1.3. The purged measure of the diaspora remains significant, and the size of the coefficient is only slightly altered (it is not significantly different from that on the endogenous diaspora measure). This suggests that there is indeed a substantial causal effect of the diaspora on the risk of conflict renewal. The result also guides our interpretation of why the risk of conflict repetition declines as peace is maintained. Recall that in principle this could be either because hatreds gradually fade, or because 'rebellion-specific capital' gradually depreciates. How might diasporas slow these processes? Diasporas preserve their own hatreds: that is why they finance rebellion. However, it is unlikely that the diaspora's hatreds significantly influence attitudes among the much larger population in the country of origin. By contrast, the finance provided by the diaspora can offset the depreciation of rebellion-specific capital, thereby sustaining conflict risk.

In Table 1.4 we turn to objective grievance as the explanation of rebellion, dropping all the economic measures of opportunity.[17] We retain the number of months since a previous conflict, since (subject to our discussion above) this can be interpreted as proxying fading hatreds. In the first column we also exclude the inequality measures due to considerations of sample size. This enables a very large sample of 850 episodes and 59 civil wars.

Table 1.4 Grievance model

	1	2	3
Ethnic fractionalization	0.010	0.011	0.012
	(0.006)*	(0.007)*	(0.008)
Religious fractionalization	–0.003	–0.006	–0.004
	(0.007)	(0.008)	(0.009)
Polarization $\alpha = 1.6$	–3.067	–4.682	–6.536
	(7.021)	(8.267)	(8.579)
Ethnic dominance (45–90%)	0.414	0.575	1.084
	(0.496)	(0.586)	(0.629)*
Democracy	–0.109	–0.083	–0.121
	(0.044)***	(0.051)*	(0.053)**
Peace duration	–0.004	–0.003	–0.004
	(0.001)***	(0.001)***	(0.001)***
Mountainous terrain	0.011	0.007	–0.0001
	(0.007)	(0.009)	(0.009)
Geographic dispersion	–0.509	–0.763	–1.293
	(0.856)	(1.053)	(0.102)
Ln population	0.221	0.246	0.300
	(0.096)**	(0.119)**	(1.133)**
Income inequality		0.015	
		(0.018)	
Land inequality			0.461
			(1.305)
N	850	604	603
No. of wars	59	41	38
Pseudo R^2	0.13	0.11	0.17
Log likelihood	–185.57	–133.46	–117.12

Notes: All regressions include a constant. Standard errors in parentheses. ***, **, * indicate significance at the 1, 5 and 10% level, respectively. Column 1: the two measures of fractionalization and ethnic dominance are not jointly significant.

The four proxies for ethnic and religious tension are surprisingly unimportant in view of the attention that the phenomenon attracts. Ethnic fractionalization is significant at 10 per cent with the expected sign. Religious fractionalization and polarization are insignificant with the wrong sign, and ethnic dominance is insignificant. Nor are the three measures jointly significant.[18] Democracy is highly significant with the expected sign—repression increases conflict risk. The time since the previous conflict is again highly significant, but we have suggested that this is more likely to be proxying rebellion-specific capital than grievance. In the second and third columns we introduce income inequality and land inequality respectively. Although the sample size is reduced, it is still substantial— over 600 episodes of which 41 (income) and 38 (land) are wars. Neither variable is close to significance.[19] All three grievance models have very low explanatory power with a pseudo R^2 of 0.17 or lower.

We now turn to the question of which model, opportunity or grievance, provides a better explanation of the risk of civil war. Since the two models are non-nested, i.e. one model is not a special case of the other, we use the J-test as suggested by Davidson and MacKinnon (1981). As shown in the first two columns of Table 1.5, we find that we cannot reject one model in favour of the other.[20] Thus, we conclude that while the opportunity model is superior, some elements of the grievance model are likely to add to its explanatory power. We therefore investigate the combination of the two models as presented in column 3 of Table 1.5.

Since this combined model includes income inequality and a lagged term, our sample size is much reduced (479 observations). In column 4 we drop inequality (which is consistently insignificant). Omitting inequality increases the sample size to 665. In this combined model neither democracy, ethnic and religious fractionalization nor the post-Cold War dummy are significant. Other variables are statistically significant or close to significance and the overall fit is reasonable (pseudo R^2 of 0.26). Since both the grievance and opportunity models are nested in the combined model, we can use a likelihood ratio test to determine whether the combined model is superior. We can reject the validity of the restrictions proposed by the grievance model, but not by the opportunity model.[21]

Although the combined model is superior to the opportunity and grievance models, several variables are completely insignificant and we drop them sequentially. First we exclude the post-Cold War dummy, then religious fractionalization, then democracy,[22] then polarization, then ethnic fractionalization and finally mountainous terrain, yielding the baseline model of column 5 and its variant with per capita income replacing secondary enrolment in column 6. No further reduction in the model is accepted, and no additions of variables included in our previous models are accepted. The baseline model and its variant yield very similar results although the variant has less explanatory power and two variables lose significance (ethnic dominance and geographic dispersion).

Our baseline model allows us to calculate the change in the probability of war-starts for different values of the explanatory variables. We present these calculations in Appendix Table A2.1. At the mean of all variables the risk of a war-start is about 11.5 per cent. Our model predicts that a hypothetical country with all the worst characteristics found in our sample would have a near-certain risk of war, while one with all the best characteristics would have a negligible risk. We now calculate how each variable affects the risk of civil war (keeping all other variables at their mean values).

The effect of primary commodity exports on conflict risk is both highly significant and considerable. At peak danger (primary commodity exports being 33 per cent of GDP), the risk of civil war is about 22 per cent, while a country with no such exports has a risk of only 1 per cent. The effect is sufficiently important to warrant disaggregation into different types of commodities. We categorized primary commodity exports according to which type of product was dominant: food, non-food agriculture, oil, other raw materials, and a residual category of 'mixed'.[23] Of the many potential

Table 1.5 Combined opportunity and grievance model

	1	2	3	4	5	6	7
Primary commodity exports/GDP	19.107 (5.996)***		37.072 (10.293)***	23.385 (6.692)***	18.937 (5.865)***	16.773 (5.206)***	50.608 (14.09)***
(Primary commodity exports/GDP)^2	-30.262 (12.008)***		-69.270 (21.697)***	-36.335 (12.998)***	-29.443 (11.781)***	-23.800 (10.040)**	-131.00 (42.93)***
Post-cold war	-0.208 (0.457)		-0.873 (0.644)	-0.281 (0.459)			
Male secondary schooling	-0.021 (0.011)**		-0.029 (0.013)**	-0.022 (0.011)**	-0.031 (0.010)***		-0.034 (0.011)***
Ln GDP per capita						-0.950 (0.245)***	
(GDP growth) $t-1$	-0.108 (0.044)***		-0.045 (0.062)	-0.108 (0.045)**	-0.115 (0.043)***	-0.098 (0.042)**	-0.113 (0.046)***
Peace duration	-0.0003 (0.002)	0.0005 (0.0014)	-0.0003 (0.0015)	-0.003 (0.001)***	-0.004 (0.001)***	-0.004 (0.001)***	-0.003 (0.001)***
Mountainous terrain	0.005 (0.010)	0.001 (0.008)	0.005 (0.012)	0.015 (0.009) $p=0.11$			
Geographic dispersion	-1.976 (1.049)*	0.053 (1.101)	-4.032 (1.490)***	-1.962 (1.149)*	-2.487 (1.005)**	-0.992 (0.909)	-2.871 (1.130)***
Ln population	0.489 (0.193)**	-0.022 (0.136)	0.927 (0.250)***	0.697 (0.181)***	0.768 (0.166)***	0.510 (0.128)***	1.123 (0.226)***
Social fractionalization	-0.0002 (0.0001)***		-0.0008 (0.0003)**	-0.0005 (0.0003) $p=0.11$	-0.0002 (0.0001)**	-0.0002 (0.0001)***	-0.0003 (0.0001)***
Ethnic fractionalization		0.008 (0.007)	0.041 (0.019)**	0.023 (0.015)			

(continued overleaf)

Table 1.5 continued

	1	2	3	4	5	6	7
Religious fractionalization		-0.005 (0.008)	0.015 (0.020)	0.014 (0.019)			
Polarization		-9.338 (8.734)	-25.276 (13.390)*	-15.992 (10.518)			
Ethnic dominance (45–90%)		1.210 (0.648)*	2.020 (0.915)**	1.592 (0.746)**	0.670 (0.354)*	0.480 (0.328) $p = 0.14$	0.769 (0.369)**
Democracy		-0.036 (0.054)	-0.018 (0.062)	-0.042 (0.054)			
Income inequality			0.025 (0.024)				
Grievance predicted value	0.765 (0.413)*						
Opportunity predicted value		1.044 (0.211)***					
Primary commodity exports/GDP* oil dummy							-28.275 (9.351)***
(Primary commodity exports/GDP)²* oil dummy							106.459 (38.704)***
N	665	665	479	665	688	750	654
No. of wars	46	46	32	46	46	52	45
Pseudo R^2	0.24	0.25	0.24	0.26	0.24	0.22	0.30
Log likelihood	-126.69	-125.29	-89.55	-124.60	-128.21	-146.84	-114.20

Notes: All regressions include a constant. Standard errors in parentheses. ***, **, * indicate significance at the 1, 5, and 10% level, respectively.

disaggregations of primary commodity exports permitted by this data, only one was significant when introduced into our baseline regression, namely oil versus non-oil. The results are reported in column 7. We add variables that interact the primary commodity export share and its square with a dummy variable that takes the value of unity if the exports are predominantly oil. Both variables are significant: oil exports have a distinct effect on the risk of conflict. However, the effect is modest: at the average value of primary commodity exports oil has the same effect as other commodities. Low levels of oil dependence are somewhat less risky than other commodities and high levels of dependence are somewhat more risky. The disaggregation slightly reduces the sample size, does not change the significance of any of the other variables, and substantially improves the overall fit of the model.[24]

Recall that the other proxies for financial opportunities, the Cold War and diasporas, are not included in this baseline. The end of the Cold War does not appear to have had a significant effect. Diasporas are excluded from the baseline purely for considerations of sample size. In the parsimonious variant in which they are included, their effect on the risk of repeat conflict is substantial: after five years of peace, switching the size of the diaspora from the smallest to the largest found in post-conflict episodes increases the risk of conflict six-fold.

The proxies for earnings foregone have substantial effects. If the enrollment rate for secondary schooling is ten percentage points higher than the average the risk of war is reduced by about three percentage points (a decline in the risk from 11.5 per cent to 8.6 per cent). An additional percentage point on the growth rate reduces the risk of war by about one percentage point (a decline from 11.5 per cent to 10.4 per cent). Our other proxy for the cost of rebellion is also highly significant and substantial. Directly after a civil war there is a high probability of a re-start, the risk being about 32 per cent. This risk declines over time at around one percentage point per year.

The only measures of rebel military advantage that survive into the baseline are population dispersion and social fractionalization. Consistent with Herbst's hypothesis, countries with a highly concentrated population have a very low risk of conflict, whereas those with a highly dispersed population have a very high risk (about 37 per cent). Consistent with the hypothesis that cohesion is important for rebel effectiveness, social fractionalization makes a society substantially safer: a maximally fractionalized society has a conflict risk only one quarter that of a homogenous society.

Only one of the proxies for grievance survives into the baseline regression, namely ethnic dominance. If a country is characterized by ethnic dominance its risk of conflict is nearly doubled. Thus, the net effect of increased social diversity is the sum of its effect on social fractionalization and its effect on ethnic dominance. Starting from homogeneity, as diversity increases the society is likely to become characterized by ethnic dominance, although this will be reversed by further increases in diversity. The risk of conflict would first rise and then fall. Note that while these measures in combination are superficially similar to the hypothesized effect of polarization, our measure of polarization itself is insignificant.

Finally, the coefficient on the scale variable, population, is highly significant and close to unity: risk is approximately proportional to size. We have suggested that proportionality is more likely if conflict is generated by opportunities than by grievances.

1.4 Robustness checks

We now test these baseline results for robustness. We consider the sensitivity both to data and to method. With respect to data, we investigate the effect of outlying observations, and of different definitions of the dependent and independent variables. With respect to method, we investigate random effects, fixed effects and rare events bias.

We investigate outlying observations using two different methods. First, we inspect the characteristics of the 46 conflict episodes used in the baseline regression and second, we use a systematic analysis of influential data points. Since our sample is unbalanced as between events and non-events, the potential problems of outliers arises predominantly among the 46 conflict episodes. Of these conflict episodes, 24 were first-time conflicts and 22 were repeat conflicts.

First, the classification of events in Romania in 1989, and in Iran in 1974, 1978, and 1981 as civil wars is in various respects questionable. They are, on our analysis highly atypical of conflict episodes. Both had secondary school enrolments much higher than the other conflict episodes, and Iran also had an atypically high primary commodity export share. In Table 1.6 column 1 we drop these doubtful observations. No results are overturned, but the performance of the regression improves and all variables are now significant at the 1 per cent or 5 per cent level.

There are four observations of highly negative growth: Angola in 1970–74, Zaïre (now the Democratic Republic of the Congo) in 1990–95, Iran in 1975–79 and Iraq in 1980–84. All of these growth collapses appear to be genuine, and they occur in different countries. We now check whether the result that the growth rate affects conflict risk is dependent upon these four observations, deleting them along with Iran and Romania (Table 1.6, column 2). Growth remains significant, and its coefficient is only slightly reduced. Hence, we can conclude that the increased risk of conflict due to slow growth is not confined to episodes of growth collapse, but is a more continuous relationship.

We next analyse whether our regression results are sensitive to the inclusion of influential data points. Based on the methods developed by Pregibon (1981)[25] we examined which observations may be influential and investigated whether omitting these observations from our baseline model changed our results. We find three influential observations: Congo 1995–99, Iran 1970–74, and Romania 1985–89. However, when we omitted these three observations from our regression, the overall fit of the regression improved (from previously

Table 1.6 Robustness checks

	1 Excluding Iran and Romania	2 Excluding Iran and Romania and growth collapses	3 Excluding influential data points	4 Excluding high primary commodity exporters	5 Peace periods of shorter than one month are treated as continuous wars	6 Peace periods of shorter than one year are treated as continuous wars
Primary commodity exports/GDP	19.696 (6.608)***	19.029 (6.671)***	28.745 (7.862)***	18.771 (6.063)***	19.147 (5.939)***	22.686 (6.718)***
(Prim. com. exports/GDP)^2	-34.090 (14.356)**	-33.250 (14.609)**	-59.818 (17.781)***	-28.466 (12.299)**	-30.150 (12.031)***	-39.053 (14.405)***
Male secondary schooling	-0.035 (0.011)***	-0.037 (0.011)***	-0.041 (0.011)***	-0.031 (0.010)***	-0.031 (0.010)***	-0.031 (0.010)***
(GDP growth) $t-1$	-0.140 (0.047)***	-0.100 (0.052)**	-0.137 (0.046)**	-0.122 (0.044)***	-0.102 (0.044)***	-0.071 (0.047)
Peace duration	-0.004 (0.001)***	-0.003 (0.001)***	-0.004 (0.0011)	-0.004 (0.001)***	-0.003 (0.001)***	-0.003 (0.001)***
Geographic dispersion	-2.114 (1.080)**	-2.272 (1.090)**	-2.890 (1.136)***	-2.449 (1.008)**	-2.541 (1.012)***	-2.953 (1.049)***
Social fractionalization	-0.0002 (0.0001)**	-0.0002 (0.0001)**	-0.0003 (0.0001)***	-0.0002 (0.0001)**	-0.0002 (0.0001)**	-0.0002 (0.0001)***
Ethnic dominance	0.727 (0.368)**	0.732 (0.370)**	0.655 (0.372)*	0.647 (0.354)*	0.732 (0.357)**	0.741 (0.362)**
Ln population	0.747 (0.174)***	0.743 (0.175)***	0.899 (0.195)***	0.772 (0.168)***	0.782 (0.167)***	0.832 (0.176)***
N	674	671	685	662	686	683
No. of wars	42	39	43	46	44	41
Pseudo R^2	0.25	0.22	0.29	0.21	0.23	0.21
Log likelihood	-118.40	-116.17	-114.04	-122.23	-126.33	-122.23

Notes: All regressions include a constant. Standard errors in parentheses. ***, **, * indicate significance at the 1, 5, and 10% level, respectively.
Column 2: We exclude the following three growth collapses: Angola 1970–74, Iraq 1980–84, and Zaire 1990–94.
Column 3: We exclude the following three influential data points: Iran 1970–74, Romania 1985–89, Congo 1995–99.
Column 4: We exclude the countries with the highest primary commodity export to GDP ratio, namely Saudi Arabia, Guyana, Oman, and Trinidad and Tobago. Their average primary commodity export to GDP ratio is 0.504 (sample average 0.158).
Column 5: We exclude the following war starts: Angola 1975 and Somalia 1988.
Column 6: We exclude the following war starts: Angola 1975, Mozambique 1976, Sierra Leone 1997, Somalia 1988 and Zaire/Democratic Rep. of Congo 1997.

$R^2 = 0.24$ to $R^2 = 0.29$) and all of the coefficients remain statistically significant (Table 1.6, column 3).

We now investigate the possibility that a few countries with a high commodity export ratio account for the non-monotonic relationship to conflict risk. This might imply that the reduction in conflict risk only occurred at extreme values of commodity dependence. Four peaceful countries have particularly high values of primary dependence: Saudi Arabia, Guyana, Oman, and Trinidad and Tobago. In Table 1.6, column 4 we present our baseline model excluding these four high primary commodity exporters. The non-monotonic relationship between primary commodity exports and the risk of conflict remains significant, as do all other results.

We next turn to questions of variable definition. The most contentious aspect of the dependent variable is distinguishing between whether a country has a single long war or multiple shorter wars interrupted by periods of peace. In the above analysis we have been guided by the judgement of the political scientists who built the original data sets. Some peace periods are, however, quite short and it might be better to conceptualize these as interludes in a single war. We first reclassified all those wars that were separated by peace periods of less than one month as continuous wars (Table 1.6, column 5). The baseline results are not altered by this redefinition. We then reclassified those wars separated by less than a year as continuous wars (Table 1.6, column 6). The only result to be affected is that the growth rate becomes marginally insignificant ($p = 0.12$), although its coefficient is little changed.[26]

We investigated how robust our results are to the definition of ethnic dominance and social fractionalization. In the baseline we define ethnic dominance as the largest ethnic group constituting 45–90 per cent of the population. We investigate other definitions that either vary the range of the population or use the share of the largest group regardless of its size. As the range is changed from 45–90 per cent the significance level and the coefficient are both reduced, while if the definition is changed more radically to being the population share of the largest group it is completely insignificant. We also find that 'social fractionalization', our measure of cross-cutting cleavages, dominates the other possible aggregation procedures for ethnic and religious diversity. When this measure of fractionalization is included with the ethnic and religious diversity indices either together or individually, it is significant whereas the underlying indices are not significant.

In the baseline we use only the most extreme measure of polarization over the range proposed by Esteban and Ray (1994). However, if this measure is replaced by either the lower bound ($\alpha = 0$), or the central measure ($\alpha = 0.8$) the results are unaffected: polarization remains insignificant and the other variables remain significant. We also experimented with the alternative measure proposed by Reynal-Querol (2002), and with the number of ethnic groups, but with the same result.[27]

In Table 1.7 we investigate a number of different estimation issues. We concentrate on the analysis of random effects, fixed effects, time effects, and a correction for rare events. We re-estimated our models using random effects. For the baseline model we find that the panel data estimator is not different from the pooled estimator, i.e. we accept the hypothesis that we can pool across the observations.[28] The estimation of fixed effects logits was only possible on a very small sub-sample of the observations. The countries for which the dependent variable does not vary over time (the majority of countries

Table 1.7 Estimation issues

	1 Random effects	2 Fixed effects	3 Pooled logit plus time dummies	4 Rare events logit
Primary commodity	18.937	35.850	18.895	17.161
exports/GDP	(5.865)***	(14.436)***	(5.988)***	(6.535)***
(Primary commodity	−29.443	−65.967	−29.815	−25.594
exports/GDP)^2	(11.782)***	(26.964)***	(12.098)***	(14.355)*
Male secondary schooling	−0.032	0.007	−0.031	−0.029
	(0.010)***	(0.033)	(0.010)***	(0.010)***
(GDP growth) $t-1$	−0.115	−0.045	−0.129	−0.110
	(0.043)***	(0.072)	(0.047)***	(0.040)***
Peace duration	−0.004	0.011	−0.004	−0.004
	(0.001)***	(0.002)***	(0.001)***	(0.001)***
Geographic dispersion	−2.487	115.363	−2.447	−2.394
	(1.005)***	(74.562)	(1.018)**	(1.085)**
Social fractionalization	−0.0002	−0.007	−0.0002	−0.0002
	(0.0001)**	(0.006)	(0.0001)**	(0.0001)**
Ethnic dominance	0.670		0.682	0.644
(45–90%)	(0.354)*		(0.359)*	(0.336)*
Ln population	0.768	0.010	0.762	0.726
	(0.166)***	(1.410)	(0.170)***	(0.151)***
*T*70–74			0.725	
			(0.602)	
*T*75–79			0.578	
			(0.608)	
*T*80–84			1.137	
			(0.602)*	
*T*85–89			−0.013	
			(0.757)	
*T*90–94			0.802	
			(0.677)	
*T*95–99			−0.492	
			(0.921)	
N	688	145	688	688
No. of wars	46	44	46	46
Pseudo *R*^{2}			0.26	
Log likelihood	−128.21	−38.18	−124.30	

Notes: All regressions include a constant. Standard errors in parentheses ***, **, * indicate significance at the 1, 5, and 10% level, respectively experienced only peace) cannot be included in the analysis. Although the fixed effects test is very severe, the non-monotonic effect of primary commodity exports remains significant. Were the effect of primary commodity exports dependent only upon cross-section data, it might suggest that the variable was proxying some other characteristic such as geography. However, the fixed effects regression uses only changes in primary commodity dependence, and so reduces the scope for alternative interpretations.[29]

We analysed whether time effects matter by including time dummies in the model. Based on a log likelihood ratio test we cannot reject the hypothesis that the time dummies are zero.[30]

Finally, in the last column of Table 1.7 we use a recently developed correction method for rare events data (King and Zeng, 2001). The event we predict (war) occurs in only about 7 per cent of our observations. King and Zeng show that standard logit estimation tends to underestimate the probability of rare events. We therefore used their correction procedure. The differences between the standard logit results and the rare events corrected results are negligible with all variables significant at the same levels. The mean of the predicted probabilities obtained from the rare events logit regression is 0.072. Thus, we find that the corrected results are very similar to the logit results.

We examined a number of different model specifications. We found that none of the following geographic and demographic characteristics were significant: forest coverage, population density and the proportion of young men aged 15 to 29.[31] We also investigated the potential endogeneity of income to civil war. Evidently since we are measuring income prior to war the endogeneity only arises if a country has more than one war. Since the first war will have reduced income, for subsequent wars the correlation between income and war could in principle reflect this reverse causation. To control for this we re-estimated excluding repeat wars. The income variable remained highly significant.

1.5 Interpretation and conclusion

Using a comprehensive data set of civil wars over the period 1960–99 we used logit regressions to predict the risk of the outbreak of war in each five-year episode. We find that a model that focuses on the opportunities for rebellion performs well, whereas objective indicators of grievance add little explanatory power. The model is robust to a range of tests for outliers, redefinitions, and alternative specifications.

One factor influencing the opportunity for rebellion is the availability of finance. We have shown that primary commodity exports substantially increase conflict risk. We have interpreted this as being due to the opportunities such commodities provide for extortion, making rebellion feasible and perhaps even attractive. An alternative explanation would be that primary commodity dependence worsens governance and so generates stronger grievances. However, we are controlling for economic performance—the level, growth, and distribution of income—and for political rights (which appear not to affect the risk of conflict). While we would not wish to discount the possibility of an effect working through corruption (for which we cannot control), there is plenty of case study evidence supporting the extortion interpretation. Another source of finance for which there is good case study evidence is diasporas. We have found that diasporas substantially increase the risk of conflict renewal, and it is hard to find an alternative explanation for this result.

A second factor influencing opportunity is the cost of rebellion. Male secondary education enrolment, per capita income, and the growth rate all have statistically significant and substantial effects that reduce conflict risk. We have interpreted them as proxying earnings foregone in rebellion: low foregone earnings facilitate conflict. Even if this is correct, low earnings might matter because they are a source of grievance rather than because they make rebellion cheap. However, if rebellion were a protest against low income, we might expect inequality to have strong effects, which we do not find.

A third aspect of opportunity is military advantage. We have found that a dispersed population increases the risk of conflict, and there is weaker evidence that mountainous terrain might also advantage rebels. It remains possible that these are correlated with unmeasured grievances.

Most proxies for grievance were insignificant: inequality, political rights, ethnic polarization, and religious fractionalization. Only 'ethnic dominance'—one ethnic group being a majority—had adverse effects. Even this has to be considered in combination with the benign effects of social fractionalization: societies characterized by ethnic and religious diversity are safer than homogenous societies as long as they avoid dominance. We have suggested that diversity makes rebellion harder because it makes rebel cohesion more costly. It would be difficult to argue that diversity reduced grievance.

Finally, the risk of conflict is proportional to a country's population. We have suggested that both opportunities and grievances increase with population. Thus, the result is compatible with both the opportunity and grievance accounts. However, grievances increase with population due to rising heterogeneity. Yet those aspects of heterogeneity that we are able to measure are not associated with an increased risk of conflict. Hence, a grievance account of the effect of population would need to explain why unobserved, but not observed, heterogeneity increases conflict risk.

One variable, the time since a previous conflict, has substantial effects: time heals. Potentially, this can be interpreted either as opportunity or grievance. It may reflect the gradual depreciation of rebellion-specific capital, and hence an increasing cost of rebellion, or the gradual erosion of hatred. However, we have found that a large diaspora slows the 'healing' process. The known proclivity of diasporas to finance rebel groups offsets the depreciation of rebellion-specific capital, and so would be predicted to delay 'healing'. The diaspora effect thus lends support to the opportunity interpretation.

Opportunity as an explanation of conflict risk is consistent with the economic interpretation of rebellion as greed-motivated. However, it is also consistent with grievance motivation as long as perceived grievances are sufficiently widespread to be common across societies and time. Opportunity can account for the existence of either for-profit, or not-for-profit, rebel organizations. Our evidence does not therefore imply that rebels are necessarily criminals. But the grievances that motivate rebels may be substantially disconnected from the large social concerns of inequality, political rights, and ethnic or religious identity.

Appendix 1.1: A simple migration model

Our estimation of migration is based on the following model

$$dias_{it} = 1.163 \cdot dias_{it} - 0.0002 \cdot \ln GDP_{i,t-1} + 0.003 \cdot war_{i,t-1} + 0.003 \cdot T_{80} + 0.005 \cdot T_{90+} \, 0.013$$
$$(0.045)^{***} \quad (0.001)^{**} \qquad\qquad (0.03) \qquad\qquad (0.002) \qquad (0.002) \qquad (0.008)$$

Where *dias* denotes diaspora which is measured as the ratio of emigrants in the USA to the total population of the country of origin. The variable *war* is a war dummy, measured at $t-1$ it takes a value of one if the country experienced a civil war in the previous period. The method of estimation is OLS. The data is measured at the beginning of each decade, i.e. 1960, 1970, 1980, and 1990. The regression includes time dummies, T, which are jointly significant.

Based on this simple migration model we estimated the size of the diaspora at time t.

$$di\hat{a}s_{it} = x_{it} \cdot \hat{\beta}$$

For countries which experienced a previous civil war we used these estimated values to correct for a possible endogeneity problem. We replaced a total of 64 observations. For countries which did not experience a civil war we use the actual diaspora data. In order to obtain values for 1965 we took the averages of this corrected diaspora data measured in 1960 and 1970, and analogously for the values for 1975 and 1985. For 1995 we use the observations measured in 1990.

Appendix 1.2: Calculating the marginal probabilities

In our regressions we estimate the probability of a war breaking out during a five-year period, and the model can be written in the following general form

$$Y_{it} = a + bX_{it} + cM_{i,t-1} + dZ_i + u_{it} \qquad\qquad (A2.1)$$

where t and i are time and country indicators. The dependent variable is a dummy variable indicating whether a war broke out during the five-year

Table 1A.1 Marginal probabilities

Variable	Coefficient	Mean of X	(1) At the mean	(2) Worst	(3) Best	(4) primary commodity/ GDP = 0.33	(5) 10% extra men in school	(6) 1% extra growth	(7) Min. peace	(8) Max. fractionalization	(9) Ethnic dominance
Primary commodity exports/GDP	18.937	0.158	2.992	6.060	0	6.060	2.992	2.992	2.992	2.992	2.992
(Primary commodity exports/GDP)^2	−29.443		−0.735	−3.015	0	−3.015	−0.735	−0.735	−0.735	−0.735	−0.735
Male secondary schooling	−0.032	44.489	−1.406	−0.032	−4.645	−1.406	−1.722	−1.406	−1.406	−1.406	−1.406
(GDP growth)$_{t-1}$	−0.115	1.618	−0.186	1.508	−1.660	−0.186	−0.186	−0.417	−0.186	−0.186	−0.186
Peace duration	−0.004	347.5	−1.286	−0.004	−2.19	−1.286	−1.286	−1.286	−0.004	−1.286	−1.286
Geographic dispersion	−2.487	0.602	−1.497	0.000	−2.415	−1.497	−1.497	−1.497	−1.497	−1.497	−1.497
Social fractionalization	−0.0002	1790	−0.376	−0.004	−1.465	−0.376	−0.376	−0.376	−0.376	−1.465	−0.376
Ethnic dominance (45–90%)	0.670	0.439	0.294	0.670	0	0.294	0.294	0.294	0.294	0.294	0.670
Ln population	0.768	30,500,000	13.230	16.049	9.136	13.230	13.230	13.230	13.230	13.230	13.230
Constant	−13.073		−13.073	−13.073	−13.073	−13.073	−13.073	−13.073	−13.073	−13.073	−13.073
$\hat{W}$			−2.043	8.160	−16.312	−1.255	−2.359	−2.273	−0.761	−3.132	−1.667
$\hat{p}$			0.115	1.000	0.000	0.222	0.086	0.093	0.318	0.042	0.159

period, so that Y_{it} is the log odds of war. The explanatory variables are either measured at the beginning of the period (for example, income per capita, primary commodity exports/GDP, population), or during the previous five-year period (for instance, per capita income growth), or are time invariant or changing slowly over time (for example, social fractionalization).

The expected probability $\hat{p}_{it}$ of a war breaking out can be calculated by using the estimated coefficients obtained from equation (A1.1):

$$\hat{a} + \hat{b}X_{it} + \hat{c}M_{i,t-1} + \hat{d}Z_i = \hat{W}_{it} \tag{A2.2}$$

$$\hat{p}_{it} = \frac{e^{\hat{W}_{it}}}{(1 + e^{W_{it}})} \cdot 100 \tag{A2.3}$$

Appendix 1.3: Data sources

Democracy   The degree of openness of democratic institutions is measured on a scale of zero (low) to ten (high). Source: http://www.cidcm.umd.edu/polity/index.html. The data are described in Jaggers and Gurr (1995).

Diaspora   We used the data on the foreign born population from the US Bureau of the Census and divided these numbers by the total population in the country of origin. http://www.census.gov/population/

Ethnic dominance   Using the ethno-linguistic data from the original data source (USSR, 1964) we calculated an indicator of ethnic dominance. This variable takes the value of one if one single ethno-linguistic group makes up 45 to 90 per cent of the total population and zero otherwise. We would like to thank Tomila Lankina for the translation of the original data source.

Forest coverage   We used the FAO measure of the proportion of a country's terrain which is covered in woods and forest. Source: http://www.fao.org/forestry.

GDP per capita   We measure income as real PPP adjusted GDP per capita. The primary data set is the Penn World Tables 5.6 (Summers and Heston, 1991). Since the data are only available from 1960–92 we used the growth rates of real PPP adjusted GDP per capita data from the World Bank's World Development Indicators 1998 in order to obtain income data for the 1990s. These GDP per capita data were used to calculate the average annual growth rate over the previous five years.

Geographic dispersion of the population   We constructed a dispersion index of the population on a country by country basis. Based on population data for 400 km² cells we generated a Gini coefficient of population dispersion for each country. A value of 0 indicates that the population is evenly distributed across the country and a value of 1 indicates that the total population is concentrated in one area. Data is available for 1990 and 1995. For years prior to

1990 we used the 1990 data. We would like to thank Uwe Deichman of the World Bank's Geographic Information System Unit for generating this data. He used the following data sources: Center for International Earth Science Information Network (CIESIN), Columbia University; International Food Policy Research Institute (IFPRI); and World Resources Institute (WRI). 2000. Gridded Population of the World (GPW), Version 2. Palisades, NY: IESIN, Columbia University. Available at http://sedac.ciesin.org/plue/gpw.

Inequality   Inequality was either measured as income inquality (source: Deininger and Squire, 1996) or as inequality in land ownership (source: Deininger and Squire, unpublished). Both inequality measures are provided as a Gini coefficient.

Male secondary school enrolment rates   We measure male secondary school enrolment rates as gross enrolment ratios, i.e. the ratio of total enrolment, regardless of age, to the population of the age group that officially corresponds to the level of education shown. Secondary education completes the provision of basic education that began at the primary level, and aims at laying the foundations for lifelong learning and human development, by offering more subject- or skill-oriented instruction using more specialized teachers. Source: World Bank Development Indicators, 1998.

Mountainous terrain   The proportion of a country's terrain which is mountainous was measured by John Gerrard, a physical geographer who specialized in mountainous terrain. His measure is based not just on altitude but takes into account plateaus and rugged uplands. The data are presented in Gerrard (2000).

Peace duration   This variable measures the length of the peace period (in months) since the end of the previous civil war. For countries which never experienced a civil war we measure the peace period since the end of World War II.

Population   Population measures the total population, the data source is the World Bank's World Development Indicators 1998.

Primary commodity exports/GDP   The ratio of primary commodity exports to GDP proxies the abundance of natural resources. The data on primary commodity exports and GDP were obtained from the World Bank. Export and GDP data are measured in current US dollars.

Social, ethnolinguistic, and religious fractionalization   We proxy social fractionalization in a combined measure of ethnic and religious fractionalization. Ethnic fractionalization is measured by the ethno-linguistic fractionalization index. It measures the probability that two randomly drawn individuals from a given country do not speak the same language. Data are only available for 1960. In the economics literature this measure was first used by Mauro (1995). Using data from Barrett (1982) on religious affiliations we constructed an analogous religious fractionalization index. Following Barro (1997) we aggregated the various religious affiliations into nine categories: Catholic, Protestant, Muslim, Jew, Hindu, Buddhist, Eastern Religions (other than Buddhist), Indigenous Religions, and no religious affiliation.

The fractionalization indices range from zero to 100. A value of zero indicates that the society is completely homogenous whereas a value of 100 would characterize a completely heterogeneous society.

We calculated our social fractionalization index as the product of the ethno-linguistic fractionalization and the religious fractionalization index plus the ethno-linguistic or the religious fractionalization index, whichever is the greater. By adding either index we avoid classifying a country as homogenous (a value of zero) if the country is ethnically homogenous but religiously divers, or vice versa.

War data   A civil war is defined as an internal conflict in which at least 1,000 battle related deaths (civilian and military) occurred per year. We use mainly the data collected by Small and Singer (1992) and according to their definitions (Singer and Small, 1984) we updated their data set for 1992–99.

Notes

1   On the analysis of the duration of civil war see Collier *et al.* (2004) and Fearon (2004).
2   By the 'Machiavelli Theorem' (Hirshleifer, 2001, pp. 10–11) no one will pass up a profitable opportunity to exploit someone else.
3   In Table 1.6 we examine whether our results are sensitive to this definition of civil war. Sambanis (2002) comes to a similar conclusion.
4   We list the data sources and definitions in Appendix 1.3.
5   The standard deviation of primary commodity exports is 0.11 for the conflict episodes and 0.19 for the peace episodes.
6   Collier (2000) provides an illustrative formal model of such a non-monotonic relationship.
7   The economic growth literature concentrates on the analysis of political instability as a determinant of economic growth (see for example Barro 1991, 1997). Alesina *et al.* (1996) estimate a simultaneous equation system of economic growth and political instability. They present support for the hypothesis that political instability reduces growth. Lower growth does not seem to cause political instability, defined as the number of government changes. However, when they define political instability more narrowly as unconstitutional government changes they find that lower growth rates are a causal factor of political instability.
8   For the calculation of the Gini coefficient we used the population data per 400 km² cell. Analogous to the income Gini coefficient, the Gini coefficient of population dispersion will be high if the population is concentrated in a relatively small area of the country.
9   If there were *e* equally sized ethnic groups and *r* equally sized religious groups, maximum potential social fractionalization would be measured simply by the product *er*. Since both the underlying indices of ethnic and religious fractionalization range on the scale 0–100, their product is zero if there is either religious or ethnic homogeneity whereas there is social homogeneity only if both indices are zero. We therefore measure social fractionalization as the product of the underlying indices plus whichever index is the greater.

10 The link from polarization to conflict is proposed by Esteban and Ray (1999) and Reynal-Querol (2000) and is common in the popular literature.

11 Our data source was *Atlas Narodov Mira*, USSR (1964). The Esteban-Ray measure includes a coefficient d that denotes the degree of antagonism between two different ethnic groups. Obviously, in large samples such as we are using this is not observed. Following Reynal-Querol (2000) we assume that the distance between any two ethnic groups is unity whereas that within the group is zero, so that d has the properties: $d = 1$ if $i \neq j$ and $d = 0$ if $i = j$.

12 For $\alpha = 0$ the polarization measure is equal to the Gini coefficient.

13 This is analogous to the theory of tax exit proposed by Buchanan and Faith (1987).

14 Mounting diversity is the offset to scale economies in the provision of public goods in the model of optimal county size proposed by Alesina and Spolaore (1997).

15 This approach contrasts with our initial work (Collier and Hoeffler, 1998) in which we used a tobit procedure to study the duration of civil war (on a much inferior data set) and argued that the same factors that determined duration would determine the risk of initiation. Collier *et al.* (2004) establishes that this is wrong: initiation and duration are radically different processes.

16 We differentiate the probability of civil war with respect to primary commodity exports and find that the risk is at its maximum at 33 per cent of primary exports in GDP ($18.149/(2*27.445) = 0.33$).

17 We retain the two geographic measures, population dispersion and mountainous terrain. Although their exclusion does not affect the results, non-economists often find the proposition that geographic opportunity affects conflict plausible and inoffensive, while contesting the role of economic opportunity. We retain population size as a scale variable.

18 At this stage we measure polarization with $\alpha = 1.6$ and define ethnic dominance as occurring when the largest ethnic group constitutes 45–90 per cent of the population. These specifications are justified in Section 1.4 where we investigate robustness to alternative definitions.

19 We also tried the ratio of the income shares of the top to the bottom quintiles. This was also insignificant.

20 The J-test is based on the following artificial nesting procedure. First we explain the risk of civil war, p, in terms of the two different models, opportunity and grievance.
(1) $p = f(\text{opportunity})$
(2) $p = f(\text{grievance})$
Based on these logit regressions we calculate the predicted probabilities and add these predicted values, $\hat{p}^{\text{opportunity}}$ and $\hat{p}^{\text{grievance}}$ to our alternative models.
(1) $p = f(\text{opportunity}, \hat{p}^{\text{grievance}})$
(2) $p = f(\text{grievance}, \hat{p}^{\text{opportunity}})$
According to the J-test the significance of the coefficients of these added variables enables us to choose between the two different models. If $\hat{p}^{\text{grievance}}$ is significant in the opportunity model we reject the opportunity model in favor of the grievance model. If $\hat{p}^{\text{opportunity}}$ is significant in the grievance model we reject the grievance model in favor of the opportunity model. As can be seen in columns 1 and 2 of Table 1.5, $\hat{p}^{\text{grievance}}$ is significant in the opportunity model and $\hat{p}^{\text{opportunity}}$ is significant in the grievance model.

21 Using the same sample as for the combined model ($n = 665$) we obtain the following results: Opportunity model versus combined model, 5 degrees of freedom, Likelihood Ratio Test (LRT) statistic 7.85 ($p = 0.165$); grievance model versus combined model, 6 degrees of freedom, LRT statistic 29.64 ($p = 0.000$).

22 We tried different specifications to test for the effect of political repression by investigating non-linear effects, by including the autocracy score instead of the democracy score, and by using the difference between the two variables as

suggested by Londregan and Poole (1996). We also tried the Freedom House measure of political freedom, but neither of these alternative political repression measures were found to be significant.

23 We would like to thank Jan Dehn for providing us with the data that enabled this disaggregation.

24 Furthermore, using data from Dehn (2000) we investigated whether contemporaneous export price changes altered the risk of conflict. We could not find any evidence to support this hypothesis.

25 Long (1997) pp. 98–101 provides a discussion of influence in limited dependent variable models.

26 We also examined the effect of time since the previous conflict in more detail by including the natural logarithm of the peace variable or its square, however, a linear decay term provides a better fit. Note that the measure of peace since the end of the civil war is somewhat imprecise since we only measure it from the end of the war to the initial year of each sub-period. A duration model of post-war peace would allow a more detailed analysis of this peace effect, however, the duration model results in Collier *et al.* (2004) support the results presented in this paper.

27 All of these robustness checks are presented in Collier and Hoeffler (2002).

28 A LRT provides a x^2 statistic of 0 ($p = 0.998$). Thus, we cannot reject the null-hypothesis that the panel data and pooled estimator provide the same results.

29 We also investigated the effect of commodity prices. Since prices are exogenous, they can be entered contemporaneous with the episode being predicted, whereas our value-based proxy has to be lagged. We experimented with both the level of export prices and with the change in prices from the previous period. However, in either form when added to the baseline regression the variable was insignificant. The fact that lagged values of exports are significant even in the fixed effects regression suggests that rebels do respond to changes in values, but the response is evidently not so rapid as to give rise to an in-period price response. Potentially, the effect on conflict risk captures the 'voracity effect' predicted by Lane and Tornell (1999) whereby an increase in the price of a natural resource export would induce more than the increment in value to be devoted to conflict. Our results suggest that there may be such an effect but that it is lagged.

30 The LRT statistic is 7.83, 6 restrictions ($p = 0.251$).

31 The proportion of the population living in urban areas was statistically significant when we excluded the geographic concentration of the population. However, when we included both proxies for the concentration of the population, the geographic concentration measure remained statistically significant while the proportion of the population living in urban areas was marginally insignificant ($p = 0.11$).

References

Alesina, A., Baqir, R., and Easterly, W. (1999). 'Public goods and ethnic divisions', *Quarterly Journal of Economics*, 114, 1243–84.

Alesina, A., Oetzler, S., Roubini, N., and Swagel, P. (1996). 'Political instability and economic growth', *Journal of Economic Growth*, 1, 189–211.

Alesina, A. and Spolaore, E. (1997). 'On the number and the size of nations', *Quarterly Journal of Economics*, 112, 1027–56.

Angoustures, A. and Pascal, V. (1996). 'Diasporas et financement des conflicts', in F. Jean and J-C. Rufin (eds), *Economie des Guerres Civiles*, Paris: Hachette.

Barro, R.J. (1991). 'Economic growth in a cross section of countries', *Quarterly Journal of Economics*, 106, 407–43.

Barro, R.J. (ed.) (1997). *Determinants of Economic Growth*, Cambridge, MA: MIT Press.

Barrett, D.B. (ed.) (1982). *World Christian Encyclopedia*, Oxford: Oxford University Press.

Buchanan, J.M. and Faith, R.L. (1987). 'Secession and the limits of taxation: towards a theory of internal exit', *American Economic Review*, 77, 1023–31.

Collier, P. (2000). 'Rebellion as a quasi-criminal activity', *Journal of Conflict Resolution*, 44, 839–53.

Collier, P. (2001). 'Ethnic diversity: an economic analysis of its implications', *Economic Policy*, 32, 129–66.

Collier, P. and Hoeffler, A. (1998). 'On the economic causes of civil war', *Oxford Economic Papers*, 50, 563–73.

Collier, P. and Hoeffler, A. (2002). 'Greed and grievance in civil war', CSAE Working Paper, WPS 2002–01, Oxford University. http://www.economics.ox.ac.uk/CSAEadmin/workingpapers/pdfs/2002–01 text.pdf.

Collier, P., Hoeffler, A., and Söderbom, M. (2004). 'On the duration of civil war.' *Journal of Peace Research*, 41, 253–73.

Davidson, R. and MacKinnon, J.G. (1981). 'Several tests for model specification in the presence of alternative hypotheses', *Econometrica*, 49, 781–93.

Dehn, J. (2000). 'Commodity price uncertainty, investment and shocks: implications for economic growth', D.Phil. thesis, University of Oxford.

Deininger, K. and Squire, L. (1996). 'A new data set measuring income inequality', *World Bank Economic Review*, 10, 565–91.

Deininger, K. and Squire, L. (1998). 'New ways of looking at old issues: inequality and growth', *Journal of Development Economics*, 57, 249–87.

Easterly, W. and Levine, R. (1997). 'Africa's growth tragedy: policies and ethnic divisions.' *Quarterly Journal of Economics*, 113, 203–49.

Esteban, J-M. and Ray, D. (1994). 'On the measurement of polarization', *Econometrica*, 62, 819–51.

Esteban, J-M. and Ray, D. (1999). 'Conflict and distribution', *Journal of Economic Theory*, 87, 379–415.

Figes, O. (1996). *A People's Tragedy: The Russian Revolution 1891–1924*, London: Pimlico.

Fearon, J. (2004) 'Why do some civil wars last so much longer than others?' *Journal of Peace Research*, 41, 275–301.

Gerrard, A.J.W. (2000). 'What is a mountain?', mimeo, DECRG, Washington, DC: World Bank.

Grossman, H.I. (1991). 'A general equilibrium model of insurrections', *American Economic Review*, 81, 912–21.

Grossman, H.I. (1999). 'Kleptocracy and revolutions', *Oxford Economic Papers*, 51, 267–83.

Hegre, H., Ellingsen, T., Gates, S., and Gleditsch, N-P. (2001). 'Toward a democratic civil peace? Democracy, political change, and civil war, 1816–1992', *American Political Science Review*, 95, 33–48.

Herbst, J. (2000). *States and Power in Africa*, Princeton NJ: Princeton University Press.

Hirshleifer, J. (1995). 'Theorizing about conflict', in K. Hartley and T. Sandler (eds), *Handbook of Defense Economics*, Vol. 1, Elsevier Science, Amsterdam, 165–89.

Hirshleifer, J. (2001). *The Dark Side of the Force: Economic Foundations of Conflict Theory*, Cambridge: Cambridge University Press.

Jaggers, K. and Gurr, T.R. (1995). 'Tracking democracy's third wave with the Polity III data', *Journal of Peace Research*, 32, 469–82.

King, G. and Zeng, L. (2001). 'Logistic regression in rare events data', *Political Analysis*, 9, 137–63.

Klare, M.T. (2001). *Natural Resource Wars: The New Landscape of Global Conflict*, New York: Metropolitan Books.

Lane, A. and Tornell, P.R. (1999). 'The voracity effect', *American Economic Review*, 89, 22–46.

Londregan, J.B. and Poole, K.T. (1996). 'Does high income promote democracy?', *World Politics*, 49, 1–30.

Long, J.S. (1997). *Regression Models for Categorical and Limited Dependent Variables*, London: Sage Publications.

Mauro, P. (1995). 'Corruption and growth', *Quarterly Journal of Economics*, 110, 681–712.

Pregibon, D. (1981). 'Logistic regression diagnostics', *The Annals of Statistics*, 9, 705–24.

Reynal-Querol, M. (2000). 'Religious conflict and growth: theory and evidence'. Ph.D. thesis, London School of Economics and Political Science.

Reynal-Querol, M. (2002). 'Ethnicity, political systems and civil war', *Journal of Conflict Resolution*, 46, 29–54.

Sachs, J. and Warner, A.M. (2000). 'Natural resource abundance and economic growth', in G.M. Meier and J.E. Rauch (eds), *Leading Issues in Economic Development*, 7th ed., Oxford: Oxford University Press.

Sambanis, N. (2002). 'What is a civil war? Conceptual and empirical complexities of an operational definition', mimeo, Yale University.

Sen, A. (1973). *On Economic Inequality*, Oxford: Clarendon Press.

Singer, D.J. and Small, M. (1994). 'Correlates of war project: international and civil war data, 1816–1992', data file, Inter-University Consortium for Political and Social Research, Michigan: Ann Arbor.

Small, M. and Singer, J.D. (1982). *Resort to Arms: International and Civil War, 1816–1980*, Beverly Hills, CA: Sage.

The Stockholm International Peace Research Institute (2002). *Yearbook of World Armaments and Disarmaments*, Oxford: Oxford University Press.

Summers, R. and Heston, A. (1991). 'The Penn World Table (Mark 5): an expanded set of international comparisons, 1950–1988', *Quarterly Journal of Economics*, 99, 327–68.

USSR (1964). *Atlas Narodov Mira*, Moscow: Department of Geodesy and Cartography of the State Geological Committee of the USSR.

World Bank (2000). *World Development Indicators*, Washington DC, data file.

2 Beyond greed and grievance

Feasibility and civil war

With Anke Hoeffler and Dominic Rohner

2.1 Introduction

Over the past half-century civil war has replaced international war as the most prevalent form of large-scale violence. Once started, civil wars are hard to stop: they persist for more than ten times as long as international wars. Their consequences are usually dire, being massively destructive to the economy, to the society, and to life itself. The prevention of civil war is therefore rightly seen as one of the key priorities for international attention. Informed strategies of prevention must rest upon an analysis of what makes situations prone to civil war. Precisely because in any particular violent conflict the issue is highly politicized, with supporters of each side proffering a litany of self-serving 'explanations', the public discourse is hopelessly contaminated by advocacy. The issue is thus particularly well-suited to statistical analysis of global data. This approach both abstracts from any particular conflict and subjects the researcher to the discipline of statistical method.

This approach to establishing the factors which make a country prone to civil war was pioneered in Collier and Hoeffler (1998, 2004). Since those papers, the literature, the data, and our own thinking have all advanced considerably. In the present chapter we revisit the issue, replicating, overturning, and extending our earlier results.

The foundation for serious quantitative analysis of civil war was laid by political scientists at the University of Michigan, the university that pioneered much quantitative political analysis, who carefully built a comprehensive global data set on civil wars, the Correlates of War Project (COW). Using this data set, its variants and now its rivals, economists and political scientists have begun to analyze the factors that might account for the onset of conflict (Collier and Hoeffler, 1998, 2004; Fearon and Laitin, 2003; Miguel, Satyanath and Sergenti, 2004). Quantitative analysis based on global data sets has its own severe limitations imposed by data constraints and so should be seen as complementing qualitative in-country research rather than supplanting it. As data constraints are periodically relaxed so opportunities for better quantitative analysis are opened. The present paper uses such an opportunity, aspiring to be definitive conditional upon the recent quantum expansion in data, both for the dependent and independent variables, in respect of quality, quantity and timeliness. One reason for a quantum expansion in the data for our analysis is an artefact of our dependent variable: the risk of civil war during a five-year period. Our previous analysis closed in December 1999 and we are now able to include a further five years. Since 2000 there has been a shift towards international intervention, notably the United Nations policy of a 'responsibility to protect' (Evans and Sahnoun, 2002) and the replacement of the Organization of African Unity, with its principle of 'non-interference', by the African Union with its principle of 'non-indifference'. These shifts in sentiment were reflected in an increase in the number of settlements of civil war that was sufficiently dramatic to suggest a significant break with past behaviour. Hence, it is of particular interest to investigate whether there was a corresponding significant change in the incidence of civil war onsets. There have also been striking advances in the quantification of potential explanatory variables. These enable us to investigate a new range of social and political variables. Using the technique of stepwise deletion of insignificant variables we arrive at a provisional core regression in which all terms are significant. We then conduct specification tests to ensure that no additional significant variable can be added. The resulting regression has a reasonable claim to be the best characterization of the data. Since we adopted this same approach in our previous study, albeit on substantially inferior data, a comparison of our results from the two studies provides some indication of how robust the present results are likely to prove to further inevitable improvements and innovations in data sets.

Our own thinking on proneness to civil war has also evolved. As implied by the title 'greed and grievance', our previous paper was still rooted in the traditional focus on the motivation for rebellion. Since then our work has increasingly called into question whether motivation is as important as past emphasis upon it had implied (Collier and Hoeffler, 2007). Instead of the circumstances which generate a rebellion being distinctive in terms of motivation, they might be distinctive in the sheer financial and military feasibility of rebellion. We have formulated this into the 'feasibility hypothesis': that where a rebellion is feasible it will occur. While in this paper the spirit of our empirical analysis is to provide a comprehensive investigation of the factors that make a country prone to civil war rather than to test a single hypothesis, along the way we will investigate whether the feasibility hypothesis can be disconfirmed.

In Section 2.2 we set out the theoretical framework for our analysis. By combining motivation and opportunity, our framework encompasses a range of political science analyses which stress various types of motivation, and economic analyses some of which focus on motives while others focus on opportunities. In Section 2.3 we discuss the data, focusing upon the major expansions and revisions since our previous article. In Section 2.4 we report our results. Although our previous results are broadly confirmed, we find three new variables to be significant. Not only are these three variables important in their own right, they provide a somewhat firmer basis for discriminating between theories. Section 2.5 concludes with a discussion of the implications for policy towards promoting civil peace.

2.2 The economic theory of civil war

Just as the quantitative study of civil war has evolved rapidly, so has its analysis using standard applications of economic theory.[1] Whereas traditional political analyses either assumed or asserted some particular 'root cause' of civil war, usually traced to an historical grievance, modern economic theory focuses on the feasibility of rebellion as well as its motivation. The defining feature of a civil war is large scale organized violence on the part of a rebel army. This is not meant to imply that the rebel side is 'to blame', but rather that since virtually all governments maintain standing armies, the distinctive feature of civil war is the existence of a non-government army. In most circumstances the establishment of a rebel army would be both prohibitively expensive and extremely dangerous regardless of its agenda. The relatively rare circumstances in which rebellion is financially and militarily feasible are therefore likely to constitute an important part of any explanation of civil war. Hirshleifer (2001), who pioneered much of the analytic research on conflict, proposed the Machiavelli Theorem, that no profitable opportunity for violence would go unused. Our variant of this theorem, the *feasibility hypothesis*, proposes that where rebellion is materially feasible it will occur. This can be expressed as the following, empirically testable hypothesis:

> Factors that are important for the financial and militarily feasibility of rebellion but are unimportant for motivation decisively increase the risk of civil war.

The feasibility hypothesis leaves the motivation of the rebel group unspecified, its initial agenda being determined by the preferences of the social entrepreneur leading whichever organization is the first to occupy the niche. Sometimes this will be a not-for-profit organization with a political or religious agenda, and sometimes a for-profit organization. Where the niche is sufficiently large several rebel groups may coexist, but the factors that explain the initial rebel agendas are incidental to the explanation of civil war. Weinstein (2005) provides an interesting extension: rather than motivation being orthogonal to the feasibility of civil war it may be determined by it. He shows that regardless of the initial agenda, where there is manifest scope for loot-seeking self-selection of recruits will gradually transform the rebel organization into one motivated by loot-seeking.

The two most obvious material conditions for rebellion are financial and military. A rebel army is hugely more expensive than a political party and faces far more acute organizational difficulties of raising voluntary contributions from within the country. For example, the Tamil Tigers, a relatively small rebel group in the small developing country of Sri Lanka, is estimated to spend between $200m and $350m per year, an amount equal to between 20 per cent and 34 per cent of the GDP of Northeast Sri Lanka, the zone it controls and for which it seeks political secession (see Strategic Foresight Group, 2006). In Britain, the leading opposition political party, unusually well-funded because it is pro-business, spends around $50m per year (see Conservative Party of Great-Britain, 2005), or about 0.002 per cent of GDP. The Tamil Tigers are far short of being the best-funded rebel group in the world: their scale of funding is probably fairly normal for a rebel group, and the Conservative Party is far from being at the impecunious end of the distribution of opposition political parties. Yet the Tamil Tigers are commanding resources at least 10,000 times greater as a share of GDP than one of the world's major political opposition parties. More generally, a rebellion cannot be regarded as a natural evolution from, or alternative to, political protest: it requires a quantum difference in financial resources. Often a rebellion will simply be beyond the financial means of those groups politically opposed to the government. Similarly, in most states rebellion is not militarily feasible: the government has effective localized control of its entire territory. Financial and military viability are evidently interdependent: conditional upon the efficacy of government security there is some minimum military scale of rebellion which is capable of survival, and this determines the height of the financial hurdle that must be surmounted by an organization that aspires to rebellion. Viability is likely to be assisted by some combination of a geography that provides safe havens and an ineffective state.

This account can be contrasted with the more traditional grievance-based explanation which proposes that objective social exclusion explains civil war. However, the grievance-based account is itself only a subset of accounts based on motivation. While for purposes of propaganda rebel leaders are indeed likely to explain their motivation in terms of grievances, other plausible motivations for organized private violence would include predation and sadism. Indeed, since the typical civil war lasts for many years and rebel victories are rare, if rebellion is rational motivations are likely to reflect benefits during conflict, rather than prospective benefits consequent upon a victory which must be heavily discounted both by time and risk. Further, if the rebellion is rationally motivated it is more likely to be due to benefits that accrue to the rebel leadership itself, rather than to the attainment of social justice for a wider group: social justice is a public good and so faces acute collective action problems. Even if these collective action problems could be overcome, during civil war civilian suffering is very widespread so that the social groups that rebel leaders claim to be fighting for are likely to lose heavily: rebellion is far more likely to deliver devastation than justice. This opens a further motive-based account of civil war: rebellions may be due to mistakes, or they may even be non-rational. The former possibility has been developed in theories analogous to the winner's curse of auction theory: rebellions occur due to military over-optimism. The latter has not been explored formally, but there is evidence that several rebel leaders have shown signs of irrationality. Based on the examples of Bosnia and Rwanda, Mueller (2004) suggests that leaders whip up hatred and recruit 'fanatics, criminals and hooligans' to commit most of the violence. A further likely example of irrationality is the Ugandan Lord's Resistance Army whose leader claims to fight for the rights of the Acholi ethnic group in Northern Uganda. This rebel organisation has killed and kidnapped many members of its own ethnic group. With its only stated goal being the establishment of rule by the Ten Commandments, it may be more closely analogous to freak religious groups such as Waco and Jones-town than to organizations of political opposition.

An implication of the wide range of possible explanations for rebellion is that the factors which potentially cause it cannot be restricted *a priori* to a narrow range of proxies for grievance. Our approach is rather to find proxies for each of the three major perspectives: feasibility, and the two main variants of motivation, greed and grievance. In practice, due to the limitations of data that are available globally for several decades, some concepts can only be proxied by variables that have more than one possible interpretation. This was, unfortunately, the case with our previous results. In the present analysis we introduce three new variables that have less ambiguous interpretations and so enable us to distinguish more readily between feasibility and motivation.

2.3 Data and method

We examine how likely it is for a country to experience an outbreak of civil war. War starts are coded as a binary variable and we analyze this risk by using logit regressions. The risk of a war start is examined in five year periods, from 1965–69 until 2000–2004. If a war breaks out during the five year period we code this as a one and zero if the country remained peaceful. We code ongoing war observations as missing because we do not want to conflate the analysis of war initiation with the analysis of its duration. Previous research indicates that the duration of a civil war is determined by different factors from their onset (Collier, Hoeffler and Söderbom 2004). In order to code civil war starts we used data provided by Kristian Gleditsch (2004), who has carefully updated the correlates of war (COW) project (Small and Singer, 1982, and Singer and Small, 1994).[2] An advantage of using this data set is that it is an update of the data used in our previous work (Collier and Hoeffler, 2004) which makes comparisons between the previous and new results relatively straightforward. We perform robustness checks on an alternative new data set. Our analysis potentially includes 208 countries and 84 civil war outbreaks. We list these wars in Table 2.1.

The COW definition of civil wars is based on four main characteristics. It requires that there is organized military action and that at least 1,000 battle

Table 2.1 List of civil wars

Country	War	Country	War	Country	War	Country	War
Afghanistan	1978–2001	DRC	1960–1965	Liberia*	1989–1990	Serbia*	1991–1992
Algeria	1962–1963	DRC*	1993	Liberia*	1992–1995	Serbia	1998–1999
Algeria*	1992–2000	DRC*	1996–2000	Liberia*	1996	Sierra Leone*	1991–1996
Angola*	1975–1991	CongoRep.*	1997–1999	Liberia	2003	Sierra Leone*	1998–2000
Angola*	1992–1994	Côte d'Ivoire*	2002–ongoing	Mozambique*	1979–1992	Somalia*	1982–1997
Angola*	1998–2001	Dom. Rep.	1965	Myanmar*	1968–1980	South Africa*	1989–1993
Azerbaijan	1991–1994	El Salvador*	1979–1992	Myanmar*	1983–1995	South Africa*	1999–2002
Burundi*	1972	Ethiopia*	1974–1991	Nepal	2002–ongoing	Sri Lanka*	1971
Burundi*	1988	Guatemala*	1966–1972	Nicaragua*	1978–1979	Sri Lanka*	1983–1993
Burundi*	1991–1992	Guatemala*	1978–1984	Nicaragua*	1982–1990	Sri Lanka*	1995–2001
Burundi	1993–1998	Guinea-Biss.*	1998	Nigeria*	1967–1970	Sudan	1963–1972
Burundi	2000–2002	India*	1985–1993	Nigeria*	1980–1981	Sudan*	1983–1992
Cambodia	1970–1975	India*	2002–ongoing	Nigeria	1984	Sudan*	1995–ongoing
Cambodia	1978–1991	Indonesia	1956–1960	Pakistan*	1971	Thailand*	1970–1973
Cambodia	1993–1997	Iran*	1978–1979	Pakistan	1973–1977	Turkey*	1991–2002
Cameroon	1959–1961	Iran*	1981–1982	Pakistan*	1994–1995	Uganda	1966
Chad*	1966–1971	Iraq	1961–1963	Peru*	1982–1995	Uganda*	1980–1988
Chad	1980–1988	Iraq*	1974–1975	Philippines*	1972–1992	Uganda*	1996–2001
Chad*	1990	Iraq*	1985–1993	Philippines*	2000–2001	Uganda*	2004–ongoing
Chile*	1973	Iraq	1996	Romania*	1989	Vietnam	1960–1965
China*	1967–1968	Jordan*	1970	Russia*	1994–1996	Yemen	1962–1969
Colombia*	1984–1993	Lao PDR	1960–1962	Russia*	1998–ongoing	Yemen	1986
Colombia*	1998–ongoing	Lao PDR	1963–1973	Rwanda*	1963–1964	Yemen	1994
		Lebanon	1975–1990	Rwanda*	1990–1993	Zimbabwe*	1972–1979
				Rwanda	1994		
				Rwanda*	1998		

Source: Gleditsch (2004).

Note: War observations marked with an asterisk are included in our core model (Table 2.3, column 4). If two wars broke out in the same five-year period we only coded one war start.

deaths resulted in a given year.[3] In order to distinguish wars from genocides, massacres and pogroms there has to be effective resistance; at least five per cent of the deaths have been inflicted by the weaker party. A further requirement is that the national government at the time was actively involved. Our alternative measure of civil war, which we use for robustness checks, is based on the 'Armed Conflict Dataset' (ACD) by Nils Petter Gleditsch *et al.* (2002). Their definition has two main dimensions. First, they distinguish four types of violent conflicts according to the participants and location: (1) extra-systemic conflicts (essentially colonial or imperialist wars), (2) inter-state wars, (3) intrastate wars and (4) internationalized intrastate wars. The second dimension defines the level of violence. *Minor* conflicts produce more than 25 battle related deaths per year, *intermediate* conflicts produce more than 25 battle related deaths per year and a total conflict history of more than 1,000 battle related deaths and lastly *wars* are conflicts which result in more than 1,000 battle related deaths per year. We coded civil wars as all armed conflicts except interstate wars, dating the war start for the first year when the violence level was coded as *war*, and the end as the first year when the armed conflict did not generate any deaths.

There are a large number of factors that may determine what makes a country more prone to a civil war. While we do not consider idiosyncratic characteristics for individual countries, such as trigger events and leadership, we have collected a wide variety of economic, political, sociological, geographic and historical variables for our global cross-country panel. We present the summary statistics in Table 2.2 and list the data sources in Appendix 2.1.

We start with a comprehensive model of factors that potentially influence the risk of rebellion. The theoretical and empirical justifications for consider-ing these factors are discussed below. We then delete stepwise the variables that are not significant to end up with our core model described in Table 2.3, column 4. We have tested different ways of excluding variables to avoid issues of path dependency. The following key variables are included in the initial model. In what follows we briefly present the variables and their expected sign. A more extensive discussion of all variables will follow in the results section.

In our initial model we include the following *economic* variables.

Ln GDP per capita This is a difficult variable to interpret since it is corre-lated with many omitted variables. There is also a potential problem of reverse causality since a high risk of rebellion will depress income. With these caveats there are two reasons to expect that low per capita income would directly increase the risk of rebellion: the opportunity cost of rebellion is lower, and the state is likely to have less control over its territory.

Growth of GDP per capita This again raises serious problems of endogene-ity. However, the expectation is that the faster the rate of growth the lower

Table 2.2 Means of key variables

	Sample	Peaceful observations	Warstart observations	Former French African colonies
War Start (dummy)	0.067	0	1	0.037
GDP per capita (US $, base year 1997)	5452	5764	1101	681
GDP per capita Growth $(t-1)$	1.844	2.011	−0.486	0.204
Primary Commodity Exports (proportion of GDP)	0.164	0.165	0.146	0.178
Years of Peace	32	33	16	32
Former French African Colony (dummy)	0.101	0.104	0.056	1
Social Fractionalization (index 0–1)	0.180	0.173	0.282	0.287
Proportion of Young Men (proportion of age 15–29 in total population)	0.129	0.129	0.133	0.128
Total Population	30.2	28.3	56.5	9.1
Mountainous (proportion of total land area)	15.779	15.442	20.484	4.538
Number of observations	1063	992	71	107

Note: Based on the sample used for our core model, Table 2.3, column 4.

the risk of rebellion. For example, the faster is growth the tighter will be the labour market and so the more difficult will it be for the rebel organization to recruit. Miguel, Satyanath and Sergenti (2004) were able to address endogeneity through instrumenting growth with rainfall shocks and found that it indeed substantially reduced risks.

Primary Commodity Exports (PCE)   Natural resources can increase the risk of rebellion because they constitute easy sources of rebel finance. This may both directly motivate rebellion and make rebellions that are motivated by other considerations more feasible. They can also sever the government from the need to tax citizens and hence indirectly produce a government that is not accountable, thereby increasing the grounds for grievance. The previous empirical evidence on natural resources is ambiguous. In our earlier work (Collier and Hoeffler, 2004) we found that the relationship between natural resources and conflict takes the form of an inverted U-shape. We suggested that this arose because if the government had very large resource revenues it could afford to buy off all of its opponents so that beyond some point additional revenue was risk-reducing. Fearon (2005) agrees that resource revenues increase the risk of rebellion but argues that the relationship is log-linear rather than quadratic. Other studies, such as Fearon and Laitin (2003) emphasize the effect of oil rather than of natural resources in general. We use the quadratic formulation for our initial model, but check the robustness of our results with respect to points raised by other studies.

Country studies of civil war invariably trace the onset of rebellion to some historical roots and so *historical conditions* should be expected to matter for the risk of conflict. We investigate the following:

Post Cold War   The impact of this variable on the conflict risk is controversial. While Kaplan (1994) predicted that the fall of the iron curtain would increase the number of conflicts, Gleditsch *et al.* (2002) argue the contrary. Thus, *a priori* the sign of this variable is ambiguous.

Previous War   We analyze the effect of previous civil war through two variables which need to be considered jointly: a dummy variable for the occurrence of a previous civil war and a continuous variable which measures the number of months since the previous war ended ('peace'). The dummy variable controls for any fixed effects that might have precipitated the initial war and also make the country prone to further wars. Having controlled for such effects, the continous variable measuring the time since the previous war, proxies legacy effects which might be expected gradually to fade. These might be psychological, such as hatreds or a sense of 'never again', material, such as stocks of weapons, and organizational, notably the rebel army. In principle the sign is ambiguous.

Former French African Colony   A security guarantee from an outside regime for the government in power can reduce the incentives for rebellion. The only nation that provided a de facto security guarantee to some of its former colonies was France between 1965 and 1999. We shall accordingly expect this dummy variable to reduce the scope for conflict.

   The composition of the *society* is also commonly invoked as an explanation for conflict. We therefore include:

Social Fractionalization   The impact of ethnic and religious social cleavages on the risk of conflict has been controversial in the literature (Collier and Hoeffler, 1998, 2004; Fearon and Laitin, 2003). Different forms of fractionalization have previously been found to increase, reduce or not affect the scope for conflict. Therefore, we do not *a priori* expect a particular sign for this variable. In the main analysis we include a variable of social fractionalization that captures various forms of cleavages. The exact definition of this variable is discussed in more detail further below.

Proportion of Young Men   We expect this variable to increase the risk of rebellion. A great availability of potential recruits as rebel soldiers makes it easier and cheaper to start a rebellion. It may also increase the alienation of youth.

Ln Population   Since our economic scale variable is per capita income, our remaining scale variable is population size. The key interest in this variable is not its sign, which is likely to be positive, but whether the marginal effects are large. If an increase in the population does not proportionately raise the risk of conflict this could be interpreted as evidence of scale economies in security. If, for example, two identical countries are merged with no underlying change in the risk in either place, r, then the measured risk of rebellion (in either location) would be $r + (1 - r)r$ and so would very nearly double. Thus, if the coefficient on population was such that risks increased proportionately this would in effect be the benchmark of size neutrality.

Geography is particularly pertinent for investigating the feasibility hypothesis. In Collier and Hoeffler (2004) we investigated both forest cover and the extent of mountainous terrain. The former was insignificant and is not investigated further here. The latter was marginally significant and was subsequently incorporated by Fearon and Laitin (2003) who extended the measure. We use that extended measure here.

The majority of the academic work on civil war is conducted by political scientists. This reflects a presumption that it is at root driven by the grievance of political exclusion. We therefore include a measure of the extent of *political rights*.

2.4 Results

Overview and descriptive statistics

Wars tend to occur in situations where data collection has already broken down and so there is a severe trade-off between the number of wars that can be included and the quality of the data on which the analysis is based. Our core regression includes 71 of the 84 wars and has 1063 observations for 172 countries. This sample is a considerable improvement on the core regression used in Collier and Hoeffler (2004) which was based on 52 wars and 688 observations. Our core sample includes some imputed data for social fractionalization, young men and mountains. For variables with missing data points we have set missing values to the mean of observed values and added a dummy variable which takes the value of unity if the data are missing.[4] This tests whether the assumption that missing observations are on average the same as actual observations is correct. When this dummy[5] variable is insignificant, so that the assumption is accepted, the dummy is then dropped from the regression. Potentially data imputation can be taken further than this and in one of our robustness checks we use the AMELIA method of multiple random imputation of all missing values of explanatory variables. This enables us to include all 84 wars and 1,472 observations.

As mentioned earlier, Table 2.1 gives an overview list of all civil wars included in the data set and Table 2.2 presents descriptive statistics of the key variables of the core model. We now turn to the regression analysis.

Core results

Our core results are developed in Table 2.3. In the first three columns we progressively eliminate insignificant variables stepwise to arrive at the core model of column 4.[6] We now discuss in detail the results for the variables included in the core model.

The key theme of our previous analysis was that three *economic character-istics* drive proneness to civil war, namely the level, growth and structure of income. Peaceful observations in our data set are characterized by a per capita *income* that is more than five times higher than in countries in which wars broke out. To reduce problems of endogeneity we measure income at the start of each five-year period. In all columns of table 3 we find that the risk of a civil war during the period is significantly greater at lower levels of initial income. It is useful to benchmark the risk of conflict in a hypothetical country with characteristics set at the sample mean. The predicted risk for such a country is 4.6 per cent.[7] If the level of per capita income is halved from this level, the risk is increased to 5.3 per cent. The effect of the level of income is also found by the other major global quantitative study, Fearon and Laitin (2003). However, even with a five-year lag there are potentially serious concerns about endogeneity. When we turn to our robustness checks we address these issues, showing that our initial results survive once income is instrumented.

Although income appears to be proxying some causal relationship, its interpretation is extremely difficult since it is correlated with so many other features of a society. Fearon and Laitin interpret it as proxying the effectiveness of the state, and thus the ability of the government to deter rebellion. In our previous work we interpreted it as proxying the opportunity cost of time and hence the cost of rebel recruitment. These interpretations need not be alternatives.

Wars often start following *growth* collapses. To reduce problems of endogeneity we measure the growth rate of GDP per capita over the five-year period prior to that for which we are estimating the risk of conflict. The growth rate during the five years prior to conflict averages –0.5 per cent, compared to 2 per cent in peaceful countries. In all the columns of Table 2.3 growth significantly reduces the risk of conflict. Again at the mean of other characteristics, if the growth rate is increased by one percentage point, the risk of conflict decreases by 0.6 percentage points to 4.0 per cent. The effect

Table 2.3 Feasibility of civil war

	(1)	(2)	(3)	(4)
Economy				
ln GDP per capita	−0.232	−0.233	−0.216	−0.216
	(1.72)*	(1.72)*	(1.74)*	(1.74)*
GDP per capita	−0.148	−0.147	−0.147	−0.144
Growth ($t-1$)	(3.69)***	(3.69)***	(3.69)***	(3.69)***
Primary Commodity	7.150	6.98	6.916	6.988
Exports (PCE)	(1.74)*	(1.76)*	(1.76)*	(1.77)*
PCE squared	−14.581	−14.245	−14.233	−14.438
	(1.77)*	(1.79)*	(1.80)*	(1.82)*
History				
Post Cold War	−0.135	−0.158	−0.138	
	(0.35)	(0.45)	(0.40)	
Previous War	−0.082			
	(0.17)			
Peace	−0.058	−0.056	−0.056	−0.056
	(3.78)***	(5.75)***	(5.77)***	(5.83)***
Former French	−1.203	−1.201	−1.231	−1.221
African Colony	(1.95)*	(1.94)*	(2.02)**	(2.00)**
Social Characteristics				
Social	2.173	2.189	2.193	2.186
Fractionalization	(2.68)***	(2.72)***	(2.72)***	(2.71)***
Proportion of	12.493	12.378	12.532	12.639
Young Men	(1.52)	(1.51)	(1.54)	(1.55) p=0.12
Ln Population	0.276	0.272	0.272	0.266
	(2.72)***	(2.76)***	(2.76)***	(2.73)***
Geography				
Mountainous	0.011	0.011	0.011	0.011
	(1.48)	(1.48)	(1.46)	(1.45)
Polity				
Democracy	0.012	0.014		
	(0.27)	(0.30)		
Observations	1063	1063	1063	1063
Pseudo R^2	0.28	0.28	0.28	0.28
Log Likelihood	−188.66	−188.68	−188.72	−188.80

Note: Logit regressions, dependent variable: war start. Absolute value of z statistics in parentheses. Asterisks (*, **, ***) indicate significance at the 10%, 5% and 1% level, respectively. All regressions include an intercept (not reported).

of the growth rate of income is also found by Miguel, Satyanath and Sergenti (2004) using Africa-only data, on which they are able ingeniously to instrument for growth by means of rainfall. This is not a feasible option for a global sample since Africa is atypical in having rain-fed agriculture as a large component of GDP. Again, growth can be interpreted in several different ways. Our own interpretation stays with the issue of rebel recruitment: growth implies job creation which reduces the pool of labour likely to be targeted by rebels. However, growth could also be an important determinant of government popularity and through this influence the willingness of the population to support rebels, or at least not inform against them.

Our final economic variable is the *structure of income*. We follow Sachs and Warner (2000) and proxy richness in natural resources by the proportion of primary commodity exports in GDP, measuring it at the start of each period. In all columns of Table 3 there is an inverted U-shaped relationship between *natural resources* and conflict, with the sign of primary commodity exports (PCE) being positive and significant and PCE squared being negative and significant. Since Fearon (2005) has argued that the relationship is log-linear rather than quadratic, we tested the log-linear specification against the quadratic, but found that the latter dominates: the risk of dependence upon primary commodity exports is at its peak when exports constitute around 25 per cent of GDP. Taking the extremes of 0 per cent and 25 per cent, the implied risks at the mean of other characteristics are 2.2 per cent and 5.0 per cent.

The channels by which primary commodities might relate to the risk of conflict have come under intense scrutiny and debate (Ross, 2004; Humphreys, 2005; Rohner, 2006). Three channels seem likely. One is that primary commodity exports provide opportunities for rebel predation during conflict and so can finance the escalation and sustainability of rebellion. The most celebrated cases are the diamond-financed rebellions in Sierra Leone and Angola. Oil also provides ample opportunities for rebel finance, whether through 'bunkering' (tapping of pipelines and theft of oil), kidnapping and ransoming of oil workers, or extortion rackets against oil companies (often disguised as 'community support'). A second channel is that rebellions may actually be motivated, as opposed to merely being made feasible, by the desire to capture the rents, either during or after conflict. A third channel is that the governments of resource-rich countries tend to be more remote from their populations since they do not need to tax them, so that grievances are stronger (see Tilly, 1975). Evidently, these three channels need not be alternatives, but a study by Lujala, Gleditsch and Gilmore (2005) helps to distinguish between them. They find that conflicts are more likely to be located in the areas of a country in which natural resources are extracted, providing some support for the rebel finance hypothesis.

Two policy implications have often been drawn from our previous results on these three economic variables. One is that economic development is critical for reducing the incidence of civil war. The other is that international trade in primary commodities carries particular risks and so warrants special measures such as the Kimberley Process and the Extractive Industries Transparency Initiative. As is evident from our above discussion, while these policies are consistent with our results they are not entailed by them: alternative interpretations could be found in which these would not be warranted. However, our present results remain consistent with these policies.

Twenty-three countries experienced repeat civil wars. Either this reflects country fixed-effects, or conflict increases the risk of further conflict. To test the latter we introduced a variable for the time that has passed since the previous conflict.[8] This is again highly significant: in all the columns of Table 2.3 risks decline as the *duration of peace* lengthens but the effect is very slow. A country only ten years post-conflict has a risk of 14.2 per cent, and one that is twenty years post-conflict has a risk of 8.6 per cent. To check that this is not proxying some unobserved fixed characteristic that makes these countries endemically prone to conflict we introduced a dummy variable that took the value of unity if the country had had a previous conflict (Table 2.3, column 1). The variable is insignificant. The high risk of repeat conflict was one component of our concept of the 'conflict trap'. Once a country stumbled into a civil war there was a danger that it would enter a dysfunctional cycle in which the legacy of war was a heightened risk of further conflict, partly because of this time effect, and partly because of the likely decline in income. The principle legacy of a civil war is a grossly heightened risk of further civil war.

We now turn to the effect of *population size*. In all columns of Table 2.3 population size increases the risk of civil war. However, the marginal effect is small. A doubling of population size increases the risk of civil war by only one fifth 20 (from 4.6 per cent to 5.5 per cent). The most plausible interpretation of this is that there are economies of scale in certain basic functions of the state, most notably the deterrence of organized violence.[9] An implication is that controlling for other characteristics, a region that is divided into many countries, such as Africa, will have considerably more conflicts that one which is divided into only a few countries, such as South Asia. This result sits uneasily with the recent international fashion for settling conflicts by the creation of new states: Eritrea and prospectively Southern Sudan in Africa, the dissolution of Yugoslavia in Europe, East Timor in Asia, the (now-dissolved) FARC mini-state in Latin America, and most recently the two Palestinian proto-states of the West Bank and Gaza in the Middle East. As the low-income world divides into more countries to settle 'historic grievances' there should be some presumption that unless these societies achieve economic development internal conflict is likely eventually to increase.

These five variables (income, growth, natural resources, peace duration, and population) constitute what is common between our previous analysis and our present results. What is different? One difference is in respect of social composition. In our previous work we found that ethnic *fractionalization* had ambiguous effects. Risks were increased by what we termed 'ethnic dominance'. By this we meant that the largest ethnic group constituted somewhere between 45 per cent and 90 per cent of the population. Other than this, we found that social and religious fractionalization tended to reduce the risk of conflict. In combination this implied a quadratic effect of ethnic fractionalization, first increasing risk and then reducing it. With our new data we find a simpler relationship: social fractionalization significantly increases risk (cf. all columns of Table 2.3). We measure social fractionalization by combining two measures of ethnic and religious diversity. The ethno-linguistic fractionalization index measures the probability of two randomly picked individuals not speaking the same language. The religious fractionalization index is constructed in a similar way. We use a combination of these two variables to capture the possible cross cutting of ethnic and religious diversity. *A priori*, ethnic and religious fractionalization can interact in various ways. If cleavages are coincident either one might be redundant. If cleavages are non-coincident they could be additive, with three ethnic groups and three religious groups generating six differentiated groups, or multiplicative, with cross-cutting cleavages generating nine groups. We found that the multiplicative specification dominated other possibilities and this is the specification adopted in our core regressions.[10] So measured, doubling social fractionalization from 18 per cent to 36 per cent, for example, raises the risk of conflict from 4.6 per cent to 6.67 per cent. The change of results from our previous analysis matters most for risk estimates in the most ethnically diverse societies, most notably much of Africa.

Three new variables enter the core regression, surviving the stepwise deletion process in Table 2.3. The first is a dummy for being a *former French colony in Africa* during the period 1965–99. This has a negative sign and is significant, as shown in Table 2.3, column 4. During this period analyzed the former French colonies of Africa had a risk of civil war that was less than a third of that which would otherwise have been predicted. They faced a risk of 2.6 per cent (given the estimated coefficient), while they would have suffered a civil war risk of 8.2 per cent if they had had the same characteristics, but without being Francophone. How might this have come about? One possibility is that the distinctive cultural and administrative traditions established by France have left a more peaceable legacy than those societies that were not colonized by France. An alternative interpretation is that during this period Francophone Africa remained under a French military umbrella, with French bases through the region providing *de facto* security guarantees. Since the security guarantees were confined to Sub-Saharan Africa, partly for logistical reasons, and to a clearly defined period, it is possible to test between these two interpretations by including both a dummy variable for all countries that were former French colonies, a dummy variable for the Francophone Sub-Saharan African countries during 1965–99, and a dummy variable for Sub-Saharan Africa. As discussed in more detail in our discussion of robustness tests, we show that it is the security interpretation which is best-supported. The French policy was in striking contrast to British post-colonial policy which very rapidly ceased to countenance military intervention. As political governance gradually became more of an issue during the 1990s, French military intervention came to be seen as unjustified since it had involved support for tainted regimes (Michailof, 1993, 2005). The decisive departure from the practice of guarantees was when the French government decided to allow the coup d'etat in Cote d'Ivoire of December 1998 to stand despite being in a position to reverse it. This was a controversial decision taken by a new President against the advice of the civil service establishment whose views reflected past practice. This decision enables the shift in policy to be precisely dated.

Paradoxically, shortly after the French government decided against further military intervention the British government introduced it, sending a substantial force into Sierra Leone to end the civil war and enforce the post-conflict peace. This British policy is evidently too recent and indeed to date too country-specific to warrant inclusion in a statistical analysis. However, we invite political scientists to construct a variable which rates for each country-year globally over this period the *de facto* security guarantees provided, whether from former colonists, superpowers, or military alliances. The introduction of such a variable into the analysis would provide a useful test of a widespread strategy.

A second new variable that we include in our core model is the *proportion of the population made up of males in the age range 15–29*. In our previous work this was insignificant but the expansion of sample and improvement in data quality bring it sufficiently close to significance to warrant inclusion (see Table 2.3, column 4). Our robustness checks, discussed below, also support the inclusion of this variable. A doubling in the proportion of the population in this category increases the risk of conflict from 4.6 per cent to 19.7 per cent. As with criminality, rebellion relies almost exclusively upon this particular segment of the population. A likely explanation for this extreme selectivity is that some young men have both an absolute advantage and a taste for violence. Some rebel groups undertake forced recruitment from among boys. A common tactic, employed for example by the Lord's Resistance Army in Uganda, was for boys to be kidnapped from schools and then required to commit an atrocity that made it impossible for them to return to their community. Another tactic, employed for example by the Revolutionary United Forces in Sierra Leone, is to target young male drug addicts who can then be controlled through drug supplies.

A third new variable is the proportion of the terrain of a country that is *mountainous*. This is a difficult concept to measure empirically because it is not well-proxied by crude objective indicators such as altitude: a high plateau is not particularly 'mountainous'. For the measure used in our previous work we commissioned a specialist geographer, John Gerrard, to code terrain globally. This has since been extended by Fearon and Laitin, who indeed found the variable to be significant in their specification, and we use these extended data. In our core specification the variable is not quite significant ($p=0.14$) but we retain it, in part because of its intrinsic plausibility. We also find the point estimate and standard error for mountainous to be very stable when we subject this core model to the various specification and robustness checks discussed below. The effect is potentially large. Taking the point estimate at face value, were Nepal flat its risk of civil war would have been 3.5 per cent based on its other characteristics. Given that 67.4 per cent of its terrain is mountainous, its risk was 7 per cent. This variable replaces our previous geographic variable, which measured the dispersion of the population over the country, which is no longer significant.

In addition to the variables listed in Table 2.3 we also tested the significance of a number of other possible determinants of war risk. None of the measures of inequality were significant, nor were literacy rates for men, political rights, checks and balances and the proportion of the country covered by forests.

Robustness checks

How robust are these results? Our procedure of stepwise deletion risks path-dependence and some of the variables are likely to be endogenous. Table 2.4 presents specification tests while Table 2.5 extends the analysis to a wider class of robustness checks.

We first test the robustness of the dummy variable for Francophone Africa during 1965–99. We add dummy variables for being a former French colony, regardless of region, and for being African regardless of colonial history. When all three variables are included (Table 2.4, column 1) none is significant, but the dummy variable for being a former French African colony has the highest z-statistics. Eliminating successively those of these three variables with the lowest z-statistics (see Table 2.4, column 2) leaves this as the only surviving, significant variable. Hence, the most reasonable interpretation is that the radically lower risk of conflict was as a result of the French security guarantee.

In column 3 we show that the number of years since independence does not significantly affect the risk of conflict. In the columns 4 and 5 we show that our measure of social fractionalization has a stronger impact than alternative measures of ethnic dominance and ethnic fractionalization. In column 6 we show that population density does not significantly affect the risk of conflict.

As mentioned, Fearon and Laitin (2003) have argued that what matters is not as much natural resources in general, but oil in particular. We therefore tested whether the relationship was more general than oil (Table 2.4, column 7). The addition of a variable for the value of fuel exports was insignificant, while the original specification of primary commodity exports and its square both remained significant.

In Table 2.5 we investigate a range of more methodological issues. In the first three columns of Table 2.5 we check the robustness of the income variable. Post-conflict countries will tend to have lower income than other countries, due to the costly effects of war, and they will also tend to have higher risks of conflict, if only because of unobserved fixed effects. This creates the possibility that the association between low income and high risk is not causal. To control for this possibility we investigate a variant in which only 'first time' civil wars are included, with post-conflict countries dropped from the sample (Table 2.5, column 1). The concept of 'first-time wars' is made much easier empirically because for several decades until the wave of decolonisation around the start of the period covered in our analysis peace was maintained through imperial rule in much of the world. With subsequent wars excluded, income remains significant. In addition, we also used more formal, econometric tests to check whether the endogeneity of income is

Table 2.4 Specification tests

	(1)	(2)	(3)	(4)	(5)	(6)	(7)
Economy							
ln GDP per capita	-0.155	-0.149	-0.256	-0.211	-0.210	-0.219	-0.212
	(1.09)	(1.05)	(1.83)*	(1.70)*	(1.67)*	(1.75)*	(1.70)*
GDP per capita Growth ($t-1$)	-0.142	-0.143	-0.141	-0.142	-0.143	-0.142	-0.144
	(3.61)***	(3.63)***	(3.57)***	(3.66)***	(3.68)***	(3.64)***	(3.69)***
PCE	7.167	7.011	6.444	7.578	6.842	6.622	7.339
	(1.80)*	(1.78)*	(1.63)	(1.89)*	(1.73)*	(1.63)	(1.80)*
PCE squared	-14.536	-14.220	-13.584	-15.328	-14.239	-13.835	-14.766
	(1.82)*	(1.80)*	(1.72)*	(1.92)*	(1.80)*	(1.72)*	(1.85)*
Fuel exports							-0.002
							(0.35)
History							
Peace	-0.056	-0.056	-0.054	-0.056	-0.056	-0.055	-0.056
	(5.82)***	(5.83)***	(5.65)***	(5.84)***	(5.83)***	(5.81)***	(5.82)***
Former French African Colony	-1.071	-1.340	-1.265	-1.144	-1.238	-1.254	-1.227
	(1.08)	(2.17)**	(2.06)**	(1.87)*	(2.03)**	(2.03)**	(2.01)**
Former French colony	-0.268						
	(0.34)						
Years since independence				0.002			
				(0.63)			
Social Character							
Social fractionalization	1.597	1.650	2.330	2.941	1.788	2.159	2.155
	(1.63)	(1.70)*	(2.76)***	(2.41)**	(1.50)	(2.66)***	(2.66)***
Ethnic fractionalization					0.372		
					(0.45)		
Ethnic dominance				-0.471			
				(0.82)			
Proportion of young men in population	12.896	13.021	13.138	13.450	12.650	12.984	12.721
	(1.60)	(1.62)	(1.61)	(1.63)	(1.54)	(1.58)	(1.55)
	0.302	0.304	0.213	0.268	0.256	0.263	0.271
	(2.83)***	(2.84)***	(1.95)*	(2.76)***	(2.57)**	(2.70)***	(2.73)***
Geography							
Mountainous	0.011	0.012	0.009	0.011	0.011	0.010	0.011
	(1.52)	(1.56)	(1.14)	(1.46)	(1.45)	(1.38)	(1.47)
Sub-Saharan Africa	0.445	0.463					
	(0.95)	(0.99)					
Population Density						-0.000	
						(0.32)	
Observations	1063	1063	996	1063	1063	1063	1063
Pseudo R^2	0.28	0.28	0.27	0.28	0.28	0.28	0.28
Log Likelihood	-188.25	-188.31	-187.95	-188.47	-188.70	-188.72	-188.74

Note: Logit regressions, dependent variable: war start. Absolute value of z statistics in parentheses. Asterisks (*, **, ***) indicate significance at the 10%, 5% and 1% level, respectively. All regressions include an intercept (not reported).

likely to cause problems with the interpretation of the results obtained from our core model. Since there are no standard endogeneity tests for logit or probit models, we re-estimate our core regression as a linear probability model, a strategy previously employed by Miguel *et al.* (2004), and instrument income. Our instruments for income are the distance from Washington

Table 2.5 Further robustness checks

	(1) First war only	*(2)* Linear	*(3)* 2SLS probability model	*(4)* ACD data set	*(5)* Fixed effects	*(6)* Random effects	*(7)* Time independence	*(8)* Post full events	*(9)* Rare	*(10)* Amelia
Economy										
ln GDP per capita	−0.311 (2.06)**	−0.011 (1.90)*	−0.025 (2.12)**	−0.117 (0.79)	−0.635 (1.39)	−0.221 (1.75)*	−0.211 (1.69)*	−0.237 (1.89)*	−0.209 (2.05)*	−0.255 (2.22)**
GDP per capita Growth $(t-1)$	−0.075 (1.41)	−0.011 (4.55)***	−0.010 (4.28)***	−0.157 (3.40)***	−0.220 (3.55)***	−0.144 (3.67)***	−0.145 (3.40)***	−0.126 (3.20)***	−0.141 (4.29)***	−0.083 (2.74)***
PCE	5.263 (1.16)	0.156 (0.87)	0.097 (0.54)	4.386 (0.95)	8.087 (1.61)	7.104 (1.78)*	6.737 (1.69)*	6.847 (1.71)*	5.980 (1.62)*	1.743 (0.858)
PCE squared	−10.157 (1.16)	−0.307 (1.20)	−0.207 (0.81)	−9.729 (1.11)	−13.154 (1.01)	−14.596 (1.82)*	−13.96 (1.74)*	−14.304 (1.77)*	−11.854 (1.63)*	−3.671 (1.31)
History										
Peace	−0.006 (0.47)	−0.004 (6.14)***	0.004 (5.77)***	−0.060 (5.01)***	0.068 (3.43)***	−0.058 (5.68)***	−0.058 (5.84)***	−0.057 (5.90)***	−0.053 (5.51)***	−0.059 (6.50)***
Former French African Colony	−1.252 (1.58)	−0.086 (3.39)***	−0.108 (3.31)***	−1.191 (1.47)	−16.206 (0.01)	−1.235 (1.99)**	−1.230 (2.01)*	−1.259 (2.05)**	−1.095 (1.89)*	−0.873 (1.517)*
Social Characteristics										
Social fractionalization	1.621 (1.56)	0.186 (3.07)***	0.153 (2.26)**	1.907 (1.96)**		2.203 (2.68)***	2.157 (2.64)***	2.084 (2.55)***	2.140 (2.80)***	2.001 (2.81)***
Proportion of young men in population	14.526 (1.63)*	0.375 (0.90)	0.302 (0.72)	15.589 (1.66)**	−37.337 (1.56)	12.463 (1.51)	12.676 (1.53)	13.659 (1.66)*	13.274 (1.70)**	18.59 (3.15)***
	0.232 (1.99)**	0.014 (2.59)**	0.012 (2.14)*	0.257 (2.07)**	0.892 (1.50)	0.273 (2.75)***	0.262 (2.61)***	0.225 (2.26)**	0.254 (3.14)***	0.316 (3.89)***
Geography										
Mountainous	0.013 (1.48)	0.003 (0.62)	0.0001 (0.20)	0.005 (0.54)		0.011 (1.44)	0.011 (1.47)	0.010 (1.40)	0.010 (1.46)	0.006 (1.20)

Table 2.5 continued

	(1)	(2)	(3)	(4)	(5)	(6)	(7)	(8)	(9)	(10)
Time dummy 1970–1974							0.798 (1.49)			
Time dummy 1975–1979							0.230 (0.39)			
Time dummy 1980–1984							0.732 (1.32)			
Time dummy 1985–1989							0.158 (0.25)			
Time dummy 1990–1994							1.038 (1.84)*			
Time dummy 1995–1999							0.452 (0.78)			
Time dummy 2000–2004							0.260 (0.40)			
Observations	1026	911	911	1045	242	1063	1063	1020	1063	1472
Pseudo R^2	0.11	0.15	0.21	0.25			0.29	0.27		0.27–0.31
Log Likelihood	−132.36			−134.43	−70.74	−188.89	−185.82	−183.11	−222.6	−236.0

Note: Logit regressions, dependent variable: war start. Absolute value of z statistics in parentheses. Asterisks (*, **, ***) indicate significance at the 10%, 5% and 1% level, respectively. All regressions include an intercept (not reported).

D.C., access to the nearest sea port, and the proportion of the country that is located in the tropics. We do not have the values for the instrumental variables for all countries and our sample size is significantly reduced from 1063 to 911 observations. In order to compare our two stage regression results we present the linear probability model estimated on this reduced sample size in Table 2.5, column 2. Compared with our core model primary commodity exports are not statistically significant. A Hausman test suggests that income may be endogenous[11] and we present our two stage least squares results in Table 2.5, column 3. The Hansen test suggests that our instruments are valid (p=0.58). Instrumented income is significant at the five per cent level and the coefficient point estimate is more than double than when income is uninstrumented. Further, all the other variables that were significant in the uninstrumented regression run on the restricted 911 observations remain significant when income is instrumented. To sum up, we find some evidence that income is endogenous but our instrumental variable results suggest that this is unlikely to mislead us in the interpretation of our results, since instrumented income has an even stronger impact on the risk of a civil war outbreak when compared with the non-instrumented model and no other variables lose significance.

In column 4 we change the definition of the dependent variable to the new Uppsala/PRIO Armed Conflict Dataset (ACD) by Gleditsch *et al.* (2002). For this regression we make a corresponding change in our measure of the time since the previous civil war, basing the estimate on the ACD. Our results are very similar, growth, peace, population and fractionalization are significant, the proportion of young men in the society now becomes significant, while income and primary commodity exports lose significance but do not change sign. In column 5 we introduce fixed effects. This leads to a loss of observations; if countries had no time variation in the dependent variable, i.e. entirely peaceful countries, they are dropped from the sample. Time-invariant variables have to be omitted from this estimation. None of the variables that change slowly over time are significant but two time-variant variables, growth and peace, are significant. The sixth column introduces random effects. The core results all remain significant. The seventh column introduces time dummies. These have little effect on the core results and only one of them is individually significant: there was a temporary increase in the risk of civil war in the first half of the 1990s. This provides some evidence for Kaplan's 'coming anarchy' hypothesis which was published in 1994. Luckily, this turned out not to be a general post-coldwar trend because the dummies for 1995–99 and 2000–04 are not statistically significant. In a further robustness check in column 8 we exclude countries if they were not fully independent at the start of the sub-period. We lose two wars (Angola and Mozambique's war starts in the 1975–79 period) and a further 41 peace observations. The results are now a little stronger than the ones obtained from our core model, all variables apart from mountains are now significant at conventional levels. In column 9 of Table 2.5 we make the standard adjustment for rare events (King and Zeng,

2001). This treatment strengthens our results. In column 10 we expand the sample to its maximum by using the AMELIA program of multiple imputation of all missing values of explanatory variables (King *et al.*, 2001). This increases our coverage of civil wars from 71 to the full 84. Again, this seems to strengthen our results. The proportion of young men in the society is now significant at the one per cent level. The level of primary commodity exports is no longer significant, but its square term remains significant at the ten per cent level. This weaker result is most likely due to the characteristics of the previously omitted conflicts. They tend to be in countries in which official data on exports radically underestimate actual transactions. For example, in Afghanistan and Cambodia, two of the omitted conflicts, there is considerable evidence that the conflict was financed partly by substantial illegal exports of drugs, gems and timber. Hence, the loss of significance for primary commodity exports may well be the result of introducing severely biased data.

Implications

We now return to our core results and focus on the implications of the three new variables. The variables, countries under the French security umbrella, the proportion of young men in the population, and the proportion of the terrain which is mountainous, all have substantial effects. Consider two hypothetical countries whose characteristics were at the mean of all the other variables but which differed substantially in respect of these three. One was under the implicit French security umbrella, had only half the average proportion of young men in its society, and had no mountainous terrain. The other was not under the security umbrella, had double the average proportion of young men in its society, and was as mountainous as Nepal. The respective risks of civil war in these two otherwise identical societies are 0.6 per cent and 32.9 per cent.

However, the key significance of these new variables is not that they have such substantial effects but that they are somewhat easier to interpret than any of the variables that were previously found to be significant. They are better proxies for distinguishing between the two key branches of the theoretical models: motivation versus feasibility. While the three economic variables, the level, growth and structure of income, can all be interpreted as either feasibility or motivation, the three new variables cannot so readily be interpreted as proxying motivation. By contrast, they all have very ready interpretations as important aspects of feasibility. The Francophone security guarantee made rebellion more dangerous and less likely to succeed. It was simply less militarily feasible. Mountainous terrain provides an obvious safe haven for rebel forces: it increases military feasibility. Finally, the proportion of young men in the society is a good proxy for the proportion of the population psychologically predisposed to violence and best-suited for rebel recruitment: again, it makes rebellion more feasible. The results are therefore consistent with the feasibility hypothesis.

However, they are still not a fully convincing test of the hypothesis because two of them can also be interpreted as affecting the motivation for rebellion. Mountainous areas might be atypically poor, and so proxy wide regional inequalities. There is a long history of cities of the plains being attacked by the marches. Similarly, in societies with a high proportion of young men youth might be the victim of exploitation by older age groups. We have not, however, been able to think of an equivalent motivation-based account for the effect of La Francophonie. If the most plausible interpretation of the importance of mountains and of the proportion of young men in the society is that they proxy important aspects of feasibility, then the results are powerful. By construction the two hypothetical countries are identical in respect of all other motivations for conflict, and differ only in these three aspects of feasibility. The implication would be that differences in feasibility are decisive for the risk of conflict.

Two other variables are perhaps also most readily interpreted as proxying feasibility, although they could be interpreted in other ways. These are population size and primary commodity exports. The fact that the marginal effect of the log of population size is relatively small reflects scale economies in security provision and so proxies military feasibility. Primary commodity exports probably proxy the scope for rebel financial predation and so proxy financial feasibility. We conclude with a refinement of our two hypothetical countries in which these two variables are added as further differences. In the former, in which rebellion is already difficult, we set the population to be 50 million, and set primary commodity exports as a share of GDP to zero. Note that all these five features that make rebellion less feasible are within the observed range. All the other characteristics of the country are at the sample mean. In the other territory, in which rebellion is easy, there are five identical countries each with a population of 10 million. Each has primary commodity exports equal to 25 per cent of GDP and also the other three features that make rebellion easy, as specified previously. Other than these characteristics each is identical to the country in which rebellion is difficult. By design, each territory has the same total population although one is divided into five small countries, and the characteristics that might affect the motive for rebellion have been kept constant at the mean of all observations. What is the risk of civil war in each of these territories? In the territory in which rebellion is difficult the risk of civil war in any five-year period is now only 0.3 per cent. In other words, rebellion does not occur because it is infeasible. In the territory in which there are fewer impediments to rebellion the risk that a civil war will erupt somewhere in the territory is now an astonishing 99.8 per cent.[12] Thus, where rebellion is feasible, it will occur without any special inducements in terms of motivation. While our five variables have broadly captured the important aspects of feasibility, namely finance, military deterrence, and the availability of suitable recruits, we have not set up an extreme situation. For example, we have not introduced anything about the level or growth of per capita income, or about the time since a previous civil war. Low per capita income, slow growth, and the organizational and armaments legacies from a previous civil war all make rebellion more feasible even though they may also increase the motivation for rebellion.

Thus, the new evidence goes considerably beyond supporting the key results of our previous work about the primacy of economic variables in the risk of civil war. While not decisive, it points clearly towards the proposition that feasibility rather than motivation is decisive for the risk of rebellion.

There are, however, severe limits to what can be concluded from the regression analysis of global data sets. Our variables are proxies for concepts that could be much better measured by purpose-design field studies. Our analysis suggests the importance of causal processes about the conditions of viability for rebellion. Oyefusi (2007) provides detailed micro-evidence on rebel recruitment in the Niger delta. In this case study the decision to join seems to be determined by personal economic characteristics rather than by group grievances. However, what is needed are more complementary economic anthropology studies that provide the basis for quantitative micro-level analysis.

2.5 Conclusion

In this paper we have analyzed empirically the causes of civil war. This is our third paper on the topic. Our first, (Collier and Hoeffler, 1998) was the first quantitative study of the topic. Our second, (Collier and Hoeffler, 2004) though a major advance on our first study, still omitted many civil wars and has been subject to considerable challenge and debate. We have attempted to make the results in this paper more definitive. The sample has nearly doubled to over 1,000 observations, the period of analysis has been brought up to end-2004, and the quality of the data has been considerably improved. Our results are important in two respects. First, despite the challenges, the core results of our previous analysis all survive. In particular, economic characteristics matter: namely, the level, growth and structure of income.

Secondly, two new variables are found to be both significant and quantitatively important. These are whether the country was under the implicit French security umbrella and the proportion of its population who were males in the age range 15–29. We also found some weaker evidence that mountainous countries are more conflict prone. Not only are these three variables important in their own right, from our perspective their key significance is that for the first time variables are significant which can reasonably be interpreted in terms of the major theoretical divisions. As we discuss in our review of theory, the basic division between theories of civil war is those that focus on feasibility, and those which focus on motivation, which in turn has two variants, 'greed' and 'grievance'. The three new variables point to the primacy of feasibility over motivation, a result which is consistent with the *feasibility hypothesis*. The feasibility hypothesis proposes that where rebellion is feasible it will occur: motivation is indeterminate, being supplied by whatever agenda happens to be adopted by the first social entrepreneur to occupy the viable niche, or itself endogenous to the opportunities thereby opened for illegal income.

An implication of the feasibility hypothesis is that if the incidence of civil war is to be reduced, which seems appropriate given its appalling consequences, it will need to be made more difficult. This is orthogonal to the rectification of justified grievances, the case for which is implied directly by the concept of 'justified grievance' without any need to invoke perilous consequences from the failure to do so.

Appendix 2.1: Data sources

Democracy   We measure democracy with the democracy indicator from the Polity IV data set. It ranges from 0 (autocratic) to 10 (fully democratic). Data source: http://www.cidcm.umd.edu/inscr/polity/

Economic growth   Using World Bank World Development Indicators (WDI) data for GDP per capita we calculated the annual growth rates (World Bank, 2006).

Former French African Colony   This dummy takes a value of one for the following countries: Benin, Burkina Faso, Cameroon, Central African Republic, Chad, Congo, Rep., Cote d'Ivoire, Djibouti, Gabon, Guinea, Madagascar, Mali, Mauritania, Niger, Senegal, Togo. This variable is zero for all countries for the last period 2000–04.

GDP per capita   We measure GDP per capita annually. Data are measured in constant 1995 US dollars and the data source is World Bank, 2006.

Peace   The number of years since the end of the last civil war. If the country never experienced a civil war we count all years since the end of World War II.

Population   Population measures the total population, in our regressions we take the natural logarithm. Data source: World Bank, 2006.

Primary Commodity Exports   The ratio of primary commodity exports to GDP proxies the abundance of natural resources. The data on primary commodity exports and GDP were obtained from the World Bank. Export and GDP data are measured in current US dollars.

Social, ethnolinguistic and religious fractionalization   We proxy social fractionalization in a combined measure of ethnic and religious fractionalization. Ethnic fractionalization is measured by the ethno-linguistic fractionalization index. It measures the probability that two randomly drawn individuals from a given country do not speak the same language. The religious fractionalization index measures this probability for different religious affiliations. The fractionalization indices range from zero to 1. A value of zero indicates that the society is completely homogenous whereas a value of 1 would characterize a completely heterogeneous society. We calculated our social fractionalization index as the product of the ethno-linguistic fractionalization and the religious fractionalization. Data source: Fearon and Laitin (2003).

Warstarts   Our main measure is based on Gleditsch (2004) and can be downloaded from http://weber.ucsd.edu/~kgledits/expwar.html (12 July 2006). Our alternative measure comes from the Armed Conflict Database (Gleditsch *et al.* 2002) and can be found on http://www.prio.no/page/CSCW_research_detail/Programme_detail_CSCW/9649/45925.html (12 July 2006).

Young Men   We define this variable as the proportion of young men aged 15–49 of the total population (%). Data Source: UN Demographic Yearbook 2005.

Notes

1 The survey in the *Handbook of Defense Economics* provides a fuller discussion of this new literature (Collier and Hoeffler, 2007).
2 Gleditsch (2004) only lists wars until 2002. For the years 2003 and 2004 we used the 'Armed Conflict Dataset' (ACD) by Gleditsch *et al.* (2002).
3 However, the COW researchers made adjustments for long conflicts. For some major armed conflicts the number of battle deaths dropped below the 1000 threshold but since the country was not at 'peace' the war is coded as ongoing. Without these adjustments many war countries would have multiple conflict spells rather than one long conflict.
4 On this treatment of missing values see Greene (2003, pp. 59–60).
5 'Dummy' refers to a dichotomous variable that can only take the values of 0 or 1.
6 This method of stepwise deletion is based on the 'general to specific' approach (Hendry, 1995, p. 270). More recently this method has also been used in a cross-section context (Hendry and Krolzig, 2004).
7 For readability, the marginal effects are not displayed in the tables.
8 If the country never experienced a civil war we count the years since the end of World War II.
9 In support of this, Collier, Hoeffler and Söderbom (2008) find that the effectiveness of international peacekeeping forces is related to their absolute size and not their size relative to population or economic activity.
10 Potentially, this implies that if a society is homogenous with respect to either religion or ethnicity then the other dimension of differentiation has no effect. In practice, the only society so characterized in our data is Mauritania.
11 Following Wooldridge (2002) we first regress income on all of the variables included in the core model and our three instruments. We then predict the residuals from this regression and include them in the core model. The coefficient on the residual is not significant (p=0.12). Thus, there is only weak evidence that income should be instrumented.
12 In each small country separately it is 28.5.

References

Collier, P., and Hoeffler, A. (1998). 'On Economic Causes of Civil War', *Oxford Economic Papers*, 50: 563–73.
Collier, P., and Hoeffler, A. (2004). 'Greed and Grievance in Civil War', *Oxford Economic Papers*, 56: 563–95.

Collier, P., and Hoeffler, A. (2004a). 'Conflicts' in: B. Lomborg (ed), *Global Crises, Global Solutions*, Cambridge UK: Cambridge University Press.

Collier, P., and Hoeffler, A. (2007). 'Civil War', Chapter 23 in: T. Sandler and K. Hartley (eds), *Handbook of Defense Economics*: 712–39, Amsterdam: Elsevier.

Collier, P., Hoeffler, A. and Söderbom, M. (2004). 'On the Duration of Civil War', *Journal of Peace Research*, 41: 253–73.

Collier, P., Hoeffler, A. and Söderbom, M. (2008). 'Post-Conflict Risks', *Journal of Peace Research* 45(4): 461–478.

Conservative Party of Great Britain. (2005). 'Annual Report and Financial Statistics for 2004', London: Conservative Party of Great Britain.

Evans, G., and Sahnoun, M. (2002). 'The Responsibility to Protect', *Foreign Affairs*, 81: 99–110.

Fearon, J. (2005). 'Primary Commodity Exports and Civil War', *Journal of Conflict Resolution*, 49: 483–507.

Fearon, J., and Laitin, D. (2003). 'Ethnicity, Insurgency, and Civil War', *American Political Science Review*, 97: 75–90.

Gerrard, A.J.W. (2000). 'What is a Mountain?', Mimeo, DECRG, World Bank.

Gleditsch, K.S. (2004). 'A Revised List of Wars Between and Within Independent States, 1816–2002', *International Interactions*, 30: 231–62.

Gleditsch, N.P., Wallensteen, P., Eriksson, M., Sollenberg, M. and Strand, H. (2002). 'Armed conflict 1946–2001: A new dataset', *Journal of Peace Research*, 39: 615–37.

Greene, W.H. (2003). *Econometric Analysis*, 5th ed, Upper Saddle River NJ: Prentice Hall.

Hendry, D.H. (1995). *Dynamic Econometrics*, Oxford: Oxford University Press.

Hendry, D.H. and Krolzig, H.J. (2004). 'We Ran One Regression', *Oxford Bulletin of Economics and Statistics*, 66: 799–810.

Hirshleifer, J. (2001). *The Dark Side of the Force: Economic Foundations of Conflict Theory*, Cambridge UK: Cambridge University Press.

Humphreys, M. (2005). 'Natural Resources, Conflict, and Conflict Resolution: Uncovering the Mechanisms', *Journal of Conflict Resolution,* 49: 508–37.

Kaplan, R. (1994). 'The Coming Anarchy', *Atlantic Monthly*, 273: 44–76.

King, G., Honaker, J., Joseph, A. and Scheve, K. (2001). 'Analyzing Incomplete Political Science Data: an Alternative Algorithm for Multiple Imputation', *American Political Science Review*, 95: 49–69.

King, G., and Zeng, L. (2001). 'Logistic Regression in Rare Events Data', *Political Analysis*, 9: 137–63.

Lujala, P., Gleditsch, N.P. and Gilmore, E. (2005). 'A diamond curse? Civil war and a lootable resource', *Journal of Conflict Resolution*, 49: 538–62.

Michailof, S. (1993). *La France et L'Afrique: vade-mecum pour un nouveau voyage*, Paris: Karthala.

Michailof, S. (2005). 'Côte d'Ivoire 2005: bienvenue sur le Titanic!', *Commentaire*, 28: 393–404.

Miguel, E., Satyanath, S. and Sergenti, E. (2004). 'Economic Shocks and Civil Conflict: An Instrumental Variables Approach', *Journal of Political Economy*, 112: 725–53.

Mueller, J. (2004). *The Remnants of War*. Ithaca, NY: Cornell University Press.

Oyefusi, A. (2007). 'Oil-dependence and Civil conflict in Nigeria', WPS/2007-09. http://www.csae.ox.ac.uk/workingpapers/wps-list.html.

Rohner, D. (2006). 'Beach holiday in Bali or East Timor? Why conflict can lead to under- and overexploitation of natural resources', *Economics Letters,* 92: 113–17.

Ross, M. (2004). 'What Do We Know about Natural Resources and Civil War?', *Journal of Peace Research,* 41: 337–56.

Sachs, J., and Warner, A.M. (2000). 'Natural Resource Abundance and Economic Growth' in: G.M. Meier and J.E. Rauch, *Leading Issues in Economic Development,* 7th ed, Oxford: Oxford University Press.

Singer, J.D., and Small, M. (1994). 'Correlates of war project: International and civil war data, 1816–1992', Ann Arbor MI: Inter-University Consortium for Political and Social Research.

Small, M., and Singer, J.D. (1982). *Resort to Arms: International and Civil War, 1816–1980,* Beverly Hills CA: Sage.

Strategic Foresight Group (2006). 'Cost of Conflict in Sri Lanka', Mumbai: Strategic Foresight Group.

Tilly, C. (ed) (1975). *The Formation of National States in Western Europe,* Princeton NJ: Princeton University Press.

Weinstein, J.M. (2005). 'Resources and the Information Problem in Rebel Recruitment', *Journal of Conflict Resolution,* 49: 598–624.

World Bank (2006). *World Development Indicators,* Washington DC: World Bank.

Wooldridge, J.M. (2002). *Econometric Analysis of Cross Section and Panel Data,* Cambridge MA: MIT Press.

3 On the duration of civil war

With Anke Hoeffler and Måns Söderbom

3.1 Introduction

This chapter explores empirically the duration of civil war. The subject is of interest both for policy and as a means of distinguishing between alternative theories of civil conflict. From the policy perspective, a distinctive feature of civil war is its persistence. The average civil war lasts over six times longer than the average international war.[1] Given the long duration of civil wars, an important policy question is how civil wars can be shortened. Fortunately, it is possible to access a comprehensive dataset of international policy interventions in civil wars, thus making it possible to investigate the efficacy of these interventions in shortening conflict. Furthermore, this article investigates the effect of changes in the price of exported primary commodities. This approximates the curtailment of rebel incomes from the plunder of natural resources. Several initiatives now have this objective, most notably the newly launched Kimberley Process of diamond certification. From the perspective of theory, this analysis casts some light on whether rebel groups regard civil war as a cost of achieving post-conflict change, or as itself constituting an improvement upon the pre-conflict state.

3.2 The duration of conflict in the literature on civil war

The literature on civil war currently offers three rival conceptualizations of rebellion. The first is rebellion-as-investment. In this approach, the payoff to rebellion, whether political or material, is treated as being contingent upon rebel victory. The articulated aspirations of rebel groups suggest that this eventual payoff is political, and a large case-study literature usually takes this at face value.[2] The celebrated model of Grossman (1991) makes the same assumption about the importance of victory, but treats the payoff as financial. These models have testable implications for the duration of conflict. Although the original Grossman model was not temporal, in a simple extension Grossman (1995) introduced a discount rate into the analysis. Building on this, Collier and Hoeffler (1998) modelled the benefits as accruing upon victory, *while during the period of fighting the rebels incurred net costs.* In this structure, the longer the expected duration of war, the higher are the costs and the more heavily discounted are the benefits. *A key prediction is that the higher the payoff from victory, the longer would be the warranted rebellion.* The payoff from victory might be narrowly self-serving, such as the capture of government revenues, or altruistic, such as the release from repression. Collier and Hoeffler (2004) have found that one of the risk factors making a country prone to civil war is the presence of primary commodity exports with large rents. If the payoff to civil war is the post-conflict control of such resources, then a testable prediction is that *the duration of civil war should be increased by the extent of pre-conflict primary commodity exports.* If, instead, the post-conflict payoff is more altruistic, such as release from repression, then a testable prediction would be that *the duration of civil war is increased by the severity of pre-conflict political repression.*

The second conceptualization is rebellion-as-mistake. Hirshleifer (2001), in particular, has stressed the scope for misperceptions: for example, analogous to the 'winner's curse', each side may overestimate its military prospects. Such misperceptions would evidently make wars more likely to start, but they might also explain why they persist. Because civil war is socially costly, it is always possible to envisage an agreed return to peace in which both protagonists are better off. However, if each side overestimates its prospects of victory, there may be no peaceful outcome in which both protagonists *recognize* that they are better off. In this case, a settlement recognized as mutually beneficial being infeasible, the conflict continues. In the sample used for this article, the mean duration of conflict is seven years, and this very persistence of costly conflicts demonstrates the considerable difficulties in achieving a settlement that both protagonists consider advantageous. In order to apply this explanation for the persistence of rebellion to *differences* in the duration of conflict, we need to establish the circumstances in which misperceptions have particularly debilitating effects on the ability to reach a settlement.

Clearly, one differentiating feature is the magnitude of the misperceptions of military prospects. Other things being equal, the larger is the mutual degree of overoptimism about military prospects, the longer will the war last. This trivial-sounding proposition turns out to have a readily testable proxy. In the context of civil war, the winner's curse implies that in those situations in which war is initiated, both parties will tend to be overoptimistic. Evidently, where both sides are overpessimistic, they will strive hard to avoid escalating the situation to the point of warfare. However, as the war proceeds, the continuing flow of new military information inconsistent with these initially over-optimistic expectations should gradually force their revision towards greater realism. As expectations converge towards reality, it becomes progressively easier to find a settlement recognized as mutually beneficial. Hence, if errors in expectations are the chief explanation for the persistence of civil war, a testable prediction is that *the probability of reaching a settlement in each time period should rise over time.* That is, the chance of ending the war would be higher in the third year than in the second, and so on.

Now consider whether, for a given degree of over-optimism about military prospects, there are other features which differentiate the duration of conflict, but which indeed depend upon some degree of over-optimism? One such feature is the cost of conflict to society. If the cost is sufficiently large, then even with substantial over-optimism, it should be possible to find a mutually beneficial settlement. The social cost of conflict is indeed likely to vary systematically across societies. One reasonable proposition is that the higher the costs of conflict, the higher is the per capita income of the society prior to the conflict, implying the testable proposition that *the duration of war would be negatively related to initial per capita income.* Unfortunately, this proposition does not distinguish the war-as-mistake approach from the other approaches. This is because a high social cost of conflict is likely also to imply a high private cost of conflict for the rebel group, and both the other approaches would predict that higher private costs of rebellion would imply shorter conflicts.

A second feature which differentiates the duration of conflict is the extent to which the share of income accruing to each protagonist depends upon victory versus defeat. If the distributional swing dependent upon the military outcome is very large, then even a modest degree of over-optimism will be sufficient to preclude a settlement recognized as mutually beneficial. A fairly good proxy for the distributional swing contingent upon the military outcome is the distribution of income in the society prior to the conflict. The more unequal is the society, then the larger are the gains from moving to the top of the ranking, which victory can be presumed to achieve, leading to the testable prediction that *initial inequality is positively related to the duration of conflict.* Again, unfortunately, this does not distinguish the conflict-as-mistake approach from the other approaches. The greater is inequality for a given level of income, the worse off are the poor and so the lower the cost of rebel recruitment. Both the other approaches would predict that the lower the costs of recruitment, the longer would be the duration of conflict.

The third conceptualization is rebellion-as-business. In this literature, the rebellion pays off through income or satisfaction *during* the fighting: rebels gain despite the costs to society. Collier (2000) models the rebellion as 'quasi-criminal', the opportunity for looting during the conflict providing the motivation.[3] Collier and Hoeffler (2004) allow the rebellion to be motivated by non-economic objectives, but with financial and military viability during conflict as the binding constraint. They suggest that all societies have at least a few hundred people attracted by the role of the rebel and willing to engage in sustained violence for hazy objectives. If such subjective grievance is indeed widespread across societies, it cannot explain why some societies experience civil wars whereas most do not. In this case, the relevant explanatory variables for the occurrence of conflict are those that determine the relatively rare conditions in which aggrieved people can combine into an organization that is financially and militarily viable. Rebellions will occur where and only where they are profitable (although they need not be motivated by profit).

They will be profitable where revenues during conflict are atypically high and costs atypically low. One component of rebel revenue stressed by Collier and Hoeffler (2004) is the extortion of revenues from primary commodity exports, most notably natural resources where the rents are often very high. A testable prediction of this approach is that the duration of conflict should be related to the world price of these exports. Like the test of the war-as-mistake approach, this has the advantage of being time-variant. That is, *prospects of peace should improve when world prices are low, implying a squeeze on rebel finances, and deteriorate when world prices are high.* The base period against which to compare prices would be the time at which the conflict started. When world prices of the commodity exported by the country are below this level, rebellion is less profitable than it was initially; when they are above this level, the rebellion is more profitable than it was initially.

In effect, whereas in the second conceptualization the persistence of rebellion reflects mistakes, now rebellions persist *unless* they are mistakes. One prediction of this approach is that unless the revenues or costs change, *the chance of peace per period will be negligible and will not change significantly.* As noted, the cost of conflict enters in all three approaches but with differences. The rebellion-as-investment approach assumes that during conflict, rebels have net costs, whereas the rebellion-as-business approach assumes that rebel revenue exceeds costs. The rebellion-as-mistake approach is concerned with the overall costs to society.

In addition to this economic analysis of the duration of conflict, different literatures have also proposed social, geographic, historical, psychological and policy influences. Although these are not integrated into a single model, they are evidently worth investigation and we briefly discuss them. Peer pressure and solidarity are critical to military effectiveness. There is some evidence that social diversity makes cooperation more difficult, leading to the prediction that *socially diverse rebellions should be shorter.*[4] A further speculation from the military literature is that some terrain is particularly suitable to sustained rebellion. The use of 'agent orange' to defoliate areas of Vietnam was a dramatic instance of the hypothesis that forest cover sustains conflict. The rise of global private and clandestine markets in both armaments and illicit primary commodities, such as 'conflict' diamonds, timber and drugs, has led some analysts to speculate that conflict has become increasingly viable and so easier to sustain.[5] Finally, international relations scholars have discussed the extent to which international policy interventions have succeeded in shortening wars (Regan, 2002).

3.3 Data and econometric model

The analysis of war duration is critically dependent upon definitions of what constitutes a war, its start and its end. Following the Correlates of War (COW) project, we define civil wars as violent conflicts that resulted in at least 1,000 battle-related deaths per annum.[6] In addition, these conflicts are internal to a country, and the nongovernmental forces are responsible for a minimum of 5 per cent of the deaths in order to distinguish civil wars from massacres. For many conflicts, the COW project offers start and end dates and thus can be used for duration analysis. Trigger events, for example the assassination of Rwanda's president on 6 March 1994, often spark a civil war. If the conflict ended in a peace treaty, ceasefire or military defeat, it is also easy to date the end of the civil war. However, often the violence escalates over some period of time before it reaches the relevant threshold and thus can be defined as a civil war. Military victories and peace treaties are also relatively rare in civil wars, and dating the end of the civil wars is often difficult. In many cases, the number of fatalities falls beneath the threshold and is thus not counted as a civil war, although the country is not at peace. Thus, higher death thresholds result in recording shorter civil wars. For example, in our dataset the mean duration of civil war is about seven years, while the civil wars in Fearon's (2004) sample have an average of about 12 years. The difference is because Fearon includes conflicts which resulted in a minimum of 1,000 deaths over their entire duration as civil wars. Furthermore, a higher threshold leads to a higher number of repeat war episodes. Take, for example, a conflict during which the number of battle-related deaths is lower than the per annum threshold for some period before the level of violence escalates again. A rigid application of the absolute threshold criterion could lead to the classification of two conflicts for a high-threshold definition and to the classification of one conflict for a low-threshold definition. By our definition, 77 civil wars started during the period 1960–99.[7]

This article uses a new dataset on international policy interventions in civil war, collected by Regan (2002).[8] His operational definition of third-party interventions in intrastate conflicts includes 'convention-breaking military and/or economic activities in the internal affairs of a foreign country targeted at the authority structures of the government with the aim of affecting the balance of power between the government and opposition forces' (Regan, 2000: 2). The notion of convention breaking allows him to discriminate between the normal course of international influence and interventions. Regan lists a number of different economic and military interventions. Economic interventions include grants, loans, non-military equipment or expertise, credits, relief of past obligations and economic sanctions. For this article, a dummy variable 'economic intervention' was created, taking a value of 1 if any of these interventions took place. Regan distinguishes between six different types of military intervention: troops, naval forces, equipment or aid, intelligence or advisers, air support and military sanctions. If any of these six interventions occurred, we classified it as a military intervention. Furthermore, he distinguishes between how the intervention is targeted: in favour of the government, in favour of the opposition, or neutrally, and we retain this disaggregation.

Our other explanatory variables are from the dataset of Collier and Hoeffler (2004). This attempts to collect socio-economic, political and geographic data for all the 77 civil wars, based on the definition discussed above. Data limitations, notably missing data on key variables, reduce the effective sample to 55 wars, which are listed in Appendix Table 3A.1. Summary definitions of the socio-economic variables are given in the Appendix. Table 3A.2 presents descriptive statistics of all the variables, giving means for all the conflicts in the sample, disaggregated into those for shorter and longer conflicts.

The regression analysis is based on maximum likelihood estimation, where the econometric specification is a hazard model of the monthly transition rates from war to peace. To illustrate the model, let $\tau = 1, ..., T$ denote calendar time (in months), where $\tau = 1$ represents January 1960 and $\tau = T$ December 1999, and let t denote the duration of a war that started at a point in time a between $\tau = 1$ and $\tau = T - 1$. We assume a proportional hazard function of exponential form:

$$h(t; x_\tau, \mu, \theta) = \exp(x_\tau \beta + \mu) h^B(t), \tag{1}$$

where x_τ is a vector of observed exogenous variables, θ is a vector of unknown parameters of which β is a sub-vector, μ is a country-specific unobserved random effect assumed orthogonal to x_τ and h^B is the baseline hazard. Subscript τ on the vector of explanatory variables indicates that the explanatory variables may be, but are not necessarily, time-varying.[9] For the baseline hazard, a piecewise exponential specification was adopted. Specifically, we divide the time axis into W intervals by the points $c_1, c_2, ..., c_W$, and constant baseline hazard rates within each interval were assumed:

$$h^B(t) = \exp\left(\alpha + \sum_{w=2}^{W} \lambda_w d_w(t)\right), \tag{2}$$

where $d_w(t)$ is a duration dummy variable equal to 1 if $c_{w-1} < t \le c_w$ for $c_0 = 0$ and $c_W = \infty$, and 0 otherwise; α is an intercept; and $\lambda_2, ..., \lambda_W$ are baseline hazard parameters to be estimated. Thus, the baseline hazard is allowed to vary freely between intervals, which imposes few restrictions on duration dependence. Because an intercept was included in the model and the first duration dummy (i.e. d_1) was excluded, negative (positive) coefficients on $\lambda_2, ..., \lambda_W$ imply that the hazard is lower (higher) than in the first interval.

Now consider the likelihood function. A completed ($\delta = 1$) or censored ($\delta = 0$) war of length t is observed with likelihood

$$L(t; x_\tau, \mu, \theta) = [h(t; x_\tau, \mu, \theta)]^\delta \cdot S(t; x_\tau, \mu, \theta) \tag{3}$$

where $S(t; \cdot) = \exp(-\Lambda(t; \cdot))$ is the survivor function and $\Lambda(t; \cdot)$ is the integral of the hazard function over time with limits $(a, a + t)$.[10] While this likelihood depends on the unobserved country random effect μ, the parameter vector θ can still be estimated consistently if μ is integrated out.[11] This is a relatively straightforward task under the maintained assumption that μ is orthogonal to x_r. If there is no unobserved heterogeneity in the data, that is, zero variance of μ, the likelihood simplifies to $L(t{:}x_r,\, \theta) = [h(t{;}x_r,\theta)]^\delta \cdot S(t{;}x_r,\, \theta)$.

The sample likelihood, finally, is simply the product of the relevant individual likelihood contributions. With N countries and $R(i)$ wars occurring in country i over the sampling period, the sample likelihood of the model with unobserved heterogeneity is

$$\lambda_{UH} = \prod_{i=1}^{N} \int \prod_{r=1}^{R(i)} L_{ir}\, (t;\, x_r, \mu,\, \theta)\, g\, (\mu)\, d\mu, \tag{4}$$

where L_{ir} is the likelihood of the rth war in country i and $g(\mu)$ is a density function. Without unobserved country heterogeneity, no integration is necessary, hence

$$\lambda = \prod_{i=1}^{N} \prod_{r=1}^{R(i)} L_{ir}\, (t;\, x_r,\, \theta). \tag{5}$$

Given the functional form of (1), this is the same likelihood as that of the ordinary exponential regression, generalized to allow for a piecewise baseline hazard.

3.4 Empirical results

As a first step, estimates of the parameters of a hazard function in which explanatory variables and unobserved heterogeneity are absent are derived:

$$h\, (t) = \exp\left(\alpha + \sum_{w=2}^{W} \lambda_w\, d_w\, (t)\right) \equiv h^B\, (t). \tag{6}$$

This, of course, is restrictive, but serves as a usual benchmark. The underlying assumption is that the monthly hazard rates are constant over a period of 12 months. Rather than reporting the estimates of the parameters, α, λ_2, ..., λ_W, Figure 3.1 shows the estimated hazard function up to 17 years.[12] The graph shows estimates based on both the full sample of 77 wars and the estimation sample of 55 wars, and the results are similar. Clearly, the hazard of peace falls quite rapidly in the early phases of war and then starts to increase after three years of war, albeit slowly. In the following discussion, the effects of including explanatory variables are considered.

Table 3.1 presents the preferred reference model of conflict duration with eight variants. The reference model is reached after a series of iterations in which insignificant variables are deleted and variants of economic, social, geographic and historical explanatory variables are then tested in turn. Given the small sample, it is desirable to keep the number of segments of the baseline hazard as small as possible without imposing too many strong restrictions on the data. Guided by Figure 3.1, the interval between 0 and 72 months was divided into three two-year periods, while beyond 72 months the hazard was assumed to be flat. Experimentation with the data showed that the main

Table 3.1 Econometric estimates of hazard function parameters

	(1)	(2)	(3)	(4)
Income inequality	-0.1244 (0.0284)***	-0.1258 (0.0283)***	-0.1186 (0.0306)***	-0.1262 (0.0289)***
Missing inequality	-5.868 (1.2774)***	-5.8717 (1.2689)***	-5.6289 (1.3644)***	-5.9118 (1.2800)***
Per capita income	0.3651 (0.1322)***	0.4043 (0.1370)***	0.4452 (0.1736)***	0.3633 (0.1332)***
Ethnic fractionalization	-0.0628 (0.0259)**	-0.0695 (0.0261)***	-0.0788 (0.0270)***	-0.0624 (0.0258)**
Ethnic fractionalization^2	0.0006 (0.003)**	0.0007 (0.0003)**	0.0008 (0.0003)***	0.0006 (0.003)**
In population	-0.3164 (0.1231)***	-0.2860 (0.1225)**	-0.2373 (0.1587)	-0.3318 (0.1325)***
1970s	0.0078 (0.4625)	0.1298 (0.4677)	0.0064 (0.5049)	0.0041 (0.4622)
1980s	-1.4202 (0.5203)***	-1.3830 (0.5256)***	-1.5404 (0.5865)***	-1.4282 (0.5202)***
1990s	-1.1621 (0.5417)**	-1.1810 (0.5405)**	-0.9705 (0.6332)	-1.1796 (0.5469)**
3rd and 4th years of war (λ_2)	-0.8067 (0.5743)	-0.8747 (0.5790)	-1.2103 (0.6590)*	-0.8146 (0.5746)
5th and 6th years of war (λ_3)	-0.0011 (0.5606)	0.0044 (0.5601)	-0.0460 (0.5619)	-0.0170 (0.5614)
7th year of war and beyond (λ_4)	0.6098 (0.4464)	0.7100 (0.4440)	0.7471 (0.4592)*	0.5966 (0.4470)
Change in commodity price index (CPI)		1.7669 (1.0629)*	2.1929 (1.0304)**	
Primary commodity exports/GDP (sxp)		10.6114 (5.9267)*	12.2126 (5.6428)**	
CPI*sxp		-11.3237 (5.8518)**	-13.2774 (5.7058)**	
Democracy				0.0189 (0.0584)
Constant	7.4331 (2.7079)***	5.2044 (3.0352)*	3.8077 (3.4190)	7.7223 (2.8481)***
Log likelihood	-80.43	-78.18	-67.05	-80.38
Number of observations	55	55	51	55

Income inequality	-0.1247 (0.0284)***	-0.1264 (0.0275)***	-0.1312 (0.0306)***	-0.1314 (0.0320)***	-0.1264 (0.0293)***
Missing inequality	-5.868 (1.2798)***	-5.7676 (1.2254)***	-6.0510 (1.3523)***	-6.1956 (1.4352)***	-6.1673 (1.3247)***
Per capita income	0.3820 (0.1401)***		0.3114 (0.1482)**	0.3581 (0.1356)***	0.4264 (0.1353)***
Ethnic fractionalization	-0.0635 (0.0260)**	-0.0685 (0.0260)***	-0.0691 (0.0270)***	-0.0647 (0.0261)***	-0.0803 (0.0273)**
Ethnic fractionalization^2	0.0006 (0.003)**	0.0007 (0.0003)**	0.0007 (0.0003)**	0.0006 (0.0003)**	0.0008 (0.0003)**

Table 3.1 continued

	(5)	(6)	(7)	(8)	(9)
In population	−0.3217	−0.4768	−0.3523	−0.3163	−0.3500
	(0.1224)***	(0.1283)***	(0.1388)***	(0.1266)***	(0.1299)***
1970s	0.0160	0.0962	0.0350	0.0844	−0.0771
	(0.4637)	(0.4586)	(0.4657)	(0.4727)	(0.4742)
1980s	−1.4021	−1.4378	−1.4530	−1.4146	−1.7871
	(0.5228)***	(0.5137)***	(0.5253)***	(0.5222)***	(0.5615)***
1990s	−1.1823	−1.2212	−1.1042	−1.1072	−1.4467
	(0.5506)**	(0.5309)**	(0.5564)**	(0.5541)**	(0.5678)***
3rd and 4th years of war (λ_2)	−0.8013	−0.8458	−0.8189	−0.8055	−0.7438
	(0.5748)	(0.5691)	(0.5759)	(0.5747)	(0.5854)
5th and 6th years of war (λ_3)	0.0072	−0.1095	−0.0334	−0.0056	0.0421
	(0.5619)	(0.5476)	(0.5597)	(0.5612)	(0.5786)
7th year of war and beyond (λ_4)	0.6176	0.4758	0.5852	0.5784	0.4948
	(0.4504)	(0.4182)	(0.4442)	(0.4514)	(0.5001)
Primary commodity exports/GDP (sxp)	−0.6079				
	(1.6205)				
Male secondary school enrollment rates		0.0272			
		(0.0092)***			
Religious fractionalization			−0.0136		
			(0.0399)		
Religious fractionalization^2			0.0001		
			(0.0006)		
Mountains				−0.0068	
				(0.0084)	
Forests				0.0011	
				(0.0094)	
Pro-government economic intervention					−0.0167
					(0.1592)
Pro-rebel economic intervention					−0.1747
					(0.4180)
Pro-government military intervention					−0.0127
					(0.0806)
Pro-rebel military intervention					0.1994
					(0.0933)**
Constant	7.5691	9.9927	8.6983	7.9985	8.3512
	(2.7225)***	(2.7974)***	(3.2204)***	(2.9428)***	(2.8474)***
Log likelihood	−80.56	−80.03	−80.09	−80.10	−76.93
Number of observations	55	55	55	55	55

Notes: z-statistics are based on asymptotic standard errors. Significance at the 10%, 5% and 1% level is indicated by *, ** and ***, respectively. All results have been calculated using Stata Release 8.0 (StataCorp, 2003).

results are robust to alternative definitions. Throughout, no evidence was found that unobserved heterogeneity was present in the data, and therefore results are shown without controls for unobserved heterogeneity.[13] The translation from the hazard (which is a density function) to a single summary number for the duration of conflict is non-trivial: an increase in the 'hazard' of peace will evidently shorten the expected duration of conflict, but the relationship is not linear. While the regression results directly report the parameters of the hazard

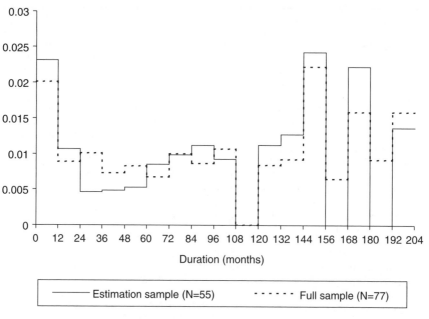

Figure 3.1 Estimates of the hazard function without controls for explanatory variables.

Notes: The hazard function is calculated using the formula exp: $[\hat{\alpha} + \Sigma_w \hat{\lambda}_w d_w (t)]$, where, $\hat{\alpha}, \hat{\lambda}_2, ...,$ $\hat{\lambda}_w$ are parameter estimates obtained by means of maximum likelihood. The underlying regression is not reported but is available on request from the authors.

function, the effects of important variables upon the expected duration of conflict are reported below.

First, the results of the reference model (column 1) are considered. The most significant variable in the model is income inequality, as measured by the Gini coefficient. Globally comparable data on income inequality are limited. To preserve sample size, missing values of the Gini coefficient were replaced by zeros and a dummy variable was added, taking the value 1 for missing observations and 0 for complete ones.[14] Income inequality, as measured by the Gini coefficient, is not just statistically highly significant, it has large effects. At the mean of other variables, a ten-point increase in the Gini coefficient (from 41 to 51) increases the expected duration of conflict from 59 months to 144 months – an elasticity of duration with respect to inequality of 4. Although income inequality is evidently important, the routes by which it affects the duration of conflict are open to multiple interpretations. It might be proxying the difference between the victory and defeat payoffs, as suggested by the rebellion-as-mistake approach. It might also be proxying the costs of recruitment: since recruits tend to come from the poor, for a given mean per capita income, the greater is inequality the lower will be recruitment costs. In turn, lower costs will imply a longer conflict in both the rebellion-as-investment and the rebellion-as-business approaches.

The next significant variable is per capita income. Higher income increases the hazard of peace and thus reduces the expected duration of conflict. A 10 per cent increase in per capita income is associated with a 5 per cent reduction in the duration of conflict, the elasticity being −0.5. Per capita income is correlated with so many other characteristics that it is difficult to interpret. However, the higher is per capita income prior to the conflict, the higher is the opportunity cost of conflict to society, and so one interpretation is that it is proxying this social cost.[15] No other variables characterizing the economy just prior to the conflict are significant in explaining the duration of conflict.[16]

Ethnic fractionalization is important for the duration of conflict. We measure it on a scale of 0 to 100. This measures the probability that two randomly drawn individuals do not belong to the same group. Thus, a value of 0 characterizes perfect homogeneity and 100 complete heterogeneity. The measure is based on the data from Atlas Narodov Mira (USSR, 1964). The effect of ethnic diversity is significant and substantial, but it is non-monotonic: the duration of conflict is at its maximum when ethnic fractionalization is around 50 on its 0–100 range. This typically occurs when the society has two or three large ethnic groups. One interpretation of this is that when there are only two major groups, one is the government side and the other is the rebel side, so that this degree of diversity at the national level actually increases social cohesion on the rebel side. Beyond this, higher levels of national diversity introduce diversity into the rebel side and so reduce cohesion. Evaluated at the mean values of the other variables, ethnic fractionalization of 50 is associated with a duration of conflict of 84 months. This falls to 59 months if the fractionalization score is 25, and to 70 months if the fractionalization score is 75. Collier and Hoeffler (2004) find a similar effect in their analysis of conflict initiation.

In addition to the social composition of the population, its size is significant: more populous countries tend to have longer wars. Doubling the population increases the duration of conflict by 18 per cent. However, this result needs to be interpreted with caution. It need not mean that any particular rebellion continues for longer in more populous countries. More populous countries tend to have more rebellions, though not necessarily more than proportionately to their population, and so may have several under way at the same time. A conflict is coded as continuing if any rebellion is continuing, so that this alone will tend to produce a correlation between country size and the duration of conflict. Hence, the results do not imply that a continent divided into many countries would have shorter wars than an otherwise identical continent divided into few countries.

Decade dummies have significant and substantial effects. At the means of other variables, the hazards of peace prevailing during the 1960s and 1970s were identical, implying an expected duration of 43 months, evaluated at the mean values of the other regressors. In the 1980s, the hazard of peace was much lower, implying an expected duration of 122 months. In the 1990s, there was a modest improvement, with the expected duration declining to 101 months. Evidently, from the model we cannot account for this large lengthening of conflict. A phenomenon stressed in the case study literature is the growing role of global markets, both for the illicit sale of natural resources by rebel groups and for the illicit purchase of armaments. These results are consistent with this literature. The small reduction in the expected duration of conflict during the 1990s is quite probably accounted for by a temporary surge in peace settlements following the end of the Cold War. During the Cold War, both superpowers had illicitly funded rebel groups opposed to governments in the rival bloc, and this source of finance rapidly declined once it was no longer useful.

The final parameter estimates in the reference model refer to the shape of the baseline hazard. As already discussed, the baseline hazard is assumed to be constant within, but potentially varying between, the intervals (0,24), (24,48) and (48,72) months, and flat beyond 72 months. Based on the estimates of the baseline, we investigate one prediction of the rebellion-as-mistake approach, namely, that the chances of peace should increase as each party is disabused of its initial military optimism. The broad pattern of the period-specific hazard is U-shaped. However, the only statistically significant component of the U-shape is that beyond six years of a conflict, where the chances of reaching peace are significantly better than during the third and fourth years.[17] This improvement over time in the chance of peace is consistent with the rebellion-as-mistake approach, but this should be set against the failure to find any more general tendency for chances to improve over time. Indeed, the more reasonable reading of the estimated baseline hazard parameters is the absence of any strong trend, something which is more consistent with the rebellion-as-business approach. We also investigated whether the characteristics that influence the duration of conflict are differentially important in different phases of conflict. For this, taking each significant variable in turn, interaction terms between the variable and the phase of conflict dummies were added but none was significant. Figure 3.2 shows the baseline hazard, evaluated at mean values of the explanatory variables. For reference, the dashed line shows the baseline hazard obtained without controls for explanatory variables. As expected, the evidence suggests that the latter exhibits some degree of bias towards negative duration dependence.

This evidence on the U-shaped path of the peace hazard can be related to the path of the risk of conflict initiation. One of the results from the analysis of the initiation of conflict is that the risk is temporarily much higher in post-conflict situations. Evidently, something happens during the conflict that increases this risk. For example, one obvious hypothesis is that since conflict causes grievances, it is these accumulated grievances that make the reversion to war more likely. Although the concept of conflict continuation

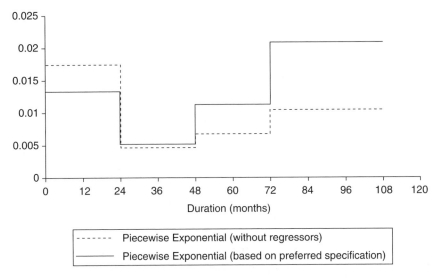

Figure 3.2 Piecewise exponential estimates of the hazard function.

Notes: The hazard function based on the preferred specification (i.e. the reference model) is calculated using the formula $\exp[\bar{x}_r \,\hat{\beta}] \cdot \exp[\hat{\alpha} + \Sigma_u \,\hat{\lambda}_w \, d_w \,(t)]$, where $\hat{\beta}, \hat{\alpha}, \hat{\lambda}_2, \ldots, \hat{\lambda}_w$ are the parameter estimates and $\bar{x}_r$ denotes a vector of sample means of the explanatory variables. The hazard function without regressors was calculated as explained in the notes to Figure 3.1. The underlying regression is not reported but is available on request from the authors.

is not the same as that of conflict re-ignition, it is reasonable to suppose that the risk of conflict re-ignition, which is latent during conflict, broadly follows the observed risk of conflict continuation. While the risk of conflict *initiation* is much higher after a conflict than before it, the risk of conflict *continuation* does not rise continuously during the conflict – indeed, if anything it declines. Hence, the latent risk of conflict re-ignition probably jumps with the onset of the conflict. This jump may be more related to the establishment of the rebel military organization than to any sudden upsurge in grievances.[18]

Columns 2 and 3 present variants of this reference model that are on the borderline of statistical significance and are pertinent for testing the rebellion-as-business approach. In these variants, we introduce data on changes in the world price of the country's primary commodity exports. The case study literature suggests that rebel groups often rely upon the plunder of natural resources and, sometimes, other primary commodities, in order to sustain conflict financially (see Klare, 2001, for a discussion). Lower world prices would therefore squeeze rebel finances and potentially shorten the conflict. Evidently, governments also get revenue from primary commodities, and the net effect in any particular instance would depend upon which party was more dependent upon commodity taxation for its finance, but a presumption might be that normally rebel groups have fewer alternative sources of finance than governments. The issue is of some policy importance since international efforts are currently underway to reduce rebel access to global commodity markets, notably for diamonds and timber. The effect of such efforts is not literally to exclude rebels from the market, but rather to create a price discount for rebel supplies – industry sources suggest that the early effects of the Kimberley Process of diamond certification have been to create a discount of around 10 per cent for illicit diamonds. A reduction in the world price to an extent simulates such rebel-specific discounts. For this analysis, a weighted export price series constructed by Dehn (2000) was used. Specific export price indices, for which the base period is the year of the onset of the conflict, were constructed.[19] The resulting indices are year-by-year time-varying (for a given war), and we are, therefore, investigating how price changes from the time of conflict initiation affect duration. Evidently, such changes in prices are only even potentially important to the extent that the country has such exports, and so the relevant concept is the price index multiplied by the pre-conflict share of primary commodity exports in GDP. To enable the interpretation of this interaction term, its two components were also separately introduced into the regression. The effect of a change in commodity prices then has to be evaluated for each particular level of commodity dependence, as the net effect of the three variables. Because Dehn's series is not available for a few countries, we investigate two approaches to missing variables. In column (2), we impose the mean value of the variable on missing observations, and in column (3) we delete missing observations. The two approaches produce very similar results, although the latter yields higher levels of statistical significance. The new variables are each significant at 5 per cent, although jointly they are not quite significant.[20] The effect of changes in world prices depends upon the initial level of a country's exports. For low levels of dependence upon primary commodity exports, world prices have no significant effect. However, taking a fairly high but not atypical initial level of such exports in GDP of 30 per cent, a sustained reduction in the world price of 10 per cent would shorten the duration of conflict by 12 per cent. This result gives some support to the rebellion-as-business approach.

The next variants consider those variables that might proxy the expected payoff to victory. Recall that this payoff may be political or financial, and according to the rebellion-as-investment approach, it should increase the duration of conflict. The expected political payoff to victory is proxied by a measure of pre-conflict political repression. If rebellions are commonly struggles to end elite oppression, which is the media image that rebel groups usually portray, it might be expected that the more severe the repression prior to the conflict, the longer would the conflict tend to persist. As a proxy for political repression, the Polity III dataset measure of the openness of the political institutions (Jaggers and Gurr, 1995) is used. The scale runs from 0 (least open) to 10 (most open). In contrast to inequality, this proxy for the political payoff to victory is insignificant (column 4).[21]

The expected financial payoff to victory is proxied by the pre-conflict share of primary commodity exports in GDP. Primary commodity exports are the most readily taxable sector of an economy, and their capture might well be the lure for victory. However, the regression results find that primary commodity exports have no significant effect on the duration of conflict (column 5). The rebellion-as-business approach would suggest that the reason for this is that the plunder of primary commodities does not require victory, but can be conducted during the conflict. Taken together, the absence of significant effects from both political repression and primary commodities casts some doubt upon the key assumption of the rebellion-as-investment approach.

In the reference model, per capita GDP is significant, and we have suggested that one interpretation of this variable is that it is proxying the social cost of conflict. In column 6, we try an alternative variable which can also be seen as proxying these costs, namely, the proportion of young males enrolled in secondary schooling. To the extent that the pertinent opportunity cost is that of rebel recruits, who are drawn predominantly from young males, this proxy may be more accurate than per capita GDP. The coefficient on school enrolment is also significant and positive: societies with higher enrolment rates for males in secondary school have higher hazards of peace and thus shorter expected conflicts. Unfortunately, per capita income and secondary school enrolment are too highly correlated to be included in the same regression, and statistically there is little to choose between them.

In column 7, religious fractionalization is introduced; the proxy is analogous to ethnic fractionalization. The religious diversity measure is based on the *World Christian Encyclopaedia* (Barrett, 1982). Unlike ethnic fractionalization, it has no significant effect, whether entered as a linear or a quadratic relationship. Possibly, religion is less useful than ethnicity as a force for military cohesion.

In column 8, proxies for geography are investigated. Specifically, the extent of forest coverage and the extent of mountainous terrain are investigated. Neither is significant. Evidently, mountains and forests offer safe havens for rebels in necessity. Perhaps, however, the results suggest that in the circumstances where it has proved feasible to escalate a conflict to a substantial scale – so that it is included in our sample – it can be sustained militarily even without favourable geography.

The final variant introduced is international policy interventions (column 9). Four types of intervention can be distinguished, according to whether they are economic or military, and according to whether they are pro-government or pro-rebel. Each intervention is dated by month. This gives the option of treating an intervention as only likely to be effective during that month, or allowing it to have a continuing effect. In the reported results, the latter was assumed although the former was also investigated. Specifically, a measure that cumulates the number of months of each type of intervention from the onset of the war (at time a) to each of the periods $(a + 1, a + 2, ..., a + t)$ was constructed. For example, sustained pro-government military assistance is therefore entered not as a constant dummy variable, but with a steadily rising value over time. Hence, our interventions variables are month-by-month time-varying. Since interventions are purposive, the results must be treated with caution. For example, interventions might be targeted on situations that had become militarily critical, so that even if they had no effect, they would be correlated with the proximate subsequent end of conflict. Similarly, interventions might have the intention of aligning the intervening power with whichever side is set to win. In the event, the economic interventions, whether pro-government or pro-rebel, are completely insignificant. It is possible that economic interventions are systematically targeted to the side in danger of defeat, so that the apparent lack of an effect is because these interventions lengthen what would otherwise be conflicts in their last stages. However, a less contrived interpretation is surely that economic interventions have not usually been large enough to have a significant effect. Military intervention on the side of the government is also ineffective. The only intervention that is significant is military intervention on the side of the rebels. A possible interpretation is that with sufficient military support for rebels, government forces can be defeated: for example, the recent US support for the Northern Alliance in Afghanistan had this effect. By contrast, because rebel groups have the option of concealment, military support for the government may not produce a decisive military outcome.

Overall, the results are not decisive between the three different approaches outlined in the theoretical framework above. However, they offer some support for both rebellion-as-mistake and rebellion-as-business, while tending to reject rebellion-as-investment. The two better-supported approaches are not incompatible, and can be synthesized into a theory suggesting that long conflicts may be persistent because they are characterized by a double-bind. First, in long conflicts rebellion is likely to be sustainable as a going concern, as implied by the rebellion-as-business approach. If the gross costs of rebellion to the rebel group are low (low opportunity costs for recruits) and if rebel revenues during conflict are high (high commodity prices), rebels may be better off than prior to the conflict and therefore under little pressure to reach a settlement. This is then compounded by the difficulty of reaching a settlement recognized as mutually advantageous. The potential mutual gains to peace are modest (per capita income is low), relative to the gap between the defeat and victory payoffs (inequality is high).[22]

Finally, the implications for policies to shorten conflict are briefly considered. The potential for shortening conflict is partly through operating on the structural variables that characterize countries prior to conflict and partly through operating on the variables that change during conflict. At the structural level, low per capita income and high inequality were identified as lengthening conflict. Hence, the results suggest some support for regarding equitable economic development as a way of reducing the duration of conflict. With regard to the variables that can be changed during conflict, the results can be interpreted as indicating three variable forces for peace: a squeeze on rebel finances (a decline in commodity prices shortens conflict); a more realistic assessment of military prospects (by the seventh year of a conflict, the chances of peace per year have risen); and an exogenous change in the balance of military power (external military support for the rebels shortens conflict). Of these, the first appears to offer the clearest opportunities for international intervention.

3.5 Conclusion

A comprehensive dataset on large-scale violent civil conflicts since 1960 was used to analyse the duration of conflict by means of estimated hazard functions. The duration of conflict is systematically related both to structural conditions prevailing prior to conflict and to circumstances during conflict. The key structural characteristics that lengthen conflict are low per capita income, high inequality and a moderate degree of ethnic division. The key variable characteristics that shorten conflict are a decline in the prices of the primary commodities that the country exports and external military intervention on the side of the rebels. The internal clock of the conflict has relatively little effect on the chances of reaching peace, but the external clock seems to have been important. The chances of peace were much lower in the 1980s and 1990s than they had been previously. It was speculated that this may reflect the easier access of rebel groups to global markets for the sale of plundered commodities and for the purchase of armaments. An attempt was made to relate these results to three different approaches to civil war: rebellion-as-investment, in which the critical incentive is the post-conflict payoff; rebellion-as-business, in which the critical incentive is the payoff during conflict; and rebellion-as-mistake, in which military optimism prevents the recognition of any mutually advantageous settlement. This article suggests that the evidence was incompatible with the first of these approaches but was consistent with the others.

Appendix 3.1

Table 3A.1 Sample of 55 wars

Country	Start of the war	End of the war
Algeria	07/62	12/62
Algeria	05/91	ongoing
Angola	02/61	05/91
Angola	09/92	ongoing
Burma/Myanmar	68	10/80
Burma/Myanmar	02/83	07/95
Burundi	04/72	12/73
Burundi	08/88	08/88
Burundi	11/91	ongoing
Chad	03/80	08/88
China	08/66	07/69
Columbia	04/84	ongoing
Cyprus	07/74	08/74
Dominican Republic	04/65	09/65
El Salvador	10/79	01/92
Ethiopia	07/74	05/91
Guatemala	07/66	07/72
Guatemala	03/78	03/84
Guinea-Bissau	12/62	12/74
India	08/65	08/65
India	84	94
Indonesia	06/75	09/82
Iran	03/74	03/75
Iran	09/78	12/79
Iran	06/81	05/82
Iraq	09/61	11/63
Iraq	07/74	03/75
Iraq	01/85	12/92
Jordan	09/71	09/71
Morocco	10/75	11/89
Mozambique	10/64	11/75
Mozambique	07/76	10/92
Nicaragua	10/78	07/79
Nicaragua	03/82	04/90
Nigeria	01/66	01/70
Nigeria	12/80	08/84
Pakistan	03/71	12/71
Pakistan	01/73	07/77
Peru	03/82	12/96
Philippines	09/72	12/96
Romania	12/89	12/89
Rwanda	11/63	02/64
Rwanda	10/90	07/94
Sierra Leone	03/91	11/96
Somalia	04/82	12/92
Sri Lanka	04/71	05/71
Sri Lanka	07/83	ongoing
Sudan	07/83	ongoing
Turkey	07/91	ongoing
Uganda	05/66	06/66
Uganda	10/80	04/88
Yugoslavia	04/90	01/92
Zaire/Dem. Rep. of Congo	07/60	09/65
Zaire/Dem. Rep. of Congo	09/91	12/96
Zimbabwe	12/72	12/79

Table 3A.2 Summary statistics: means and standard deviations

	All wars, N = 55	Wars ≤ 48 months, N = 22	Wars > 48 months, N = 33
Income inequality	40.7	36.3	44.51
(Gini coefficient)	(8.9)	(7.0)	(8.8)
Per capita income, 1985	1707	2202	1376
constant US$	(1411)	(1759)	(1022)
Male secondary school	29.2	35.7	24.9
enrollment rates (%)	(23.3)	(25.8)	(20.7)
Primary commodity	0.15	0.14	0.15
exports/GDP	(0.13)	(0.12)	(0.14)
Commodity price	1.28	1.10	1.38
index (CPI)	(0.64)	(0.27)	(0.76)
Democracy, index 1–10	1.97	2.1	1.9
	(3.2)	(3.4)	(3.1)
Ethnic fractionalization,	51.9	42.3	58.3
index 1–100	(29.2)	(31.4)	(26.2)
Religious fractionalization,	35.5	31.4	38.3
index 1–100	(24.8)	(24.4)	(25.1)
ln population	16.48	16.41	16.53
	(1.47)	(1.72)	(1.31)
Mountainous terrain (%)	24.5	28.6	21.7
	(23.4)	(25.1)	(22.1)
Forest coverage (%)	23.6	13.8	30.1
	(18.8)	(11.0)	(20.2)
Economic pro-government	0.42		
interventions (months)	(1.08)		
Economic anti-government	0.15		
interventions (months)	(0.52)		
Military pro-government	1.84		
interventions (months)	(3.03)		
Military anti-government	1.71		
interventions (months)	(3.07)		

Note: Standard deviations in parentheses.

Appendix 3.2: Data sources

Commodity Price Index Weighted export price series compiled by Jan Dehn, based on the methodology developed in Deaton and Miller (1996). Source: Dehn (2000).

Democracy The degree of openness of democratic institutions is measured on a scale of 0 (low) to 10 (high). Source: http://www.cidcm.umd.edu/polity/index.html. The data are described in Jaggers and Gurr (1995).

Ethno-linguistic and Religious fractionalization We proxy social fractionalization in a combined measure of ethnic and religious fractionalization. Ethnic fractionalization is measured by the ethno-linguistic fractionalization index. It measures the probability that two randomly drawn individuals from a given country do not speak the same language. Data are available only for 1960. In the economics literature, this measure was first used by Mauro (1995). Using data from Barrett (1982) on religious affiliations, we constructed an analogous religious fractionalization index. Following Barro (1997), we aggregated the various religious affiliations into nine categories: Catholic, Protestant, Muslim, Jew, Hindu, Buddhist, Eastern Religions (other than Buddhist), Indigenous Religions and no religious affiliation.

The fractionalization indices range from 0 to 100. A value of 0 indicates that the society is completely homogenous whereas a value of 100 would characterize a completely heterogeneous society.

We calculated our social fractionalization index as the product of the ethno-linguistic fractionalization and the religious fractionalization index plus the ethno-linguistic or the religious fractionalization index, whichever is the greater. By adding either index, we avoid classifying a country as homogenous (a value of 0) if the country is ethnically homogenous but religiously diverse, or vice versa.

Forest Coverage   We used the FAO measure of the proportion of a country's terrain which is covered in woods and forest. Source: http://www.fao. org/forestry.

GDP per capita   We measure income as real PPP adjusted GDP per capita. The primary dataset is the Penn World Tables 5.6 (Summers and Heston, 1991). Since the data are available only from 1960–92, we used the growth rates of real PPP adjusted GDP per capita data from the World Development Indicators (World Bank, 1998) in order to obtain income data for the 1990s.

Income Inequality   Income Inequality is measured by the Gini coefficient. Source: Deininger and Squire (1996).

Interventions   We used Patrick Regan's data on interventions. He defines third-party interventions in intrastate conflicts as 'convention breaking military and/or economic activities in the internal affairs of a foreign country targeted at the authority structures of the government with the aim of affecting the balance of power between the government and opposition forces'. Economic interventions include: grants, loans, nonmilitary equipment or expertise, credits, relieve past obligations and economic sanctions; and military interventions include: troops, naval forces, equipment or aid, intelligence or advisers, air support and military sanctions. Furthermore, he distinguishes between different targets, in favour of the government, in favour of the opposition and neutral interventions. Data can be downloaded from http:// bingweb.binghamton.edu/~pregan/.

Male Secondary School Enrolment Rates   We measure male secondary school enrolment rates as gross enrolment ratios, that is, the ratio of total enrolment, regardless of age, to the population of the age group that officially corresponds to the level of education shown. Secondary education completes the provision of basic education that began at the primary level and aims at laying the foundations for lifelong learning and human development by offering more subject- or skill-oriented instruction using more specialized teachers. Source: World Bank (1998).

Population   Population measures the total population. The data source is World Bank (1998). Again, we measure population at the beginning of each sub-period.

Primary Commodity Exports/GDP   The ratio of primary commodity exports to GDP proxies the abundance of natural resources. The data on primary commodity exports as well as GDP were obtained from the World Bank. Export and GDP data are measured in current US dollars.

War Duration   A civil war is defined as an internal conflict in which at least 1,000 battle-related deaths (civilian and military) occurred per year. We use mainly the data collected by Singer and Small (1994), and according to their definitions (Small and Singer, 1982) we updated their dataset for 1992–99.

Notes

1 Civil wars last on average seven years, while Bennett and Stam (1996) find that international wars last for about 11 months.
2 For a recent collection of the literature which brings out these rival conceptualizations, see Berdal and Malone (2000).
3 Indeed, the payoff may even depend upon the continuation of a state of lawlessness. For example, the drug revenues received by several rebel groups depend upon their controlling territory outside the control of a recognized government.
4 See Collier (2001) for a discussion of the evidence relating to the difficulties of cooperation posed by ethnic diversity.
5 See Le Billon, Sherman and Hartwell (2002) for a review.
6 The COW dataset is available from Singer and Small (1994), and a detailed discussion of their definition can be found in Small and Singer (1982).
7 For a discussion of data issues in the study of civil war, see Collier and Hoeffler (2002).
8 Data can be downloaded from http://bingweb.binghamton.edu/~pregan/.
9 In the empirical analysis, one category of variables is time-varying both across and within wars; a second category is time-varying across, but time-invariant within, wars (typically measured at the start of each war or where this is not possible, for the period closest to this date); and a third category is time-invariant.
10 See Chapter 2 in Lancaster (1990) for details on the relations between the hazard function, the integrated hazard and the survivor function.
11 It is well known that if there is unobserved heterogeneity in the data and this is not controlled for, this will result in spurious negative duration dependence and biased parameter estimates for the explanatory variables (see e.g. Lancaster, 1990: ch. 4).
12 Only 4 of the 77 wars in the full sample last longer than 17 years.
13 To test for unobserved country heterogeneity, we used a semi-parametric approach, proposed by Heckman and Singer (1984), in which $g(\mu)$ is approximated by a discrete multinomial distribution. This is a flexible approach (Mroz and Guilkey, 1995; Mroz, 1999). Allowing for two mass points in the distribution of μ, we never obtained a significant increase in the log likelihood compared to the

model without heterogeneity. Thus, the assumption that the variance of μ is zero is not rejected by the data.

14 This procedure is known as a modified zero-order regression (Greene, 2003: 60). The estimates of the coefficients on inequality and on the dummy for missing inequality can be used to determine what the value of the inequality measure would have to be to produce the same hazard rate as that conditional on inequality missing, all other factors held constant. Specifically, dividing the coefficient on the dummy by the coefficient on inequality gives the hypothetical value of inequality conditional on which the hazard rate equals the hazard rate conditional on missing data on inequality, all other factors equal. Thus, if this hypothetical value is very different from the sample mean of the observed data on inequality, this indicates that countries with missing data on Gini, for one reason or another, record atypically long or short durations, conditional on the other explanatory variables in the model.

15 We have tested for the significance of non-linear income effects on the hazard. The estimated coefficients on income squared and income interacted with inequality (as pointed out by one of the referees, inequality tends to be relatively high in middle-income countries, and so it could be that the inequality effect proxies a middle-income effect) are both insignificant at the 10 per cent level.

16 Using a different dataset and model, Fearon (2004) reaches a similar conclusion.

17 The hypothesis that $\lambda_2 = \lambda_4$ is rejected at the 5 per cent level of significance.

18 Glaeser (2002) presents a political economy model of hatred and argues that hatred is not the result of past grievances but generated by political entrepreneurs to achieve their own goals. Our empirical evidence provides some support for this hypothesis.

19 That is, the index is equal to 1 at the onset of the conflict and then takes (during the course of the war) subsequent values determined by the changes in the original Dehn of series since the onset of the conflict.

20 A log likelihood ratio test of the hypothesis that the three commodity price and primary exports coefficients are jointly zero can be carried out, based on the log likelihood values for specifications (1) and (2). The test statistic is $2[80.43 - 78.18] = 4.5$ and so, with three degrees freedom, the associated p-value is 0.21.

21 We have also tested for a quadratic effect of the openness of political institutions. We find no evidence for quadratic effects as the estimated coefficient on openness of political institutions squared is far from significant.

22 With respect to the interventions effects, our results are quite different from those reported by Regan (2002), despite the fact that we use his data on interventions. Regan's results 'suggest that third-party interventions tend to extend expected durations rather than shorten them' (Regan, 2002: 55). Using Weibull duration regressions, Regan reports very large positive effects of interventions on the expected duration of war (see Table I in the paper). However, the empirical specification assumes that interventions have contemporaneous effects only, which, with monthly data, we think is too restrictive. Looking closer at Regan's data, it is clear that there are no observations for which an economic intervention, or an intervention opposing the government, coincides with the end of a war in the same month. This explains the very large estimates of the interventions coefficients reported by Regan. If, as seems plausible, the effects of interventions operate with a lag of at least a month, then Regan's specification is likely to give misleading results. Our method of cumulating interventions in order to allow for dynamic effects should be more robust to such timing errors. Further, it is also the case that Regan's sample, which includes 150 conflicts during the period 1945–99, is rather different from ours, which could be another reason why our results differ.

References

Barrett, David B., ed., 1982. *World Christian Encyclopaedia*. Oxford: Oxford University Press.

Barro, Robert J., ed., 1997. *Determinants of Economic Growth*. Cambridge, MA: MIT Press.

Bennett, D. Scott and Alan C. Stam III, 1996. 'The Duration of Interstate Wars, 1816–1985', *American Political Science Review* 90(2): 239–257.

Berdal, Mats and David Malone, eds, 2000. *Greed and Grievance: Economic Agendas in Civil Wars*. Boulder, CO: Lynne Rienner.

Collier, Paul, 2000. 'Rebellion as a Quasi-Criminal Activity', *Journal of Conflict Resolution* 44(6): 839–853.

Collier, Paul, 2001. 'Ethnic Diversity: An Economic Analysis of Its Implications', *Economic Policy* 16(32): 129–166.

Collier, Paul and Anke Hoeffler, 1998. 'On the Economic Causes of Civil War', *Oxford Economic Papers* 50(4): 563–573.

Collier, Paul and Anke Hoeffler, 2002. 'Data Issues in the Study of Conflict', *CSAE Econometric and Data Discussion Paper* 2002–01. Oxford: Centre for the Study of African Economies, Department of Economics, University of Oxford (http://www. csae.ox.ac.uk/).

Collier, Paul and Anke Hoeffler, 2004. 'Greed and Grievance in Civil War', *Oxford Economic Papers*, forthcoming.

Deaton, Angus and Ron Miller, 1996. 'International Commodity Prices, Macro-economic Performance and Politics in Sub-Saharan Africa', *Journal of African Economies* 5(3): 99–191.

Dehn, Jan, 2000. *Commodity Price Uncertainty, Investment and Shocks: Implications for Economic Growth*. D.Phil thesis. Oxford: University of Oxford.

Deininger, Klaus and Lyn Squire, 1996. 'A New Data Set Measuring Income Inequality', *World Bank Economic Review* 10(3): 565–591.

Fearon, James D., 2004. 'Why Do Some Civil Wars Last So Much Longer Than Others?', *Journal of Peace Research* 41(3): 275–301.

Glaeser, Edward L., 2002. 'The Political Economy of Hatred', *NBER Working Paper* 9171. Cambridge, MA: National Bureau of Economic Research (http://www.nber. org/papers/w9171).

Greene, William H., 2003. *Econometric Analysis*, 5th edn. Upper Saddle River, NJ: Prentice-Hall.

Grossman, Herschel I., 1991. 'A General Equilibrium Model of Insurrections', *American Economic Review* 81(4): 912–921.

Grossman, Herschel I., 1995. 'Insurrections', in Keith Hartley and Todd Sandler, eds, *Handbook of Defense Economics* 1. Amsterdam, New York and Oxford: Elsevier Science (191–212).

Heckman, James and Burton Singer, 1984. 'A Method for Minimizing the Impact of Distributional Assumptions in Econometric Models for Duration Data', *Econometrica* 52(2): 271–320.

Hirshleifer, Jack, 2001. *The Dark Side of the Force: Economic Foundations of Conflict Theory*. Cambridge: Cambridge University Press.

Jaggers, Keith and Ted Robert Gurr, 1995. 'Tracking Democracy's Third Wave with the Polity III Data', *Journal of Peace Research* 32(4): 469–482.

Klare, Michael T., 2001. *Natural Resource Wars: The New Landscape of Global Conflict*. New York: Metropolitan.

Lancaster, Tony, 1990. *The Econometric Analysis of Transition Data*. Econometric Society Monographs No. 17. Cambridge: Cambridge University Press.

Le Billon, Philippe; Jake Sherman and Marcia Hartwell, 2002. *Controlling Resource Flows to Civil Wars: A Review and Analysis of Current Policies and Legal Instruments*. New York: International Peace Academy.

Mauro, Paolo, 1995. 'Corruption and Growth', *Quarterly Journal of Economics* 110(3): 681–712.

Mroz, Thomas A., 1999. 'Discrete Factor Approximations in Simultaneous Equation Models: Estimating the Impact of a Dummy Endogenous Variable on a Continuous Outcome', *Journal of Econometrics* 92(2): 233–274.

Mroz, Thomas A. and David Guilkey, 1995. *Discrete Factor Approximations for Use in Simultaneous Equation Models with Both Continuous and Discrete Endogenous Variables*. Mimeo. Chapel Hill, NC: University of North Carolina.

Regan, Patrick M., 2000. *Users' Manual for Pat Regan's Data on Interventions in Civil Conflicts*. Mimeo. Binghamton, NY: Binghamton University.

Regan, Patrick M., 2002. 'Third-Party Interventions and the Duration of Intrastate Conflicts', *Journal of Conflict Resolution* 46(1): 55–73.

Singer, J. David and Melvin Small, 1994. *Correlates of War Project: International and Civil War Data, 1816–1992*. Ann Arbor, MI: Inter-University Consortium for Political and Social Research.

Small, Melvin and J. David Singer, 1982. *Resort to Arms: International and Civil War, 1816–1980*. Beverly Hills, CA: Sage.

Summers, Robert and Alan Heston, 1991. 'The Penn World Table (Mark 5): An Expanded Set of International Comparisons, 1950–1988', *Quarterly Journal of Economics* 106(2): 327–368.

StataCorp, 2003. *Stata Statistical Software: Release 8.0*. College Station, TX: Stata Corporation.

USSR, 1964. *Atlas Narodov Mira*. Moscow: Department of Geodesy and Cartography of the State Geological Committee of the USSR.

World Bank, 1998. *World Bank Indicators 1998*. Washington, DC: World Bank.

4 Post-conflict risks

With Anke Hoeffler and Måns Söderbom
(in collaboration with the United Nations Department of
Peacekeeping Operations and the World Bank)

4.1 Introduction

Post-conflict societies face two distinctive challenges: economic recovery and
risk reduction. Conflict will usually have severely damaged the economy.
Supporting the recovery was the founding objective of the World Bank, and
both aid and policy reforms have been found to be highly effective in the post-
conflict context (Collier and Hoeffler, 2004). In this chapter we study the other
challenge, risk reduction. The post-conflict peace is typically fragile: around
half of all civil wars are due to post-conflict relapses (Collier *et al.* 2003). Both
external actors and the post-conflict government must therefore give priority to
reducing the risk of conflict. The two objectives of economic recovery and risk
reduction are likely to be complementary: economic recovery may reduce
risks, and risk reduction may speed recovery. However, this complementarity
between objectives does not imply coincidence of instruments: the instruments
that are effective for risk reduction may be quite distinct from those for
economic recovery.

Although there is now a large case study literature on post-conflict situations, there are few quantitative comparative studies of post-conflict risks.
Indeed, until recently there were insufficient data to support such a study.
Our approach is to estimate hazard functions on a comprehensive sample of
post-conflict situations. In Section 4.2 we discuss the hypotheses that underpin current international practice in post-conflict situations. These hypotheses are not explicitly derived from political or economic theory, but rather
have emerged over the past fifteen years of practitioner experience. We
suggest that to an extent they contrast with theory-based hypotheses. In
Section 4.3 we discuss our methodology and our sources of data. There are
various often difficult choices that must be made in building a data set of
post-conflict experiences that is comprehensive, up-to-date, and satisfactorily
delineated so as to exclude circumstances that do not really reflect the end of
a civil war. In Section 4.4 we present our results, showing how the hazard of
conflict reversion is affected both by the initial post-conflict characteristics
and with time-varying characteristics. Section 4.5 concludes with a discussion
of the implications for international policy.

4.2   Post-conflict risks: current policy and recent research

Post-conflict policy has only arisen as a practical international concern since the end of the Cold War. Since then very substantial international resources have been devoted to post-conflict situations, often under intense media scrutiny. The predominant learning process has been practitioner-based. Because it is a recent phenomenon, academic research has taken time to address the subject, and inevitably until recently the only feasible approach was through case studies. Paris (2004) and Stedman *et al.* (2003) provide a comprehensive overview of peace building during the 1990s. Only recently has an academic literature developed based on theory and quantitative analysis. We first review practitioner learning, and then turn to the academic literature.

Current policy models

Until the end of the Cold War the international community was not in a position to intervene in post-conflict situations. As a consequence there was little call for analysis. With the end of the Cold War numerous opportunities for intervention rapidly arose, and this yielded a phase in which practitioners had little choice but to learn by doing. One of the conventional wisdoms that emerged from this experience was that there were enormous differences among post-conflict situations, so that any generalization was dangerous. However, the decision of the United Nations in September 2005 to establish a Peace-Building Commission reflected a growing sense that it is time to introduce a greater degree of standardization. For example, one by-product of the 'every situation is unique' doctrine was that the amount spent on peacekeeping forces has varied enormously between different post-conflict situations with little apparent relation to need. In the absence of fresh evidence, the most likely outcome is that the Peace-Building Commission will itself attempt to codify current practices. Thus, at the risk of imposing a greater commonality on practice than exists, it is useful to suggest what such a codification is likely to yield in terms of a few rules-of-thumb. At a minimum, an effort to summarize conventional wisdom into a few rules of thumb may, through inaccuracies, provoke a more authoritative succinct statement from practitioners themselves.

The first stage in the sequence of international post-conflict practice starts while the conflict is still continuing. This is to achieve a *negotiated settlement* rather than allow the conflict to drag on to the point of victory for one or other of the parties. This has been a highly successful strategy, yielding resolutions to several wars.

The second stage is a relatively *light presence of peacekeeping troops*, the typical level where such troops are provided being around $5 per head of the population.

The third stage is to encourage a constitution which provides for a degree of democracy. Intervention is seen essentially as *pump-priming democracy*.

The degree of decentralization of power envisaged in the constitution varies. The settlement in the Sudan provides considerable autonomy for the South, but more usually it favours a fairly *unified state*.

The fourth stage is that during its period of presence in the country international intervention should be conducted in such a way as to leave a *'light footprint'*. A key implication is to allow the pace of reform to be set by the government. This is partly due to sensitivity over issues of sovereignty, and partly due to a concern that since post-conflict situations are fragile, reform could easily be destabilizing. Most post-conflict situations commence with extremely poor levels of governance and economic policy. For example, on the World Bank's five-point rating system, the Country Policy and Institutional Assessment, the typical post-conflict country starts with a rating of only 2.41, a level far below the minimum level regarded as adequate for development (Collier and Hoeffler, 2004). Since post-conflict situations are typically characterized by power struggles, the reform of economic policy is seldom treated as a high priority by governments themselves.

The fifth stage is to gain acceptance for the settlement through *post-conflict elections*. Elections are seen as legitimating both the settlement itself and the authority of the government and so help to reduce tensions.

The sixth stage is the *withdrawal of international peacekeeping troops*. Sometimes the election is treated as the milestone for this withdrawal. Just as international intervention is seen as pump-priming democracy, it is seen as pump-priming peace, with *initial tensions being swiftly reduced by time*.

These conventional rules of thumb guide our empirical enquiry. We will attempt to test whether international peacekeeping troops are effective, and try to get some measure of appropriate levels of provision. We will try to assess the extent to which pump-priming democracy is likely to strengthen post-conflict peace, and the consequences of different degrees of decentralization. We will measure whether economic issues can safely be left on the back-burner whilst more pressing political issues are pursued. Finally, we will attempt to assess whether elections are effective in strengthening peace.

Going beyond these rules of thumb, we will also try to get some sense of how post-conflict risks vary according to simple and observable initial characteristics that the Peace-Building Commission could use, without controversy, to allocate the resources available for post-conflict situations more effectively.

Theory and quantification

There is as yet no academic consensus on the causes of violent conflict, let alone an agreed theory that is specific to post-conflict. However, the predominant recent theoretical position as described in the survey of civil war in the *Handbook of Defence Economics*, has been to emphasize the conditions that determine the feasibility of rebellion as being more important than those that influence motivation (Collier and Hoeffler, 2007). The defining feature of civil war is the emergence and durability of a private rebel army, and under most conditions such organizations are likely to be neither financially nor militarily feasible. Somewhat analogous to Hirshleifer's 'Machiavelli Theorem' (Hirshleifer, 2001), the feasibility thesis suggests that where insurrection is feasible it will occur, with the actual agenda of the rebel movement being indeterminate. There is now reasonable empirical support for this thesis. Three recent quantitative studies of the causes of civil war find that variables that are most readily interpreted as indicators of feasibility are important, namely low per capita income, slow economic growth, and large exports of natural resources (Fearon and Laitin, 2003; Miguel *et al.*, 2004; Collier and Hoeffler, 2004a). Low per capita income is interpreted by Fearon and Laitin as proxying the incapacity of the state to maintain effective control over its territory. Both low income and slow growth can be interpreted as lowering the recruitment cost of rebel troops, and the predation of natural resources can provide rebel organizations with finance.

There has been little application of this work to the post-conflict situation. Within the framework of their logit model of the causes of conflict, Collier and Hoeffler (2004a) investigated the effect of the passage of time since the most recent previous conflict. They found that risks fall with time, implying that the post-conflict decade is unusually risky. This high risk is indeed consistent with the feasibility thesis. By revelation, post-conflict societies are societies in which rebellion had proved to be feasible. This is somewhat analogous to the celebrated prediction from the economic theory of crime that criminals would have a high rate of recidivism (Becker, 1968). Further, during conflict one, or often several, rebel organizations are assembled, and stocks of armaments are amassed. Both of these are legacies that lower the cost of rebellion in the post-conflict period.

The feasibility theory can be contrasted with the current policy model. As discussed above, currently policy addresses post-conflict risks primarily through political design. Underlying this is an implicit theory of the causes of conflict which gives precedence to motivation and in particular to grievances based on political exclusion. If instead feasibility is the decisive factor, then economic and military instruments might be more important. To date the only aspect of post-conflict risk that has been modelled is the effect of military spending by the government, which has been found to have a differential effect in post-conflict situations (Collier and Hoeffler, 2006a, 2006b). Typically, post-conflict governments maintain military spending at a very high level, in part as a response to the high risk of further conflict. However, uniquely in post-conflict situations, allowing for the interdependence between risks and spending, such spending is counter-productive. Collier and Hoeffler attempt to explain this through a game-theoretic model in which high military spending by the government inadvertently signals an intention on the part of the government to exploit the potential time-inconsistency of any peace agreement, by reneging on the terms of settlement.

4.3 Methodology and data

The approach adopted in the previous empirical analyses of the causes of conflict discussed above was that of logit analysis or its variants. Such an approach cannot investigate in any depth either the distinctive structure of post-conflict risks or how they evolve as a result of policy choices. In this paper our approach is to estimate a hazard function of the risk of conflict reversion on a sample confined to post-conflict countries. We assume the hazard is exponential and proportional:

$$h(x_\tau, \beta; t) = \exp(x_\tau \beta) h^B(t), \tag{1}$$

where t denotes the duration of a post-conflict peace period, x_τ is a vector of exogenous variables observed at calendar time τ, β is a vector of unknown parameters and h^B is the baseline hazard.[1] With this specification, $\beta_j > 0$ implies that an increase in the associated explanatory variable $x_{\tau j}$ leads to an increase in the hazard of war, and a reduction in the expected duration of peace; and vice versa if $\beta_j < 0$. For the baseline hazard $h^B(t)$ we adopt a piece-wise exponential model, which is quite flexible. Our starting point is a specification where we divide the time axis into W intervals by the points $c_1 c_2 ,...,$ c_W and assume constant baseline hazard rates within each interval:

$$h^B(t) = \exp\left(\alpha + \sum_{w=2}^{W} \lambda_w d_w(t)\right), \tag{2}$$

where $d_w(t)$ is a duration dummy variable equal to one if $c_{w-1} < t \le c_w$ for $c_0 = 0$ and $c_W = \infty$, and zero otherwise; α is an intercept; and $\lambda_2 ,..., \lambda_W$ are baseline hazard parameters. Thus the baseline hazard is allowed to vary freely between intervals, which imposes few restrictions on duration dependence. We include an intercept in the model and exclude the first duration dummy (i.e. d_1), which implies that negative (positive) coefficients on $\lambda_2 ,..., \lambda_W$ imply that the hazard is lower (higher) than in the first interval.

A useful metric in discussing post-conflict risks is the average risk that the peace will collapse. In our sample of 68 post-conflict episodes, 31 reverted to war, so that the average risk was 46 per cent. Since our focus is going to be on the first post-conflict decade, it is useful to consider those reversions that occurred during that decade. This reduces the proportion to 40 per cent. This serves as a benchmark for calibrating the importance of each explanatory variable. With our modelling framework, the likelihood that a country 'survives' the first decade of peace is given by the survival function evalutated at $t = 10$ years:

$$S(10) = \exp\left(-\int_{u=0}^{10} h(.;u)du\right),$$

and so the risk of a collapse is given by $F(10) = 1 - S(10)$.

The limitation of the hazard approach is that by dint of the sample it cannot make comparisons either with risks in countries that are not post-conflict or with risks that prevailed in the post-conflict country prior to conflict. However, it enables us to be much more precise in our investigation of what determines the initial risk of conflict reversion, of how that risk evolves naturally simply by the passage of time, and of how its evolution is affected by interventions during the post-conflict period. We have previously used this approach to investigate the duration of civil war (Collier, Hoeffler and Söderbom, 2004).

For the analysis of post-conflict risks we need to date both the end of conflict and, should the society revert to conflict, the end of peace. Dating the start, and more importantly for this paper, the end of the conflict is often difficult. Trigger events can be dated, but often the violence escalates over some period of time before it reaches the threshold relevant for it to be classified as a civil war. Wars end either with a military victory, settlement or truce. About half of all civil wars end in the military defeat of one party (Sambanis, 2000). This makes dating the ending of wars somewhat easier than using the dates of peace agreements, some of which may not have resulted in an end to military action. The duration of the war does not only depend on being able to date a start and end but also on the definition of violence thresholds. Data sets which define a civil war by 1,000 battle related deaths per year have on average shorter wars than data sets with lower thresholds. Consider, for example, a war with more than 1,000 battle-related deaths during the first year. If the number of such deaths falls beneath the threshold in the second year but reaches it again during the third year a rigid application of the 1,000 deaths criterion leads to the episode being classified as a failed post-conflict situation. If, however, a lower threshold is used to define the restoration of peace then the episode might be treated as a continuous war. Thus, the problems with respect to dating the start and end of the conflict are not only of importance for the analysis of the duration of conflicts but also for the analysis of post-conflict risks.

The two most commonly used data sets are the Correlates of War (COW) project initiated by Singer and Small (1984, 1992) and updated by Gleditsch (2004), and the Armed Conflict Dataset (ACD) by Gleditsch *et al.* (2002). The COW definition of civil wars is based on four main characteristics. It requires that there is organized military action and that at least 1,000 battle deaths resulted. In order to distinguish wars from genocides, massacres and pogroms there has to be effective resistance, at least five per cent of the deaths have been inflicted by the weaker party. The definition of war as used in ACD has two main dimensions. First, they distinguish four types of violent conflicts according to the participants and location: (1) extra-systemic conflicts (essentially colonial or imperialist wars), (2) interstate wars, (3) intrastate wars and (4) internationalized intrastate wars. The second dimension defines the level of violence. *Minor* conflicts produce more than 25 battle related deaths per year, *intermediate* conflicts produce more than 25 battle related deaths per year and a total conflict history of more than 1,000 battle related deaths and lastly *wars* are conflicts which result in more than 1,000 battle related deaths per year.

ACD does not report end dates to the conflicts and for the present analysis we use the updated COW data.[2]

4.4 The hazard generated by conflict legacy

We now estimate a standard hazard function on our data. Our core regression is shown in Table 4.1, column 1. In subsequent columns we investigate variations.

Table 4.1 Duration of post-war peace

	(1)	(2)	(3)	(4)
Economic				
Per capita income	−0.427*	−0.431*	−0.422*	−0.551**
	(0.085)	(0.086)	(0.089)	(0.044)
Per capita income growth	−3.549**	−3.716**	−3.613**	−4.184**
	(0.027)	(0.022)	(0.025)	(0.018)
Political				
Democracy	1.231**	0.989**	1.224**	1.515***
	(0.015)	(0.047)	(0.016)	(0.004)
Democracy missing (dummy)	1.752***	1.726***	1.754***	1.798***
	(0.007)	(0.008)	(0.007)	(0.006)
Regional autonomy	−1.561	−1.318	−1.318	−1.148
	(0.154)	(0.182)	(0.182)	(0.323)
Regional autonomy missing (dummy)	−0.253	−0.253		
	(0.620)	(0.622)		
Election shift	−0.709**			−0.754**
	(0.049)			(0.041)
1st election		−0.495		
		(0.517)		
Year following 1st election		0.997*		
		(0.088)		
Subsequent elections		−0.318		
		(0.675)		
Year following sub. Elections		0.787		
		(0.180)		
1st election shift			−0.820*	
			(0.085)	
Subsequent elections shift			−0.593	
			(0.226)	
ln Economic Freedom				−0.336
				(0.235)
Economic Freedom missing (dummy)				−2.757**
				(0.047)

(continued overleaf)

Table 4.1 continued

	(1)	(2)	(3)	(4)
Social				
ln Diaspora	−0.333***	−0.345***	−0.337***	−0.259**
	(0.005)	(0.004)	(0.005)	(0.036)
Diaspora missing (dummy)	3.465**	3.585**	3.503**	−2.626*
	(0.014)	(0.012)	(0.013)	(0.067)
Ethnic diversity	−1.038	−1.068	−1.035	−1.439
	(0.215)	(0.204)	(0.216)	(0.090)
Ethnic diversity missing (dummy)	−13.154	−14.263	−14.209	
	(0.988)	(0.992)	(0.992)	
Peacekeeping				
ln UN peacekeeping expenditure	−0.405**	−0.414**	−0.407**	−0.478***
	(0.017)	(0.016)	(0.016)	(0.009)
No UN PKO	−3.886**	−3.842**	−3.738**	−4.735**
	(0.036)	(0.027)	(0.029)	(0.013)
UN data missing (dummy)	−3.886**	−3.992**	−3.915**	−4.919**
	(0.036)	(0.033)	(0.035)	(0.013)
Time				
Years 4+ of peace	−0.475	−0.464	−0.454	−0.392
	(0.264)	(0.301)	(0.289)	(0.374)
Nobs	825	825	825	825
Number of episodes	74	74	74	74
Number of failures	33	33	33	33
Log likelihood	−66.821	−66.539	−66.759	−63.041

Note: z-values in parentheses.

The factors that influence, or might influence post-conflict risks can be grouped into temporal, economic, political, social, and military. We consider the variables in these groupings.

Temporal effects

Part of the rationale for short periods of peacekeeping, often merely two years, is that it is the initial post-conflict period during which risks are highest. In our previous work using logistical techniques we found that post-conflict risks indeed fall over time. Our present hazard function enables us to investigate this using a different approach, the key difference being that we are looking more intensively at a shorter period, the post-conflict decade, as opposed to a gradual and prolonged return to normality over several decades.

We again find that there is some very weak tendency for time to reduce risk, but the reduction is not as continuous as implied by our previous results, it is not large, and it is not statistically significant. To the extent that there is a systematic effect, the nearest the data gets to any significant change in the level of risk is between the first four years and the subsequent six. The risk during the first four years is 23 per cent, and during the remaining six years it is 17 per cent, conditional upon the first four years having been peaceful. For policy purposes the key conclusion is that there is no 'safe period' during the decade. The entire post-conflict decade faces a high level of risk.

Economic influences

The first significant economic influence is the level of income. To reduce the problem of endogeneity we introduce this variable with a two-year lag. The variable is time-varying: the society can do nothing about the level of income it inherits at the start of the peace, but its choices will influence how the level of income evolves during the decade. Income matters: it is highly significant and the effect is large. Benchmarked on the 40 per cent risk at mean characteristics, if the initial level of income is twice the mean and all other characteristics are held constant, then the decade-risk falls to 31 per cent. This has two powerful implications. One is that risks are considerably higher in low-income countries: DRC, Liberia, and East Timor are all much more alarming situations than Bosnia, other things equal. The other implication is that economic performance during the decade is likely to matter, if only because higher income will bring risks down.

In fact, the importance of economic performance is considerably greater than this, because growth itself matters. Faster growth directly and significantly reduces risk in the year in which it occurs, as well as cumulating into a higher level of income. To reduce the problem of endogeneity we lag the growth rate by one year. These effects are entirely consistent with results on the initial causes of conflict (Collier and Hoeffler, 2004a; Miguel *et al.*, 2004; Fearon and Laitin, 2003), however, it should be stressed that the present results are specific to post-conflict and generated by an entirely different statistical process to that used in the analysis of initial causes. To get a sense of the importance of growth, we return to the 40 per cent benchmark risk and vary the growth rate. Post-conflict societies have an immensely wide range of growth experience: outcomes are radically more dispersed than in normal growth situations (Collier and Hoeffler, 2004). Some post-conflict economies grow rapidly, others continue to fall apart. If the economy remains stagnant through the decade the decade-risk is 42.1 per cent. If, instead, it grows at 10 per cent per year, which is fast but not without precedent, the decade-risk falls to 26.9 per cent. For completeness, we might note that this massive reduction is split almost equally between the direct contribution of growth to risk reduction in the year in which it occurs, and its cumulative contribution via its legacy of higher levels of income.

The evident implications of the economic variables is that, other things equal, international post-conflict efforts should be concentrated disproportionately in the poorest countries, and should focus heavily upon economic recovery.

A summary measure of the sort of growth-promoting policies, institutions and governance favoured by the World Bank is its Country Policy and Institutional Assessment (CPIA). A high CPIA rating is generally associated with faster growth and in the post-conflict context its affect on growth is atypically strong (Collier and Hoeffler, 2004). Since growth is risk-reducing, there may thus be some presumption that an improvement in the CPIA would indirectly be risk-reducing. A potentially important issue is whether this is offset or indeed accentuated by any direct effects of the CPIA on risk. In a variant we therefore added the CPIA to the core regression, which of course already controls for the growth rate. The CPIA was completely insignificant and the sign of the effect was peace-promoting. While there is always a danger that particular policies will be growth-promoting but inadvertently exacerbate risk, the statistical evidence does not indicate that this is usually the case.

Political variables

We next turn to the political variables.[3] We first consider the degree of democracy. We rely upon the standard classification of countries on a scale of autocracy and democracy, that of Polity IV. Because the scale is ordinal it is inappropriate to treat it as a continuous variable. Rather, we search for significant break points. We find only one such break point, namely within the range of autocracy. There is a significant difference between states in which the polity is highly repressive, with an autocracy ranking of worse than –5, and all other states. Other than this the degree of democracy or autocracy has no significant effects. Unfortunately, severe autocracy appears to be highly successful in maintaining the post-conflict peace. Again using our benchmark of 40 per cent risk, if the polity is highly autocratic the risk is only 24.6 per cent, whereas if it is not highly autocratic the risk more than doubles to 62 per cent. Clearly, we do not wish to advocate severe autocracy. However, it is important to recognize two uncomfortable implications. First, when the international community exerts effective influence to prevent autocracy it is likely to be substantially increasing risks of further violence, and so other measures will be needed to offset this effect. Second, it suggests that international pressure for democracy should be justified by criteria other than peace-strengthening. Democracy does not appear to be an instrument for enhancing the durability of post-conflict peace.

Our next political variable is post-conflict elections. Evidently, these are a very high profile international policy and so it is of particular interest to investigate their effect on risk. We find that post-conflict elections have statistically significant effects, but these are not straightforward. Elections *shift* the risk between years rather than either raising or lowering it. Specifically, an election reduces risk in the year of the election, but increases it in the year following the election. Presumably, in the election year antagonists divert their efforts from violence to political contest, whereas once the election is concluded the losers have a stronger incentive to return to violence. To illustrate the magnitude of the effect, consider an election held in year 3. This reduces the risk in the year of the election from around 6.2 per cent to around 3.4 per cent. However, in the following year the risk is increased from around 5.2 per cent to around 10.6 per cent. Evidently, the net effect taking the two years together is modestly to increase risk.

In our core regression (column 1) the election variable imposes the same coefficient but with opposite sign in the year of the election and in the subsequent year. We arrive at this specification through various steps. First, we allow the coefficients to be different for the two years, and also distinguish between the first election and subsequent elections since there is speculation in the practitioner literature that this distinction is important (Table 4.1, column 2). If anything, it is the adverse effect of elections in the year following the election that is significant, rather than the favourable effect in the year of the election. However, both for the first election and subsequent elections the pattern is similar: a favourable effect followed by an adverse effect. In column 3 we combine the election year and the subsequent year by imposing a sign-reversal and investigate whether the first election differs from subsequent elections. The hypothesis that these two coefficients are the same cannot be rejected at conventional levels of significance. In further variants we have investigated whether any of the years prior to the election year also show significant effects. Since a post-conflict election usually takes two years to organize, the event must be known to citizens well in advance. However, prior to the year of the election there is no effect on risk. Possibly, there is so much uncertainty and fluidity in post-conflict situations that pre-announced events with a long lead-time are heavily discounted. We also investigated whether the shifting effect depended upon the level of income of the society or its ethnic composition. Neither was significant.

There are three important policy implications of this result. First, elections should not be treated as a systemic solution to the acute problem of post-conflict risk.[4] Second, as with democracy itself, post-conflict elections should be promoted as intrinsically desirable rather than as mechanisms for increasing the durability of the post-conflict peace. Third, they generate a misleading signal of calm. During the year of the elections the society experiences a lull, but this is followed by a resurgence of risk. Post-conflict elections are thus precisely the wrong 'milestone' on which to base international exit strategies.

Our final political variable is post-conflict constitutional architecture. Most post-conflict constitutions adopt a broadly unitary state, but a few constitutions grant substantial regional autonomy. Evidently, the granting of such autonomy is endogenous. However, we might expect that the normal preference on the part of the politically powerful is for a unitary state so that regional autonomy is only granted in situations that are too demanding for this to be realistic. Thus, our priorities are that the underlying risk is likely to be greater in contexts in which autonomy is granted. Because there are few cases of autonomy, the variable is not statistically significant at conventional levels: in our core regression it is only significant at 15 per cent. However, the effect is very large. Without autonomy the decade-risk is 46.2 per cent, whereas with autonomy the risk falls to 12.2 per cent. This may be a chance result, or it may be because situations where autonomy is granted are already fundamentally safer. However, the result is at least suggestive that autonomy can be a helpful constitutional design feature in post-conflict situations.

We have investigated a range of other aspects of political design, but not found any to be even marginally significant. In Table 4.1 we report one such variant, an index of economic freedom.

Social variables

Since issues of ethnicity loom large in post-conflict discourse we investigated a range of variables that describe the ethnic composition of the society. None of these variables was significant. In Table 4.1 we report the most familiar measure, ethnic diversity. Like the other measures this is insignificant, but to the extent that it has an effect it is favourable: societies that are more diverse have lower risks.

The other variable we investigated was the size of the diaspora. We measured only the diaspora in the USA, and took this as a percentage of the population of the post-conflict country. The rationale for confining the measure to the USA is partly that of consistent data, and partly that it avoids the problem of having to aggregate immigrants across distinct cultural, economic and legal environments. A large diaspora is sometimes a consequence of a past history of conflict but in this paper we have made no allowance for this endogeneity. At least superficially, one might expect that larger diasporas proxy more severe conflicts which in turn might have higher risks of conflict reversion. In fact, we find that diasporas significantly reduce post-conflict risks and this result seems less likely to be a spurious consequence of endogeneity. The result is somewhat surprising since diasporas tend to be a source of finance for politically more extreme organizations. The effect is quite large, doubling the diaspora reduces risk from 40 per cent to 32.8 per cent.

Military variables

Finally, we introduce military variables. Recall that military spending by the post-conflict government has been found to be counter-productive (Collier and Hoeffler, 2006). For the present study the United Nations has supplied us with comprehensive and detailed data on the deployment of international peacekeeping troops in post-conflict situations. From this we have constructed a variable on the expenditure per year on peacekeeping troops, measured as the logarithm of dollars spent per year. Potentially peacekeeping expenditures could be measured either in absolute terms or relative to the size of the society (its population or its economy). We find that it is far more significant when measured in absolute terms. Underlying this choice is some characterization of the deterrence of rebellion. That it is the absolute size of military deployment that matters suggests that the size of the potential rebel force is not strongly related to the size of the society so that deterrence has strong economies of scale. Virtually all rebellions have to go through a phase of being small even if they subsequently grow to very different sizes. In this incipient phase they can perhaps be deterred by a peacekeeping force of given absolute size.

In some post-conflict situations peacekeeping forces are not deployed and so deployment is potentially biased according to the level of risk. To an extent we are able to control for this by including a dummy variable which takes the value of unity if troops are not deployed. This variable is significant and negative: troops are posted to environments that are intrinsically more risky. Similarly, the scale of deployment may be systematically related to the level of risk. We have attempted to find good instruments for these decisions but have failed to do so. We therefore enter the expenditure on peacekeepers directly as an explanatory variable, recognizing that there are remaining dangers of endogeneity.[5] If endogeneity is a problem the likely direction of bias is presumably that more peacekeepers may tend to be deployed where the risks are greater: this would clearly be the implication of the dummy variable for non-deployment. Thus, if peacekeepers were ineffective there would be a spurious correlation in which they appeared to be increasing the risk of peace collapse. An apparently unfavourable effect of peacekeepers might therefore be spurious, and an apparently favourable effect is likely to be biased downwards.

We find that peacekeeping expenditures significantly reduce the risks of further conflict, the effect being significant at 2 per cent. The effect is large: doubling expenditure reduces the risk from 40 per cent to 31 per cent.

Comparing two packages

As will be evident from our results, political design does not appear to reign supreme as the mechanism for post-conflict peace. We first simulate a policy package in which political design has primacy in the peace strategy and which might be thought of as 'business as usual'. The political design is for a unitary state which adopts sufficiently democratic structures to avoid severe autocracy, and holds elections in the third post-conflict year. External peacekeeping expenditure is set at the mean for post-conflict situations, but economic issues are relegated to the back-burner so that the economy is stagnant. All other variables are set at the same levels as for our other simulations. The risk of reversion to conflict within the first decade is predicted to be astonishingly high, at 75.4 per cent. We then investigate the risk of a package which might be thought of as 'politics supported'. In this package the political variables are the same as in the 'business as usual package' package, but external military assistance and economic recovery are also given priority. Spending on external military peacekeeping is set at four times the average and the economy is given priority, achieving growth of 10 per cent per year. The risk of conflict reversion falls dramatically to 36.7 per cent. The decline in risk is achieved by the combination of policies. Economic growth without military intervention would bring risks down quite substantially, but leave them dangerously high at 55.2 per cent. While the 'politics supported' package is at the high end of both observed post-conflict growth and observed post-conflict peacekeeping, neither is an extrapolation beyond the range of observed experience. We should note that even with the 'politics supported' package, risks of conflict reversion are high: unitary states with non-autocratic regimes are inherently fragile in these settings. As a portfolio decision lending into such risks is daunting. However, given the enormously high costs of conflict, the risk-reduction that economic reconstruction and military peacekeeping provide are likely to be very cost-effective (Collier and Hoeffler, 2004b).

4.5 Conclusion and implications

In this paper we have used all available historical cases of post-conflict episodes to investigate the risks of conflict reversion by means of hazard functions. Even with this comprehensive coverage the past may not be a very accurate guide to the future: a changed international environment may be making peace more secure. Nevertheless, the past is all that we have to guide policy: unchained from experience, international action may generate risks as well as reducing them.

Our approach has been exclusively statistical. This has evident limitations. Our results are best interpreted in conjunction with in-depth case study evidence, the two approaches being complementary. Nevertheless, the statistical approach does add value, in part because the case study approach provides excessive license both to interpret particular situations according to the priorities of the particular researcher, and to generalize in an unwarranted manner from the particular. Indeed, since most conflict case studies are done by political scientists, there is a natural tendency to over-emphasize political choices as explanations. Lest we should be accused of an equivalent bias towards economics, we should note that our biases are constrained by our method.

Post-conflict situations are typically fragile. This conclusion does not need any advanced statistical methods, it is apparent from the raw numbers. We have benchmarked on the average risk that a post-conflict society reverts to conflict within the decade, namely 40 per cent. This is far higher than the risk faced by the typical low-income country, and so the international community is correct to focus explicitly on post-conflict situations as warranting distinctive engagement.

In Section 2 we attempted to deduce the rules-of-thumb which characterize current practice. These rules-of-thumb essentially reflect an implicit practitioner model of the causes of conflict which stresses motivation: grievances must be addressed by a political arrangement in order to avoid conflict reversion. In contrast to this interpretation of conflict as being explicable in terms of motive, recent theories of conflict have emphasized feasibility: rebellions happen where they are feasible. This theory would explain the high rate of reversion to conflict in post-conflict situations as reflecting its atypical feasibility, and prioritize economic and military instruments for security as necessary supplements to the political solutions sought by practitioners.

To the extent that our characterization is reasonable, our results give cause for concern. It is, of course, entirely commendable that the international community should encourage inclusive political arrangements in post-conflict situations: democracy and elections are intrinsically desirable. However, the systematic effect of such political arrangements is not peace-enhancing, and indeed leaves the typical post-conflict society severely exposed to the risk of further conflict.

An implication of our analysis is that the political solutions need to be supplemented by robust economic and military external assistance. Economic development does substantially reduce risks, but it takes a long time. International forces appear to be very effective in maintaining peace, but the actual scale of provision is low relative to what appears warranted given the high costs of conflict reversion. Unpalatable as it may be, peace appears to depend upon an external military presence sustaining a gradual economic recovery, with political design playing a somewhat subsidiary role.

We have also found a simple and statistically strong relationship between the severity of post-conflict risks and the level of income at the end of the conflict. This provides a clear and uncontroversial principle for resource allocation that might be of use to the new Peace-Building Commission of the United Nations: resources per capita should be approximately inversely proportional to the level of income in the post-conflict country. To date, allocations have been massively deviant from this simple principle.

We should stress that any statistical analysis such as our own needs to be supplemented before applied in any particular situation by appropriate contextual knowledge. There are limits as to how much the past can be a guide to the future, and even greater limits as to how much a statistical analysis can extract from this past experience. Nevertheless, because post-conflict issues are so burdened with ideology and political glamour, an analysis based on statistics can be a useful antidote to other potent influences.

Appendix 4.1: Data sources

CPIA We measure policy by the World Bank's Country Policy and Institutional Assessment indicator (CPIA). It ranges from 1 (poor) to 5 (good). The CPIA measure of policy has 20 equally weighted components divided into four categories: (1) Macroeconomic Management and sustainability of reforms (2) Structural policies (3) Policies for social inclusion (4) Public sector management.

Democracy 'Democracy' is a dummy which takes a value of one if the polity score takes a value of greater than -5. Source for the polity data: http://www.cidcm.umd.edu/inscr/polity/

Diaspora We used the data on the foreign born population in the US and divided these numbers by the total population in the country of origin. Source: US Census; US Yearbook of Immigration Statistics 2004.

Economic growth Using WDI 2005 data for GDP per capita we calculated the annual growth rates.

Economic freedom Index ranging from 0 (low) to 10 (high). Source: http://www.freetheworld.com/

Elections Source: Banks' Cross-National Time-Series Data Archive http://www.scc.rutgers.edu/cnts/about.cfm

Ethnic fractionalization The ethnicity variable involves a weighted combination of racial and linguistic characteristics.The fractionalization variable is computed as one minus the Herfindahl index of group shares, and reflects the probability that two randomly selected individuals from a population belonged to different groups. Source: Alesina *et al.* (2003) http://www.nber.org/papers/w9411

GDP per capita We measure GDP per capita annually. Data are measured in constant 1995 US dollars and the data source is WDI 2005.

Primary Commodity Exports The ratio of primary commodity exports to GDP proxies the abundance of natural resources. The data on primary commodity exports and GDP were obtained from the World Bank. Export and GDP data are measured in current US dollars.

UN expenditure UN via World Bank: data available from the authors.

Notes

1 We use a τ subscript on the vector of explanatory variables to indicate that the explanatory variables may be, but are not necessarily, time varying.
2 Data are described in Gleditsch (2004) and are available from http://weber.ucsd.edu/~kgledits/expwar.html
3 Sometimes there are missing data on these variables. Rather than lose observations we set missing observations to zero and introduce a dummy variable which takes the value of unity if the data are missing. See (Greene, 2003, p. 60) for details on this procedure, known as a modified zero-order regression.
4 Caplan (2005) considers elections in post-conflict situations. He suggests that if local elections precede national parliamentary elections, national elections are less likely to generate a focus for violence and thus a breakdown of the peace.
5 Doyle and Sambanis (2006) examine the endogeneity of UN interventions. Their IV estimations indicate that the impact of UN interventions is similar to the one

obtained from the uninstrumented regression models. They tentatively conclude 'that bargaining inside the UN is too complex to respond in a straightforward manner to a particular logic of intervention' in other words UN interventions can be treated as exogenous.

References

Alesina, A., Devleeschauwer, A., Easterly, W., Kurlat, S. and Wacziarg, R. (2002). Fractionalization, NBER Working Paper 9411, Cambridge, MA.

Becker, G. (1968). 'Crime and Punishment: An Economic Approach', *The Journal of Political Economy* 76: 169–217.

Caplan, R. (2005). *International Governance of War-Torn Territories: Rule and Reconstruction.* Oxford UK: Oxford University Press.

Collier, P., L. Elliot, H. Hegre, A. Hoeffler, M. Reynal-Querol and N. Sambanis (2003) *Breaking the Conflict Trap: Civil War and Development Policy, World Bank Policy Research Report.* Oxford, UK: Oxford University Press.

Collier, P. and A. Hoeffler (2004). 'Aid, Policy and Growth in Post-Conflict Societies', *European Economic Review.*

——. (2004a). 'Greed and Grievance in Civil War', *Oxford Economic Papers.*

——. (2004b). 'Conflicts', in Bjorn Lomborg, ed., *Global Crises: Global Solutions*, Cambridge University Press.

——. (2007). 'Civil War', in K. Hartley and T. Sandler (eds), *Handbook of Defence Economics*, North Holland.

——. (2006a). 'Military Expenditure in Post-Conflict Societies', *Economics of Governance*, 7, 89–106.

——. (2006b). 'Unintended Consequences? Does Aid Fuel Arms Races?' *Oxford Bulletin of Economics and Statistics.*

Collier, P., A. Hoeffler and M. Söderbom (2004). 'On the Duration of Civil War', *Journal of Peace Research.*

Fearon, J. and D. Laitin (2003). 'Ethnicity, Insurgency, and Civil War', *American Political Science Review* 97 (1): 75–90.

Gleditsch, K.S. (2004). 'A Revised List of Wars Between and Within Independent States, 1816–2002', *International Interactions* 30: 231–262.

Gleditsch, N.P., P. Wallensteen, M. Eriksson, M. Sollenberg and H. Strand (2002). 'Armed Conflict 1946–2001: A New Dataset', *Journal of Peace Research* 39(5): 615–637.

Hirshleifer, J. (2001). *The Dark Side of the Force*, Cambridge: Cambridge University Press.

Greene, William H. (2003). *Econometric Analysis*, New Jersey: Prentice-Hall.

Miguel, E., S. Satyanath and E. Sergenti (2004). 'Economic Shocks and Civil Conflict: an Instrumental Variables Approach', *Journal of Political Economy*, 112. 725–54.

Paris, R. (2004). *At War's End: Building Peace after Civil Conflicts.* Cambridge, UK: Cambridge University Press.

Sambanis, N. and M. W. Doyle (2006). Short-Term and Long-Term Effects of United Nations Peace Operations, mimeo.

Small, M. and J.D. Singer (1982). *Resort to Arms: International and Civil War, 1816–1980.* Beverly Hills: Sage.

Stedman, S.J., Rothchild, D. S. and E. M. Cousens (2002). *Ending Civil Wars: The Implementation of Peace Agreements.* Boulder, CO: Lynne Rienner.

5 Military expenditure in post-conflict societies

With Anke Hoeffler

5.1 Introduction

During civil war, government military spending rises sharply as a share of GDP. In previous work we have modelled military spending and find that on average a civil war raises it by about 1.8 percentage points (Collier and Hoeffler, 2004). This figure of course understates total military spending during conflict since it omits rebel expenditures. With the reversion to peace, the society therefore has the potential for a substantial 'peace dividend'. Indeed, taking into account rebel spending, the scope for a peace dividend from reduced military spending is likely usually to be even more substantial once a civil war has ended than after an international war. However, peace after a civil war is often fragile. Using our model of the risk of civil war (Collier *et al.*, 2003), we estimate that during the first five years post-conflict there is a 44 per cent risk of reversion to conflict. Any sensible government facing such high risks of civil war would tend to be cautious about rapid reductions in military spending. Further, post-conflict societies inherit at least one powerful military lobby, and quite possibly two if the rebel group is brought into government. Controlling for other characteristics, military dictatorships spend two percentage points of GDP on the military in excess of what fully democratic countries choose to spend, suggesting that where the military is powerful it lobbies for its own interest. Hence, the case for military spending based on prudent deterrence is likely to be reinforced by the atypical power of the military lobby.

Whether for reasons of prudence or due to the power of the military lobby, the typical post-conflict country maintains military spending at a high level – the average post-conflict level of military spending is 4.7 per cent of GDP. This is only a little less than the 5.2 per cent of GDP of military spending during civil war and far above the 3.3 per cent spent in peaceful societies. *Thus, the government typically foregoes over three-quarters of the potential military expenditure peace dividend that would accrue were it to revert to the pre-conflict level of military expenditure.* The issue we explore is whether high military spending is indeed prudent in post-conflict societies.

The issue is an empirical one because it is possible to construct plausible theories that predict opposing effects. Evidently, the most obvious effect of high military spending is deterrence through reduced prospects of military success for rebel groups. This is reflected in standard military success functions which model the chances of rebel success as a decreasing function of the size of government forces relative to rebel forces (Skaperdas, 1996). However, offsetting this counter-insurgency to suppress a rebel movement in its early stages is much more difficult militarily than conventional warfare and risks alienating the local population. Incipient rebel groups often attempt to provoke the government military into 'atrocities' that can be used to strengthen recruitment.

In our previous study of military spending we found that the net effect of these opposing influences on the efficacy of military expenditure was for high military spending to exacerbate the risk of civil war. When military spending was instrumented and entered into a conflict risk regression it was found significantly to increase the risk. In that work, however, we did not make allowance for the relatively rare and distinctive circumstances of post-conflict situations. Such situations are distinctive in at least two offsetting respects. On the one hand, as noted, they face radically higher risks of civil war and so may well be in the range in which military deterrence becomes effective. Especially where the civil war has ended in a decisive military victory, the post-conflict government may have learnt how to make high military spending effective. On the other hand, many civil wars end in negotiated settlements, often informal (Doyle and Sambanis, 2003). As Walter (1997) has argued, in contrast to international wars, the parties to a civil war usually lack effective means of binding themselves to respect the terms of such settlements. We argue that this creates a special role for post-conflict military spending as a signal of government intentions. We set out this theory in Section 5.2. In Section 5.3 we test the effect of military spending during different phases of post-conflict on the risk of conflict renewal. We find that the effects during the post-conflict phase are distinctive and powerful, and are consistent with a role of military spending as a signal of whether the government plans to adhere to the settlement. Section 5.4 concludes.

5.2 Military spending as a signal

Why do post-conflict peace settlements often collapse? If all conditions remained constant presumably the agreement would be maintained. Hence, in accounting for the collapse of a peace agreement, we need to look for changes in circumstances. Yet, the most evident change in circumstances is the economic recovery that commonly occurs post-conflict, and this should tend to reinforce the peace, giving both parties a stronger interest in avoiding disruption by raising its costs.

One likely cause of renewed conflict is if the balance of power changes between the government and the rebels, so that what was mutually advantageous at the time of the settlement comes to be excessively favourable to the weakened party. During the post-conflict phase a shift in relative military power is indeed likely. Maintaining a private army is expensive: the viability of a rebel group as an organization depends upon its continued access to finance. Typically, during a conflict, rebel groups use their capacity for violence to raise revenue: a common approach is through extortion rackets or other forms of predation on the high rents earned from natural resource exports. Once a settlement has been reached with the government it becomes much harder to sustain the rebel group as a fighting force. The leadership of a rebellion may well have been accommodated with positions in the government, prestige and income, but lower down the rebel organization fighters are in effect made redundant, usually with some payoff. As a result, the longer the peace lasts the more the military capability of the rebel organization decays. This decay is much more pronounced than for the government army. After all, the normal state of government armies is to be at peace. They are organized so as to be financed without the need to fight, and to maintain a degree of combat effectiveness through training. By contrast, there is no example in history of a rebel army sustaining itself financially and militarily as a combat-ready force through a prolonged period of peace.

A consequence of this differential erosion of military capability is that rebel bargaining power relative to the government gradually diminishes during the post-conflict period. This gives rise to a standard time-consistency problem: the government has an incentive to offer peace terms that, if the rebel group accepts, it is subsequently rational to renege upon. In her study of the difficulties of reaching sustainable peace settlements of civil wars, Walter (1997) concludes that it is the lack of mechanisms for the enforcement of the terms of proposed settlements that is the chief problem. The astute rebel group recognizes the potential for time inconsistent peace offers on the part of the government and so does not accept proffered peace terms, this being one reason why civil wars on average last more than ten times as long as international wars. However, the time-consistency problem not only prolongs civil war, it contributes to the fragility of peace settlements. If rebels are insufficiently astute they can get caught out by the incentive of the government to over-promise. This need not literally be a matter of 'credulous' rebel leaders being fooled by a 'sly' government. The government leaders of the time may honestly offer terms that they intend to keep, but the next generation of government leaders may not feel bound by these terms, perhaps regarding previous leaders as foolishly generous in not anticipating how circumstances would change. Hence, a rebel group can find itself accepting a settlement that is subsequently modified against its interests.

Perception is important here. As Hirshleifer (2001) has stressed, one cause of conflict is differences in perceptions between the parties: for example, each may be too optimistic about its own military prospects. By the end of a long conflict, perceptions may have been realigned closer to reality. However, if the balance of power shifts during the post-conflict phase, the range of mutually advantageous terms changes in favour of the strengthening party and this opens the possibility of new errors in perceptions. The party that is becoming stronger may overestimate the new advantage and unilaterally change the settlement to the point at which the weakened party resumes the conflict. Or, the party that is becoming weaker might fail to appreciate the extent to which its power has eroded, and refuse to accept worsened terms that are still objectively mutually beneficial.

If the military position of a rebel group post-conflict is gradually deteriorating, it needs to anticipate the extent to which this will be exploited by the government. At one extreme the government may be keen fully to exploit the potential for changing the settlement to its own advantage. At the other extreme the government might continue to adhere to the settlement despite the change in power. This could arise because the government perceives the costs of reneging upon a settlement as high: for example, it might fear that donors would reduce their aid. Alternatively, it could arise because during the peace the government gradually becomes more averse to war. For example, the composition of the government is likely to change from those with military interests to those with interests in economic and social development.

Because these attitudes of the government are difficult to forecast, at the time of the peace proposal the rebel group does not know whether the proposal is time-inconsistent. The rebel group will use whatever signals of government intentions are available to screen out proposals with low credibility. Those conflicts that reach a settlement imply that at the time of the settlement the rebel group attached some credibility to the government proposal. However, given that the settlement is potentially time-inconsistent due to the erosion of rebel military capabilities, the rebel group will undertake a continuous process of post-settlement screening in order to get early warning of government intentions to renege.

Many aspects of government behaviour post-conflict can potentially be used by the rebel group for screening. For example, the government's rhetoric can be more or less inclusive. However, the level of government military spending is likely to be a powerful signal. If post-conflict government chooses sharply to reduce such spending, using revenues for other purposes, this may reasonably be seen as an irreversible decision. This action would be consistent with a government intention to honour the terms of the settlement, but may not be rational for a government intending to renege on the settlement. Thus, the choice of the level of post-conflict government military spending may well be characterized by a separating equilibrium, with a high level signalling an intention to renege, and a low level signalling an intention to honour the settlement.

If post-conflict military spending is a revealing signal then high spending might then be associated with a heightened risk of renewed conflict in three ways. First, high spending will be correlated with an intention to renege on the settlement, and reneging is likely to increase the risk of a return to conflict. This association will hold even if the rebel group does not use the level of military spending as a screening device. In this case, high spending would not directly cause a high risk of conflict renewal. Secondly, however, the rebel group might rationally use military spending for screening purposes. High spending would then indicate a government intention to renege on the settle-ment and the rebel group might then rationally pre-empt this intention before its military power deteriorates further. Third, recognizing that the rebel group would rationally screen by military spending, a peace-loving govern-ment might rationally signal its intentions by deliberately reducing military spending. In the two latter cases, a reduction in military spending directly causes a reduction in the risk of conflict.

This signalling role of military spending post-conflict may potentially offset the deterrent effect. In the next section we investigate it empirically. In order to get as close as possible to the pure signalling effect, we control for the beneficial effects of reduced military spending on the economy. Evidently, due to these effects high military spending would indirectly tend to increase the risk of conflict. The issue is whether the direct effect – deterrence versus signal – reduces or increases the risk of conflict.

We now formalize the above discussion. Consider a two-round game between the government and the rebel organization in a post-conflict setting. In the first round the government adheres to the peace settlement but chooses the level of military spending – high (H) or low (L). This sets the level of military spending not only for the first round but also for the second, reflect-ing constraints on the ability to make high frequency changes in spending. Following the government's decision, the rebel organization decides whether to resume conflict. It chooses to resume conflict with a probability P. If it chooses to resume conflict, the war persists through both periods. Conditional upon the rebel movement having chosen to continue the peace, in the second round the government chooses whether to continue adhering to the settlement (A), or to renege (R).

The government may have an incentive to renege on the settlement, because the rebel movement is militarily weakened by the act of settlement. Whether it has such an incentive depends upon its preferences which are not directly observable by the rebels. Thus, depending upon these unobservable preferences, the settlement may be time-inconsistent. Following this decision, the rebel movement can again decide whether to continue the peace or to revert to war.

In accordance with standard military success functions (Skaperdas, 1996), we assume that in the event of combat, military prospects are increasing in military spending. If military expenditure is low rather than high we assume that any government incurs the extra costs of D in the case of war.

The post-conflict government is potentially of two types: it may be indifferent to war or it may be highly averse to war. In comparison with the war-indifferent government the war-averse government faces additional costs of conflict, C.

Thus, the peace can collapse in either period, or it can persist through both periods. The risk of reversion to war in each period, P_{ij}, is conditional upon whether the government adheres to the settlement or reneges (i = A,R), and upon the level of military spending (j = L,H). Recall that necessarily in the first period the government adheres to the settlement and in the second period it maintains the military spending chosen in the first period. If the government reneges on the settlement it can capture a bonus, B.

First, we assume that if the government reneges on the settlement that this increases the risk of reversion to war conditional upon the level of military spending. There are various reasons why reneging on the settlement might increase the risk of war: the rebels might adopt a tit-for-tat strategy, or as discussed above, one side or other might be making a mistake. Thus:

$$P_{RL} > P_{AL} \tag{1}$$

$$P_{RH} > P_{AH}. \tag{2}$$

Second, we allow military spending to have a deterrence effect, conditional upon the provocation that the government reneges on the settlement. If the government reneges, there will surely be pressures within the rebel movement for a return to fighting, but a sufficiently high level of military spending may intimidate the rebels and so preserve the peace. Thus:

$$P_{RL} > P_{RH}. \tag{3}$$

Third, we assume that the rebels use the government's choice of military spending as a screening device to infer government intentions, conditional upon it being rational to do so. If the rebels behave in this way, then low military spending will deter the rebels from a return to combat so that:

$$P_{AH} > P_{AL}. \tag{4}$$

Our approach now is to determine the conditions under which the level of military spending can indeed support a separating equilibrium so that a rational rebel group would use it as a screening device.

The government thus faces the choices of high or low military spending, and adherence to the settlement or reneging. We now set out the conditions under which a war-averse government will prefer low military spending and continued adherence to the settlement, whereas a war-indifferent government will prefer to renege upon the settlement *and therefore will choose high military spending, even though this reveals its type.*

We first consider the payoffs to different strategies for the war-indifferent government. By construction, these are straightforward and yield a clear dominant strategy. The baseline strategy, which yields a payoff of zero, is to adopt a high level of military spending but to adhere to the settlement. The strategy option is to adhere to the settlement and adopt a low level of military spending. The expected payoff to the government is negative:

$$-2 \cdot P_{AL} \cdot D \tag{5}$$

This second strategy is thus dominated by the first.

The third option is to renege upon the peace agreement while maintaining high military spending. This yields the bonus, B, with no offsetting costs. This strategy thus dominates the first strategy.

Finally, the government could renege on the settlement while maintaining low military spending. This would yield the payoff:

$$B - P_{AL} \cdot D - P_{RL} \cdot D. \tag{6}$$

This is strictly less than the third strategy. Hence, the war-indifferent government will adopt high military spending and renege on the settlement as its preferred strategy.

Now consider the payoffs to the same four options for the war-averse government. Unlike the war-indifferent government, no strategy is unambiguously dominant; the best strategy depends upon the degree of aversion to war.

If the government adheres to the settlement and adopts a high-level of military spending, the payoff is:

$$-2 \cdot C \cdot P_{AH}. \tag{7}$$

If the government adheres to the settlement but adopts a low level of military spending the payoff is:

$$-2 \cdot (C + D) \cdot P_{AL} \tag{8}$$

The strategy of low military spending dominates if:

$$D/C < (P_{AH} + P_{AL}) / P_{AL}. \tag{9}$$

The RHS is the effectiveness of low military expenditure as a signal. As the government is made more averse to war – larger values of C – and as the signal of low military expenditure is made more effective, (9) becomes increasingly likely to hold.

If the government continues to choose low military spending but reneges upon the peace agreement the payoff is:

$$B - (C+D) \cdot P_{AL} - (C+D) \cdot P_{RL}. \tag{10}$$

The strategy of low military spending and adherence to the settlement dominates this strategy if:

$$B < (C+D) \cdot (P_{RL} - P_{AL}) \tag{11}$$

According to (1) the RHS is positive. The likelihood of this condition holding is therefore increasing in the costs of war, C.

Finally, if the government reneges upon the peace agreement and has high military spending the payoff is:

$$B - C \cdot P_{AH} + C \cdot P_{RH} \tag{12}$$

The strategy of low military spending and adherence to the settlement dominates this strategy if:

$$2 \cdot D \cdot P_{AL} + B < C \cdot (P_{AH} + P_{RH} - 2 \cdot P_{AL}). \tag{13}$$

From (2) and (4) the bracketed term on the RHS is strictly positive, so (13) becomes increasingly likely to hold as C increases.

Hence, if the war-averse government incurs sufficiently high costs from conflict, there is a separating equilibrium in which it chooses low military spending and adheres to the settlement, while the war-indifferent government chooses high military spending and reneges. The level of military spending in this case reveals the type of the government. The war-indifferent government chooses high military spending even if it knows that this will reveal its type. The rebels can therefore use the level of military spending as a screening device, and the war-averse government can therefore choose low military spending as a signal.

Of course, the analysis does not demonstrate that post-conflict military spending is necessarily used for screening and signalling. But it does show that if a war-averse post-conflict government is sufficiently averse to renewed war, and a war-indifferent government gets sufficiently large benefits from reversion to conflict, the chosen level of military spending will be a good screening device for rebel organizations to distinguish between the two extremes.

5.3 Empirical testing of the effect of military spending post-conflict

Approach

Our approach follows that of Collier and Hoeffler (2004). In that paper we also investigated the effect of military spending on conflict risk but without distinguishing between post-conflict and other situations. As in that study, we utilize our model of the risk of civil war (Collier and Hoeffler, 2004a). This predicts the risk during a five-year period based on characteristics at the beginning of the period in question. The data are global subject to data constraints, for the period 1960–99, and includes 55 civil wars which in effect have to be assigned by the model across 750 country-periods.

Military spending may also affect the risk of conflict indirectly, via its effects on the economy. Knight *et al.* (1996) find that during peace military spending tends to reduce growth. In turn, we find that growth reduces the risk of conflict both directly and cumulatively, through raising the level of income

(Collier and Hoeffler, 2004a). While these two results suggest that this is one route by which military spending increases the risk of conflict, in this paper our focus is only upon the net effect of deterrence and signalling. The test conducted in this section is consistent with this focus since the growth rate (lagged) and the initial level of income, are both included directly as explanatory variables. Any remaining effect of military expenditure thus controls for the effect upon growth and income.

Military spending is likely to be endogenous to the risk of conflict: where the risk is high, governments tend to increase spending. In our previous work we have indeed found evidence for such an effect: the lagged predicted risk of conflict significantly and substantially increases military spending. Hence, there will be a positive association between military spending and conflict risk even if such spending has no effect on the risk. In our previous paper we deployed a new technique which enables the instrumental variables approach to be used in a probit regression (Keshk, 2003). In the first stage the endogenous variable is regressed on the instruments as well as the exogenous variables, and in the second stage these estimates are used in a probit regression. The coefficient estimates are consistent and the standard errors are corrected.

Were there no problem of endogeneity, the investigation of military spending in post-conflict situations would be straightforward. A term interacting a dummy variable for post-conflict status with military spending would simply be added to the regression. However, the use of such an interaction term in the context of a two-stage probit least square (2SPLS) is currently not feasible in IV programs. We therefore implement the IV approach manually, each step in turn. For the second stage this produces identical point estimates of the coefficients to those that generated through IV programs, but the standard errors are not corrected. As we show, however, our approach is likely to be a good approximation to the corrected standard errors.

Results

In column 1 of Table 5.1 we reproduce the core logit regression of the risk of civil war (Collier and Hoeffler, 2004a). For present purposes the most important explanatory variable is 'peace' – the number of months since any previous conflict. This is negative and significant – conflict risk is much higher in the early years of peace. Just prior to a conflict, the typical country that experiences a civil war has an estimated risk of 22 per cent in the ensuing five years. In the first five years of post-conflict peace the country's estimated risk of renewed conflict rises to 44 per cent. All of the variables are fully discussed in Collier and Hoeffler (2004a) and will only be discussed here as warranted. In order to use a two-stage IV approach we switch from a logit to a probit estimation. In our case the first stage regression assumes normality in the error term (OLS), thus running a probit rather than a logit is the logical choice. In column 2 we reproduce the core regression as a probit: the change in functional form has little effect.

Table 5.1 The impact of military expenditure on the risk of civil war in post-conflict countries

	(1)	(2)	(3)	(4)	(5)	(6)	(7)
Estimation methods	Logit	Probit	Probit (2SPLS)	Probit (2SPLS)	Probit (2SPLS)	Probit (2SPLS)	Probit (2SPLS)
ln GDP per capita	-0.950	-0.460	-0.607	-0.607	-0.619	-0.610	-0.620
	(0.245)***	(0.124)***	(0.149)***	(0.149)***	(0.153)***	(0.150)***	(0.151)***
(GDP growth)$_{t-1}$	-0.098	-0.051	-0.026	-0.026	-0.027	-0.030	-0.020
	(0.041)**	(0.022)**	(0.026)	(0.026)	(0.027)	(0.027)	(0.026)
Primary comm. exports/GDP	16.773	7.407	10.325	10.325	10.179	10.219	10.276
	(5.206)***	(2.456)***	(3.227)***	(3.154)***	(3.205)***	(3.171)***	(3.170)***
(Primary comm. exports/GDP)^2	-23.800	-10.160	-15.904	-15.904	-15.655	-15.787	-15.582
	(10.040)**	(4.630)**	(6.448)**	(6.370)**	(6.525)**	(6.432)**	(6.414)**
Social fractionalization	-0.0002	-0.0001	-0.0001	-0.0001	-0.0001	-0.0001	-0.0001
	(0.0001)***	(0.0001)***	(0.0001)***	(0.0001)***	(0.0001)***	(0.0001)***	(0.0001)***
Ethnic dominance	0.480	0.257	0.296	0.296	0.335	0.308	0.306
	(0.328)	(0.168)	(0.194)	(0.191)	(0.194)*	(0.192)	(0.192)
Peace	-0.004	-0.002	-0.002	-0.002	-0.003	-0.002	-0.002
	(0.001)***	(0.001)***	(0.001)***	(0.001)***	(0.001)***	(0.001)***	(0.001)***
Geographic concentration	-0.992	-0.428	-0.937	-0.937	-1.016	-0.961	-0.973
	(0.909)	(0.450)	(0.522)*	(0.506)*	(0.519)*	(0.509)*	(0.514)*
ln population	0.510	0.247	0.305	0.305	0.318	0.306	0.315
	(0.128)***	(0.063)***	(0.083)***	(0.082)***	(0.082)***	(0.082)***	(0.082)***
Military expenditure			0.033	0.033	0.008	0.027	0.017
			(0.035)	(0.034)	(0.040)	(0.035)	(0.036)
Post-conflict (1–10 yrs)					-0.969		
					(0.436)**		

(continued overleaf)

Table 5.1 continued

	(1)	(2)	(3)	(4)	(5)	(6)	(7)
Milex*post-confl. (1–10 yrs)					0.121 (0.070)*		
Post-conflict (1–5 yrs)						−0.522 (0.520)	
Milex*post-confl. (1–5 yrs)						0.068 (0.090)	
Post-conflict (6–10 yrs)							−0.895 (0.522)*
Milex*post-confl. (6–10 yrs)							0.146 (0.088)*
Pseudo R^2	0.22	0.25	0.25	0.25	0.26	0.25	0.26
Observations	750	750	563	563	563	563	563

Notes: Dependent variable is a bivariate indicator of an outbreak of civil war in any given sub-period 1965–69, ..., 1995–99. Following Keshk (2003) we correct the standard errors according to his two stage Probit least squares (2SPLS) procedure (column 3 only). All regressions include a constant. Standard errors in parentheses. ***, **, * indicate significance at the 1, 5 and 10 per cent level, respectively.

In column 3 we introduce military expenditure. As in Collier and Hoeffler, (2004), we follow the instrumental variables approach, using five instruments for military expenditure. Three dummy variables proxy external threats: current engagement in international war, past engagement in the period since 1945, and finally the Cold War period. A fourth proxy for external threats is the average military spending of neighbouring countries, weighted by their GDP. The fifth instrumental variable measures the extent of democracy. Although democracy is generally not significant in the risk of civil war, it strongly influences the level of military spending: where the military runs the country military spending rises by around two percentage points of GDP. Column 3 reports the two stage IV regression with corrected standard errors (for details of the procedure see Keshk, 2003). So instrumented, military spending is insignificant.

In column 4 we repeat the regression of column 3 using the procedure which we will subsequently be using to investigate post-conflict effects. The purpose of the column 4 regression is to establish that this procedure produces very similar results to the IV methodology. The only difference between the IV approach and that used in column 4 is that the standard errors are uncorrected. The same first-stage regression has been used to estimate military expenditure, and the results from this regression again inserted into the second-stage regression. As can be seen by comparing the two columns, the standard errors generated by this approach are very close to those of the IV approach. This gives us some reassurance that the estimated standard errors for the subsequent results will not be too inaccurate.

In column 5 we investigate post-conflict effects. We define post-conflict as being the first ten years after the end of a conflict. We include a dummy variable which takes the value of unity if the five-year period under consideration includes years which are post-conflict. The dummy variable is significant and negative. This does not mean that post-conflict societies are at less risk than other societies, since the much higher risk that they face is captured by the variable 'peace'. Rather, it is necessary to include the dummy variable itself in order to be able to interpret the next variable. This, the key variable of interest, is the interaction term between the post-conflict dummy and the military expenditure variable. This term is positive and significant, implying that in post-conflict situations military spending increases the risk of a reversion to conflict. The addition of these two post-conflict terms does not affect either the military expenditure variable or any other variable. This implies that in the post-conflict context military spending is significantly *more* adverse in its effect upon the risk of civil war than in more normal situations. Recall that the standard errors for this term are uncorrected and so, although they are likely to be close to their true values, there is a need for caution in the interpretation of the result.

In columns 6 and 7 we try to pin down when during the first post-conflict decade this effect is most pronounced. We therefore divide the decade into its two five-year sub-periods and create dummies for each period. In column 6 we repeat the analysis using only the first five-year sub-period. The signs of the coefficients remain the same as in column 5, but the variables lose statistical significance. Potentially, this is either because of something genuinely different about the first five-years of post-conflict, or because the sample size of pertinent episodes is necessarily approximately half that used when the post-conflict dummy is defined over a period of a decade. In column 7 we repeat the regression with the post-conflict dummy redefined on the second five-year period post-conflict. Now the coefficient on military spending is again significant. We do not regard these results as very robust in view of the reduced sample size once the post-conflict period is divided, but if anything, they suggest that the problems induced by high military spending post-conflict become more important with time.

Interpretation

Our intention has been to test the hypothesis that military spending post-conflict is used by rebel groups to screen government intentions and is used by governments to signal their intentions. Although the above results do not directly substantiate this hypothesis, they are clearly consistent with that interpretation. Any alternative interpretations must accommodate two somewhat surprising findings.

Firstly, the adverse effect of military spending *is significantly stronger in post-conflict situations*. This eliminates as explanations for our result most of the obvious routes by which military spending might be counter-productive. For example, a common argument is that because counter-insurgency is very difficult, military attempts to suppress rebellion tend to backfire: the government army commits atrocities against the civilian population and this facilitates rebel recruitment. Such an argument is implausible as an account of why spending in post-conflict situations is differentially counter-productive. Indeed, if anything, we might expect that over the typically long period of a civil war the government military would have acquired differential effectiveness. The signalling hypothesis accommodates this distinctiveness: both the role of military spending as a signal of government intentions, and the need for an identifiable rebel group to anticipate those intentions are far more likely in post-conflict situations.

Secondly, the adverse effect of military spending on post-conflict risk *becomes increasingly important* during the decade. This eliminates as explanations for our result several other potential routes. For example, it is plausible to imagine that a military presence in fragile post-conflict situations randomly generates confrontations that trigger renewed conflict. The larger the military presence, the greater the risk of such events. However, as the 'peace' variable finds in our regressions, the overall risks of peace gradually decline during the decade. Were a military presence simply randomly exacerbating these risks, then its effects would be larger during the first five years of peace than during the second. Again, the signalling hypothesis accommodates this effect. During the first five years post-conflict, the level of military spending – at least as measured in our data set – is likely to be a less reliable screen of government intentions than during the second. First, an initial phase of high military spending may be necessary to cover the one-off costs of demobilization of combatants (Colletta, Kostner and Wiederhofer, 1996). Evidently, rebels should be able to distinguish between high spending for demobilization and high spending for combat capability, but we cannot: our data are for the level of military spending, not its composition. Secondly, high spending might simply indicate inertia. In most post-conflict societies governments have poor policies and weak institutions across a wide range of issues, and so the failure to change a particular component of government spending in the first few years is not a good guide to intentions. However, if military spending persists in being high over the decade, it will increasingly stand out as an exception to a general pattern of reform: policies are not inert in post-conflict societies. A useful measure of policy and institutional change is the Country Policy and Institutional Assessment of the World Bank, which is an annual rating of countries on a five-point scale. It finds that over the course of the first post-conflict decade the CPIA typically improves from 2.14 to 3.00. This is a very substantial change, approximately equivalent to the difference between the average Sub-Saharan African country and the average South-Asian country. Hence, the signal value of continued high spending increases over time.

A simulation

How powerful is the signal transmitted by the military spending decision? To simulate this we take the characteristics of the mean post-conflict country during the post-conflict decade: the period during which low military spending appears to be effective as a signal. At the beginning of the decade the average risk of conflict is 44 per cent. Recall that for the typical post-conflict country military spending is only reduced by one-quarter of the increase in spending that occurred during the conflict. Specifically, average post-conflict spending is 4.7 per cent whereas average peace spending was 3.3 per cent and spending during conflict was 5.2 per cent. Now consider the risks generated by the high-spending and low-spending strategies (see Table 5.2). We represent the 'high-spending' strategy by the decision not to reduce spending at all from the level prevailing during the conflict. Thus, the high-spending strategy involves an addition 0.5 per cent military spending relative to the mean post-conflict country. Applying the coefficient on military spending found in Table 5.1, column 5, this would raise the risk of conflict from 44 per cent to 47 per cent. We contrast this with a 'low-spending' strategy in which the government reduces spending to the level of the average peaceful country. By the same procedure this reduces military spending by 1.4 per cent relative to the mean post-conflict country, and hence reduces the risk to 38 per cent. Thus, comparing the two signals, the high-spending strategy raises the risk of

Table 5.2 Simulation of risks for high and low military expenditure strategies

Variable	(1) Regression coefficients	(2) Regression coefficients adjusted	(3) Mean	(4) Average milex	(7) High milex	(8) Low milex
Ln GDP per capita	−0.6191	−0.9906	779	−6.5952	−6.5952	−6.5952
(GDP growth)$_{t-1}$	−0.0267	−0.0427	1.46	−0.0624	−0.0624	−0.0624
Primary Com. exports/GDP	10.1789	16.2862	0.131	2.1335	2.1335	2.1335
Primary Com. exports/GDP$_2$	−15.6546	−25.0474		−0.4298	−0.4298	−0.4298
Ln population	0.3184	0.5094	23million	8.64	8.64	8.64
Social fractionalization	−0.0001	−0.00016	3200	−0.512	−0.512	−0.512
Ethnic dominance	0.3354	0.53664	0.429	0.2302	0.2302	0.2302
Geographic concentration	−1.0163	−1.6261	0.563	−0.9155	−0.9155	−0.9155
Peace duration	−0.0028	−0.0045	1	−0.0045	−0.0045	−0.0045
Constant	−1.3269	−2.1230	19.8	−2.1230	−2.1230	−2.1230
Military expenditure	0.0078	0.0125	4.7	0.0587	0.0412	0.0649
Milex* post-conflict	0.1212	0.1939		0.9114	0.6399	1.0084
Post-conflict1–10	−0.9692	−1.5507		−1.5507	−1.5507	−1.5507
Sum of X-coefficients				−0.2238	−0.5127	−0.1206
Estimated risk of war				44.43	37.46	46.99

Notes: *Simulation technique used for Table 5.2.*
In Collier and Hoeffler (2004a) we estimate the probability of a war breaking out during a five-year period, and the model can be written in the following general form:

$$Y_{it} = a + bX_{it} + cM_{i,t-1} + dZ_i + u_{it}, \qquad (A1)$$

where t and i are time and country indicators. We use a logit to estimate the parameters. The dependent variable is a dummy variable indicating whether a war broke out during the five-year period, so that Y_{it} is the log odds of war. However, in this paper we use a probit to estimate the model and we apply Amemiya's parameter to convert the probit estimates into approximate logit coefficients. Specifically, divide the probit estimates by 0.625 (Amemiya, 1981). The explanatory variables X_{it} are either measured at the beginning of the period (for example, income per capita, primary commodity exports/gross domestic product [GDP], population), or during the previous five-year period, M_{it-1}, (for instance, per capita income growth, or are time invariant or changing slowly over time, Z_i, (for example, social fractionalization). The error term is denoted by u_{it}.
   The expected probability $\hat{p}_{it}$ of a war breaking out can be calculated by using the estimated coefficients obtained from equation (A1):

$$\hat{a} + \hat{b}X_{it} + \hat{c}M_{i,t-1} + \hat{d}Z_i = \hat{W}_{it} \qquad (A2)$$

$$\hat{p}_{it} = \frac{e^{\hat{W}_{it}}}{(1 + e^{\hat{W}_{it}})} \cdot 100. \qquad (A3)$$

We calculate probabilities for hypothetical observations. For example, we find the average values for $\bar{X}_{it}$, $\bar{M}_{i,t-1}$, $\bar{Z}_i$ for post-conflict observations. We then calculate the risk of a conflict breaking out in a post-conflict country, $\hat{p}_{it}$, by applying equation (A3).

reversion to conflict by around 25 per cent relative to the low-spending strategy.

5.4 Conclusion

In this paper we have investigated the effect of government military spending on conflict risk in post-conflict situations. During a civil war government military spending is naturally high – typically around 5.2 per cent of GDP, as opposed to 3.3 per cent in societies with otherwise similar characteristics but a history of internal peace. The restoration of peace thus represents an opportunity for a peace dividend. However, in practice governments tend not to take most of this dividend. In post-conflict situations the risk of renewed conflict is disturbingly high – much higher than in countries with similar characteristics but a history of peace. Governments tend to respond to a high risk of civil war with a high level of military spending and post-conflict governments follow this pattern, presumably maintaining spending at high levels in an attempt to deter renewed conflict.

We have found that such a strategy is worse than ineffective. Far from deterring conflict, high post-conflict military spending actually significantly increases the risk of renewed conflict. This result controls for the endogeneity of military spending to conflict risk and so cannot be accounted for as a spurious result of reverse causality. Further, this adverse effect of military spending is distinctive to post-conflict societies.

Since we control for the level and growth of per capita income, the adverse effect of post conflict military spending cannot be due to its adverse effects on the economy. Though such effects indeed exist, they are additional to the effect that we have identified. We suggest that a possible mechanism by which military spending might be having these peculiar and distinctive effects

Table 5.3 Descriptive statistics

	Sample (n = 563)		post-conflict 1–10 yrs (n = 60)	
	mean	*Std Dev*	*mean*	*Std Dev*
War starts	0.078	0.269	0.217	0.415
GDP per capita (const US$)	4246	4095	1824	1513
(GDP growth)$_{t-1}$	1.704	3.458	1.161	4.969
Primary comm. exports/GDP	0.149	0.135	0.134	0.089
Social fractionalization	1744	2023	2231	2317
Ethnic dominance	0.425	0.498	0.433	0.500
Peace duration	327.7	147.739	50.55	38.53
Population (millions)	25.7	80.2	61.7	136.8
Geographic concentration	0.610	0.198	0.600	0.170
Military expenditure	3.355	3.312	4.037	3.387

in post-conflict situations is because of its role as a signal of government intentions. Specifically, military spending may be characterized by a separating equilibrium in which low spending signals a government intention to adhere to the terms of the settlement, while high spending signals an intention to take advantage of the absolute deterioration in rebel military capabilities that occurs while the peace is maintained.

Our results are of both practical and analytic interest. At the practical level they suggest that post-conflict governments might well be misguided if they perceive high military spending as an effective deterrent. Our results in fact underestimate the contribution of reduced military spending to peace. Other research has established that high military spending reduces growth, while growth tends to reduce the risk of conflict. Thus, the overall effect of taking a peace dividend by sharply reducing military spending is partly the direct effect on risk estimated in this paper, and partly the indirect effect via the beneficial effects on the economy.

At the analytic level, our interpretation of our results, emphasizing the time consistency problems that may be inherent in the negotiated settlement of a civil war, meshes closely with the work of Walter (1997) on the difficulties of concluding a settlement. She argues that the critical and distinctive difficulty in restoring peace during civil wars is the lack of credible commitment technologies: neither party can trust the terms of a proposed settlement even though it might be mutually advantageous. This in turn has practical implications for post-conflict situations. To the extent that the key problem is that the government lacks credible incentives to adhere to a settlement, the international donor community may be able to provide a solution. On standard grounds of poverty reduction there is a good case for substantial aid inflows during the first post-conflict decade (Collier and Hoeffler, 2004b). These aid inflows have the potential to serve a double purpose if 'peace conditionality' is incorporated. As suggested by Boyce (2002), aid conditionality could be used to reinforce adherence to the terms of a settlement.

Appendix 5.1: Data sources

Most of the data used in this paper can be downloaded at http://users.ox.ac. uk/~ball0144.

Democracy   Measures the general openness of the political institutions, it ranges from zero (low) to ten (high). The data source is the Polity III data set as discussed by Jaggers and Gurr (1995).

Ethnic dominance   Using the ethno-linguistic data from the original data source (Atlas Narodov Mira, 1964) we calculated an indicator of ethnic dominance. This variable takes the value of one if one single ethno-linguistic group makes up 45 to 90 per cent of the total population and zero otherwise. We would like to thank Tomila Lankina for the translation of the original data source.

External threat Is a dummy variable which takes a value of one once a country was involved in an international war. Here we consider all international wars after WWII. The main data source is Singer and Small (1984, 1994). We updated this data set by using Gleditsch *et al.* (2002), this resulted in the addition of two international wars (Ethiopia – Eritrea, 1998 ongoing as of the end of 1999) and India and Pakistan (1999-ongoing as of the end of 1999).

GDP per capita We measure income as real PPP adjusted GDP per capita. The primary data set is the Penn World Tables 5.6 (Summers and Heston, 1991). Since the data are only available from 1960–92 we used the growth rates of real PPP adjusted GDP per capita data from the World Bank's World Development Indicators in order to obtain income data for the 1990s.

Geographic dispersion of the population We constructed a dispersion index of the population on a country by country basis. Based on population data for 400km^2 cells we generated a Gini coefficient of population dispersion for each country. A value of 0 indicates that the population is evenly distributed across the country and a value of 1 indicates that the total population is concentrated in one area. Data is available for 1990 and 1995. For years prior to 1990 we used the 1990 data. We would like to thank Uwe Deichman of the World Bank's Geographic Information System Unit for generating this data. He used the following data sources: Center for International Earth Science Information Network (CIESIN), Columbia University; International Food Policy Research Institute (IFPRI); and World Resources Institute (WRI). Gridded Population of the World (GPW), Version 2. Palisades, NY: IESIN, Columbia University. Available at http://sedac.ciesin.org/plue/gpw.

International war Is a dummy variable which takes a value of one if the country experienced an international war during the period. The main data source is Singer and Small (1984, 1994). We updated this data set by using Gleditsch *et al.* (2002), this resulted in the addition of two international wars (Ethiopia – Eritrea, 1998-ongoing as of the end of 1999) and India and Pakistan (1999-ongoing as of the end of 1999).

Military expenditure Military expenditure is measured as a proportion of GDP, also commonly referred to as the defense burden. Data for 1960–90 was obtained from the Stockholm International Peace Research Institute (SIPRI) and we used data from the Global Development Network for 1991–1999. We measure military expenditure is measured as the average over five year periods, 1960–1964, 1965–69, ..., 1990–95. http://www.worldbank.org/research/growth/GDNdata.htm

Peace duration This variable measures the length of the peace period (in months) since the end of the previous civil war. For countries which never experienced a civil war we measure the peace period since the end of World War II.

Population   Population measures the total population, the data source is the World Bank's World Development Indicators 1998.

Primary commodity exports/GDP   The ratio of primary commodity exports to GDP proxies the abundance of natural resources. The data on primary commodity exports and GDP were obtained from the World Bank. Export and GDP data are measured in current US dollars.

Social, ethnolinguistic and religious fractionalization   We proxy social fractionalization in a combined measure of ethnic and religious fractionalization. Ethnic fractionalization is measured by the ethno-linguistic fractionalization index. It measures the probability that two randomly drawn individuals from a given country do not speak the same language. Data are only available for 1960. In the economics literature this measure was first used by Mauro (1995). Using data from Barrett (1982) on religious affiliations we constructed an analogous religious fractionalization index. Following Barro (1997) we aggregated the various religious affiliations into nine categories: Catholic, Protestant, Muslim, Jew, Hindu, Buddhist, Eastern Religions (other than Buddhist), Indigenous Religions and no religious affiliation.

The fractionalization indices range from zero to 100. A value of zero indicates that the society is completely homogenous whereas a value of 100 would characterize a completely heterogeneous society.

We calculated our social fractionalization index as the product of the ethno-linguistic fractionalization and the religious fractionalization index plus the ethno-linguistic or the religious fractionalization index, whichever is the greater. By adding either index we avoid classifying a country as homogenous (a value of zero) if the country is ethnically homogenous but religiously divers, or vice versa.

War start   We use mainly the data collected by Singer and Small (1994) and Small and Singer (1982). War start is a dummy variable, it takes a value of one if the country was a peace at the beginning of the period and war broke out during following five years, 1960–64, 1965–69 … 1995–99. If the country remained at peace during the entire period we record a value of zero. A missing value is recorded if the country was at war at the beginning of the period. We record 78 outbreaks of civil war but cannot use all of these observations in our regressions due to missing data for some of the explanatory variables.

References

Amemiya, T. (1981). 'Qualitative Response Model: A Survey'. *Journal of Economic Literature* 19: 481–536.

Barro, R.J., ed. (1997). *Determinants of Economic Growth*. Cambridge, Massachusetts and London: MIT Press.

Barrett, D.B., ed. (1982). *World Christian Encyclopedia*. Oxford: Oxford University Press.

Boyce, J.K. (2002). *Investing in Peace: Aid and Conditionality after Civil Wars*, International Institute for Strategic Studies, Adephi Paper 351, Oxford: Oxford University Press.

Colletta, N.J., M. Kostner and I. Wiederhofer. (1996). Case Studies in War-to-Peace Transition: The Demobilization and Reintegration of Ex-Combatants in Ethiopia, Namibia, and Uganda. World Bank Discussion Paper No 331. Washington, DC: The World Bank.

Collier, P. and A. E. Hoeffler. (2004). Military Expenditure: Threats, Aid and Arms Races, mimeo, Centre for the Study of African Economies, Oxford.

—— (2004a). 'Greed and Grievance in Civil War.' *Oxford Economic Papers* (forthcoming).

—— (2004b). 'Aid, Policy and Growth in Post-Conflict Societies', *European Economic Review* (forthcoming).

Collier, P., L. Elliott, H. Hegre, A. Hoeffler, M. Reynol-Querol, and N. Sambanis. (2003). *Breaking the Conflict Trap: Civil War and Development Policy*, New York: Oxford University Press, and World Bank.

Doyle, M.W. and N. Sambanis. (2003). 'Alternative Measures and Estimates of Peacebuilding Success', processed, Department of International Relations, Yale, New Haven.

Gleditsch, N.P., Wallensteen, P., Eriksson, M., Sollenberg, M. and H. Strand. (2002). 'Armed Conflict 1946–2001: A New Dataset'. *Journal of Peace Research* 39: 615–637.

Hirshleifer, J. (2001). *The Dark Side of the Force: Economic Foundations of Conflict Theory*, Cambridge: Cambridge University Press.

Keshk, O.M.G. (2003). 'CDSIMEQ: A Program to Implement Two-stage Probit Least Squares'. *Stata Journal*, 3(2), 157–167.

Knight, M., N. Loayza, and D. Villanueva. (1996). 'The Peace Dividend: Military Spending Cuts and Economic Growth.' *IMF Staff Papers* 43(1):1–37.

Mauro, P. (1995). 'Corruption and Growth'. *Quarterly Journal of Economics* 110: 681–712.

Small, M. and J.D. Singer. (1982). *Resort to Arms: International and Civil War, 1816–1980*. Beverly Hills: Sage.

Singer, J.D. and M. Small. (1994). *Correlates of War Project: International and Civil War Data 1816–1992*. Inter-University Consortium for Political and Social Research, Michigan: Ann Arbor (data file).

Summers, R., and A. Heston. (1991). 'The Penn World Table (Mark 5): An Expanded Set of International Comparisons, 1950–1988'. *Quarterly Journal of Economics* 99:327–68.

Skaperdas, S. (1996). 'Contest Success Functions'. *Economic Theory* 7: 283–90.

USSR. (1964). *Atlas Narodov Mira*, Moscow: Department of Geodesy and Cartography of the State Geological Committee of the USSR.

Walter, B.E. (1997). 'The Critical Barrier to Civil War Settlement', *International Organization*, 51, 335–65.

6   Aid, policy, and growth in post-conflict societies

With Anke Hoeffler

6.1 Introduction

In January 2002 the international donor community pledged $4.5bn in aid to Afghanistan for post-conflict reconstruction. This follows similarly substantial donor responses in East Timor and Bosnia. By contrast, donor responses to the end of some other conflicts have been modest, with the international financial institutions sometimes constrained by the problem of arrears of debt, precluding renewed lending. Evidently, the enormous variation in response is because post-conflict situations are sometimes highly politicized. However, since the needs of post-conflict situations compete for the same pool of resources devoted to aid for development, it is useful to benchmark the efficacy of aid in post-conflict situations relative to development assistance more generally.

The general effectiveness of aid in reducing poverty can be benchmarked using the analysis of Collier and Dollar (2002). They first estimate a relationship between aid, policy and growth. They find that aid is subject to diminishing returns, but that absorptive capacity is dependent upon the level of policy and institutions as measured by the World Bank's annual rating, the Country Policy and Institutional Assessment (CPIA). They then estimate a relationship between growth and poverty reduction: the reduction in poverty depends upon the extent of poverty and upon the distribution of income. From these relationships they estimate a 'poverty-efficient' allocation of aid between countries, this being the allocation that would maximize the reduction in poverty for a given overall aid budget. The World Bank's allocation rules for IDA, its concessional lending to low-income countries, now reflect this framework, as increasingly does the allocation of bilateral aid. However, post-conflict situations are not explicitly considered in the Collier-Dollar analysis: 'poverty-efficient' aid for post-conflict countries makes no allowance for their special circumstances other than what is already reflected in the CPIA rating. The economic circumstances of post-conflict societies are distinctive in several respects (Collier, 1999). Typically, opportunities for recovery enable a phase when growth is supra-normal. The need to restore infrastructure, juxtaposed against the collapse of revenue, tend to make aid unusually productive. However, offsetting this, during civil war the normal incentive to maintain a reputation for honesty is often disrupted, switching the society into a persistent high-corruption equilibrium (Tirole, 1992). This, together with the weakening of civil administration, can make aid less effective. Hence, *a priori*, aid might be more or less productive in post-conflict societies.

Reflecting the presumed need for differential treatment, the IDA allocation formula has recently been revised to allow post-conflict countries to receive additional temporary resources. However, at present this is based on judgment rather than quantitative analysis. The primary purpose of this chapter is to bring post-conflict situations explicitly into the poverty-efficiency framework of aid allocation. The resulting benchmarks are all the more necessary given the highly politicized nature of aid allocation in post-conflict situations. Of course, aid in post-conflict situations has legitimate objectives other than poverty reduction. There is a considerable risk that conflict will resume and aid might directly reduce this risk beyond any effects via growth and poverty reduction. However, a benchmark in terms of the objective of poverty reduction can at least provide guidance to donors as to the lower bound for appropriate response. Since aid tends, through its growth effects, to reduce the risk of conflict (Collier and Hoeffler, 2002), the aid allocation warranted on the criterion of poverty reduction will also contribute to peace-building.

A second purpose of the paper is to investigate whether and how priorities for the reform of policies, governance and institutions might differ in post-conflict societies from those in other developing countries. At the most obvious level, priorities might differ because some problems are atypically severe. For example, if inflation were to be atypically high in post-conflict situations then improved macroeconomic management would be atypically important. Less obviously, some reforms might be atypically important not because the attained level of performance is worse than in other societies, but because the economy is atypically sensitive to them. We use a new data set on disaggregated ratings of different aspects of policy, governance and institutions to test for differential priorities.

In Section 6.2 we focus upon the pattern of post-conflict economic recovery. We find that there is typically a brief phase of supra-normal growth. In Section 6.3 we investigate whether aid affects growth differently in post-conflict situations, and from this estimate the volume of aid that is appropriate in post-conflict situations on the criterion of poverty-reduction. We show that historically, the actual donor response to post-conflict situations has not been poverty-efficient. In Section 6.4 we turn to policy, investigating how priorities between broad categories of policy – macroeconomic, structural, social and governance – should be distinctive in post-conflict situations. We find that historically there has been no tendency of policies to reflect these priorities.

6.2 The pattern of post-conflict recovery

We first investigate whether there are exogenous forces for economic recovery from conflict, in the sense that growth is more rapid during the post-conflict phase controlling for policies and for aid inflows.

For the growth relationship we rely upon the analysis and database used in the Collier-Dollar growth regression (Collier and Dollar, 2002). This analyzes the per capita growth rate over each four-year period from 1974 to 1997 for 62 countries. We introduce conflicts into this analysis using the database of Collier and Hoeffler (2002a), which provides a comprehensive listing and dating of civil wars for 1960–99. They use a definition of civil war that is conventional in the academic literature: namely, an internal conflict between a government and an identifiable rebel organization that results in at least 1,000 combat-related deaths, of which at least 5 per cent must be incurred on each side. Most of these 73 wars did not end within the period analyzed by Collier and Dollar, or, due to data limitations, were in countries other than the 64 included in their analysis. Table A1 lists all those post-civil war situations in the Collier and Hoeffler data set that fall within the 1974–97 period analyzed by Collier and Dollar, and shows which of them have sufficient data to be included in the present analysis.

The Collier–Dollar regression analyzes growth averaged over four-year periods, thereby abstracting from short-term fluctuations, generating 344 growth episodes. We wish to analyze the after-effects of conflict for around the first decade of peace. We therefore consider three episodes: that in which the conflict ends, which we refer to as peace onset, and the two following periods. When these three episodes are pooled we have 34 observations for which we have complete data. When we look at individual episodes for some purposes we increase the number of observations by dropping some data-constraining variables. At the maximum our analysis uses 48 post-conflict episodes.

The first column of Table 6.1 reproduces the core Collier–Dollar regression.[1] The regression captures the effects of policy, institutions, governance and aid, while controlling for the initial level of income, the region, and the time period. Policy and institutions, as measured by the CPIA, and governance, as measured by the ICRGE, both directly contribute to growth. Aid is subject to diminishing returns, but the absorptive capacity for aid is dependent upon policy and institutions – the better are policy and institutions, the more aid can be absorbed before the marginal contribution of aid to growth falls to zero.

In the second column of Table 6.1 we introduce a dummy variable for countries that are in any of the three post-conflict episodes. Thus, if a conflict ended in 1975, the post-conflict dummy variable would take the value of unity for each of the growth episodes 1974–77, 1978–81, and 1982–85. Thereafter, the dummy would revert to zero, the country being treated as 'post-post-conflict'. The dummy is significant: controlling for policy, institutions,

Table 6.1 The pattern of post-conflict recovery

	(1)	(2)	(3)	(4)	(5)
Initial per	0.725	0.738	0.699	0.727	0.717
capita income	(0.620)	(0.619)	(0.623)	(0.619)	(0.620)
Governance	0.146	0.232	0.136	0.212	0.175
(ICRGE)	(0.159)	(0.156)	(0.160)	(0.155)	(0.160)
CPIA	1.027	0.959	1.006	0.957	0.992
	(0.396)***	(0.396)**	(0.392)**	(0.392)**	(0.397)**
(ODA/GDP) ×	0.145	0.157	0.142	0.151	0.150
CPIA	(0.065)**	(0.065)**	(0.066)**	(0.064)**	(0.065)**
(ODA/GDP)^2	−0.029	−0.031	−0.029	−0.030	−0.029
	(0.013)**	(0.013)**	(0.013)**	(0.012)**	(0.013)**
South Asia	2.657	2.488	2.691	2.572	2.569
	(0.623)***	(0.627)***	(0.629)***	(0.626)***	(0.620)***
East Asia	2.886	2.823	2.952	2.891	2.870
	(0.662)***	(0.660)***	(0.652)***	(0.662)***	(0.659)***
Sub-Saharan	−0.502	−0.612	−0.514	−0.589	−0.578
Africa	(0.812)	(0.807)	(0.816)	(0.797)	(0.811)
Middle East/	1.546	1.516	1.569	1.543	1.512
North Africa	(0.554)***	(0.562)***	(0.556)***	(0.565)***	(0.554)***
Europe/Central	−0.347	−0.440	−0.287	−0.436	−0.387
Asia	(1.055)	(1.046)	(1.063)	(1.053)	(1.050)
Post-conflict		1.133			
0–2		(0.605)*			
War months			−0.007		
			(0.011)		
Peace-onset			0.113		
			(1.114)		
Post-conflict 1				1.889	
				(0.763)**	
Post-conflict 2					1.158
					(0.815)
Observations	344	344	344	344	344
Post-conflict	34	34	13	13	8
observations					
R^2	0.37	0.37	0.37	0.37	0.37

Note: Robust standard errors in parentheses. * significant at 10%; ** significant at 5%; *** significant at 1%. All regressions include time dummies which are jointly significant.

governance and aid, post-conflict countries on average grew 1.13 per cent more rapidly than other countries. Since the growth rate for the average country in the whole sample was only 1.65 per cent, this increment is substantial.

We next investigate whether this additional growth has any temporal pattern. For example, it might be concentrated in the initial post-conflict years as the economy bounces back. Alternatively, following Olson's classic analysis of how episodes of conflict can break the gridlock of pressure groups, rapid growth might be sustained over many years. We first focus on the peace-onset episode. This is made up of two distinct sub-periods, that during which the war is being fought, and that during which peace has been re-established. The net effect on growth during the episode is therefore the combination of a war-effect that is likely to be negative, and a peace-onset effect that may be positive. Hence, in column 3 we introduce two additional variables. The first measures the number of war months during each episode ('warmonths'), and the second measures the number of months of peace during the peace-onset episode ('peace-onset'). The latter variable tests whether growth is distinctive following the onset of peace. Although these variables have the expected signs, neither is significant (nor are they significantly different from each other). Evidently the adverse effects of war on growth are largely captured by the deterioration in the CPIA, and there is no significant bounce-back in the early post-conflict years other than through effects captured in the improvement in the CPIA.

In column 4 we focus on the second post-conflict episode, this being the first full period of peace. Here, we use a dummy variable to test for whether growth during this period is distinctive. To maintain comparability with the Collier–Dollar results we revert to the regression of column 2, dropping the two insignificant variables added in column 3. The dummy variable is significant and substantial – during this period the growth rate is nearly two percentage points above normal. In column 5 we replace this dummy with one for the third post-conflict episode. Both statistical and economic significance are now reduced: supra-normal growth is 1.2 per cent.

These results suggest that post-conflict deviations from the normal growth relationship follow an inverted-U pattern over the first post-conflict decade. However, since the dating of the four-year growth episodes in the Collier–Dollar analysis is exogenous, the above approach lacks precision: the first post-conflict period may contain anything from zero to 47 months of peace, and although the second post-conflict period will always contain 48 months of peace, these may range from starting in the second month of peace, through to starting in the 48th month. To try to get more precision as to when in the post-conflict period growth is supra-normal, in Table 6.2 we therefore replace the period dummies with eight variables defined in terms of the time that has lapsed since the end of the conflict. Thus, 'Year 1' measures the number of months in the growth episode that meet the criterion of being during the first 12 months of the end of the war. Similarly, 'Year 2' measures the number of months during the growth episode that meet the criterion of being between the 13th and the 24th month after the end of the war. The variables between them span the first eight years post-conflict. Given these definitions, the values of the variables are logically interdependent. For example, if 'Year 4' takes the value of 12, then 'Year 8' must take the value of zero, while 'Year 5' is highly likely to be non-zero. This interdependence makes it inappropriate to enter the variables into the regression collectively, and in colums 1–8 we enter them individually. Even so the interpretation of the variables must be treated with caution: for example, the coefficient on 'Year 4' will capture not

Table 6.2 Year-by-year examination of post-conflict recovery

	(1)	(2)	(3)	(4)	(5)	(6)	(7)	(8)	(9)
Initial per capita income	0.727	0.722	0.728	0.733	0.727	0.726	0.723	0.731	0.718
	(0.620)	(0.622)	(0.622)	(0.620)	(0.619)	(0.619)	(0.619)	(0.621)	(0.618)
Governance (ICRGE)	0.158	0.143	0.156	0.187	0.212	0.228	0.194	0.180	0.236
	(0.161)	(0.160)	(0.155)	(0.156)	(0.155)	(0.155)	(0.160)	(0.158)	(0.156)
CPIA	1.034	1.025	1.019	0.986	0.957	0.931	0.979	1.009	0.954
	(0.395)***	(0.395)***	(0.397)***	(0.393)**	(0.392)**	(0.393)**	(0.396)**	(0.396)**	(0.391)**
(ODA/GDP) × CPIA	0.146	0.145	0.147	0.151	0.151	0.154	0.152	0.150	0.155
	(0.065)**	(0.066)**	(0.066)**	(0.065)**	(0.064)**	(0.063)**	(0.064)**	(0.066)**	(0.063)**
(ODA/GDP)^2	-0.029	-0.029	-0.029	-0.030	-0.030	-0.030	-0.030	-0.029	-0.031
	(0.013)**	(0.013)**	(0.013)**	(0.013)**	(0.012)**	(0.012)**	(0.012)**	(0.013)**	(0.012)**
South Asia	2.669	2.657	2.660	2.612	2.572	2.559	2.551	2.653	2.573
	(0.626)***	(0.624)***	(0.622)***	(0.624)***	(0.626)***	(0.626)***	(0.624)***	(0.625)***	(0.618)***
East Asia	2.857	2.891	2.887	2.893	2.891	2.905	2.864	2.852	2.869
	(0.665)***	(0.665)***	(0.663)***	(0.662)***	(0.662)***	(0.661)***	(0.657)***	(0.666)***	(0.656)***
Sub-Saharan Africa	-0.494	-0.504	-0.507	-0.558	-0.589	-0.618	-0.604	-0.529	-0.615
	(0.813)	(0.812)	(0.811)	(0.807)	(0.797)	(0.796)	(0.810)	(0.811)	(0.801)
Middle East/North Africa	1.569	1.547	1.548	1.545	1.543	1.538	1.514	1.542	1.535
	(0.553)***	(0.554)***	(0.556)***	(0.562)***	(0.565)***	(0.553)***	(0.554)***	(0.559)***	(0.562)***
Europe/Central Asia	-0.351	-0.345	-0.359	-0.400	-0.436	-0.439	-0.410	-0.382	-0.449
	(1.054)	(1.058)	(1.053)	(1.051)	(1.053)	(1.062)	(1.047)	(1.054)	(1.045)
First post-conflict year	0.071								
	(0.131)								
Second post-conflict year		-0.017							
		(0.110)							
Third post-conflict year			0.029						
			(0.098)						

(continued overleaf)

Table 6.2 continued

	(1)	(2)	(3)	(4)	(5)	(6)	(7)	(8)	(9)
Fourth post-conflict year				0.099 (0.064)					
Fifth post-conflict year					0.157 (0.064)**				
Sixth post-conflict year						0.182 (0.058)***			
Seventh post-conflict year							0.143 (0.062)**		
First three post-conflict years								0.674 (0.821)	
Fourth–seventh post-conflict year									1.464 (0.573)**
Observations	344	344	344	344	344	344	344	344	344
Post-conflict observations	13	13	13	13	13	13	13	13	13
R^2	0.37	0.37	0.37	0.37	0.37	0.38	0.37	0.37	0.37

Note: Robust standard errors in parentheses. * significant at 10%; ** significant at 5%; *** significant at 1%. All regressions include time dummies which are jointly significant.

only the effect of the fourth year of peace, but also the effects of those years for which the other year variables are likely to be non-zero. With these caveats, the variables representing the first four years of peace are insignificant (with the fourth being borderline), the variables representing the fifth through the seventh year are all significant, with the size of the coefficient rising through to the sixth year and then declining in the seventh. The variable for the eighth year reverts to insignificance. This suggests that the peak phase for supra-normal growth is between the fourth or fifth and seventh years of post-conflict peace. We test this further by replacing the year variables by two dummy variables. The first takes the value of unity if the growth episode contains any months that fall within the first three years of peace (that is, if any of the first three 'Year' variables are non-zero). The second dummy variable takes the value of unity if and of the 'Year' variables 4 through 7 are non-zero. The results are shown in column 9. The first variable is insignificant, whereas the second variable is significant and substantial – the supra-normal growth rate is 1.5 per cent.

To summarize, we have investigated the time-profile of post-conflict growth through two approaches. The first defines three four-year episodes: peace onset and the two subsequent periods. The second allows us to date the onset of peace more precisely but encounters some difficulties of interpretation. Both approaches reveal an inverted-U pattern. On the first approach supra-normal growth peaks in the second period. This period will range from being virtually the first four years of peace to virtually the second four years of peace. The second approach dates the peak growth phase more precisely as being from the fourth to the seventh year of peace. Such a pattern of recovery is not *a priori* surprising. In the immediate aftermath of conflict there are probably many uncertainties, and basic functions of government have yet to be re-established. If peace is maintained there is then a phase of catch-up, but this peters out and the economy reverts to its long-run growth rate.

6.3 Aid during recovery

Thus, for a relatively short phase post-conflict, growth is supra-normal. We now investigate the contribution of aid, especially during this phase. The Collier–Dollar analysis of growth found that growth is augmented both by aid and by policy, supporting, with a broader measure of policy, the prior analysis of Burnside and Dollar (2001). The supra-normal growth phase could be due to a changed relationship between aid, policy and growth: most notably for our present purposes it could be because aid is atypically effective. However, it could also be because of some effect exogenous to both aid and policy: for example, peace simply enables normal economic activity to be resumed so that the economy bounces back.

We decompose supra-normal growth by introducing terms that interact the aid and policy variables with the post-conflict dummies for each of the three episodes. In the baseline Collier–Dollar model there are three such potential interactions – with aid, with policy, and with the policy-aid interaction.[2] We initially focus on the first full four-year period of peace, since this is the period during which growth is supra-normal. We introduce all three interaction terms and proceed with stepwise reduction to those that are significant. This is shown in the first four columns of Table 6.3. The stepwise reduction eliminates the direct effect of post-conflict on growth as insignificant. Supra-normal growth is not due to automatic 'bounce-back'. The final regression (column 4) retains only one route by which post-conflict effects growth, namely the interaction between the post-conflict dummy and the aid-policy interaction variable. This new double interaction term is highly significant both in the statistical sense and in the economic sense.

The coefficient on the new term has important implications for aid absorption post-conflict. The Collier–Dollar analysis finds that aid is subject to diminishing returns, so that at some point – the *saturation point* – aid becomes ineffective in raising growth. The saturation point depends upon policy – the better is policy the greater the amount of aid that can be productively absorbed. The growth regression takes the form:

$$g = a + bAP - cA^2 \tag{1}$$

where:

g = the growth rate
A = aid (as a share of GDP)
P = policy and institutions (as measured by the CPIA).

The contribution of aid to growth is thus:

$$dg/dA = bP - 2cA \tag{2}$$

so that the saturation point, A^S, is defined by:

$$A^S = (b/2c)P. \tag{3}$$

In the baseline Collier–Dollar regression reported in Table 6.1, column 2, the coefficients imply that the saturation point is 2.5 times the CPIA score. A typical CPIA score is around three, so that the result implies that normal absorptive capacity for aid has a limit of around 7.5 per cent of GDP. It is important to note that in the Collier–Dollar analysis aid is measured at purchasing power parity prices. With the more conventional measure of aid at prevailing exchange rates, this would translate into around 20 per cent of GDP.

The results of Table 6.3, column 4, decompose the saturation point into that which applies in the first full period of post-conflict peace, and all other observations. The introduction of the post-conflict term slightly reduces the

Table 6.3 Interaction effects

	(1)	(2)	(3)	(4)	(5)	(6)	(7)	(8)
Initial per capita income	0.718 (0.627)	0.715 (0.621)	0.717 (0.618)	0.712 (0.617)	0.718 (0.629)	0.719 (0.627)	0.715 (0.625)	0.711 (0.624)
Governance (ICRGE)	0.196 (0.160)	0.197 (0.157)	0.198 (0.157)	0.172 (0.155)	0.158 (0.160)	0.158 (0.160)	0.153 (0.161)	0.147 (0.160)
CPIA	0.991 (0.397)**	0.991 (0.396)**	0.988 (0.390)**	1.021 (0.392)***	0.996 (0.402)**	0.999 (0.401)**	1.017 (0.396)**	1.017 (0.396)**
ODACPIAC	0.134 (0.066)**	0.134 (0.066)**	0.134 (0.065)**	0.127 (0.064)*	0.151 (0.066)**	0.148 (0.066)**	0.148 (0.066)**	0.147 (0.065)**
(ODA/GDP)^2	−0.028 (0.012)**	−0.028 (0.012)**	−0.028 (0.012)**	−0.028 (0.012)**	−0.029 (0.013)**	−0.029 (0.013)**	−0.029 (0.013)**	−0.028 (0.013)**
South Asia	2.614 (0.644)***	2.611 (0.639)***	2.619 (0.625)***	2.662 (0.620)***	2.605 (0.629)***	2.623 (0.629)***	2.618 (0.630)***	2.633 (0.626)***
East Asia	2.891 (0.663)***	2.889 (0.660)***	2.884 (0.660)***	2.880 (0.660)***	2.847 (0.668)***	2.855 (0.667)***	2.866 (0.668)***	2.883 (0.664)***
Sub-Saharan Africa	ms0.440 (0.821)	ms0.442 (0.817)	ms0.442 (0.816)	ms0.366 (0.809)	ms0.569 (0.830)	ms0.545 (0.827)	ms0.556 (0.820)	ms0.550 (0.817)
Middle East/North Africa	1.590 (0.568)***	1.591 (0.567)***	1.589 (0.567)***	1.606 (0.563)***	1.506 (0.552)***	1.515 (0.554)***	1.520 (0.556)***	1.524 (0.553)***
Europe/Central Asia	−0.400 (1.059)	−0.402 (1.056)	−0.403 (1.054)	−0.365 (1.053)	−0.353 (1.074)	−0.355 (1.068)	−0.354 (1.067)	−0.352 (1.064)
Post-conflict 1	1.385 (3.237)	1.445 (3.073)	0.913 (0.755)					
Post-conflict 1 × CPIA	−0.186 (1.011)	−0.180 (1.019)						
Post-conflict 1 × (ODA/GDP)^2	−0.009 (0.102)							
Post-conflict 1 × (ODA/GDP) × CPIA	0.168 (0.330)	0.141 (0.442)***	0.139 (0.041)***	0.186 (0.046)***				

(continued overleaf)

Table 6.3 continued

	(1)	(2)	(3)	(4)	(5)	(6)	(7)	(8)
Peace-onset × (ODA/GDP)²					0.033 (0.231)	−0.031 (0.027)	−0.033 (0.021)	−0.027 (0.019)
Peace-onset					−0.594 (5.531)	−1.102 (5.579)	0.352 (1.179)	
Peace-onset × CPIA					0.502 (1.648)	0.516 (1.691)		
Peace-onset × (ODA/GDP) × CPIA					−0.223 (0.800)			
Post-conflict 2								
Post-conflict 2 × CPIA								
Post-conflict 2 × (ODA/GDP)²								
Post-c.2 × (ODA/GDP) × CPIA								
Observations	344	344	344	344	344	344	344	344
Post-conflict observations	13	13	13	13	13	13	13	13
R²	0.38	0.38	0.38	0.38	0.37	0.37	0.37	0.37

Note: Robust standard errors in parentheses. * significant at 10%; ** significant at 5%; *** significant at 1%. All regressions include time dummies which are jointly significant.

estimate of the saturation point in normal circumstances to 2.27 times the CPIA. However, the estimate of the saturation point during post-conflict is dramatically larger, at 5.59 times the CPIA. Thus, conditional upon policy and institutions, post-conflict countries have more than double the absorptive capacity for aid of that in more normal circumstances.

It does not necessarily follow from this that post-conflict countries should get more aid than other countries with similar levels of poverty. Allowance must be made for the unsurprising fact that policies and institutions tend to be less satisfactory in post-conflict situations. Hence, the greater absorptive capacity conditional upon policy, is qualitatively offset by worse policy: To quantify this, for the 1990s we compare the average CPIA score for all countries with that for those countries in their first full period of post-conflict peace. The former is 3.00 and the latter is 2.88. The typical country in its first full four-year period of post-conflict peace thus has a saturation point around 2.36 times that for the typical country in other circumstances.[3]

To summarize, during the first full period of post-conflict, the typical country experiences a temporary growth spurt of around two percentage points per year in excess of normal growth. This growth spurt is largely, or entirely, dependent upon aid: for given policies aid is more than twice as productive in post-conflict circumstances, and so at normal levels of aid, growth is higher. In the absence of aid there would be no growth spurt.

We next consider whether these effects of aid are distinct to the first full period of post-conflict peace. To investigate the effects of peace onset we use the 'peace-onset' variable analogously to our previous use of the dummy for the first full episode of peace, again using a stepwise process of reduction. The results, reported in Table 6.3 columns 5–8, show that there is no significant growth effect through any route during the peace onset period. Recall that there is also no supra-normal growth in this period. To investigate the effects during the second full peace episode is problematic: there are only seven countries in the Collier–Dollar sample that have completed this peace period and such a sample is evidently too small for meaningful analysis. Recall that there are indications that after the first full peace period the supra-normal growth effect starts to fade. Presumably, post-conflict countries gradually revert to the normal growth relationships.

To summarize, the end of a civil war creates a temporary phase during which aid is particularly effective in the growth process. Our results suggest that during the first full peace period the absorptive capacity for aid is around double its normal level. As with aid in more normal circumstances, absorptive capacity depends upon policy, but, conditional upon policy, aid is considerably more effective. Although policy is worse in post-conflict societies than in most other societies, this is insufficient to offset the greater absorptive capacity, so that post-conflict societies constitute an important exception to the proposition that for given levels of poverty, aid should be lower in societies with worse policies.

Our results also suggest that the increased scope for effective aid absorption does not occur immediately. There is neither a supra-normal growth effect nor a supra-normal effect of aid in the peace onset period. Since the moment of peace onset is randomly distributed across the four-year peace-onset episode, its average length is two years. We have also found that there appears to be no supra-normal growth effect during the first three years of peace, or beyond the seventh year of peace. Hence, there is some presumption that the key period during which aid absorption is exceptionally high is approximately between the fourth and the seventh year of peace. From the perspective of effective use of aid for economic recovery, aid volumes should gradually build up during the first few years of peace, and gradually revert to normal levels after around a decade. We should stress that these results are tentative: as data for the episode 1998–2001 become available, the sample of post-conflict countries will increase and the results should be re-assessed.

With this caveat we now compare the proposed pattern of aid to post-conflict situations with the actual pattern. In Table 6.4 we change the dependent variable from growth to aid. In the baseline regression (column 1) aid is investigated as a function of per capita income, total population, region, policy, time period, and 'warmonths'. Unsurprisingly, donors sharply reduce aid during periods of active conflict. In the next three columns we introduce in turn variables for the three post-conflict episodes. The number of peace-onset months is positive but insignificant, suggesting that donors rapidly restore aid once peace is restored, at least to normal levels and perhaps in excess of normal levels. The dummies for the first and second full peace periods are negative and large with the latter being significant. Donors are at most funding at normal levels and, after an initial spurt, are phasing aid out even during this first decade of peace, reducing it below levels normal for other countries with similar circumstances.

An implication of the above analysis is that donors have not responded appropriately to post-conflict situations. The initial response during the peace-onset period – typically the first two years – has indeed restored lending, perhaps (on the narrow criterion of poverty reduction) even excessively, but thereafter aid should have continued to taper in whereas it has tended to taper out. This is consistent with other evidence that suggests that historically donors have not been very responsive to growth opportunities (Alesina and Dollar, 2000). The recent experiences of Afghanistan and East Timor suggest that donor behavior may be changing: the volume of aid allocated to post-conflict situations may well have increased substantially, which on our analysis would be appropriate. However, the timing of the inflow may not be appropriate, arriving too soon and tapering out too early. For example, the present rules concerning IDA allocation to post-conflict allow for supranormal aid allocations only in the first three years of peace, which on our analysis is too early for effective absorption. Of course, the benchmarks provided by regression analysis, especially on such a small sample of episodes, can provide only limited guidance. Each situation will appropriately be assessed using much richer country-specific information. However, given the

Table 6.4 Aid allocation

	1	(2)	(3)	(4)
Initial per capita income	−2.329	−2.329	−2.324	−2.304
	(0.241)***	(0.241)***	(0.242)***	(0.239)***
In population	−0.717	−0.719	−0.712	−0.708
	(0.080)***	(0.081)***	(0.081)***	(0.080)***
Governance (ICRGE)	0.001	0.005	−0.013	−0.025
	(0.082)	(0.082)	(0.082)	(0.083)
CPIA	0.274	0.277	0.282	0.288
	(0.126)**	(0.126)**	(0.124)**	(0.127)**
South Asia	−0.203	−0.205	−0.187	−0.119
	(0.274)	(0.272)	(0.280)	(0.279)
East Asia	0.061	0.054	0.065	0.095
	(0.206)	(0.208)	(0.206)	(0.205)
Sub-Saharan Africa	0.376	0.378	0.390	0.432
	(0.370)	(0.370)	(0.376)	(0.369)
Middle East/North Africa	0.655	0.661	0.653	0.679
	(0.319)**	(0.321)**	(0.317)**	(0.317)**
Europe/Central Asia	0.275	0.284	0.296	0.318
	(0.292)	(0.298)	(0.293)	(0.294)
War months	−0.011	−0.012	−0.012	−0.013
	(0.005)**	(0.005)**	(0.005)**	(0.005)**
Peace-onset		0.287		
		(0.438)		
Post-conflict 1			−0.407	
			(0.607)	
Post-conflict 2				−1.058
				(0.376)***
Observations	354	354	354	354
Post-conflict observations		14	13	8
R^2	0.63	0.63	0.63	0.63

Note: Dependent variable: ODA/GDP. Robust standard errors in parentheses. * significant at 10%; ** significant at 5%; *** significant at 1%. All regressions include time dummies which are jointly significant.

highly politicized context of aid allocations in post-conflict situations, it would not be surprising if historically they have not been appropriately aligned with the opportunities for reinforcing economic recovery.

6.4 Policy priorities during recovery

We now turn to the question of whether policy priorities for growth should be distinctive in post-conflict societies. The previous analysis has already implicitly answered this at the aggregate level of policy captured by the overall CPIA rating, which is an average over ratings of twenty different particular policies. Since the effect of aid is dependent upon policy, as measured by the CPIA, the better is policy, the larger is the growth spurt. Thus, when policy reform is coordinated with aid flows, it is atypically effective in promoting growth in post-conflict situations. The previous analysis has also found that the interaction term between policy and the three post-conflict variables is insignificant. Hence, other than through its effects on enhancing aid absorption, policy is neither more nor less important for growth in post-conflict situations than in other situations. Policy matters more in post-conflict situations because it differentially augments the effectiveness of aid.

We now investigate whether *particular* policies are differentially important in post-conflict situations. For this we disaggregate the overall policy rating into four components: macro, structural, social and governance. This disaggregation is dictated by the availability of data, but it corresponds to important broad categories of policy and so is potentially useful. The data on macro, structural and social policies are from the components of the CPIA ratings and are available since 1990. Prior to this the CPIA was only an aggregate indicator of policy. Within the CPIA each of these three components is scored on a scale, 1–5. Thus, if one component has a lower score than another this has no intrinsic meaning. However, in practice, the mean values of the three components are all very similar: during the 1990s the average rating for macro policies was 4 per cent higher than for structural policies, and 6 per cent higher than for social policies. This suggests that each component of the scale was approximately ordinal, with a country that was average for macroeconomic policies, getting approximately the same rating on these policies as the rating for social policies for a country that was average for those policies. In addition to the CPIA, which is measured on a common basis by World Bank staff, the ICRGE is used to measure governance. Again, this is a subjective assessment on a scale of 1–6.

In Table 6.5 we compare post-conflict countries with all countries in respect of these four aspects of policy for the 1990s. The macro, structural and social policy scores are shown as relative to the overall CPIA score.

Unsurprisingly, post-conflict societies have worse CPIA scores than other societies. The scores by post-conflict episode reveal a steady improvement as long as peace is maintained. In the peace-onset period the CPIA

Table 6.5 Means of policy and governance variables

	All countries	Post-conflict countries			
		Period 1	Period 2	Period 3	All periods
Policy (CPIA)	3.00	2.41	2.88	3.05	2.67
Macro policy*	1.03	1.05	1.02	1.08	1.04
Structural policy*	0.99	0.98	1.01	0.94	0.98
Social policy 1*	0.97	0.97	0.98	0.98	0.98
Governance (ICRGE)	4.73	3.67	3.61	3.47	3.60

Note: *Relative to the average of macro, structural and social policies.

is only 2.41, in the first full period of peace it is 2.88, and in the second full peace period it has risen to 3.05 and so is in effect back to normal. Hence, the phase of distinctively problematic policy is the first 4–8 years post-conflict. However, although the level of overall policy is distinctively poor during this period, there appears to be no systematic difference between policies. Macro, structural and social policy scores are all equally discounted in post-conflict countries and show fairly uniform improvements during the three post-conflict periods. Governance, as measured by the ICRGE, is markedly worse during the peace onset period, than other developing countries. However, in contrast to the CPIA components, it actually appears to deteriorate over the ensuing decade.

We now return to the regression analysis, introducing terms which interact each of the four components of policy with a post-conflict dummy variable. This tests whether any of these policies is differentially important for growth in post-conflict situations and hence provides some guidance as to priorities for policy improvement. Since our analysis can only be conducted for the period since 1990, the number of post-conflict observations is too small to permit disaggregation into the three distinct post-conflict episodes analyzed above so that the post-conflict dummy refers to all three episodes.

In Table 6.6, column 1 we add the interaction term for governance. The interaction term is insignificant, so that governance is approximately as important for growth in post-conflict situations as in other contexts.

Macro, structural and social policy scores on the CPIA are too highly correlated with the overall CPIA to be entered together in the same regression. To overcome this problem, we measure each relative to the average CPIA score. Thus, we retain the overall CPIA score in the regression and add variables showing how the components deviate from the overall score. Evidently, since the overall score is simply the average of its three components, once the deviation of any two of the components from the average is specified, the deviation of the third component is also determined. Hence, only two of the deviations in the components can be entered together in the regression. In Table 6.6, column 2 we introduce the deviations for the macro and social components of the CPIA as additional variables, and also the interactions of these terms with the post-conflict dummy, so that structural policies are the excluded term and so the benchmark.

Since the regression is run for all episodes since 1974, but the disaggregated CPIA data is only available for the 1990s, we initially include both a dummy variable for the 1990s and an interaction of this dummy with the overall CPIA score. This allows both that exogenous growth might have been different during this period and that the effect of policy might have been different. Without these terms the CPIA component terms might be spuriously picking up such effects. In the event, neither term is significant and they are dropped from the regression.

The regression includes the direct effect of the macro and social components of the CPIA (i.e. without being interacted with the post-conflict

Table 6.6 Policy priorities

	(1)	*(2)*
Initial per capita income	0.747	0.657
	(0.622)	(0.651)
Governance (ICRGE)	0.225	0.270
	(0.162)	(0.159)*
CPIA	0.962	1.034
	(0.396)**	(0.401)**
ODA/GDP × CPIA	0.157	0.143
	(0.065)**	(0.063)**
(ODA/GDP)^2	−0.031	−0.029
	(0.013)**	(0.012)**
Post-conflict 0–2	0.738	0.644
	(2.813)	(0.855)
Post-conflict 0–2 × Governance	0.109	
	(0.676)	
South Asia	2.465	2.542
	(0.624)***	(0.670)***
East Asia	2.824	2.623
	(0.661)***	(0.683)***
Sub-Saharan Africa	−0.608	−0.595
	(0.811)	(0.845)
Middle East/North Africa	1.502	1.384
	(0.562)***	(0.542)**
Europe/Central Asia	−0.431	−0.266
	(1.048)	(1.060)
Macro Policy		5.038
		(3.711)
Social Policy		0.282
		(3.671)
Post-conflict 0–2 × Macro policy		−13.162
		(3.582)***
Post-conflict 0–2 × Social policy		16.167
		(3.778)***
Observations	344	341
Post-conflict observations	34	34
R^2	0.37	0.39

Note: Robust standard errors in parentheses. * significant at 10%; ** significant at 5%; *** significant at 1%. All regressions include time dummies which are jointly significant.

dummy). These terms are necessary in order to determine how the effects of these components of policy are distinctive in post-conflict situations, through their interaction with the post-conflict dummy. However, the temptation to interpret these direct effects as showing which components of policy are most important for growth outside the context of post-conflict should be resisted. All they show is what would happen if the three component parts of the CPIA score were to be varied in such a way as to keep the aggregate score constant. At the most, these results will tell us that the reforms represented *by a one point increase* in one component are more valuable for growth than the reforms represented by *a one point increase* in another component. They are therefore a comment not upon the relative importance of macro, structural and social policies, but upon the scoring systems for them. There is no reason why a one point change in one component should be in any sense commensurate with a one point increase in another component.

While the direct effects of the three policy components must therefore be dismissed, the variables generated by interacting the policy components with the post-conflict dummy are readily interpretable. They test for whether policy priorities should be distinctive in post-conflict situations when compared to other circumstances. Both the interaction terms are significant, with macro negative and social positive. Further, the coefficients on both terms are large. Given the objective of promoting growth, consider priorities as between macro, structural and social reforms in two societies with identical CPIA scores on each component, one society being post-conflict and the other having no history of conflict. The results tell us that the post-conflict society should pay more attention to improvements in social policy than the other society, and less attention to improvements in macro policy. This formulation of the result is not only meaningful, it is pertinent. Post-conflict situations constitute only a small minority of the situations on which IFI experience is based. Hence, in the absence of such knowledge, IFI staff are likely to advise for post-conflict situations those policy priorities that are effective in normal circumstances. While the broad direction of such advice might be correct, our results suggest that priorities based on general experience are likely to be misplaced. For example, suppose that a post-conflict society starts with each component – macro, structural and social – rated at 2.5, and the matter for judgment is whether a small improvement in social policies at the expense of a small deterioration in macroeconomic policies would be advisable from the perspective of growth. To be specific, let these small changes in policy amount to an improvement in social policies to 2.6 and a deterioration in macroeconomic policies to 2.4. The coefficients on the direct effects of these components of policy suggest that were the situation not post-conflict, such a change would reduce growth. By contrast, in a post-conflict situation growth would be increased by around one percentage point.

We can also distinguish to an extent between the two possible ways by which policy priorities might be distinctive – differential severity of policy problems and differential effects of policies. Recall that the three components of the CPIA are all equally poor in post-conflict situations. There does not appear to be differential deterioration. Hence, it appears that the differential importance of social policy is not because social policies are differentially bad in post-conflict situations, but rather that they are differentially important. This is indeed consistent with much of the practical policy work in post-conflict situations which tends to prioritize social issues. However, recall from Table 5 that the policy ratings tend to improve through the various phases of post-conflict in tandem. Our analysis suggests that it would be desirable if social policy could improve at a faster rate than structural policy, which in turn should improve at a faster rate than macro policy. This is decidedly not to say that macro does not matter. In post-conflict, as elsewhere, everything matters. But the practical process of reform is always a matter of priorities.

6.5 Conclusion

Countries coming out of conflict are in atypical need of both financial resources and policy advice. Their societies are often extremely fragile and so it is important that the response of the international development community should be as appropriate as possible. Although such situations are becoming more common, they still constitute a small minority of development experience, and so there is a danger that they will receive both finance and advice that largely ignores their special characteristics. Most donors now have units specially dedicated to post-conflict, but to date the learning process has largely been highly context-specific. Indeed, a common assessment from policy practitioners is that each situation is so distinctive that there are no general lessons. In this paper we have investigated post-conflict economic recovery statistically, using all episodes for which data are available. Since the number of such observations is quite limited, the degree of confidence in the results must be correspondingly discounted. The basis for our analysis has been to incorporate post-conflict situations explicitly into the existing analysis of the relationship between aid, policy and growth as undertaken in Collier and Dollar (2002). Two general patterns have emerged from this analysis.

First, we find that aid is considerably more effective in augmenting growth in post-conflict situations than in other situations. For 'poverty efficiency', aid volumes should be approximately double those in other situations. The pattern of aid disbursements should probably gradually rise during the first four years, and gradually taper back to normal levels by the end of the first post-conflict decade. Actual aid practice has not, historically, followed this pattern.

Second, we find that among policies the key priorities for improvement, relative to an otherwise similar society without a history of recent conflict, should be social policies first, sectoral policies second, broadly with the same priority as in other contexts, and macro policies last. Again, actual improvements in policies during the first decade of peace do not appear to reflect these priorities: all policies other than governance appear to improve more or less in tandem.

Appendix 6.1: Data sources

Sample The core sample contains 349 observations from the following 62 countries: Algeria, Argentina, Bahamas, Bangladesh, Bolivia, Botswana,

Brazil, Cameroon, Chile, Colombia, The Democratic Republic of the Congo, Costa Rica, Cote d'Ivoire, Dominican Republic, Ecuador, Egypt, El Salvador, Ethiopia, Gabon, Gambia, Ghana, Guatemala, Guyana, Haiti, Honduras, Hungary, India, Indonesia, Jamaica, Kenya, South Korea, Madagascar, Malawi, Malaysia, Mali, Mexico, Morocco, Nicaragua, Niger, Nigeria, Pakistan, Panama, Paraguay, Peru, Philippines, Senegal, Sierra Leone, Singapore, South Africa, Sri Lanka, Sudan, Syria, Tanzania, Thailand, Togo, Trinidad and Tobago, Tunisia, Turkey, Uruguay, Venezuela, Zambia and Zimbabwe.

Variable definitions   We use information from two data sets for this paper. The economic and policy data was taken from Collier and Dollar (2001) and the conflict data is based on the Collier and Hoeffler (2002a) data set. We list all civil wars in Table 6A.1.

The Collier and Dollar data set is a panel, spanning 12 four year periods (1966–69, 1970–73, …, 1994–98) for 199 countries, thus it contains 2,388 potential observations. In their analysis Collier and Dollar use data for the six most recent periods (1974–77, …, 1994–97). Due to missing data their sample size is 349 observations.

Growth   The average annual growth rate of per capita GDP. Source: Collier and Dollar (2001).

Initial per capita income   Per capita income measured at the beginning of each sub-period (1974, 1978, …, 1994). Data are in 1990 constant US dollars. Source: Collier and Dollar (2001).

Policy   The Policy measure used is the World Bank's Country Policy and Institutional Assessment (CPIA). It ranges from 1 (poor) to 5 (good). The CPIA measure of policy has 20 equally weighted components divided into four categories as follows:

A. Macroeconomic Management and Sustainability of Reforms

1. General Macroeconomic Performance
2. Fiscal Policy
3. Management of External Debt
4. Macroeconomic Management Capacity
5. Sustainability of Structural Reforms

B. Structural Policies for Sustainable and Equitable Growth

1. Trade Policy
2. Foreign Exchange Regime
3. Financial Stability and Depth
4. Banking Sector Efficiency and Resource Mobilization
5. Property Rights and Rule-based Governance
6. Competitive Environment for the Private Sector
7. Factor and Product Markets
8. Environmental Policies and Regulations

Table 6A.1 Civil wars

Country	Start of the war	End of the war	Peace-onset	Post-conflict 1	Post-conflict 2
Angola	11/75	05/91			
Burundi	04/72	12/73		*	
Burundi	08/88	08/88		*	
Chad	03/80	08/88		*	*
Congo	97	10/97			
El Salvador	10/79	01/92	*	**	
Ethiopia	07/74	05/91	*	**	
Guatemala	07/66	07/72		**	
Guatemala	03/78	03/84	*	*	**
Guinea-Bissau	12/62	12/74		**	*
India	84	94	*		
Indonesia	06/75	09/82	*	**	**
Iran	06/81	05/82			*
Jordan	09/70	09/70		*	*
Morocco	10/75	11/89	*	**	**
Mozambique	07/76	10/92		*	
Nicaragua	10/78	07/79	*		
Nicaragua	03/82	04/90	*	**	
Nigeria	01/66	01/70		**	
Nigeria	12/80	08/84	*	**	**
Pakistan	01/73	07/77	*	**	**
Peru	03/82	12/96	*		
Philippines	09/72	12/96	*		
Romania	12/89	12/89		*	
Russia	12/94	08/96			
Rwanda	10/90	07/94			
Somalia	05/88	12/92	**		
Sri Lanka	04/71	05/71		**	**
Sudan	10/63	02/72		**	**
Uganda	10/80	04/88		*	*
Zimbabwe	12/72	12/79	*	**	**

Note: Columns 2 and 4: two stars indicate that the post-conflict observations are included in the 344 sample, one star indicates that the observation was also included in the 532 sample.

C. Policies for Social Inclusion

  1. Poverty Monitoring and Analysis
  2. Pro-poor Targeting and Programs
  3. Safety Nets

D. Public Sector Management

  1. Quality of Budget and Public Investment Process
  2. Efficiency and Equity of Revenue Mobilization
  3. Efficiency and Equity of Public Expenditures
  4. Accountability of the Public Service

Governance We measure governance with the International Country Risk Guide (ICRG) data, it is a composite index and ranges from 1(poor) to 6 (good). Source: Collier and Dollar (2002).

Overseas Development Assistance Overseas Development Assistance (ODA) is measured as a percentage of GDP. Source: Collier and Dollar (2002).

Post-conflict Is a dummy variable, taking the value of one for the three periods after the war ended, i.e. if the war ended in 1975 the dummy takes the value one for the following periods: 1974–77, 1978–1981 and 1982–85.

Post-conflict 0 Is a dummy variable, taking the value one for the period in which the war ended, i.e. if the war ended in 1975 the dummy takes the value one for the period: 1974–77.

Post-conflict 1 Is a dummy variable, taking the value one for the period after the war ended, i.e. if the war ended in 1975 the dummy takes the value one for the 1978–1981 period.

Post-conflict 2 Is a dummy variable, taking a value of one for the second period after the war ended, i.e. if the war ended in 1975 the dummy takes the value one for the 1982–1985 period.

Warmonths Is the sum of months at war during the period.

Peace-onset Is the number of months after the conflict end. We only consider the immediate post conflict period. For example if the war ended in June 1975 this variable takes a value of 18 for period 1974–77 and zero for all other periods.

Post-conflict year Post-conflict year indicates how many post-conflict years there are in each sub-period. We measure the number of months in the period that fall into the following category: first 12 months post-conflict, second 12 months post-conflict etc. We consider the first eight years since the end of the conflict. As an example take a war that ended in June 1976:

for period 1974–77 yr1=6, yr2=12, yr3=0 ... yr8=0
for period 1978–81 yr1=0, yr2=0, yr3=12, yr4=12, yr5=12, yr6=12, yr7=0, yr8=0
for period 1982–85 yr1=0 ... yr6=0, yr7=12, yr8=12

1st–3rd post-conflict year Is a dummy variable which takes the value of one if either post-conflict year variables for years 1–3 are positive.
4th–7th post-conflict year Is a dummy variable which takes the value of one if either post-conflict year variables for years 4–7 are positive.

Notes

1 Five observations were mis-coded in the original regression, missing CPIA values being coded as zeros. This is corrected in the present regression which accounts for the slight differences with the published version.

2 Potentially, aid can enter the regression twice, both directly and squared. The squared term is necessary to capture diminishing returns, but, given the inclusion of the aid-policy interaction term, whether a separate term for the direct effect of aid is needed is entirely an empirical matter. Collier and Dollar (2002) show that when such a term is included it is insignificant and so it is dropped from their core regression.

3 $(2.88/3.00).(5.59/2.27) = 2.36.$

References

Alesina, Alberto and David Dollar. (2000). 'Who Gives Foreign Aid to Whom and Why?' *Journal of Economic Growth*, 5: 33–63.

Burnside, Craig and David Dollar. (2001). 'Aid, Policy and Growth,' *American Economic Review*, 90: 847–868.

Collier, Paul. (1999). 'On the Economic Consequences of Civil War,' *Oxford Economic Papers*, 51: 168–183.

Collier, Paul and David Dollar. (2002). 'Aid Allocation and Poverty Reduction,' *European Economic Review,* 46: 1475–1500.

Collier, Paul and Anke Hoeffler. (2002). 'Aid, Policy and Peace: Reducing the Risks of Civil Conflict,' *Journal of Defense Economics and Peace* (forthcoming).

——. (2002a). 'Greed and Grievance in Civil War.' WPS 2002–01, Centre for the Study of African Economies Working Paper.

Tirole, Jean. (1992). 'Persistence of Corruption, Institute for Policy Reform,' Working Paper 55, Washington DC.

7   Post-conflict monetary
       reconstruction

With Christopher Adam and
Victor A.B. Davies

War is expensive and so has powerful economic consequences. Civil war—now by far the most common form of war—is particularly damaging, reducing income, increasing capital flight, and diverting activity into subsistence. All of these effects can be expected to reduce the demand for money. The resulting decline in seigniorage revenue collides with increased government fiscal needs, with both effects tending to raise inflation. A likely economic legacy of war is thus a deterioration in the tradeoff between seigniorage and inflation. Just as the postwar government faces a hard choice between continued military spending and the reconstruction of infrastructure, so too it faces a choice between continued inflation and the "reconstruction" of the monetary base.

Section 7.1 of this chapter sets out the decision problems facing households and governments. The demand for money on the part of households is the constraint against which the government maximizes. Section 7.2 applies the model to the data. The expansion in data on civil wars has recently made it a researchable phenomenon using standard quantitative techniques (Miguel, Satyanath, and Sergenti 2004; Collier and Hoeffler 2004b). Estimates are made of both how money demand is affected by civil war and its aftermath and how the revealed preferences of governments change when governments are faced with new constraints and needs. Potentially, the harsh policy tradeoffs that governments face in post-conflict situations can be alleviated by aid—indeed, this is the context for which aid was invented. Section 7.3 introduces aid into the analysis, estimating how it affects constraints and choices and showing the path of inflation, money demand, and seigniorage with and without post-conflict aid. Section 7.4 discusses the policy implications of the results.

7.1 The government decision

Assume that before civil war, the government conducts its monetary policy on a sustainable basis. This may well involve the choice of a positive rate of inflation; it does not, however, involve the government attempting to fool private agents by delivering more inflation than they expect. The government is not assumed necessarily to try to maximize social welfare. The actual choice of inflation will depend on how costly it is to the government relative to other sources of revenue, where the costs taken into account by the government may differ from those that concern society.

Civil war takes the society and the government by surprise. This is a reasonable characterization because, although civil wars can to some extent be expected, no model has been able to predict the actual outbreak of civil war with any certainty: the main news occurs around the outbreak.

Consider the effect of the outbreak of civil war on private agents. Civil war reduces GDP growth. A typical estimate of the economic loss is that growth is reduced by about 2.3 per cent over a period of seven years (Collier 1999). Heightened insecurity tends to divert economic activity toward relatively sheltered sectors, notably subsistence, and agents attempt to protect assets through capital flight. In the post-conflict decade the economy usually recovers, but slowly, with GDP typically growing about 1.1 per cent more than normal (Collier and Hoeffler 2004a). Hence, for a prolonged period, the demand for money is likely to be reduced both directly, as a result of the fall in income, and indirectly, as a result of activity and asset substitution.

The decline in the demand for money exacerbates the seigniorage-inflation tradeoff facing the government. However, the government will want to increase its spending for the duration of the conflict. Military spending typically increases by nearly 2 per cent of GDP during civil war (Collier and Hoeffler 2007). This need for increased military spending raises the government discount rate. Because borrowing is difficult during civil war, the government chooses a higher rate of inflation.

This government's problem can be set out more formally using a simple model in which a forward-looking government chooses how much conflict-related expenditure is to be financed at the margin through seigniorage. The model, built around a simple Cagan (1956) characterization of the private sector's demand for money, is similar to that found in Bruno and Fischer (1990), Adam (1995), and Marcet and Nicolini (2003).

A number of simplifying assumptions are made to sharpen the exposition. First, and least important, private income and other sources of financing are held constant, except for the direct changes caused by war itself. The discussion thus abstracts from broader questions of the optimal fiscal response to expenditure shocks (see, for example, Mankiw 1987; Cashin, Ul Haque, and Olekalns 2002).[1]

Second, a simple monetarist framework is assumed, in which the authorities' monetary instrument is the volume of nominal base money, which is the only domestic financial liability. Money is held by both the bank and non-bank private sectors. In the empirical analysis seigniorage earned on currency in circulation is distinguished from seigniorage earned on bank reserves; without loss of generality the two are combined in the model presented in this section.

Third, the private sector's inflation expectations are assumed to be formed adaptively, albeit in a manner consistent with learning. Given the context, this has an intuitive appeal, because private agents could be expected to respond with a lag, possibly a very short one, to conflict-related changes in public expenditure. Employing an adaptive expectations framework has other merits. Specifically, given the Cagan-form money demand function, inflation equilibria on the 'good side' of the seigniorage Laffer curve are dynamically stable under the assumption of adaptive expectations, whereas those on or above the top of the Laffer curve are unstable. As Bruno and Fischer (1990) show, the opposite holds under rational expectations, a feature that gives rise to the 'high inflation trap' analyzed in their article.[2] Given that the analysis here starts from a position at which the economy is in an initial equilibrium on the 'good side' of the Laffer curve, it makes sense that this initial equilibrium is dynamically stable.

Finally, time-inconsistency problems are assumed away, in the strict sense that the initial and any subsequent long-run inflation equilibria are credible.

The model

Government preferences are defined as

$$V = V(g(\pi_t), k(\pi_t)) \tag{1}$$

where g denotes government expenditure, π_t the inflation rate at time t, and $k(\pi_t)$ the discounted future costs of current inflation distinct from the inflation-tax distortion on the demand for money. For example, $k(\pi_t)$ could reflect the reduction in investment efficiency associated with higher inflation. The model assumes that $V_g > 0$, $V_k < 0$, and $k'(\pi_t) > 0$. Both $g(.)$ and $k(.)$ are measured as shares of GDP.

The government's period budget constraint in normal terms is given by

$$G_t = \Delta M_t + A_t + T_t \tag{2}$$

where M_t denotes the nominal base money, A_t the domestic value of aid inflows, and T_t conventional tax revenues. Dividing through by nominal GDP, $Y_t = P_t y_t$, allows equation (2) to be expressed as

$$g_t - a_t - \tau_t = \Delta m_t + \left(\frac{\pi_t}{1 + \pi_t}\right) m_{t-1} \tag{3}$$

where g_t denotes the real value of government expenditure, a_t real aid, τ_t real conventional taxation, while the terms on the right side denote total seigniorage (consisting of the growth in real money balances plus the inflation tax).

Aid and tax revenue are treated as fixed, so that at the margin, changes in government expenditure are financed by changes in domestic deficit financing. The private sector's demand for money is characterized by a Cagan money demand function of the form

$$m_t = c_t y_t \exp(-\alpha \tilde{\pi}_t^e) \tag{4}$$

where c denotes a constant that may shift over time (in response to the onset or cessation of conflict, for example), π_t^e denotes expected inflation, and $\tilde{\pi}_t^e = \pi_t^e/(1 + \pi_t^e)$.[3] Defined in this manner, the inflation term, $\tilde{\pi}_t$, is bounded above by 1 as the conventional measure of inflation becomes arbitrarily large, giving it a natural interpretation as a tax rate at which a value of 1 implies complete confiscation.

The private sector adjusts its inflation expectations, defined in terms of the inflation factor $\tilde{\pi}_t^e$, in response to the deviation of actual inflation from the level anticipated in the previous period:

$$\dot{\tilde{\pi}}_t^e = \beta_t \, (\pi_t - \pi_t^e). \tag{5}$$

where a dot ($\cdot$) denotes the derivative with respect to time and $0 < \beta_t < 1$ measures the speed of adjustment, which could vary over time, as a result of learning, for example. See Marcet and Nicolini (2003) for a discussion of alternative learning algorithms. For the most part, β_t is assumed to equal β.

Equilibrium

The government's problem is to maximize equation (1) subject to equations (2) and (4). Given the assumption that the government can credibly commit to a given inflation rate, in equilibrium inflation expectations are correct. Assuming no growth in real income, this implies a constant rate of inflation $\tilde{\pi}_{t+1}^e = \tilde{\pi}_{t+1} = \tilde{\pi}_t$ and hence a constant growth rate of the money supply. From equation (5) it follows that $\dot{\tilde{\pi}}_{t+1}^e = 0$. In these circumstances the first-order condition with respect to inflation is given by

$$\frac{- V_k k'(\tilde{\pi}_t)}{V_g} = m_t \, (1 - \alpha \, \tilde{\pi}_t) \tag{6}$$

The solution to equation (6) defines the optimal (constant) inflation rate, $\tilde{\pi}_t^* = \tilde{\pi}_0^*$, and hence the optimal rate of growth of the money supply. Substituting equation (6) into equations (4) and (3) yields optimal seigniorage, shown as point A in Figure 7.1.

The right side of equation (6) is simply the slope of the seigniorage Laffer curve defined by the demand for money, equation (4). The seigniorage revenue–maximizing point is attained at $\tilde{\pi}^{\max} = 1/\alpha - \hat{y}$, where $\hat{y}$ denotes the growth rate of real income. The left side of equation (6) is the slope of the government's indifference curve, measuring the rate at which the government trades off present government consumption against future damage to the economy. This can be thought of as a quasi-discount rate. It follows from equation (6) that

$$\frac{\partial \tilde{\pi}_t^*}{\partial V_g} > 0 \text{ and } \frac{\partial \tilde{\pi}_t^*}{\partial V_k} < 0. \tag{7}$$

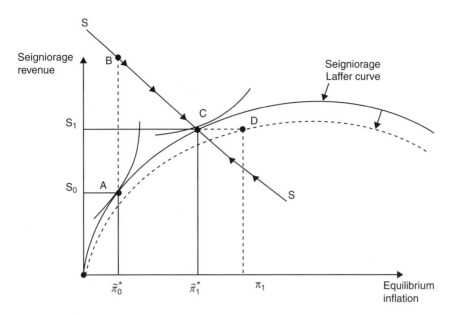

Figure 7.1 Inflation and seigniorage revenue during conflict.

Dynamics

The short-run dynamics of the model in response to anticipated and unanticipated changes in the fiscal deficit emerge directly from equations (3)–(5). The model assumes that in the short run, c_t in equation (4) is constant. Taking the log derivative with respect to time and substituting yields

$$\frac{d\ln m_t}{dt} = \hat{m}_t = \hat{y}_t - \alpha\dot{\hat{\pi}}_t^e. \tag{8}$$

where a hat (^) represents a proportionate change. Using the definition $\hat{M}_t = (\hat{m}_t + \pi_t + \hat{y}_t)$ and denoting the growth in the nominal money supply by $\sigma_t = \hat{M}_t$ allows inflation to be expressed as

$$\pi_t = \sigma_t + \alpha\dot{\hat{\pi}}_t^e - \hat{y}_t \tag{9}$$

Substituting equation (9) into equation (5) leads to the following differential equation for inflation expectations:

$$\dot{\pi}_t^e = \left(\frac{\beta}{1-\alpha\beta}\right)(\sigma_t - \pi_t^e - \hat{y}_t). \tag{10}$$

When inflation expectations adjust sufficiently slowly, such that $\beta < 1/\alpha$, equation (10) is dynamically stable and the economy's adjustment to an increase in the nominal growth of the money supply is denoted by the saddle path SS in Figure 7.1.

Responses during conflict

During conflict the government faces increased pressure to spend in order to confront its opponents. At the same time, however—and not necessarily independently—private sector demand for money declines.

Consider first the government's choice, assuming for the moment no change in the private sector's demand for money. Additional expenditure needs temporarily increase the marginal utility of government consumption, V_g. This implies an increase in the quasi-discount rate for the duration of the conflict, and, from equation (7), a higher optimal rate of inflation, chosen in order to generate a higher rate of seigniorage. Thus, the government seeks to move along the Laffer curve. It does so by increasing the growth of the money supply, which generates an initial jump in seigniorage to point B. From equation (5), expected inflation rises, inducing a decline in real money balances. This continues along SS to the new equilibrium at C, at which point inflation expectations have fully adjusted, such that $\tilde{\pi}_t^e = \tilde{\pi}_1^*$. The initial real resource flow at B occurs regardless of how rapidly inflation expectations subsequently adjust, because the increased growth in the money supply is exchanged for real private resources at the price level prevailing in the initial equilibrium. How much additional transitional seigniorage revenue accrues thereafter depends on the private sector's speed of adjustment: the more slowly inflation expectations adjust to the new rate of growth of the money supply, the larger the windfall.

Extracting this higher level of seigniorage assumes, however, no change in the underlying demand for money. For the reasons noted in the introduction, however, this is unlikely. Conflict reduces incomes: it therefore lowers the demand for money and hence seigniorage for any inflation rate. But conflict also induces private agents to disengage from the formal economy and to seek opportunities for capital flight and currency substitution, entailing both an autonomous shift out of domestic currency (a decline in c_i in equation (4)) and an increase in the inflation semi-elasticity of the demand for money, α. These effects on private sector money demand combine to unambiguously shift the Laffer curve downward, so that the level of seigniorage previously feasible at point C cannot now be achieved at inflation rate $\tilde{\pi}_1^*$. This level could be generated at a higher rate of inflation, such as that prevailing at D, but clearly the shift inward could be sufficiently large as to render this level of seigniorage infeasible in equilibrium, forcing the government to accept a lower (credible) seigniorage yield.[4]

Learning

The onset of conflict often comes as a surprise. However, it is reasonable to assume that as conflict endures, the private sector learns about the government's policy rule and adjusts its expectation algorithms accordingly (see, for example, Marcet and Nicolini 2003). Learning algorithms are not explicitly introduced here, but those considered in the literature would be consistent with a gradual increase in β_t in the face of rising inflation. As learning progresses, inflation expectations adjust more rapidly, the saddle path in Figure 7.1 gets steeper (more so if at the same time the semi-elasticity of money demand increases), and the transitional seigniorage revenue shrinks. Eventually, when $\beta_t \geq 1/\alpha$, the polarity of the saddle path reverses and the economy suddenly experiences an explosive path for inflation expectations.[5]

Post-conflict responses

The post-conflict period is in some respects a halfway house between peace and war. Although GDP starts to recover, the process takes many years; given the legacy of conflict, money demand is likely to remain below its peace-time level. Moreover, there is evidence that episodes of the loss of fiscal control tend to reduce the post-crisis income elasticity of the demand for money, thereby slowing the remonetization of the economy once inflation pressures have passed and growth has recovered (Adam and Bevan 2004). Similar patterns are likely to be present in the wake of conflict-induced increases in inflation.

While the constraint on raising seigniorage remains tight, government spending needs remain higher than before the war and are indeed likely to increase. Post-conflict reconstruction cannot generally be financed by a fiscal peace dividend, because the high risk of conflict reversion typically keeps military spending close to wartime levels (Collier and Hoeffler 2006). Both the persistence of the reduced demand for money and the increased demand for spending imply that the government would choose a higher rate of inflation, such as that entailed by a point in the region of D on the new Laffer curve in Figure 7.1.

7.2 Empirical analysis

The empirical analysis uses annual data for a panel of 66 developing economies, 30 of which experienced at least one episode of civil war between 1964 and 2002 (Table 7A.1). Organization for Economic Co-operation and Development countries are excluded, because they are generally free of civil war and tend not to rely on seigniorage to nearly the same extent as other countries. Former communist countries are also excluded, principally because of lack of data. Finally, countries in currency unions are excluded, because union membership constrains their scope for seigniorage. (South Africa is retained, because its dominant role in the Common Monetary Agreement of Southern Africa means that it enjoys de facto full monetary independence.)

Countries with more than 1,000 battle-related deaths are classified as being in a state of civil war in that year.[6] A recent innovation in data on civil war has been the development of measures of conflict intensity based on the extent of combat-related mortality (Lacina and Gleditsch 2005). *A priori*, it is unclear whether the monetary effects of a conflict will be more closely related to a measure of its intensity (such as combat-related mortality) or to a state-dependent measure. The core results reported here are based on a state-dependent measure, on the grounds that it better reflects the quantum effects a shift from a state of peace to a state of war may have on expectations relevant for asset demands. (The robustness of the results is tested to alternative measures of conflict; see Table 7A.2.)

Four stylized facts characterize the data (Table 7.1). On average, inflation rises during conflict and falls following conflicts, but it remains higher than before the conflict. Seigniorage follows a similar pattern, rising by more than 1 full percentage point of GDP during the conflict (against a pre-conflict level of 1.8 per cent of GDP) before falling back toward, but not quite achieving, its pre-conflict level. The composition of seigniorage revenue changes markedly. During conflict, governments rely more heavily on seigniorage raised through reserve requirements on the banking system. The differential responses of the (unconstrained) non-bank private sector and the (highly constrained) bank sector are reflected in the summary statistics on real balances. Currency holdings of the non-bank private sector fall from 8.2 per cent to 6.2 per cent of GDP, while bank reserves rise by almost 3 percentage points of GDP. As a result, the average seigniorage yield on bank reserves rises sharply during conflict. Following a conflict, both revert toward their pre-conflict values.

Table 7.1 Descriptive statistics (means)

Statistic	Full sample (1964–2002)	Prewar	War	Postwar
Inflation (per cent per year)	14.3	13.3	20.4	15.3
Reserve money (per cent of GDP)	11.4	10.7	11.6	11.7
Currency	6.6	8.2	6.2	6.8
Reserves	4.8	2.6	5.4	4.8
Seigniorage (per cent of GDP)	2.1	1.8	3.0	2.3
Currency	1.0	1.2	1.2	1.1
Reserves	1.0	0.5	1.8	1.2
Aggregate GDP growth (per cent per year)	3.6	4.4	2.6	4.5
Per capita GDP growth (per cent per year)	1.2	1.9	0.4	2.3
Aid (per cent of GDP)	6.0	4.5	4.6	6.5

Source: See Table 7A.3.

Money demand

The regression analysis begins with money demand, which constitutes the constraint on government choices. Currency in circulation and reserve holdings by the banking system are distinguished, because reserve holdings may be subject to government control rather than being a choice variable for the private sector. Cagan-style money demand functions of the form

$$
\begin{aligned}
\ln(m)_{it} = {} & \gamma_0 + \gamma_1 \ln(y)_{it-1} + \gamma_2 \ln(pop)_{it} \\
& + \gamma_3 \tilde{\pi}_{it-1} + \gamma_4 war_{it} + \gamma_5 postwar_{it} \\
& + \gamma_6 [\ln(y)_{it-1} \cdot war_{it}] + \gamma_7 [\ln(y)_{it-1} \cdot postwar_{it}] \\
& + \gamma_8 [\tilde{\pi}_{it-1} \cdot war_{it}] + \gamma_9 [\tilde{\pi}_{it-1} \cdot postwar_{it}] + \varepsilon_{it}
\end{aligned}
\tag{11}
$$

are estimated (Table 7.2), where countries are denoted by i and time by t. The dependent variable, corresponding to each of the measures of money, is defined as a share of GDP. The analysis expands on the specification in equation (4) by allowing for the possibility that the per capita income elasticity of the demand for money deviates from 1: it thus includes population (*pop*) and real income (*y*) as regressors. To avoid potential problems of endogeneity, $\ln(y)$ enters equation (11) with a lag. Inflation, $\tilde{\pi}$, is as defined in equation (4). The dummy variable *war* takes the value of 1 if country i is in a state of civil war at time *t* and 0 otherwise; *postwar* takes the value of 1 in the first 10 years following the ending of hostilities. The equation residual $\varepsilon_{it} = \mu_i + \omega_t + \nu_{it}$ is a conventional two-way error component residual. Each equation is estimated using a within-groups/fixed-effects estimator with a full set of common time and year dummies. Pooling tests reject the null hypothesis of a common intercept.[7]

Controlling for income and inflation, the analysis first introduces civil war and its aftermath as dummy variables (columns 1–3). Both are highly significant and negative for reserve money as a whole and for each of its components. Over and above any effects through income and inflation, conflict reduces the demand for money. More surprisingly, this direct erosion in the demand for money appears to intensify during the post-conflict decade, when money demand declines by 19 per cent relative to peacetime and 6 per cent relative to wartime. The decline relative to wartime is statistically significant, overall and for currency demand.

Bank reserves are not a direct choice variable for the private sector; they are determined by the interaction of government policy on reserve requirements, the banking sector's liquidity preference, and the private sector's demand for inside money. It is, then, not surprising that except for the autonomous *war* and *postwar* shift effects, the results for bank reserves are weak: neither income nor inflation is statistically significant, and the overall fit of the equation is markedly lower than for currency demand. What follows therefore concentrates on the demand for currency (the question of how the authorities balance their seigniorage extraction between these two sources is returned to later).

Table 7.2 Fixed-effects estimates of log money demand (per cent of GDP). OLS estimates

Variable	Log reserve money (1)	Log currency (2)	Log bank reserves (3)	Log currency (4)	Log currency (5)	Log bank reserves (6)
Constant	-1.690 (9.67)	-1.953 (8.21)	-5.130 (15.80)	-2.700 (11.88)	-2.640 (11.85)	-4.975 (12.11)
Log real GDP				0.007 (2.21)	0.005 (1.87)	0.008 (1.09)
lrgdp* war				-0.007 (0.93)	-0.008 (1.01)	-0.008 (0.48)
lrgdp* postwar				-0.054 (4.59)	-0.025 (2.06)	-0.018 (0.92)
Log population	-0.020 (0.32)	0.190 (2.16)	-0.122 (1.07)	0.449 (5.34)	0.432 (5.21)	-0.168 (1.14)
infl	-0.239 (2.77)	-0.541 (8.72)	-0.026 (0.17)	-0.484 (7.06)	-0.461 (6.60)	-0.204 (1.07)
infl* war				-0.337 (2.53)	-0.257 (1.92)	0.745 (2.36)
infl* postwar				0.089 (0.49)	0.036 (0.22)	0.416 (1.32)
war	-0.126 (3.89)	-0.074 (2.73)	-0.251 (4.28)	0.044 (0.62)	-0.038 (0.50)	-0.268 (1.79)
postwar	-0.189 (6.14)	-0.178 (5.38)	-0.287 (5.33)	0.264 (2.53)	-0.019 (0.18)	-0.167 (0.93)
aid* war					1.001 (6.74)	-0.098 (0.15)
aid* postwar					0.831 (4.40)	-0.679 (1.74)
Pooling F-test (country = 0) Probability	124.4 (0.000)	213.97 (0.000)	55.71 (0.000)	202.36 (0.000)	208.6 (0.000)	53.116 (0.000)
F-test (war = postwar)	3.5 (0.0129)	8.65 (0.003)	0.4 (0.529)	3.59 (0.058)	0.02 (0.882)	0.24 (0.626)
F-test (infl* war = infl* postwar)				4.52 (0.034)	2.59 (0.107)	0.66 (0.417)
F-test (lrgdp* war = lrgdp* postwar)				12.06 (0.001)	1.35 (0.245)	0.22 (0.643)
F-test (aid* war = aid* postwar)				0.56 (0.456)	0.62 (0.431)	
R-squared	0.704	0.832	0.607	0.848	0.855	0.612
Number of observations	2,009	2,004	2,004	1,925	1,908	1,908

Source: Authors' calculations based on analysis in text.

Note: All specifications include country and year dummy variables. infl denotes inflation factor. The interaction effect between log real GDP and the war dummy is denoted lrgdp* war and similarly for all other interaction effects. Figures in parenthesis beside coefficient estimates are t-statistics; figures in parenthesis beside F-statistics are probability values.

To investigate the transmission paths for this erosion in the private sector's money demand, interaction terms are introduced between both the *war* and *postwar* dummy variables and inflation (column 4). Similarly, the possibility that the income elasticity of money systematically differs from unity during and after conflict is allowed for. With the introduction of these interaction terms, the direct effects of both dummies cease to be significant. As suggested by the model in section I, the wartime erosion of currency demand works principally through a heightened sensitivity to inflation: not only does the (absolute) inflation semi-elasticity rise significantly during war, the increase in inflation generates a disproportionate reduction in money demand. Postwar the inflation semi-elasticity of demand is not significantly different from the prewar environment. However, the decline in the income elasticity of money demand, as attested by the postwar interaction term, means that the recovery in postwar income does not rebuild money demand proportionally, because the private sector continues to reduce its need for currency per unit of income.

These results are tested for robustness to various measures of the intensity of conflict (the results are reported in appendix Table 7A.2). Columns 1–3 in Table 7A.2, in which conflict is measured directly by the number of combat-related deaths, correspond directly to the same columns in Table 7.2. The wartime dummy variable is replaced by the number of deaths in each year, and the postwar dummy variable is replaced by the cumulated number of these deaths during the preceding conflict. In columns 4–6 a variant is investigated in which the number of deaths is scaled by population. For both specifications the new variables are significant, the size of the effect on money demand being very close to that found using the dummy variables. Non-nested encompassing tests suggest that from a purely statistical perspective, no measure of conflict dominates. Changing the way in which conflict is measured does not affect the other determinants of money demand, in particular the inflation semi-elasticity, which is the focus here. Column 7 in Table 7A.2 extends the robustness check by interacting the combat death measure of conflict with inflation, with the same results as in Table 7.2, column 4. What follows therefore relies on the results of Table 7.2, in which conflict is treated as a state variable.

The government's choice of seigniorage

In raising seigniorage, the government has two instruments at its disposal, the supply of currency and the reserve requirements on the banking system. The supply of currency induces inflation; the reserve requirement is a tax on the banking system, which is liable to reduce the allocative efficiency of finance. The government's chosen level of seigniorage can be expressed as:

$$s_{it} = \beta_0 + \beta_1 war_{it} + \beta_2 postwar_{it} + \lambda_1 \ln(m)_{it} + u_{it}, \tag{12}$$

where *s* is the seigniorage revenue corresponding to the three measures of money, expressed as percentage points of GDP, and u_{it} is a two-way error term, as defined above. Substituting for ln(*m*) from the money demand equations allows choices to be expressed as determined by the direct and indirect "structural" effects of war and postwar. Collecting the war and postwar terms allows seigniorage outcomes to be expressed as follows:

$$s_{it} = (\hat{\beta}_0 + \hat{\lambda}_1 \hat{\gamma}_0) + \hat{\lambda}_1 [\hat{\gamma}_1 \ln(y)_{it-1} + \hat{\gamma}_2 \ln(pop)_{it} + \hat{\gamma}_3 \pi_{it-1}]$$
$$+ [\hat{\beta}_1 + \hat{\lambda}_1 (\hat{\gamma}_4 + (\hat{\gamma}_1 + \hat{\gamma}_6) \ln(y)_{it-1} + (\hat{\gamma}_3 + \hat{\gamma}_8) \tilde{\pi}_{it-1})] \, war_{it}$$
$$+ [\hat{\beta}_2 + \hat{\lambda}_1 (\hat{\gamma}_5 + (\hat{\gamma}_1 + \hat{\gamma}_7) \ln(y)_{it-1} + (\hat{\gamma}_3 + \hat{\gamma}_9) \tilde{\pi}_{it-1})] \, postwar_{it} + w_{it} \quad (13)$$

where w_{it} is the composite error term from regressions 11 and 12. The parameters $\hat{\beta}_1$ and $\hat{\beta}_2$ reflect the direct 'choice' effects; the terms multiplied by $\hat{\lambda}_1$ reflect the indirect effects of war and postwar on the demand for money.

Consider the combined seigniorage from currency in circulation and bank reserves. Columns 1–3 in Table 7.3 report the results of the seigniorage regressions. Controlling for the level of real money balances, regressions introduce dummy variables for the war and postwar periods. Both are highly significant: wartime and postwar governments resort more to seigniorage than peacetime governments do. The coefficients on the two dummies are not significantly different from each other: postwar governments are as desperate for revenue as wartime governments. Conditional on the level of the constraint, war conditions increase seigniorage extraction by about 1.1 per cent of GDP. Given that prewar seigniorage is about 1.8 per cent of GDP (see Table 7.1), this is a substantial increase in needs. In the post-conflict decade the direct effect is virtually as large as during the war, at 0.8 per cent of GDP. This is consistent with the observed continuing high levels of government military spending in post-conflict conditions.

While the total direct effects of wartime and postwar conditions on the government's resort to seigniorage are the same, their composition differs. During war governments rely predominantly on taxing the banking system, with four-fifths of total seigniorage generated from this source. Postwar, although taxation of the banking system still dominates, there is some shift toward greater reliance on printing currency. This shift may be appropriate: because of the collapse of investment, allocative financial efficiency may temporarily be unimportant during conflict.

War and postwar conditions alter seigniorage not only through direct effects on government choices but also through their effects on income and money demand. While government needs increase pressure to resort to seigniorage, the tightening of the constraint resulting from lower income and the erosion in the demand for money reduces the amount of seigniorage that can be raised. The direct effect combined with the two offsetting indirect effects determines the overall effect of war and its aftermath on seigniorage. The decline in overall seigniorage between war and postwar noted in table 1

Table 7.3 Fixed-effects estimates of seigniorage choice (per cent of GDP)

Variable	Seigniorage from reserve money (ordinary least squares) (1)	Seigniorage from currency (ordinary least squares) (2)	Seigniorage from bank reserves (ordinary least squares) (3)	Seigniorage from reserve money (instrumental variable) (4)	Seigniorage from reserve money (instrumental variable) (5)	Seigniorage from currency (instrumental variable) (6)	Seigniorage from currency (instrumental variable) (7)
Constant	0.069 (10.65)	0.039 (11.88)	0.062 (7.44)	0.068 (9.60)	0.068 (9.59)	0.037 (10.65)	0.070 (5.90)
war	0.011 (3.83)	0.003 (3.00)	0.008 (3.24)	0.009 (0.96)	0.008 (3.29)	0.002 (1.41)	0.011 (3.03)
postwar	0.008 (3.38)	0.002 (1.78)	0.006 (3.05)	0.027 (1.78)	0.027 (2.02)	0.007 (1.18)	0.016 (1.30)
ln money demand	0.030 (8.38)	0.008 (6.56)	0.013 (8.28)	0.027 (7.15)	0.027 (7.54)	0.008 (5.62)	0.012 (6.78)
aid* war				−0.024 (0.15)			
aid* postwar				−0.320 (1.23)	−0.332 (1.50)	−0.087 (0.93)	−0.198 (0.88)
Pooling F-test (country = 0)	6.04 (0.000)	7.71 (0.000)	3.1 (0.000)	5.31 (0.000)	5.28 (0.000)	9.28 (0.000)	2.97 (0.000)
F-test (war = postwar)	1.35 (0.246)	1.16 (0.283)	1.08 (0.299)	0.67 (0.414)	2.58 (0.108)	1.04 (0.306)	0.22 (0.636)
R-squared	0.348	0.377	0.284	0.2453	0.2404	0.3195	0.2381
Number of observations	2,200	2,193	2,193	2,003	2,003	1,996	1,652
Cragg-Donald Identification Test (Ho: underidentified)				(0.008)	(0.000)	(0.0004)	(0.0005)
Shea Weak Instrument Test (Ho: instrument is weak)							
aid* war				0.0227 (0.000)	0.0177 (0.0396)		
aid* postwar				0.0177 (0.0396)	0.0148 (0.0742)	0.0148 (0.0742)	0.0092 (0.0178)

Source: Authors' calculations based on analysis in text.

Note: All specifications include country and year dummy variables. The interaction effect between aid and the war dummy and between aid and the postwar dummy are denoted aid* war and aid* postwar respectively. These variables are treated as endogenous regressors and are instrumented. See text for details. Figures in parenthesis beside coefficient estimates are t-statistics; figures in parenthesis beside F-statistics and tests for identification and weak instruments are probability values.

reflects both a decline in needs, of about 0.3 percentage points of GDP on average, and a reduction in the seigniorage tax base of about the same amount (Table 7.4).

7.3 Post-conflict assistance

During the postwar period, the government is faced with a harsh tradeoff. The need for revenue increases, but the capacity to raise it through seigniorage deteriorates, as the demand for money erodes. From the long-run perspective there is a case for reducing resort to seigniorage, thereby investing in the reconstruction of money demand and so restoring the future potential for sustainable seigniorage. From the short-run perspective there is a case for further resort to seigniorage, despite its rising cost in terms of inflation and damage to the banking system. Does aid resolve this dilemma?

Post-conflict reconstruction is the original rational for aid. Indeed, the original name for the World Bank was the International Bank for Reconstruction; the words 'and Development' were added as an afterthought. Following the end of conflict, there is typically a surge in aid, as donors respond to perceived post-conflict needs. Aid has indeed been found to be significantly more effective in enhancing growth during the post-conflict decade than at other times (Collier and Hoeffler 2004a). Postwar aid can also have monetary effects, which can affect the government's need for seigniorage.

Aid and the government choice of seigniorage

Aid, expressed as a share of GDP, is introduced into the seigniorage regression as follows:

$$s_{it} = \beta_0 + \beta_1 war_{it} + \beta_2 postwar_{it} + \beta_3[aid_{it} \cdot war_{it}] + \beta_4[aid_{it} \cdot postwar_{it}] + \lambda_1 \ln(m)_{it} + u_{it} \tag{14}$$

Table 7.4 Decomposition of war and postwar seigniorage yields (per cent of GDP)

Period/cause of change in seigniorage	Reserve money	Currency	Bank reserves
War			
Direct needs	1.10	0.30	0.80
Constraint shift	−0.34	−0.06	−0.33
Net seigniorage	0.76	0.24	0.47
Postwar			
Direct needs	0.80	0.20	0.60
Constraint shift	−0.59	−0.14	−0.37
Net seigniorage	0.21	0.06	0.23
Mean prewar seigniorage	1.80	1.20	0.50

Source: Authors' calculations based on analysis in text.

The supply of aid cannot be assumed to be exogenous to government fiscal choices: donors might plausibly either increase aid flows in response to fiscal desperation or reduce them in response to fiscal irresponsibility. Aid is therefore instrumented using a vector of political, cultural, and economic measures of distance between each recipient country and its principal Development Assistance Committee aid donors (see Tavares 2003).[8] The underlying idea is that to some extent, bilateral donor governments provide aid based on historical ties and domestic budgetary circumstances that are unrelated to circumstances in the recipient country. As the instrument validity tests reported at the bottom of Table 7.3 suggest, the instrumenting strategy adopted here appears reasonably robust.

Columns 4 and 5 in Table 7.3 introduce aid instrumented in this way into the seigniorage regression for reserve money. During wartime aid is unsurprisingly negligible; instrumented aid is therefore insignificant when interacted with the wartime dummy variable. In effect, the aversion of donors to funding warfare overrides the proclivities of bilateral donors to provide aid. When the interaction of aid with this wartime dummy variable is dropped, the interaction between aid and the postwar dummy variable is negative and substantial. Although it is only on the borderline of significance, it is fully consistent with theory: it is not surprising that aid reduces the resort by government to seigniorage. An increase in aid equivalent to 1 percentage point of GDP reduces seigniorage by about 0.33 percentage points of GDP.

Because aid usually surges following the end of conflict, the addition of aid makes a substantial difference to the other components of the regression. In particular, the direct effect of the postwar dummy variable is now about four times its previous value. Although the regression involves a small reduction in the sample, this is not the explanation for the change.[9] Thus, controlling for aid, postwar governments appear to be far more desperate for revenue even than they are during war. The surge in aid postwar accommodates these needs and thereby reduces resort to seigniorage.

Columns 6 and 7 in Table 7.3 again show how the resort to seigniorage is split between currency and bank reserves, in this case controlling for post-conflict aid. Although the differences between seigniorage extracted from currency and from bank reserves seen in columns 2 and 3 remain, there is no statistically significant difference in the impact of post-conflict aid.

Aid and money demand

Because aid reduces the resort to seigniorage, it reduces inflation. Indirectly, aid therefore raises the demand for money. Aid also significantly augments growth in the postwar context (Collier and Hoeffler 2004a), which directly raises the demand for money. The theoretical specification of the demand function suggests that conditional on income and inflation, aid should have no direct effect on private sector demand for money. However, in the context of the aftermath of civil war, there may be such an effect. One likely explanation for the severe erosion of the demand for money in the postwar period is a 'peso effect,' in which the high risk of a reversion to conflict supports expectations of further inflation in excess of that directly implied by current experience. Conceivably, large aid programs might help reassure citizens, thereby directly increasing the demand for money. This hypothesis is tested, by modifying the demand for money function as follows:

$$\ln(m)_{it} = \gamma_0 + \gamma_1 \ln(y)_{it-1} + \gamma_2 \ln(pop)_{it} + \gamma_3 \tilde{\pi}_{it-1}$$
$$+ \gamma_4 war_{it} + \gamma_5 postwar_{it}$$
$$+ \gamma_6[\ln(y)_{it-1} \cdot war_{it}] + \gamma_7 [\ln(y)_{it-1} \cdot postwar_{it}]$$
$$+ \gamma_8 [\tilde{\pi}_{it-1} \cdot war_{it}] + \gamma_9 [\tilde{\pi}_{it-1} \cdot postwar_{it}]$$
$$+ \gamma_{10}[aid_{it} \cdot war_{it}] + \gamma_{11}[aid_{it} \cdot postwar_{it}] + \varepsilon_{it}. \qquad (15)$$

In a reduced-form regression of the type estimated here, any impact of aid inflows must reflect a direct effect, because the regression controls for the indirect effects.

It is reasonable to assume that aid is weakly exogenous with respect to private sector demand for money; aid is therefore introduced into the demand for money functions using ordinary least squares (Table 7.2, columns 5 and 6). Aid has a small and statistically insignificant effect on the demand for reserve money (not shown in Table 7.2), but this is because it has strong but offsetting effects on the two components of money. Aid significantly increases the demand for currency in circulation both during war and in the post-conflict period (column 5); it also reduces the demand for bank reserves by the same order of magnitude (column 6). The 'demand' for bank reserves in the context of civil war and its aftermath is most reasonably interpreted as being a coerced demand: banks must comply with central bank regulations. Hence, the decline in 'demand' as a result of postwar aid is likely to reflect the reduced pressure for government revenue. These aid effects are not large, but they are significant: as the regression controls for both income and inflation, the result is consistent with the hypothesis that aid reassures and so reduces the 'peso problem' arising from fears of collapse.

The inclusion of aid in the money demand regression changes the direct effect of the postwar dummy variable quite substantially. In the analysis of Section II, which omitted aid, it appeared that the demand for money eroded considerably more during the postwar period than during the war itself. Controlling for aid, this is no longer the case. The 'pure' effect of the postwar period on money demand continues to be substantially adverse in comparison to the prewar peace, but it is now significantly and substantially better than during the war itself.

Postwar aid 'reconstructs' the demand for money and hence seigniorage capacity through three distinct routes. First, post-conflict aid directly substitutes for seigniorage revenue, enabling the government to reduce its reliance on inflationary finance and thereby stimulating recovery in the demand for money. Second, post-conflict aid restores money demand indirectly, through its effect on income growth. While the overall effect of aid on growth is controversial, there is evidence that it is particularly effective in postwar situations (Collier and Hoeffler 2004a). Finally, as the regression results suggest, aid also appears to play a role in supporting a modest portfolio shift in favor of domestic money demand.

Applications to post-conflict monetary reconstruction

The regression results are applied to two pertinent questions concerning post-conflict aid. The first concerns the marginal effects of post-conflict aid; the second concerns the paths of reconstruction of the monetary base post-conflict, with and without aid.

The analysis draws on the evidence from the seigniorage and money demand regressions, combined with evidence from Collier and Hoeffler (2004a), to simulate the marginal impact on inflation and money demand of an increase in post-conflict aid. Given the peculiar nature of the demand for bank reserves, the focus here is exclusively on currency demand. Using the sample estimates for the levels of inflation and money demand at the start of the post-conflict period, the analysis measures the marginal impact of an increase in aid of 1 percentage point of GDP, sustained over a 10-year period. The impact consists of two distinct components. The first is the change in inflation arising from the aid-induced fall in seigniorage needs, which determines the end-of-conflict demand for currency (this represents a movement along the immediate post-conflict Laffer curve). The second is the improvement in post-conflict currency demand, including the induced effect of the further fall in inflation associated with rising currency demand given the marginal change in seigniorage needs. The results (Table 7.5) suggest that if the fall in desired seigniorage noted in Table 7.3 were sustained over the 10-year postwar period, the aid inflow would lead to a substantial restoration in real money balances of about 2.9 percentage points of GDP (an increase of almost 50 per cent over the end-of-conflict level) and an almost halving of inflation, from about 20 per cent to just over 10 per cent a year (Table 7.5).

The regression results are also used to track the evolution of the monetary base, inflation and seigniorage for the typical conflict-affected country under two scenarios: no aid and aid at the level typical of post-conflict situations. Each dynamic simulation is computed as a recursive forecast (Figures 7.2–7.4). Exploiting the adaptive inflation expectations specification used in the estimations, and given exogenous paths for real income growth (from Tables 7.1 and 7.5), the demand for currency at time t is predetermined, given the relevant coefficient values from Table 7.3. With currency demand predetermined, changes in seigniorage needs from Table 7.2 then imply changes in inflation and the current seigniorage yield. The change in inflation is used to update the demand for money in $t + 1$ and so forth. The coefficients on the war and post-conflict dummy variables are derived from a cross-section of observations; they therefore only approximate a genuinely dynamic analysis. In

Table 7.5 Marginal impact of 1 per cent increase in aid sustained over 10-year period

Channel	Impact	Seigniorage (per cent of GDP)	Inflation (per cent per year)	Money demand (per cent of GDP)
Inflation effect				
Impact of aid on aggregate seigniorage needs[a]	−0.33			
Decline in seigniorage from currency[b]		−0.12		
Initial post-conflict currency balances[c]	6.20			
Inflation (factor)[c]	0.20			
Inflation semi-elasticity[d]	−0.72			
Change in annual inflation			−3.08	
Induced increase in currency demand				0.10
Income effect				
Impact of aid on post-conflict growth (per cent per year)[e]	0.26			
Postwar income elasticity of currency demand[d]	0.98			
Increase in currency demand	0.26			2.56
Postwar inflation semi-elasticity of currency demand[d]	−0.43			
Change in annual inflation	−0.88			
Change in inflation over 10-year post war period			−677	
Induced increase in currency demand				0.14
Portfolio effect				
Portfolio shift coefficient[d]	0.83			
Currency balances, including Inflation effect[f]	6.30			
Increase in currency demand				0.05
Change in inflation over 10-year post war period			−0.18	
Induced increase in currency demand				0.00
Total effects				
Total direct reduction in seigniorage requirements		−0.12		
Total postwar increase in money demand				2.86
Total postwar reduction in inflation			−10.04	

Source: Authors' calculations based on analysis in text.

Notes

[a] Table 7.3, column 5.
[b] Assumes that 36 per cent of seigniorage revenue is to be raised from currency in circulation.
[c] Table 7.1.
[d] Table 7.2, column 5.
[e] From Collier and Hoeffler (2004a).
[f] Includes increase in currency demand due to initial post-conflict inflation reduction.

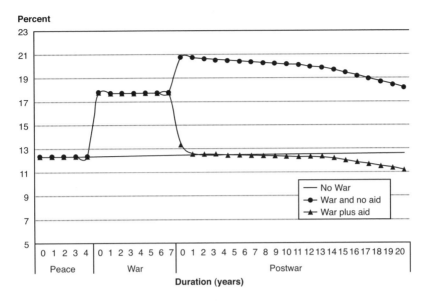

Figure 7.2 Impact of post-conflict aid on inflation (per cent per year).

particular, they produce discrete jumps upon the onset and end of war that exaggerate the likely actual speed of adjustment. These artificial jumps are juxtaposed against more genuinely dynamic adjustments to inflation and income.

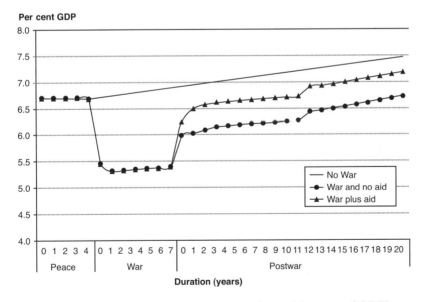

Figure 7.3 Impact of post-conflict aid on currency demand (per cent of GDP).

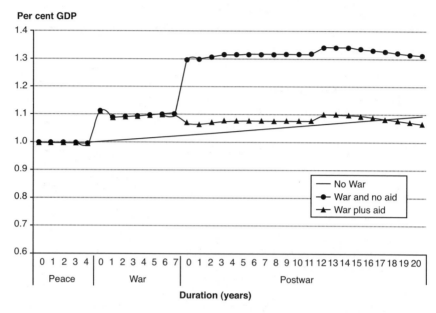

Figure 7.4 Impact of post-conflict aid on seigniorage (per cent of GDP).

Figure 7.2 plots the rate of inflation. The typical country in the sample had a pre-conflict rate of inflation of about 12 per cent. During war this rate rises to about 18 per cent, although not as abruptly as depicted in the figure. In the absence of aid the regressions reported in Tables 7.2 (column 5) and 7.3 (column 6) imply that there would be a substantial increase in inflation to 21 per cent with the onset of peace, an adjustment that is likely to be more gradual than depicted. This increase reflects the heavy fiscal needs facing post-conflict governments. Post-conflict aid at typical levels is sufficient not only to meet these needs but to enable the government to invest in monetary reconstruction. The inflation rate with aid rapidly reverts to its peacetime level and indeed starts to dip below it, as is necessary to rebuild money demand. As post-conflict aid typically surges immediately after the end of conflict, this fiscally driven effect may well be rapid.

Figure 7.3 plots the consequences for the demand for currency as a share of GDP. During war currency demand collapses from about 6.7 per cent to about 5.3 per cent of GDP. In the absence of aid currency demand nevertheless rebounds somewhat following the end of the conflict, to about 6 percentage points of GDP, but thereafter it stalls near this level: money demand is never rebuilt to its pre-conflict level. The rebound followed by stall is likely to be a spurious artefact of the post-conflict dummy variable; the fact that the ceiling to the recovery is well short of the pre-conflict level is not. With aid the initial post-conflict rebound is a little higher, at about 6.5 per cent of GDP; the key difference is that thereafter it gradually recovers toward its peacetime level. Even after a decade, recovery is not complete, but it is substantially accomplished.

Figure 7.4 tracks seigniorage from currency as a per cent of GDP. Such seigniorage increases during the war; if post-conflict aid is not forthcoming, a dramatic exploitation of the currency occurs with the onset of peace. While the speed of the increase is surely exaggerated by the dummy variable, the onset of increased fiscal needs is indeed liable to be rapid. Aid enables the government not only to avoid this jump in seigniorage but gradually to bring its taxation of the currency down to its peacetime level. The process of reversion is slow, taking almost 20 years.

7.4 Conclusion

Post-conflict situations are characterized by an unusually wide range of outcomes. While on average economies rebound from wartime decline, decline continues in some countries, and about 40 per cent of countries revert to conflict within a decade. Policy choices concerning the economic recovery of these hopeful but fragile situations have received far less attention than issues of political design and humanitarian needs.

Seigniorage is strategic, both because as revenue of last resort it reveals government preferences and because the ability to raise it reflects the degree of confidence of private actors in a fundamental government commitment. The results imply a rationale for aid that is peculiar to the post-conflict macroeconomic situation. In effect, just as infrastructure needs to be reconstructed, so too does the demand for money. Even controlling for inflation and income, private demand for money erodes sharply in the postwar period. Yet in the absence of aid, post-conflict governments resort to seigniorage far more heavily after war than during it.

While the restoration of the demand for money is beyond the capacity of the typical post-conflict government to finance out of its own resources, it is both an important objective in itself and a useful indicator of the broader restoration of confidence. Aid is effective in reconstructing the long-term scope for seigniorage, acting through three distinct routes. The most obvious one is that for which aid is primarily intended: it raises the growth of income, thereby raising the demand for money. Unfortunately, this effect is relatively weak in postwar conditions, because the income elasticity of the demand for money is lower than in normal times. However, two other effects occur. First, aid reduces the need for the government to resort to seigniorage and so reduces inflation. Second, and more surprisingly, over and above the effects through income and inflation, postwar aid has a direct effect, perhaps through strengthening confidence in the maintenance of peace. This article treats aid as a single aggregate, abstracting from different types and uses. The core result, however, implies that it is aid to the budget that achieves monetary reconstruction. This need not necessarily imply the superiority of budget support. Because much project aid is likely to be fungible, it indirectly relieves the budget, even though it is ostensibly earmarked.

Post-conflict aid is decisive in achieving monetary reconstruction. Rather than deteriorating, inflation and seigniorage—the monetary variables under the control of the government—revert to peacetime levels. The demand for currency, which is the constraint on government choices, takes longer to recover, because civil war severely damages confidence in the currency. Aid helps facilitate a gradual recovery. These monetary effects of post-conflict aid have been an unsung success: attention has focused on the more televisual roles of aid in humanitarian relief and the reconstruction of physical infrastructure. The effects on monetary reconstruction are no less real or substantial.

Appendix 7.1

Table 7A.1 Civil war episodes in sample countries

Country	Years
Algeria	1991 – present
Argentina	1973–77
Bangladesh	1985–92
Burundi	1995 – present
Colombia	1978 – present
Egypt, Arab Republic of	1967, 1969–70
El Salvador	1979–91
Ethiopia	1966–91 2002 – present
Guatemala	1966–95
India	1985 – present
Indonesia	1975–92, 1997 – present
Iran	1966–68, 1979–88, 1990–93, 1996–97, 1999–2001
Israel	1964 – present
Lebanon	1975–91
Morocco	1975–89
Nepal	1999 – present
Nicaragua	1978–79, 1981–89
Nigeria	1966–70
Pakistan	1971, 1974–77
Peru	1980–99
Philippines	1970 – present
Rwanda	1991–94, 1997–2002
Sierra Leone	1992–2000
South Africa	1975–88
Sri Lanka	1971, 1983–2001
Sudan	1963–72, 1983 – present
Syria	1979–82
Thailand	1974–82
Uganda	1978–79, 1981–91, 1994 – present
Zimbabwe	1974–79

Source: Gleditsch and others 2002.

Note: Non-conflict countries in the sample include Bahrain, Barbados, Belize, Bhutan, Bolivia, Botswana, Brazil, Cape Verde, Chile, Costa Rica, Ecuador, Fiji, The Gambia, Ghana, Haiti, Honduras, Jamaica, Jordan, Kenya, Kuwait, Madagascar, Malawi, Mauritius, Oman, Paraguay, Saudi Arabia, the Seychelles, the Solomon Islands, Suriname, Tonga, Trinidad and Tobago, Tunisia, Uruguay, Vanuatu, República Bolivariana de Venezuela, and Zambia.

Table 7A.2 Robustness of money demand results to alternative measures of conflict (per cent of GDP)

Variable	Battle deaths			Battle deaths per capita			Battle deaths
	Log reserve money (1)	Log currency (2)	Log bank reserves (3)	Log reserve money (4)	Log currency (5)	Log bank reserves (6)	Log currency (7)
Constant	−1.634 (24.07)	−1.880 (7.80)	−5.064 (15.15)	−1.590 (9.03)	−1.930 (8.27)	−4.960 (11.74)	−1.880 (7.76)
log population	0.002 (4.72)	0.184 (2.10)	−0.113 (0.99)	−0.037 (0.59)	0.177 (2.05)	−0.164 (1.10)	0.188 (2.12)
infl	−0.245 (2.91)	−0.547 (8.76)	−0.050 (0.33)	−0.242 (2.86)	−0.571 (8.98)	−0.034 (0.23)	−0.594 (9.44)
infl* war							0.001 (0.67)
infl* postwar							0.008 (1.56)
war	−0.004 (3.11)	−0.002 (2.05)	−0.004 (1.96)	−0.028 (2.28)	0.001 (0.02)	−0.043 (2.78)	−0.003 (2.08)
postwar	−0.004 (2.85)	−0.004 (2.56)	−0.003 (1.58)	−0.038 (2.72)	−0.020 (1.53)	−0.048 (2.70)	−0.005 (2.86)
F-test (war = postwar)	0.02 (0.8853)	1.59 (0.207)	1.13 (0.288)	4.58 (0.033)	19.2 (0.000)	0.57 (0.449)	2.57 (0.109)
F-test (infl* war = infl* postwar)							1.54 (0.215)
R-squared	0.703	0.829	0.604	0.704	0.834	0.613	0.831
Number of observations	1,973	1,968	1,968	1,973	1,968	1,892	1,968
Encompassing test Ho: M2 encompasses M1	9.31	5.57	42.9	21.76	44.51	60.05	5.98

Source: Authors' estimates based on analysis in text.

Note: All specifications include country and year dummies. The interaction effect between inflation and the war dummy and between inflation and the postwar dummy are denoted infl* war and infl* postwar respectively. Figures in parenthesis beside coefficient estimates are t-statistics; figures in parenthesis beside F-statistics and tests for identification and weak instruments are probability values. The Cox test is distributed $N(0, 1)$ under the null.

Table 7A.3 Variable definitions and data sources

Variable	Meaning	Definition and source
m	Money aggregate (per cent of GDP)	Defined for reserve money (IMF 2006 linc 14) and its components, currency in circulation (IMF 2006 line 14a) and bank reserves (IMF 2006 line 20), all measured as share of current price GDP in local currency (World Bank 2006)
s	Seigniorage (per cent of GDP)	Defined for each money aggregate as $s_t = (M_t - M_{t-1})/((1/2)(Y_t + Y_{t+1}))$ for nominal money aggregate, *M*, and nominal GDP, *Y*.
y	Real GDP	Constant price GDP (World Bank 2006)
pop	Population (millions)	World Bank (2006)
$\tilde{\pi}$	Inflation factor	Defined as $\tilde{\pi} = \pi/(1 + \pi)$, where π denotes annual change in consumer price index (World Bank 2006)
war	Civil war indicator	See text for explanation (Gleditsch and others 2002)
postwar	Postwar indicator	See text for explanation (Gleditsch and others 2002)
aid	Aid (per cent of GDP)	Net official development assistance (excluding technical assistance) as per cent of GDP (World Bank 2006)

Source: Authors' compilation.

Notes

1 Equivalently, the government's problem can be characterized in terms of the change in expenditure requirements net of other financing items.
2 This property of adaptive expectations is replicated under rational expectations if there is lagged adjustment of money demand.
3 Calvo and Leiderman (1992) show that under specific restrictions on functional form, equation (4) derives directly from the dynamic first-order condition for a representative agent maximizing utility of the form $U = \int_{t=0}^{\infty} |u(c_t) + v(m_t)|e^{-pt} dt$.
4 Depending on the precise changes in the demand for money, the seigniorage-maximizing rate of inflation may increase or decrease. As noted earlier, this inflation rate is defined as $\tilde{\pi}^{\max} = (1/\alpha) - \hat{y}$. Whether it rises or falls during and after conflict depends on the inflation semi-elasticity of money demand, the income elasticity of demand, and the growth of income.
5 Marcet and Nicolini (2003) use adaptive learning algorithms of this class to analyze hyperinflations in Latin America, which tend to follow the same trajectory of periods of high but stable inflation followed by hyperinflationary bursts that are brought under control by aggressive exchange rate–based stabilization.
6 All war-related data are from the Uppsala Conflict Data Program/International Peace Research Institute Armed Conflict Dataset Version 4–2006 (see Gleditsch and others 2002).
7 Whether behaviour differed between the first and second five-year post-conflict subperiods was investigated. Because the data do not reject pooling across the subperiods, however, only a single 'postwar' effect is reported.
8 The aid instrument is defined as $\tilde{a}_{it} = \Sigma_i \theta_{ij} A_{ji}$, where $\tilde{a}_{it}$ denotes instrumented aid for recipient *i* in period *t*; $\theta_{ij} = (1/D_{ij}, L_{ij}, R_{ij})$ is a vector of time-invariant measures of

'distance' between donor j and recipient i, where D_{ij} is the distance between the capital cities of i and j; L_{ij} is a dummy variable taking the value of 1 when i and j share the same official language and 0 otherwise; R_{ij} is a dummy variable taking the value of 1 when i and j share the same dominant religion and 0 otherwise; and A_{jt} is donor i's aid to GNI ratio in time t. This measure is calculated for the five principal aid donors: the United States, the United Kingdom, Japan, France, and Germany.

9 Reestimating the regression in column 1 on the reduced sample does not significantly affect the coefficient estimates.

References

Adam, Christopher. (1995). 'Fiscal Adjustment, Financial Liberalization and the Dynamics of Inflation: Some Evidence from Zambia.' *World Development* 23(5):735–50.

Adam, Christopher, and David Bevan. (2004). 'Fiscal Policy Design in Low-Income Countries.' In Tony Addison and Alan Roe eds., *Fiscal Policy for Development: Poverty, Reconstruction and Growth*. London: Palgrave Macmillan.

Bruno, Michael, and Stanley Fischer. (1990). 'Seigniorage, Operating Rules and the High Inflation Trap.' *Quarterly Journal of Economics* 105(2):353–74.

Cagan, Philip. (1956). 'The Monetary Dynamics of Hyperinflation.' In Milton Friedman, ed., *Studies in the Quantity Theory of Money*. Chicago: University of Chicago Press.

Calvo, Guillermo, and Leonardo Leiderman. (1992). 'Optimal Inflation Tax under Pre-Commitment: Theory and Evidence.' *American Economic Review* 82(1):179–94.

Cashin, Paul, Nadeem Ul Haque, and Nils Olekalns. (2002). 'Tax Smoothing, Tax Tilting and Fiscal Sustainability in Pakistan.' *Economic Modelling* 20(1):47–67.

Collier, Paul. (1999). 'On the Economic Consequences of Civil War.' *Oxford Economic Papers* 51(1):168–83.

Collier, Paul, and Anke Hoeffler. (2004a). 'Aid, Policy and Growth in Post-Conflict Societies.' *European Economic Review* 48(4):1125–45.

Collier, Paul, and Hoeffler Anke. (2004b). 'Greed and Grievance in Civil War.' *Oxford Economic Papers* 56(4):563–95.

———. (2006). 'Military Spending in Post-Conflict Societies.' *Economics of Governance* 7(1):89–107.

———. (2007). 'Unintended Consequences: Does Aid Finance Military Spending?' *Oxford Bulletin of Economics and Statistics* 69(1):1–27.

Gleditsch, Nils Petter, Peter Wallensteen, Mikael Eriksson, Margareta Sollenburg, and Havard Strand. (2002). 'Armed Conflict 1956–2001: A New Data Set.' *Journal of Peace Research* 39(5):615–37.

IMF (International Monetary Fund). (2006). *International Financial Statistics*. Washington, D.C.

Lacina, Bethany, and Nils Petter Gleditsch. (2005). 'Monitoring Trends in Global Combat: A New Dataset of Battle Deaths.' *European Journal of Population* 21(2–3):2–3.

Mankiw, Gregory, (1987). 'The Optimal Collection of Seigniorage: Theory and Evidence.' *Journal of Monetary Economics* 20(2):327–41.

Marcet, Albert, and Juan Nicolini. (2003). 'Recurrent Hyperinflations and Learning.' *American Economic Review* 93(5):1476–98.

Miguel, Edward, Shanker Satyanath, and Ernest Sergenti. (2004). 'Economic Shocks and Civil Conflict: An Instrumental Variables Approach.' *Journal of Political Economy* 112(112):725–54.

Tavares, Juan. (2003). 'Does Foreign Aid Corrupt?' *Economic Letters* 79(1):99–106.

World Bank. (2006). *World Development Statistics*. Washington, DC.

8   On economic causes of civil war

With Anke Hoeffler

8.1 Introduction

This chapter investigates whether civil wars have economic causes. Explanations of particular civil wars often invoke such causes. For example, the war in Rwanda has been attributed to pressure on land, while that in Angola has been interpreted as a contest for natural resources. The subject has not, to our knowledge previously been investigated. A related study by Bennett and Stam (1996) investigates the duration of international wars in terms of political and military variables. We utilize a comprehensive data set of civil wars (Singer and Small, 1982, 1994) and attempt to explain why they occurred in terms of underlying economic variables. Section 8.2 discusses the variables used in the analysis, basing them on a simple analytic framework. Section 8.3 presents the results, and Section 8.4 concludes.

8.2 Analytic framework

We first set out an analytic framework for the occurrence of civil war, drawing upon Grossman (1995) and Azam (1995). War occurs if the incentive for rebellion is sufficiently large relative to the costs. Both authors propose that in part these will be determined by distributional considerations: a government which rewards its supporters by exploiting a section of the population will increase the incentive for rebellion. However, there is insufficient data to introduce distributional considerations into the empirical analysis, as we discuss below. We therefore focus on those analytic causes of civil war other than distribution.

The objective of rebellion is either to capture the state or to secede from it. In general, the incentive for rebellion is the product of the probability of victory and its consequences. We first consider the determinants of the probability of rebel victory. Abstracting from distributional considerations, the probability of victory depends upon the capacity of the government to defend itself. As Grossman argues, typically, the military technology options available to rebels are fairly narrow, whereas the government faces a wide range of possible technological responses of increasing cost. For example, rebels seldom have the option of aerial combat. The government has the airfields from which to mount such combat and its capacity to use them depends upon its financial resources. In the limit, for a given population the military capability of rebellion is unrelated to the domestic economy (for example, being financed externally), whereas the military capability of the government depends upon its military expenditure. Since both military expenditure and tax rates are endogenous to the risk of rebellion, it is necessary to use some exogenous indicator of the capacity for military expenditure, such as the taxable base. Hence, the probability of rebel victory, p, would be diminishing in the per capita taxable base of the economy, T.

Following Grossman, the incentive for rebellion conditional upon victory, is determined by the capacity of a future rebel government to reward its supporters. If the objective of the rebellion is to capture the state, then (again abstracting from distributional considerations), this capacity will be dependent upon the potential revenue of the government and hence of the taxable base, T. Hence, the incentive for rebellion is an increasing function of $p(T) \cdot T$. Since T both reduces the probability of victory and increases the gain in the event of victory, its net effect on the risk of war is *a priori* ambiguous.

If the objective of the rebellion is secession then the taxable base of the pre-secession state is not the determinant of the gains conditional upon victory and distributional considerations are intrinsic. For example, secession might be motivated because the region is atypically well-endowed with resources, or because the preferences of the region are under represented in the government. Although there is insufficient data to introduce geographic inequality as an explanatory variable, one variable which is likely to capture the desire for secession is the size of the population *(P)*. The effect of population size on the desire for secession is most apparent when considered at the extremes. Were the global population contained within a single nation, linguistic and cultural disparities would be likely to generate continuous violent conflicts. By contrast, were there as many nations as socio-cultural groups, the desire for secession would presumably be much diminished.

Although any particular rebel group may be motivated only by one of the potential benefits, state capture and secession, in practice rebellions may consist of groups with each objective. For example, the civil war in Ethiopia included as allies the Tigrean People's Liberation Front, which upon victory took over the state, and the Eritrean People's Liberation Front, which upon victory seceded from the state. Both potential gains may therefore motivate the same rebellion. The gains from rebellion are thus an increasing function of both $p(T) \cdot T$ and P.

We now turn to the costs of rebellion. First, the actual conduct of civil war is costly to the rebels. This is due partly to the opportunity cost of rebel labour and partly to the disruption to economic activity caused by warfare. Both of these costs can be expected to increase with per capita income: a high income population has more to lose than a low income population during rebellion. These costs of rebellion increase with the duration of the conflict. The expected duration of the conflict also affects the gains from rebellion through the discount factor as modelled by Grossman. Hence, the probability of war is diminishing in both the expected duration of conflict (D) and the per capita income of the population (Y). We model the expected duration of warfare not as a choice variable for the rebels, but rather as being determined by the military capability of the government (proxied by the taxable capacity of the economy). Thus, a certain expected minimum duration of warfare will be necessary to achieve rebel objectives with the anticipated probability.

The above framework treats the rebels as a single agent. Hirshleifer (1987), while modelling rebellion in this way, acknowledges that it is a deficiency since war-making is the decision of a collective, so that the passage from individual interests to collective decisions should be incorporated. We therefore introduce the costs of coordination into the model. These can be regarded as a transactions cost. We discuss proxies for these transactions costs below.

Formally, the rebel decision on whether to embark on civil war can be set out as

$W = 1$ if $U_w > 0$, else $W = 0$

where $W = 1$ is war and $W = 0$ is peace, and U_w is the rebel utility function.
Rebel utility can be specified as

$$U_w = \int_{t=D}^{\infty} \frac{p(T) \cdot G(T, P)}{(1+r)^t} \, dt - \int_{t=0}^{t=D} \frac{(f(Y) + C)}{(1+r)^t} \, dt \tag{1}$$

where p = the probability of rebel victory, T = the taxable capacity of the economy, G = gain conditional upon victory, P = the size of the population, D = expected duration of warfare, Y = per capita income, C = coordination costs, and r = the discount rate.

Linearizing and treating the process as stochastic, a civil war will occur if

$$a \cdot p(T) \cdot T + b \cdot P - c \cdot D - d \cdot Y - e \cdot C > \eta \tag{2}$$

The maximum expected duration of a civil war conditional upon its occurrence follows from the same formulation

$$D < (a \cdot p(T) \cdot T + b \cdot P - d \cdot Y - e \cdot C - \eta)/c \tag{3}$$

Hence, if rebels have perfect foresight, so that the expected duration coincides with the actual duration, the observed duration of civil wars will be an increasing function of $p(T) \cdot T$ and P, and a decreasing function of Y and C, just as the probability of the occurrence of war. The resulting formulation makes both the probability of war and its duration outcomes of a single decision process in which they are each a function of $p(T) \cdot T$, P, Y, and C. Each potential rebel group faces the choice between remaining peaceful and fighting a war with a particular probability of success and a particular expected duration which is necessary to achieve the outcome with the expected probability. Since rebel groups in different countries face different benefits from victory, they will be prepared to accept wars of differing expected durations. Thus, although no single rebel group chooses the duration of war, across all potential rebellions there will be a relationship between the benefits of victory and the necessary duration of warfare which rebels find an acceptable price for victory. This enables us to test the model using both dichotomous data on whether civil wars occur and continuous data on their duration. Since civil wars are infrequent, their econometric analysis solely on the basis of dichotomous information suffers from the low number of observations and so the introduction of a continuous variable should strengthen the results.

If rebels have rational expectations but not perfect foresight then the observed duration of war is a biased predictor of the expected duration. Errors of optimism on the part of rebels will tend to induce war by mistake, and errors of pessimism will tend to produce peace by mistake. Hence, where the expectation is erroneously of a very long war the observation will be war of length zero. Thus, in the extreme case in which rebels always made massive, though unbiased, errors in their forecasts of the duration of warfare, the actual duration would be negatively correlated with the expected duration. If, empirically, the four explanatory variables T, P, Y, and C have the same effects on duration and occurrence this is reasonable evidence that the two are caused by the same underlying process and that errors in expectations of duration are not massive. If the explanatory variables differ as between duration and occurrence the results could variously be interpreted as a rejection of the underlying theory or as indicating large errors in rebel expectations.

We now turn to the construction of proxies for the hypothesized variables.

First consider gains to rebellion, made up of the probability of rebel victory and the gains conditional upon victory. We have suggested that the probability of victory is decreasing in government military expenditure per capita, which is in turn a function of the per capita taxable capacity of the economy. We proxy taxable capacity by per capita income and the natural resource endowment, since the latter is more readily taxable than other components of income. We use the Perm World Tables estimates of per capita income in 1960. These correct for international differences in the cost of living. We measure the natural resource endowment by the share of primary exports in GDP, this being the proxy for natural resources used by Sachs and Warner (1995).

Taxable capacity, thus proxied, also enters as the incentive for rebellion, conditional upon the probability of victory, so that its net effect on the probability of war need not be monotonic. We have proposed that a proxy for the benefits of secession is the size of the population.

Now consider the costs of rebellion, namely the loss of income sustained during the conflict and the costs of coordination. The loss of income caused by the conflict, which is essentially the opportunity cost of labour, is proxied by per capita income, measured as above. The costs of coordination are likely to be important because the normal transactions costs associated with collective action are increased in the case of rebellion by the need for secrecy, and the consequent premium upon trust. We proxy the transactions costs of coordinated action partly by cultural distinctness and partly by size. Cultural distinctness is measured by an index of ethno-linguistic fractionalization. This variable measures the probability that any two citizens will be drawn from a different ethno-linguistic group. The variable is re-scaled so that complete homogeneity scores zero and maximum fragmentation scores 100. It was first utilized by Mauro (1995) to explain the rate of growth. We hypothesize that coordination costs would be at their lowest when the population is polarized between an ethnic group identified with the government and a second, similarly sized ethnic group, identified with the rebels. Rebel coordination would be more difficult both in societies in which the entire population was from the same group, so that there was no obvious distinction between government and rebel supporters, and in societies which were so highly fractionalized that rebellion required coordination across multiple distinct groups. Mapped into the index of ethno-linguistic fractionalization, this would imply that coordination costs were at their minimum (and hence the risk of civil war at its maximum) in the middle range of the index. The second proxy for the costs of coordination is the size of the population. A rebellion covering a given proportion of the population (and thus, *ceteris paribus,* standing the same change of success), will require communication between a larger number of people in a country with a larger population.

To summarize, we propose a formulation in which both the probability of civil war and its duration are a function of the gains from rebellion, made up of the probability of rebel victory and the gains from victory (state capture or secession), and the costs of rebellion, made up of the opportunity costs of conflict and the cost of coordination. We have proposed four proxies for these variables, namely per capita income, the natural resource endowment, population size, and the extent of ethno-linguistic fractionalization. The first three proxies represent more than one variable so that only their net effect can be measured, and this need not be monotonic.

8.3 Results

The dependent variables are the occurrence and the duration of civil war. We use the Singer and Small (1982, 1994) data set on civil wars from 1816–1992. Singer and Small (1982) provide an operational definition of civil war. The authors define wars in terms of violence, not in terms of the goals of the protagonists or the results of the war. A civil war in Singer's and Small's (1982) typology is based on four dimensions. First, one of the primary actors in any conflict identified as a civil war must be the national government in power at the time hostilities begin. Secondly, the concept of war requires that both sides have the ability to inflict death upon each other. As a rule of thumb Singer and Small (1982) define that in a civil war the stronger forces must sustain at least 5 per cent of the number of fatalities suffered by the weaker forces. This rule enables them to distinguish genuine war situations from massacres, pogroms, and purges. Thirdly, significant military action must take place. Only civil wars that resulted in at least 1,000 battle related deaths per year are included in the data set. This figure includes civilian as well as military deaths. Fourthly, the war must be internal to the country. On the Singer and Small definition of internality this produces some important exclusions. Wars which they regard as being between a country and dependent territories, such as those in Angola, Mozambique, and Eritrea prior to formal independence, are classified by Singer and Small not as civil wars but as a subcategory of international wars termed 'extra-systemic'. However, since they are in many respects more akin to civil wars, being fought entirely within national boundaries, for our purposes we have included them in our sample.

While the series built by Singer and Small gives the potential for an analysis over a period of more than a century, and enables us to measure the period since the previous civil war without significant truncation, data on the other variables is only available for more recent periods. Data on per capita income and population size for the full sample is available from 1960 and for natural resources from 1965. Ethno-linguistic fractionalization is measured as of the early 1960s. This yields a sample of 98 countries of which 27 had civil wars of varying durations during the period.

We use probit and tobit regressions to investigate whether the above variables explain the occurence and duration of civil war during the period 1960–92.

The results are presented in Table 8.1. The tobit utilizes more information than the probit and so is the better form for assessing whether variables are significant. However, in order to interpret the effect of a variable it is more natural to focus not upon the duration of war but on the probablity of its occurrence.

All variables are significant in the tobit. In the probit, which uses less information, the index of ethno-linguistic fractionalization loses significance but is still sufficiently close to significance for their coefficients to be useful in interpreting the effect of the variable on the risk of war.[1]

Higher per capita income reduces the duration of civil war and the probability of its occurrence. These effects are very powerful. At the mean of other variables the probability of civil war is 0.63 if the country has half mean income but only 0.15 if the country has double mean income. Similarly, the predicted duration of civil war is much shorter if income is higher. Civil war is overwhelmingly a phenomenon of low income countries.

The effect of natural resources is non-monotonic. The possession of natural resources initially increases the duration and the risk of civil war but then reduces it. The maximum occurred at 27 per cent for the risk of war and at 24 per cent for its duration. The average share for the 98 countries was

Table 8.1 Determinants of the occurrence and duration of civil war

Variable	Probit of occurrence		Tobit of duration	
	Coefficient	t-ratio	Coefficient	t-ratio
income	−0.001	2.70	−0.069	2.39
primary	16.16	2.56	1957.6	2.49
primary^2	−29.47	2.28	−4106.0	2.42
ELF	0.0329	1.35	5.582	2.00
ELF^2	−0.0004	1.60	−0.065	2.02
population	0.0003	2.39	0.0086	2.31
sigma	–	–	135.45	6.49

| | | Predicted | | log likelihood: −193.62 | |
		0	1		
Actual	0	65	6		
	1	13	14		

Notes: Income = PPP adjusted per capita income in 1960
primary = share of primary commodity exports to GDP in 1965
ELF = index of ethno-linguistic fractionalization in 1960, ranges from 1–100
population = population in 1960 in 10,000

15 per cent and the maximum was 67 per cent. In effect, possessing natural resources made things worse, unless there were plenty of them. The effect is again quite strong. At the means of other variables, a country with the worst amount of natural resources has a probability of war of 0.56 as against one without natural resources of only 0.12.

Both per capita income and natural resources proxy the taxable base, whereas per capita income also proxies the opportunity cost of rebellion. Thus, income could potentially predominantly proxy either variable. However, the effect of the taxable base should be non-monotonic, whereas that of the opportunity cost of rebellion should be monotonic. Were income predominantly proxying the taxable base, then it would enter as a quadratic, as do natural resources. In fact the square of income is not significant, so that the results are consistent with income being predominantly a proxy for the opportunity cost effect.

Countries with larger populations have higher risks of war and these wars last longer. We interpret this as the greater attraction of secession. A country with double mean population has an increased probability of war of 0.56 at the means of other variables, and an increased duration of war of 12 months compared with one with mean population. While potentially the effect of population size is ambiguous, since it also proxies coordination costs, evidently, the increased desire for secession predominates.

The effect of ethno-linguistic fractionalization is also non-monotonic. We interpret this as proxying the costs of coordination. The probability of civil war reaches its peak when the index takes the value 38 (on the range 0–100)

in the probit, and at value 43 in the tobit. At the peak value of 38 a country with otherwise mean characteristics has a risk of war of 0.44. By contrast, both completely homogeneous societies (such as South Korea) and highly fractionalized ones (such as Indonesia with a value of 76) with otherwise mean characteristics have a risk of only 0.30. Hence, it is not ethno-linguistic fractionalization which is damaging to societies but that degree of fractionalization which most facilitates rebel coordination.

Between them, these four variables make a substantial difference to the chances of civil war. Consider two societies, one ideally endowed in terms of the four variables and the other catastrophically endowed. The ideal society would have the maximum income found in our sample ($9,895), a natural resource endowment of 0.67, the maximum ethno-linguistic fractionalization (93), and the smallest population (17.6). It would have a risk of civil war of 0.0000017. The catastrophic society would have the lowest income found in the sample ($257), a relatively high natural resource endowment (24 per cent), a near-average degree of ethno-linguistic fractionalization (38), and the largest population (43,485). It would have a risk of civil war of 0.99.

We have tested for robustness of the results by experimenting with several other variables, namely, population growth, population density, years since independence, and income inequality. None of these is significant in both the tobit and the probit and their inclusion leaves the core variables significant with largely unaltered coefficients.

Hence, the variables in the core regression were robust to changes in the specification.

In conclusion we apply the results to the specific problem of civil war in Africa. In 1960 Africa on average was characterized by conditions which made it prone to civil war. It was a very low income continent. It had a share of primary exports to GDP of 17 per cent, higher than the world average but insufficient to reach the range in which natural resources purchase government security. The most favourable aspects of Africa's inheritance as of 1960 was that it had high coordination costs of civil war, both because of its very high ethno-linguistic fractionalization (a mean of 67) and because societies were usually not polarized by recent previous wars: there had been only two

Table 8.2 Africa compared with other developing countries

	Sample	Sub-Saharan Africa	Other developing countries
Number of civil wars	27	12	15
Average duration in months	112	111	113
Income in 1960 in const. 1985 US$	2,378	845	1,880
Primary	0.15	0.17	0.16
Population in 10,000	1,854	595	2,412
ELF	42	65	36
N	98	32	40

civil wars in the previous decade. Thus, that Africa has had many civil wars since 1960, is, on our analysis, due not to its ethno-linguistic factionalization, but to its poverty.

8.4 Conclusion

We have investigated the generic causes of civil wars, building upon a simple theoretical framework based upon Hirshleifer (1987), Grossman (1995), and Azam (1995). The incentive for rebellion was increasing in the probability of victory, and in the gains conditional upon victory, and decreasing in the expected duration of warfare and the costs of rebel coordination. For any potential rebellion there is therefore a critical expected duration of warfare (which may be negative) at which rebellion becomes rational. Both the probability of civil war and its duration can therefore potentially be explained on a common set of variables.

We used data on the occurence and duration of civil wars 1960–92 for probit and tobit regressions. We have found that four variables are significant and strong determinants of both the duration and the probablity of civil wars. The higher is per capita income on an internationally comparable measure, the lower is the risk of civil war. We interpret this as being due to the effect of higher income on the opportunity cost of rebellion. The effect of natural resource endowments is non-monotonic. Initially, increased natural resources increase the risk of war. We interpret this as being due to the taxable base of the economy constituting an attraction for rebels wishing to capture the state. However, at a high level, natural resources start to reduce the risk of war. We interpret this as being due to the enhanced financial capacity of the government, and hence its ability to defend itself through military expenditure, gradually coming to dominate. The larger is the population the greater is the risk of war. We interpret this as being due to the increased attraction of secession.

We postulated that the extent of the coordination problem faced by potential rebels would influence the risk of war. We proxied coordination costs by ethno-linguistic fractionalization, and by population size. Perhaps our most interesting result concerns ethno-linguistic fractionalization, measured by an index on the range 0 to 100. Both economists and political scientists have postulated that such fractionalization is unambiguously conflict-enhancing. Easterly and Levine (1997) have established that greater fractionalization reduces growth, but have interpreted this as being due to the greater risk of conflict in fractionalized societies. Analogously, ethnic division is the most common political explanation for civil war. We have found that these interpretations are incorrect. While ethno-linguistic fractionalization is significant, more fractionalized societies are not more prone to civil war. The relationship is a quadratic which peaks when the index is 38. The index would take the value of 100 when each individual was in a different ethno-linguistic group. It would take the value 38 when, for example, there were two similarly-sized ethno-linguistic groups. Highly fractionalized societies are no more prone to war than highly homogeneous ones. The danger of civil war arises when the society is polarized into two groups. The effect is again powerful. Polarized societies have around a 50 per cent higher probability of civil war than either homogeneous or highly fractionalized societies. Thus, a country with two similarly sized ethno-linguistic groups could reduce the risk of civil war either by partition or equally well by union with other countries. We interpreted the greater safety of highly fractionalized societies as being due to the high coordination costs of rebellion when the potential rebels are themselves fractionalized.

We investigated several other variables but found the above formulation to be robust. It is striking that between them these four make a very large difference to the risk of civil war. A hypothetical country endowed with the most favourable of each of these five characteristics found in our sample would have had a risk of war during the period 1960–92 of one in a million. A hypothetical country with the least favourable of each would have a risk of 99 per cent.

Appendix 8.1: Data sources

Sample Sample includes the following countries: Algeria*, Argentina, Australia, Austria, Barbados, Benin, Bolivia, Brazil, Burkina Faso, Burundi*, Cameroon, Canada, Central African Republic, Chad*, Chile, Congo, Costa Rica, Denmark, Dominican Republic*, Ecuador, Egypt, El Salvador*, Ethiopia*, Finland, France, Gabon, Gambia, Germany, Ghana, Greece, Guatemala*, Guyana, Haiti, Honduras, Hong Kong, Iceland, India*, Indonesia*, Iraq*, Ireland, Israel, Italy, Cote d'Ivoire, Jamaica, Japan, Kenya, Korea, Liberia*, Madagascar, Malawi, Malaysia, Mali, Malta, Mauretania*, Mauritius, Mexico, Morocco*, Mozambique*, Myanmar*, Nepal, Netherlands, New Zealand, Nicaragua*, Niger, Nigeria*, Norway, Pakistan*, Panama, Papua New Guinea, Paraguay, Peru*, Philippines*, Saudi Arabia, Senegal, Sierra Leone, Singapore, Somalia*, South Africa, Spain, Sri Lanka*, Sudan*, Sweden, Switzerland, Syria, Tanzania, Thailand, Togo, Trinidad and Tobago, Tunisia, Turkey*, UK, USA, Uganda*, Uruguay, Venezuela, Zaire*, Zambia, Zimbabwe*.

An asterisk indicates that the country experienced a civil war during 1960–92.

Variables *Income:* real GDP for 1960 from Penn World Table Mark 5.6 (RGDPCH) (Summers and Heston, 1991).

Share of Primary Exports in GDP (Primary): share of primary exports in GDP in 1965 was obtained from the World Bank 'World Data' CD-ROM. The export of primary products (TX VAL RAWP CD) is the sum of the categories 'non fuels' covering SITC categories, 0, 1, 2, 4, and 68 and 'fuels' covering category 3. The data, as well as GDP (NYGDP MKTP CD), is measured in current US dollars.

Population: population data for 1960 was obtained from the World Bank 'World Data' CD-ROM (SP POP TOTL).

Ethnolinguistic Fractionalization Index (ELF): Index as used by Mauro (1995). This variable measures the probability that any two citizens will be drawn from a different ethno-linguistic group. The variable is re-scaled so that complete homogeneity scores zero and maximum fragmentation scores 100.

Note

1 In the probit ELF is only significant at 17 per cent and the square of ELF is significant at 11 per cent.

References

Azam, J.-P. (1995). 'How to pay for the Peace? A theoretical framework with references to African countries', *Public Choice*, 83, 173–84.

Bennett, S.D. and Stam III, A.C. (1996). 'The Duration of Interstate Wars, 1816–1985', *American Political Science Review*, 90, 239–57.

Easterly, W. and Levine, R. (1997). 'Africa's Growth Tragedy: Policies and Ethnic Divisions', *Quarterly Journal of Economics*, 112, 1203–50.

Grossman, H.I. (1995) 'Insurrections', in K. Hartley and T. Sandier (eds), *Handbook of Defence Economics*, Vol. I, Amsterdam: Elsevier Science B.V.

Hirshleifer, J. (1987). 'Conflict and Settlement', in J. Eatwell, M. Milgate, and P. Newman (eds) *New Palgrave, A Dictionary of Economics*, London: Macmillan Press.

Mauro, P. (1995). 'Corruption and Growth', *Quarterly Journal of Economics*, 110, 681–712.

Sachs, J.D. and Warner, A. (1995). 'Economic Reform and the Process of Global Integration', *Brooking: Papers on Economic Activity* Iss. 1, 1–118.

Singer, J.D. and Small, M. (1994). *Correlates of War Project: International and Civil War Data, 1816–1992 (Computer file)*, Inter-University Consortium for Political and Social Research, Michigan: Ann Arbor.

Small, M. and Singer, J.D. (1982). *Resort to Arms: International and Civil War, 1816–1980*, Beverly Hills: Sage.

Summers, R. and Heston A. (1991). 'The Penn World Table (Mark 5): An Expanded Set of International Comparisons, 1950–1988', *Quarterly Journal of Economics*, 99, 327–68.

9 Unintended consequences

Does aid promote arms races?

With Anke Hoeffler

9.1 Introduction

Military expenditure in developing countries constitutes a substantial claim on government budgets. The opportunity cost in terms of foregone social and growth-promoting expenditures is evident. As donors provide substantial finance to budgets, either directly or as a result of fungibility, there is also a widespread fear that aid intended for poverty reduction may in fact be financing the military. Governments nevertheless choose to spend substantial resources on the military. The most reasonable motivation is the need for security. Historically for most countries the main security threat was external – the country may need to fight an international war. However, international wars are now very rare. For developing countries, the main security threat is likely to be internal. For example, during 2002 there were 21 large-scale violent conflicts of which only one was international (Stockholm International Peace Research Institute, SIPRI, 2003). As the social and economic consequences of internal conflict are often appalling, governments may reasonably conclude that money spent on reducing the risk of internal conflict is well spent despite its high direct opportunity costs for social and economic development.[1]

In this chapter, we investigate both the revealed motivation for military spending in developing countries and its effectiveness in deterring internal conflict. We find that the risk of internal conflict is indeed one important motivation for military spending, but that other less reasonable pressures are also present – for example, the political power of the military lobby affects the defence budget. Further, we find that military spending is at best ineffective in reducing the risk of internal conflict. Governments do not, in fact, face the hard choice between internal security and social expenditures that they imagine.

While from the perspective of internal security, military spending appears to be merely unproductive, once external security considerations are introduced such spending becomes positively harmful. We find that there are neighbourhood arms race effects, which turn military spending into a regional public 'bad', inflicting negative externalities across borders.

Finally, budgets in most developing countries are partially financed by aid, either directly through budget support, or indirectly because of the fungibility of projects. There is a widespread concern that inadvertently aid is financing military spending. We investigate whether aid indeed leaks into military budgets.

Section 9.2 provides the foundations for the study by estimating a military expenditure function that attempts a comprehensive coverage of motivations, incorporating both external and internal threats. In Section 9.3, we develop one important implication of the regression analysis, the existence of neighbourhood arms races. This quantifies the 'regional public bad' nature of military expenditure. To the extent that military expenditure is driven by local arms races, a neighbourhood reduction in spending would presumably be without serious social cost. However, to the extent that it is effective in deterring internal rebellion, military spending can have substantial benefits. Indeed, as rebellion in one country hurts the economies of neighbouring countries, effective deterrence of internal rebellion may be a regional public good. In Section 9.4, we therefore investigate whether military expenditure is effective in deterring rebellion. Section 9.5 discusses the implications for international action towards the control of military spending.

9.2 Modelling military expenditure

Previous studies of the determinants of military expenditure are reviewed by Hartley and Sandler (1990, 2001, Vol. 1, Chap. 2) and Smith (1995). The main focus of the literature has been on military expenditure by developed countries during the Cold War, which was dominated by an arms race between NATO and the Warsaw Pact. This phenomenon generated both a theoretical and an empirical literature.

The canonical theoretical model of the arms race is that of Richardson (1960), more recent work being surveyed in Smith and Dunne (forthcoming). Following Smith (1989) and Skaperdas (1996), we hypothesize that military expenditure, M, is an input to security, S. That is, it reduces the bargaining power of those external and internal enemies who are willing to resort to violence. Conventional military contest success functions posit that in the event of a conflict the chances of success, P, depend upon the balance of forces, typically:

$$P = P(M_g/(M_g + M_e)) \tag{1}$$

where g stands for government forces and e enemy forces.

Such a functional form implies that an increase in the size of enemy forces raises the marginal productivity of government forces, $(d(dP/dM_g)/dM_e > 0)$, and so provides the underpinnings for an arms race.[2]

Spending can be adjusted in response to changes in need. Spending will thus be higher during wartime than during peace. However, because spending can only be adjusted slowly, the credibility of a military deterrent depends upon the level of spending during peacetime. By reducing the chances of enemy victory in the event of military conflict, peacetime military spending deters military challenges by enemies – thus producing security. In addition to the current level of the forces of potential enemies, other external factors, E, also influence the need for security. Together with the contest function, this implies a security function of the form:

$$S = S(M_g, M_e, E). \tag{2}$$

Security enters the welfare function along with non-military expenditures, C. Welfare is given by:

$$W = W(S, C, I) \tag{3}$$

where I are exogenous internal political influences which parameterize shifts in the objective function. The welfare function is maximized subject to a budget constraint:

$$Y \geq P_m M_g + P_c C \tag{4}$$

where P_m, P_c are prices.

Maximization of equation (3) subject to equations (2) and (4) then implies a demand function for military spending:

$$M_g = M_g(Y, P_m, P_c, M_e, E, I). \tag{5}$$

The empirical literature has also been dominated by attempts to estimate the arms race during the Cold War (Smith, Dunne and Nikolaidou, 2000). It naturally deployed the time-series econometric approach. A smaller literature focuses on developing countries, which are our primary interest. Deger and Somnath (1991) survey this literature which uses a cross-sectional approach (see, for example, Maizels and Nissanke, 1986; Looney, 1989; Gyimah-Brempong, 1989). The dependent variable is the ratio of military spending to GDP, commonly referred to as the 'defence burden'. The explanatory variables include a range of political and economic factors, but, in contrast with the NATO–Warsaw Pact literature, arms races are not analysed.

As our focus is on developing countries, and upon how military spending changes during development, we use a pooled cross-sectional approach, with a global coverage of countries during the period 1960–99, divided into eight sub-periods. Although this approach has been conventional in much of the growth literature, it has only just begun to be applied to the phenomenon of military spending (Dunne and Perlo-Freeman, 2003). Specifically, we have data for 161 countries, averaged over each 5-year period 1960–64, ..., 1995–99. Our regression analysis pools the data over countries and periods, yielding 563 observations for which we have complete data on the dependent and explanatory variables. As discussed below, an important advantage of this approach is that it enables us to introduce a measure of internal threat, constructed for precisely corresponding periods.

We now attempt to estimate a regression that approximates as closely as possible to the theoretical model specified in equation (5). The dependent variable in equation (5), military expenditure, is specified in absolute terms. However, because absolute levels of military spending are highly correlated with the level of development, it is more revealing to define the dependent variable as the share of military spending in GDP. The dependent variable is nevertheless problematic because data on military expenditure are unreliable, as discussed by Brzoska (1995). Here we use data from the SIPRI for the period 1960–90, updated with data from the *Global Development Indicators*. So measured, on average countries spend around 3.4 per cent of GDP on the military, but around this average there is enormous variation, ranging from 0.1 per cent to 46 per cent.[3]

Our core regression is presented in Table 9.1, column 1. Our dependent variable is the logarithm of the defence burden (military spending as a share of GDP). Our explanatory variables attempt to proxy those included in equation (5). We are able to develop satisfactory proxies for Y, M_e, E and I, but not for the relative price of military services. Generating a satisfactory relative price series would be a major undertaking.[4] Evidently, as the dependent variable is expenditure rather than the quantity of purchases, the sign of the price response is *a priori* ambiguous, depending upon whether the quantity response is greater than or less than minus unity. In effect, our analysis assumes the special case in which price effects wash out because the coefficient is not significantly different from zero. As our focus is on neighbourhood arms races rather than time trends the omission is unlikely to be important. We discuss our proxies for the other explanatory variables in turn.

The need for security

As discussed above, one part of the demand for military forces is the need to maintain external and internal security. The most evident need for military expenditure is during periods of active warfare. We introduce dummy variables for participation in an international war, and for civil war, both proxying E, external factors influencing the level of the threat from enemies. Unsurprisingly, both these variables are significant.[5] International war raises expenditure by 1.5 per cent of GDP, and civil war by about 1 per cent of GDP.

We next introduce proxies for the risk, while at peace, of participation in international warfare. One potential indicator of the current risk of such participation is the history of participation. Past involvement in a war may indicate either a hostile relationship with a neighbour, or an international security role. For example, the participation of Australia in the Korean War set a precedent for its subsequent involvement in East Asian conflicts, notably the

Table 9.1 Determinants of military expenditure

	1	2	3	4
International war	0.448 (0.127)***	0.476 (0.133)***	0.560 (0.161)***	0.577 (0.154)***
Civil war	0.297 (0.124)**	0.305 (0.125)***	0.294 (0.142)**	0.215 (0.145)
				$P = 0.145$
External threat	0.520 (0.078)***	0.595 (0.090)***	0.503 (0.108)***	0.468 (0.108)***
(Neighbours' military expenditure)$_{t-1}$	0.098 (0.012)***	0.098 (0.012)***	0.126 (0.018)***	0.114 (0.019)***
ln population	-0.042 (0.024)*	-0.042 (0.024)*	-0.119 (0.033)***	-0.077 (0.040)*
Internal threat	0.735 (0.450)*	1.004 (0.533)*	1.041 (0.552)*	1.191 (0.498)**
1995–99	-0.358 (0.108)***	-0.358 (0.010)***	-0.232 (0.146)	-0.273 (0.148)**
Democracy	-0.059 (0.010)***	-0.058 (0.010)***	-0.061 (0.013)***	-0.066 (0.013)***
ln GDP per capita	0.237 (0.043)***	0.234 (0.045)***	0.232 (0.068)***	0.388 (0.108)***
Israel	1.332 (0.276)***	1.265 (0.279)***	1.279 (0.310)***	1.213 (0.312)***
Internal threat */external threat		-1.168 (0.750) $P = 0.12$		
Aid/GDP			0.005 (0.007)	0.033 (0.017)**
N	482	482	339	339
R^2	0.44	0.44	0.47	0.45

Notes: Dependent variable is the logarithm of the defence burden. All regressions include a constant. Robust standard errors in parentheses; values are significant at ***1%, **5% and *10% levels. Results for column 4 were obtained by using two stage least squares (2SLS) estimation, first-stage regression results are reported in Table 9A.3. Allowing for heteroscedasticity in the error terms, we use a Hansen test as an overidentification test of the instruments and obtain a test-statistic of $Z_3^2 = 3.28$ ($P = 0.35$).

Vietnam War, which in turn set a precedent for its current involvement in East Timor and the Solomon Islands. Hence, participation in a war may change both the perceived level of threat, and the obligation to participate in international security provision. We measure the previous history of participation by a dummy variable which takes the value of unity if the country has been involved in an external war prior to the period in question but subsequent to 1945, this being a further proxy for E. The dummy is positive for around 20 per cent of our observations. It is highly significant, raising spending by around 1.8 per cent. Presumably this risk fades with time, but we could not find any significant rate of decay over the observed period, so possibly the process of decay is very slow.[6]

A second historical variable of evident significance for military expenditure is the ending of the Cold War. This defused both the arms race between NATO and the Warsaw Pact, and several of the proxy wars in developing countries. Again, this proxies the concept E. There is no unambiguous precise dating for the end of the Cold War – the failure of the communist coup d'état in August 1991 is sometimes seen in retrospect as the decisive end of the period of confrontation. However, during the early years of Yeltsin the reversion to hard line Soviet leadership could not be discounted. As our data is organized into 5-year sub-periods, our effective options are that the end of the Cold War should have had significant effects on military spending in either the entire period January 1990 to December 1999, or only during the shorter period January 1995 to December 1999. This is again an empirical matter. We find that if the end of the Cold War is defined on the entire decade of the 1990s there is no significant effect, whereas if it is defined on the shorter period since 1995 it significantly reduced military spending by 1.3 per cent of GDP. One possible reason for this apparent delay in the effect of the ending of the Cold War is that around 1991 global military spending temporarily surged because of the war in Kuwait. However, it is also possible that the combination of initial uncertainty as to the evolution of events in the former Soviet Union, and bureaucratic inertia in budget reductions, should produce a relatively long lag between the headline political events such as the dismantling of the Berlin wall, and actual military spending.

We now introduce the current military capacity of potential enemies, M_e, in equation (5). For developing countries, currently, most potential external threats are from neighbours and in the present analysis, we use the military spending of neighbours as a proxy for the potential threat. While this is evidently only an approximation to the countries that actually constitute threats, it has the advantage of being entirely exogenous. A more politically informed identification of threatening countries may be endogenous to chosen spending levels: for example, a country with a large military capability is likely to adopt a more aggressive foreign policy. Thus specified, the demand for security is related to the military spending levels of neighbours – the classic situation posited in neighbourhood arms races. Countries may be influenced by the expenditure of neighbours for reasons other than military threat. In the absence of clear indicators of military need, governments may base their judgment on the behaviour of their neighbours: emulation might account for what appears to be rivalry.

Somewhat surprisingly, in view of the focus of the developed country literature upon arms races, there are few studies in the empirical developing country literature that analyse the expenditure of neighbours as an explanatory variable. Dunne and Perlo-Freeman (2003) are a notable exception. There are various ways in which the military spending of neighbours can be specified. To distinguish between threat and emulation effects we create two distinct measures. If the military spending of neighbours poses a threat then presumably what matters is the absolute level of such spending, rather than the proportion of GDP which the neighbour devotes to such spending. Thus, if a small country (say Eritrea) is concerned about the threat posed by a larger neighbour (Ethiopia), it will aspire, if possible, to match the absolute level of its neighbour's forces, not the share of GDP devoted to the military. As our dependent variable is the share of GDP that the country devotes to military spending, we can express this aspiration as being the absolute level of the neighbour's military spending *as a share of home country GDP*. If, by contrast, international threats are seen as negligible, the choices of a neighbour may still be influential in the internal budget struggle between the Ministries of Finance and Defence because of emulation, but in this case the relevant influence will be the military spending of the neighbour relative to its own GDP.

Most countries have multiple neighbours. We therefore measure both the neighbourhood threat and emulation variables as aggregates. The threat variable is the sum of neighbours' military spending, divided by home country GDP, and the emulation variable is the sum of neighbours' military spending divided by the sum of neighbours' GDP. Thus, for example, although India has borders with both Nepal and China, the level of threat that it faces is dominated by the military spending of China.

Empirically, the behaviour of neighbours is important. To reduce the econometric problem of interdependence, we introduce neighbour's military spending with a lag.[7] When both the threat and emulation variables are entered into the regression, the former is completely insignificant whereas the latter is significant. The emulation variable remains significant when the threat variable is eliminated. This suggests that genuine international threats are largely captured by the history of past international conflict, already included in the regression, whereas other neighbourhood influences are predominantly peer-group effects.

We now turn to the analogous risk of internal rebellion which is a further proxy for E. The incidence of civil war is around 10 times greater than that of international war, and so the risk of rebellion is potentially considerably more important as an influence on military expenditure than is the fear of international war. To our knowledge this has not previously been investigated. For the dominant developed country literature on military expenditure, it is clearly irrelevant as the risk of civil war is negligible in these societies. For developing countries, where internal security is potentially important, there has been no empirical model of the threat. Recently, however, several models have been developed to estimate such risks. We use our own model, which we have already applied in other contexts (Collier and Hoeffler, 2002a,b, 2004a). The key features of the model are that risks are related to the level, growth and structure of income. Social, historical and geographic characteristics are also included: for example, ethnic and religious diversity. Other models of the risk of internal conflict use similar explanatory variables, although differing in detail (Fearon and Laitin, 2003; Hegre *et al.*, 2001). Our modelled risk of civil war does not take into account high-frequency 'triggering' events such as political protests or assassinations. Although these might be good indicators of imminent conflict, we are not attempting to model the short-term escalation of military spending in the run-up to civil war. Rather, we are trying to explain the average level of military spending over a 5-year period in terms of slower changing risk factors that prevailed prior to the period. Our model estimates the risk of civil war that prevails on average during each 5-year period.

We introduce this predicted risk of civil war into the regression. As it is a generated regressor we correct standard errors accordingly.[8] The risk is significant in the regression and its effect is fairly substantial. The typical low-income country at peace has a risk of internal conflict of 13.8 per cent in any 5-year period (Collier and Hoeffler, 2004b). A doubling of this risk would raise military expenditure by 10 per cent. The variable is potentially endogenous: higher levels of military spending might reduce the risk of civil war. In Section IV we investigate this further. However, such endogeneity would tend to produce a *negative* association between spending and risk whereas we find a positive one.

Although both external and internal risks increase military spending, it is unlikely that the two effects are additive. Just as the same alarm may protect against two distinct risks of fire, so the same army may protect against two distinct risks of war. At one extreme, the two risks could be entirely uncorrelated, be sufficiently low that they are highly unlikely to occur together, and be capable of being met by the same military provision. Thus, having made provision for the higher of the two risks, the lower risk would not increase the need for military spending. This is the case of full complementarity. Such complementarity would be reduced were the two risks are highly covariant. Generally this is not the case: civil wars are concentrated in the poorest countries whereas participation in international wars is not. However, sometimes a hostile neighbour might encourage an internal insurgency: for example, the government of India perceives this to have been a tactic of past Pakistani governments in Kashmir. Conversely, the existence of an internal insurgency occasionally tempts neighbours into opportunistic attacks, as when Somalia invaded Ethiopia during its prolonged civil war. Complementarity would also be reduced if the type of military spending required to meet an external threat differed substantially from that needed to meet an internal threat: for example, jet fighters vs. helicopters. Hence, the complementarity of military provision against the two risks cannot be assumed *a priori*, but is an empirical matter. We investigate it by including an interaction term between our measure of internal risk and our measure of external risk. If complementarity is substantial this should be significantly negative, as the separate effects of each component of risk would exaggerate actual military needs. The interaction term with our proxy for external threat, previous international war, is negative and significant at about 12 per cent (Table 9.1, column 2). According to the coefficients, a country with both a past history of international war and a 50 per cent risk of civil war spends no more on the military than were either one of these risks set to zero (although it spends a lot more than were *both* risks set to zero). There is thus some basis for thinking that military provisions for internal and external threats are complements. Consistent with our interpretation of the influence of neighbours' military spending being because of emulation rather than threat, the interaction between our measure of internal threat and our measure of neighbours' military spending is insignificant.

As our dependent variable is military spending relative to GDP, it is neutral with respect to the size of the society. Yet potentially, the production of security may be subject to scale economies or diseconomies. We investigate such potential scale effects by including the logarithm of the population of the country. The variable is indeed negative – larger countries have less need for military spending relative to their GDP.[9]

The lobbying of interested parties

In addition to security needs, military expenditure may be influenced by domestic political interests, as hypothesized in equation (5) through the variable *I*. The most evident beneficiary of military expenditure is the military itself. A high level of expenditure enables a larger size of the military, implying better prospects of promotion, higher salaries and larger bureaucratic empires. While the interest of the military in military expenditure is probably broadly similar across societies, the ability of the military to influence budgetary decisions differs considerably. We might expect that the greater the political power of the military interest, the higher would be military expenditure. The actual expenditures incurred as a result of such influence may have little or no relation to military capability. For example, during a long period of military government in Nigeria, the navy gradually accumulated more admirals than it had ships. This high expenditure on admirals is more plausibly explained by the position of senior naval officers in the government than by the distinctive operational needs of the Nigerian navy. Indeed, it was promptly rectified upon the resumption of civilian rule. We proxy differences in the ability of the military interest to secure patronage-motivated expenditures by the extent to which the government is democratic. We postulate that the less democratic the government, the more reliant it is upon the military and so the higher will be patronage expenditures for a given level of risk. We use the

Polity III measure[10] of the degree of democracy, which rates the general openness of political institutions on a scale of 0 (low) to 10 (high). The variable is highly significant and the coefficient is substantial: a dictatorial society will spend 2 per cent of GDP more on the military, controlling for other characteristics, than a fully democratic society. In an attempt to control for endogeneity, we instrumented democracy with its lagged value. The results were unaffected.

The financial resources of government

Finally, we turn to proxies for the ability to pay, which is the variable Y in equation (5). There is no reason to expect military spending to rise proportionately with per capita income. Superficially, security might be expected to be a necessity, so that it would rise less than proportionately with income. In fact, security appears to be a luxury as the share of GDP devoted to military spending is strongly increasing in the level of per capita income. This is less surprising than it might first appear. Military spending is a component of government expenditure, and total government expenditure as a share of GDP is strongly increasing in income. The explanation for this may simply be that the capacity for the state to tax and to borrow increases with development.

Countries may be able to spend beyond the level implied by their income because they receive money from foreign governments. Usually, such aid is intended for the purposes of development, and then the issue is whether donors are able to enforce their intentions on recipient governments. However, in rare cases finance is explicitly earmarked for military purposes. Globally, by far the most notable instance of explicit finance for military expenditure is the support provided by the USA for Israel. We would therefore expect to find that the level of Israeli military expenditure has exceeded that implied by its level of security threat and its income. To test for this, we introduce a dummy variable for Israel. It is highly significant and very large: Israeli military expenditure is almost 8 per cent of GDP larger than implied by its other characteristics (including the military expenditure of its neighbours).

More usually, foreign financial assistance is targeted to development rather than security. Such aid is earmarked, usually through being tied to projects. However, evidence suggests that earmarked aid can be highly fungible within a budget. For example, Feyzioglu, Swaroop and Zhu (1998) find that with the exception of transport (where projects tend to be very large), the sector to which aid is ostensibly tied does not influence the sectoral composition of government expenditure. There is thus a real possibility that development finance inadvertently ends up funding increased military spending. However, precisely because donors understand this possibility and are particularly sensitive to it, they try to depress military expenditure.[11] The agency problem in inhibiting fungibility of aid *into* military expenditure is much easier than that of inhibiting fungibility of aid *out of* development projects. If military spending increases coincident with an increase in aid but with tax revenue constant, then donors will reasonably interpret this as evidence of abuse. By contrast, as long as the development project is completed, the counterfactual that it would have been undertaken even without aid is unobservable. Thus, donors could fail to achieve their earmarked expenditures and yet be successful in curtailing military expenditure: governments could increase expenditures in less sensitive areas. We test for this by including aid as a percentage of GDP, averaged over the 5-year period, as an explanatory variable. As reported in column 3, aid is insignificant. At first sight, donors thus appear to be successful in preventing aid from leaking into military expenditure. However, an alternative interpretation of this result is that donors maintain the integrity of their aid budgets in aggregate by reducing aid *ex ante* to countries that adopt high levels of military spending. That is, aid may be endogenous to the government's chosen level of military spending.

To allow for this possibility we instrument aid. In our methodology, we broadly follow Tavares (2003). He argues that the aid outflows from the individual donor countries are good instruments: when a donor country changes its total outflow, which is usually for domestic budgetary reasons, recipient countries that are culturally and geographically closer to that donor country experience an exogenous change in aid inflows. Hence, much of the variation in a country's aid receipts is exogenous to its own actions.

Our sample consists of 85 aid recipient countries and we used the Organisation for Economic Co-operation and Development (OECD) aid outflows to construct instrumental variables. We concentrate on bilateral outflows from the five largest donors: Japan, the USA, France, Germany and the UK. In 1999, about 52 per cent of global aid was provided by these five donors. The data source for the aid outflows is the OECD (2001) database. We then generate four variables to capture the political, geographic and cultural distance of each donor from each recipient. For political distance we use an index of UN voting affinity (Gartzke and Jo, 2002). The values for the affinity data range from -1 (least similar interests) to 1 (most similar). We proxy geographic proximity by the inverse of the distance in kilometres between capitals of the recipient and donor countries. Cultural distance is captured by dummy variables for a common language and for a common principal religion. All our distance indicators are invariant over time but vary across countries, while the aid outflow variables are invariant across recipient countries but vary over time. The aid inflows vary both across recipient countries and over time. We regress the aid inflows on all the exogenous variables and the product of the aid outflows times the four distance indicators. For our five donor countries we can potentially use 20 instruments. However, no recipient country shares a common language with Japan. We then follow the instrumental variable (IV) approach, reducing the set of 20 IVs stepwise. The resulting first stage results are reported in Table 9A.1. Using a Hausman test we reject ordinary least square (OLS) in favour of IV estimation, i.e. aid is endogenous and should be instrumented in our model.[12]

The coefficient on instrumented aid is significant and positive. Thus, corrected for endogeneity, aid does appear to be fungible into military spending. During the Cold War some aid was provided on the basis of political allegiance. We would expect this to be much more pronounced on the part of the superpowers. Soviet aid is already excluded from our data, but the US aid was at times substantial. We therefore repeat the analysis of the effect of aid on military spending, excluding the US aid. The results were in fact marginally more significant. Hence, the result that aid has financed military spending cannot be attributed to such intentional funding on the part of the US government.

The coefficient shows that on average a 1 percentage point increase in aid as a share of GDP would increase military spending by 3.3 per cent. As military spending, in our sample, averaged 3.355 percentage points of GDP, this implies that on average around 11.4 per cent of development aid leaks into military budgets. While this is quite a modest level of leakage, it would imply that for large aid recipients a substantial part of their military budgets are inadvertently financed by aid. For example, on average, African countries receive a net aid inflow of 11.1 percentage points of their GDP and spend 3.17 percentage points of GDP on the military. Hence, to the extent that they conform to the global pattern of aid leakage, around 40 per cent of African military spending is inadvertently financed by aid. However, the absence of a significant relationship when aid is not instrumented suggests that, anticipating such a leakage, donors divert funds *ex ante* from those governments with particularly large military budgets.

The models of Table 9.1 are parsimonious, yet they provide quite a reasonable level of explanatory power with around 40 per cent of the variance explained. We experimented with variants without disturbing these core results. The model has both implications and applications. In Section 9.3 we turn to an implication, the existence of regional arms races, and in Section 9.4 to an application, an analysis of the effectiveness of military spending.

9.3 An implication: neighbourhood arms races

Our core regression finds that in determining the level of military spending, governments respond to the level set by their neighbours. We have suggested that the motivation underlying this interdependent behaviour is usually emulation rather than threat. This may make mutual de-escalation of military budgets less sensitive.

The analytics of a neighbourhood arms race are straightforward. Each country's defence burden, m_i, is determined by an exogenous component, a_i, plus an endogenous response to the expenditure of its neighbours:

$$m_i = a_i + b \sum_{j=1}^{n} m_j, \quad \text{where } i \neq j \quad \text{and } n = 1, \dots, N. \tag{6}$$

We first consider a simple two-country case. Assume that an island is divided into two countries, so that each country only has the other as a neighbour. The analysis is depicted graphically in Figure 9.1 showing the military expenditure response functions for two countries, A and B. The initial equilibrium is at E_1. First, consider the case in which this is disturbed by a *unilateral* decision of country A to increase its military expenditure. The new equilibrium levels of spending will rise to E_2 in which, because country B has responded to the initial increase, country A finds that it must further increase its own budget. Next consider the case in which the exogenous component of military expenditure is common to both neighbours ($a_1 = a_2 = a$). In this case any initial increase is common, and this triggers responses that raise the new equilibrium levels of spending to E_3.

These two cases illustrate two multiplier processes. For each it is straightforward to calculate the eventual effect of an exogenous increase in military spending. In the second case, in equilibrium the two countries have the same defence burden. Elementary rearrangement of equation (6) yields:

$$m_i = \frac{a}{(1-b)}.$$

(7)

Differentiating equation (7) with respect to a shows the extent to which a common exogenous increase in military spending escalates as a result of interdependence. We term this the *arms race multiplier* (ARM):

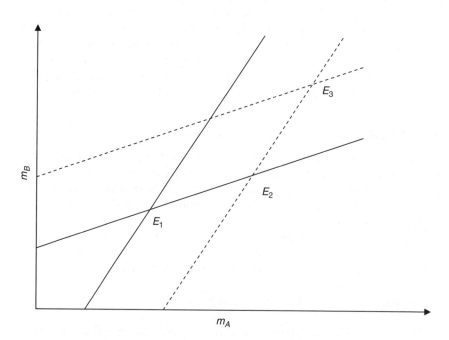

Figure 9.1 Military expenditure reaction functions.

$$ARM = \frac{1}{(1-b)}. \qquad (8)$$

The ARM applies only if both the country and its neighbours experience a common exogenous increase in military expenditure. If only one country exogenously increases its expenditure, as illustrated in the first case, then there are two ARMs, that for the country with the initial increase (the arms race multiplier for own expenditure, ARMOE), and that for the neighbour (ARMNE). Again, the multipliers can be derived straightforwardly from appropriate rearrangement of equation (6) as:

$$ARMOE = \frac{1}{(1-b^2)} \quad \text{and} \quad ARMNE = \frac{b}{(1-b^2)}. \qquad (9)$$

Equation (5), which we have estimated in Table 9.1, column 1, is an elaboration of equation (6). The coefficient on the military expenditure of neighbours, which is found empirically to be 0.1, is an estimate of b. As in the regression military expenditure is measured as a logarithm, the coefficient is an elasticity: a 1 per cent increase in the spending of neighbours raises own expenditure by 0.1 per cent. The ARM is thus 1.11. That the ARM is greater than unity suggests that where common exogenous influences are important, there is a difference between the uncoordinated (arms race) level of military expenditure and the level that would be chosen through coordination. There are several circumstances in which neighbouring countries indeed face a common exogenous increase in their military spending. We now consider a particularly important one, namely, if neighbours have a war with each other. Recall that our core regression finds that once a country has participated in an international war, it exogenously chooses a considerably higher level of military spending, specifically, an increase of 40 per cent. This exogenous increase is augmented by the ARM, so that the equilibrium increase is 44 per cent. In turn, this has implications for the cost of warfare: in the absence of negotiated reductions in post-conflict military spending, *much of the true cost of an international war might accrue after it is over*. As an illustration, the brief war between Ethiopia and Eritrea in 2000 has currently left a legacy of military spending far above international norms in both countries. If these high levels of spending persist, their present value could easily exceed the costs incurred during the war. Although both countries have other neighbours, for military purposes each country may regard the other as the only pertinent neighbour for determining the appropriate level of military spending, so that chosen spending is highly interdependent.

Although we have illustrated the ARM through a two-country model, it applies wherever neighbouring countries face a common exogenous shock to their military spending, regardless of the number of countries involved. However, the same does not apply to the ARMOE and the ARMNE. As the number of pertinent neighbours increases, the ARMOE and the ARMNE decline. Generalizing to the n-*country* case:

$$\text{ARMOE} = \frac{1}{\left(1 - \left(\frac{b}{n-1}\right)^2\right)} \tag{10}$$

and

$$\text{ARMNE} = \frac{\frac{b}{n-1}}{\left(1 - \left(\frac{b}{n-1}\right)^2\right)}. \tag{11}$$

Thus, as the number of neighbours increases, these ARMs converge to the following values: $\text{ARMOE} \to 1$ as $n - 1 \to \infty$ and $\text{ARMNE} \to 0$ as $n - 1 \to \infty$. This convergence is quite rapid as shown in Figures 9.2 and 9.3. Given our estimate of b, neighbourhood arms races are thus only of importance in the case of common shocks to the region; spending increases by individual 'rogue' governments do not generate significant neighbourhood effects.

While an international war is intrinsically multicountry, a civil war may be confined to a single country. However, the risk of civil war might rise across a region. For example, during the social breakdown in Albania the huge government stores of military equipment were ransacked, and this made rebellion easier over the entire Balkan area. We thus consider the effect of an increase in the risk of civil war of 10 percentage points across a neighbourhood. Such an increase in risk would directly raise military spending in each country by around 7.3 per cent. This would in turn be increased through the ARM to around 8.1 per cent. Hence, through its effect on the military spending of neighbours, the risk of civil war is a regional public bad.

So far we have considered common adverse shocks: international war and the risk of civil war. We now consider a common favourable shock: aid. Specifically, suppose that aid to Africa was doubled. Recall that about

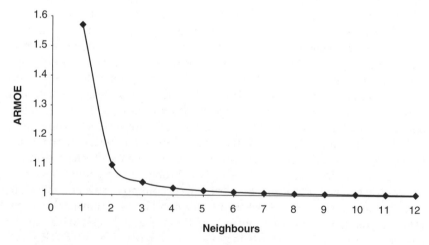

Figure 9.2 Arms race multiplier own expenditure (ARMOE).

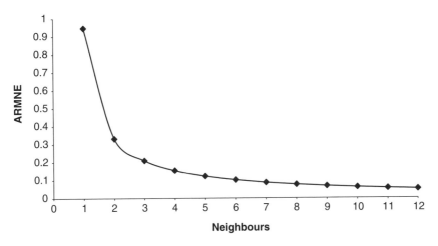

Figure 9.3 Arms race multiplier neighbour expenditure.

40 per cent of African military spending appears to be inadvertently financed by aid. Hence, unless behaviour patterns were to change, a doubling of aid would approximately directly increase military spending by 40 per cent. The ARM would then increase this further to 44 per cent. Equivalently, almost half of current African military spending is either financed by aid or induced by the arms race triggered by this additional finance.

9.4 An application: the effectiveness of military expenditure

In Section III we quantified the effects of regional military expenditure as if it were entirely a regional public bad. We found that high spending by one country increases spending by neighbours. However, military spending might be socially beneficial if it deters civil war and we now investigate whether there is such an offsetting benefit. Civil war can reasonably be seen as a regional public bad: it reduces growth rates across the region (Murdoch and Sandler, 2002; Collier and Hoeffler, 2004b), and spreads disease (Collier *et al.*, 2003). In Section 9.2, we found that governments respond to the risk of civil war by increasing their military expenditure. If this is effective as a deterrent then there is an offsetting positive externality from military spending, generated by the reduction in the risk of civil war. Potentially, military expenditure is therefore a regional public *good*. In determining the net regional externality of military spending – public good or public bad – the key unknown is the efficacy of military spending as a deterrent of civil war. This is the task of the present section.

In Table 9.2, column 1, we report for ease of reference our core logit regression of the risk of civil war (Collier and Hoeffler, 2004a). We cannot simply

Table 9.2 Deterrence effects of military expenditure on rebellion

Estimation method	1 Logit	2 Probit	3 Probit 2SLS	4 Probit 2SLS
ln GDP per capita	-0.950 (0.245)***	-0.460 (0.124)***	-0.649 (0.166)***	-0.622 (0.149)***
(GDP growth)$_{t-1}$	-0.098 (0.041)**	-0.051 (0.022)**	0.030 (0.027)	-0.027 (0.025)
Primary commodity exports/GDP	16.773 (5.206)***	7.407 (2.456)***	10.306 (3.353)***	10.648 (3.226)***
(Primary commodity exports/GDP)^2	-23.800 (10.040)**	-10.160 (4.630)**	-15.622 (6.625)**	-16.867 (6.480)***
Social fractionalization	-0.0002 (0.0001)***	-0.0001 (0.0001)**	-0.0002 (0.0001)***	-0.0001 (0.0001)**
Ethnic dominance (45–90%)	0.480 (0.328)	0.257 (0.168)	0.365 (0.210)*	0.345 (0.193)*
Peace duration	-0.004 (0.001)***	-0.002 (0.001)***	-0.002 (0.001)***	-0.002 (0.001)***
ln population	0.510 (0.128)***	0.247 (0.063)***	0.245 (0.090)***	0.277 (0.085)***
Geographic concentration	-0.992 (0.909)	-0.428 (0.450)	-0.972 (0.569)*	-1.236 (0.547)**
Military expenditure			0.338 (0.233) $P = 0.148$	0.452 (0.248)*
N	750	750	482	570
Pseudo R^2	0.22	0.22	0.27	0.26
Log likelihood	-146.84	-147.48	-96.53	-115.33

Notes: Dependent variable is a bivariate indicator of an outbreak of civil war in any given sub-period 1965–69, ..., 1995–99. The probit 2SLS procedure is as described in Keshk (2003). All regressions include a constant. Standard errors in parentheses. Values are significant at ***1%, **5% and *10% levels. While there is no standard over-identification test for 2SLS probits, we re-estimated columns 3 and 4 as a linear probability model. These models satisfy the Hansen test, we obtained $Z_4^2 = 4.481$ ($P = 0.35$) for the model in column 3 and $Z_3^2 = 4.588$ ($P = 0.205$) for the model in column 4.

introduce military spending into this regression because we have already established that it is endogenous to the risk of civil war, rising in correct anticipation of rebellion. Unless this effect is controlled for, military spending will spuriously appear to increase the risk of rebellion. To allow for this endogeneity, we instrument for military expenditure, adopting an IV procedure. Our first stage, the estimation of the military expenditure function, uses OLS. Assuming normality the natural choice for the second stage is a probit, rather than a logit regression. We apply the two-stage probit least squares procedure as suggested by Keshk (2003). In Table 9.2, column 2, we repeat our core regression of the risk of civil war using a probit instead of a logit. The regression is scarcely altered by this change in functional form. We then select instruments for military expenditure. Fortunately, as established in Section II, there are some powerful influences on military expenditure which can reasonably be seen as unrelated to the risk of rebellion. All the variables included in our core regression of Table 9.1, with the evident exceptions of being at civil war and the risk of civil war, are reasonable candidates as instruments. For example, as countries differ enormously in the extent of external threats, they differ considerably in their predicted levels of military expenditure. The two-stage results generated by including all the variables of Table 9.1, column 1, as instruments, less the two noted exceptions, are shown in Table 9.2, column 3.

So instrumented, the coefficient on military expenditure is insignificant. As, however, it is close to being significant, it is worth considering its sign, which is positive, implying that if anything, military spending *increases* the risk of civil war. As discussed in section 9.2, the military spending of neighbours might potentially be endogenous to the risk of civil war. In Table 9.2, column 4, we therefore repeat the IV procedure, dropping this variable as an instrument. Far from this amendment rehabilitating the deterrence effect, the sign of the military spending variable remains positive and it becomes significant at 10 per cent: if anything, high military spending aggravates the risk of civil war. The complete absence of any deterrent effect is quite striking as the instruments themselves seem to be good. We would therefore expect, that were military expenditure to have a substantial deterrence effect, it would be observable in this regression. We also experimented with nonlinear effects in case there should be some optimal level of deterrence, but found no significant relationship.

Thus, although governments increase military spending in an effort to deter rebellion, the expenditure appears to be at best ineffective. Both economics and political science offer possible explanations for this apparently perverse result. Mehlum and Moene (2006) analyse the effect of incumbent military advantage on the incentive to rebel and show that it is *a priori* ambiguous. Although greater government advantage reduces the prospects of success, as in equation (1), it increases the value of success because of the reduced danger of challenge. An increase in government military equipment can thus induce rebellion instead of deterring it. Fearon and Laitin (2003) emphasize the sheer difficulty of military deterrence of rebellion. During the inception stage of rebellion, a large military response might be ineffective, or even counterproductive: excessive repression by government forces assists rebel recruitment and appears to be a common error of counterinsurgency. Finally, military spending might inadvertently increase the risk of conflict through its adverse effect on economic growth. Knight, Loayza and Villanueva (1996) find that military expenditure significantly reduces growth, while Miguel, Satyanath and Segenti (2004) show that growth reduces the risk of rebellion. In a companion paper (Collier and Hoeffler, 2006), we investigate the deterrence effects of military spending further by distinguishing post-conflict societies. We show that the post-conflict context is distinctive, with military spending having significantly *adverse* effects. Any deterrence effect is more than offset by other effects. However, even with this postconflict effect separately distinguished, in other contexts military spending still has no significant deterrence effect.

9.5 Conclusion: some implications for policy

We have found that the level of military expenditure chosen by a government is influenced both by aid and by the level of spending chosen by neighbouring governments. Where aid is common across a region, as in Africa, it thereby inadvertently has the effect of escalating a regional arms race. Taking the two effects together, we estimate that in Africa military spending is almost double its level in the absence of aid. Although this is ostensibly a detrimental effect, the increased level of military spending may potentially have helped both to maintain international peace and to reduce the incidence of rebellion. However, we found that the influence of the military spending of neighbours worked through emulation rather than threat, suggesting that the deterrence of international war is usually unimportant as a rationale for military spending. Further, we found that while military spending indeed responds to the objective risk of civil war, it is not effective in reducing that risk: military spending does not deter rebellion.

The conjunction of an arms race effect with the absence of a deterrence effect suggests that military expenditure is a regional public 'bad', and so will be oversupplied by national-level decisions. Despite this scope for regional coordination of military spending, such agreements are rare. An important obstacle to reaching an agreement is the low observability of military expenditure. In this situation, the international financial institutions may have a facilitating role as neutral but privileged observers, and may even have a role as external enforcers of regional agreements (see Murshed and Sen, 1995, for a discussion of the scope for International Financial Institutions (IFI) peace conditionality).

The donor community has a further interest in the reduction of military expenditure in aid-recipient countries as, on our evidence, aid leaks into the finance of military spending and inadvertently fuels an arms race. Hence, donors might quite reasonably attempt to reduce the level of military expenditure by aid recipients. Our analysis has suggested a further justification for such efforts, namely as a coordinating device that a region can itself use for reciprocal reductions in expenditure. In the absence of a natural regional leader willing to incur the costs of such leadership, a donor norm can supply a credible common target. Finally, we should note that it may be necessary to spend so as to save. Reducing military spending in developing countries will usually involve demobilizing soldiers and this is likely to require initial expenditures on severance packages.[13] Hence, a donor policy of imposing a cap on military spending might have the inadvertent consequence of inhibiting expenditure reduction.

Appendix 9.1

Table 9A.1 Descriptive statistics

	Mean	SD	Min.	Max.	N
Military expenditure	3.355	4.275	0.1	45.96	563
International war	0.073	0.260	0	1	563
Civil war	0.078	0.269	0	1	563
External threat	0.226	0.418	0	1	563
Neighbours' military expenditure	3.578	3.488	0	22.211	563
ln population	15.984	1.42	12.716	20.773	563
Internal threat	0.053	0.075	0	0.608	563
Democracy	4.195	4.370	0	10	563
ln GDP per capita	7.853	1.050	5.403	9.852	563
Aid/GDP$_{t-1}$	4.608	6.278	−0.047	55.240	382

Table 9A.2 Correlation coefficients

	Ex. Milieux	Ex. threat	ln GDP	Neighb. milieux	ln pop.	Dem.	Int. threat	Int. war	Civ. war
Ex. threat	0.330	1							
ln GDP	0.114	0.200	1						
N. milieux	0.665	0.264	0.090	1					
ln pop	−0.015	0.283	0.015	0.039	1				
Dem.	−0.167	0.123	0.678	−0.198	0.017	1			
Int. threat	−0.031	−0.048	−0.447	−0.024	0.194	−0.321	1		
Int. war	0.346	0.307	0.005	0.226	0.081	−0.052	0.054	1	
Civ. war	0.091	0.065	−0.215	−0.001	0.147	−0.134	−0.207	0.122	1
Israel	0.359	0.208	0.115	0.273	−0.059	0.125	−0.075	0.154	−0.033

Table 9A.3 First stage regression

International war	−0.634 (1.121)
Civil war	2.502 (1.043)**
External threat	1.342 (0.767)*
(Neighbours' military expenditure)$_{t-1}$	0.285 (0.133)
ln population	−1.752 (0.237)***
Internal threat	−6.424 (3.588)
1995–99	1.618 (1.118)
Democracy	0.136 (0.096)
ln GDP per capita	−5.881 (0.396)***
Israel	6.934 (2.395)***
UK* Aid language	−0.0012 (0.0005)***
UK* Aid religion	−0.0016 (0.0008)***
US* Aid political similarity	−0.0006 (0.0001)***
Japan Aid* 1/distance	−2.8339 (0.9999)**
N	339
R^2	0.52

Notes: First stage results for the 2SLS results presented in Table 9.1, column 4. Dependent variable is aid/GDP. The regression includes a constant. Standard errors in parentheses. Values are significant at ***1%, **5% and *10% levels.

Data   The model presented in Table 9.2 primarily uses data from Collier and Hoeffler (2002b) and the data can be obtained from Anke Hoeffler's website: http://users.ox.ac.uk/~ball0144.

Aid/GDP   We measure aid as the percentage of official overseas development assistance and official aid in GDP. Aid and GDP are measured in current US dollars and we use the average percentage over the 5-year period. Data sources: World Development Indicators (2003) and OECD (2001).

Civil war   It is a dummy variable which takes a value of one if the country experienced a civil war during the period. A civil war is defined as an internal conflict in which at least 1,000 battle related deaths (civilian and military) occurred per year. We use mainly the data collected by Small and Singer (1982) and Singer and Small (1994) and according to their definitions Nicholas Sambanis updated their data set for 1992–99.

Democracy   It measures the general openness of the political institutions, it ranges from zero (low) to 10 (high). The data source is the Polity III data set as discussed by Jaggers and Gurr (1995).

Ethnic dominance (45–90 per cent)   Using the ethno-linguistic data from the original data source (Department of Geodesy and Cartography of the State Geological Committee of the USSR, 1964) we calculated an indicator of ethnic dominance. This variable takes the value of one if one single ethno-linguistic group makes up 45–90 per cent of the total population and zero otherwise.

External threat   It is a dummy variable which takes a value of one once a country was involved in an international war. Here we consider all international wars after WWII. The main data source is Small and Singer (1982) and Singer and Small (1994). We updated this data set by using Gleditsch *et al.* (2002). This resulted in the addition of two international wars: Ethiopia and Eritrea (1998 – ongoing as of the end of 1999) and India and Pakistan (1999 – ongoing as of the end of 1999).

(GDP growth)$_{t-1}$ Using the above income per capita measure we calculated the average annual growth rate as a proxy of economic opportunities. This variable is measured in the previous 5-year period.

Geographic concentration   We constructed a dispersion index of the population on a country-by-country basis. Based on population data for 400 km^2 cells we generated a Gini coefficient of population dispersion for each country. A value of 0 indicates that the population is evenly distributed across the country and a value of 1 indicates that the total population is concentrated in one area. Data is available for 1990 and 1995. For years prior to 1990 we used the 1990 data.

Internal threat   It is the predicted probability of a civil war breaking out. This prediction is based on the core model as presented in Collier and Hoeffler (2002b).

International war   It is a dummy variable which takes a value of one if the country experienced an international war during the period. The main data source is Small and Singer (1982) and Singer and Small (1994). We updated this data set by using Gleditsch *et al.* (2002). This resulted in the addition of two international wars: Ethiopia and Eritrea (1998 – ongoing as of the end of 1999) and India and Pakistan (1999 – ongoing as of the end of 1999).

ln GDP per capita   We measure income as real PPP-adjusted GDP per capita. The primary data set is the Penn World Tables 5.6 (Summers and Heston, 1991). As the data is only available from 1960 to 1992, we used the growth rates of real PPP-adjusted GDP per capita data from the World Bank's World Development Indicators (2002) to obtain income data for 1995. Income data is measured at the beginning of each sub-period, 1965, 1970, …, 1995.

ln population   Population measures the total population, the data source is the World Bank's World Development Indicators (2002). Again, we measure population at the beginning of each sub-period.

Israel   It is a dummy variable which takes the value of one for Israel and zero for all other countries.

Military expenditure   Military expenditure is measured as a proportion of GDP, also commonly referred to as the defence burden. Data for 1960–90 was obtained from the SIPRI and we used data from the Global Development Network for 1991–99 (http://www.worldbank.org/research/growth/GDNdata.htm).

Neighbours' military expenditure   For country i we calculated the weighted average of the neighbours' defence burden by dividing the sum of the neighbours' total military expenditure, M_i, by the sum of the neighbours' total national income, Y_i:

$$m_i = \frac{\sum_{j=1}^{N} M_j}{\sum_{j=1}^{N} Y_j} \cdot \text{ where } i \neq j \text{ and } n = 1, \ldots, N.$$

For our analysis we excluded countries for which we had no military expenditure data. We are grateful to James Murdoch and Todd Sandler who made their data set on neighbours available to us (Murdoch and Sandler, 2002). Income data was obtained from the Penn World Table (see data source for ln GDP per capita). We multiplied the RGDPCH series by the total population to calculate total income.

Peace duration   This variable measures the length of the peace period as the end of the previous civil war. For countries which never experienced a civil war we measure the peace period as the end of World War II until 1962 (172 months) and add 60 peace months in each consecutive 5-year period.

Primary commodity exports/GDP   The ratio of primary commodity exports to GDP proxies the abundance of natural resources. The data on primary commodity exports as well as GDP was obtained from the World Bank. Export and GDP data are measured in current US dollars. The data is measured at the beginning of each sub-period, 1965, 1970, ..., 1995.

Social fractionalization   We proxy social fractionalization in a combined measure of ethnic and religious fractionalization. Ethnic fractionalization is measured by the ethno-linguistic fractionalization index. It measures the probability that two randomly drawn individuals from a given country do not speak the same language. Data is only available for 1960. In the economics literature, this measure was first used by Mauro (1995). Using data from Barro (1997) and Barrett (1982) on religious affiliations, we constructed an analogous religious fractionalization index. Following Barro (1997), we aggregated the various religious affiliations into nine categories: Catholic, Protestant, Muslim, Jew, Hindu, Buddhist, Eastern Religions (other than Buddhist), Indigenous Religions and no religious affiliation. Data is available for 1970 and 1980 and the values are very similar. For 1960, 1965 and 1970, we used the 1970 data and for 1980, 1985, 1990 and 1995 we use the 1980 data. For 1975 we use the average of the 1970 and 1980 data.

The fractionalization indices range from zero to 100. A value of zero indicates that the society is completely homogenous whereas a value of 100 would characterize a completely heterogeneous society. We calculated our social fractionalization index as the product of the ethno-linguistic fractionalization and the religious fractionalization index plus the ethno-linguistic or the religious fractionalization index, whichever is greater. By adding either index, we avoid classifying a country as homogenous (a value of zero) if the country is ethnically homogenous but religiously diverse, or vice versa.

War starts The dependent variable in Table 9.2, 'war starts', takes a value of one if a civil war started during the period and zero if the country is at peace. If a war started in period t and continues in $t + 1$ we record the value of the war started value as missing. A civil war is defined as an internal conflict in which at least 1,000 battle-related deaths (civilian and military) occurred per year. We use mainly the data collected by Small and Singer (1982) and Singer and Small (1994) and according to their definitions updated for 1992–99.

1995–99 It is a dummy variable which takes a value of one for the time period 1995–99 and zero for all other periods.

Notes

1 On the social and economic consequences of internal conflict see Collier *et al.* (2003).
2 Contest success functions can take various forms. The ratio of forces, used here, is probably the most common, but alternative specifications can sometimes have significantly different implications. See Konrad and Skaperdas (1998).
3 SIPRI has recently updated its publicly available information on military spending. To determine whether this updating materially affected our results we checked the correlation between the data set used in the present analysis and the newly updated figures. The two data sets were correlated at 0.98, suggesting that none of our results would be significantly altered.
4 For example, actual payments to military personnel are clearly in part endogenous. Changes in the price of military equipment are highly dependent upon its composition: prices of small arms tended to decline, whereas prices for advanced technology probably tended to rise.
5 We also investigated variables measuring the months of international and civil war during the period. The dummy variables outperform these measures, implying that military expenditure does not usually jump in the month that war starts, nor sharply decline the month after it stops, but rather is also high shortly prior to, and shortly after wars.
6 Specifically, we introduced a variable on the duration of the period since the last international conflict, but this was insignificant.
7 As we regress a country's defence burden on the lagged neighbours' weighted defence burden, we avoid the simultaneity issues arising from neighbourhood effects. For a detailed discussion, see Manski (1993) and Anselin, Florax and Rey (2004).
8 We would like to thank Brian Poi (Stata Corp.) for help with the programming. We follow the method developed by Murphy and Topel (1985).
9 We also investigated other specifications of population, notably population relative to that of the largest neighbour. However, we found no specification that outperformed the simple inclusion of the above population variable.
10 See Jaggers and Gurr (1995) for a full description.
11 For example, such was British pressure on the government of Uganda that in 2001 when the President wished to increase the military budget beyond planned levels he first wrote to the British Minister of International Development. He received a strong rebuttal.
12 We obtained a t-statistic of 1.67.

13 However, our results are not contaminated by these demobilization expenditures as they are excluded from the SIPRI definition that we adopt.

References

Anselin, L., Florax, R. and Rey, S. (eds) (2004). *Advances in Spatial Econometrics, Methodology, Tools and Applications*. Berlin: Springer-Verlag.

Barrett, D. B. (ed.) (1982). *World Christian Encyclopedia*, Oxford: Oxford University Press.

Barro, R. J. (ed.) (1997). *Determinants of Economic Growth*, Cambridge, MA, and London: MIT Press.

Brzoska, M. (1995). 'World military expenditures', in Hartley K. and Sandler T. (eds), *Handbook of Defense Economics*, Vol. 1, pp. 46–67, Oxford: Elsevier.

Collier, P. and Hoeffler, A. (2002a). 'On the incidence of civil war in Africa', *Journal of Conflict Resolution*, Vol. 46, pp. 13–28.

Collier, P. and Hoeffler, A. (2002b). 'Aid, policy and peace: reducing the risks of civil conflict', *Defence and Peace Economics*, Vol. 13, pp. 435–450.

Collier, P. and Hoeffler, A. (2004a). 'Greed and grievance in civil war', *Oxford Economic Papers*, Vol. 56, pp. 563–595.

Collier, P. and Hoeffler, A. (2004b). 'Conflict', in Lomborg B. (ed.), *Global Crises, Global Solutions*, Cambridge: Cambridge University Press, pp. 129–156.

Collier, P. and Hoeffler, A. (2006). 'Military expenditure in post-conflict societies', *Economics of Governance*, Vol. 7, pp. 89–107.

Collier, P., Elliott, V. L., Hegre, H., Hoeffler, A., Reynal-Querol, M. and Sambanis, N. (2003). *Breaking the Conflict Trap: Development Policy and Civil War*, Oxford: Oxford University Press.

Deger, S. and Somnath, S. (1991). 'Military expenditure, aid and economic development', in Summers L. and Shah S. (eds), *Proceedings of the World Bank Annual Conference on Development Economics*, pp. 159–186, Washington DC: World Bank.

Department of Geodesy and Cartography of the State Geological Committee of the USSR (1964). *Atlas Naradov Mira*, Moscow.

Dunne, P. and Perlo-Freeman, S. (2003). 'The demand for military spending in developing countries', *International Review of Applied Economics*, Vol. 17, pp. 23–48.

Fearon, J. and Laitin, D. (2003). 'Ethnicity, insurgency, and civil war', *American Political Science Review*, Vol. 97, pp. 75–90.

Feyzioglu, T., Swaroop, V. and Zhu, M. (1998). 'A panel data analysis of the fungibility of foreign aid', *World Bank Economic Review*, Vol. 12, pp. 29–58.

Gartzke, E. and Jo, D.-J. (2002). The Affinity of Nations Index, 1946–1996. Version 3.0. http://www.columbia.edu/~eg589/datasets.html.

Gleditsch, N. P., Wallensteen, P., Eriksson, M., Sollenberg, M. and Strand, H. (2002). 'Armed conflict 1946–2001: a new dataset', *Journal of Peace Research*, Vol. 39, pp. 615–637.

Gyimah-Brempong, K. (1989). 'Defense spending and economic growth in sub-Saharan Africa: an econometric investigation', *Journal of Peace Research*, Vol. 26, pp. 79–90.

Hartley, K. and Sandler, T. (eds) (1990). *The Economics of Defence Spending: An International Survey*, London: Routledge.

Hartley, K. and Sandler, T. (eds) (2001). *The Economics of Defence*, 3 Vols, Cheltenham, UK: Elgar.

Hegre, H., Ellingsen, T., Gates, S. and Gleditsch, N.-P. (2001). 'Toward a democratic civil peace? Democracy, political change, and civil war, 1816–1992', *American Political Science Review*, Vol. 95, pp. 33–48.

Jaggers, K. and Gurr, T. R. (1995). 'Tracking democracy's third wave with the Polity III data', *Journal of Peace Research*, Vol. 32, pp. 469–482.

Keshk, O. M. G. (2003). 'CDSIMEQ: a program to implement two-stage probit least squares', *Stata Journal*, Vol. 3, pp. 157–167.

Knight, M., Loayza, N. and Villanueva, D. (1996). 'The peace dividend: military spending cuts and economic growth', *IMF Staff Papers*, Vol. 43, pp. 1–37.

Konrad, K. A. and Skaperdas, S. (1998). 'Extortion', *Economica*, Vol. 65, pp. 461–477.

Looney, R. E. (1989). 'Internal and external factors in effecting third world military expenditures', *Journal of Peace Research*, Vol. 26, pp. 33–46.

Maizels, A. and Nissanke, M. K. (1986). 'The determinants of military expenditure in developing countries', *World Development*, Vol. 14, pp. 1125–1140.

Manski, C. F. (1993). 'Identification of endogenous social effects: the reflection problem', *Review of Economic Studies*, Vol. 60, pp. 531–542.

Mauro, P. (1995). 'Corruption and growth', *Quarterly Journal of Economics*, Vol. 110, pp. 681–712.

Mehlum, H. and Moene, K. (2006). 'Fighting against the odds', *Economics of Governance*, Vol. 7, pp. 75–87.

Miguel, E., Satyanath, S. and Segenti, E. (2004). 'Economic shocks and civil conflict: an instrumental variable approach', *Journal of Political Economy*, Vol. 112, pp. 725–753.

Murdoch, J. C. and Sandler, T. (2002). 'Economic growth, civil wars, and spatial spillovers', *Journal of Conflict Resolution*, Vol. 46, pp. 91–110.

Murphy, K. M. and Topel, R. H. (1985). 'Estimation and inference in two-step econometric models', *Journal of Business and Economic Statistics*, Vol. 3, pp. 370–379.

Murshed, S. M. and Sen, S. (1995). 'Aid conditionality and military expenditure reduction in developing countries: models of asymmetric information', *The Economic Journal*, Vol. 105, pp. 498–509.

OECD (2001). Overseas Development Assistance, data-file (CD-ROM), OECD, Paris.

Richardson, L. F. (1960). *Arms and Insecurity*, Chicago: The Boxwood Press.

Singer, D. J. and Small, M. (1994). *Correlates of War Project: International and Civil War Data, 1816–1992*. Inter-University Consortium for Political and Social Research, Michigan: Ann Arbor.

SIPRI (The Stockholm International Peace Research Institute) (2003). *Yearbook of World Armaments and Disarmaments*, Oxford: Oxford University Press.

Skaperdas, S. (1996). 'Contest success functions', *Economic Theory*, Vol. 7, pp. 283–290.

Small, M. and Singer, J. D. (1982). *Resort to Arms: International and Civil War, 1816–1980*, Beverly Hills: Sage.

Smith, R. P. (1989). 'Models of military expenditure', *Journal of Applied Econometrics*, Vol. 4, pp. 345–359.

Smith, R. P. (1995). 'The demand for military expenditure', in Hartley K. and Sandler T. (eds), *Handbook of Defense Economics*, pp. 70–87, Amsterdam: Elsevier.

Smith, R. P. and Dunne, P. J. (forthcoming). 'The econometrics of military arms races', in Hartley K. and Sandler T. (eds), *Handbook of Defense Economics*, 2nd edn, Amsterdam: Elsevier.

Smith, R. P., Dunne, P. J. and Nikolaidou, E. (2000). 'The econometrics of arms races', *Defence and Peace Economics*, Vol. 11, pp. 31–43.

Summers, R. and Heston, A. (1991). 'The Penn World Table (Mark 5): an expanded set of international comparisons, 1950–1988', *Quarterly Journal of Economics*, Vol. 106, pp. 327–368.

Tavares, J. (2003). 'Does foreign aid corrupt?', *Economics Letters*, Vol. 79, pp. 99–106.

World Bank World Development Indicators (2002). *Data File*, Washington, DC: World Bank.

Part II

The political economy of democracy

10 Democracy, development and conflict

With Dominic Rohner

10.1 Introduction

Many low-income countries are periodically beset by political violence. Since the fall of the Soviet Union the dominant international strategy for promoting peace in these societies has been democracy. The rationale for this strategy, over and above the intrinsic desirability of democracy, is that by making the government more accountable, citizens will have less cause for violent opposition. While such an *accountability effect* is indeed plausible, democracy may also have other effects on the risk of violence. In particular, accountability may curtail some government strategies that are effective in maintaining security. For example, unconstrained by accountability, both Stalin and Saddam Hussein were able to maintain peace through intense repression despite manifest reasons for popular grievance. In both societies, more democratic successor governments have faced more violence because accountability to the law has limited what security services are permitted to do. Democracy thus generates *technical regression in repression*, which can potentially more than fully offset accountability, so that democracy increases the risk of violence.

A priori the relative potency of these opposing effects of democracy is ambiguous and in this paper we investigate it empirically. However, we suggest that the accountability effect becomes more potent as income rises. Hence, while the net effect is ambiguous, it is systematically related to income. A corollary is the possibility that there is a threshold level of income at which the net effect is zero, being differently signed above and below this threshold.

Why might we expect the accountability effect to vary with the level of income? First, as income increases the structure of the economy changes with a rising share of government spending. This can be expected to enhance the importance of the accountability effect of democracy since accountability can be presumed to increase the efficiency of government spending. As this efficiency bonus of democracy will be proportionately more important at higher levels of income, rebellion-for-democracy will tend to have a larger payoff. This in turn implies that democracy might be more peace-promoting at higher levels of income.

A second change in the structure of the economy as income rises is that the share of primary commodities declines. This is important because primary commodities generate 'loot-seeking' opportunities which are one motivation for rebellion (Collier and Hoeffler, 2004). If at low levels of income 'loot-seeking' rather than accountability is the predominant motivation for rebellion, enhanced accountability due to democracy may have little effect.

Third, as income increases individual preferences change. Inglehart (1997) finds that the 'instrumental' goal of material reward becomes less important relative to the more abstract goals of ideology and identity. A corollary is that 'loot-seeking' opportunities will become less valued relative to accountability: a lack of democracy will be more provoking at higher levels of income.

Finally, as shown by Weinstein (2005), even for a given set of individual preferences the aggregate preferences of the rebel organization are endogenous to the structure of economic opportunities. Where loot-seeking opportunities are prominent, adverse selection in recruitment ensures that the goals of the rebel organization become instrumental. Hence, the preferences of the rebel organization give more weight to abstract goals such as that of democratic accountability at higher levels of income.

An implication of each of these four mechanisms is that the accountability effect of democracy, whereby the incentive for political violence is reduced, becomes more potent as income rises. Indeed, as income rises, not only might democracies become safer, but the greater weight placed upon the goal of accountability might make autocracies absolutely more prone to violence.

Having suggested that the net effect of democracy on political violence is *a priori* ambiguous, and that it will vary systematically with income, we now investigate the relationship empirically. First, we substantiate the regression-in-repression effect: democracies are indeed constrained in deploying a key standard technique of suppressing political violence. We take the accountability effect of democracy to be uncontroversial so that the substantiation of regression-in-repression is sufficient to make the net effect of democracy on violence ambiguous. Second, we show that across all the main types of political violence, and across all the main quantitative models, the net effect of democracy on violence improves with income and that *below a threshold level of income democracy increases violence*. In this chapter we do not aspire to establish which of the various possible mechanisms are responsible for the changing net effect of democracy. Given that democracy has a regression-in-repression effect alongside its effect on accountability, a shift in the balance between these two is a potential explanation. However, our empirical results are likely to be consistent with others.

Our results are superficially troubling for the agenda of promoting democracy in low-income societies. However, democracy may still be highly desirable because of its intrinsic merits. An implication is that in low-income societies that democratize additional strategies may be needed to secure peace.

10.2 Empirical evidence

We first investigate in Table 10.1 whether democracy generates technical regress in state repression. We measure government repression by purges, these being an archetypical aspect of the technology of repression. The main independent variable of interest is the level of democracy. For this our under-lying measure is the Polity IV scale (from CIDCM, 2007), but since this is an ordinal measure, we transform it into a dummy variable which partitions the sample at a threshold. To avoid an arbitrary choice of control variables, method and estimation approach we rely upon those adopted in the influen-tial study of Fearon and Laitin (2003).[1] Data are discussed in Appendix 10.1.

We find that democracy indeed significantly reduces the scope for govern-ment repression. We investigate seven different specifications and in all of them the effect of democracy is negative, highly significant and substantial. In columns (1) and (2) the baseline model without and with interaction term is performed. The purges-reducing effect of democracy is also robust to the inclusion of time effects and country fixed effects in the columns (3) and (4), to the instrumentation of income and the interaction term in column (5),[2] and to performing logit and probit estimations in the columns (6) and (7).[3,4]

At the mean of characteristics, an undemocratic government is predicted to have a 29-fold greater propensity to purge than a democratic government. If purges are an effective technology of repression this is sufficient to make the net effect of democracy on political violence *a priori* ambiguous.

We now turn to the core issue, whether the net effect of democracy is to reduce or increase political violence and whether this is related to the level of income. To our knowledge this issue has not yet been addressed in the pub-lished literature.[5] In Table 10.2 we focus on rebellion and in Table 10.3 extend the analysis to a wider range of political violence.

We measure rebellion both by the number of incidents of guerrilla warfare (columns 1–6) and by the COW classification of civil wars (column 7). In column (1) we present a conventional specification of the effect of democracy without any interaction with income. In this and the next five columns the control variables are again as in Fearon and Laitin (2003). In column (1) development significantly reduces guerrilla rebellion but democracy is not sig-nificant. In column (2) we introduce the interaction term between democracy and income. Now both it and the direct effect of democracy become signifi-cant but with opposite signs. The direct effect is to increase the incidence of rebellion, consistent with technological regression in repression. This is offset by a favourable interaction with income, creating a threshold level of income per capita at around $2,750 below which the net effect of democracy is to increase the incidence of rebellion. In the columns (3) to (7) we investigate a variety of robustness checks. Column (3) introduces time dummies and column (4) instruments for GDP per capita. Columns (5) and (6) replace the OLS with logit and probit specifications in which the dependent variable takes the value of unity if there is any guerrilla activity in the year. In column (7) we

Table 10.1 The impact of development and democracy on government repression

	(1) Normal term	(2) Interaction effects	(3) Time effects	(4) Fixed	(5) 2SLS – logit	(6) Dummy – probit	(7) Dummy
GDP per capita (−1)	−0.000 (1.98)**	0.000 (0.05)	0.000 (0.08)	0.000 (0.13)	0.000 (1.76)*	−0.000 (0.14)	−0.000 (0.28)
Democracy (−1)	−0.134 (5.93)***	−0.118 (4.64)***	−0.094 (3.67)***	−0.194 (5.23)***	−0.084 (2.01)**	−1.598 (5.86)***	−0.696 (6.07)***
GDP per capita (−1)* Democ (−1)		−0.000 (1.38)	−0.000 (1.29)	−0.000 (1.50)	−0.000 (1.99)**	−0.000 (2.66)***	−0.000 (2.48)**
Population (−1)	0.038 (5.49)***	0.040 (5.65)***	0.046 (6.54)***	−0.197	0.047 (5.90)***	0.341 (6.94)***	0.167 (6.69)***
Mountainous Territory	−0.000 (0.90)	−0.000 (0.75)	0.006 (0.68)	−0.007 (0.04)	−0.000 (0.35)	0.001 (0.16)	−0.000 (0.10)
Noncontigous Territory	0.029 (1.00)	0.032 (1.10)	0.006 (0.20)	−0.019 (0.06)	0.033 (1.02)	0.747 (3.54)***	0.276 (2.58)***
Oil Exporter	−0.074 (2.65)***	−0.082 (2.88)***	−0.061 (2.14)**	−0.063 (1.05)	−0.120 (3.30)***	−1.097 (4.23)***	−0.490 (4.18)***
New State	−0.029 (0.25)	−0.031 (0.26)	0.006 (0.05)	−0.030 (0.25)	−0.031 (0.25)		
Instability (−1)	0.056 (1.41)	0.054 (1.35)	0.047 (1.18)	0.053 (1.25)	0.047 (1.12)	0.470 (1.91)*	0.210 (1.68)*
Ethnic Fraction	−0.151 (3.76)***	−0.147 (3.67)***	−0.137 (3.44)***	−0.177 (0.09)	−0.110 (2.38)**	−0.895 (3.25)***	−0.379 (2.82)***
Religious Fraction	−0.009 (0.19)	−0.007 (0.14)	0.007 (0.15)		−0.115 (0.22)	−0.868 (2.26)**	−0.383 (2.07)**
Constant	−0.390 (3.44)***	−0.425 (3.66)***	−0.606 (4.70)***	3.549 (1.54)	−0.571 (4.19)***	−7.344 (8.85)***	−3.806 (9.20)***
Estimation method	OLS	OLS	OLS	OLS	2SLS	Probit	Logit
Observations	4379	4379	4379	4379	4228	4348	4348
(Pseudo) R-squared	0.02	0.02	0.05	0.02	0.02	0.14	0.13

Note: Dependent variable: Purges. Abs. value of z statistics in parentheses. *, **, *** = significant at 10%, 5%, 1% respectively. (−1) – first lag. Instruments included in column (5) for the instrumentation of GDP per capita and of the interaction term: Post Cold War, Rural Population, Distance from USA, Land in Tropics, Island, Number Neighbours, Population in Tropics, Coast (all variables are explained in detail in the Appendix).

Table 10.2 The impact of development and democracy on rebellion

	(1) Normal	(2) Interaction term	(3) Time effects	(4) 2SLS	(5) Dummy – logit	(6) Dummy – probit	(7) Civil War data
GDP per capita (−1)	−0.000 (5.30)***	0.000 (1.76)*	0.000 (1.87)*	0.000 (3.71)***	−0.000 (1.37)	−0.000 (1.47)	0.069 (0.37)
Democracy (−1)	**−0.014** (0.69)	**0.046** (1.97)**	**0.078** (3.44)***	**0.134** (3.52)***	**0.263** 2.15**	**0.152** (2.28)**	**4.462** 2.36**
GDP per capita (−1)* Democ (−1)		**−0.000** (5.63)***	**−0.000** (5.79)***	**−0.000** (5.03)***	**−0.000** (1.97)*	**−0.000** (1.92)*	**−0.609** (2.22)**
Population (−1)	0.046 (7.18)***	0.052 (8.05)***	0.059 (9.37)***	0.058 (7.99)***	0.283 (8.60)***	0.158 (8.64)***	0.197 (1.76)*
Mountainous Territory	0.001 (2.75)***	0.001 (3.33)***	0.001 (3.47)***	0.002 (3.86)***	0.010 (4.35)***	0.005 (4.20)***	0.019 (2.34)**
Noncontiguous Territory	0.231 (8.80)***	0.242 (9.21)***	0.214 (8.40)***	0.273 (9.26)***	1.228 (9.99)***	0.663 (9.48)***	
Oil Exporter	−0.035 (1.38)	−0.066 (2.52)**	−0.039 (1.56)	−0.135 (4.04)***	−0.363 (2.47)**	−0.180 (2.30)**	
New State	−0.119 (1.12)	−0.125 (1.19)	−0.073 (0.69)	−0.130 (1.18)			
Instability (−1)	0.049 (1.35)	0.041 (1.11)	0.036 (1.02)	0.027 (0.71)	−0.230 (1.21)	−0.139 (1.35)	
Ethnic Fraction	(3.60)***	0.132 (3.96)***	0.145 (4.47)***	0.158 (4.44)***	0.187 (4.06)***	0.762 (4.03)***	0.417
Religious Fraction	−0.235 (5.22)***	−0.226 (5.03)***	−0.209 (4.82)***	−0.198 (4.20)***	−1.007 (4.33)***	−0.560 (4.35)***	
Other control variables	No	No	No	No	No	No	Cf. note
Constant	−0.542 (5.22)***	−0.674 (6.35)***	−0.884 (7.69)***	−0.837 (6.72)***	−6.635 (11.96)***	−3.748 (12.33)***	−7.974 (2.80)***
Estimation method	OLS	OLS	OLS	2SLS	Logit	Probit	Logit
Observations	4379	4379	4379	4228	4348	4348	871
(Pseudo) R-squared	0.06	0.07	0.14	0.05	0.12	0.12	0.25

Note: Dependent variable: Guerrilla warfare. Abs. value of z statistics in parentheses. *, **, *** = significant at 10%, 5%, 1% respectively; (−1) = first lag. Instruments included in column (4) for the instrumentation of GDP per capita and of the interaction term: Post Cold War, Rural Population. Distance from USA, Land in Tropics, Island, Number Neighbours, Population in Tropics, Coast (all variables are explained in detail in the Appendix). In column (7) the other control variables of the core model of Collier, Hoeffler and Rohner (2006) have been included (not displayed): Growth, Primary Co. Exports (PCE), PCE squared, Peace, Former French colonies, Social fractionalization, Young men.

replace guerrilla incidents by whether there is an outbreak of civil war, the specification and control variables following those of Collier, Hoeffler and Rohner (2006). Throughout all specifications the interaction term of income has a negative sign and is significant, implying that *democracy has more benign effects in richer countries*. Further, again in all specifications that include this interaction, the direct effect of democracy is positive and significant. This suggests that democracy *reduces* rebellion in rich countries, while *increasing* it in poor countries. There is also some indication that the direct effect of income is positive. Once the interaction term is included, income has a positive sign in all specifications in which it is significant and becomes highly significant once income is instrumented. This suggests that although income growth makes democracies safer, it increases proneness to violence in autocracies.

The marginal effects show the impact of democracy on guerrilla warfare to be substantial and that it varies considerably depending on the level of income. At the mean of other variables and a GDP of $200 per capita, a democracy is predicted to face 0.237 guerrilla acts, whereas an autocracy faces 0.195. In contrast, at a GDP of $10,000 per capita a democracy faces a sharply reduced number of 0.119 attacks, whereas an autocracy faces 0.238 attacks.

In Table 10.3 we investigate whether the results hold for other forms of political violence. We consider riots, coups, revolutions, assassinations, political strikes and demonstrations. In each case the interaction term of democracy and income is negative and in all but one it is highly significant. Conversely, the direct effect of democracy is positive in the four cases in which it is significant. The direct effect of income is less clear, although the predominant pattern is again for the effect to be positive and significant. Thus, casting the net effect of political violence wider suggests that our core results are not an artefact of one particular measure.

10.3 Conclusion

Since the fall of the Soviet Union democracy has been widely promoted in low-income countries. We have investigated both theoretically and empirically whether democracy is peace-promoting in these countries. We have suggested that the increased accountability and consequent diminished reasons for legitimate grievance inherent in democracy may be offset by the inability of democratic governments to use techniques of repression that autocracies find effective and we showed empirically that democracies indeed appear to be much more constrained than autocracies in using one key technique of repression. If democracy indeed generates these two opposing effects on proneness to political violence, its net effect is *a priori* ambiguous. However, we suggested why the net effect is likely to be systematically related to the level of income. Potentially, this implies an income threshold below which democracy makes societies more prone to political violence. We have found that empirically across a wide variety of forms of political violence there

Table 10.3 The impact of development and democracy on other forms of political violence related to rebellion

	(1) Riots	(2) Coups	(3) Revolutions	(4) Assassinations	(5) Strikes	(6) Demos
GDP per capita (–1)	0.000	–0.000	–0.000	0.000	0.000	0.000
	(3.08)***	(1.78)*	(1.36)	(1.40)	(2.30)**	(3.15)***
Democracy (–1)	**0.456**	**–0.287**	**–0.010**	**0.252**	**0.222**	**0.241**
	(5.77)*	(0.90)	(0.50)	**(6.15)***	**(9.84)***	**(3.43)***
GDP per capita (–1)* Dem. (–1)	**–0.000**	**–0.000**	**–0.000**	**–0.000**	**–0.000**	**–0.000**
	(5.62)*	(1.35)	**(2.65)***	**(4.47)***	**(4.69)***	**(4.60)***
Population (–1)	0.328	–0.082	0.029	0.073	0.055	0.331
	(14.83)***	(1.18)	(5.23)***	(6.33)***	(8.76)***	(16.81)***
Mountainous Territory	0.000	0.004	0.002	0.005	0.001	0.002
	(0.18)	(0.94)	(4.41)***	(6.04)***	(1.54)	(1.55)
Noncontig. Territory	0.481	–0.356	0.081	0.163	0.031	0.471
	(5.36)***	(0.85)	(3.59)***	(3.50)***	(1.20)	(5.90)***
Oil Exporter	–0.199	–0.551	–0.005	0.008	–0.032	0.219
	(2.23)**	(1.63)	(0.20)	(0.18)	(1.27)	(2.76)***
New State	0.013	0.786	0.192	–0.087	–0.064	0.216
	(0.03)	(1.05)	(2.11)**	(0.46)	(0.62)	(0.67)
Instability (–1)	–0.152	0.252	0.053	0.212	0.097	0.088
	(1.22)	(0.80)	(1.69)*	(3.28)***	(2.74)***	(0.79)
Ethnic Fraction	0.489	0.828	0.161	0.031	0.090	–0.003
	(3.90)***	(2.04)**	(5.10)***	(0.47)	(2.51)**	(0.02)
Religious Fraction	–0.212	–0.776	–0.058	–0.418	–0.391	–0.145
	(1.38)	(1.61)	(1.49)	(5.25)***	(8.94)***	(1.07)
Constant	–5.064	–1.820	–0.335	–0.968	–0.711	–4.788
	(13.95)***	(1.60)	(3.66)***	(5.13)***	(6.87)***	(14.84)***
Estimation method	OLS	Logit	OLS	OLS	OLS	OLS
Observations	4379	4374	4379	4379	4379	4380
(Pseudo) R-squared	0.08	0.09	0.05	0.05	0.07	0.10

Note: Dependent variable: Cf. second row. Abs. value of z statistics in parentheses. *, **, *** = significant at 10%, 5%, 1% respectively. (–1) = first lag.

appears to be such a threshold. While income growth makes democracies safer, we have also found some evidence that it makes autocracies not just relatively but absolutely more prone to violence.

While these results are troubling, they do not necessarily call into question the promotion of democracy. Rather, they might imply that in low-income countries international promotion of democracy needs to be complemented by international strengthening of security.

Appendix 10.1: Data sources

Assassinations   Number of politically motivated murders, from Banks (2005).
Coast   Percentage of land within 100 km of ice-free coast, from Gallup, Mellinger and Sachs (2001).
Coups   Dummy variable being 1 if a coup occurred, recoded of Banks (2005).
Democracy   Dummy variable, based on Polity IV scores, from CIDCM (2007). Coded as democracy for scores higher or equal to 6.
Demonstrations   Number of anti-government demonstrations, cf. Banks (2005).
Distance from USA   Distance (km) from capital city to Washington DC, from Gleditsch and Ward (2001).
Ethnic fractionalization   Updated variable from Fearon and Laitin (2003).
GDP per capita   Per capita GDP in current US$, from World Bank (2006).
GDP growth   percentage change on previous year's GDP per capita (as defined above).
Guerrilla warfare   Number of any armed activity, sabotage, or bombing aimed at the overthrow of the present regime, from Banks (2005).
Instability   Following Fearon and Laitin (2003)'s definition, updated using Polity IV scores, from CIDCM (2007).
Island   Dummy taking a value of 1 for islands. From Hoeffler (2007).
Land in Tropics   Percentage of land area in geographical tropics, from Gallup, Mellinger and Sachs (2001).
Mountainous territory   Percentage of the territory that is mountainous, updated variable from Fearon and Laitin (2003).
New state   Dummy variable taking a value of 1 when a state was founded in the previous two years, updated from Fearon and Laitin (2003).
Non-contiguous states   Dummy variable taking a value of 1 when a state is not contiguous, updated variable from Fearon and Laitin (2003).
Number of neighbours   Number of neighbouring states, from Hoeffler (2007).
Oil exporter   Dummy variable taking a value of 1 when a country year had greater than 33 per cent fuel exports, updated variable from Fearon and Laitin (2003).
Population   From World Bank (2006).
Population in Tropics   Percentage of population in the geographical tropics, from Gallup, Mellinger and Sachs (2001).
Post Cold War   Dummy variable being 1 for the years 1991 or later.

Purges Number of any systematic elimination by jailing or execution of political opposition within the regime or the opposition. From Banks (2005).
Religious fractionalization Updated variable from Fearon and Laitin (2003).
Revolutions Number of revolutions. From Banks (2005).
Riots Number of violent demonstrations and clashes. From Banks (2005).
Rural population Percentage of population living in rural areas, World Bank (2006).
Strikes Number of general strikes of 1,000 or more workers, cf. Banks (2005).

Notes

1 In particular, in the baseline model we address endogeneity concerns with lagged variables.
2 We have checked that all instruments are valid and not explanatory factors of purges and guerrilla warfare. The first stage regressions are available from the authors on request.
3 The dummy variable of purges in the columns (6) and (7) in Table 1 takes a value of 1 if at least one purge occurs and 0 otherwise.
4 Ai and Norton (2003) have shown that interpreting the interaction terms for non-linear models such as logit or probit is not straightforward and that the magnitude of the coefficient varies for each observation. We have applied their program "Inteff" and have checked that for all our specifications with logit or probit models all or the overwhelming majority of observations have a negative interaction term.
5 The only related work which we could find is an unpublished political science paper by Hegre (2003) who, in an empirical investigation of civil war, finds an income-democracy interaction to be significant.

References

Ai, Chunrong, and Edward Norton. (2003). 'Interaction terms in logit and probit models', *Economics Letters*, 80, 123–9.
Banks, Arthur. (2005). 'Cross-National Time-Series Data Archive', Binghamton NY, Databanks International, data file.
CIDCM. (2007). 'Polity IV project', University of Maryland, data file.
Collier, Paul and Anke Hoeffler. (2004). 'Greed and grievance in civil war', *Oxford Economic Papers*, 56, 563–95.
Collier, Paul, Anke Hoeffler and Dominic Rohner. (2006). 'Beyond Greed and Grievance: Feasibility and Civil War', CSAE Working Paper 2006–10, University of Oxford.
Fearon, James and David Laitin. (2003). 'Ethnicity, Insurgency, and Civil War', *American Political Science Review*, 97, 75–90.
Gallup, John, Andrew Mellinger and Jeffrey Sachs. (2001). 'Geography Datasets', avail. on http://www.cid.harvard.edu/ciddata/geographydata.htm.
Gleditsch, Kristian and Michael Ward. (2001). 'Minimum Distance Data', available on http://privatewww.essex.ac.uk/~ksg/mindist.html.
Hegre, Havard. (2003). 'Disentangling Democracy and Development as Determinants of Armed Conflict', mimeo, PRIO.
Hoeffler, Anke. (2007). 'Geographical dataset', mimeo, University of Oxford.

Inglehart, Ronald. (1997). *Modernization and Postmodernization: Cultural, Economic, and Political Change in 43 Societies*, Princeton NJ: Princeton University Press.

PRIO. (2006). *Data on Armed Conflicts*, Oslo, PRIO, data file.

United Nations. (2002). *UN Demographic Yearbook*, New York: UNO.

Weinstein, Jeremy. (2005). 'Resources and the Information Problem in Rebel Recruitment', *Journal of Conflict Resolution*, 49, 598–624.

World Bank. (2006). *World Development Indicators*, Washington DC: World Bank, data file.

11 Testing the neocon agenda

Democracy in resource-rich societies

With Anke Hoeffler

11.1 Introduction

Many resource-rich countries have suffered from the 'resource curse': the failure to harness commodity revenues for sustained growth. In this chapter we investigate analytically and empirically whether this curse is ameliorated by democracy. The question is at the intersection of two large and active literatures, one accounting for the resource curse and the other investigating the economic consequences of democracy. On the intersection, however, there is to date very little. Yet the intersection is of considerable practical concern. The recent rise in commodity prices has generated revenue booms in commodity exporters that were last experienced in the 1970s. The widespread failure to harness those booms for sustained growth is the empirical basis for the resource curse: hence, whether the present booms will repeat history is of first order importance for a large group of low-income societies. Between the two resource booms one striking institutional change has occurred: resource-rich countries are now on average more democratic.[1] The importance of institutions and the scope for changing them are now central controversies in development economics. Thus, our investigation of the economic consequences of democratization in resource-rich countries nests within this larger debate.

The 'neocon agenda' of the United States, combined with two other influences, has increased the prevalence of resource-rich democracies. The agenda diagnosed the perceived ills of the Middle East as being due to its lack of democracy. Thus, Selden (2004) defines the neocon agenda as using:

> American power to reshape the global environment in the name of a set of liberal democratic ideals. It is their belief that this will make the United States more secure by reducing the seemingly intractable problems of the Middle East, thus getting at some of the root causes of terrorism.

Democracy as promoted by the American government partly by hard power, as in Iraq, and partly by soft power, exemplified by the first multiparty Egyptian elections held in 2005. The lack of democracy in the Middle East is itself related to the resource abundance of the region: Ross (2001) shows that resource-rich countries are systematically less democratic. In addition to the neocon agenda the 'third wave' of democratization following the fall of the USSR spread to some resource-rich countries. Additionally, some of the resource discoveries triggered by high prices have been in countries that had already democratized.

The concept of the resource curse was initially triggered by particular graphic instances such as Nigeria. There is now a substantial literature exploring both the evidence for the curse and the mechanisms by which it is generated (for example Sachs and Warner (2005), Auty (2001), Gylfason (2001)). There is overwhelming statistical evidence that countries rich in natural resources experienced lower growth rates since 1960. Although the initial statistical evidence was based on cross-section, it is now supported by time series analysis of panel data (Collier and Goderis, 2007, 2007a). The explanation for the curse has also evolved. The initial explanation was the purely economic process of Dutch disease (Corden and Neary, 1982) whereas more recent explanations have been framed in terms of political economy. Tornell and Lane (1999) proposed a 'voracity effect' whereby the high value of resource rents would induce competing political groups to 'gauge' in the process not merely wasting the rents as in conventional rent-seeking, but actually reducing income. The celebrated work of Acemoglu, Johnson and Robinson (2000) also featured a key adverse role for resource rents: inducing institutions suited to extracting rents rather than to the provision of public goods. They proposed that these types of institutions were both distinctive and highly persistent, generating divergent paths of economic development. The two articles to which our work is most closely related are Robinson, Torvik and Verdier (2006) and Mehlum, Moene and Torvik (2006) since they address not only why political processes might be dysfunctional in the context of resource rents, but suggest that this may be remedied through appropriate institutions. Robinson, Torvik and Verdier develop a theory of patronage politics in the context of resource wealth and suggest that this dysfunctional behaviour may be restrained by good institutions. Mehlum, Moene and Torvik find some empirical support for the idea that institutions are particularly important in the context of natural resources but do not investigate specifically which institutions are important. Both articles rely upon the Sachs and Warner cross-section data set. The present paper extends these studies both analytically, by proposing a more detailed mechanism of political failure, and empirically by using a panel data set and unbundling the concept of 'institutions'.

While the resource curse literature has thus evolved to the stage where institutional weaknesses are regarded as central to the explanation of the curse, it has not yet specifically related these weaknesses either to whether the polity is autocratic rather than democratic, or to variations in democratic design. Yet, as we have noted, democratization has been the main recent institutional innovation in resource-rich countries and in other contexts its effects on economic performance, including the effects of variations in its design, and the possibility of reverse causality from development to democracy, have been intensively studied (Lipset, 1959; Przeworski and Limongi, 1993; Acemoglu, Johnson, Robinson, and Yared, 2008). Overall, the net effect of democracy on economic development is far from clear-cut. Drazen (2000) concludes from a survey of the literature that there is no clear effect. Acemoglu *et al.* (2008) suggest that different countries are on different long term trajectories, some of which lead to both development and democracy, whereas others lead to development without democracy. They do not find any evidence of a causal link between income and democracy but provide some statistical evidence to show that omitted variables, most likely historical variables, jointly determine the political as well as economic development paths. Barro (1996) finds evidence for a non-linear effect: democracy is beneficial at 'intermediate levels'.

None of this literature considers resource rents. For example, it is entirely omitted in the comprehensive survey of theory and evidence by Feng (2003). Yet this neglect is surprising. One of the few clear results of the literature on the economic effects of democracy has been to highlight the problem posed by the shortening of government horizons introduced by the elections for those public decisions that require a long-term view. For example, Tavares and Warziarg (2001) find that democracies have systematically lower investment than autocracies. High investment is central to economic management in resource-rich countries since extraction depletes assets which must be replaced if increased consumption is to be sustained. While this suggests that democracy might be problematic for resource-rich countries, this adverse effect might be overwhelmed by both the enhanced accountability of public revenues, and by the widening of the power base that democracy facilitates. Or the two opposing effects might broadly neutralize each other, leaving no clear relationship between democracy and economic performance in resource-rich countries.

In Section 11.2 we consider the mechanisms by which resource rents might either enhance or undermine the contribution of democracy to economic development. We show that *a priori* either is possible so that the issue can only be resolved empirically.

In Section 11.3 we explain a new empirical measure of the rents from natural resource exports, country-by-country, for the period 1970–2001. This is a substantial advance on the empirical proxy that has been standard in the literature, namely the value of primary commodity exports. Evidently, rents differ radically both between different commodities and are not proportional to changes in prices. In Section 11.4 we use this measure to investigate whether the effect of democracy upon growth is altered by the presence of natural resource rents. We find a large adverse interaction of natural resource rents and electoral competition and a large positive interaction of natural resource rents and checks and balances. We then investigate the routes by which electoral competition and checks and balances might have these effects, and finally show that over the long term checks and balances are endogenous to resource rents. Section 11.5 concludes.

11.2 How might resource rents affect the economic consequences of democracy?

Potentially democracy might be either more or less advantageous for economic performance if a society has large natural resources. While in the long run democracy is itself liable to be endogenous to resource rents, Smith (2004) plausibly suggests that because institutions usually pre-exist resource discoveries, the effects of the rents are likely to be dependent upon this prior institutional variation. We consider some possible mechanisms that would work in each direction.

Mechanisms that enhance the benefits of democracy

We suggest two mechanisms by which democracy might lead to a differential improvement in economic performance. Both the economic consequences of autocracy may be made absolutely worse by resource rents, and the economic consequences of democracy may be made absolutely greater.

Autocrats may be particularly predatory in the presence of resource rents. The reasoning is analogous to the famous distinction made by Olson between the roving and the stationary bandit (Olson, 1993). Whereas the roving bandit snatches whatever he can without regard to future consequences for the economy, the stationary bandit must limit predation to a rate that is sustainable. The same argument applies if bandit actions can extend to investments that expand the economy: the roving bandit does not invest, but the stationary bandit invests. Being atypically immobile and highly taxable, natural resource rents reduce the need for an autocrat to invest in the growth of the non-resource private economy. This is indeed close to the explanation of Acemoglu, Johnson and Robinson (2000) as to why autocratic colonial governments were made dysfunctional by the presence of resource rents. An autocrat in resource-scarce economies, whether the British government in colonial Kenya or the communist government of modern China, must develop the private economy if it is to generate significant tax revenues and for this it must provide public goods. In contrast, an autocrat in resource-rich central Africa, whether King Leopold or President Mobutu, can generate revenues without the provision of public goods.

Conversely, democratic governments may be particularly useful in societies with large resource rents. With the sole exception of America, such rents accrue in large part to the government so that resource-rich states have an atypically high level of public spending. Suppose, not implausibly, that democracy enhances the accountability of public spending to citizens, preventing it from being captured by powerful minorities. In this case, the pay-off to democracy will be approximately proportional to the share of public spending in GDP and so differentially greater in resource-rich societies. Accountable public spending would be far more beneficial to Angola, where resource revenues alone are a more than half GDP, than to Uganda where public spending in total is only a fifth of GDP.

While we do not develop further these sketches of why democracy might be particularly valuable for resource-rich countries, they do not seem to be readily dismissible as possibilities.

Mechanisms that undermine the benefits of democracy

We now develop at greater length an exposition of a mechanism that works in the opposite direction. We devote greater length to it partly because it is less obvious than the above mechanisms and also because, based on the results of Section 11.4, it appears more likely to be correct.

We focus on the functioning of democracy and consider how politicians use public resources subject to restraints. Potentially, these resources can be used either for the provision of public goods or for private patronage. In a well-functioning polity politicians who divert public resources into private patronage suffer both electoral defeat and prosecution. We develop a simple model of these restraints, showing how they may be undermined by natural resource rents.

In the absence of effective legal restraint political parties face a choice of technologies in how they attract votes. They can adopt the conventional mode of presenting programs to voters which commit to the provision of public goods. Alternatively, they can directly buy votes. In mature democracies vote-buying is not a viable electoral strategy for four reasons. Contracts with voters would be non-enforceable due to secret ballots. Bribe transactions would be liable to criminal prosecution. They would antagonize other voters. Finally, they would be too expensive to be affordable by political parties. However, in the conditions typical of developing countries these four inhibitions may not apply. Bribe contracts may indeed be enforceable because they fit naturally into a prevailing culture of reciprocal exchange: bribes are regarded as gifts which rightly attract obligations (Githongo, 2006). The police and courts may not be sufficiently independent of the political process to prosecute vote-buying. In a prevailing atmosphere of political corruption even electors may find vote-buying acceptable: it is the only benefit they can realistically expect from participation in the democratic process. Finally, political parties may have access to very large sources of finance.

Vote-buying is indeed common in developing countries so political parties evidently regard it as cost-effective. Vicente (2007) conducts a unique randomized analysis of vote-buying in the resource-rich country of São Tomé, Principe, and finds that it is both widespread and effective in inducing voters to change allegiance. Another widespread strategy that is analytically similar to vote-buying is for the politician to hire a militia which then targets opposition supporters, discouraging them from voting. Since the act of voting is readily observable and identity politics increases the observability of allegiance, targeted intimidation may also be a cost-effective use of political finance.

Besley (2006) shows analytically that the weaker is voter information about government performance, and the more that voting is pre-determined by identity, the less traction is available to an honest politician whose intentions are congruent with voters. In these conditions corrupt politicians with dissonant intentions may find vote-buying and intimidation highly effective. They can be targeted to the minority of swing voters. Indeed, if many voters follow the instructions of community leaders, by bribing them politicians can purchase votes 'wholesale'. A core argument of Besley is that the motivation of politicians is endogenous to these underlying electoral conditions: where honest politicians with congruent intentions stand little chance of election they will not come forward as candidates. We imagine a political contest in which the underlying conditions completely discourage honest politicians: all the candidates have dissonant intentions and are prepared to be dishonest. Expenditure on bribery and intimidation is cost-effective in election campaigns and will predominate to the extent permitted by political finance. This in turn depends upon how much public revenue can be embezzled from its proper uses. To the extent that public spending cannot be embezzled, even corrupt politicians will find themselves presiding over systems which deliver public goods since these provide some electoral advantage, *despite* rather than because of their intentions. In effect, public revenues have two different degrees of electoral potency: embezzled money is high-powered because it can be used for bribes, while money that cannot be embezzled can only be used for the less cost-effective strategy of providing public goods. Thus, given our assumptions, public goods are provided not because politicians need to do so in order to win votes, but because the checks and balances present in the system prevent them from diverting all revenues to patronage.

Hence, the key issue is the determination of the checks and balances that limit the embezzlement of public resources. Effective checks and balances are themselves a type of public good: to be effective, restraints need to be implemented through a continuous process of public scrutiny. To endogenize this process we introduce a relationship in which citizens are provoked into scrutiny by taxation. This relationship is exemplified in the central demand of the American revolution: 'no taxation without representation'. As a proposition in political science it is most closely identified with Tilly (1975), being central to his celebrated explanation of the emergence of government accountability to citizens in Europe. More recently the proposition has been central to the work of Moore (see, for example, Moore, 1998). Brautigam and Knack (2004) provide a clear recent application in their discussion of the problems associated with aid: 'when revenues do not depend on the taxes raised from citizens and businesses, there is less incentive for government to be accountable to them' (p. 265). Resource rents are a non-tax revenue somewhat analogous to aid. Ross (2004) investigates empirically the link between taxation and representation. Consistent with the Tilly hypothesis he finds that the larger is the share of government expenditure which is financed through taxation the more likely is the government to become representative.

We now develop a simple model that incorporates the above behavioural relationships. Politicians would like to tax heavily in order to generate revenue for patronage, but they are constrained from doing so because high taxation provokes intense scrutiny.

Patronage expenditures are determined by the product of the tax rate, t, taxable income, Y, and the proportion of revenue which can be embezzled for patronage, e. In turn, the rate of embezzlement is constrained by the degree of scrutiny, which is determined by the rate of taxation.

This implies a maximum revenue available for patronage, somewhat analogous to a Laffer curve. The maximum is determined by:

$$P^{max} = \text{Max } e{\cdot}t{\cdot}Y.$$
$$\text{wrt } t \tag{1}$$

subject to $e = e(t)$, $e'<0$.

To see the implication at its simplest, we linearize the inverse relationship between the embezzlement rate and the tax rate:

$$e = \alpha(1-t). \tag{2}$$

The society has an underlying rate of embezzlement, α, which is curtailed by taxation. This underlying rate may differ greatly between societies, being determined by culture and history. Our analysis is pertinent in those societies where α is sufficiently high that taxation is material. However, evidence on public corruption (Friedman, Johnson, Kaufmann and Zoido-Lobaton, 2004) suggests that many societies do not have strong intrinsic defenses.

The decision problem for the corrupt politician is thus:

$$\text{max: } \alpha(1-t){\cdot}t{\cdot}Y.$$
$$\text{wrt } t \tag{3}$$

At the patronage-maximizing tax rate, $t^* = 0.5$, the resources available for patronage are:

$$P = Y\alpha/4, \tag{4}$$

Thus, in this simple model, in a society with no intrinsic defences ($\alpha = 1$) a dishonest politician would set taxes so as to generate public revenues that were half of GDP, and half of these revenues would be embezzled for political patronage. The scrutiny provoked by this level of taxation would defend the remaining half of the revenues from embezzlement and the politician would, albeit reluctantly, find that the most electorally cost-effective remaining use for these revenues was to spend them on the provision of public goods. More generally, the provision of public goods is:

$$G = (2 - \alpha)Y/4. \tag{5}$$

Competitive electoral politics drives parties to adopt the most cost-effective strategy of winning votes, subject to the constraint imposed by endogenous scrutiny. Although politicians would like to retain the rents for themselves, in a competitive equilibrium parties must embezzle as much public revenue as possible and use it to bribe voters.

Hence, (4) and (5), though extremely simple, describe the equilibrium outcome of electoral competition with the restraint of scrutiny endogenized.

The simplicity of the analysis enables the complication of resource rents to be introduced without the model becoming either intractable or opaque. We denote resource rents as a proportion of income by, r. The rents accrue directly to the government, augmenting its revenue from the taxation of citizens. We assume that the government is not able to ring-fence the revenue from resource rents from the prevailing public scrutiny of its tax revenue. This is not an unreasonable assumption. Citizen scrutiny amounts to the creation of processes such as budgets and audits which apply to all revenues regardless of their source: the government cannot choose which revenues are subject to scrutiny and which are not. The government is thus not free simply to spend all the resource rents on patronage. However, unlike taxation, the resource rents do not themselves provoke citizen scrutiny. This assumption is precisely analogous to that made in respect of aid by Brautigam and Knack (2004) and Moore (1998): *citizens are only provoked into scrutiny by having money taken from them by government.* Government revenue thus becomes:

$$[t(1-r)+r]\cdot Y, \tag{6}$$

and the maximum patronage resources available to the government become:

$$\max \alpha (1-t)\cdot[t(1-r)+r]\cdot Y \tag{7}$$

wrt t

The patronage-maximizing tax rate is now:

$$t^{**} = (1-2r)/(2-2r). \tag{8}$$

A corollary of (8) is that *the higher is revenue from resource rents the lower is the tax rate.* This relationship is manifest in developing countries: for example, the oil-rich economies have very low non-oil taxation. While this is usually interpreted as reflecting the reduced *need* for such taxation, it is notable that the same relationship does not seem to hold in the oil-rich developed economies. For example, Norway, which is the most oil-rich society in the OECD, has among the highest rates of non-oil taxation. Our model provides an alternative explanation for the phenomenon: where α is high (unlike in Norway), governments of oil-rich countries consciously set low tax rates so as not to provoke scrutiny of the oil revenues.[2] In turn, this implies that the level of scrutiny is lower and so the rate of embezzlement is higher. More surprisingly, total chosen revenue as a share of income, v, is constant over the entire range $0 \leq r \leq 0.5$:

$$v^{**} = t^{**} (1 - r) + r = [(1 - 2r)/(2 - 2r)] \cdot [(1 - r) + r] = 0.5 \qquad (9)$$

That is, until taxation is driven down to zero which occurs once resource rents exceed half of GDP. For a given total income, revenue for patronage rises as a result of resource rents not because the government commands more money, but because it is able to raise the same money while arousing less public scrutiny. As a result, less needs to be diverted to the provision of public goods. A corollary of this is that over this range of resource rents, *comparing two societies with the same level of income but with different shares of natural resource rents, the one with the higher share will have the worse provision of public goods.*

Whether a resource discovery which augments income will nevertheless worsen the provision of public goods depends upon the scale of the resource discovery, r, and the value of α. To see this it is useful to consider a resource discovery which precisely doubles national income, so that once the society gets the resource rents $r = 0.5$. From (8) at this point the tax rate on the non-rent economy has been driven down to zero. Total government revenue has thus doubled: the state previously received half of national income and now it receives all the rents, worth the entire previous national income, but nothing else. The demise of taxation increases the rate of embezzlement from $\alpha/2$ to α. Hence, public goods provision in the presence of the rents, G^r is:

$$G^r = (1 - \alpha)2Y. \qquad (10)$$

Comparing this with (5), there is a critical level of α above which public goods provision actually deteriorates, the critical rate being $\alpha = 0.857$. For resource discoveries beyond $r = 0.5$ there is no further scope for the reduction in taxation (unless, for example, sinecures in public employment are introduced), and so public goods provision unambiguously begins to improve. As noted, Norway is an example of a relatively small resource discovery in a society with a strong prior tradition of scrutiny, so that α was very small. Saudi Arabia is an example of a society were the resource discovery is so large that even though α is high, the provision of public goods has improved. Nigeria is an example of a society with a moderate-size discovery and a high initial value of α, where the discovery has indeed probably worsened public goods provision: across a range of social indicators Nigeria is ranked below other African economies without resource rents.

While the direct focus of this model is on the provision of public goods, it has a ready extension to a more general measure of economic performance. Public goods are not predominantly consumed, they are in large measure capital expenditures which cannot easily be substituted by the private sector, such as education and infrastructure. Further, the entire model could readily be reformulated to include the provision of public *policies* which do not require expenditure but do require political effort. Politicians with dissonant interests would prefer the easy life but can be disciplined by tax-provoked scrutiny to supply good policies. In democracies without resource rents the costs of political effort become costs such politicians have to pay in order to raise revenues, some of which can then be embezzled. In equivalent resource-rich democracies politicians get the same total revenue with lower taxes and so are able to get away with lower policy effort. Thus, the result that for given income those resource-rich democracies that lack exogenously given scrutiny mechanisms (a low value of α), will have inferior public goods to similar resource-scarce democracies, readily extends to the entire range of public policies. A corollary is that *ceteris paribus* they would have inferior economic growth performance. Growth performance thus provides the most general testable formulation of our model. It predicts that, in the absence of exogenously low values of α, resource-rich democracies would have significantly slower growth than resource-scarce democracies. Further, since autocracies are freed from the electoral competition that remorselessly drives such democracies to an equilibrium in which public goods and policies are inferior, resource-rich autocracies might out-perform equivalent democracies. These are the propositions which we now test.

11.3 Natural resource rents and democracy: descriptive statistics

In order to test the relationship between resource rents, democracy, and growth, it is necessary to have a measure of resource rents. Usually, this concept has been proxied in the literature by primary commodity exports. However, this is a highly imperfect approximation and data are now available to enable the construction of a more accurate measure. In this Section we describe how this measure can be built, country-by-country and year-by-year, for the period 1970–2001. We then match this data against a quantitative measure of political rights for the same period.

Since we try to proxy 'rents' we did not want to rely on the commonly used Sachs-Warner measure of natural resources which is the ratio of primary commodity exports to GDP. Evidently, the share of export earnings accruing as rents differs radically both between commodities and over time depending upon the level of world prices. For example, when world coffee prices are low coffee exports will not generate rents whereas when oil prices are high most of the revenue will be rents. We therefore adopted a more precise measure of rents, using environmental economic data from the World Bank which included both costs of production and prices and so enabled us to calculate natural resource rents as a percentage of GDP.[3] This calculation included several different steps. First, we defined rents as the difference between the natural resource price and the extraction costs. For example, for oil the World Bank database provides the average of four spot crude oil prices. Prices are global, thus they vary over time but are the same across countries. Extraction costs on the other hand vary over time as well as across countries. In a second step, we multiplied the natural resource rents per unit of output by the total volume extracted. We then added these total rents for a variety of natural resources: oil, gas, coal, lignite, bauxite, copper, iron, lead, nickel, phosphate, tin, zinc, silver and gold.[4] For each year we divided the sum of resource rents by GDP. Our regression analysis uses four year averages, so we averaged the data over 8 sub-periods: 1970–73, 1974–77, ..., 1998–2001. We were able to construct this rent variable for 969 panel data observations. A histogram of the natural resource rents as a percentage of GDP shows a heavily skewed frequency. A number of countries did not extract any of these natural resources (158 observations) and a large number only had small rents of less than one per cent (363 observations). For 180 observations the natural resource rents were between one and five per cent and 79 observations had rents between five and ten per cent. We define countries with a natural resource rent percentage of ten or higher as high rent countries. Only 187 observations were in this range.[5]

We proxy democracy by the Polity IV scoring of 'Democracy'. This is an 11 point ordinal scale, ranging from zero to ten. Higher values indicate a greater competition and openness of the democratic process. Although the measure is termed 'democracy', its criteria are essentially focused on electoral processes. Data are available for 1,004 observations. We measure democracy at the beginning of each sub-period. Since the democracy score is ordinal, all uses that treat it as cardinal are at best approximations. In our subsequent regression analysis we check the robustness of results that assume cardinality by replacing the democracy score with a binary measure partitioned by a threshold. Nevertheless, descriptive statistics that assume cardinality are a convenient introduction to the data. In Table 11.1 we show the means and standard deviations for the democracy scores. The first row provides these

Table 11.1 Democracy scores

Period	Sample	High natural rents countries
1970–1998	4.03 (4.26)	1.46 (3.11)
1970	3.29 (4.16)	0.96 (2.56)
1974	3.08 (4.22)	0.89 (2.56)
1978	3.18 (4.28)	1.32 (3.09)
1982	3.43 (4.29)	1.76 (3.41)
1986	3.72 (4.35)	1.28 (3.08)
1990	4.52 (4.27)	1.89 (3.49)
1994	5.29 (3.96)	2.00 (3.48)
1998	5.26 (3.98)	1.92 (3.43)

Note: Standard deviation in parentheses.

descriptive statistics for the entire sample period (1970–1998). The average democracy score for the entire sample is about 4, whereas for countries with a high percentage of natural resources it is only around 1.5. However, the standard deviation is large compared with the entire sample, indicating that there is a wide dispersion of democracy scores among these countries. On average democracy scores have increased over time: for the entire sample the biggest increase occurred between 1986 and 1990 with the collapse of the Eastern Block. For the natural resource rich economies the increases have been less marked: by the end of the period their score was still only 1.9 as compared with 5.3 for the average country.

11.4 Empirical analysis

Whether resource rents enhance or undermine the economic consequences of democracy is *a priori* ambiguous. We now use our measure of rents to investigate the issue empirically. We adopt the medium-term growth rate of the economy as our measure of economic performance. Since resource rents are largely depletable, the central policy issue in resource-rich societies is the transformation of depleting rents into more sustained forms of income. We take four-year periods as our units of observation to smooth out the noise of annual observations of growth rates. Evidently, in addition to any interaction effects with the political process, natural resource rents can be expected to have direct effects on growth and we will control for them.

We start from a simple specification which includes only the variables directly of interest – the level of natural resource rents, and the level of democracy – and a single conditioning variable, the level of per capita income (Table 11.2, column 1). Countries with an initially higher democracy score have on average higher growth rates. The coefficient on natural resource rents is insignificant. From this base we introduce the interaction term rents democracy which is the focus of our analysis (column 2). The interaction term is negative and significant at the ten per cent level. Democracy appears to enhance growth except in the presence of substantial natural resources. Around this simple specification we first investigate three variants. We allow for the possibility of diminishing returns to rents (column 3) but find no evidence of such non-linear effects. Second, we allow for lagged effects. The large case-study literature on natural resource rents has many examples of public expenditure being increased to unsustainable levels. When we lagged resource rents as a further explanatory variable (column 4), the term is significant, negative and substantial: resource rents indeed appear to generate unsustainable increases in the level of output. Third, since contemporaneous natural resource rents have no significant direct effect in this regression we investigate dropping the term in favour of this lagged effect (column 5). At this stage the interaction of democracy and resource rents is negative but not significant at conventional levels (p = 0.166).

While democracy is most commonly understood in terms of competitive elections which determine how a government acquires power, a mature

Table 11.2 Growth, democracy and natural resource rents

	(1)	(2)	(3)	(4)	(5)	(6)	(7)	(8)	(9)	(10)
ln GDP	-0.045 (0.702)	-0.130 (0.284)	-0.118 (0.333)	-0.254 (0.041)**	-0.183 (0.146)	-0.216 (0.115)	-0.219 (0.104)	-0.137 (0.259)	-0.274 (0.043)**	-0.223 (0.083)*
Nat. Resources	-0.027 (0.154)	-0.013 (0.572)	0.027 (0.538)	0.053 (0.140)						-0.036 (0.280)
Democracy	0.089 (0.036)**	0.131 (0.005)***	0.141 (0.003)***	0.162 (0.001)***	0.129 (0.005)***	0.151 (0.005)***	0.145 (0.002)***	0.971 (0.364)***	0.119 (0.012)**	0.167 (0.000)***
NatRes·Dem		-0.007 (0.096)*	-0.010 (0.028)**	-0.009 (0.054)*	-0.005 (0.166)	-0.020 (0.003)***	-0.020 (0.002)***	-0.136 (0.047)***	-0.018 (0.004)***	-0.020 (0.002)***
NatRes²			-0.001 (0.432)							
NatRes$_{t-1}$				-0.055 (0.016)**	-0.026 (0.067)*	-0.052 (0.044)**	-0.051 (0.042)**	-0.051 (0.038)**	-0.070 (0.002)**	
Checks						-0.024 (0.805)				
NatRes·Checks						0.034 (0.043)**	0.033 (0.033)**	0.027 (0.055)*	0.035 (0.024)**	0.029 (0.082)*
East Asia	3.080 (0.000)***	2.989 (0.000)***	2.943 (0.000)***	3.055 (0.000)***	3.113 (0.000)***	2.905 (0.000)***	2.901 (0.000)***	2.918 (0.000)***	3.451 (0.000)***	2.994 (0.000)***
E&C Europe	0.688 (0.212)	0.545 (0.318)	0.541 (0.326)	0.649 (0.271)	0.719 (0.228)	0.645 (0.293)	0.648 (0.292)	0.595 (0.333)	0.156 (0.822)	0.563 (0.330)
MEast&NAfrica	0.708 (0.124)	0.476 (0.326)	0.462 (0.341)	0.226 (0.647)	0.577 (0.206)	0.144 (0.770)	0.155 (0.750)	0.168 (0.730)	-0.628 (0.281)	0.111 (0.828)
South Asia	0.683 (0.169)	0.433 (0.382)	0.498 (0.317)	0.556 (0.240)	0.700 (0.142)	0.499 (0.329)	0.476 (0.333)	0.598 (0.216)	0.302 (0.556)	0.587 (0.228)
SSAfrica	-0.763 (0.063)*	-0.921 (0.024)**	-0.888 (0.031)**	-1.038 (0.015)**	-0.933 (0.030)**	-1.199 (0.006)***	-1.198 (0.006)***	-1.156 (0.009)	-1.152 (0.018)**	-1.047 (0.016)**
Observations	858	858	858	760	760	720	720	720	720	729
R-squared	0.138	0.142	0.145	0.149	0.142	0.159	0.159	0.154	0.337	0.149

Notes: Dependent variable: average annual growth. Robust p values in parentheses. * significant at 10%; ** significant at 5%; *** significant at 1%, regressions include time dummies (not reported).

democracy also includes checks and balances which in various degrees constrain how a government can use power. This distinction is indeed central to the theory of Section 11.2. With an unconstrained government, electoral competition drives an economy into patronage politics. Only the checks and balances that are provoked by taxation force political actors to compete through the effective provision of national public goods. The role of taxation is important for the emergence of checks and balances because, unlike electoral competition, these themselves are public goods that are otherwise likely to be radically under-supplied. Elections are easy to introduce, as is evident from those held under the precarious conditions of Afghanistan and Iraq in 2005. This is partly because they are one-off events, and also because the incentives for parties to participate are strong: participation is the route to power. By contrast, checks and balances are not events but processes which must function continuously and so do not lend themselves to short but focused efforts. Further, not only are they public goods that nobody has a strong incentive to provide, but the actors with the power to create them have an active interest to resist them. Precisely because checks and balances are far more difficult to provide than electoral competition, democracies differ considerably in the balances between these two defining features. We therefore introduce a specific measure of checks and balances into the analysis in addition to the more general measure of democracy. We proxy the power of checks and balances by a measure used by Keefer and Stasavage (2004) termed 'checks'. As implied, this focuses on the ability of other agents to restrain the government. The index ranges from one (few veto players) to 17 (high number of veto players). Unlike the democracy index it is in principle cardinal, being a count of the number of veto players. Although the democracy score and the checks variable are correlated ($\rho = 0.72$), there is sufficient variation to include the two indices in the same regression. As can be seen from Figure A1 in the Appendix 11.1 and consistent with our hypothesis that checks are considerably more difficult to provide than elections, there are no countries which have a low democracy score and a high number of checks. However, there is considerable variation across countries with above average democracy scores. Some have few or no veto players, whereas others have many: the country with the highest number of checks (17) is India, which also has a high democracy score.

Having distinguished between the two aspects of democracy we introduce an additional interaction term between resource rents and checks and balances. We also add the variable 'checks' itself, to control for any direct effect that it might have other than through its effect on the utilization of resource rents, the results being shown in Table 11.2, column 6. While the direct effect of checks is insignificant, the interaction of resource rents with checks and balances is positive and significant. Further, the adverse interaction effect of democracy and natural resources now becomes highly significant. Thus, whereas democracy *per se* is distinctively detrimental for resource-rich countries, checks are distinctively beneficial. In column 7 we drop the insignificant direct effect of checks with no change in the overall results. We now subject these results to four tests for robustness.

First, we replace democracy as a continuous variable with a dummy which takes the value of unity if the democracy score is greater than or equal to five (column 8). Our results remain unaffected: in particular, the interaction between democracy and natural resource rents is still negative and significant at the one per cent level.

Second, we control for fixed effects. Since our model contains time invariant variables (continent dummies) and variables which are in general only changing slowly over time (political economy variables) we cannot estimate this model by conventional fixed effects. However, the technique of least squares dummy variables is equivalent to fixed effects (Hendry, Johansen and Santos, 2004). Following this procedure, we first included one third of all country dummies in our model as presented in column 7 and then repeated the estimation with each of the other thirds of the country dummies. Based on these three regressions we gathered all those country dummies which were significantly different from zero and re-estimated the model.[6] These results are shown in column 9. The coefficients and standard errors are similar to our pooled OLS regression and our core results remain significant at the one per cent level. The main difference between the pooled results and the one including country dummies is that the coefficient on GDP per capita is slightly larger and the standard error is smaller, making GDP significant at the five per cent level.

Third, we re-introduce the contemporaneous, direct effect of resource rents (column 10). Although our baseline regression of column 7 is *close* to being a differences-in-differences specification, the direct effect of natural resource rents is only included with a lag whereas the interaction term measures resource rents contemporaneously. We therefore replace lagged by contemporaneous natural resources so that the requirements for differences-in-differences are fully met. The coefficient on the interaction term is unchanged and is again statistically significant at one per cent.

Fourth, we attempt to allow for the potential endogeneity of democracy. We should note that since we are only concerned with the interaction effect of democracy, rather than its direct effect, this problem is less serious than were we attempting to infer a direct causal connection from democracy onto some outcome. The interaction effect is analogous to a difference-in-differences approach: does a difference in democracy have a different effect depending upon resource rents? However, to address remaining concerns we instrument for democracy. We use as an instrument the historical data on settler mortality (Acemoglu, Johnson and Robinson, 2000). Although Acemoglu, Johnson and Robinson use settler mortality to instrument for other types of institutions, settlers had an interest in encouraging political institutions that were representative of their interests, and as elsewhere, such institutions invite subsequent pressure to expand the franchise. Indeed, in their more recent work they argue that democracy is the outcome of a long institutional trajectory,

238 The political economy of democracy

rather than being generated by economic development (Acemoglu *et al.*, 2008). Because of data limitations this instrumentation drastically reduces the size of our sample and so we economize on other variables. Nevertheless, so instrumented, the interaction of democracy and natural resource rents is negative and significant (Table 11.3).[7]

We also examined the possible endogeneity of our natural resource measure. An unobserved variable may be causing slow growth and low GDP. Since we measure natural resource rents as a percentage of GDP, it is possible that our estimates suffer from endogeneity bias. We tried two different approaches to tackle this issue. First, we use total rather than relative resource rents. The interaction term with democracy is negative and significant while the interaction term with checks and balances is positive and significant. Second, we use a product of a commodity price index and the quantity of sub-soil assets (Collier and Goderis, 2007a) as an instrument for natural resource rents. They argue that prices and the occurrence of natural resources can be considered as exogenous. Using this instrument the interaction terms are significant and have the same signs as before.[8]

Table 11.3 Growth, democracy and natural resource rents – 2SLSQ

	1st stage	2nd stage
Dependent Variable ln GDP	Democracy	Growth
	0.977	−0.495
	(0.000)***	(0.370)
Nat. Res.	0.019	0.036
	(0.294)	(0.161)
Democracy		0.542
		(0.156)
ln Settler Mortality	−0.560	
	(0.004)***	
NatRes·Democracy		−0.011
Residual		(0.012)**
		−0.486
		(0.207)
East Asia	−3.963	5.406
	(0.000)***	(0.000)***
Middle East and	−4.903	2.908
North Africa	(0.000)***	(0.116)
South Asia	1.606	0.244
	(0.025)	(0.817)
Sub-Saharan Africa	−1.876	−0.079
	(0.000)***	(0.935)
Observations	435	434
R-squared	0.49	0.19

Notes: 2SLQ regression. Robust p values in parentheses,* significant at 10%; ** significant at 5%; *** significant at 1%, regressions include time dummies (not reported).

These checks suggest that there is indeed a causal mechanism from the interaction of natural resources and democracy onto growth as hypothesized in Section 11.2, and provide some support for our choice of the model in column 7 as our baseline. Applying the coefficients on the two critical interaction terms, in a developing country at the 75th percentile of the democracy score, (9), but with no checks and balances, each additional percentage point of GDP from natural resource rents reduces growth by 0.23 percentage points. For a given level of checks and balances, resource rents are more damaging if the country is democratic: taking a developing country with resource rents equal to 20 per cent of GDP, if the country is switched from being at the 75th percentile of the democracy score (9) to the 25th percentile (0), its growth rate increases by 2.2 percentage points. By contrast, again for a given level of checks, in the absence of resource rents democracy is good for growth: taking a developing country without resource rents, if it is switched from the 25th percentile of the democracy score to the 75th percentile, its growth rate increases by 1.31 percentage points. The critical level of natural resource rents beyond which democracy becomes dysfunctional for growth, for given checks, is 7.44 per cent of GDP. While these are the central estimates from variables that are statistically significant, we should note that the confidence intervals are nevertheless substantial. For example, the reduction of 0.23 percentage points due to an additional one per cent resource rents has a 95 per cent confidence interval of 0.12 to 0.34 percentage points.

Within the basic structure of electoral competition being distinctively detrimental and checks and balances being distinctively beneficial, we now investigate the routes by which resource rents undermine the economy and hence the behaviour that checks and balances inhibits. Our approach is to control for possible routes to see whether the interaction effects lose economic and statistical significance. The regressions with these controls are presented in Table 4, and for ease of reference Table 11.4, column 1 repeats are baseline regression.

It is known that democracy tends to reduce the share in investment in GDP (Tavares and Wacziarg, 2001) and that countries with a high dependency on natural resources have a low investment share (Gylfason and Zoega, 2006). Since investment is likely to be central to the transformation of resource rents into sustained growth, potentially democracy is detrimental due to underinvestment. To test this we control for the share of investment in GDP (Table 11.4, column 2). Unsurprisingly, investment is positive and significant at the one per cent level. However, its inclusion has virtually no effect. The coefficients on both the democracy·rents interaction and the checks·rents interaction barely change value and remain significant. Thus, to the extent that growth is driven by investment, democracy must be undermining growth in the resource-rich countries through the quality of investment rather than its quantity.

We next control for public consumption (Table 11.4, column 3). As is commonly found in the growth literature, government consumption expenditure is negative. However, this has no effect on either the significance of the

Table 11.4 Growth, democracy and scrutiny

	(1)	(2)	(3)	(4)	(5)
ln GDP	−0.219	−0.511	−0.160	−0.166	−0.216
	(0.104)	(0.001)***	(0.269)	(0.240)	(0.106)
Nat. Resources$_{t-1}$	−0.051	−0.052	−0.050	−0.050	−0.051
	(0.042)**	(0.105)	(0.052)*	(0.044)**	(0.044)**
Democracy	0.145	0.147	0.152	−0.049	0.142
	(0.002)***	(0.003)***	(0.003)***	(0.486)	(0.003)***
NatRes·Dem	−0.020	−0.018	−0.020	−0.020	−0.035
	(0.002)***	(0.002)***	(0.001)***	(0.003)***	(0.264)
NatRes·Checks	0.033	0.032	0.034	0.035	0.033
	(0.033)**	(0.036)**	(0.029)**	(0.036)**	(0.034)**
ln Investment		1.485			
		(0.000)***			
Gov cons.			−0.034		
			(0.216)		
Ethnicity				−3.901	
				(0.000)***	
Ethnicity·Dem				0.401	
				(0.001)***	
NatRes*Dem^2					0.002
					(0.584)
East Asia	2.901	2.173	2.811	2.954	2.959
	(0.000)***	(0.000)***	(0.000)***	(0.000)***	(0.000)***
E&C Europe	0.648	0.299	0.721	0.528	0.717
	(0.292)	(0.633)	(0.243)	(0.390)	(0.225)
MEast&NAfrica	0.155	0.135	0.320	−0.037	0.173
	(0.750)	(0.771)	(0.520)	(0.939)	(0.721)
South Asia	0.476	0.158	0.412	0.604	0.503
	(0.333)	(0.747)	(0.403)	(0.244)	(0.300)
SSAfrica	−1.198	−0.723	−1.053	−0.244	−1.175
	(0.006)***	(0.103)	(0.024)**	(0.598)	(0.007)***
Observations	720	686	713	718	720
R-squared	0.159	0.197	0.163	0.181	0.159

Notes: Dependent variable: average annual growth. Robust p values in parentheses, * significant at 10%; ** significant at 5%; *** significant at 1%, regressions include time dummies (not reported).

core interaction terms, or the magnitude of their coefficients. Thus, the route by which democracy undermines the growth effects of resource rents is not that public spending becomes inflated. Again, to the extent that public spending matters for the growth process, resource rents must be undermining the quality of spending rather than inflating its quantity. This result is consistent with the somewhat counter-intuitive theoretical prediction of (9) above: resource rents induce a shift in the composition of public spending away from public goods towards patronage goods, rather than an increase in overall spending. These results are also consistent with the corollary proposition that resource rents are used to reduce taxation.

We next control for the effect of ethnic diversity. Previous studies have found that ethnic diversity is detrimental to growth (Easterly and Levine, 1997), but that this effect is reduced by democracy (Collier, 2000). This benign interaction effect of democracy is thus the opposite of the malign effect we have so far found. A probable explanation for it is that autocracy is liable to be particularly damaging in the context of ethnic diversity: if power is narrowly based on an ethnic support group redistribution dominates the public good of growth. We now bring the two effects together (Table 11.4, columns 6–9). We use a new measure of diversity proposed by Alesina *et al.* (2003), which classifies ethnic groups according to their racial and linguistic characteristics. Consistent with previous research, the direct effect of ethnic diversity on growth is adverse, and its interaction with democracy is positive. However, controlling for these effects has no effect on either the significance or the size of the coefficients of the two core interaction terms. Thus, whatever the route by which natural resource rents undermine the growth process in a democracy, it does not run through ethnic diversity.

Finally, we test our results against the superficially similar 'voracity effect' of Tornell and Lane (1999). They also predict adverse consequences of resource rents on growth in the context of patronage politics. However, in their model the problem is generated by the uncoordinated 'gauging' of multiple powerful groups, restrained only by concern for a participation constraint. Resource rents ease the participation constraint and induce an increase in gauging greater than the value of the rents, this being the voracity effect. A testable difference between the two explanations is that the voracity effect is at its peak when there are only *two* powerful groups in the society, each able to gauge. In this situation the cost of rent extraction is predicted to be double the value of the rents themselves. There is no voracity effect either when the political system is autocratic, or when it is fully competitive with multiple groups each holding some power. In contrast, our model predicts that as electoral competition increases the costs of resource rents continue to mount. The Tornell-Lane model thus predicts that the effect of the political system on the use of resource rents is non-monotonic. We test for this by adding the square of the democracy score interacted with resource rents as an additional variable (Table 11.4, column 5). Evidently, since the democracy score is ordinal, all rank-preserving transformations have equal validity. However, for the Tornell-Lane hypothesis to hold this term should be significantly positive. In fact it is completely insignificant. We have also tested using dummy variables to capture break points in the democracy scores and found no evidence that the relationship is non-monotonic. There is no sign that as political competition intensifies the problem of resource rents is diminished, rather it continues to get worse.

We now turn to our prediction that in resource-rich democracies the mechanisms of scrutiny would be systematically weakened: due to low taxation citizens would not be provoked into supplying the public good of scrutiny. We test whether checks and balances are differentially eroded by resource rents. For completeness, we also analyze whether resource rents tend to reduce democracy itself, an effect already established for oil economies by Ross (2001).

We begin with a simple OLS specification in which the level of checks and balances and democracy are each explained by the level of per capita GDP, and time dummy variables, and the lagged value of natural resource rents (Table 11.5a,b). For both checks and balances and democracy the lagged value of resource rents is highly significant and negative. Further, as the lag is progressively lengthened from one period (four years) to two periods (eight years) to seven periods (28 years), the significance level and the size of the coefficient increase. The effects are large: after 28 years a country with mean income but with resource rents worth 30 per cent of GDP would have a checks score in the 22th percentile instead of in the 34th percentile, and a democracy score in the 25th percentile instead of in the 40th percentile.

Table 11.5a Checks and natural resource rents

	(1)	(2)	(3)	(4)	(5)	(6)	(7)
ln GDP	0.511						
	(0.000)***						
NatRes	−0.029						
	(0.000)***						
ln GDP_{t-1}		0.495					
		(0.000)***					
$NatRes_{t-1}$		−0.023					
		(0.000)***					
ln GDP_{t-2}			0.496				
			(0.000)***				
$NatRes_{t-2}$			−0.030				
			(0.000)***				
ln GDP_{t-3}				0.466			
				(0.000)***			
$NatRes_{t-3}$				−0.031			
				(0.000)***			
ln GDP_{t-4}					0.417		
					(0.000)***		
$NatRes_{t-4}$					−0.035		
					(0.000)***		
ln GDP_{t-5}						0.322	
						(0.001)***	
$NatRes_{t-5}$						−0.036	
						(0.000)***	
ln GDP_{t-6}							0.179
							(0.229)
$NatRes_{t-6}$							−0.037
							(0.000)***
Observations	758	645	518	402	294	191	96
R-squared	0.306	0.279	0.259	0.225	0.172	0.117	0.059

Notes: Dependent variable: Checks. Robust p values in parentheses, * significant at 10%; ** significant at 5%; *** significant at 1%, regressions include time dummies (not reported).

Table 11.5b Democracy and natural resource rents

	(1)	(2)	(3)	(4)	(5)	(6)	(7)
ln GDP	1.682						
	(0.000)***						
NatRes	−0.068						
	(0.000)***						
ln GDP$_{t-1}$		1.701					
		(0.000)***					
NatRes$_{t-1}$		−0.065					
		(0.000)***					
ln GDP$_{t-2}$			1.717				
			(0.000)***				
NatRes$_{t-2}$			−0.092				
			(0.000)***				
ln GDP$_{t-3}$				1.688			
				(0.000)***			
NatRes$_{t-3}$				−0.098			
				(0.000)***			
ln GDP$_{t-4}$					1.649		
					(0.000)***		
NatRes$_{t-4}$					−0.112		
					(0.000)***		
ln GDP$_{t-5}$						1.528	
						(0.000)***	
NatRes$_{t-5}$						−0.124	
						(0.000)***	
ln GDP$_{t-6}$							1.586
							(0.000)***
NatRes$_{t-6}$							−0.144
							(0.000)***
Observations	762	635	506	393	287	186	91
R-squared	0.487	0.493	0.518	0.528	0.524	0.488	0.515

Notes: Dependent variable: Democracy. Robust p values in parentheses, * significant at 10%; ** significant at 5%; *** significant at 1%, regressions include time dummies (not reported).

While the OLS results are suggestive, they are open to multiple interpretations. In Table 11.6a,b we check robustness by switching the dependent variable to the *changes* in checks and democracy, respectively, over various periods, controlling for both their initial level and per capita GDP. Again, resource rents significantly erode both checks and democracy. These results are consistent with the predictions of the model and also with Ross (2001).

Overall, our results suggest that the form of democratic polity best-suited to resource-rich countries is one with checks and balances that are strong relative to electoral competition. This is indeed the form of democracy in the most striking exception to generally adverse combination of democracy and resource rents, namely Botswana. Electoral competition is in practice quite limited: the government has never been defeated at the polls. Yet, perhaps because the democracy has been continuous since independence, the legal

Table 11.6a Change in checks and natural resource rents

	(1) Checks – Checks$_{t-1}$	(2) Checks – Checks$_{t-2}$	(3) Checks – Checks$_{t-3}$	(4) Checks – Checks$_{t-4}$	(5) Checks – Checks$_{t-5}$	(6) Checks – Checks$_{t-6}$
ln GDP$_{t-1}$	0.157 (0.003)***					
Checks$_{t-1}$	–0.384 (0.000)***					
NatREs$_{t-1}$	–0.012 (0.000)***					
ln GDP$_{t-2}$		0.214 (0.004)***				
Checks$_{t-2}$		–0.500 (0.000)***				
NatREs$_{t-2}$		–0.017 (0.000)***				
ln GDP$_{t-3}$			0.234 (0.010)**			
Checks$_{t-3}$			–0.563 (0.000)***			
NatREs$_{t-3}$			–0.022 (0.000)***			
ln GDP$_{t-4}$				0.222 (0.066)*		
Checks$_{t-4}$				–0.617 (0.000)***		
NatREs$_{t-4}$				–0.025 (0.000)***		
ln GDP$_{t-5}$					0.120 (0.574)	
Checks$_{t-5}$					–0.608 (0.018)**	
NatREs$_{t-5}$					–0.022 (0.014)**	
ln GDP$_{t-6}$						–0.112 (0.766)
Checks$_{t-6}$						–0.415 (0.292)
NatREs$_{t-6}$						–0.016 (0.352)
Observations	626	497	381	272	168	77
R-squared	0.182	0.200	0.190	0.191	0.197	0.139

Notes: Dependent variable: Change in Checks. Robust p values in parentheses, * significant at 10%; ** significant at 5%; *** significant at 1%, regressions include time dummies (not reported).

and bureaucratic procedures that constitute checks and balances have been maintained. Other examples of democracies that have had relatively strong checks and reasonable economic performance are Papua New Guinea, Chile and Mexico. These polities contrast with many of the 'instant' and often

Table 11.6b Change in democracy and natural resource rents

	(1) Dem– Dem$_{t-1}$	(2) Dem– Dem$_{t-2}$	(3) Dem– Dem$_{t-3}$	(4) Dem– Dem$_{t-4}$	(5) Dem– Dem$_{t-5}$	(6) Dem– Dem$_{t-6}$	(7) Dem– Dem$_{t-7}$
ln GDP$_{t-1}$	0.372 (0.000)***						
Democracy$_{t-1}$	−0.212 (0.000)***						
NatRes$_{t-1}$	−0.025 (0.000)***						
ln GDP$_{t-2}$		0.636 (0.000)***					
Democracy$_{t-2}$		−0.390 (0.000)***					
NatRes$_{t-2}$		−0.045 (0.000)***					
ln GDP$_{t-3}$			0.905 (0.000)***				
Democracy$_{t-3}$			−0.545 (0.000)***				
NatRes$_{t-3}$			−0.071 (0.000)***				
ln GDP$_{t-4}$				1.083 (0.000)***			
Democracy$_{t-4}$				−0.642 (0.000)***			
NatRes$_{t-4}$				−0.084 (0.000)***			
ln GDP$_{t-5}$					1.172 (0.000)***		
Democracy$_{t-5}$					−0.721 (0.000)***		
NatRes$_{t-5}$					−0.094 (0.000)***		
ln GDP$_{t-6}$						1.161 (0.000)***	
Democracy$_{t-6}$						−0.752 (0.000)***	
NatRes$_{t-6}$						−0.106 (0.000)***	
ln GDP$_{t-7}$							1.238 (0.000)***
Democracy$_{t-7}$							−0.745 (0.000)***
NatRes$_{t-7}$							−0.124 (0.000)***
Observations	710	579	472	368	268	176	86
R-squared	0.149	0.243	0.349	0.420	0.463	0.478	0.488

Notes: Dependent variable: Change in Democracy. Robust p values in parentheses, *significant at 10%; **significant at 5%; ***significant at 1%, regressions include time dummies (not reported).

externally driven democracies that swept across Africa and Central Asia following the collapse of the Soviet Union. .

11.5 Conclusion

Resource-rich countries have tended to be autocratic and also have tended to use their resource wealth badly. The neoconservative agenda of promoting democratization in resource-rich countries thus offers the hopeful prospect of a better use of their economic opportunities. Our analysis has tested whether this hopeful prognosis is likely to be borne out.

We first showed that *a priori* the effect of natural resources on the economic consequences of democracy is ambiguous. While there are plausible mechanisms that would support the proposition that resource rents enhance the benefits of democracy, the opposite might also hold. We set out a simple model of democratic politics in which we distinguish between two dimensions of democracy, electoral competition and checks and balances. By undermining checks and balances, resource rents unleash patronage politics and in these conditions electoral competition is economically damaging.

Using new data on the value of resource rents, we then tested these propositions. We found that in developing countries the combination of resource rents and democracy has been significantly growth-reducing. In the absence of resource rents democracies outperform autocracies, in the presence of large resource rents autocracies outperform democracies. We found that this result was robust to controlling for the potential endogeneity of democracy and was also robust to fixed effects. We found that the antidote to these adverse effects of democracy was intensified checks and balances. While countries with large resource rents need checks and balances, this is not what they get. Resource rents tend gradually to undermine checks and balances. Thus, in those developing societies where the state has most command over resources, the democratic process has been least effective at controlling them for the public good. The implication for the neoconservative agenda is that it either needs to be scaled down or scaled up. On the criterion of economic performance targeting electoral competition on the resource-rich societies appears to be particularly inappropriate unless it is complemented by checks and balances. Unfortunately, whereas electoral competition is easy to establish since there are strong incentives for participation, checks and balances are public goods liable to be undersupplied.

Appendix 11.1 Descriptive statistics for the core model

Table 11A.1: Means

Variable	Obs	Mean	Std. Dev.	Min	Max
Growth	720	1.29	3.64	−16.23	20.29
ln GDP	720	7.48	1.62	4.57	10.73
Nat. Resources	720	5.99	11.84	0	80.60
Nat. Res.$_{t-1}$	720	6.30	12.92	0	106.60
Democracy	720	4.51	4.28	0	10
Checks	720	2.54	1.77	1	17
Ethnic	718	0.46	0.26	0.012	0.93
ln Investment	686	2.57	0.62	0.60	4.03
Gov. Cons.	713	15.66	6.81	3.67	74.32

Table 11A.2: Correlation coefficients

	Growth	ln GDP	Nat. Res.	Nat. Res.$_{t-1}$	Democr.	Checks	Ethnic	ln Inv.
ln GDP	0.115	1						
Nat. Res.	−0.101	−0.068	1					
Nat. Res.$_{t-1}$	−0.142	−0.077	0.819	1				
Democracy	0.160	0.683	−0.219	−0.202	1			
Checks	0.161	0.505	−0.145	−0.138	0.716	1		
Ethnic	−0.236	−0.512	0.172	0.131	−0.427	−0.326	1	
ln Investment	0.278	0.687	−0.029	−0.056	0.448	0.358	−0.469	1
Gov. Cons.	−0.081	0.354	0.065	0.064	0.232	0.181	0.130	0.192

Table 11A.3: Checks scores

Period	Sample	High natural rents countries
1975–1998	2.34 (1.72)	1.54 (1.34)
1974	1.74 (1.41)	1.03 (0.16)
1978	1.89 (1.35)	1.26 (0.70)
1982	2.08 (1.51)	1.46 (1.10)
1986	2.17 (1.59)	1.48 (1.43)
1990	2.41 (1.89)	1.64 (1.89)
1994	2.97 (1.87)	2.40 (2.00)
1998	2.88 (1.87)	2.04 (1.59)

Note: Standard deviation in parentheses.

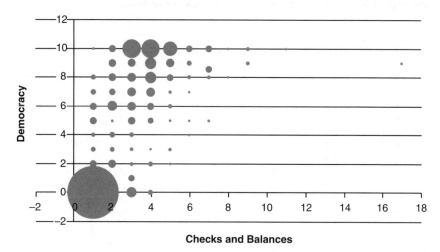

Figure A1: Checks and balances and democracy.

Sample:

Albania, Algeria, Angola, Argentina, Armenia, Australia, Austria, Azerbaijan, Bangladesh, Belarus, Belgium, Benin, Bolivia, Botswana, Brazil, Bulgaria, Burkina Faso, Burundi, Cameroon, Canada, Central African Republic, Chad, Chile, China, Colombia, Dem. Rep. Congo, Rep. Congo, Costa Rica, Cote d'Ivoire, Croatia, Czech Republic, Denmark, Dominican Republic, Ecuador, Egypt, El Salvador, Eritrea, Estonia, Ethiopia, Fiji, Finland, France, Gabon, The Gambia, Georgia, Germany, Ghana, Greece, Guatemala, Guinea, Guinea-Bissau, Haiti, Honduras, Hungary, India, Indonesia, Iran, Ireland, Israel, Italy, Jamaica, Japan, Jordan, Kazakhstan, Kenya, Kuwait, Kirguiz Rep., Laos, Latvia, Lesotho, Macedonia, Madagascar, Malawi, Malaysia, Mali, Mauritania, Mauritius, Mexico, Moldova, Mongolia, Morocco, Mozambique, Namibia, Nepal, Netherlands, New Zealand, Nicaragua, Niger, Nigeria, Norway, Oman, Pakistan, Panama, Papua New Guinea, Paraguay, Peru, Philippines, Poland, Portugal, Romania, Russian Federation, Rwanda, Saudi Arabia, Senegal, Sierra Leone, Singapore, Slovak Republic, Slovenia, South Africa, Sri Lanka, Sudan, Sweden, Syrian Arab Republic, Tanzania, Thailand, Togo, Trinidad and Tobago, Tunisia, Turkey, Turkmenistan, Uganda, Ukraine, United Kingdom, United States, Uruguay, Uzbekistan, Venezuela, Vietnam, Yemen, Zambia, Zimbabwe.

Appendix 11.2: Data description and sources

Economic Growth   We used WDI 2003 data for GDP and population. GDP is measured in constant 1995 US dollars, we divided GDP by the population to calculate per capita GDP. We approximated the growth of per capita GDP by taking the log differences at the beginning and end of each sub period (1970–73, 1974–77, …, 1998–2001) and divided this difference by the number of years, four, and multiplied this by 100.

GDP per capita   We measure GDP per capita at the beginning of each sub-period (1970–73, 1974–77, …, 1998–2001). Data are measured in constant 1995 US dollars and the data source is WDI 2003.

Natural Resource Rents   Using data from the World Bank's adjusted savings project we calculated the rents for each commodity by subtracting the cost from the commodity price. We then multiplied the rents per unit by the amount extracted and summed across the different commodities. We then calculated the share of rents in GDP. Since the rents are provided in current US dollars we used the WDI 2003 GDP in current dollars to calculate this share. Natural resources for which rent data were available are: oil, gas, coal, lignite, bauxite, copper, iron, lead, nickel, phosphate, tin, zinc, silver and gold. The data are described in Hamilton and Clemens (1998) and available from http://lnweb18.worldbank.org/ESSD/envext.nsf/44ByDocName/GreenAccountingAdjustedNetSavings

Democracy   The degree of competition for executive power is measured on a scale of zero (low) to ten (high). We used the Polity IV score at the beginning of each sub-period (1970–73, 1974–77, …, 1998–2001). Source: http://www.cidcm.umd.edu/polity/index.html. The data are described in Jaggers and Gurr (1995).

Investment   We used total investment as a percentage of GDP and averaged and logged over each sub-period (1970–73, 1974–77, …, 1998–2001). Data source: PWT as described in Heston, Summers and Aten (2002).

Checks   This variable captures the number of veto players. This variable is built from several other variables, two of which are the legislative and the executive indices of electoral competitiveness. The checks and balances index ranges from 1 to 17 with higher numbers indicating a higher number of veto players. Data Source: DPI2000, data are described in Beck *et al.* (2001) and Keefer and Stasavage (2003) and are available from http://econ.worldbank.org/view.php?type=18&id=25467

Ethnic Diversity   Diversity is a measure of ethnic fractionalization is measured as the probability of two random people not belonging to the same ethnic group. This measure of ethnic fragmentation is based on a broad classification of groups, taking into account not only language but also other cleavages such as racial characteristics. Data source: Alesina *et al.* (2003).

Regional Dummies   The regional dummies were obtained from Collier and Dollar (2001).

Sub-Saharan Africa   Angola, Burundi, Benin, Burkina Faso, Central African Republic Cote Congo, Rep Cape Verde, Djibouti, Eritrea, Ethiopia, Gabon, Ghana, Guinea, The Gambia, Guinea-Bissau, Equatorial Guinea, Kenya, Liberia, Lesotho, Madagascar, Mali, Mozambique, Mauritania, Mauritius, Malawi, Namibia, Niger, Nigeria, Rwanda, Sudan, Senegal, Sierra Leone, Somalia, São Tomé and Principe, Swaziland, Seychelles, Chad, Togo, Tanzania, Uganda, South Africa, Congo, Dem. Rep., Zambia and Zimbabwe.

South Asia Afghanistan, Bangladesh, Bhutan, India, Sri Lanka, Maldives, Nepal and Pakistan.

East Asia China, Indonesia, Japan, Korea, Rep., Malaysia, Philippines, Singapore and Thailand.

Middle East and North Africa United Arab Emirates, Bahrain, Algeria, Egypt, Arab Rep., Greece, Iran, Islamic Rep., Iraq, Israel, Jordan, Kuwait, Lebanon, Libya, Morocco, Malta, Oman, Portugal, Qatar, Saudi Arabia, Syrian Arab Republic, Tunisia and Yemen, Rep.

Eastern and Central Europe Albania, Armenia, Azerbaijan, Bulgaria, Bosnia and Herzegovina, Belarus, Czech Republic, Estonia, Georgia, Croatia, Hungary, Kazakhstan, Kyrgyz Republic, Lithuania, Latvia, Moldova, Macedonia, FYR, Poland, Romania, Russian Federation, Slovak Republic, Slovenia, Tajikistan, Turkmenistan, Turkey, Ukraine, Uzbekistan and Yugoslavia (Serbia/Montenegro).

Notes

1 During the resource boom of the 1970s, the average resource-rich country scored only 0.96 on the Polity IV scale of political rights (the scale ranges 0–10). By the mid-1990s the score had risen to 3.47. The scale ranges from 0–10. Details of these figures are given in Section 3.

2 Half of all Nigerian oil revenues accrue to the Governors of the 36 states, all of which also have powers of local taxation: differences among states thus constitute a 'natural experiment'. In 2006 the Chief Economic Advisor to the President observed to Collier that the more corrupt the Governor the lower the tax rate he chose to set.

3 This data set has now been used by a number of studies, for example Ross (2006) analyzes the link between the resource rents from oil and civil war.

4 A notable omission from our coverage is diamonds. As Olsson (2007) shows diamonds have adverse effects on economic growth conditional upon poor institutions, a result entirely consistent with our subsequent results.

5 For two observations this average is larger than 100. This is possible because the numerator and denominator are based on different measurement concepts, rents and value added. In any case in our regression analysis we could not use these observations because other data were missing.

6 We would like to thank David Hendry for this suggestion. Country dummies included are: Armenia, Australia, Azerbaijan, Botswana, Central African Republic, Chile, China, Dominican Republic, Egypt, Estonia, Georgia, Guinea, Haiti, Ireland, Jamaica, Japan, Lesotho, Lithuania, Latvia, Madagascar, Macedonia, Mauritius, Niger, Nicaragua, Norway, Oman, Peru, Philippines, Portugal, Sierra Leone, Tunisia, Uzbekistan, Vietnam, Democratic Republic of the Congo and Zambia.

7 Due to the democracy interaction term our model is non-linear in the variables and we use the test for endogeneity as described in Wooldridge (2002). We calculate the residuals from the first stage regression and include them in the second stage regression. A zero coefficient on the residual is interpreted as an indication that endogeneity does not pose major problems and that OLS regression can be used. This approach is sometimes referred to as the 'control function' approach. A recent application can be found in Söderbom *et al.* (2006, section V).

8 Results available upon request.

References

Auty, R. (ed.) (2001). *Resource Abundance and Economic Development*. Oxford: Oxford University Press.

Acemoglu, D., S. Johnson and J. Robinson. (2000). 'The Colonial Origins of Comparative Development: An Empirical Investigation', *American Economic Review* 91: 1369–1401.

Acemoglu, D., S. Johnson, J. A. Robinson and P. Yared. (2008). 'Income and Democracy'. *American Economic Review*, forthcoming.

Alesina, Alberto, Arnaud Devleeschauwer, William Easterly, Sergio Kurlat, and Romain Wacziarg. (2003). 'Fractionalization'. *Journal of Economic Growth* 8 (2): 155–194.

Alesina, Alberto, and Eliana La Ferrera. (2004). 'Ethnic Diversity and Economic Performance'. *Journal of Economic Literature* 43:762–800.

Barro, R. J. (1996). 'Democracy and growth'. *Journal of Economic Growth* 1: 1–27.

Beck, T., G. Clarke, A. Groff, P. Keefer and P. Walsh. (2001). 'New tools in comparative political economy: The Database of Political Institutions'. *World Bank Economic Review* 15(1): 165–176.

Besley, T. (2006), *Principled Agents?* New York: Oxford University Press.

Brautigam, D. and S. Knack. (2004) 'Foreign Aid, Institutions and Governance in Sub-Saharan Africa', *Economic Development and Cultural Change* 52: 255–285.

Collier, Paul. (2000). 'Ethnicity, Politics and Economic Performance'. *Economics and Politics* 12 (3): 225–245.

Collier, Paul and Benedikt Goderis. (2007). 'Prospects for Commodity Exporters: Hunky Dory or Humpty Dumpty?' *World Economics* 8:1–15.

Collier, Paul and Benedikt Goderis. (2007a). 'Commodity Prices, Growth, and the Natural Resource Curse: Reconciling a Conundrum'. University of Oxford. Mimeo.

Corden, W. Max, and J. Peter Neary, 'Booming Sector and De-Industrialization in a Small Open Economy,' *The Economic Journal* 92 (1982), 825–848.

Drazen, A. (2000). *Political Economy in Macroeconomics*. Princeton, New Jersey: Princeton University Press.

Easterly, William and Ross Levine. (1997). 'Africa's Growth Tragedy: Politics and Ethnic Divisions'. *Quarterly Journal of Economics* 112:1203–50.

Feng, Y. (2003). *Democracy, Governance and Economic Performance: Theory and Evidence*, MIT Press: Boston, Mass.

Friedman, E., S. Johnson, D. Kaufmann and P. Zoido–Lobaton. (2004). 'Dodging the grabbing hand: the determinants of unofficial activity in 69 countries'. *Journal of Public Economics* 76 (2000) 459–493.

Githongo, J. (2006). 'Inequality, Ethnicity and the Fight against Corruption in Africa: A Kenyan Perspective'. Forthcoming in *Economic Affairs*.

Gylfason, T. (2001). 'Natural resources, education,and economic development'. *European Economic Review* 45: 847–859.

Gylfason, T. and G. Zoega. (2006). 'Natural Resources and Economic Growth: The Role of Investment'. *The World Economy* 29: 1091–1115.

Hamilton, K. and M. Clemens. (1998). Genuine Saving Rates in Developing Countries, Worldbank, Washington DC available on http://lnweb18.worldbank.org/ESSD/envext.nsf/44ByDocName/GreenAccountingAdj ustedNetSavings

Hendry, D. F., S. Johansen and C. Santos. (2004). 'Selecting a Regression Saturated by Indicators', unpublished paper, Economics Department, University of Oxford.

Heston, A., Summers, R. and B. Aten. (2002). PWT 6.1. Center for International Comparisons at the University of Pennsylvania (CICUP), October 2002. http://pwt.econ.upenn.edu/

Jaggers, Keith, and Ted Robert Gurr. (1995). 'Tracking Democracy's Third Wave with the Polity III Data'. *Journal of Peace Research* 32: 469–482.

Keefer, P. and D. Stasavage. (2003). 'The Limits of Delegation: Veto Players, Central Bank Independence and the Credibility of Monetary Policy'. *American Political Science Review* (August).

Lipset, S. M. (1959). 'Some Social Requisites of Democracy: Economic Development and Political Legitimacy'. *American Political Science Review* 53: 69–105.

Mehlum, Halvor, Karl Moene, and Ragnar Torvik. (2006). 'Institutions and the Resource Curse'. *Economic Journal* 116: 1–20.

Moore, Mick, (1998), 'Death without Taxes: Democracy, State Capacity and Aid Dependence in the Fourth World', in *Towards a Democratic Developmental State*, eds. Gordon White and Mark Robinson, Oxford: Oxford University Press.

Olson, M. (1993). 'Dictatorship, Democracy, and Development'. *American Political Science Review* 87: 567–576.

Olsson, O. (2007). 'Conflict Diamonds'. *Journal of Development Economics* 82: 267–286.

Przeworski, A. and F. Limongi. (1993). 'Political Regimes and Economic Growth'. *The Journal of Economic Perspectives* 7: 51–69.

Robinson, James A., Ragnar Torvik, and Thierry Verdier. (2006). 'Political Foundations of the Resource Curse'. *Journal of Development Economics* 79: 447–468.

Ross, M. L. (2001). 'Does Oil Hinder Democracy?' *World Politics* 53 (April): 325–61.

Ross, M. L. (2004). 'Does Tax lead to Representation?' *British Journal of Political Science* 34: 229–249.

Ross, M. L. (2006). 'A Closer Look at Oil, Diamonds, and Civil War'. *Annual Review of Political Science* 9: 263–300.

Sachs, Jeffrey D., and Andrew M. Warner. (2005). 'Natural Resource Abundance and Economic Growth.' In *Leading Issues in Economic Development*, ed. G. M. Meier and J. E. Rauch. 8th edition. New York: Oxford University Press.

Smith, B. (2004). 'Oil Wealth and Regime Survival in the Developing World', 1960–1999, *American Journal of Political Science* 48 (2): 232–246.

Selden, Z. (2004). Neoconservatives and the American Mainstream. *Hoover Institution Policy Review*, April 2004.

Söderbom, M., Teal, F., Wambugu, A. and G. Kahyarara. (2006). 'The Dynamics of Returns to Education in Kenyan and Tanzanian Manufacturing', *Oxford Bulletin of Economics and Statistics* 68: 261–288.

Tavares, J. and R. Wacziarg. (2001), 'How Democracy Affects Growth', *European Economic Review* 45: 1341–1378.

Tilly, Charles. (1975), *The Formation of National States in Western Europe*, Princeton: Princeton University Press.

Tornell, Aaron and Philip Lane. (1999). 'The Voracity Effect', *American Economic Review* 89: 22–46.

Vicente, P. (2007). Does Oil Corrupt? Evidence from a Natural Experiment in West Africa, Centre for the Study of African Economies. http://users.ox.ac.uk/~econ0192/oil.pdf

Wooldridge, J. M. (2002). *Econometric Analysis of Cross Section and Panel Data*. Cambridge MA: MIT Press.

12 Elections and economic policy in developing countries

With Lisa Chauvet

12.1 Introduction

This chapter investigates whether elections in developing countries have improved economic policies and economic governance. Both casual empiricism and casual theorizing suggest that they have done so. As contested elections have become more common since the 1990s, the policy ratings from the World Bank and the International Country Risk Guide have both improved markedly. These improvements accord with the fundamental notion that elections discipline governments into good performance.

Yet this view from on high often collides with the actual experience of individual elections. The Kenyan election of December 2007 triggered a catastrophic implosion of the society, polarizing it on ethnic lines. To date, the legacy of that election is a policy paralysis: for example, the number of government ministers has been doubled with a resulting loss of policy coherence. In Zimbabwe the prospect of contested elections in 2002 and 2008 clearly failed to discipline President Mugabe into adopting good economic policies: he chose hyperinflation, using the revenues to finance patronage. The most celebrated economic reform episode in Africa is Nigeria 2003–6, when a group of technocrats led by Ngozi Nkonjo-Iweala as Minister of Finance turned the economy around. This episode was ushered in by the replacement of a military dictator, General Abacha, with an elected president, Obasanjo, suggesting that elections indeed improved government performance. However, reform only began in Obasanjo's second and *final* term, when he no longer faced the discipline of an election. He told Nkonjo-Iweala that the window for reform was only three years, not the full four years of his term: as he said, 'the last year will be politics'.[1] Indeed, that Nigeria failed to harness the first oil boom was primarily the responsibility of a democratic government, elected in 1978. That government adopted very poor economic policies, including borrowing heavily in order to finance public consumption; it was also famously corrupt. Despite its disastrous performance it was re-elected in 1983. As these examples suggest, in the conditions typical of many developing countries, elections may be two-edged swords.

The effect of elections on policy in low-income countries is of considerable importance. Since aid was first used conditionally to promote 'Structural Adjustment' in the 1980s the international community has recognized that policy improvement is fundamental to development. During the 1990s the approach to *how* good policies should be promoted shifted from conditionality, which was increasingly seen as both ineffective and unacceptable, to the promotion of democracy. Electorates rather than donors would coerce governments into good performance. At the core of the promotion of democracy was the promotion of elections: for example, in 2006 donors provided $500m to finance elections in the Democratic Republic of the Congo. Yet the premise that elections are effective in such conditions has yet to be evaluated. At a more pragmatic level, since elections periodize political decision taking, they might also periodize policy reform: some times might be ripe for good policy. For example, it would be useful both to political leaders and to donors to know whether the year just prior to an election is indeed unsuited to policy reform as President Obasanjo evidently thought.

There is a large general literature on the relationship between democracy and economic performance but it does not provide much guidance as to these questions. The conclusion from the literature is that any such relationship is weak (Drazen, 2000; Feng, 2003; Przeworski *et al.*, 2000). However, these studies do not focus specifically on the characteristics prevalent in developing countries many of which democratized during the 1990s. Several recent studies find that democracy has distinctive effects in the context of such characteristics. Alesina and La Ferrara (2005) and Collier (2001) focus on the consequences of ethnic diversity for growth. They find that diverse societies benefit significantly more from democracy than homogenous societies. Collier and Rohner (2008) focus on the relationship between democracy and the risk of large-scale political violence. They find that whereas in developed economies democracy increases security, below an income threshold of around $2,700 per capita it significantly increases the risk of political violence. Finally, Collier and Hoeffler (2008) focus on the relationship between democracy and the economic performance of resource-rich countries. They find that whereas below a threshold of resource wealth democracy is significantly beneficial, above the threshold it significantly worsens performance. These results suggest that no simple model of how democracy affects economic policy may be globally applicable. Models designed to describe how elections affect political incentives in OECD societies may prove seriously misleading if applied to contexts such as Afghanistan and the Democratic Republic of the Congo. Our purpose in this paper is to investigate empirically the various effects of elections. As we discuss in Section 12.2, since there are potentially several distinct and offsetting effects, an appropriate empirical strategy needs to distinguish between them: simple composite empirical measures are likely to be misleading.

In many developing countries governments are failing to provide their citizens with the rudiments of social provision and economic opportunities now considered both normal and feasible. A reasonable inference is that in such states the ruling politicians are either ill-motivated or incompetent. We focus directly on policies rather than on economic outcomes. The typical developing country is subject to large shocks that introduce much noise into the mapping from policy choices to outcomes and we are concerned with the variables that are more directly under the control of politicians. The direct observation of policies is difficult, but in this respect the researcher is at an advantage over the electorate. We rely upon two international data sets which rate economic policies and governance, neither of which has been available to citizens of rated countries. Hence, while citizens must largely rely upon observable economic performance, we are able to observe policies directly, albeit with the limitations implied by these international rating systems. In Section 12.2 we discuss the theory which informs our empirical analysis. We show that while democracy may have both structural and cyclical effects on policy, *a priori* there are offsetting effects so that the net effect is ambiguous: the issue must therefore be resolved empirically. In Section 12.3 we discuss our empirical strategy: no one approach is ideal and so we test the robustness of each against the reasonable alternatives. In Section 12.4 we present our core results, subjecting them to a range of robustness tests in Section 12.5. Section 12.6 extends the analysis to those developing countries at the extremes of poverty and poor policies, and investigates possible interactions between elections and other political variables. Section 12.7 draws out the implications for policy, both in terms of international support for the process of policy reform, and for the better functioning of the new low-income democracies.

12.2 A theoretical overview

Elections can affect economic policy both through their effect on the incentives facing politicians and through selection. By making politicians accountable to citizens they increase the incentive to adopt socially beneficial economic policies. Selection is both a direct consequence of electoral choice and, more fundamentally, because if politicians are accountable the profession becomes more attractive for people who aspire to further the public good and less attractive for people who are ill-motivated (Besley, 2006). Hence, through both incentives and selection elections may enhance political motivation to adopt good policies. Further, an elected government may face lower costs of doing so. By conferring legitimacy elections might make it easier to face down vested interests that oppose reform.

However, in addition to the structural change of accountability, elections introduce friction. Elections are periodic events the timing of which may affect the incentives facing politicians. In particular, elections as events may disrupt policy. If elections affect policies both structurally and cyclically the empirical relationship between elections and policies may appear confused because of opposing effects. Elections may improve the average level of policies, yet worsen them in the short run. In this paper we try to disentangle the two effects.

12.2.1 Cyclical effects of elections

Elections are periodic events. One effect of an election is to create a discrete difference between the period prior to the election during which the government is in power and on which it may be judged by voters, and the period after the election when it may not be in power. This introduces an incentive for the government to improve its record by transferring resources from expenditures that only generate observable benefits after the election to those that generate observable benefits prior to the election. There is indeed some evidence in support of the short-term bias of democratic governments: they invest less than autocracies (Tavares and Wacziarg, 2001). Reform, by its nature, is a form of investment: short term political costs are incurred for longer term benefits. An implication is that as an election approaches the ratio of pre-election to post-election effects of policy reform falls and so the incentive to reform diminishes. Hence, the pace of reform might slow, or even become negative, as the election approaches. For example, in run-up to the Zambian election of 1991 President Kaunda increased the money supply by 400 per cent, and in the run-up to the Zimbabwean election of 2008 President Mugabe confiscated foreign currency bank accounts and distributed the proceeds.

Elections are fought not just on the past record of the government but on promises: they are occasions when politicians make future policy commitments. In many developing countries the electorate lacks both the education and information properly to evaluate these commitments: the media are both highly partisan and lack the capacity for specialist analysis of economic policy, and in any case many voters are illiterate. Elections thus expose the society to the risk of political promises based on economic populism. For example, in South Africa in 2008 the electoral contest between Jacob Zuma and Thabo Mbeki for the leadership of the ruling ANC clearly pitched economic populism versus economic prudence: populism won by 9:1. A legacy of an election may therefore be a period in which policy reform is hamstrung by the need to implement some of these commitments.

Each of these short term effects of elections would give rise to a cycle, potentially in either the level of policy or the pace of reform. The shortening horizon would predict a gradual deterioration as the next election approached, while the legacy of populist commitments would predict gradual policy improvement. Empirically, there are four possibilities. Neither of the effects might be significant in which case there would be no electoral policy cycle. The shortening horizons effect might predominate, in which case the policy cycle would be a saw-tooth of post-election deterioration. The populist legacy effect might predominate, in which case the saw-tooth would have the opposite slope, with gradual post-election improvement. Finally, the potency of each effect might recede with the time to the pertinent election, forward-looking for shortening horizons, backward-looking for populist legacies. Thus, the shortening horizons effect might matter most in the period immediately prior to an election, as our examples illustrate, while the populist legacy effect might matter most in the period immediately after an election. In this case, rather than a saw-tooth, there would be a genuine cycle in which the level or pace of improvement of policy was at its peak around the mid-point between elections.

The relative importance of the two effects also determines how elections should be dated in empirical analysis. If the only significant effect is that of shortening horizons then the theory implies that the empirical measure should be forward-looking: the time to the next election. In this case, if data are organized as annual observations, an election in January has virtually no effect in the year of the election and elections in the first half of the year are better reassigned to the previous year. Conversely, if the only significant effect is populist legacy, elections in the second half of the year are better reassigned to the next year. Only if the two effects are similarly potent is the election best left in the year in which it occurred.

The evidence on whether political cycles are important is mixed. In developed countries, where democracies are more mature and information is good, the consensus is that there is no cycle. However, there is some evidence that cycles are significant in developing countries. To date, work has focused on budget deficits. Shi and Svensson (2006) find that political budget cycles are significantly more pronounced in developing than in developed countries. Similarly, Brender and Drazen (2005) show that in their sample of developed and developing economies political budget cycles are confined to the 'new democracies'. Block (2002) finds that in developing countries the fiscal deficit increases in election years and is followed by post-election retrenchments.

12.2.2 *Structural effects*

Democracy is widely seen as the best system of government despite such cyclical effects. The case for democracy rests on its structural effects: increasing the accountability and legitimacy of government. The accountability effect is straightforward: faced with an election, a government may need to attract votes by adopting policies which are good for citizens, or at least good for the median voter. The legitimacy effect is not usually modelled but may also be important. It is that a government which has acquired power through winning an election has a *mandate* to implement its commitments and the wide recognition of this mandate reduces the ability of those opposed to these policies to block them.

Although elections hold government to account and confer legitimacy, they only do so periodically. The periodicity of elections is likely to affect the intensity of these effects as well as introducing the possibility of a cycle. A plausible hypothesis is that the greater the frequency of elections the more closely is the government held to account and the greater its legitimacy in enacting its policies. Variations in the frequency of elections thus provide an empirical measure of these structural effects.

While the 'accountability and legitimacy' model may be applicable, it is by no means inevitable. We now consider how it might be undermined, ultimately to the point at which elections have adverse structural effects on policy.

Voter ignorance

Information about economic policy is costly and because of the free-rider problem individual voters have very little incentive to acquire it. As a result voters may not be able to monitor government performance. Besley (2006) rigorously analyzes this problem. Observable economic outcomes may be dependent upon many influences outside the control of the politician, a condition likely in the shock-prone and media-scarce conditions of many developing countries. As the ability of voters to monitor the politician deteriorates, at some point the electoral advantage from good policies becomes too small to offset the rent-seeking advantages which a dishonest politician would value. Crucially, once this point is reached, rent-seekers are attracted to politics, honest people are consequently discouraged, and the pool of candidates deteriorates: voters end up merely choosing among rent-seekers.

Identity voting

Voters may hold strong ethnic allegiances which predetermine their support, making votes unresponsive to performance (Bossuroy, 2007; Fridy, 2007). This in turn weakens the incentive for governments to depart from patronage politics to provide the national public good of policy reform. For example, consider the elections of December 2007 in Kenya, which has long been regarded as one of the more successful and advanced African economies. The presidential election pitted an incumbent Kikuyu against a Luo challenger. Even among Luo voters President Kibaki had a remarkably high approval rating: those giving him a favourable rating outnumbered those disapproving by 44 per cent:14 per cent (Dercon *et al.*, 2008). Yet 98 per cent of Luo intended to vote for the Luo candidate. Evidently, the need to win an election provided President Kibaki little incentive to adopt policies other than those that favoured the Kikuyu. Similarly, in a remarkable field experiment in Benin in which candidates varied their electoral message randomly across localities, Wantchekon (2003) found that promises of ethnic patronage were more effective than promises of national public goods in attracting votes.

Many developing countries, especially in Africa, are highly ethnically diverse and these sub-national identities trump the relatively recent introduction of national identities (Collier, 2009). As with poor voter information, above some threshold of identity voting, the difference between good and bad policies has too little effect on voting to deter 'unprincipled' politicians from seeking office and so the pool of candidates deteriorates.

Illicit tactics

Governments may win elections through illicit strategies such as ballot fraud, bribery and intimidation. Recent analysis of the Nigerian election by Collier and Vicente (2008) has shown that all three features were not just widespread but were used strategically. Through a randomized experiment that succeeded in reducing violence in selected locations, they are also able to show that where a party adopted the strategy of violence it was effective, reducing the turnout of those who support other parties. Similarly, in a randomized experiment in São Tomé, Vicente (2007) was able to show that bribery was effective.

These illicit strategies may well be more than convenient supplements to the desired strategy of adopting good economic policies. If politicians are ill-motivated and wish to maintain dysfunctional policies which are personally advantageous, they may adopt the illicit strategies in order to free themselves from the need for good policies.

Whether governments are able to resort to illicit tactics depends upon dimensions of democracy other than elections. Whereas elections describe the technology by which a government *acquires* power, checks and balances determine how government *uses* power. The new democracies tend to have lop-sided democracy because elections, being discrete events, can be introduced much more readily than checks and balances, which are continuous processes. Further, the private incentive for political parties to contest elections is considerable, whereas checks and balances are public goods and so likely to be under-provided by private action. The under-provision of checks and balances is compounded because governments have an incentive not to substitute for the lack of private provision. The implication is that many of the new low-income democracies may lack the social and constitutional pre-conditions for elections to provide an effective discipline on government performance. The most damaging scenario would be if in order to adopt the illicit strategies the government undermines the rule of law: in this case elections would induce policy deterioration. From the perspective of an ill-motivated incumbent the switch from autocracy to electoral competition may be viewed as technical regress in the retention of power. The privately optimal response may be to adopt more costly means of power retention.

Where these illicit strategies are rife an election may fail to establish the accountability of government for its performance. It may also *reduce* the perceived legitimacy of government. For example, once President Kibaki was perceived to have won the Kenyan election through ballot fraud, opposition to his regime was far stronger than that against the former Kenyan autocrats, Kenyatta and Moi. Combined with the undermining of checks and balances as incumbents resort to more costly strategies of power retention, elections might therefore *retard* reform. A recent result by Kudamatsu (2007) provides some support for this hypothesis that the consequences of elections depend upon how they are conducted. Using changes in infant mortality as a measure of the performance of African governments, he finds that only in those rare cases in which the incumbent government has lost the election does performance improve. Since the illicit tactics greatly favour incumbents, those elections in which the incumbent loses are likely to have been relatively free of such tactics.

12.2.3 Implications

The above discussion has three implications for an empirical strategy of the effect of elections on policy. First, political cycles are complicated: neither the dating of observations nor the functional form of any relationship can be determined *a priori*. Second, the structural effect of democracy in the conditions prevailing in many developing countries is *a priori* ambiguous: the triumph of accountability cannot simply be assumed. Third, if elections have both cyclical and structural effects, neither can be investigated in isolation.

As noted, in most low-income countries contested elections are recent and follow a phase of autocracy in which economic policies were highly dysfunctional. Of course, the apparent association between democracy and policy improvement may be coincidental. An alternative simple interpretation is that elites have learnt from past failure. Even if in the long run democracy leads to a better *level* of policy, the recent observed phase may be a gradual adjustment out of disequilibrium: the observable relationship may be between democracy and the rate of policy improvement towards an equilibrium level. Hence, we will investigate both the relationship in levels (and its transformation into the relationship between changes in democracy and changes in policy), and the adjustment relationship between the level of democracy and the change in policy conditional upon the attained level of policy.

12.3 Empirical strategy and presentation of the data

12.3.1 Estimation method

The dependent variable in our analysis is economic policy and governance rather than economic performance. This has the important advantage of being under the direct control of the government, but it poses a distinct set of difficulties. Economic policies and governance are multidimensional and so must be aggregated. Some of these dimensions are not readily mapped onto a cardinal scale. Our core measure is the Country Policy and Institutional Assessment (CPIA) of the World Bank. A precise definition of the CPIA is presented in Appendix 1. It is an annual rating system for twenty different aspects of economic policy and institutions that covers around 130 countries since 1977. This has several important advantages and some severe disadvantages.

It is available for a long period, 1977–2004, and is intended to be comparable across countries and, with minor qualifications, over time. It is intended to assess the overall economic efficacy of government choices regarding policies and institutions. The CPIA also has strong disadvantages. Although clear criteria are set out for the ratings, it is subjective. The ratings are given annually by economists who are staff of the World Bank specialized on the country. More senior economics staff then adjust these ratings so as to be comparable both within and across regions. A common objection to the CPIA is that it inadvertently incorporates growth outcomes: staff working on a rapidly growing economy will tend to assess policies and institutions more favourably than objectively similar policies and institutions in a slow-growing economy. A second common criticism is that the ratings reflect World Bank opinions about policy which are at times contentious. This is likely to be more serious in some contexts than others. In the range of very poor economic policies common during the 1980s in much of Africa the direction of change in World Bank ratings is likely to be fairly uncontroversial. An example is Uganda during the 1990s. There is good objective evidence of major policy improvement during this period. In the first years of the decade the Ministry of Finance lost control of the economy and inflation reached 230 per cent. This persuaded President Museveni to replace his economic team with a group of technocrats who had previously been critics of policy. As this group gradually gained the confidence of the president they were able to implement a widening agenda of economic policy reforms. Most notably, public spending was restrained through a 'cash budget'; the administered exchange rate was replaced first by an auction and then by an inter-bank market; the state bank was privatized; and the state monopoly on transporting coffee exports was lifted. These improvements were recognized in the international private sector: the country's rating by *Institutional Investor*, based on a poll of informed observers, rose from around 6/100 to over 20/100. The CPIA fully reflected these improvements, rising from a low level of 2.5 early in the decade to 4.0. The ICRG, which we will use as a robustness check, also improves from 30/100 to 60/100. All these reforms were entirely in line with standard economic analysis and so could not reasonably be seen as contentious within the profession, although they were of course contentious politically. The CPIA is likely to be more contentious within the economics profession where reforms involve a complex transition such as that which occurred in Eastern Europe. Since there were at the time open professional disputes about the pace and sequencing of reform the CPIA must be seen as merely reflecting one institutional position.

The CPIA is ordinal in nature. Each of its twenty components is rated on a scale from 1 to 6. Because it is an average of twenty components the CPIA can take all the values within this range, as illustrated by Table 12.1. Our core use of this ordinal variable is to create a dummy variable which takes the value of unity in any year in which the CPIA has improved relative to the previous year. Another approach we adopt is to classify the CPIA into nine

Table 12.1 Country policy and institutional assessment, 1978–2004, 82 countries

CPIA	Ordered CPIA	Observations	of which CPIA equals	Observations	Percentage
[1 – 1.5]	1	65	1	43	66.2
[1.5 – 2]	2	46			
[2 – 2.5]	3	216	2	50	23.1
[2.5 – 3]	4	360			
[3 – 3.5]	5	589	3	157	26.7
[3.5 – 4]	6	313			
[4 – 4.5]	7	193	4	60	31.1
[4.5 – 5]	8	48			
[5 – 5.5]	9	19	5	12	63.2
		1849		322	

bands as shown in Table 12.1 and assign a ranking with which we estimate an ordered probit. Both of these approaches involve a loss of information. This is the price to be paid for respecting the ordinal nature of the variable: there is little sense in which an improvement from 2 to 3 is equivalent to an improvement from 3 to 4. However, the maximum potential information is to be achieved from ignoring these concerns and treating the CPIA as though it were cardinal. We therefore also investigate these variants, both in levels and in differences.

In our cardinal treatment of the CPIA we first estimate a model of the following form:

$$CPIA_{i,t} = CPIA_{i,t-1} + X'_{i,t}\beta + Election'_{i,t}\theta + \varphi_i + \tau_t + \varepsilon_{i,t}, \qquad (1)$$

where i ($i = 1 \dots N$) denote countries and t ($t = 1 \dots T$) denote years. $X_{i,t}$ and $Election_{i,t}$ are respectively a set of control and election variables. φ_i and τ_t are respectively country fixed effects and years dummies.

The first way to estimate equation (1) is to use a *Within* estimator, which is asymptotically biased on finite T (Nickell, 1981; Sevestre and Trognon, 1985). However, our sample is large (more than 1,000 observations) and the average T is 23 years (the maximum being 27 years), suggesting that the bias plaguing the *Within* estimator is close to zero (Judson and Owen, 1999). The second way of estimating equation (1) is to transform the model in first-difference. OLS estimations of the first-difference transformation of equation (1) may still be biased because of the correlation between the lagged endogenous variable and the error term. An alternative is to use the application of the Generalized Method of Moments proposed by Arellano and Bond (1991) and to instrument $\Delta CPIA_{i,t-1}$ by its lagged values in level starting from t–2.

One of our ordinal strategies is to estimate an *ordered probit* model of the following form:

$$CPIA^*_{i,t} = CPIA_{t-1} + X'_{i,t}\beta + Election'_{i,t}\theta + \varphi_i + \tau_t + \varepsilon_{i,t}, \qquad (2)$$

$$\text{where } CPIA^*_{i,t} = \begin{cases} 1 \text{ if } \mu_1 < CPIA_{i,t} \leq \mu_2 \\ 2 \text{ if } \mu_2 < CPIA_{i,t} \leq \mu_3 \\ \dots \\ J \text{ if } \mu_J < CPIA_{i,t} \leq \mu_{J+1} \end{cases}.$$

The other ordinal strategy is to explain positive changes in the CPIA by means of a *logit* model of the following form:

$$Change_{i,t} = CPIA_{i,t} + X'_{i,t}\beta + Election'_{i,t}\theta + \varphi_i + \tau_t + \varepsilon_{i,t}, \qquad (3)$$

$$\text{where } Change_{i,t} = \begin{cases} 1 & \text{if } \Delta CPIA_{i,t} > 0 \\ 0 & \text{if } \Delta CPIA_{i,t} \leq 0 \end{cases}.$$

Because equation (3) links the changes in the CPIA to level variables it may omit some important control variables. Changes in the CPIA may be more related to changes in $X_{i,t}$ than to the level of $X_{i,t}$. Equation (3) can therefore be augmented in the following way:

$$Change_{i,t} = CPIA_{i,t} + X'_{i,t}\beta + \Delta X'_{i,t}\gamma + Election'_{i,t}\theta + \varphi_i + \tau_t + \varepsilon_{i,t}, \qquad (4)$$

Of the three empirical strategies, we use the third one as our core analysis and test its robustness using the two other strategies. The choice of one strategy over the other crucially depends on how ordinal the CPIA is considered to be. The advantage of the third strategy is to respect the ordinal nature of the CPIA without making any strong econometric assumptions as to the ordinality/cardinality of the CPIA.

Finally, the choice of the CPIA as our core dependent variable is crucial to our analysis, and as noted above is not without raising substantial conceptual and econometric issues. We therefore test the robustness of our baseline model using the ICRG (International Country Risk Guide). The ICRG is a rating of countries according to their economic and political environment, which reflects the feeling of private investors. The ICRG is an alternative measure of policy and institutions which gives more weight than the CPIA to the quality of institutions (corruption, rule of law, quality of bureaucracy, etc.). As such, it is both an interesting robustness check and a good complement to our analysis using the CPIA.

12.3.2 Variables and data

Policy and institutions depend on a set of control variables, $X_{i,t}$, and on a set of variables relating to politics, $Election_{i,t}$. $X_{i,t}$ include conventional development indicators: the level of income and its square, population and education. It also includes more structural characteristics such as the share of the natural resource rents in GDP, and whether the country is at war. These variables and their sources are presented in detail in Appendix 12.2.

Election$_{i,t}$ is a set of variables relating to the timing of elections. Data on elections are from the Database on Political Institutions (DPI) of the World Bank. To test the robustness of our results, we also use the database on elections used by Brender and Drazen (2005) and provided by Allan Drazen. Since our analysis is based on annual observations elections that occur early in the year may be more appropriately assigned to the previous year. We discuss this issue more fully in Section 12.4.

Knowing election years we construct four variables to precisely capture the characteristics of the electoral timing and test the cyclical and structural effects of elections raised in section 12.2. The first one, FREQUENCY of election, is the number of years between the current election and the previous election. We lag this variable because of its potential endogeneity with respect to the chances of reform. By lagging, we mean that if an election occurs in year t, FREQUENCY is equal to the number of years between election in year t and the previous election. This number is reported for each year of the mandate starting in year t.[2]

To construct FREQUENCY, the country obviously needs to have held at least two elections. FREQUENCY is therefore equal to 0 if the country never had an election as well as during the mandate following the first elections. To control for this characteristic of FREQUENCY, we construct two dummy variables: NEVER, which is equal to 1 for the period during which the country never had an election – knowing that we have information on elections since 1975 – and FIRST which is equal to one during the first mandate.

The fourth variable captures the political cycle. CYCLE is constructed as the number of years that separate year t from the nearest election, whether this is the previous election or the next election. So if an election occurs in years t and $t + 4$, CYCLE is equal to 0 in both years t and $t + 4$; it is equal to 1 in years $t + 1$ and $t + 3$; and it is equal to 2 in year $t + 2$.

Table 12.2 provides some summary statistics on the dependent variables, on $X_{i,t}$ and on the various variables included in *Election$_{i,t}$*.

12.4 Estimation of the baseline model

We now turn to our results. We investigate whether elections create pressures for better policies and governance on a sample of 82 developing countries on annual data from 1978 to 2004. *A priori* no single statistical approach dominates and so we present results using four different ones. Similarly, there are two distinct data sets on policy and governance, two data sets on elections, and potentially three different options for assigning elections to calendar years. Since the number of possible permutations of these options is considerable we

Table 12.2 Descriptive statistics, 1978–2004, 82 countries

Averages on the sample		Obs.	Mean	St. Devia.	Minimum	Maximum
Dependent	CPIA	1849	3.13	0.78	1	5.5
	ICRG	1273	60.1	12.5	13	83.5
Election$_{i,t}$	ELECTION	1849	0.17	0.37	0	1
	NEVER	1849	0.18	0.38	0	1
	FIRST	1849	0.20	0.40	0	1
	FREQUENCY	1849	3.19	2.99	0	19
	CYCLE	1849	0.86	1.23	0	11
	QUALITY	1849	3.31	3.05	0	7
$X_{i,t}$	Ln income p.c.. lagged	1849	7.98	0.86	5.14	9.82
	Income p.c. lagged	1849	4059	3205	171	18390
	Secondary education. lagged	1849	7.26	8.19	0.10	110.08
	Ln population. lagged	1849	16.13	1.65	11.76	20.98
	Population. lagged (in thousands)	1849	49600	164000	127.8	1290000
	Natural resource rent. lagged	1849	5.94	9.01	0	74.78
	Dummy AT WAR	1849	0.11	0.32	0	1
Averages by countries						
Election$_{i,t}$	Average nb of elections	82	3.77	1.97	0	8
	Average nb of years before the 1st election	82	4.00	6.58	0	27
	Average nb of years of the 1st mandate	82	4.48	3.12	0	18
	Average FREQUENCY[1]	82	3.37	1.49	0	8
	Average CYCLE[1]	82	0.90	0.60	0	4.44
	Average QUALITY[1]	82	3.54	2.06	0	7

Notes: (1): calculated on the period following the first mandate. Our sample of 1,849 observations contains 82 developing countries on a period from 1978 to 2004. When we use the ICRG, this sample is reduced to 1,273 observations on 70 countries on a period from 1985 to 2005.

proceed by presenting first a 'core' regression and then progressively introducing alternatives. While not all permutations are presented, all have been investigated and we note in the text those which are significantly different. Complete results are available from the authors.

In Table 12.3 we explore the factors that lead to a year-on-year improvement in the CPIA. We estimate Equations (3) and (4). Since the CPIA is not a cardinal variable, we analyze its change by creating a dummy variable which takes the value of unity if it has improved relative to the previous year and estimate the probability of improvement through a logit regression. Subsequently we investigate a cardinal treatment of the CPIA.

Table 12.3 Logit estimations of the baseline model, 1978–2004, 82 countries

Dummy = 1 if $\Delta CPIA>0$	(1)	(2)	(3)	(4)	(5)	(6)
Dummy ELECTION (datation 1)	-0.102 (0.68)	-0.091 (0.58)				
Dummy NEVER had an election			-0.978 (2.98)***	-0.986 (2.96)***	-0.847 (2.02)**	-0.827 (1.95)*
Dummy FIRST election			-1.019 (3.46)***	-1.026 (3.47)***	-0.893 (2.28)**	-0.872 (2.19)**
CYCLE			0.208 (2.01)**	0.204 (1.92)*	0.208 (2.01)**	0.203 (1.92)*
CYCLE squared			-0.040 (3.68)***	-0.041 (3.65)***	-0.040 (3.70)***	-0.041 (3.67)***
FREQUENCY of elections			-0.153 (4.68)***	-0.155 (4.70)***	-0.113 (1.12)	-0.106 (1.03)
FREQUENCY squared					-0.003 (0.44)	-0.003 (0.52)
CPIA in level, lagged	-1.402 (8.11)***	-1.476 (8.35)***	-1.466 (8.55)***	-1.545 (8.76)***	-1.469 (8.47)***	-1.548 (8.68)***
Ln income p.c., lagged	3.760 (1.63)	4.623 (1.71)*	3.275 (1.43)	4.055 (1.51)	3.282 (1.44)	4.065 (1.52)
Ln income p.c. squared, lagged	-0.269 (1.75)*	-0.328 (1.83)*	-0.247 (1.60)	-0.300 (1.66)*	-0.247 (1.61)	-0.300 (1.67)*
Secondary education, lagged	-0.007 (0.66)	-0.003 (0.14)	-0.000 (0.01)	0.001 (0.03)	-0.001 (0.06)	-0.000 (0.01)
Ln population, lagged	-1.109 (0.92)	-0.962 (0.83)	-0.728 (0.59)	-0.583 (0.49)	-0.748 (0.60)	-0.605 (0.50)
Resource rent, lagged	0.031 (1.87)*	0.028 (1.64)	0.031 (1.93)*	0.028 (1.68)*	0.031 (1.91)*	0.028 (1.63)
Dummy AT WAR	-0.784 (3.21)***	-0.788 (3.17)***	-0.758 (2.93)***	-0.761 (2.89)***	-0.757 (2.93)***	-0.760 (2.88)***
Δ Ln income p.c., lagged		-14.305 (2.64)***		-15.079 (2.91)***		-15.046 (2.92)***
Δ Ln income p.c. squared, lagged		1.088 (2.86)***		1.136 (3.03)***		1.134 (3.05)***
Δ Secondary education, lagged		-0.038 (0.20)		-0.002 (0.01)		-0.002 (0.01)
Δ Ln population, lagged		6.095 (0.97)		7.037 (1.09)		7.111 (1.10)

Δ Resource rent, lagged		0.003 (0.15)		0.002 (0.09)		0.003 (0.11)
Constant	3.525 (0.21)	−1.531 (0.09)	6.505 (0.37)	−1.636 (0.09)	3.192 (0.19)	−1.782 (0.10)
Observations	1849	1849	1849	1849	1849	1849
Countries	82	82	82	82	82	82
Turning point in CYCLE (years)			2.6	2.5	2.6	2.5
Income threshold (in logarithm)	6.99	7.05	6.63	6.76	6.64	6.78

Notes: Robust z statistics in parentheses. Standard errors are adjusted for intra-country correlation.
* significant at 10%; ** significant at 5%; *** significant at 1%.

DEPENDENT VARIABLE:	Dummy = 1 when Δ CPIA is strictly positive.
ESTIMATION METHOD:	Logit with country fixed effects and year dummies.
DATING OF ELECTIONS:	The electoral dummy equals one in an election year and zero otherwise, no matter when during the year the election occurred. NEVER, FIRST, CYCLE and FREQUENCY are constructed according to this dating of elections.

The first two columns provide baseline logit regressions with fixed effects and year dummies. Elections are introduced in the simplest possible form, namely a dummy variable which takes the value of unity if there is an election during the year. As with the other regressions in this table the election is assigned to the calendar year in which it occurs. The other explanatory variables are the CPIA, income and its square, secondary education, the size of the population, and the value of natural resource rents, all these variables being lagged. A dummy variable takes the value of unity if the country is at war. The regression in column (1) only the levels of these explanatory variables are included, whereas in (2) the changes in these variables are included along with their levels.

In both regressions the dummy variable for elections is completely insignificant. Elections, the key institutional technology of democracy, appear to wash over the society without affecting economic policy. However, as we will show, this result is spurious and misleading. It may compound offsetting cyclical and structural effects, or it may reflect endogeneity. The better is the CPIA the harder it is to improve it further, the result being highly significant in both regressions. Per capita income has non-linear effects that are borderline significant: reform is most likely at around $1,150 per capita. Out of the 82 countries in our sample, only 17 have a per capita income lower than this threshold, all but Nepal in Africa. Low income thus appears to be a stimulus to change. Somewhat surprisingly, natural resource rents have positive effects that are borderline significant. This may appear to run counter to the resource curse literature. However, that literature is concerned with the long term effects and the short term effects may be benign. Unsurprisingly, civil wars have a significantly negative impact on the probability that policy and institutions will improve. Annual time dummies (not reported) suggest that policies are getting better over time. While this may reflect nothing more than grade inflation on the part of World Bank staff, it is reasonable to expect that in countries which mostly only became independent during the 1960s governments would go through a gradual learning process.

The regressions of columns 3 and 4 introduce the variables that are consistent with the discussion of theory in Section 12.2. Four new variables between them characterize elections. As discussed in Section 12.3, one is a dummy variable characterizing countries which up to the year being considered have never had an election during the period 1978–2004. A second is a dummy variable for those observations in which there has been only one prior election in the country. The third variable – CYCLE – is the time in the electoral cycle as measured by the number of years that separate the year in question from the *nearest* election, whether this is the previous election or the next election. Note that this conflates two potentially distinct distances: forward-looking and backward-looking. Thus, in this regression we treat the shortening horizon effect and the populist legacy effect as symmetrical. In subsequent analysis we test whether this conflation is warranted on the data. Both CYCLE and its square are included. As discussed in Section 12.2, the effect of the time from the nearest election is unlikely to be monotonic. While in the vicinity of the election greater distance from it might improve policy, if the nearest election is very distant then the accountability of government to the electorate may be weakened. The final new variable – FREQUENCY – captures the frequency of elections. It is measured by the length of time between the most recent previous election and the one prior to that. Hence, the higher is the value of the variable the *less* frequent are elections.

The control variables are the same as in the first two regressions. The regression of column (3) includes only the levels of these variables whereas that of column (4) also includes their changes. As previously, all these variables are lagged. The introduction of the new variables for elections does not significantly change the coefficients or significant levels of these control variables and so we focus on the election variables themselves.

In contrast to the naïve approach of columns (1) and (2), all the elections variables are now significant. The inclusion of the changes in the control variables in addition to their levels makes virtually no difference to either coefficients or significance levels, nearly all of which are at one per cent. What do the coefficients imply?

The dummy for those countries which never held an election prior to the year under observation has a large negative coefficient. This is consistent with the hypothesis that elections introduce accountability, although the interpretation need not be causal. An alternative interpretation is that the absence of elections is a symptom of a more fundamental problem that prevents improvements in economic policy and governance rather than being its explanation. However, in addition to the control variables, recall that this regression includes fixed effects so that for all countries which did not have an election over the entire period 1978–2004 any effects of the absence of elections are subsumed in the fixed effect. Essentially, the variable NEVER is picking up the difference between periods prior to the first election and those subsequent to it: periods subsequent to elections are much more likely to have improvements in economic policy. The coefficient on observations in which the previous election was the first election is also large and negative, and statistically indistinguishable from that on the dummy for countries that never held elections. The most reasonable interpretation is that a single election is insufficient to change the behaviour of a government.

The remaining three variables, CYCLE, its square, and FREQUENCY, exclude the first election. We start with FREQUENCY which is the structural relationship. Recall that the variable measures the number of years between the two previous elections. Hence, an increase in the variable is a *reduction* in the frequency of elections. The negative coefficient therefore implies that the more frequent are elections the more likely is the CPIA to improve. This is consistent with the accountability and legitimacy theory of democracy. As with the two dummy variables for countries which have never held elections or have only held one, the frequency of elections may itself proxy some characteristics not included in our control variables, but the deep and unchanging characteristics are all subsumed by means of fixed effects.

Taken together with the negative and highly significant coefficients on the dummy variables, the negative and highly significant coefficient on FREQUENCY suggests that sustained elections really do have a structural effect on economic policy and governance, over the observed period increasing the chance of policy improvement and presumably in the long run improving the level of policy. Despite the reasons to fear that in developing countries governments might be able to win elections without regard to policy, democracy appears to work.

We now turn to CYCLE and its square. Both are significant, and whereas if the squared term is excluded CYCLE itself loses significance. CYCLE is positive and its square is negative: what does this mean? Recall that CYCLE measures the time until the nearest election, either viewed back to the previous one or forward to the next. An important issue is going to be whether this conflation of effects is warranted on the data, but for the moment we will focus on what it implies if it is warranted. The positive coefficient on CYCLE implies that the further away is an election the better are the chances of policy reform. This indicates a tension between elections as important structural instruments of democracy and as periodic events which interrupt the normal business of government. Because both effects matter, any measure which conflates them is liable to be misleading. The negative coefficient on the square of CYCLE indicates that as the distance from an election increases at some point the benefits of further distance are exhausted and go into reverse. Since FREQUENCY is included, the periodicity of elections is already controlled for. However, it implies that if the periodicity is infrequent then the mid-term is not a good time for policy reform. This becomes clearest if elections are very infrequent, such as once-a-decade. In such a case it is indeed plausible that at the midterm the government would be less conscious of accountability to citizens.

The socially optimal periodicity of elections implied by these results depends upon the three variables in combination. This is explored further in Section 12.7. However, here we pose a seemingly simple question: if elections increase accountability can elections be too frequent? As the periodicity is increased there are opposing effects. The direct effect of an increased value of FREQUENCY is adverse. However, a longer periodicity also changes the average composition of the years within each period: proportionately less time is very close to an election. Up to a point, this effect is benign. Hence, for the social optimum the net effect must be calculated and this is taken up in Section 12.7.

The inclusion of the square of CYCLE but not the square of FREQUENCY may appear arbitrary. We first provide a degree of reassurance by adding the square of FREQUENCY in columns (5) and (6): the square is insignificant. There is indeed a good reason other than this result for the core regression to take the form of (3) and (4). Given that the structural and cyclical effects of elections are qualitatively offsetting, the minimum specification that can hope to capture optimality must include at least one squared term (or adopt some other function form which allows non-linearity). If, as appears to be the case, as periodicity is increased beyond a point the chances of reform in the mid-term period deteriorate, this can be captured better by including the square of CYCLE than the square of FREQUENCY. However, to include the square of both terms would build in redundancy.

A fundamental aspect of the variable CYCLE is that it combines the backward and forward-looking effects of elections. In Tables 12.4 and 12.5 we investigate whether this is warranted. The conventional political economy analysis of elections is forward-looking: as the election approaches the government is less inclined to invest in policy reform because a higher proportion of the benefits will accrue after the election. If this is the only effect of elections on policy then an implication is that if analysis is based on annual observations those elections that occur in the first half of the year should be re-assigned to the previous year. For example, almost all of the effects of an election held in January will be on policy decisions in the previous year. We now investigate whether such reassignment is superior to the strategy adopted in Table 12.3. In Table 12.4 we introduce dummy variables according to whether the election is in the first or second half of the year and interact them with the election variables. The key new variables are the interactions with CYCLE and its square. Evidently, since the cyclical effects are now spread over four variables instead of two, each pair with only around half as many observations, we might expect some loss of significance. However, the loss of significance is considerably more severe for the elections occurring in the first half of the year than in the second. This result suggests that the forward-looking effect of elections may be the only one of importance in which case the dating

Table 12.4 Baseline model, splitting the timing of elections, 1978–2004, 82 countries

Dummy = 1 if ΔCPIA>0	(1)	(2)	(3)	(4)	(5)	(6)
Dummy NEVER had an election		−1.159 (3.44)***	−1.169 (3.43)***	−0.970 (2.21)**	−0.949 (2.13)**	

Variables in interaction with a dummy FIRST HALF of the year

	(1)	(2)	(3)	(4)	(5)	(6)
Dummy ELECTION	0.044 (0.21)	0.068 (0.32)				
Dummy FIRST election			−0.868 (2.85)***	−0.871 (2.87)***	−0.691 (1.64)	−0.665 (1.56)
CYCLE			−0.008 (0.03)	−0.036 (0.16)	0.021 (0.09)	−0.008 (0.03)
CYCLE squared			0.073 (0.95)	0.075 (1.01)	0.067 (0.89)	0.069 (0.95)
FREQUENCY of elections			−0.149 (4.16)***	−0.150 (4.13)***	−0.114 (1.12)	−0.105 (1.00)
FREQUENCY squared					−0.001 (0.25)	−0.002 (0.34)

Variables in interaction with a dummy SECOND HALF of the year

	(1)	(2)	(3)	(4)	(5)	(6)
Dummy ELECTION	−0.250 (1.09)	−0.252 (1.06)				
Dummy FIRST election			−1.506 (4.05)***	−1.522 (4.03)***	−1.315 (2.79)***	−1.297 (2.67)***
CYCLE			0.143 (1.01)	0.154 (1.06)	0.128 (0.87)	0.139 (0.92)
CYCLE squared			−0.038 (2.69)***	−0.041 (2.83)***	−0.037 (2.52)**	−0.039 (2.66)***
FREQUENCY of elections			−0.206 (4.25)***	−0.211 (4.33)***	−0.120 (0.83)	−0.113 (0.77)
FREQUENCY squared					−0.008 (0.70)	−0.009 (0.76)
CPIA in level, lagged	−1.402 (8.09)***	−1.477 (8.33)***	−1.489 (8.66)***	−1.564 (8.88)***	−1.491 (8.63)***	−1.566 (8.84)***
Ln income p.c., lagged	3.774 (1.65)*	4.650 (1.73)*	3.002 (1.31)	3.862 (1.44)	2.962 (1.31)	3.800 (1.43)
Ln income p.c. squared, lagged	−0.270 (1.77)*	−0.331 (1.84)*	−0.228 (1.48)	−0.287 (1.58)	−0.226 (1.48)	−0.284 (1.58)
Secondary education, lagged	−0.006 (0.63)	−0.003 (0.13)	0.000 (0.05)	0.004 (0.17)	−0.001 (0.06)	0.002 (0.10)
Ln population, lagged	−1.126 (0.93)	−0.985 (0.84)	−0.764 (0.61)	−0.627 (0.52)	−0.836 (0.65)	−0.702 (0.57)
Resource rent, lagged	0.032 (1.87)*	0.028 (1.65)*	0.035 (2.22)**	0.032 (2.01)**	0.034 (2.19)**	0.032 (1.95)*
Dummy AT WAR	−0.792 (3.22)***	−0.798 (3.19)***	−0.772 (2.89)***	−0.779 (2.90)***	−0.775 (2.90)***	−0.779 (2.90)***

(continued overleaf)

Table 12.4 continued

Dummy = 1 if ΔCPIA>0	(1)	(2)	(3)	(4)	(5)	(6)
Δ Ln income p.c., lagged		−14.576 (2.74)***		−14.972 (2.87)***		−14.569 (2.84)***
Δ Ln income p.c. squared, lagged		1.107 (2.96)***		1.124 (2.99)***		1.100 (2.97)***
Δ Secondary education, lagged		−0.037 (0.19)		−0.031 (0.16)		−0.027 (0.14)
Δ Ln population, lagged		6.098 (0.97)		7.164 (1.06)		7.453 (1.08)
Δ Resource rent, lagged		0.003 (0.14)		0.002 (0.07)		0.003 (0.12)
Observations (countries)	1849 (82)	1849 (82)	1849 (82)	1849 (82)	1849 (82)	1849 (82)

Notes: Robust z statistics in parentheses. Standard errors are adjusted for intra-country correlation. * significant at 10%; ** significant at 5%; *** significant at 1%. DEPENDENT VARIABLE: Dummy = 1 when ΔCPIA is strictly positive. ESTIMATION METHOD: Logit with country fixed effects and year dummies, constant included but not shown. DATING OF ELECTIONS: The electoral dummy equals one in an election year and zero otherwise, no matter when during the year the election occurred. NEVER, FIRST, CYCLE and FREQUENCY are constructed according to this dating of elections. The dummies FIRST and SECOND half of the year are equal to one if the elections were held, respectively, before and after June. This dummy is equal to one during the whole duration of the mandate.

Table 12.5 Baseline model, alternative dating of elections, 1978–2004, 82 countries

Dummy = 1 if ΔCPIA>0	(1)	(2)	(3)	(4)	(5)	(6)
Dummy ELECTION (datation 2)	−0.246 (1.53)	−0.244 (1.48)				
Dummy NEVER had an election			−0.674 (2.07)**	−0.663 (2.03)**	−0.422 (1.09)	−0.391 (1.01)
Dummy FIRST election			−0.725 (2.47)**	−0.719 (2.46)**	−0.479 (1.33)	−0.451 (1.24)
CYCLE			0.217 (1.98)**	0.221 (1.99)**	0.216 (1.97)**	0.220 (1.97)**
CYCLE squared			−0.039 (3.12)***	−0.040 (3.16)***	−0.039 (3.14)***	−0.040 (3.17)***
FREQUENCY of elections			−0.141 (4.97)***	−0.142 (4.95)***	−0.059 (0.75)	−0.053 (0.64)
FREQUENCY squared					−0.005 (1.21)	−0.006 (1.29)
CPIA, lagged	−1.401 (8.09)***	−1.475 (8.34)***	−1.444 (8.68)***	−1.522 (8.92)***	−1.450 (8.59)***	−1.529 (8.83)***

	(1)	(2)	(3)	(4)	(5)	(6)
Ln income p.c., lagged	3.728	4.610	3.434	4.259	3.493	4.323
	(1.63)	(1.71)*	(1.51)	(1.60)	(1.56)	(1.65)*
Ln income p.c. squared, lagged	−0.267	−0.328	−0.255	−0.312	−0.259	−0.315
	(1.74)*	(1.83)*	(1.66)*	(1.73)*	(1.70)*	(1.78)*
Secondary education, lagged	−0.008	−0.004	−0.002	−0.000	−0.003	−0.002
	(0.73)	(0.18)	(0.24)	(0.00)	(0.34)	(0.08)
Ln population, lagged	−1.143	−1.003	−0.913	−0.782	−0.963	−0.832
	(0.94)	(0.86)	(0.76)	(0.67)	(0.79)	(0.70)
Resource rent updated, lagged	0.032	0.029	0.033	0.030	0.032	0.029
	(1.89)*	(1.66)*	(2.07)**	(1.83)*	(2.02)**	(1.74)*
Dummy AT WAR	−0.790	−0.795	−0.750	−0.756	−0.748	−0.752
	(3.22)***	(3.19)***	(2.90)***	(2.88)***	(2.89)***	(2.86)***
Δ Ln income p.c., lagged		−14.553		−14.999		−14.933
		(2.74)***		(2.94)***		(2.95)***
Δ Ln income p.c. squared, lagged		1.103		1.134		1.130
		(2.95)***		(3.08)***		(3.10)***
Δ Secondary education, lag		−0.039		−0.021		−0.016
		(0.20)		(0.11)		(0.08)
Δ Ln population, lagged		6.164		6.859		6.964
		(0.98)		(1.06)		(1.08)
Δ Resource rent, lagged		0.003		0.002		0.003
		(0.14)		(0.08)		(0.12)
Constant	4.023	−0.828	7.750	2.201	4.175	−0.617
	(0.24)	(0.05)	(0.46)	(0.12)	(0.26)	(0.04)
Observations	1849	1849	1849	1849	1849	1849
Countries	82	82	82	82	82	82
Turning point in CYCLE (years)			2.8	2.8	2.8	2.8

Notes: Robust z statistics in parentheses. Standard errors are adjusted for intra-country correlation.
* significant at 10%; ** significant at 5%; *** significant at 1%.

DEPENDENT VARIABLE: Dummy = 1 when Δ CPIA is strictly positive.

ESTIMATION METHOD: Logit with country fixed effects and year dummies.

SECOND DATING: The electoral dummy equals one in an election year if the election occurs after June and in the year before the election year it the election occurs before June. It is equal to zero otherwise. NEVER, FIRST, CYCLE and FREQUENCY are constructed according to this dating of elections.

of elections should be changed accordingly. In Table 12.5 we therefore re-run the regressions of Table 3 but with the revised dating and compare it with Table 12.3. There is little to choose between the two sets of regressions. On the criterion of the *p*-values of the two cyclical variables judged on the two core regressions of columns (3) and (4) the original dating slightly outperforms: three of the four *p*-values are higher. On the criterion of the other election variables the preference for the original dating is a little stronger: in particular, the *p*-values on the two election dummy variables drop considerably with when elections in the first half of the year are re-assigned to the previous year. Fortunately, the actual coefficients on the election variables are virtually unaltered. We therefore retain the calendar dating of elections, thereby implicitly giving legacy effects similar weight to anticipation effects. Quite possibly the anticipation effects are stronger than the legacy effects but not the entire story.

12.5 Robustness checks

In this section, we provide a set of robustness checks of our baseline model. The CPIA has often been contested and the first robustness check is therefore to estimate the baseline model using the ICRG as an alternative measure of policy and institutions. Moreover, the chosen empirical strategy potentially loses information by treating the CPIA as ordinal. Our second set of robustness checks therefore explores alternative estimation methods using equations (1) and (2). A third set of robustness checks provides estimations of our baseline model using Allan Drazen's database of elections. Using this dataset also allows to explore the potential endogeneity issue of our elections variables by distinguishing between constitutionally predetermined elections and endogenous elections. Finally, our fourth set of robustness checks focuses more specifically on the CYCLE variable and proposes alternative ways of measuring political cycles.

12.5.1 Estimations using the ICRG

Our first variant on these core results is to switch from the CPIA as a measure of policy improvement to the ICRG rating. Recall that the ICRG is a commercial rating and so is subject to the discipline of the market. However, it covers fewer countries than the World Bank rating and only a period starting in 1985.[3] Further, as the recent travails of the credit rating agencies indicate, the discipline of the market may in practice produce worse quality than that of an impartial public bureaucracy.

Table 12.6 reproduces the regressions of Table 12.3 with the dependent variable being a dummy which is equal to one when changes in the ICRG are positive. Among the control variables, it agrees with the World Bank data in finding that there has been an improvement in policy year-by-year that is unrelated to the other explanatory variables (the time dummies are not shown in the table). Hence, our former result is unlikely to be fully explained by grade inflation among World Bank staff. The result is important because it severs the secular improvement in policy from the spread of democracy.

As to our election variables, it finds the same cyclical and structural effects as using the CPIA data. Although CYCLE is not individually significant its square is and so the two variables should be assessed in terms of their joint

Table 12.6 Robustness checks using ICRG, 1985–2005, 70 countries

Dummy = 1 if ΔICRG>0	(1)	(2)	(3)	(4)	(5)	(6)
Dummy ELECTION	0.013 (0.07)	0.009 (0.05)				
Dummy NEVER had an election			−0.867 (1.09)	−0.939 (1.15)	−1.905 (2.00)**	−1.905 (1.93)*
Dummy FIRST election			−0.331 (0.63)	−0.419 (0.81)	−1.319 (1.81)*	−1.338 (1.81)*
CYCLE			0.083 (0.68)	0.087 (0.68)	0.074 (0.61)	0.078 (0.62)
CYCLE squared			−0.029 (2.04)**	−0.026 (1.82)*	−0.027 (1.95)*	−0.024 (1.70)*
FREQUENCY of elections			−0.019 (0.34)	−0.027 (0.45)	−0.337 (2.01)**	−0.323 (2.00)**
FREQUENCY squared					0.021 (2.08)**	0.020 (2.12)**
ICRG in level, lagged	−0.125 (6.93)***	−0.141 (7.42)***	−0.130 (7.32)***	−0.146 (7.83)***	−0.129 (7.21)***	−0.144 (7.74)***
Ln income p.c., lagged	0.951 (0.21)	0.791 (0.22)	0.471 (0.11)	0.440 (0.12)	0.733 (0.17)	0.611 (0.17)
Ln income p.c. squared, lagged	−0.033 (0.11)	−0.028 (0.12)	0.002 (0.01)	−0.001 (0.01)	−0.016 (0.06)	−0.015 (0.06)
Secondary education, lagged	−0.002 (0.06)	0.008 (0.20)	0.007 (0.17)	0.019 (0.46)	0.023 (0.55)	0.033 (0.79)
Ln population, lagged	−0.165 (0.10)	−0.624 (0.39)	0.289 (0.18)	−0.093 (0.06)	0.324 (0.20)	−0.097 (0.06)
Resource rent, lagged	0.026 (0.80)	0.025 (0.86)	0.021 (0.72)	0.020 (0.75)	0.021 (0.72)	0.020 (0.76)
Dummy AT WAR	−1.039 (2.56)**	−0.894 (1.97)**	−1.021 (2.59)***	−0.877 (1.99)**	−1.041 (2.69)***	−0.895 (2.06)**
Δ. Ln income p.c., lagged		10.492 (1.11)		9.946 (1.06)		9.708 (1.01)
Δ. Ln income p.c. squared, lagged		−0.297 (0.49)		−0.270 (0.45)		−0.249 (0.40)
Δ. Secondary education, lagged		0.128 (0.47)		0.135 (0.51)		0.109 (0.42)
Δ. Ln population, lagged		21.013 (3.00)***		21.138 (3.17)***		20.664 (3.19)***
Δ. Resource rent, lagged		0.046 (1.60)		0.049 (1.73)*		0.048 (1.70)*
Constant	5.244 (0.26)	12.929 (0.58)	1.733 (0.09)	7.951 (0.35)	1.065 (0.05)	8.231 (0.37)
Observations	1273	1273	1273	1273	1273	1273
Countries	70	70	70	70	70	70
Turning point in CYCLE (years)			1.4	1.7	1.4	1.6

(continued overleaf)

Table 12.6 continued

Dummy = 1 if ΔCPIA>0	(1)	(2)	(3)	(4)	(5)	(6)
Joint significance of CYCLE and its square (*p*-value)			0.019	0.033	0.025	0.049

Notes: Robust z statistics in parentheses. Standard errors are adjusted for intra-country correlation.
* significant at 10%; ** significant at 5%; *** significant at 1%.

DEPENDENT VARIABLE:	Dummy = 1 when Δ ICRG is strictly positive.
ESTIMATION METHOD:	Logit with country fixed effects and year dummies.
DATING OF ELECTIONS:	The electoral dummy equals one in an election year and zero otherwise, no matter when during the year the election occurred. NEVER, FIRST, CYCLE and FREQUENCY are constructed according to this dating of elections.

significance. The last row of Table 12.6 reports that CYCLE and its square are jointly significant at 5 per cent.

The ICRG gives more weight to institutions – rule of law, corruption, quality of bureaucracy, etc. – than the CPIA which is primarily focused on economic policy and structural economic reforms. A minor difference between Tables 12.3 and 12.6 is that FREQUENCY only becomes significantly negative once its square is introduced. Although the squared term is positive, within the relevant range of the data it almost never predominates. The turning point is in excess of 8 years which is found only in Liberia, Sierra Leone and Togo. The results are thus consistent with those of Table 12.3.

Finally, NEVER and FIRST have the same negative coefficient as in Table 12.3, but are less robustly significant.

12.5.2 Robustness of the estimation method: estimation of equations (1) and (2)

We next turn to robustness checks of the estimation method. More specifically, Table 12.7 presents the estimations of Equation (1) – assuming continuous CPIA – using three different estimation methods: within estimator, OLS on first-difference, and Arellano and Bond (1991) GMM estimator. It also presents the estimations of Equation (2) – assuming ordered CPIA – using an ordered probit model.

These results are presented in Table 12.7. The most striking result is the robustness of the CYCLE effect. In Table 12.7, the turning point is relatively stable, between 1.7 and 2.3, and close to that of Table 12.3. The coefficients on FREQUENCY, NEVER and FIRST are all always negative, as in Table 12.3, but they are each only significant in two of the regressions. Among the control variables, although the square of income is only significant in four of the regressions, it is always negative, as in Table 12.3.

Table 12.7 Robustness checks of the estimation method, 1978–2004, 82 countries

Estimation method	WITHIN		FIRST-DIFFERENCE		A&B GMM		ORDERED PROBIT	
	(1)	(2)	(3)	(4)	(5)	(6)	(7)	(8)
Dummy NEVER had an election	−0.093 (2.08)**	−0.144 (2.27)**	−0.083 (1.01)	−0.095 (0.74)	−0.028 (0.26)	−0.075 (0.42)	−0.126 (0.71)	−0.331 (1.38)
Dummy FIRST election	−0.075 (1.77)*	−0.125 (2.09)**	−0.080 (1.19)	−0.092 (0.78)	−0.031 (0.34)	−0.078 (0.47)	−0.080 (0.50)	−0.278 (1.29)
CYCLE	0.027 (1.97)*	0.027 (1.98)*	0.034 (2.24)**	0.034 (2.24)**	0.030 (1.68)*	0.030 (1.68)*	0.094 (1.71)*	0.092 (1.68)*
CYCLE squared	−0.006 (4.12)***	−0.006 (4.17)***	−0.010 (2.58)**	−0.009 (2.57)**	−0.007 (1.97)**	−0.007 (1.96)**	−0.021 (2.19)**	−0.020 (2.17)**
FREQUENCY of elections	−0.010 (1.74)*	−0.025 (1.49)	−0.013 (1.44)	−0.017 (0.54)	−0.008 (0.67)	−0.023 (0.55)	−0.029 (1.45)	−0.091 (1.66)*
FREQUENCY squared		0.001 (0.98)		0.000 (0.15)		0.001 (0.42)		0.004 (1.32)
CPIA, lagged	0.726 (36.73)***	0.727 (36.89)***	−0.049 (1.71)*	−0.049 (1.71)*	0.606 (11.49)***	0.605 (11.48)***	2.260 (19.46)***	2.264 (19.57)***
Ln income p.c., lagged	0.616 (1.86)*	0.612 (1.85)*	0.428 (0.63)	0.428 (0.63)	2.425 (2.65)***	2.440 (2.68)***	1.049 (0.88)	1.052 (0.88)
Ln income p.c. squared, lagged	−0.048 (2.08)**	−0.048 (2.07)**	−0.020 (0.42)	−0.020 (0.42)	−0.193 (3.05)***	−0.194 (3.08)***	−0.091 (1.12)	−0.091 (1.12)
Secondary education, lag	0.002 (1.81)*	0.002 (1.95)*	0.006 (0.91)	0.006 (0.91)	0.002 (0.43)	0.003 (0.47)	0.004 (1.09)	0.005 (1.27)
Ln population, lagged	−0.118 (0.77)	−0.112 (0.73)	−0.470 (0.76)	−0.468 (0.76)	−0.351 (0.59)	−0.344 (0.58)	−0.763 (1.60)	−0.740 (1.56)
Resource rent, lagged	−0.000 (0.14)	−0.000 (0.13)	0.004 (1.35)	0.004 (1.34)	0.006 (1.57)	0.006 (1.57)	−0.008 (1.22)	−0.008 (1.20)

(continued overleaf)

Table 12.7 continued

Estimation method	WITHIN		FIRST-DIFFERENCE		A&B GMM		ORDERED PROBIT	
	(1)	(2)	(3)	(4)	(5)	(6)	(7)	(8)
Dummy AT WAR	-0.119	-0.120	-0.096	-0.096	-0.052	-0.054	-0.283	-0.285
	(2.94)***	(2.97)***	(1.60)	(1.60)	(0.73)	(0.75)	(1.90)*	(1.91)*
Constant	1.205	1.171	0.045	0.045				
	(0.45)	(0.44)	(3.14)***	(3.12)***				
Observations (countries)	1849 (82)	1849 (82)	1771 (82)	1771 (2)	1771 (82)	1771 (82)	1849 (82)	1849 (82)
Turning point in CYCLE (years)	2.3	2.3	1.7	1.9	2.1	2.1	2.2	2.3
AR(1) [AR(2)] p-values					0.00 [0.23]	0.00 [0.23]		
Hansen test p-value [nb of instruments]					1.00 [97]	1.00 [97]		

Notes: Robust z statistics in parentheses. Standard errors are adjusted for intra-country correlation. * significant at 10%; ** significant at 5%; *** significant at 1%.

Columns (1) and (2): Within estimations of equation (1); dependent variable is continuous CPIA; estimations include year dummies.

Columns (3) and (4): Estimations in first-difference of equation (1); dependent variable is continuous ΔCPIA; estimations include year dummies.

Columns (5) and (6): Arellano and Bond GMM estimation of equation (1) transformed in first-difference; dependent variable is continuous ΔCPIA; estimations include year dummies; two-step estimator, using levels of CPIA from $t-2$ to $t-4$ as instruments for $\Delta CPIA_{i,t}$.

Columns (7) and (8): Estimation of ordered probit; the CPIA is ordered from 1 to 9 every 0.5 increment in the CPIA: estimations include year and country dummies.

Dating of elections: The electoral dummy equals one in an election year and zero otherwise, no matter when during the year the election occurred. NEVER, FIRST, CYCLE and FREQUENCY are constructed according to this dating of elections.

12.5.3 *Predetermined versus endogenous elections*

Our third set of robustness checks of the core results is to switch from the DPI data on elections to that used by Brender and Drazen (2005) and provided by Allan Drazen on his website. The switch to Drazen's data considerably shrinks the sample (see Appendix 12.3), however, it has one key advantage. Drazen distinguishes between those elections which were the result of a constitutionally mandated period between elections and those which were not. The former can be regarded as predetermined events whereas the latter are potentially far more seriously contaminated by endogeneity than the lagged elections used in our core analysis. The Drazen data thus enable us to test whether our core results are likely to be spurious. We first briefly discuss the results for all elections and then distinguish between predetermined and endogenous elections focusing upon the former.

Table 12.8 reproduces our core regression using Drazen's database. It reproduces the significant cyclical effects but the effects of FREQUENCY are not as robust. NEVER and FIRST still have negative coefficients in all columns but are not significant.

Within the set of all elections some can be considered as predetermined and other as potentially endogenous. Columns (1) and (2) of Table 12.9 distinguish between the two. Predetermined elections are those which are held within the expected year of the constitutionally fixed term (Brender and Drazen, 2005). Although there is a striking difference between the results for the exogenous and potentially endogenous elections, it is not troubling for our core results. The exogenous elections have results very similar to those of our core regressions. CYCLE is significantly positive, its square is significantly negative, and FREQUENCY or its square are negative and either significant or nearly so. It is the potentially endogenous elections which fail to generate significant results. This suggests that our core results are not the spurious consequence of endogeneity.

In columns (3) and (4) of Table 12.9, we turn back to using the DPI database and provide an alternative test of the distinction between predetermined and potentially endogenous elections. Unfortunately, the DPI database does not provide this kind of distinction. However, we can account for the regularity of elections. Regularly held elections are more likely to be predetermined than endogenous. We therefore construct a dummy REGULAR, which is equal to one for the countries which have had the same FREQUENCY of elections during the whole period following the first mandate. We then multiply this dummy with CYCLE and FREQUENCY. The interaction terms do not alter the results for CYCLE. The number of years away from elections which maximizes the chances of policy change is 2.7, close to the results of Table 12.3. In column (3), which replicates the form of our core regressions, the interaction terms are never significant, suggesting that the potential endogeneity of some elections is not an important issue in the regression. In column (4), where we introduce the square of FREQUENCY, its interaction

Table 12.8. Robustness checks using Drazen's database, 1978–2001, 39 countries

Dummy = 1 if $\Delta CPIA>0$	(1)	(2)	(3)	(4)
Dummy NEVER had an election	-0.887	-0.354	-0.641	-0.124
	(1.13)	(0.41)	(0.91)	(0.16)
Dummy FIRST election	-0.820	-0.336	-0.894	-0.427
	(1.84)*	(0.57)	(2.12)**	(0.75)
CYCLE	0.296	0.296	0.291	0.291
	(2.32)**	(2.33)**	(2.30)**	(2.30)**
CYCLE squared	-0.044	-0.044	-0.045	-0.045
	(2.66)***	(2.63)***	(2.61)***	(2.57)**
FREQUENCY of elections	-0.060	0.104	-0.060	0.099
	(1.76)*	(0.72)	(1.81)*	(0.69)
FREQUENCY squared		-0.006		-0.006
		(1.27)		(1.24)
CPIA, lagged	-1.997	-2.042	-1.976	-2.019
	(7.20)***	(7.32)***	(7.05)***	(7.15)***
Ln income p.c., lagged	-12.606	-12.437	-10.113	-9.897
	(1.26)	(1.27)	(1.11)	(1.10)
Ln income p.c. squared, lagged	0.640	0.635	0.495	0.487
	(1.07)	(1.08)	(0.90)	(0.90)
Secondary education, lagged	-0.015	-0.029	-0.002	-0.014
	(0.24)	(0.44)	(0.03)	(0.23)
Ln population, lagged	-6.426	-6.441	-5.245	-5.239
	(2.00)**	(2.06)**	(2.12)**	(2.17)**
Resource rent, lagged	-0.008	-0.010	-0.004	-0.007
	(0.26)	(0.37)	(0.15)	(0.24)
Dummy AT WAR	-0.909	-0.978	-0.956	-1.023
	(1.90)*	(1.97)**	(2.01)**	(2.09)**
Δ Ln income p.c., lagged	19.294	18.905	15.676	15.278
	(0.97)	(0.95)	(0.85)	(0.83)
Δ Ln income p.c. squared, lagged	-0.845	-0.828	-0.622	-0.605
	(0.72)	(0.71)	(0.57)	(0.56)
Δ Secondary education, lagged	0.609	0.646	0.542	0.575
	(1.68)*	(1.73)*	(1.50)	(1.55)
Δ Ln population, lagged	37.357	32.709	31.387	26.702
	(0.71)	(0.60)	(0.62)	(0.50)
Δ Resource rent, lagged	-0.015	-0.012	-0.015	-0.012
	(0.30)	(0.24)	(0.31)	(0.25)
Constant	156.388	155.092	128.638	124.969
	(2.14)**	(2.17)**	(2.23)**	(2.20)**
Observations	772	772	782	782
Countries	39	39	39	39
Turning point in CYCLE (years)	3.4	3.4	3.2	3.2

Notes: Robust z statistics in parentheses. Standard errors are adjusted for intra-country correlation. * significant at 10%; ** significant at 5%; *** significant at 1%. DEPENDENT VARIABLE: Dummy = 1 when Δ CPIA is strictly positive. ESTIMATION METHOD: Logit with country fixed effects and year dummies. ELECTION VARIABLES: From Drazen's database. Columns (1) and (2) restrict the sample to countries included in estimations using DPI database. Columns (3) and (4) are not restricted to a sub-set of our main database which uses DPI; this leads to adding information on more years for three countries (Hungary, Romania and Poland). DATING OF ELECTIONS: The electoral dummy equals one in an election year and zero otherwise, no matter when during the year the election occurred. NEVER, FIRST, CYCLE and FREQUENCY are constructed according to this dating of elections.

Table 12.9. Logit estimations of the baseline model, 1978–2001/2004, 39/82 countries

Dummy = 1 if ΔCPIA>0	DRAZEN		DPI	
	(1)	*(2)*	*(3)*	*(4)*
Dummy NEVER had an election	–0.643 (0.74)	0.703 (0.64)	–0.822 (2.04)**	–0.641 (1.37)
Dummy FIRST election	–0.604 (1.36)	0.638 (0.95)	–0.905 (2.82)***	–0.711 (1.71)*
Predetermined CYCLE	0.387 (2.50)**	0.360 (2.30)**		
Predetermined CYCLE squared	–0.057 (2.14)**	–0.050 (1.83)*		
Predetermined FREQUENCY of elections	–0.053 (1.52)	0.289 (1.79)*		
Predetermined FREQUENCY squared		–0.012 (2.26)**		
Endogenous CYCLE	0.116 (0.45)	0.156 (0.61)		
Endogenous CYCLE squared	–0.026 (1.08)	–0.031 (1.25)		
Endogenous FREQUENCY of elections	0.116 (0.82)	1.132 (2.15)**		
Endogenous FREQUENCY squared		–0.159 (1.60)		
CYCLE			0.235 (2.10)**	0.239 (2.13)**
CYCLE squared			–0.043 (3.79)***	–0.044 (3.86)***
FREQUENCY of elections			–0.153 (4.63)***	–0.098 (0.94)
FREQUENCY squared				–0.003 (0.54)
REGULAR × CYCLE			–0.183 (0.54)	–0.205 (0.60)
REGULAR × CYCLE squared			0.012 (0.22)	0.017 (0.32)
REGULAR × FREQUENCY of elections			0.094 (0.98)	0.895 (2.16)**
REGULAR × FREQUENCY squared				–0.165 (1.87)*
CPIA, lagged	–2.028 (7.15)***	–2.089 (7.07)***	–1.554 (8.55)***	–1.563 (8.46)***
Ln income p.c., lagged	–11.989 (1.20)	–15.557 (1.50)	4.097 (1.41)	4.066 (1.42)
Ln income p.c. squared, lagged	0.603 (1.01)	0.815 (1.32)	–0.305 (1.56)	–0.300 (1.55)
Secondary education, lagged	–0.002 (0.02)	–0.024 (0.37)	0.001 (0.04)	0.000 (0.01)
Ln population, lagged	–6.326 (1.95)*	–6.528 (2.04)**	–0.662 (0.55)	–0.636 (0.52)

(continued overleaf)

Table 12.9 continued

Dummy = 1 if ΔCPIA>0	DRAZEN		DPI	
	(1)	*(2)*	*(3)*	*(4)*
Resource rent, lagged	−0.002	−0.007	0.028	0.027
	(0.06)	(0.26)	(1.68)*	(1.57)
Dummy AT WAR	−0.973	−1.001	−0.767	−0.772
	(2.02)**	(2.02)**	(2.89)***	(2.90)***
Δ Ln income p.c., lagged	19.824	21.027	−15.053	−14.739
	(1.01)	(1.09)	(2.90)***	(2.83)***
Δ Ln income p.c. squared, lagged	−0.880	−0.958	1.136	1.114
	(0.75)	(0.84)	(3.03)***	(2.97)***
Δ Secondary education, lagged	0.614	0.606	−0.009	−0.009
	(1.70)*	(1.70)*	(0.05)	(0.05)
Δ Ln population, lagged	38.473	39.895	7.115	7.048
	(0.74)	(0.74)	(1.12)	(1.10)
Δ Resource rent, lagged	−0.017	−0.017	0.001	0.002
	(0.34)	(0.34)	(0.05)	(0.10)
Constant	152.100	174.355	−0.858	−1.350
	(2.06)**	(2.26)**	(0.05)	(0.07)
Observations (countries)	772 (39)	772 (39)	1849 (82)	1849 (82)

Notes: Robust z statistics in parentheses. Standard errors are adjusted for intra-country correlation. * significant at 10%; ** significant at 5%; *** significant at 1%. DEPENDENT VARIABLE: Dummy = 1 when Δ CPIA is strictly positive. ESTIMATION METHOD: Logit with country fixed effects and year dummies. DATING OF ELECTIONS: The electoral dummy equals one in an election year and zero otherwise, no matter when during the year the election occurred. NEVER, FIRST, CYCLE and FREQUENCY are constructed according to this dating of elections.

with the dummy for regular elections is borderline significant and negative, suggesting that endogeneity may perhaps be weakening the adverse effects of infrequent elections

12.5.5 *Alternative measures of CYCLE*

Finally our last set of robustness checks focuses on CYCLE. In the way we construct CYCLE, we implicitly assume some symmetry between the backward and forward-looking effects of elections discussed in Section 12.2. CYCLE is a mix of two variables: the time since the last election and the time to the next election. In the first column of Table 12.10 we reproduce the estimation of our baseline model. In columns (2) and (3), while retaining the composite CYCLE variable and its square, we add one of the two components, namely the number of years since the last election and its square. By introducing one of the two, we allow for some asymmetry in the treatment of these two components of CYCLE. If the two components had very different effects we would expect this to be revealed by significant coefficients on the added variable, positive or negative according to which component was key. In fact, adding these two variables does not alter the CYCLE result, nor the optimal year for policy change (around 2.8 years), and the added variables are insignificant.

Finally, in column (4), we disaggregate CYCLE into four dummy variables. The first one is equal to one in the year following and in the year preceding an election. The second dummy is equal to one in the second years following and preceding an election. Because the average FREQUENCY of elections in our sample is lower than 4 years, we create four dummies of this kind. However, adding more of them does not alter the results of column (4). The coefficients of these four variables gradually increase up to the third dummy and start decreasing for the fourth one. Consistently with our previous results, three years away from elections seems to be the best timing for policy improvement. However, this set of dummies is not significant. Only the third one is close to significance with a *p*-value of 0.11.

Table 12.10 Robustness to alternative measures of CYCLE, 1978–2004, 82 countries

Dummy = 1 if ΔCPIA>0	*(1)*	*(2)*	*(3)*	*(4)*
Dummy NEVER had an election	−0.986	−0.991	−0.988	−0.960
	(2.96)***	(2.96)***	(2.94)***	(2.83)***
Dummy FIRST election	−1.026	−1.038	−1.035	−0.982
	(3.47)***	(3.46)***	(3.42)***	(3.30)***
FREQUENCY of elections	−0.155	−0.156	−0.157	−0.155
	(4.70)***	(4.67)***	(4.67)***	(4.55)***
CYCLE	0.204	0.243	0.231	
	(1.92)*	(2.14)**	(1.84)*	
CYCLE squared	−0.041	−0.043	−0.042	
	(3.65)***	(3.75)***	(3.64)***	
Number of years since last election		−0.029	−0.016	
		(0.71)	(0.18)	
Number of years since last election, squared			−0.001	
			(0.25)	
One year away from past and next election				0.193
				(1.02)
Two years away from past and next election				0.252
				(1.36)
Three years away from past and next election				0.607
			(*p*-value = 0.114)	(1.58)
Four years away from past and next election				0.295
				(0.84)
CPIA, lagged	−1.545	−1.540	−1.540	−1.525
	(8.76)***	(8.76)***	(8.75)***	(8.87)***
Ln income p.c., lagged	4.055	3.624	3.527	4.324
	(1.51)	(1.22)	(1.19)	(1.68)*
Ln income p.c. squared, lagged	−0.300	−0.274	−0.269	−0.316
	(1.66)*	(1.40)	(1.38)	(1.80)*
Secondary education, lagged	0.001	0.000	0.001	0.001
	(0.03)	(0.02)	(0.03)	(0.03)
Ln population, lagged	−0.583	−0.532	−0.506	−0.712
	(0.49)	(0.45)	(0.42)	(0.61)

(continued overleaf)

Table 12.10 continued

Dummy = 1 if ΔCPIA>0	(1)	(2)	(3)	(4)
Resource rent, lagged	0.028	0.028	0.028	0.029
	(1.68)*	(1.62)	(1.61)	(1.78)*
Dummy AT WAR	−0.761	−0.749	−0.746	−0.784
	(2.89)***	(2.88)***	(2.84)***	(3.02)***
Δ Ln income p.c., lagged	−15.079	−15.086	−14.982	−13.550
	(2.91)***	(2.87)***	(2.80)***	(2.61)***
Δ Ln income p.c. squared, lagged	1.136	1.137	1.131	1.036
	(3.03)***	(3.00)***	(2.94)***	(2.76)***
Δ Secondary education, lagged	−0.002	−0.001	−0.002	−0.010
	(0.01)	(0.00)	(0.01)	(0.05)
Δ Ln population, lagged	7.037	6.759	6.739	6.236
	(1.09)	(1.05)	(1.05)	(0.98)
Δ Resource rent, lagged	0.002	0.002	0.002	0.002
	(0.09)	(0.10)	(0.09)	(0.07)
Constant	−1.636	−0.396	2.274	−1.346
	(0.09)	(0.02)	(0.12)	(0.08)
Observations	1849	1849	1849	1849
Countries	82	82	82	82
Turning point in CYCLE (years)	2.5	2.8	2.8	

Notes: Robust z statistics in parentheses. Standard errors are adjusted for intra-country correlation. * significant at 10%; ** significant at 5%; *** significant at 1%. DEPENDENT VARIABLE: Dummy = 1 when Δ CPIA is strictly positive. ESTIMATION METHOD: Logit with country fixed effects and year dummies. DATING OF ELECTIONS: The electoral dummy equals one in an election year and zero otherwise, no matter when during the year the election occurred. NEVER, FIRST, CYCLE and FREQUENCY are constructed according to this dating of elections.

12.6 Extensions

We now extend the analysis to investigate whether there are significant differences in our results according to the characteristics of countries.

Doubts over the efficacy of elections in developing countries are particularly centred on the scope for subverting them. Incumbents can resort to several illicit means of retaining power. Our results so far have suggested that accountability works: by requiring governments to attract votes, elections induce them to adopt improved economic policies and governance. Potentially, if governments can retain power by other means they need not adjust policies to those wanted by the electorate but not by politicians themselves. We first investigate whether there is any quantitative evidence that the conduct of elections indeed affects economic policy. For this we rely upon an ordinal indicator of the quality of elections (see Appendix 12.2 for a precise definition). As might be expected, this indicator is itself of doubtful value. In particular, it does not use the assessment of external monitors who now often rate elections according to whether they are 'free and fair'. However, it does assess them by the objective indicator of the proportion of seats won by the opposition. Unfortunately, while this is an indicator of whether the election was conducted in a manner than enabled the opposition to gain seats, it is also one that is evidently endogenous to government performance. Other things equal, an opposition will be more likely to win seats if the government has adopted, or looks likely to adopt, very poor economic policies. Hence, the quality indicator will be high not only in situations in which the electorate can indeed discipline the government by voting, but in situations in which the government has particularly failed to deliver what voters want. While we would expect the former effect to produce a positive link between the measured quality of elections and the chance of good policy, the latter effect is liable to produce the opposite association due to reverse causality. This provides an important caveat: our measure, QUALITY, is likely to be biased against clear results.

Table 12.11 presents the results. We introduce QUALITY both directly and interacted with the structural political variable FREQUENCY across all seven of our approaches. The direct effect of QUALITY is significant in two of these regressions when using the ICRG as dependent variable, in both being positive. The more important issue is whether, controlling for this direct effect, QUALITY affects the structural efficacy of elections. In three of the seven regressions the interaction is significant, and in a fourth it is close to being so, in all four cases being negative. Further, in all four the coefficient on FREQUENCY now changes sign and becomes positive, sometimes significantly so. Yet more striking, in two of the remaining three regressions where the interaction is not significant, its addition destroys the significantly negative direct effect of FREQUENCY, this being the channel that captures the structural accountability effect of elections. Only in the regression of column (1) in which the dependent variable is the direction of change in the CPIA does it survive, but this is contradicted by the ordered probit results for the CPIA in column (7), which arguably captures more information from the CPIA data, where the coefficient switches to being positive.

Taking these results as reliable for the moment, the meaning of this conjunction of coefficients is that frequent elections that are not of reasonable quality do not induce good economic policies and governance. On the contrary, they are more likely to lead to deterioration. It is only well-conducted elections that have the favourable structural effects on policy and governance. With the favourable structural effect lost, the only remaining effect of elections is cyclical: the further away is the society from an election the more likely is the government to improve policy and governance. However, this conclusion comes with a double caveat. The effect of QUALITY is notably less robust than our core results, and the variable, by its definition, is problematic.

Finally, we investigate whether our results hold for the particular circumstances of low-income countries and most especially, for those among them

Table 12.11 Quality of elections, 1978–2004 on 82 countries for CPIA, 1985–2005 on 70 countries for ICRG

Dependent variable Estimation method	Dummy = 1 when Δ>0 LOGIT + FE		Continuous WITHIN		Continuous FIRST-DIFFERENCE		Ordered CPIA (0–9) ORDERED PROBIT
	CPIA (1)	ICRG (2)	CPIA (3)	ICRG (4)	CPIA (5)	ICRG (6)	CPIA (7)
Dummy NEVER had an election	-0.766 (1.26)	-0.179 (0.16)	-0.002 (0.02)	0.301 (0.30)	-0.093 (0.85)	-0.027 (0.02)	0.432 (1.40)
Dummy FIRST election	-0.738 (1.20)	0.298 (0.29)	0.027 (0.30)	0.209 (0.22)	-0.090 (0.84)	-0.118 (0.10)	0.534 (1.70)*
CYCLE	0.218 (2.02)**	0.062 (0.49)	0.029 (2.11)**	-0.068 (0.47)	0.034 (2.18)**	0.104 (0.77)	0.102 (1.86)*
CYCLE squared	-0.042 (3.70)***	-0.024 (1.68)*	-0.006 (4.22)***	-0.028 (1.80)*	-0.009 (2.52)**	-0.054 (1.81)*	-0.022 (2.30)**
FREQUENCY of elections	-0.177 (2.12)**	0.181 (1.34)	-0.001 (0.09)	0.330 (2.44)**	-0.014 (0.70)	0.240 (1.43)	0.041 (0.95)
QUALITY of elections (1–7)	0.055 (0.50)	0.159 (0.99)	0.022 (1.38)	0.310 (1.76)*	-0.002 (0.12)	0.266 (1.39)	0.131 (2.25)**
FREQUENCY × QUALITY	0.007 (0.37)	-0.045 (1.81)*	-0.002 (0.69)	-0.090 (3.03)***	0.000 (0.08)	-0.077 (2.47)**	-0.015 (1.58) (p-value= 0.113)
Dependent variable in level, lagged	-1.569 (8.51)***	-0.146 (7.76)***	0.725 (35.94)***	0.799 (38.46)***	-0.049 (1.70)*	0.152 (4.97)***	2.258 (19.43)***
Ln income p.c., lagged	3.925 (1.45)	0.438 (0.12)	0.604 (1.79)*	1.750 (0.35)	0.428 (0.63)	20.359 (1.58)	1.059 (0.85)
Ln income p.c. squared, lagged	-0.295 (1.63)	0.001 (0.00)	-0.047 (2.04)**	-0.171 (0.51)	-0.020 (0.42)	-1.042 (1.22)	-0.092 (1.09)
Secondary education, lagged	0.001 (0.04)	0.025 (0.60)	0.002 (1.92)*	0.039 (0.70)	0.006 (0.90)	0.099 (0.55)	0.006 (1.38)

	(1)	(2)	(3)	(4)	(5)	(6)	(7)
Ln population, lagged	−0.549	13.216	−0.473	1.610	−0.076	−0.075	−0.393
	(1.13)	(1.42)	(0.77)	(0.87)	(0.49)	(0.05)	(0.32)
Resource rent, lagged	−0.008	0.169	0.004	0.051	−0.000	0.019	0.028
	(1.34)	(3.92)***	(1.35)	(1.26)	(0.18)	(0.71)	(1.72)*
Dummy AT WAR	−0.269	−1.635	−0.096	−1.216	−0.117	−0.894	−0.749
	(1.81)*	(2.59)**	(1.60)	(1.79)*	(2.90)***	(2.03)**	(2.82)***
Δ. Ln income p.c., lagged						9.177	−14.794
						(0.95)	(2.92)***
Δ. Ln income p.c. squared, lagged						−0.223	1.123
						(0.36)	(3.05)***
Δ. Secondary education, lagged						0.129	−0.003
						(0.49)	(0.02)
Δ. Ln population, lagged						20.044	7.408
						(3.17)***	(1.13)
Δ Resource rent updated, lagged						0.049	0.003
						(1.72)*	(0.15)
Constant		0.515	0.045	−20.575	0.472	6.848	−0.037
		(2.58)**	(3.12)***	(0.78)	(0.17)	(0.31)	(0.00)
Observations (countries)	1849 (82)	1206 (70)	1771 (82)	1273 (70)	1849 (82)	1273 (70)	1849 (82)

Notes: All regressions include year dummies. Robust z statistics in parentheses. Standard errors are adjusted for intra-country correlation. * significant at 10%; ** significant at 5%; *** significant at 1% The electoral dummy equals one in an election year and zero otherwise, no matter when during the year the election occurred. NEVER, FIRST, CYCLE and FREQUENCY are constructed according to this dating of elections. (1): p-value.

which have had a phase of very poor policies and governance. In Table 12.12, columns (1) to (4) the sample is restricted to low-income countries. We might expect that with the reduction in sample size there would be some loss of significance and this is indeed the case. However, in the core regression of column (1) the three key election variables all remain significant and their coefficients are virtually identical to the results from the full sample of developing countries. Hence, there appears to be no important distinctive effect of low income.

In regressions (5) to (8) we further restrict the sample to 'failing states', these being countries which at some time during the observed period had very poor policies, defined as a CPIA score below 2.5. This level is commonly recognized by World Bank staff as being a threshold below which policies and governance are seen as overall highly problematic. Column (5) reruns our core regression. All five election variables remain significant. This is an important result in that it suggests that our analysis is applicable in these contexts in which the improvement of economic policies and governance is most needed. The coefficient on FREQUENCY, which we have suggested captures the structural effect of accountability to the electorate, is virtually identical to that for the entire sample: elections appear to produce accountability over a wide range of economic development. The coefficients on CYCLE and its square are both somewhat larger than those for the full sample. Since the full sample of course contains this sub-sample it suggests that the cyclical effects may be more pronounced in failing states than in other developing countries.

The final results concern the effects of adding QUALITY interacted with FREQUENCY to the regressions, both for low-income countries in general and failing states in particular. As we have just seen in Table 12.11, in our core CPIA regession (though in that alone) on our full sample of developing countries the direct effect of FREQUENCY remains significant. Now, on both our sub-samples, (columns (3) and (7)) it completely loses significance. The interaction terms themselves are not significant either in these two regressions, so not too much can be made of them. However, we may conclude weakly that in these societies there is little basis for believing that elections are structurally effective in disciplining governments into good policies regardless of their conduct.

12.7 Implications and conclusions

Economic policy is critical for prosperity and so how it is shaped is of enormous importance for developing societies. It is now widely accepted that the struggle for good economic policies and governance is predominantly an internal process within these societies rather than something that can be imposed from outside by means of policy conditionality.

Since the fall of the Soviet Union both pressure from the international community and internal pressures within these societies have promoted elections. This first wave of change is now largely complete: almost all societies have

Table 12.12 Estimation on failing states and low income countries

Dummy = 1 if ΔCPIA/ΔICRG >0	LOW-INCOME				FAILING STATES			
	(1)	(2)	(3)	(4)	(5)	(6)	(7)	(8)
	CPIA	ICRG	CPIA	ICRG	CPIA	ICRG	CPIA	ICRG
Dummy NEVER had an election	-0.612 (1.26)	-0.565 (0.48)	0.335 (0.28)	1.106 (0.65)	-0.797 (1.78)*	-1.431 (0.99)	-0.444 (0.54)	-1.188 (0.60)
Dummy FIRST election	-0.561 (1.29)	-0.531 (0.58)	0.413 (0.37)	1.178 (0.68)	-0.757 (2.03)**	-1.216 (1.33)	-0.365 (0.48)	-1.018 (0.56)
CYCLE	0.240 (1.71)*	0.124 (0.65)	0.242 (1.59)	0.095 (0.48)	0.316 (2.19)**	0.043 (0.27)	0.327 (2.18)**	0.031 (0.19)
CYCLE squared	-0.044 (3.33)***	-0.032 (1.56)	-0.044 (3.10)***	-0.031 (1.52)	-0.052 (3.69)***	-0.021 (1.27)	-0.053 (3.65)***	-0.020 (1.22)
FREQUENCY of elections	-0.157 (3.12)***	0.040 (0.50)	-0.012 (0.06)	0.371 (1.81)*	-0.157 (4.00)***	0.060 (0.73)	-0.128 (1.04)	0.132 (0.61)
QUALITY of elections (1–7)			0.263 (1.00)	0.439 (1.72)*			0.099 (0.67)	0.050 (0.18)
FREQUENCY × QUALITY			-0.042 (0.69)	-0.088 (2.03)**			-0.007 (0.22)	-0.019 (0.43)
Dependent in level, lagged	-1.421 (5.84)***	-0.128 (4.28)***	-1.421 (5.70)***	-0.133 (4.17)***	-1.461 (5.52)***	-0.134 (4.65)***	-1.463 (5.40)***	-0.136 (4.55)***
Ln income p.c., lagged	7.555 (2.05)**	-8.556 (1.09)	7.656 (2.21)**	-7.533 (0.91)	4.232 (1.25)	-8.252 (1.13)	4.100 (1.24)	-7.095 (0.88)
Ln income p.c. squared, lagged	-0.561 (2.09)**	0.644 (1.16)	-0.567 (2.23)**	0.582 (0.98)	-0.304 (1.23)	0.611 (1.20)	-0.299 (1.23)	0.532 (0.95)
Secondary education, lagged	).006 (0.13)	0.052 (0.56)	0.001 (0.03)	0.086 (0.76)	-0.037 (0.66)	-0.017 (0.17)	-0.041 (0.70)	-0.013 (0.12)
Ln population, lagged	3.444 (1.50)	-8.461 (2.00)**	3.553 (1.52)	-8.044 (1.79)*	4.242 (1.86)*	-8.874 (1.90)*	4.288 (1.86)*	-8.599 (1.80)*

(continued overleaf)

Table 12.12 continued

Dummy = 1 if ΔCPIA/ΔICRG >0	LOW-INCOME				FAILING STATES			
	(1)	(2)	(3)	(4)	(5)	(6)	(7)	(8)
	CPIA	ICRG	CPIA	ICRG	CPIA	ICRG	CPIA	ICRG
Resource rent, lagged	0.050	0.064	0.049	0.060	0.033	0.049	0.034	0.047
	(2.71)***	(1.11)	(2.83)***	(0.93)	(1.92)*	(1.02)	(2.03)**	(0.95)
Dummy AT WAR	-0.358	-0.478	-0.372	-0.584	-0.562	-0.609	-0.550	-0.610
	(0.76)	(0.72)	(0.79)	(0.86)	(1.18)	(0.94)	(1.16)	(0.95)
Δ Ln income p.c., lagged	-5.187	13.769	-5.761	11.451	-5.300	2.918	-4.289	2.034
	(0.49)	(0.79)	(0.45)	(0.71)	(0.53)	(0.19)	(0.39)	(0.14)
Δ Ln income p.c. squared, lagged	0.336	-0.536	0.369	-0.382	0.358	0.200	0.285	0.263
	(0.43)	(0.46)	(0.40)	(0.35)	(0.49)	(0.19)	(0.36)	(0.27)
Δ Secondary education, lagged	-0.383	0.709	-0.302	0.938	-0.111	0.406	-0.043	0.388
	(1.00)	(0.79)	(0.79)	(1.04)	(0.36)	(0.49)	(0.13)	(0.48)
Δ Ln population, lagged	18.126	36.626	17.505	36.222	13.228	42.179	13.249	41.664
	(1.91)*	(3.68)***	(1.77)*	(3.69)***	(1.42)	(2.42)**	(1.42)	(2.39)**
Δ Resource rent, lagged	-0.013	0.016	-0.011	0.016	-0.004	0.026	-0.004	0.026
	(0.44)	(0.34)	(0.41)	(0.30)	(0.13)	(0.52)	(0.13)	(0.52)
Constant	-70.753	215.105	-73.745	193.769	-70.895	155.325	-72.105	147.270
	(2.59)***	(2.69)***	(2.31)**	(2.43)**	(2.71)***	(2.74)***	(2.45)**	(2.64)***
Observations (countries)	834 (35)	509 (27)	834 (35)	509 (27)	811 (34)	488 (26)	811 (34)	488 (26)
Joint-significance of CYCLE and its square	0.000	0.041	0.000	0.035	0.000	0.057	0.000	0.052
Turning point in CYCLE (years)	2.7	1.9	2.8	1.5	3.0	1.0	3.1	0.8

Notes: Robust z statistics in parentheses. Standard errors are adjusted for intra-country correlation. * significant at 10%; ** significant at 5%; *** significant at 1%.
DEPENDENT VARIABLE: Dummy = 1 when ΔCPIA / ΔICRG is strictly positive.
ESTIMATION METHOD: Logit with country fixed effects and year dummies.
DATING OF ELECTIONS: The electoral dummy equals one in an election year and zero otherwise, no matter when during the year the election occurred. NEVER, FIRST, CYCLE and FREQUENCY are constructed according to this dating of elections.

elections. Potentially, elections are the key institutional technology of democracy than enables citizens to hold governments to account. While the potential may seem self-evident, quantitative political science research has become rather sceptical of the efficacy of democracy in improving economic performance: the broad conclusion is that there is little if any overall relationship. This paper has revisited the relationship, focusing upon policy choices instead of economic performance, and on elections as events instead of generalized ratings of the extent to which the country is democratic. We have investigated whether elections have forced governments into policy improvement.

We have found that elections have two offsetting effects. Because they are offsetting, unless they are distinguished the results are liable to be confused. Indeed, we showed that with a naïve approach of introducing a dummy variable for elections into a regression, elections appear to have no effect: as with the political science literature, this key aspect of democracy washes over the process of policy setting without trace. We might note that it is probably only by focusing on developing countries that these two effects can be distinguished: in developed countries there is liable to be too little variation, especially over time.

However, once the two effects are separately distinguished, each is clear and robust. Elections in developing countries have cyclical effects on policy. The instinct of President Obasanjo of Nigeria that 'the last year would be politics' was quite consistent with our results: periods in the vicinity of elections are less propitious for policy improvement. How powerful is the cycle. In Figure 12.1 we show the probability of policy improvement year-by-year at the mean of other characteristics for an electoral cycle of six years. The probability increases from 0.37 in the year of the election to 0.44 during the mid-term. Hence, the effect is not large but worth bearing in mind: by choosing the right moment for change the probability of success is increased by around 20 per cent. In this sense, elections are bad news for policy improvement, but not very bad news.

More important than this cyclical effect is the structural effect of elections. They indeed produce accountability of government to citizens. The degree to which they do this depends upon their frequency: the more frequent the better. The net effect of higher frequency has to be computed while allowing for the implications of each frequency for the cyclical effects: a lower frequency reduces the adverse effect of an election year compared to the mid-terms. The net effect of different frequencies on the probability of policy improvement is shown in Figure 12.2. The effects are large: taking the extremes of the range, shifting from an election once a decade to an election each year would almost double the chance of policy improvement in the average year. Since our core results are robust whether they are done in levels or differences, this statement about policy improvement can be reformulated as one about the eventual level of policy: frequent elections produce better policy.

Does this mean that concerns about elections are unwarranted? Our extension of the analysis to allow for variations in the quality of the conduct of

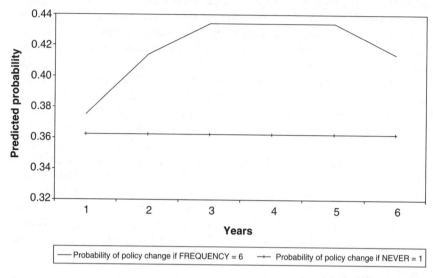

Figure 12.1 Predicted probability of policy change when FREQUENCY is six years.

elections suggests that there is indeed a sound basis for concern. While the results are less robust, there is a reasonable basis for concluding that if elections are badly conducted they lose their structural efficacy for policy improvement. This is surely what would be expected. Where governments resort to illicit means of securing electoral victory, such as bribery, ballot fraud and voter intimidation, they are released from the discipline of adopting good policies in order to win votes. Indeed, in order to resort to such strategies they may well need to adopt bad policies. An election which is not

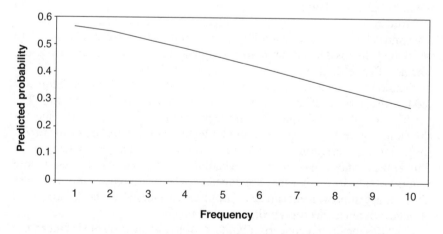

Figure 12.2 Predicted probability of policy change depending on FREQUENCY.

'free and fair' is a broken technology: it cannot be expected to hold governments accountable to citizens.

Hence, the overall conclusion from our analysis is that the frequency and conduct of elections matter. Of course, accountability to citizens can reasonably be viewed as a good in itself. However, our results suggest that it is also efficacious for economic policy and that elections are a key instrument in achieving accountability. Elections fail to achieve accountability if they are infrequent, and if they are mis-conducted.

For international policy to promote development the results have an important, if uncomfortable, implication. It is widely accepted that good economic policy is critical to successful development. In the past the main approaches to foster good policy have been donor policy conditionality and technical assistance for 'capacity-building' but neither of these has had much success. Our results suggest that the route to policy improvement is through accountability of governments to their citizens through proper elections. To the extent that this process has failed it is because governments have subverted the electoral process. Hence, the international community needs to use its influence to reinforce the regular holding of elections and ensure that they are conducted to high standards. The development discourse of the last decade, replete with expressions such as 'partnership', 'country-led', and 'clients', has critiqued the previous emphasis of the World Bank on good economic policies as measured by the CPIA as being incompatible with the preferences of these societies themselves: local preferences were being overridden. Yet when citizens are able to hold their governments to account, they appear to want a better CPIA. The task for the international community is thus to promote the effective accountability of government to citizen. For example, conditioning aid upon the proper conduct of regular elections appears, on the basis of our evidence, to be a reasonable use of aid for development.

Appendix 12.1: Definition of the Country Policy and Institutional Assessment (CPIA)

A. Economic management
  1. Management of inflation and macroeconomic imbalances
  2. Fiscal policy
  3. Management of external debt
  4. Management and sustainability of the development program

B. Structural policies
  1. Trade policy and foreign exchange regime
  2. Financial stability and depth
  3. Banking sector efficiency and resource mobilization
  4. Competitive environment for the private sector
  5. Factor and product markets
  6. Policies and institutions for environmental sustainability

C. Policies for social inclusion / equity
   1. Gender
   2. Equity of public resource use
   3. Building human resources
   4. Social protection and labour
   5. Monitoring and analysis of poverty outcomes and impacts

D. Public sector management and institutions
   1. Property rights and rule-based governance
   2. Quality of budgetary and financial management
   3. Efficiency of revenue mobilization
   4. Quality of public administration
   5. Transparency, accountability and corruption in the public sector

---

Note: Each of the 20 components of the CPIA is rated on a scale of 1–6.

Appendix 12.2: Sources for Data

CPIA   Country Policy and Institutional Assessment (World Bank). See Appendix 1.

ICRG   Composite indicator of political stability, economic stability and financial stability. It is rated from 0 (bad policy and institutions) to 100 (good policy and institutions). Source: International Country risk Guide, Political Risk Services. http://www.prsgroup.com/

Income per capita   Real gross domestic product per capita ($ in 1996 constant prices), Penn World Tables 6.1. http://pwt.econ.upenn.edu/

Population   World Development Indicators of the World Bank (2005).

Secondary education   R. Barro and J.W. Lee (2000) dataset. Percentage of the population who completed secondary education (population aged 25 and above). http://www.cid.harvard.edu/ciddata/ciddata.html

Resource Rents   Natural resource rents (percentage of GDP). Resource Rents are calculated by summing the total value of rents for all extractive (i.e. non agricultural) resources. These values are in current US$ and are then divided by GDP in current US$. Source: Collier and Hoeffler (2005).

Dummy at war   Dummy equals one during civil war. Correlates of War (Singer and Small, 1994; Small and Singer, 1982). http://www.correlatesofwar. org/. It is updated using the PRIO database (www.prio.no/CSCW/Datasets/ Armed-Conflict/)

Elections   Database of Political Institutions (Beck *et al.*, 2001) of the World Bank. http://econ.worldbank.org/WBSITE/EXTERNAL/EXTDEC/ EXTRESEARCH/0,,contentMDK:20649465~pagePK:64214825~piPK: 64214943~theSitePK:469382,00.html

We use executive elections for presidential systems and legislative elections for parliamentary systems.

FREQUENCY: the number of years between election in year *t* and the previous election. This number is reported for each year of the mandate.

CYCLE: the number of years that separate year *t* from the nearest election, whether this is the previous election or the next election.

NEVER: dummy which is equal to one if the country never had an election.

FIRST: dummy which is equal to one during the first mandate.

QUALITY: quality of previous election. It is constructed using the EIEC and LIEC variables of the DPI database (respectively Executive and Legislative Indices of Electoral Competitiveness). It takes the values: 1: No legislature; 2: Unelected legislature; 3: Elected, 1 candidate; 4: 1 party, multiple candidates; 5: multiple parties are legal but only one party won seats; 6: multiple parties did win seats but the largest party received more than 75 per cent of the seats; 7: largest party got less than 75 per cent. If, for example, elections occur in years *t* and *t+4*, we report the value of EIEC/LIEC in *t* (depending on whether the political system is presidential or parliamentary) during the whole duration of the mandate starting in *t+4*.

We also use the database on elections used by Brender and Drazen (2005). http://www.econ.umd.edu/~drazen/

Appendix 12.3: Sample

Developing countries in the main sample	*Using ICRG data*	*Using DRAZEN data*
Algeria	x	x
Argentina	x	x
Barbados		
Belize		
Bolivia	x	x
Botswana	x	
Brazil	x	x
Bulgaria	x	x
Chile	x	x
China	x	
Colombia	x	x
Costa Rica	x	x
Croatia	x	
Czech Republic	x	x
Dominican Rep.	x	x
Ecuador	x	x
El Salvador	x	x
Fiji		x
Guatemala	x	x
Hungary	x	x
India	x	x

(continued overleaf)

Appendix 12.3: continued

Developing countries in the main sample	Using ICRG data	Using DRAZEN data
Jamaica	x	
Jordan	x	
Kenya	x	
Korea	x	x
Malawi	x	
Malaysia	x	x
Mauritius		x
Mexico	x	x
Panama	x	x
Paraguay	x	x
Peru	x	x
Philippines	x	x
Poland	x	x
Romania	x	x
Russia	x	x
Slovakia	x	x
South Africa	x	x
St. Lucia		
Swaziland		
Syria	x	
Thailand	x	
Trinidad and Tobago	x	x
Tunisia	x	
Turkey	x	x
Uruguay	x	x
Venezuela	x	x
Western Samoa		

Failing States in the main sample	Using ICRG data	Using DRAZEN data
Bangladesh	x	
Benin		
Burundi		
Cameroon	x	
Central African Rep.		
Congo, Rep.	x	
Democratic Rep. Of Congo	x	
Egypt	x	
Ethiopia	x	
Gambia	x	
Ghana	x	
Haiti	x	
Honduras	x	x
Indonesia	x	
Lesotho		
Liberia	x	
Mali	x	x
Mauritania		
Mozambique	x	
Nepal		x

Nicaragua	x	x
Niger	x	
Papua New Guinea	x	x
Pakistan	x	x
Rwanda		
Senegal	x	
Sierra Leone	x	
Sri Lanka	x	x
Sudan	x	
Togo	x	
Uganda	x	
Vietnam		
Zambia	x	
Zimbabwe	x	

Notes

1 Personal communication to one of the authors.
2 We also reconstruct FREQUENCY of elections using Drazen's database. This further allows us to tackle the endogeneity issue of the timing of elections by distinguishing between predetermined and endogenous elections (see Section 12.5 on robustness checks).
3 Three countries are in the ICRG database but not in the CPIA one: Bahrain, Iran and Iraq. We ran the estimations with and without these countries and it did not change our results. Moreover, the ICRG is available for more recent years than the CPIA. Therefore Table 12.6 covers 2005, while Table 12.3 stopped in 2004.

References

Alesina A. and E. La Ferrara (2005). 'Ethnic Diversity and Economic Performance'. *Journal of Economic Literature* XLIII(3), 762–801.
Arellano M. and S. Bond (1991). 'Some Tests of Specification for Panel Data: Monte Carlo Evidence and an Application to Employment Equations'. *Review of Economic Studies* 58, 277–297.
Barro R.J. and J-W. Lee (2000). *International Data on Educational Attainment: Updates and Implications.* CID Working Paper 42, Harvard University.
Besley T. (2006). *Principled Agents?* Princeton NJ: Princeton University Press.
Block S. A. (2002). 'Political Business Cycles, Democratization, and Economic Reform: the Case of Africa'. *Journal of Development Economics* 67, 205–228.
Bossuroy T. (2007). *Voting in an African Democracy: Does only Ethnicity Rule?* EHESS, Paris School of Economics, DIAL, mimeo.
Brender A. and A. Drazen (2005). *Political Budget Cycles in New versus Established Democracies.* Bank of Israel Discussion Paper 2005.04.
Collier, P. (2001). 'Implications of Ethnic Diversity'. *Economic Policy* 16, 127–166.
Collier P. and A. Hoeffler (2008). 'Testing the Neocon Agenda: Democracy in Resource-Rich Societies', *European Economic Review.*
Collier P. and D. Rohner (2008). 'Democracy, Development and Conflict', *Journal of the European Economic Association.*

Collier P. and P. C. Vicente (2008). *Votes and Violence: Experimental Evidence from a Nigerian Election*, Department of Economics, Oxford University, CSAE, mimeo.

Collier P. (2009). *Wars, Guns and Votes: Democracy in Dangerous Places*, New York: Random House.

Dercon S., M. Bratton, M. Kimenyi, R. Gutierrez-Romero and T. Bold (2008), Ethnicity and the 2007 Elections in Kenya, mimeo, Centre for the Study of African Economies, Oxford.

Drazen, A. (2000). *Political Economy in Macroeconomics*. Princeton NJ: Princeton University Press.

Feng Y. (2003). *Democracy, Governance and Economic Performance: Theory and Evidence*. Cambridge, MA: MIT Press.

Fridy K. (2007). 'The Elephant, Umbrella and Quarrelling Cocks: Disaggregating Partisanship in Ghana's Fourth Republic'. *African Affairs* 106, 423.

Beck T., Clarke G., Groff A., P. Keefer and P. Walsh (2001). 'New Tools in Comparative Political Economy: The Database of Political Institutions'. *World Bank Economic Review* 15(1), 165–176.

Judson R.A. and A.L. Owen (1999). 'Estimating Dynamic Panel Data Models: A Guide for Macroeconomists'. *Economic Letters* 65, 9–15.

Kudamatsu M. (2007). 'Has Democracy Reduced Infant Mortality in sub-Saharn Africa?' LSE, mimeo.

Nickell S. (1981). 'Biases in Dynamic Modems with Fixed Effects'. *Econometrica* 49, 1417–1426.

Przeworski A., M.E. Alvarez, J.A. Cheibub, F. Limongi (2000). *Democracy and Development: Political Institutions and Wellbeing in the World, 1950–90*. Cambridge: Cambridge University Press.

Tavares J. and R. Wacziarg (2001). 'How Democracy Affects Growth'. *European Economic Review* 45, 1341–1378.

Sevestre P. and A. Trognon (1985). 'A Note on Autoregressive Error-Components Models'. *Journal of Econometrics* 29, 231–245.

Singer J. D. and M. Small (1994). *Correlates of war project: International and civil war data, 1816–1992*. Ann Arbor MI: Inter-University Consortium for Political and Social Research.

Shi M. and J. Svensson (2006). 'Political Budget Cycles: Do They Differ Across Countries and Why?' *Journal of Public Economics* 90, 1367–1389.

Small M. and J.D. Singer (1982). *Resort to Arms: International and Civil War, 1816–1980*, Beverly Hills CA: Sage.

Vicente P. (2007). Is Vote-Buying Effective? Evidence from a Randomized Experiment in West Africa. Mimeo, CSAE, Oxford.

Wantcheckon L. (2003). 'Clientalism and Voting Behaviour: Evidence from a Field Experiment in Benin'. *World Politics* 55, 399–422.

Part III
Aid and trade

13 Aid allocation and poverty reduction

With David Dollar

13.1 Introduction

The allocation of aid among countries can legitimately reflect multiple objectives. Aid may be used to rebuild post-conflict societies, to meet humanitarian emergencies, or to support the strategic or commercial interests of the aid-giver. However, one core objective most commonly cited to support aid programs is poverty reduction. In this chapter, we estimate the allocation of aid that would maximize the reduction in poverty and compare it to actual allocations. Our principal finding is that the poverty impact of aid could be roughly doubled if donors made use of recent research findings on the impact of aid in deciding their aid allocation. To the extent that donors are interested in poverty reduction, the estimated 'poverty-efficient' allocation is directly useful for policy-makers. But, even where donors wish to pursue other objectives, this allocation is also useful, because it provides information on the opportunity cost (in terms of poverty reduction) of pursuing other objectives with aid resources.

The recent results that donors need to take account of are that:

- the impact of aid on growth depends on the quality of economic policies and is subject to diminishing returns (Isham and Kaufmann, 1999; Burnside and Dollar, 2000);
- there is a wide range of different evidence that the quantity of aid does not systematically affect the quality of policies – even with 'conditionality' (Collier, 1997; Williamson, 1994; Rodrik, 1996; Alesina and Dollar, 2000); and
- aid resources are typically fungible, so that it is difficult for donors to target them to particular groups or use them to alter the distribution of income (Pack and Pack, 1993; Feyzioglu *et al.*, 1998).

In Section 13.2 we revisit the first result above, using a broad measure of policy and a larger number of countries than covered in previous analyses. We confirm that the marginal efficiency of aid in terms of increases in income depends on the quality of policies and on the amount of aid that a country is receiving (diminishing returns). In Section 13.3 we consider the donor's optimization problem, if the objective is to reduce poverty and if the donor takes as given the quality of policies and the distribution of income in aid-receiving countries. We derive an algorithm for the 'poverty-efficient' allocation of aid among countries that has a simple, intuitive logic: holding the level of poverty constant, aid should increase with policy (because it has a larger growth impact in the better policy environment); and, holding policy constant, it should increase with poverty (because the poverty impact of growth is higher). What defines the poverty-efficient equilibrium is that the marginal impact of an additional million dollars in aid is equalized across aid-receiving countries.

In Section 13.4 we subject the estimated poverty-efficient allocation to a number of sensitivity analyses. The estimated coefficients from the growth analysis play a role in the algorithm, and we vary these coefficients by a standard deviation in either direction to investigate the practical importance of imprecision in the estimates. In addition, there are a number of different poverty measures that could be targeted by donors (headcount, poverty gap, or squared poverty gap). We examine the impact of shifting from one measure to another, and from a $1 per day poverty line to a $2 per day poverty line. Our benchmark allocation of aid is correlated 0.89 or above with any of the alternative estimates that arise from this sensitivity analysis. The actual allocation of aid is correlated only 0.57 with our benchmark allocation. We conclude from the sensitivity analysis that significant changes in the estimated parameters or in the poverty measure of choice lead to only minor variations in the 'poverty-efficient' allocation – variations that are minor especially in comparison to the difference between our benchmark and the actual allocation of aid. In this sense, the poverty-efficient allocation is quite robust.

The fifth section of the paper examines in more detail the extent to which the actual allocation of aid deviates from the poverty-efficient allocation. We show that aid has the 'wrong' relationship with policy, after controlling for poverty. Precisely, in the range of policy in which aid becomes increasingly effective in poverty reduction, aid is currently lower the better is policy. In short, aid is being tapered out with reform, when it should be tapered in with reform. We estimate that in our sample of countries aid as currently allocated sustainably lifts 10 million people per year out of poverty. The same volume of assistance, allocated efficiently, would lift an estimated 19 million people out of poverty. Thus, the productivity of aid could be nearly doubled if it were allocated more efficiently.

13.2 The mapping from aid to growth

Our objective in this section is to arrive at estimates of the impact of aid on growth for a large number of countries, as a first step toward estimating the impact of aid on poverty reduction. Burnside and Dollar (2000) have shown that the impact of aid on growth depends on the quality of the incentive regime.[1]

However, their study – and in particular the policy measure that they use – has two limitations for the practical application of the results to aid allocation.

First, Burnside and Dollar confined their measurement of policies to three readily quantifiable macroeconomic indicators. It is implausible that these are the only policies which matter for growth and, as acknowledged by the authors, they are likely to be proxying a much broader range of policies for which comparable quantitative measures were lacking. We address this problem by utilizing as our measure of the policy environment the World Bank's Country Policy and Institutional Assessment. This measure has 20 different, equally weighted components covering macroeconomic issues, structural policies, public sector management, and policies for social inclusion (Appendix 13A, Table 13.8). Each of the 20 components is rated ordinally by country specialists, on a scale of 1–6, using standardized criteria. Considerable care is taken to ensure that the ratings are comparable both within and between regions. While the scores include an irreducible element of judgement, they have a reasonable claim to being the best consistent and comprehensive policy data set. The World Bank policy ratings are available for the period 1974–97 and from this we construct four-year averages beginning in 1974–77 and ending in 1994–97.

Secondly, the Burnside–Dollar study covered only 56 countries and so cannot provide comprehensive guidance on aid allocation. By switching to more comprehensive data sets, we are able to re-estimate the aid-growth relationship over a larger number of observations (we have 349 growth-aid-policy episodes of four years each, compared to Dollar–Burnside's 275).

To start, we use the expanded data set to revisit the core Burnside–Dollar results. These are (1) that the efficacy of aid in the growth process depends upon the policy environment (aid is more effective in raising growth the better is the policy environment) and (2) that aid is subject to diminishing marginal returns. Thus, growth (G) is a function of exogenous conditions (X), the level of policy (P), the level of net receipts of aid relative to GDP (A), the level of aid squared, and the interaction of policy and aid:[2]

$$G = c + b_1 X + b_2 P + b_3 A + b_4 A^2 + b_5 AP. \qquad (1)$$

The coefficient on the interaction term, b_5, addresses the hypothesis that the effectiveness of aid depends on the policy environment, while the coefficient on the quadratic, b_4, will pick up any diminishing returns to aid. The co-efficient on aid, b_3, may be positive, negative or zero depending upon the importance of policy for aide effectiveness. When it is zero it implies that in the best policy environments, scored as 6, the initial contribution of aid to growth is 6 times as large as in the worst policy environments, scored as 1. When it is positive it implies that the growth differential is less than six, and when it is negative it implies that the differential is greater than six. Thus, unlike the other variables, neither its sign nor its significance constitute tests of the hypotheses.

Table 13.1, column 1 presents the OLS results for the estimation of (1) on our data set. To capture initial conditions we have initial income (Summers

Table 13.1 Aid, growth, and policies (OLS, panel regressions)[a,b]

	(1)	*(2)*	*(3)*	*(4)*	*(5)*
Initial per capita GNP	0.67	0.85	0.55	0.64	0.49
	(1.08)	(1.49)	(0.79)	(1.03)	(0.71)
Institutional quality (ICRGE)	0.28	0.27	0.35	0.43	0.52
	(1.67)	(1.61)	(1.90)	(2.39)	(2.67)
Policy (CPIA)	0.46	0.64	0.45	0.39	0.38
	(1.65)	(2.26)	(1.55)	(1.44)	(1.36)
ODA/GDP	−0.54	–	−0.58	−0.33	−0.32
	(1.40)		(1.24)	(0.79)	(0.68)
(ODA/GDP)^2	−0.02	−0.04	−0.01	−0.03	−0.01
	(1.60)	(3.07)	(0.64)	(1.74)	(0.53)
CPIA×ODA/GDP	0.31	0.18	0.28	0.36	0.33
	(2.94)	(3.06)	(2.29)	(3.53)	(2.77)
ICRGE×ODA/GDP	—	—	—	−0.08	−0.10
				(1.69)	(1.76)
Log (inflation + 1)	—	—	0.02	—	−0.12
			(0.04)		(0.26)
Openness (X + M/GDP)	—	—	−0.22	—	−0.22
			(0.39)		(0.39)
Gov Cons/GDP	—	—	−0.02	—	−0.01
			(0.32)		(0.29)
South Asia	2.59	2.76	2.41	2.65	2.44
	(4.10)	(4.62)	(3.59)	(4.17)	(3.61)
East Asia	3.28	3.27	3.33	3.25	3.27
	(5.49)	(5.46)	(4.86)	(5.53)	(4.83)
Sub-Saharan Africa	−0.75	−0.72	−0.79	−0.60	−0.59
	(0.91)	(0.87)	(0.84)	(0.72)	(0.61)
Middle East/North Africa	1.49	1.50	1.72	1.57	1.78
	(2.69)	(2.76)	(2.54)	(2.84)	(2.64)
Europe/Central Asia	0.11	0.33	−0.11	−0.22	−0.48
	(0.12)	(0.33)	(0.11)	(0.22)	(0.48)
# of Observations	349	349	302	349	302
R^2	0.37	0.36	0.35	0.37	0.36
Adjusted R^2	0.34	0.33	0.31	0.34	0.31

Notes: (a) Dependent variable growth rate of per capita GNP. (Four-year averages, 1974–77 to 1994–97, 59 countries.) (b) *t*-Statistics in parentheses (calculated with robust standard errors).

and Heston, 1991), a measure of institutional quality (ICRGE) from Knack and Keefer (1995), and regional dummies.[3] There are also period dummies to account for the world business cycle (not reported). The most significant variable in the regression is the interaction of aid and policy, with a positive coefficient, significant at the 1 per cent level. Hence, the core Burnside–Dollar result was not due to its particular choice of policy variables and is robust to the inclusion of more countries and of more recent years. The CPIA measure of policy also enters directly with a positive coefficient, and marginal significance. Aid and aid squared both enter with negative coefficients and are jointly significant. However, the coefficient on aid itself, b_3, is not significantly different from zero. In a second specification, reported in column 2, the aid term is dropped in the interest of parsimony (recall that it is not intrinsic to the main hypotheses). In this second specification, the t-statistics on policy, the policy–aid interaction, and aid squared all increase, with the two latter being significant at 1 per cent.

We subject this result to several types of sensitivity analysis. First, we add three other policy-related variables commonly used in the empirical growth literature: the inflation rate, government consumption relative to GDP, and the measure of openness used by Frankel and Romer (1999): exports plus imports relative to GDP. It can be seen in column (3) that none of these variables adds any information, beyond what is already contained in the CPIA measure. It is the case, however, that the measure of institutional quality is close to significant, and it is possible that the effectiveness of aid depends on this element rather than on policies. Hence, in columns (4) and (5) we add aid interacted with the institutional quality variable to check whether the aid–policy interaction might be proxying for this instead. Column (4) otherwise reverts to the variables in our baseline regression (1), whereas (5) adds in the objectively measured macroeconomic variables of (3). In both variants, the interaction of aid and policy continues to be statistically highly significant and economically substantial. By contrast, the added interaction term between institutional quality and aid is statistically only marginally significant and its economic effect is small and negative. Thus, in all these variants, the policy environment significantly and substantially determines how rapidly diminishing returns eliminate the marginal contribution of aid to growth. Specifically, the marginal impact of aid on growth is

$$G_a = b3 + b5* P + 2*b4* A. \tag{2}$$

where we have consistently estimated $b5$ to be positive and $b4$ to be negative.

For our benchmark estimate of (2), we are going to use the coefficients from column 1 in Table 13.1. But, inevitably the relationship is estimated with some imprecision, so it is important to look as well at variants of the estimated relationship. Variant II uses the coefficients in column 2. Variants III and IV change the estimated coefficients from column 1 by one standard deviation as follows:

III: $b3$ – s.d.: $b5$ + s.d.:

IV: $b3$ + s.d.: $b5$ – s.d. .

Obviously, there are a large number of possible permutations. For sensitivity analysis, we choose the two above for the following reasons. For countries at the same level of poverty, the key to aid allocation will be to give aid up to the point that the marginal dollar has the same effect on growth. Relative to the benchmark, Variant III increases the importance of policy differences. G_a is an increasing function of policy, and Variant III makes the slope of that relationship steeper. In contrast, Variant IV might be called the 'egalitarian' variant because it makes the G_a-policy relationship relatively flat.

In Table 13.2 we evaluate the derivative at different levels of aid and of policy for all four variants. The mean level of aid in the data set is 2.15 per cent of real PPP GDP. The mean level of CPIA is 3.04. For a country with mean policy and mean aid, an additional 1 per cent of GDP in aid would add between 0.27 (Variant IV) and 0.39 (Variants II and IV) percentage points to the growth rate (equivalent to a 20–30 per cent rate of return, after adjusting for depreciation). At the mean, all four variants provide similar estimates of the effect of aid. They all have the property that this impact increases with policy and decreases with the level of aid. However, it can be seen that Variants III and IV provide rather different estimates when one moves away from the means. The table shows the estimated derivatives evaluated at CPIA plus or minus one standard deviation from the mean, and at aid plus one standard deviation from the mean and aid equals zero. Aid minus a standard deviation would lead to a negative number, which would take the analysis into an economically uninteresting range. Instead, by evaluating the derivative at Aid = 0, we investigate the economically interesting question of the productivity of the first dollar of aid.

The reason why it is important to consider these different variants is straightforward. If the estimated 'poverty efficient' allocation of aid varies significantly based on small changes in the estimated coefficients in the

Table 13.2 Aid impact on growth

			CPIA		
			Derivative of the growth rate with respect to 1% of GDP in aid, evaluated at:		
			2.16	3.04	3.91
Aid/GDP	0	I	0.13	0.40	0.67
		II	0.39	0.55	0.70
		III	−0.01	0.36	0.72
		IV	0.29	0.47	0.65
	2.15	I	0.04	0.32	0.59
		II	0.23	0.39	0.55
		III	−0.10	0.27	0.64
		IV	0.20	0.39	0.56
	4.70	I	−0.06	0.21	0.48
		II	0.05	0.21	0.37
		III	−0.20	0.17	0.53
		IV	0.10	0.28	0.46

growth regression, then the practical utility of this approach would be questionable.

13.3 The poverty-efficient allocation of aid

The results above suggest that donors can affect growth through their allocation of aid; growth in turn will typically lead to poverty reduction in low-income countries. Dollar and Kraay (2001) show that on average growth of per capita GDP is translated into proportional growth of income of the poor. Furthermore, the policies that are good for growth (and are measured by the CPIA) are good to the same extent for income of the poor. The intuition of our approach for allocating aid is straightforward: to maximize the reduction in poverty, aid should be allocated to countries that have large amounts of poverty and good policy. The presence of large-scale poverty is obviously necessary if aid is to have a large effect on poverty reduction. The good policy ensures that aid has a positive impact. In the remainder of this paper we formalize this idea, subject it to sensitivity analysis, examine the extent to which donors are already behaving optimally, and estimate the gains in poverty reduction that could be achieved through a more efficient allocation of existing aid volumes.

To formalize these ideas, we consider a world in which aid is given with the purpose of maximizing the reduction in poverty. Aid affects growth, but we take it that policy and the distribution of income within recipient countries are exogenous from the point of view of aid donors.[4] That is, the objective function of donors is to allocate aid among countries so as to

Max poverty reduction $\qquad \sum_i G^i z^i h^i N^i$

subject to $\qquad \sum_i A^i y^j N^i = \bar{A}, A^i \geqslant 0.$ $\qquad$ (3)

where y is per capita income, $\bar{A}$ is the total amount of aid, h is a measure of poverty (headcount index or other measures), z is the elasticity of poverty reduction with respect to income, N is population, and the superscript 'i' indexes countries. As in the previous section, growth is a function of a country's policy and the amount of aid it receives.

Note that this problem has some formal similarity to the literature that analyzes the optimal allocation of an anti-poverty budget (Bourguignon and Fields, 1990; Kanbur, 1987). That literature considers the optimal way to allocate transfers *among households* within a country. Bourguignon and Fields show that, in solving that problem, it makes a large difference whether the poverty measure is the headcount index or an alternative poverty measure such as the poverty gap. If one targets the headcount, then in general the transfers should be given to household just below the line; whereas if the poverty objective is a measure that puts more weight on the lower tail of the distribution, then the transfers would go there.

In the tradition of that literature, we will consider the impact of choosing alternative measures of poverty (headcount, the poverty gap, and the squared poverty gap). However, note that there is an important difference between our problem and that considered by the earlier literature. We are interested in allocating a fixed aid budget across countries, *assuming that donors have no influence on the within-country distribution of income*. Thus, donors cannot target their money to particular households. They can only affect poverty by raising aggregate income. For our problem it is not obvious that the choice of poverty measure will matter as much as in the household transfer literature. One way to interpret the optimization problem, (3), is that donors desire to allocate aid among countries to maximize a weighted average of their growth rates, where the weights are population times a measure of poverty. The practical issue, then, is whether the cross-country weights obtained by using different poverty measures differ to any significant extent. A final point is that, if the poverty measure is the headcount index, this maximization has a particularly simple interpretation: allocate aid so that the marginal aid cost of lifting someone above the poverty line is the same in each aid-receiving country.

Considering for the moment only interior solutions (in which each country gets some aid), the first order conditions for a maximum are

$$G_a^i z^i h^i \, N^i = \lambda y^j N^i, \tag{4}$$

where λ is the shadow value of aid. Using the estimate of G_a from (2) above (Variant I coefficients), we can solve explicitly for each country's aid receipts as a function of its policy, poverty level, per capita income, and elasticity of poverty with respect to income:

$$A^i = 13.5 + 7.8 \, p^i - \frac{\lambda}{0.04 z^i} \left(\frac{h^i}{y^i}\right)^{-1} \tag{5}$$

The basic properties of the equilibrium can be easily illustrated. Assume for simplicity that the elasticity of poverty reduction with respect to income is constant across countries. Then the equilibrium conditions define a set of relationships among aid, policy, and the poverty measure divided by per capita income – relationships that can be shown in two dimensions if we hold each variable constant in turn. For example, holding aid constant, we have the relationship between policy and (poverty divided by per capita income) shown in Figure 13.1a. Each isoquant shows combinations of policy and poverty that would justify a certain level of aid (given the shadow value of aid). The poorer a country, the lower is the policy quality required to justify a certain volume of aid. Intuitively, the aid will have less growth impact because of the weaker policies, but the poverty impact of a unit of growth is higher. The isoquant for Aid = 0 is the dividing line between countries that receive aid in the efficient allocation and countries that receive none. We also show the isoquant for an aid level of two per cent of GDP.

Holding policy constant, the relationship between aid and poverty is upward-sloping, but with diminishing returns to aid (Figure 13.1b). For a given poverty level, on the other hand, the optimal relationship between aid and policy is linear but kinked (Figure 13.1c). There will be a threshold of policy below which even the first dollar of aid is not sufficiently productive in terms of poverty reduction. Above the threshold the poverty-efficient aid allocation is monotonic in policy and happens to be linear. The reason for this is that, with poverty constant, the relationship shows combinations of aid and policy that maintain G_a at a constant level. This maps a linear relationship. An increase in the level of poverty shifts the schedule to the left.

The general point is that the optimal allocation of aid for a country depends on its level of poverty, the elasticity of poverty with respect to income, and the quality of its policies. In order to calculate a poverty-efficient allocation of aid we need to specify a measure of poverty and estimate the elasticity of poverty with respect to income for a large number of countries. We are going to start with a benchmark estimate based on the headcount poverty rate calculated on a $2 per day poverty line, and then in the next section experiment with other poverty measures in order to investigate the extent to which the choice of poverty measure affects the allocation.

If the distribution of income is constant, the elasticity of the headcount with respect to mean income is a complicated function that requires full knowledge of the density function. One question we are interested in is whether a simple approach to calculating the poverty-efficient allocation of aid yields results similar to a more sophisticated approach. So, when using the head-count measure, we are going to assume that the elasticity with respect to mean income is the same everywhere and equal to 2.0. This number is the median estimate of the elasticity from Ravallion and Chen (1997), who have looked at the relationship between headcount poverty and mean income in a large sample of countries.[5] In our sensitivity analysis, we will examine how this simple approach fares relative to a more complicated analysis that uses information about how the growth elasticity of poverty varies across countries.

We restrict our analysis to 59 developing countries for which high-quality information on the distribution of income is now available. Table 13.3 lists the countries and the different poverty measures that we will consider: headcount poverty for a $1 per day poverty line (*h*1); the poverty gap corresponding to that line (*pg*1); the squared poverty gap corresponding to that line (*s pg*1); the headcount for a $2 per day poverty line (*h*2); the poverty gap corresponding to that line (*pg*2); and the squared poverty gap corresponding to that line (*s pg*2).

These data are reported in the *World Development Indicators 1999*. The underlying source of the information in each case is a nationally representative survey of consumption at the household level. The surveys are from different years in the 1990s, and the year of the survey is reported in *WDI*. Where surveys are based on income rather than consumption, an adjustment is made. The international poverty line (either $1 per day or $2 per day) is

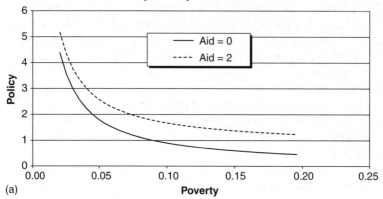

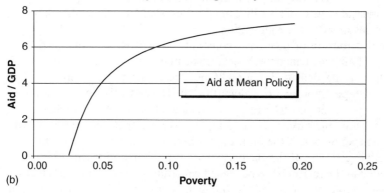

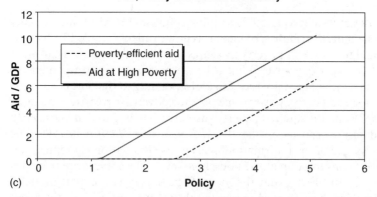

Figure 13.1 Policy, poverty and aid.

Table 13.3 Aid allocation and measures of poverty

Country	Poverty measures					
	Pop < $1 a day (%)	Pov gap $1 day (%)	Pov gap Sq $1 day (%)	Pop < $2 a day (%)	Pov gap $2 day (%)	Pov gap Sq $2 day (%)
Uganda	69.3	29.1	15.1	92.2	56.6	38.5
Ethiopia	46.0	12.4	4.7	89.0	42.7	23.8
Zambia	84.6	53.8	39.3	98.1	73.4	59.4
Tanzania	10.5	2.1	0.6	45.5	15.3	6.8
Lesotho	48.8	23.8	14.6	74.1	43.5	30.3
Rwanda	45.7	11.3	3.7	88.7	42.3	23.2
Senegal	54.0	25.5	15.1	79.6	47.2	32.7
Niger	61.5	22.2	10.5	92.0	51.8	32.9
Guinea-Bissau	88.2	59.5	45.5	96.7	76.6	64.2
Madagascar	72.3	33.2	18.9	93.2	59.6	42.0
Kyrgyz Rep.	18.9	5.0	1.8	55.3	21.4	10.8
Honduras	46.9	20.4	11.3	75.7	41.9	27.7
Vietnam	69.3	29.1	1.5	80.0	56.6	12.7
Mauritania	31.4	15.2	10.5	68.4	33.0	21.4
Kenya	50.2	22.2	12.6	78.1	44.4	29.7
Pakistan	11.6	2.6	1.0	57.0	18.6	8.3
Nicaragua	43.8	18.0	9.6	74.5	39.7	25.4
Cote d'Ivoire	17.7	4.3	1.5	54.8	20.4	10.0
Nepal	50.3	16.2	6.9	86.7	44.6	26.6
Nigeria	31.1	12.9	7.0	59.9	29.8	18.7
India	52.5	15.6	6.2	88.8	45.8	26.9
Algeria	1.0	0.3	0.1	17.6	4.4	1.6
Belarus	1.0	0.0	0.0	6.4	0.8	0.2
Botswana	33.0	12.4	6.0	61.0	30.4	18.7
Brazil	23.6	10.7	6.3	43.5	22.4	14.6
Bulgaria	2.6	0.8	0.5	23.5	6.0	2.4
Chile	15.0	4.9	2.3	38.5	16.0	8.8
China	22.2	6.9	2.9	57.8	24.1	13.0
Colombia	7.4	2.3	1.0	21.7	8.4	4.4
Costa Rica	18.9	7.2	3.7	43.8	19.4	11.4
Czech Rep.	3.1	0.4	0.1	55.1	14.0	4.8
Ecuador	30.4	9.1	3.6	65.8	29.6	16.5
Egypt	7.6	1.1	0.3	51.9	15.3	6.0
Estonia	6.0	1.6	0.7	32.5	10.0	4.5
Guatemala	53.3	28.5	19.0	76.8	47.6	34.7
Guinea	26.3	12.4	7.7	50.2	25.6	16.8
Hungary	1.0	0.3	0.2	10.7	2.1	0.8
Indonesia	11.8	1.8	0.4	58.7	19.3	8.2
Jamaica	4.3	0.5	0.1	24.9	7.5	3.0
Jordan	2.5	0.5	0.2	23.5	6.3	2.4
Kazakhstan	1.0	0.1	0.0	12.1	2.5	0.7
Lithuania	1.0	0.0	0.0	18.9	4.1	1.2
Malaysia	5.6	0.9	0.2	26.6	8.5	3.6
Mexico	14.9	3.8	1.9	40.0	15.9	8.2

(continued overleaf)

Table 13.3 continued

Country	Poverty measures					
	Pop < $1 a day (%)	Pov gap $1 day (%)	Pov gap Sq $1 day (%)	Pop < $2 a day (%)	Pov gap $2 day (%)	Pov gap Sq $2 day (%)
Moldova	6.8	1.2	0.3	30.6	9.7	4.2
Morocco	1.0	0.1	0.0	19.6	4.6	1.5
Panama	25.6	12.6	8.2	46.2	24.5	16.6
Philippines	28.6	7.7	2.7	64.5	28.2	15.2
Poland	6.8	4.7	0.0	15.1	7.7	5.9
Romania	17.7	4.2	1.6	70.9	24.7	11.5
Russia	1.0	0.1	0.0	10.9	2.3	0.7
Slovak Rep.	12.8	2.2	0.7	85.1	27.5	11.3
South Africa	23.7	6.6	2.3	50.2	22.5	12.4
Sri Lanka	4.0	0.7	0.2	41.2	11.0	4.1
Thailand	1.0	0.2	0.0	23.5	5.4	1.6
Tunisia	3.9	0.9	0.4	22.7	6.8	2.9
Turkmenistan	4.9	0.5	0.1	25.8	7.6	3.0
Venezuela	11.8	3.1	1.1	32.2	12.2	6.0
Zimbabwe	41.0	14.3	6.3	68.2	35.5	21.8

Country	Elasticity measures					
	Elasticity: Pop < $1 day	Elasticity: Pov gap $1 day	Elasticity: Pov Gap Sq $1 day	Elasticity: Pop < $2 day	Elasticity: Pov Gap $2 day	Elasticity Pov Gap Sq $2 day
Uganda	2	1.4	1.84	2	0.6	0.94
Ethiopia	2	2.7	3.23	2	1.1	1.59
Zambia	2	0.6	0.74	2	0.3	0.47
Tanzania	2	4.0	4.55	2	2.0	2.48
Lesotho	2	1.1	1.26	2	0.7	0.87
Rwanda	2	3.0	4.06	2	1.1	1.65
Senegal	2	1.1	1.37	2	0.7	0.88
Niger	2	1.8	2.21	2	0.8	1.15
Guinea-Bissau	2	0.5	0.61	2	0.3	0.39
Madagascar	2	1.2	1.52	2	0.6	0.84
Kyrgyz Rep.	2	2.8	3.61	2	1.6	1.95
Honduras	2	1.3	1.61	2	0.8	1.03
Vietnam	2	1.4	38.11	2	0.4	6.91
Mauritania	2	1.1	0.90	2	1.1	1.09
Kenya	2	1.3	1.52	2	0.8	0.99
Pakistan	2	3.5	3.13	2	2.1	2.51
Nicaragua	2	1.4	1.75	2	0.9	1.12
Cote d'Ivoire	2	3.1	3.84	2	1.7	2.08
Nepal	2	2.1	2.71	2	0.9	1.36
Nigeria	2	1.4	1.68	2	1.0	1.20
India	2	2.4	3.04	2	0.9	1.41
Algeria	2	2.3	3.29	2	3.0	3.47
Belarus	2	24.0	0.29	2	7.0	6.89

Botswana	2	1.7	2.14	2	1.0	1.26
Brazil	2	1.2	1.41	2	0.9	1.07
Bulgaria	2	2.3	1.07	2	2.9	2.96
Chile	2	2.1	2.35	2	1.4	1.63
China	2	2.2	2.68	2	1.4	1.70
Colombia	2	2.2	2.51	2	1.6	1.78
Costa Rica	2	1.6	1.86	2	1.3	1.41
Czech Rep.	2	6.8	5.62	2	2.9	3.82
Ecuador	2	2.3	3.04	2	1.2	1.58
Egypt	2	5.9	6.18	2	2.4	3.08
Estonia	2	2.8	2.30	2	2.3	2.49
Guatemala	2	0.9	1.00	2	0.6	0.74
Guinea	2	1.1	1.23	2	1.0	1.05
Hungary	2	2.7	0.30	2	4.1	3.42
Indonesia	2	5.6	6.49	2	2.0	2.69
Jamaica	2	7.6	11.16	2	2.3	2.98
Jordan	2	4.0	4.62	2	2.7	3.27
Kazakhstan	2	9.3	2.85	2	3.8	4.96
Lithuania	2	24.0	0.29	2	3.6	4.71
Malaysia	2	5.2	5.66	2	2.1	2.73
Mexico	2	2.9	2.10	2	1.5	1.89
Moldova	2	4.7	6.70	2	2.2	2.60
Morocco	2	5.8	5.35	2	3.3	3.97
Panama	2	1.0	1.09	2	0.9	0.95
Philippines	2	2.7	3.71	2	1.3	1.71
Poland	2	0.4	0.00	2	1.0	0.63
Romania	2	3.2	3.12	2	1.9	2.31
Russia	2	7.1	7.54	2	3.7	5.06
Slovak Rep.	2	4.8	3.99	2	2.1	2.88
South Africa	2	2.6	3.65	2	1.2	1.64
Sri Lanka	2	4.7	3.96	2	2.7	3.43
Thailand	2	4.3	7.40	2	3.4	4.67
Tunisia	2	3.3	2.96	2	2.3	2.68
Turkmenistan	2	8.8	9.90	2	2.4	3.04
Venezuela	2	2.8	3.63	2	1.6	2.08
Zimbabwe	2	1.9	2.56	2	0.9	1.26

Country	*Poverty-efficient aid*		*Actual-aid*	
	Realloc. Aid Pop < $2 (%GDP)	*Marg eff Pop < $2 (people $ mn)*	*1996 Aid Gdp (%)*	*Marg eff Pop < $2 (people $ mn)*
Uganda	11.4	285.1	3.34	1001.5
Ethiopia	10.7	285.1	2.90	1654.8
Zambia	8.8	285.1	7.53	421.6
Tanzania	7.0	285.1	4.46	449.4
Lesotho	6.1	285.1	3.09	416.8
Rwanda	6.0	285.1	15.75	−1071.1
Senegal	5.6	285.1	4.03	358.0
Niger	5.0	285.1	2.97	484.0
Guinea-Bissau	4.9	285.1	15.67	−700.8

(continued overleaf)

Table 13.3 continued

Country	Poverty-efficient aid		Actual-aid	
	Realloc. Aid Pop < $2 (%GDP)	Marg eff Pop < $2 (people $ mn)	1996 Aid Gdp (%)	Marg eff Pop < $2 (people $ mn)
Madagascar	4.7	285.1	2.84	470.3
Kyrgyz Rep.	4.0	285.1	2.45	325.4
Honduras	3.8	285.1	2.82	318.3
Vietnam	3.5	285.1	0.78	414.9
Mauritania	3.4	285.1	6.15	185.8
Kenya	3.3	285.1	1.91	380.2
Pakistan	3.0	285.1	0.41	376.2
Nicaragua	2.9	285.1	10.21	23.7
Cote d'Ivoire	2.8	285.1	3.91	250.5
Nepal	2.5	285.1	1.70	347.3
Nigeria	2.4	285.1	0.19	430.9
India	0.13	670.6	0.13	670.6
Algeria	0.0	33.5	0.22	32.7
Belarus	0.0	3.0	0.16	2.8
Botswana	0.0	134.9	0.71	129.2
Brazil	0.0	89.5	0.04	89.2
Bulgaria	0.0	34.1	0.46	31.7
Chile	0.0	67.4	0.12	67.0
China	0.0	237.4	0.06	236.3
Colombia	0.0	47.2	0.10	46.9
Costa Rica	0.0	98.7	−0.03	98.9
Czech Rep.	0.0	77.8	0.11	77.3
Ecuador	0.0	63.2	0.44	57.6
Egypt	0.0	214.3	1.31	190.6
Estonia	0.0	119.3	0.91	113.0
Guatemala	0.0	227.2	0.51	217.2
Guinea	0.0	247.4	2.45	178.9
Hungary	0.0	27.8	0.26	27.4
Indonesia	0.0	144.3	0.16	141.5
Jamaica	0.0	68.1	0.66	63.5
Jordan	0.0	81.9	3.26	61.0
Kazakhstan	0.0	45.1	0.23	44.3
Lithuania	0.0	58.1	0.54	55.8
Malaysia	0.0	35.6	−0.20	36.1
Mexico	0.0	61.4	0.04	61.2
Moldova	0.0	148.0	0.59	135.8
Morocco	0.0	71.7	0.70	67.7
Panama	0.0	102.6	0.46	99.6
Philippines	0.0	260.9	0.36	254.2
Poland	0.0	44.9	0.36	44.0
Romania	0.0	118.1	0.21	114.9
Russia	0.0	18.9	0.00	18.9
Slovak Rep.	0.0	151.9	0.35	147.9
South Africa	0.0	98.2	0.13	97.4
Sri Lanka	0.0	222.8	1.16	202.2

Thailand	0.0	44.0	0.20	43.3
Tunisia	0.0	80.0	0.29	78.6
Turkmenistan	0.0	8.7	0.26	5.4
Venezuela	0.0	34.7	0.02	34.6
Zimbabwe	0.0	266.1	1.45	223.3

based on 1993 consumption purchasing power parity estimates from the World Bank. For most countries, the poverty measures are calculated from the full distribution in the nationally represented sample. In a minority of cases, only consumption shares for deciles or quintiles are available, in which case the Lorenz curve is estimated from these points. See Chen and Ravallion (2000) for the details of how these poverty measures are estimated.[6]

The optimization problem above results in equating the marginal productivity of aid (people lifted out of poverty per million dollars) across countries receiving aid. As a point of departure, it is useful to look at the actual estimated marginal productivities based on the allocation of aid in 1996. For the $2 per day headcount measure (with an elasticity assumed equal to 2), the estimated marginal productivities are shown in the last column of the table. That the 1996 allocation of aid was inefficient can be seen in the large variations in these estimates. For some countries receiving extremely large amounts of aid, the estimated marginal productivity is negative. In India, Ethiopia, and Uganda, on the other hand, the estimated marginal impact of aid is high, reflecting the fact that these countries are characterized by large poverty, reasonably good policies, and modest amounts of aid in 1996. In Ethiopia, for example, the estimated marginal productivity is 1,655 people per million dollars; that is, the one-time cost of lifting a person out of poverty is about $600.

Making aid more efficient in poverty reduction requires reallocating among countries to equalize these marginal productivities. The first thing that we learned trying this approach is that India is seriously under-funded. Since India is so large, the 'optimal' allocation of aid would give about two-thirds of all aid to that one country. While this result is of interest, telling us that under any politically realistic aid allocation India will be under-funded on the criterion of poverty reduction, it does not provide a good basis for discrimination between other environments and so does not guide marginal improvements in aid allocation. We therefore constrain India to its actual level of aid, and investigate poverty-efficient allocation among remaining countries.

Our benchmark allocation of aid, with India constrained at its actual level of aid, is shown in Table 13.3. (The total amount in the allocation is the $28 billion in aid that these countries actually received in 1996.) For all of the countries receiving positive amounts of aid, the marginal productivity of aid is 285 people per million dollars (or, $3,509 per person). The countries that receive zero aid are ones in which the productivity of the first dollar of aid does not meet that threshold. In general, these are middle-income countries. Our algorithm puts a large weight on poverty. The correlation between our poverty efficient allocation and headcount poverty is 0.64, compared to a correlation of 0.50 between the 1996 allocation of aid and headcount poverty. Thus, it is possible to make the allocation of aid more sharply targeted to poverty and more sharply targeted to good policy, *simultaneously*. The large gainers in our reallocation are a number of low-income countries that have reformed their economic policies but have only received modest amounts of aid (Uganda, Ethiopia, Vietnam). A final point that we will come back to in the next section is that the correlation between our benchmark allocation and actual aid allocation is 0.57.

13.4 Sensitivity analysis

How sensitive is our estimated poverty-efficient allocation of aid to variations in the parameter estimates from our growth regressions and to the choice of poverty measure? These are the questions that we turn to in this section.

We explained in Section 13.2 that we would investigate four different variants of the estimated impact of aid on growth. It is straightforward to recalculate the poverty-efficient allocation in Table 13.3 using the different parameter estimates. Table 13.4 shows the correlations among the resulting allocations. The key point here is that our benchmark is correlated 0.97 or 0.98 with each of the variants. Thus, changing the key parameter estimates by one standard deviation, does not result in any large change in the allocation of aid. The biggest difference in the allocations is between Variants III and IV, which by construction are meant to be very different. The resulting allocations have a positive correlation of 0.91, distinctly higher than the correlation between our benchmark and the actual allocation of aid.

While the allocations are highly correlated, it is nevertheless interesting to see where the differences lie (Table 13.5). Putting less weight on policy takes aid away from well-known reformers such as Uganda or Kyrgyz Republic and reallocates it to poor-policy countries such as Kenya. Still, it can be seen that the changes are not large. Furthermore, for 52 of the 59 countries the actual allocation of aid is either entirely above or entirely below all five variants, so that the desirable direction of change is unambiguous.

Table 13.4 Correlation matrix among allocations using different parameter estimates

Variant	I	II	III	IV
I	1			
II	0.97	1		
III	0.98	0.91	1	
IV	0.97	0.98	0.91	1

Table 13.5 Allocations of aid based on different parameter estimates or poverty measures (aid as a per cent of GDP)

	Actual Aid 1996	Benchmark	Variant III	Variant IV	$2PGS	$1 Headcount
Uganda	3.34	11.42	12.46	9.86	11.16	12.71
Ethiopia	2.90	10.67	10.84	10.18	10.70	10.91
Zambia	7.53	8.77	8.67	8.44	7.53	10.01
Tanzania	4.46	6.98	6.96	6.35	6.79	3.57
Lesotho	3.09	6.15	6.71	4.67	5.07	8.37
Rwanda	15.75	6.00	4.77	6.89	6.25	6.46
Senegal	4.03	5.58	5.75	4.57	4.65	7.68
Niger	2.97	4.99	3.75	5.80	4.87	5.93
Guinea-Bissau	15.67	4.95	3.77	5.67	3.03	6.56
Madagascar	2.84	4.70	3.36	5.62	4.37	5.93
Kyrgyz Rep.	2.45	3.96	5.36	1.71	3.56	1.55
Honduras	2.82	3.76	4.08	2.37	2.72	5.99
Vietnam	0.78	3.50	2.93	3.26	7.35	6.63
Mauritania	6.15	3.37	3.53	2.15	1.53	3.65
Kenya	1.91	3.32	2.04	4.01	2.83	4.64
Pakistan	0.41	2.98	3.04	1.86	1.68	0
Nicaragua	10.21	2.91	2.92	1.86	2.05	4.80
Cote d'Ivoire	3.91	2.82	3.19	1.27	1.81	0
Nepal	1.70	2.47	0.62	3.81	2.43	3.29
Nigeria	0.19	2.37	0.77	3.38	1.78	2.96
India	0.13	0.13	0.13	0.13	0.13	0.13
Algeria	0.22	0	0	0	0	0
Belarus	0.16	0	0	0	0	0
Botswana	0.71	0	0	0	0	0
Brazil	0.04	0	0	0	0	0
Bulgaria	0.46	0	0	0	0	0
Chile	0.12	0	0	0	0	0
China	0.06	0	0	0	0	0
Colombia	0.10	0	0	0	0	0
Costa Rica	−0.03	0	0	0	0	0
Czech Rep.	0.11	0	0	0	0	0
Ecuador	0.44	0	0	0	0	0
Egypt	1.31	0	0	0	0	0
Estonia	0.91	0	0	0	0	0
Guatemala	0.51	0	0	0	0	2.21
Guinea	2.45	0	0	0	0	0.22
Hungary	0.26	0	0	0	0	0
Indonesia	0.16	0	0	0	0	0
Jamaica	0.66	0	0	0	0	0
Jordan	3.26	0	0	0	0	0
Kazakhstan	0.23	0	0	0	0	0
Lithuania	0.54	0	0	0	0	0
Malaysia	−0.20	0	0	0	0	0
Mexico	0.04	0	0	0	0	0
Moldova	0.59	0	0	0	0	0

(continued overleaf)

Table 13.5 continued

	Actual Aid 1996	Benchmark	Variant III	Variant IV	$2PGS	$1 Headcount
Morocco	0.70	0	0	0	0	0
Panama	0.46	0	0	0	0	0
Philippines	0.36	0	0.07	0	0	0
Poland	0.36	0	0	0	0	0
Russia	0.21	0	0	0	0	0
Romania	0.00	0	0	0	0	0
Slovak Rep.	0.35	0	0	0	0	0
South Africa	0.13	0	0	0	0	0
Sri Lanka	1.16	0	0	0	0	0
Tunisia	0.20	0	0	0	0	0
Thailand	0.29	0	0	0	0	0
Turkmenistan	0.26	0	0	0	0	0
Venezuela	0.02	0	0	0	0	0
Zimbabwe	1.45	0	0	0	0	1.95

The next step in the sensitivity analysis is to see if the results change signicantly when an alternative measure of poverty is used. For a given distribution of income, there are simple formulae for the elasticities of the poverty gap and the squared poverty gap with respect to mean income (Datt and Ravallion, 1993):

$$x_{pg} = (pg - h)/pg, \tag{6}$$

$$x_{s\,pg} = 2(spg - pg)/spg. \tag{7}$$

Table 13.3 reports the poverty measures and the associated elasticities calculated from both the $2 per day poverty line and the $1 per day poverty line.[7]

Any of these poverty measures with its associated elasticity can be used in the aid allocation equation, (5). (In each case we are reallocating a constant volume of aid, and the parameter λ adjusts endogenously.)

With three different poverty measures and two different poverty lines, we have six variations of a poverty-efficient allocation of aid. Table 13.6 shows that these are highly correlated. For a particular poverty line ($1 or $2), the allocations based on the three different measures are generally correlated 0.9 and above. Thus, once we have settled on a poverty line, each of the measures provides similar cross-country information about which countries are poor. Furthermore, using the country-specific elasticities based on the Lorenz curves does not result in any significant difference from the allocation based on the simple assumption that the elasticity is the same everywhere.

Table 13.6 also shows the correlations among the allocations based on the $2 per day lines and the $1 per day lines. Where the same measure is used, the correlations range from 0.82 to 0.94.

Table 13.6 Correlation matrix of allocations of aid using different measures of poverty

		$2 Day			$1 Day		
		Head count	Poverty gap	Poverty gap squared	Head count	Poverty gap	Poverty gap squared
$2 Day	Head count	1					
	Poverty gap	0.93	1				
	Poverty gap squared	0.97	0.89	1			
$ 1 Day	Head count	0.94	0.77	0.93	1		
	Poverty gap	0.96	0.82	0.96	0.98	1	
	Poverty gap squared	0.89	0.69	0.90	0.98	0.96	1
	Actual aid	0.57	0.44	0.49	0.57	0.53	0.52

At first glance it may seem surprising that our results are so different from the literature that considers how to optimally allocate transfers among households. There, measures that put different weights on different households lead to very different results on how to allocate transfers among households. In our problem, donors cannot target assistance to particular households; they can only affect the poor through generalized growth. The weight that we put on growth in different countries is indexed by (the elasticity times the poverty measure).

Referring back to Table 13.3, we can find countries (such as Rwanda and Guinea-Bissau) that have similar $2/day headcount poverty but very different poverty gaps squared. One might think then that shifting to the poverty gap squared would be an advantage for Guinea-Bissau. Note, however, that the elasticity of the poverty gap squared is extremely low in Guinea-Bissau. The same high inequality among the poor that gives it a large poverty gap squared also gives it a small elasticity. And, since it is the product of the poverty measure and the elasticity that enters into the allocation rule, the end result is less alteration in the allocation than one might expect.

The allocation with the $2 per day poverty gap squared is shown in Table 13.5. Rwanda gets about the same as in the benchmark. Guinea-Bissau gets somewhat less because its elasticity is so low. The table also shows the allocation with the $1/day headcount. Note that there are a few significant changes from our benchmark. Honduras and Vietnam are about equally poor on the $2 per day poverty line. But Vietnam has a more equal distribution of income and that results in it getting a lot more aid in the allocation based on the poverty gap squared (because Vietnam has such a large elasticity). Thus, while our different allocations are highly correlated, donors may nevertheless want to put some thought into which concept of poverty they are actually targeting.

In summary, our benchmark allocation is correlated 0.89 or above with any plausible alternatives (based on different coefficient estimates, different measures of poverty, country-specific elasticities, or a lower poverty line), far higher than its 0.57 correlation with the actual allocation of aid. We conclude from this that were donors to adopt our benchmark, they would probably be closer to the 'true' poverty-efficient allocation than if they continue current practice.

13.5. Reallocating aid for poverty reduction

We now consider in more detail how the actual allocation of aid compares to the allocation that maximizes poverty reduction and quantify the gains from moving from the current allocation to our benchmark allocation.

In our model of efficient aid, what a country receives relative to GDP should be a monotonic but non-linear increasing function of the headcount index divided by per capita income (which we will denote POV). It should be a monotonic increasing function of policy (CPIA). The actual allocation of aid in 1996 across 106 countries has a broadly appropriate relationship to poverty (Table 13.7, regression 1). However, there is no significant linear relationship to policy. One possible reason might be that in practice countries with small populations receive higher per capita aid and this may be disguising the true aid–policy relationship. When population is added to the equation it is indeed highly significant, but there is still no significant linear relationship between policy and aid (regression 2). Nor is the absence of a significant relationship caused by outliers. Omitting three outliers with aid to GDP above 20 per cent does not change this result (regression 3).[8]

Table 13.7 Dependent variable: ODA as a per cent of GDP – 1996[a]

	(1)	(2)	(3)	(4)
Constant	–0:43	11.8	9.7	5.26
	(0.26)	(5.09)	(6.04)	(1.93)
POV	78.2*	81.9*	61.9*	57.0*
	(3.90)	(4.85)	(5.21)	(4.78)
POV²	–217.2***	–213.8**	–143.2***	–122.3***
	(1.73)	(2.02)	(1.93)	(1.66)
CPIA	0.24	0.39	0.18	3.28**
	(0.58)	(1.13)	(0.75)	(2.11)
CPIA²	—	—	—	–0.49**
				(2.02)
Ln (POP)	—	–0.81*	–0.62*	–0:63*
		(6.52)	(7.10)	(7.29)
N	106	106	103	103
R²	0.35	0.54	0.60	0.62

Notes:
a *t*-Statistics in parentheses.
*Significant at the 1 per cent level.
**Significant at the 5 per cent level.
***Significant at the 10 per cent level.

Nevertheless, there is a significant relationship between policy and aid, but it is non-monotonic. Regression 4 shows that policy is significant once it is included as a quadratic. For a given level of poverty, in the range between bad policies and mediocre policies aid is positively related to policy. However, still controlling for poverty, in the range between mediocre policies and good policies aid sharply *declines*. Thus, just as policy moves into the realm in which aid becomes effective in reducing poverty, aid starts to be phased out. Whereas the efficient aid-poverty mapping would require that aid should *taper in* with policy reform, actual donor behavior is for aid to *taper out* with reform. Evidently, if policy is treated as exogenous to aid, this represents a large misallocation of aid on the criterion of poverty reduction.

Clearly, one rationale for the present aid allocation rule is that aid is being used to induce policy change. This is one reason why it is concentrated over the range of policy in which there is the most scope for improvement. Were policy highly responsive to aid then this assignment might be poverty-efficient even though, for given policy environments, it is inefficient. However, Burnside and Dollar (2000) find that increases in the amount of aid do not typically result in better policy. Although there are undoubtedly particular instances where aid does induce reform, there are also cases where it delays reform. Their econometric results are consistent with the larger literature on aid and the political economy of reform (Collier, 1997; Killick, 1991; Rodrik, 1996; Williamson, 1994). Unfortunately, this ineffective use of aid to induce policy change has had a high opportunity cost. As can be seen from Figure 13.1, the optimal relationship between aid and policy is the opposite of the actual. While aid has apparently been ineffective at inducing sustained policy change in poor policy environments, it is proving highly effective in reducing poverty in the newly reformed environments.

What kind of efficiency gains could we expect if donors used the available results on aid effectiveness to allocate aid? Given current practice, there is no *single* marginal productivity of aid. We have shown that it varies enormously across developing countries. But, weighted by aid dollars the average marginal productivity in 1996 was 235 people per million dollars (or, a marginal cost of \$4,250). Contrast that with the estimate that the marginal productivity of aid in Ethiopia was 1,655 people per million dollars. Thus, a million dollars allocated to Ethiopia would have had 7 times as much poverty impact as a million dollars allocated in proportion to existing volumes.

That first move from an inefficient situation, of course, has the highest payoff. A rough estimate of the overall impact of allocating aid efficiently can be gained through the following counterfactual calculations. We estimate that the effect of eliminating aid for one year would be to increase poverty in our sample countries (excluding India) by 10 million people; that is, the actual average cost of poverty reduction is estimated to be \$2,650 per person. If the same volume of aid were allocated to these countries efficiently, an additional 9.1 million would be lifted out of poverty (virtually cutting the average cost in half, to \$1,387 per person). Thus, the productivity of aid could be doubled.

Clearly, there is quite a bit of uncertainty about this point estimate, but it is large enough to make us confident that the effectiveness of aid could be increased quite dramatically through reallocation.

13.6 Conclusion

Although aid may be allocated coherently, it is allocated inefficiently with respect to poverty reduction. At present, aid is allocated partly as an inducement to policy reform and partly for a variety of historical and strategic reasons. This produces a pattern in which aid is targeted to weak policy environments and to countries which do not have severe poverty problems. The diversion of aid from poverty reduction to policy improvement would be justifiable were there evidence that the offer of finance is effective in inducing policy improvement. However, the evidence suggests that finance is ineffective in inducing either policy reform or growth in a bad policy environment.

Even with the current inefficiencies, we estimate that in our sample of countries the present allocation of aid lifts 10 million people permanently out of poverty each year. With a poverty-efficient allocation this would increase to 19 million per year. Hence, the attempt over the past decades to use aid to induce policy reform has come at a large cost.

Table 13.8 The CPIA measure of policy

A. Macroeconomic management and sustainability of reforms
  1. General macroeconomic performance
  2. Fiscal policy
  3. Management of external debt
  4. Macroeconomic management capacity
  5. Sustainability of structural reforms

B. Structural policies for sustainable and equitable growth
  1. Trade policy
  2. Foreign exchange regime
  3. Financial stability and depth
  4. Banking sector efficiency and resource mobilization
  5. Property rights and rule-based governance
  6. Competitive environment for the private sector
  7. Factor and product markets
  8. Environmental policies and regulations

C. Policies for social inclusion
  1. Poverty monitoring and analysis
  2. Pro-poor targeting and programs
  3. Safety nets

D. Public sector management
  1. Quality of budget and public investment process
  2. Efficiency and equity of revenue mobilization
  3. Efficiency and equity of public expenditures
  4. Accountability of the public service

Appendix 13 A: *Components of the CPIA measure*

The CPIA measure of policy has 20 equally weighted components divided into four categories (Table 13.8). As shown in the text, when the CPIA is included in a growth regression, along with variables commonly used in the growth literature to capture different policies, the CPIA has statistical significance, whereas the other policy measures do not. We take this as evidence that it is a good summary indicator of the overall policy environment for growth.

Notes

1 Earlier literature generally did not find any robust effect of aid on investment or growth (Boone, 1994; Levy, 1987; White, 1992). The Burnside-Dollar result is consistent with this earlier literature in that during the 1970s and 1980s their estimate of the effect of aid on growth in a country with mean policy level is not significantly different from zero.

2 In this formulation we make use of two other results from Burnside and Dollar. First, they consider the possibility that policy is endogenous and in particular is influenced by the level of aid, but they find no significant effect of the amount of aid on policy. Our specification for growth makes use of this information, that the policy measure is not affected by the level of aid and can be taken as independent of it. Second, Burnside and Dollar consider the possibility that aid is correlated with the error term in the growth regression and instrument for it. Their OLS and 2SLS regressions are essentially the same, indicating that there is no significant correlation between aid and the error term. In light of this, we use OLS to estimate the growth equation.

3 Data on official development assistance are from the OECD. We divide aid by real PPP GDP per capita from Summers and Heston. Data on growth rates, inflation, government consumption, trade volumes, and population are from the World Bank's *World Development Indicators*.

4 In some cases aid may change the distribution of income. Indeed, donor projects will often attempt to target the poor. However, in aggregate aid tends to be fungible (Pack and Pack, 1993; Feyzioglu *et al.*, 1998) and so has distributional consequences which are similar to a general increase in public expenditure combined with a general decrease in taxation. Such evidence as there is on the distributional incidences of public expenditure and taxation in developing countries suggests that on average such changes will not be distributionally progressive to any great extent. The incidence of public spending in developing countries is mildly progressive (van de Walle, 1995; Devarajan and Hossain, 1998). However, the tax reduction effect of aid is likely to be regressive. Furthermore, there is evidence that the distribution of income is fairly stable over time in a majority of countries (Li *et al.*, 1998). We therefore assume that the net effect of aid is distributionally neutral.

5 Bourguignon (2000) finds an empirical income elasticity of headcount poverty ($1 per day line) of -1.9 in a cross section of countries. He also shows that the absolute value of the elasticity varies positively with per capita income and negatively with initial income inequality. If the distribution of income is log-normal, there is an exact expression for the elasticity as a function of initial per capita income and inequality.

6 In a few cases we were able to receive more recent estimates from Chen and Ravallion; these will appear in future editions of *World Development Indicators*.

7 Note that there are a number of upper-middle income countries (Thailand is an example) that have virtually no poverty using the $1 per day poverty line. The

World Bank data arbitrarily sets a lower limit of 1 per cent for this measure, and the estimated poverty gap and poverty gap squared are close to zero. For these observations, the elasticities of the poverty gap and the poverty gap squared are not likely to be reliably estimated, because they depend on the shape of the Lorenz curve at the very bottom tail of the distribution. However, this imprecision in the estimates of the elasticities for the upper-middle income countries does not affect our allocations. Basically, these countries have no poverty by the $1 per day measure, and hence they will receive no aid in any of the allocations regardless of the size of the elasticity.

8 Our objective here is not to estimate a full behavioural model of aid allocation, but simply to look at whether the allocation of aid meets the efficiency condition that we have established. Alesina and Dollar (2000) show that much of the allocation of aid can be explained by strategic–political variables such as colonial past or UN voting patterns.

References

Alesina, A., Dollar, D. (2000). 'Who gives aid to whom and why?' *Journal of Economic Growth* 5 (March) 33–63.

Boone, P. (1994). The impact of foreign aid on savings and growth. London School of Economics, London, Mimeo.

Bourguignon, F. (2000). The pace of economic growth and poverty reduction, DELTA, Paris, Mimeo.

Bourguignon, F., Fields, G. (1990). 'Poverty measures and anti-poverty policy'. *Recherche Economiques de Louvain* 56 (3/4), 409–427.

Burnside, C., Dollar, D. (2000). (Aid, policies, and growth). *American Economic Review* 90 (4), 847–868.

Chen, S., Ravallion, M. (2000). How did the World's poorest fare in the 1990s. Policy research working paper no. 2409, Washington, DC: World Bank.

Collier, P. (1997). 'The failure of conditionality'. In: Gwin, C., Nelson, J. (eds.), *Perspectives on Aid and Development*. Washington, DC: Overseas Development Council.

Datt, G., Ravallion, M. (1993). 'Regional disparities, targeting, and poverty in India'. In: Lipton, M., van der Gaag, J. (eds.), *Including the Poor*. Washington, DC: World Bank.

Devarajan, S., Hossain, S.I. (1998). 'The combined incidence of taxes and public expenditures in the Philippines'. *World Development* 26 (6), 963–977.

Dollar, D., Kraay, A. (2001). Growth is good for the poor. Policy research working paper no. 2587, Washington, DC: World Bank.

Feyzioglu, T., Swaroop, V., Zhu, M. (1998). 'A panel data analysis of the fungibility of foreign aid'. *World Bank Economic Review* 12 (1), 29–58.

Frankel, J.A., Romer, D. (1999). 'Does trade cause growth?' *American Economic Review* 89, 379–399.

Isham, J., Kaufmann, D. (1999). 'The forgotten rationale for policy reform: The impact on projects'. *Quarterly Journal of Economics* 114, 149–184.

Kanbur, R. (1987). Measurement and alleviation of poverty. IMF Staff Papers (34) 60–85.

Killick, T. (1991). The developmental effectiveness of aid to Africa. World Bank working paper no. 646.

Knack, S., Keefer, P. (1995). 'Institutions and economic performance: Cross-country tests using alternative institutional measures'. *Economics and Politics* 7 (3), 207–227.

Levy, V. (1987). 'Does concessionary aid lead to higher investment rates in low-income countries?' *Review of Economics and Statistics* 69, 152–156.

Li, H., Squire, L., Zou, H. (1998). 'Explaining international and intertemporal variations in income inequality'. *The Economic Journal* 108, 1–18.

Pack, H., Pack, J.R. (1993). 'Foreign aid and the question of fungibility'. *Review of Economics and Statistics* 75, 258–265.

Ravallion, M., Chen, S. (1997). 'What can new survey data tell us about recent changes in distribution and poverty?' *World Bank Economic Review* 11 (2), 357–382.

Rodrik, D. (1996). 'Understanding economic policy reform'. *Journal of Economic Literature* XXXIV, 9–41.

Summers, R., Heston, A. (1991). 'The Penn world table, version V'. *Quarterly Journal of Economics* 106, 1–45.

van de Walle, D. (1995). 'The distribution of subsidies through public health services in Indonesia, 1978–87': in van de Walle, Nead (eds.), *Public Spending and the Poor*. Johns Hopkins University Press for the World Bank.

White, H. (1992). 'The macroeconomic analysis of aid impact'. *Journal of Development Studies* 28, 163–240.

Williamson, J. (ed.) (1994). *The political economy of policy reform*. Washington, DC: Institute for International Economics.

14 The complementarities of poverty reduction, equity, and growth

A perspective on the *World Development Report 2006*

With Stefan Dercon

14.1. Introduction

In a celebrated psychology test, an audience is shown a short film of a basketball game and asked to count the number of passes (Simons and Chabris 1999). Typically, around 90 per cent of the audience give the correct answer but completely fail to notice that a large gorilla walks slowly through the players: attention to detail has an opportunity cost. Perhaps something like this has happened in the development discourse on poverty.

Over the past decade the predominant metric of progress in development has come to be the reduction of absolute poverty. The choice of absolute poverty was essentially a political solution to a range of political problems. One problem was that the popular image of the World Bank had been so badly damaged by public perceptions of 'structural adjustment' that the agency needed an objective that signaled that it 'cared.' A second problem was that there was a clear need for some reasonably specific and measurable objective to assess agency performance. By the 1990s those electorates that funded aid were highly doubtful that it was effective, and, as a result, aid finance was in rapid decline. Further, poverty reduction offered an objective that could be embraced by the entire pantheon of development agencies and so offered the prospect of coordination that had otherwise proved elusive. Beyond these, the overriding problem was that the left, which was the only part of the political spectrum that favoured aid, was mainly concerned about inequality within societies while being deeply suspicious of the normal process of economic growth: a focus on 'the poor' offered the possibility of compromise with this critical lobby.

The privileging of poverty reduction worked well in terms of the first three objectives: the image of the World Bank improved; agency performance became more oriented to the 'result' of poverty reduction; and all agencies signed up to the Millennium Development Goals, of which poverty reduction was the overarching objective. Since the absolute number of those in poverty was still rising, the need for aid was evidently increasing, and aid flows duly reversed their rapid decline. Only the fourth problem remained elusive: the critics of a market-oriented development paradigm remained largely unreconciled to growth, wanting to bring social inequality to the fore as the central challenge of development.

The *World Development Report 2006: Equity and Development* (*WDR*) of the World Bank (2005) represents, in the political sense, a further effort to build a bridge toward this critical lobby. It offers the convenient proposition that whether or not the reduction of social inequality is viewed as an objective, it is advisable because it is an obstacle to growth. Hence, the choice of objective can be sidestepped. The inequality in question is not of outcomes but of opportunities: the 'level playing field' becomes the objective around which both those who broadly trust market processes and those who broadly distrust them can unite: an 'unlevel' field is both unjust and inefficient. At the same time, and unlike most recent *World Development Reports*, much effort is devoted to documenting the scale of inequalities within countries and across the world. The *Human Development Report, 2005* of the UN Development Program (UNDP 2005), published around same time as the *WDR*, while not exclusively focusing on inequality, also emphasizes the scale of inequalities and touches on the case for growth benefits of reduced inequality.

In this chapter, we do not intend to question the proposition that there are relevant circumstances in which this is correct so that equity can indeed be reconciled with efficiency. Understanding these processes remains a fruitful area of research, not least at the empirical level. But as general metrics of progress in development, neither poverty nor equity is adequate: both individually and jointly they are liable to induce strategic errors. They may well be politically convenient for aid agencies, but their elevation to the status of ultimate goals comes at a cost. Just as we may fail to spot the gorilla running through the crowd, this new consensus among the aid community may take away our focus from those factors that will ultimately best serve the citizens of the developing world in terms of sustained improvements in their standard of living.

The structure of the chapter is as follows: in Section 14.2 we discuss how donors have used 'poverty' and 'inequality' for their own purposes. In effect, policy implications have been derived casually but predictably from these concepts. This is not, of course, a critique of the academic literature on these matters, but it is something of which academics should be aware. In Section 14.3 we turn to *World Development Report 2006* and the way it uses the academic literature itself. We suggest that the *WDR* stretches the term 'equity,' making three unhelpful conceptual conflations. Again, these lead to misleading inferences about policy.

14.2 Donor use and abuse of 'poverty' and 'inequality'

The focus on poverty and inequality is not a self-evident choice for assessing the success of the development process. We first discuss the normative base and then turn to the opportunity costs of a narrow focus on poverty and inequality.

The normative base

Both absolute poverty and inequality are legitimate metrics of the distribution of income and wealth in a country or across countries. It is useful information and tells us something about what is going on. How much importance one wants to give them is, however, a normative choice.

Agreements about the norm of absolute poverty are driven by a strange coalition. For 'progressives' it is viewed as part of a battle that is not confined to the poorest countries. For 'conservatives,' who have deep suspicions of aid in general, spending on 'the poor' or for 'humanitarian reasons' is seen as a solution to a political dilemma. Both views are potentially deeply patronizing, since any sense of a social contract between a government and its citizens—a domestic social welfare function—is shelved. A social welfare function that only attends to the concerns of the poor is not a necessary, or even a likely, outcome of democracy. Both theory and the domestic spending priorities observed in the richer democracies point to the clear dominance of the median voter and not to an exclusive focus on the poor. For good reason, the international community advocates democracy. A corollary is surely that the society should be left free to determine its own social welfare function, which is unlikely to be exactly coincident with the minimization of poverty.

Thinking about a social welfare function in the context of growth would involve some sort of weighting of the growth incidence curve (Ravallion and Chen 2003). The democratic political process generates such a weighting. Alternatively, at the moment the international donor community imposes one without recourse to any democratic involvement of the affected population. If, as is typical in many low-income countries, around 40 per cent of the population falls below the poverty line, the democratic process is unlikely to ignore the 'nonpoor' majority. Indeed, different democracies are likely to produce very different weightings of the growth incidence curve, as is evident from a comparison of the choices of Swedes and Americans. Donor governments are exhibiting policy incoherence in advocating democracy while trying to impose their own weightings.

Against our view, it is sometimes argued that in 'signing up' for the Millennium Development Goals (MDGs) all governments have in some way committed themselves to the acceptance of donor policy priorities regarding poverty reduction. Similarly, donor agencies sometimes suggest that their emphasis on social participation in the Poverty Reduction Strategy Papers (PRSP) reconciles the process of domestic choice with donor priorities. The reality is that recipient countries are ranged along a continuum of democratization. Approaches that are legitimate in countries radically lacking in democracy are illegitimate in countries with functioning democracies. In the former, *faux de mieux*, the international community may need to act on behalf of ordinary citizens, so that insisting on the MDGs and the participation of social groups in PRSP consultations is better than nothing. In the latter, it is a cynical abuse of donor power to suggest that signing up to the MDGs overrides the democratic choices of the society: signing up was something that no government of a small and poor country could in practice avoid since it was linked to the promise of aid.

The opportunity costs

The move from the Copenhagen Social Summit of 1995 to the Millennium Development Goals of 2000, of which poverty is explicitly a part, in one sense marks an important advance in policy awareness from focusing on inputs to focusing on outcomes. However, it has three opportunity costs.

First, the presence of explicit targets creates a demand for measurement. The myriad complications of the measurement of poverty and inequality risk crowding out a focus on the processes of income generation and hence how poverty arises. While measurement can be a useful component of understanding these processes, it is neither necessary nor sufficient and so, given the scarcity of analytic resources, comes with an opportunity cost. The point is not that measurement is unimportant: time and energy should indeed be devoted to it since concepts of poverty and inequality contain information. But its relative dominance of the discourse distracts from understanding how absolute poverty or even inequalities emerge.

Second, and more important, the focus on identifying 'the poor' creates the impression that the most efficient policies to reduce poverty and inequality are self-evident: what appear to be required are simply redistributive transfers to 'the poor'. In a more subtle way, government budgets and aid strategies come to be evaluated in terms of whether they directly contribute to poverty reduction. Similarly, reducing inequality is implicitly treated as costless: redistribution has no adverse general equilibrium or political economy effects. The implicit analytic framework is comparative statics: more equal societies do better than less equal societies, therefore the less equal societies should become more equal. But here lies the problem: even if more equal societies do better, there are few institutional contexts where redistribution can be done 'painlessly'. Banerjee, Gertler, and Ghatak (2002) analyze one such case, the redistribution of tenancy rights through Operation Barga in West Bengal. However, such stable institutional contexts are rare. In Ethiopia the land reform of 1976, while perhaps sensible in isolation, was part of a more fundamental upheaval that created a collapse of the entire rural economy. In Kenya and Tanzania the state was insufficiently effective to implement changes in land rights on the ground: the radically different government strategies of land titling and collectivization in the 1970s, respectively, appear to have had no effect (Pinckney and Kimuyu 1994) and have now been unwound (Ensminger 1997). Indeed, the same sort of statistical evidence that suggests that more equal societies grow faster also suggests that changes in inequality—even equalizing changes—are detrimental (Banerjee and Duflo 2003).

Third, and most crucial, development is about long-run growth in living standards for ordinary people. If policies are assessed on the criterion of short-run reductions in poverty, large errors are likely. Even were the appropriate metric of development success to be poverty reduction, its measurement should be dynamic. That is, the best development path would be that which minimized the discounted sum of future poverty. The growth strategy that achieves this minimization is likely to be substantially different from a strategy that minimizes poverty in the short run. A clear way of bringing down absolute poverty today is to change policies in such a way that current household consumption is higher at the expense of future consumption. Conversely, a widely spread tax, the revenue from which is used to build roads, will increase both poverty and growth. In any particular context the key components of a successful development strategy might be clear enough: it may, for example, be investment in the infrastructure needed by firms in new export activities. However, the short-term payoff in terms of poverty reduction may be negligible, and it may increase inequality, while the long term payoffs are inevitably uncertain. It will always be possible to find alternative uses of resources that in the short term are manifestly more 'poverty focused' and hence yield more reliable 'results'. An emphasis on 'poverty' and 'results' thus biases development strategies away from growth in living standards.

Taken together, these three biases promote policies that redistribute both from the future and from the majority of the economy, to those who are currently poor. Such redistributions are doubtless capable of reducing current poverty and, indeed, quite possibly of eliminating it. The great historical example of this prioritization is obviously Cuba. More populous and current examples are Venezuela under President Chavez and much of North Africa. Through their redistributive strategies Cuba and North Africa have largely eliminated poverty, and Venezuela may well do so. These are, however, not models to be emulated but rather disastrous development cul-de-sacs.

That Cuba, North Africa, and Venezuela are not development models is not merely the judgment of economists. Despite the elimination of poverty, Cubans and North Africans vote with their feet to get out, and those who leave do not return. Emerging evidence suggests that the low-income countries to which citizens are most willing to return once they have left are China and now, but strikingly only very recently and tentatively, India. Obviously, despite its acute increase in inequality in recent years and its political context, China offers hope that the future will be prosperous for ordinary people: that the lives of their children and grandchildren will not be fundamentally more limited if they live in China than if they live elsewhere. It is this credible prospect of international convergence that is in our view what ordinary citizens of developing countries want. Offering a credible future for developing societies is what development agencies should have as their objective.

14.3 Is equity instrumental?

We now turn to the core thesis of the *World Development Report 2006*, namely, that equity is instrumental in the growth and development process.

The concept of equity used for this thesis in the *WDR* is equality of opportunity, although it has to be said that a large majority of its examples of inequality actually concern outcomes.

The general argument is that 'greater equity can in the longer term underpin faster growth' (*World Development Report 2006* [2005, 70]). This thesis is overarching: it is applied in radically different contexts. One of these is the efficiency of resource utilization within an economy. Another is the application to issues of inequality between countries. A third context is its application to issues of political inequality. We will argue that so applied, the thesis is radically overextended. While the thesis is robust when applied to the analysis of inequality of opportunity in particular contexts, notably the credit market and blatant cases of stigmatization and discrimination, it cannot credibly offer a more general account of the instrumental role of equity. We take these three conceptual conflations in turn.

The efficiency–equity trade-off within a market economy

Economic theory has in recent years clarified the circumstances in which the standard neoclassical trade-off between efficiency and equity does not apply. A necessary condition is that particular markets are imperfect. As is well known, the presence of market failure may justify welfare-improving interventions. To do so, the market failure needs to interact with inequalities in such a way that those with low wealth are more severely constrained in their behaviour than those with higher wealth. A consequence is that efficiency losses are more substantial for low-wealth groups than for high-wealth groups. In this situation redistribution of wealth could be efficiency improving.

The standard example is the functioning of credit markets. Constraints of information or enforcement may induce lenders to use wealth as collateral, thereby restricting credit for the low-wealth group. For non-increasing returns to scale and common technology this would imply that the marginal return to capital for the low-wealth group is higher than for the high-wealth group. This implies that there are opportunities for redistribution that would also generate gains in overall efficiency as returns to capital are equalized. The *World Development Report 2006* carefully develops this example in chapter 5, 'Inequality and Investment'. In the development of the overall conclusions, in the overview chapter, it is reiterated, and the example becomes a central part of the argument for the instrumental role of inequality.

Even in the credit market these conditions can easily be violated. As the *WDR* acknowledges (*World Development Report 2006* [2005, 102]), low-wealth households may face entry costs or thresholds to the more productive technologies, thereby undermining the efficiency case for marginal redistributions. How relevant is the example of the credit market for other factor markets? Widespread risk and the failure of insurance markets may fit the credit market case, since credit can provide an obvious insurance substitute. Furthermore, the ability to cope with risk is closely linked to wealth. Consider, however, whether the argument extends from financial capital to human capital. The report opens with a resounding example of educational inequality: in the same society one child will complete tertiary education and another will have next to no education. This may well be unjust, but under what circumstances is it an opportunity for efficiency-enhancing redistribution of education?

There can indeed be such circumstances. From the point of view of the child with no education the lack of opportunity is likely to be linked with a lack of wealth. Education is an investment with a high sunk cost so that low-wealth households may not be able to finance it. The credit market failure as described above is then relevant, and redistributive policies would allow a more efficient use of the human potential of the low-wealth household. However, this only considers the benefits to the low-wealth household. The redistribution must imply reducing the educational achievement of the high-wealth household. Any efficiency argument will have to take this into account. One way in which there could be net efficiency gains from such redistribution is if there are ability differences between households. Provided that these differences are unrelated to wealth, redistribution would better align educational opportunities with abilities and so increase the efficiency of educational resource allocation.

In effect, this argument is analogous to the 'threshold' effect of differences in technologies discussed above in the context of the credit market but with the reverse implication. Whereas low-wealth households may be excluded from the more productive technologies, now it is the high-wealth households that are using education less productively because at the margin they are conferring education on less able children. Any tendency of wealth and inherited ability to be correlated would, of course, undermine this argument. Further, the argument is still dependent on non-increasing returns to common technology, and in the case of human capital this is far more contentious than in the case of physical capital. The *WDR* quotes mean rates of return to education (*World Development Report 2006* [2005, 101]) to suggest that returns to education are substantial. However, this misses the point. The key issue is the shape of the returns function within an economy. At least for Africa there is systematic evidence that private returns are convex: in other words, there are increasing returns to education (Söderbom *et al.* 2006; for the United States, see Belzil and Hansen [2002]). Convex private returns do not necessarily imply convex social returns. However, in small, badly governed societies the social return to creating a critical mass of people with sufficient education to devise and implement strategies for change may be enormous. It is clear that under increasing social returns to education, redistributing education from the highly educated to the less educated, while enhancing equity, unambiguously reduces efficiency. The parable of efficiency-enhancing equity does not even readily extend from the market for financial capital to the market for human capital. Over the past decade the priorities of 'education for all' have indeed shifted spending from tertiary to primary education: this is a practical example of the power of the poverty and equity metrics. Whether this shift was either efficient or beneficial for longer term development is unclear.

Of course, it may well be appropriate to expand educational opportunities at the bottom without reducing them at the top. The *World Development Report 2006* nowhere specifically argues for redistribution of education from the rich as the appropriate policy mechanism to increase the education for the poor. However, in this case redistribution and equity are an inappropriate banner under which to promote a simple point: that increasing the total stock of human capital may well increase efficiency and that educating the poor is an obvious choice for boosting the total stock, with a beneficial poverty reduction and equity impact. This has little to do with redistribution. It also avoids the question whether educating a few more people to a high level may be better than educating a lot more at low levels.

Not only does the example of efficiency-promoting equity not readily generalize from the financial market to other factor markets, even in respect of the financial market but also the proposition does not usually constitute a case for redistribution. The lack of an efficiency-equity trade-off in particular circumstances stems from the interaction of inequalities with market failures. Redistribution is at best a second-best policy response from an efficiency point of view: addressing the underlying market failures should normally be the priority. For example, the key lesson of successful microfinance institutions is not that it is worthwhile to offer credit to poor people in any form but rather that particular institutional arrangements, with sensible incentive and enforcement structures, succeed in remedying market failures affecting the poor.

Domestic versus global inequality

The *World Development Report 2006* excels in presenting evidence of inequalities across the world, both between and within countries. Reducing domestic and global inequities—offering a level playing field both within societies and internationally—are seen as complementary measures with potentially substantial growth impacts. We will argue that this conceptual conflation of domestic and global inequity is misleading and misses the point.

Statistics of global poverty and inequality levels miss a key part of the development catastrophe of the past 30 years. This is that a large group of low-income countries, largely in Africa, and with a combined population of around 1 billion, have failed to grow for a variety of reasons. Meanwhile, in the rest of the developing world, which is to say a large majority of it, growth has been accelerating, decade by decade. Since 1980 the stagnant billion have been diverging from the other 4 billion at an average rate of around 5 per cent per year. The result has been an astounding rate of divergence, resulting in a massive absolute inequality between the stagnant poor countries and the rest, with a gap in the order of magnitude of 5:1. Whether per capita incomes have been slightly in decline or slightly increasing in the countries stuck at the bottom is a second order issue, as is their trend in absolute poverty: the vital fact is of radical divergence. Quite evidently, it is not viable in a world with easy international mobility to have a billion people at the bottom in countries that are diverging from the rest of the world. Both for their sake and for the sake of everybody else, international action will have to change this situation, and it will be difficult because it has been so persistent. This is the overwhelming challenge of development in the coming decades.

Convergence is clearly about inequality: if convergence is the objective, international inequality most certainly matters. Superficially, this sounds like at least part of the message of the *World Development Report 2006*, but it is not. Although the *WDR* includes international inequality, it is overwhelmingly concerned with social inequality—inequality within societies. Further, it defines this concern as equality of opportunity, not of outcomes, and then extends this concern to the international scene: poor countries are poor relative to rich countries because they are not facing a level playing field of opportunities. This conflation of international and social inequality is dysfunctional. The inequality that matters internationally is about outcomes, irrespective of the extent to which they are explained by unlevel international playing fields. It is the brute fact of the failure of countries such as Sierra Leone and Zambia to grow that is the problem, regardless of its cause. Furthermore, the contribution of unjust international rules to the dreadful circumstances of the poorest countries is utterly minor: Sierra Leone exports diamonds, as does the fabulously more successful Botswana. Zambia exports copper as does the fabulously more successful Chile. The overemphasis of international injustice in the *WDR* feeds the paranoia that has been so disempowering within stagnant economies. Local elites are only too willing to accept that international injustice is the cause of the problems of their economies, since it provides an easy alibi. Of course many of the rules and structures of the international economic and political system are unfair, or more usually unheeding, of the needs of these countries. Of course something should be done about it, not least since it will offer better growth opportunities. But as an explanation for the failure of the growth process in them it is quite inadequate.

So far we have set aside the question as to why some states have suffered persistent failure of the growth process whereas most have not. There is no one 'trap' that accounts for all failures. But understanding that there are traps is critical in understanding what we can do to break out of stagnation. The *WDR* considers divergence only in the most superficial way. For example, it investigates what the numbers show if China and India are excluded. But the developing world minus China and India is not a meaningful aggregate: it is not based on any characteristics that could be used to diagnose the nature of a problem. It is merely a crude bit of statistical fishing around.

The countries where the development process has failed do not need a level playing field, they need large and sustained affirmative action. Some of this, as we will discuss, involves a degree of injustice to more successful though still poor developing countries: expediency, not justice, is the honest basis for much of the necessary international action. We will here take one example of a policy that exemplifies the difference between a focus on growth convergence as opposed to the international level playing field. It is trade. The *WDR* goes through the usual litany of trade inequities, with all of which any reasonable economist should concur. Agricultural subsidies and protection should be eliminated; intellectual property rights should not be extended to low-income countries in such a way as to produce an income transfer from them. But do these measures get to the heart of the problems of the stagnant countries? We think that one important class of such countries has 'missed the boat' of breaking into Organization for Economic Cooperation and Development (OECD) markets for manufactured and service exports. Such diversification, where it is feasible, is massively advantageous for development: globally, it is the coastal, resource-scarce countries that have developed most rapidly, since these are the countries that are not debarred from export diversification either by Dutch disease or transport costs.

The great moment for breaking into world markets was the 1980s. It is now surely much harder because the low-income Asian economies are already established in these markets. That is, they have already accumulated the agglomeration economies that were for many years so critical in maintaining the competitiveness of the OECD economies despite their high wages. The latecomers do not yet have markedly lower wages than Asia, and so their lack of agglomeration economies makes them uncompetitive. Protection of their domestic markets is, of course, at best irrelevant: their tiny markets dominated by low-income consumers are not a viable preparation for exports to OECD markets. Yet to break into OECD markets the countries that have missed the boat do need temporary protection—but from Asia. That is, countries such as Kenya, Ghana, Madagascar, and Senegal need protection in OECD markets from Asian competition. This cannot, except by violence to language, be described as levelling the playing field, or 'trade justice'. The most reasonable description is that it is expedient. The OECD is currently only operating such preferences as gestures: the Africa Growth and Opportunity Act in the United States, Everything but Arms in the European Union (EU), and nothing equivalent even to those seriously flawed schemes in high-income Asia. Probably what is needed is an OECD-wide scheme, with a timeframe of around a decade, and rules of origin that can be fine tuned to achieve rapidly rising targets of manufactured exports from the stagnating countries.

Contrary to the *WDR*, the rapid divergence of some poor economies therefore does not imply the need for 'equality of opportunity' but rather for affirmative action to reduce inequality in outcomes. Further, the importance of reversing this international divergence breaks the link that the report suggests exists between international inequality and domestic (social) inequality. Reversing international divergence is likely to require widening inequality within the societies stuck at the bottom.

It is the educated who are becoming globally more mobile, rather than the uneducated. Skill shortages in richer economies actively and increasingly offer opportunities to highly educated and skilled people. The societies at the bottom are chronically short of skilled people, and to keep them they will increasingly need to offer incomes that are at least loosely related to global levels. In the context of divergence this implies that the higher-income groups must be offered increasingly wide differentials from the rest of society. Social inequality in these societies is a partial consequence of their overall economic failure, as only a minority attains the lifestyles that are normal in other societies. Suppose that the educated minority in a low-income society is willing to make modest but not large sacrifices in order to stay resident. To give a realistic but painful example, it may demand educational provision for its children that is far too expensive for the society to adopt as a norm. Those societies that choose equity, or have equity imposed upon them by international priorities, may then lose their educated people and perhaps never accumulate the critical mass needed for change. Even global equity is not served by such an outcome: the educated are better off as a result of migrating. The possibility of a sharp trade-off between equity and development in the societies that are poor and stagnant is certainly uncomfortable. It runs radically against the grain of the consensus-building political discourse that the development agencies have learned to adopt. But it should surely have been explored.

In one sense, this dilemma is indeed generated by an inequality in opportunity at the international level, stimulated by migration policies: educated and wealthy people find it much easier to emigrate to rich countries than do the uneducated. But the policy reversal implied by the 'equality of opportunity' principle, that rich countries should open their doors so that everyone should be able to leave the failing societies, is not politically feasible; it may also not be desirable. The normative consequences of the loss of entire societies cannot be adequately captured by the conventional economic calculus of gains to individuals: if the entire population of Africa were successfully absorbed in the United States, there would be a loss. Development policies should attach some weights to sustaining distinct societies.

The reality of global inequality offers few alternatives. Offering a credible future to skilled people in developing societies creates the basis for change and development. When taking into account international migration possibilities, promoting equality in these societies could thus reinforce their stagnation. If their economies grow sufficiently rapidly, that growth may increasingly create equalizing opportunities, but it is convergence that will create the possibility of equality rather than equality that will create convergence.

Economic versus political inequality

Some aspects of equity are indeed fundamental to the success of the failing societies, but they are primarily political and legal. The lack of government accountability and weaknesses in the rule of law have been at the heart of the growth failure in many countries. While in some ethnically homogeneous societies, notably China, autocracy has been consistent with rapid development and may even have assisted it, in more diverse societies it has usually been disastrous. In other words, and powerfully argued in the *WDR*, basic political equality and equality before the law often appear to be essential features for successful development.

The conflation of accountability and the rule of law with other aspects of equity is, however, again misleading. There can be trade-offs both between democracy and economic equity and between the rule of law and economic equity. When Cuba eventually democratizes it will most surely become more unequal, as would many societies if they succeeded in transforming themselves into replicas of the United States or even Sweden. The core aspect of the rule of law emphasized in economic development is the defence of property rights. By definition, property rights reflect existing, and possibly highly unequal, distributions of income. The strengthening of property rights, a strategy indeed important for development, is likely to inhibit moves to economic equity: indeed, the proposition is scarcely controversial. That the *WDR* could so gracefully elide between its espousal of equity and its espousal of property rights is thanks to the helpful phrase 'equality before the law'. But such language is surely more reasonably seen as papering over a trade-off than as demonstrating a complementarity.

14.4 Conclusion

Concern with poverty and inequality is not misplaced, but donors have over-extended its role in different ways. They implicitly subscribe to a selective normative view of other societies. This view is unlikely to be consistent with those generated within the societies themselves through democratic processes. It is not even a view to which the electorates of the donor countries usually subscribe when choosing their own governments. The imposition of these priorities is at once too radical and too conservative. It is too radical in that its imposition on the societies that are poor and stagnant risks removing any remaining incentives for the skilled population of these failing economies to seek a future in their own societies. It is too conservative in that the agenda of an international 'level playing field' is liable to be hopelessly inadequate to reverse the catastrophe of the divergence of these economies at the bottom from the rest of mankind. Furthermore, the focus on monitoring poverty outcomes has contributed to the impression that once 'the poor' have been identified, the strategy by which both governments and donors can best address poverty and the lack of opportunities for the poor is self-evident. The goal of targeted transfers has crowded out genuinely strategic thinking about the complex processes of growth in living standards.

The *World Development Report 2006* has tried to offer a balanced discussion on the role of inequality in a range of development issues by drawing on careful analysis with an eye for detail. But by making inequality a central, overarching framework for understanding the lack of growth, the *WDR* has overextended the instrumental role of inequality and thereby inadvertently reinforced the weaknesses of the current development discourse.

References

Banerjee, Abhijit, and Esther Duflo. (2003). 'Inequality and Growth: What Can the Data Say?' *Journal of Economic Growth* 8, no. 3:267–99.

Banerjee, Abhijit, Paul Gertler, and Maitreesh Ghatak. (2002). 'Empowerment and Efficiency: Tenancy Reform in West Bengal.' *Journal of Political Economy* 110, no. 2:239–80.

Belzil, Christian, and Jörgen Hansen. (2002). 'Unobserved Ability and the Return to Schooling.' *Econometrica* 70, no. 5:2075–91.

Ensminger, Jean. (1997). 'Changing Property Rights: Reconciling Formal and Informal Rights to Land in Africa.' In *The Frontiers of the New Institutional Economics*, ed. J. N. Drobak and V. C. Nye, 165–96. New York: Academic Press.

Pinckney, Thomas C., and Peter K. Kimuyu. (1994). 'Land Tenure Reform in East Africa: Good, Bad or Unimportant?' *Journal of African Economies* 3, no. 1:1–28.

Ravallion, Martin, and Shaohua Chen. (2003). 'Measuring Pro-Poor Growth.' *Economics Letters*, 78:93–99.

Simons, Daniel J., and Christopher F. Chabris. (1999). 'Gorillas in Our Midst: Sustained Inattentional Blindness for Dynamic Events.' *Perception* 28:1059–74.

Söderbom, Måns, Francis Teal, Anthony Wanbugu, and Godius Kahyara. (2006). 'The Dynamics of Returns to Education in Kenyan and Tanzanian Manufacturing.' *Oxford Bulletin of Economics and Statistics* 68 (June 2006): 261–88.

UNDP (UN Development Program). (2005). *Human Development Report, 2005*. Oxford: Oxford University Press for UNDP.

World Bank. *World Development Report 2006*. (2005). Oxford: Oxford University Press for the World Bank.

15 Does aid mitigate external shocks?

With Benedikt Goderis

15.1 Introduction

This chapter empirically investigates the role of aid in mitigating the adverse effects of commodity export price shocks on growth in commodity-dependent countries. Adverse price shocks can have negative effects, both *ex ante* and *ex post*. *Ex ante*, proneness to shocks increases uncertainty about future returns, which might reduce investment and hence growth, a problem sometimes referred to as *vulnerability*. *Ex post*, realized shocks can harm economic growth in the short run through their effect on aggregate demand or a government's fiscal position.

Aid might mitigate these effects through two distinct routes. Where aid can be made shock-continent, it acts like insurance. However, even if aid is not responsive to the realization of shocks, it might finance precautionary expenditures which make the economy more resilient to shocks, a proposition first seriously advanced by Guillaumont and Chauvet (2001). Potentially, each form of aid might mitigate either effect. Aid as insurance directly compensates realized adverse shocks whereas aid for precautionary spending reduces their cost to the economy. Both thereby make the economy less vulnerable.

Since insurance is the most appropriate solution to risk where it is feasible, shock-contingent aid has some evident attractions. However, it faces three impediments. First, administratively it is generally only feasible to compen sate the *government* of the country suffering the adverse shock. Where the shock affects the private sector such as export agriculture, compensation to government will cushion the macro economy but, through the exchange rate effect, it will compound the shock to its primary recipients. Second, aid disbursements are generally slow, so that entitlements triggered by a shock are only likely to reach the economy some years later. This was exemplified by the STABEX shock-contingent instrument of the European Commission, the disbursements from which were so heavily lagged that they were on average *pro*-cyclical. Third, shock-contingent aid would only reduce the costs of vulnerability if it was regarded as a credible long-term commitment, yet aid policies are widely perceived to be subject to fashion.

If adverse shocks generate substantial economic costs, aid might more feasibly address them through precautionary effects which depend upon the level of aid rather than its responsiveness. One straightforward precautionary effect is that the higher is aid the less exposed is the economy to import compression resulting from a shock to commodity export earnings: a given absolute shock will require a smaller proportionate reduction in imports. Aid might also finance liquidity, both higher levels of foreign reserves and greater financial depth, which can then be used to cushion shocks to external income. Aid might also finance investments that enhance the flexibility of the economy. For example, by financing human capital it might make the workforce more adaptable, and by financing infrastructure it might make factors more mobile.

In our analysis we first test to what extent shocks matter for growth, both through increased vulnerability (*ex ante*), and through the realization of shocks (*ex post*). We then investigate whether either the level of aid, or shock-contingent aid, mitigate the negative effects of shocks.

We allow for exchange rate flexibility as an alternative or additional instrument to mitigate shocks. Broda (2004) finds that the short-run output response to terms-of-trade changes is significantly smaller in countries with flexible exchange rate regimes than in those with fixed regimes. The underlying argument is that when economies are hit by real shocks and prices are sticky, the exchange rate can play a crucial role in smoothening quantity responses by allowing for a quicker adjustment of relative prices. We test the robustness of Broda's results for commodity export price shocks. In addition, we investigate whether exchange rate flexibility and aid are potentially substitutes. In particular, we test whether the effect of aid is different in countries with fixed exchange rates, which do not have an automatic alternative line of defence, than in countries with flexible exchange rates.

Using data for 100 countries from 1971 till 2003, we find that negative commodity export price shocks matter substantially for short-term growth, while the *ex ante* risk of shocks does not seem to matter for long-run GDP. We also find that both the *level* of aid and exchange rate flexibility substantially lower the adverse effect of shocks. *Incremental*, shock-contingent aid, does not seem to mitigate the effect of shocks. While the level of aid mitigates shocks, regardless of a country's exchange rate regime, the mitigating effect seems to be somewhat smaller for countries with flexible exchange rates, suggesting that aid and exchange rate flexibility are partly substitutes. Having established that aid can be effective in shock-prone countries, we then investigate whether aid has historically been targeted at such countries, but find no evidence that this is the case. This suggests that donors could increase aid effectiveness by redirecting aid towards countries that suffer from a high incidence of commodity export price shocks.

This paper is related to the literature on terms-of-trade shocks and aid effectiveness. It is most closely related to Collier and Dehn (2001), who show that the adverse effects of negative shocks can be mitigated by offsetting increases in aid. This paper improves upon their study by using instrumental variables for aid, applying several alternative dynamic panel estimation techniques, and allowing the effect of shocks to be proportional to commodity exports. We also test the importance of the *ex ante* risk of shocks as well as the realized shocks, and investigate the role of a country's exchange rate regime. In addition, we look at whether aid and exchange rate flexibility are substitutes or complements and we use a much larger and richer dataset.

The remainder of this paper is organized as follows. Section 15.2 describes data, methodology, and the construction of variables, and deals with the endogeneity of aid. Section 15.3 presents the main findings. Section 15.4 provides sensitivity analysis. Section 15.5 investigates whether aid has historically been targeted at shock-prone countries. Section 15.6 concludes.

15.2 Data and methodology

Our estimation strategy involves two steps. We first test the importance of commodity export price shocks and commodity export price uncertainty as determinants of GDP. Having established which of these have negative effects on GDP, we then investigate the potential role of foreign aid in mitigating these negative effects. The effects of shocks and uncertainty, as well as the mitigating effect of aid are analyzed using the following error-correction model:[1]

$$\Delta y_{i,t} = \alpha_i + \delta_t + \lambda y_{i,t-1} + \beta_1' x_{i,t-1} + \sum_{q=1}^{k} \beta_2 \Delta y_{i,t-q} + \sum_{m=1}^{n} \beta_3' \Delta x_{i,t-m}$$

$$+ \sum_{h=0}^{w} \beta_4' s_{i,t-h} + \sum_{j=0}^{i} \beta_5' p_{i,t-j} + \sum_{r=1}^{v} \beta_{6r}' (x_{i,t-1})(p_{i,t-1,r}) + \sum_{h=0}^{w} \sum_{r=1}^{v} \beta_{7r}'$$

$$(s_{i,t-h})(p_{i,t-h,r}) + u_{i,t} \tag{1}$$

where $y_{i,t}$ is log real GDP per capita in country i in year t and α_i and δ_t are country-specific and year-specific fixed effects, respectively. $x_{i,t-1}$ is a $z \times 1$ vector of z variables that are expected to affect GDP both in the short run and long run. This vector includes our indicator of commodity export price uncertainty to test its long-run effect on GDP. In addition, we include several controls. Four variables are taken from the empirical growth literature: i) trade openness, measured as the ratio of trade to GDP, ii) external debt to GNI, iii) inflation, measured as the consumer price index (cpi), and iv) financial development, measured as the ratio of M2 to GDP. Following Collier and Goderis (2007), we also include indices of commodity export prices and oil import prices to control for the long-run effect of commodity prices on GDP. Section 15.2.1 explains how these variables were constructed.

$s_{i,t-h}$ is an $l \times 1$ vector of l variables that are expected to have a short-run effect on growth. We first include our indicators of commodity export price shocks (see Section 15.2.1) to estimate the effects of large changes in commodity export prices. In addition, we include measures of geological, climatic, and human disasters (Raddatz, 2007), and dummy variables for civil wars and coup d'états as controls.

$p_{i,t-j}$ is a vector of $v \times 1$ vector of v variables that could mitigate the adverse effects of commodity export price shocks and uncertainty. First, we include a dummy variable which takes a value of 1 for a *de facto* flexible exchange rate, and 0 for a *de facto* fixed exchange rate. Second, we include both the level and the first difference of the log of (1 + foreign aid), where foreign aid is measured as a percentage of GNI.[2] We refer to the variable "log (1 + foreign aid)" as "aid". In Section 15.2.2 we discuss the endogeneity of aid. The interactions of $x_{i,t-1}$ and $s_{i,t-h}$ with $p_{i,t-j}$ are used to test the central hypotheses: if commodity export price shocks and commodity export price uncertainty harm economic performance, the losses will be smaller for countries that receive more aid.

Our dataset consists of all countries and years for which data are available, and covers 100 countries between 1971 and 2003. Table 15.1 reports summary

Table 15.1 Summary statistics

	Obs	Mean	St dev	Min	Max
GDP per capita (log)	2319	6.80	1.12	4.31	9.17
Trade to GDP (log)	2306	4.05	0.57	1.84	5.43
External debt to GNI (log)	2317	3.90	0.84	−0.11	7.10
CPI (log)	2312	2.52	4.27	−26.98	7.00
M2 to GDP (log)	2317	3.31	0.55	1.41	5.02
Commodity export price index (log)	2319	43.19	39.36	0.04	205.39
Commodity exports to GDP	2319	9.42	8.83	0.01	44.61
Export price uncertainty (log)	2319	0.09	0.19	0.00	3.70
Oil import price index (log)	2319	3.27	1.85	0	4.96
Flexible exchange rate	1736	0.62	0.49	0	1
Aid (log)	2311	1.57	1.05	−1.17	4.59
Δ GDP per capita (log)	2319	0.01	0.05	−0.36	0.30
Δ Trade to GDP (log)	2306	0.01	0.14	−1.20	1.40
Δ CPI (log)	2312	0.17	0.37	−0.14	5.48
Δ Aid (log)	2310	−0.01	0.27	−1.38	1.62
Coup d'etat	2319	0.03	0.18	0	2
Civil war	2319	0.10	0.30	0	1
Geological shocks	2319	0.06	0.24	0	2
Climatic shocks	2319	0.27	0.52	0	3
Humanitarian shocks	2319	0.03	0.16	0	2

Export price shocks					
	Number	Mean	St dev	Min	Max
Positive shocks	223	0.34	0.16	0.12	1.03
Negative shocks	231	0.31	0.13	0.15	0.81

Notes: This table reports summary statistics for all observations used in estimation.

Table 15.2a List of countries and their shares of commodity exports in GDP (%)

Albania (3)	Congo, D.R. (9)	India (1)	Pakistan (2)	Tonga (0)
Algeria (15)	Congo, Rep. (29)	Indonesia (15)	Panama (5)	Tr. & Tob. (19)
Angola (35)	Costa Rica (11)	Iran (14)	P. N. Guin. (18)	Tunisia (6)
Argentina (3)	Cote d'Ivoire (14)	Jamaica (18)	Paraguay (12)	Turkey (1)
Bangladesh (1)	Dominica (19)	Kenya (6)	Peru (6)	Uganda (4)
Barbados (2)	Dom. Rep. (7)	Laos (1)	Philippines (3)	Uruguay (4)
Belize (13)	Ecuador (21)	Lesotho (0)	Poland (3)	Vanuatu (5)
Benin (0)	Egypt (2)	Lithuania (0)	Romania (1)	Venezuela (32)
Bolivia (12)	El Salvador (6)	Madagascar (2)	Rwanda (4)	Vietnam (18)
Botswana (7)	Eq. Guinea (6)	Malawi (20)	Samoa (1)	Yemen (1)
Brazil (2)	Ethiopia (2)	Malaysia (21)	Senegal (6)	Zambia (35)
Bulgaria (2)	Fiji (12)	Maldives (2)	Seychelles (0)	Zimbabwe (9)
Burkina Faso (3)	Gabon (31)	Mali (7)	Sierra Leone (7)	
Burundi (6)	Gambia (4)	Mauritania (25)	Sol. Islands (8)	
Cambodia (3)	Ghana (11)	Mauritius (15)	South Africa (3)	
Cameroon (15)	Grenada (4)	Mexico (4)	Sri Lanka (7)	
Cape Verde (1)	Guatemala (8)	Morocco (4)	Sudan (2)	
C. Afr. Rep. (2)	Guin.-Bissau (1)	Mozambique (1)	Swaziland (22)	
Chad (6)	Guyana (45)	Nepal (0)	Syria (15)	
Chile (16)	Haiti (1)	Nicaragua (17)	Tanzania (5)	
China (2)	Honduras (20)	Niger (0)	Thailand (4)	
Colombia (11)	Hungary (2)	Nigeria (35)	Togo (14)	

Table 15.2b List of commodities

Non-agricultural				
Aluminium	Gasoline	Natural gas	Phosphatrock	Uranium
Coal	Ironore	Nickel	Silver	Urea
Copper	Lead	Oil	Tin	Zinc
Agricultural				
Bananas	Cotton	Oliveoil	Pulp	Sugar
Barley	Fish	Oranges	Rice	Sunfloweroil
Butter	Groundnutoil	Palmkerneloil	Rubber	Swinemeat
Cocoabeans	Groundnuts	Palmoil	Sisal	Tea
Coconutoil	Hides	Pepper	Sorghum	Tobacco
Coffee	Jute	Plywood	Soybeanoil	Wheat
Copra	Maize	Poultry	Soybeans	Wool

statistics. Table 15.2a lists the countries and their share of commodity exports in GDP. The Appendix 15A describes data and sources.

15.2.1 *Constructing indicators of commodity export prices, shocks, and uncertainty*

The commodity export price index was constructed using the methodology of Deaton and Miller (1996), Dehn (2000), and Collier and Goderis (2007). We collected data on world commodity prices and commodity export values for as many commodities as data availability allowed. Table 15.2b lists the 58 commodities in our sample. For each of the countries, we calculate the total value of 1990 commodity exports and construct weights by dividing the 1990 export values for each commodity by this total. These weights are held fixed over time and applied to the world price indices of the same commodities to form a country-specific geometrically weighted index.

It is important that the commodity export price index is exogenous, i.e. not correlated with the error term in equation (1). As argued by Deaton and Miller (1996), one of the advantages of using international commodity prices is that they are typically not affected by the actions of individual countries. Also, by keeping the weights constant over time, supply responses to price changes are not included. As a result, we believe the index to be exogenous with respect to GDP or the determinants of GDP. In our estimation, we use the log of the commodity export price index, weighted by the level of commodity exports over GDP as of 1990 (per cent), which allows the impact of commodity prices to be proportional to a country's commodity exports.

We next use the unweighted logged index to construct indicators of commodity export price shocks and uncertainty. Following Collier and Dehn (2001), we identify shocks by differencing the commodity export price index to make it stationary, and then removing predictable elements from the stationary process by running the following basic annual forecasting model:

$$\Delta I_{i,t} = \alpha_0 + \alpha_1 t + \beta_1 \Delta I_{i,t-1} + \beta_2 I_{i,t-2} + \varepsilon_{i,t} \tag{2}$$

where $I_{i,t}$ is the log commodity export price index and t is a linear time trend. We collect the residuals $\varepsilon_{i,t}$ from (2) and derive the 10th and 90th percentile of their distribution. We next define positive and negative commodity export price shock episodes as the observations with residuals above the 90th percentile or below the 10th percentile, respectively.[3] Having identified the shock episodes, we construct 2 variables. The first captures *positive* commodity export price shocks and equals the first log difference of the commodity export price index for the *positive* shock episodes, and 0 otherwise. The second captures *negative* commodity export price shocks and equals minus the first log difference of the commodity export price index for the *negative* shock episodes, and 0 otherwise. Table 15.1 provides summary statistics. The sample contains 223 positive and 231 negative shocks. We perform one further procedure. Any impact of commodity price shocks is likely to be bigger for more commodity-dependent countries. We therefore use the logged difference of the index, *weighted by the (log of the) share of commodity exports in GDP as of 1990*. This allows the effect of export price shocks to be logged linearly proportional to a country's exposure.

In addition to actual shocks, we also include a measure of export price *uncertainty*. Following Dehn (2000), we use a GARCH (1,1) model in which the actual volatility in a country's commodity export prices is explained by past volatility and past expected volatility:

$$\Delta I_t = \alpha_0 + \alpha_1 t + \beta_1 \Delta I_{t-1} + \beta_2 I_{t-2} + \beta_3 D_t + \varepsilon_t$$

$$\sigma_t^2 = \gamma_0 + \gamma_1 \varepsilon_{t-1}^2 + \gamma_2 \sigma_{t-1}^2 \qquad (3)$$

where I_t is the log commodity export price index in quarter t, t is a linear time trend, D_t is a vector of quarterly dummies to remove seasonal effects, and σ_t^2 denotes the variance of, ε_t, conditional upon information up to period t. We use the fitted values of the second equation in (3) as a measure of commodity export price uncertainty, since it captures the 'predicted' variance of the innovations in commodity export prices from past actual and expected volatility. Intuitively, this makes use of the concept of volatility clustering: big shocks tend to be followed by big shocks in either direction. This implies that historical information about the volatility in commodity prices can be used to predict future volatility. It is the (log) of the predicted future volatility that we use as a measure of uncertainty. Again, to allow the effect of commodity price uncertainty to be (log linearly) proportional to the importance of commodity exports, we weigh the indicator of uncertainty by the (log of the) share of commodity exports to GDP as of 1990.

The oil import price index was constructed by taking a logged index of world oil prices and interacting it with a dummy for net oil importers. This variable is important as oil enters the commodity export price index but is at the same time likely to affect oil importers as well. Failing to control for this effect would therefore have the consequence that the coefficient on the commodity export price index, instead of capturing the effect of higher oil prices for oil exporters, would capture the difference between the effects on oil exporters and importers.

15.2.2 The endogeneity of aid: using instrumental variables

Aid is likely to be endogenous with respect to growth. Past growth or even expected future growth of recipient countries may affect the aid allocation decisions of donors. These decisions may also be correlated with omitted variables that affect growth. In both cases the OLS estimator is biased. To address this problem, we use instruments for aid in all our specifications. Tavares (2003) argues that, 'when an OECD country increases its total aid outflows, developing countries that are culturally and geographically closer to that donor country experience an exogenous increase in aid inflows as a share of their GDP'. We follow Tavares by constructing aid instruments as follows. We collect total bilateral aid outflows from the five largest OECD donors: France, Germany, Japan, the UK, and the US, and express them as a proportion of GNI. In 2003 about half of total global aid was provided by these five donors. We then generate four variables that capture the political, geographical, and cultural distance for each donor/recipient combination. For political distance we use an index of UN voting affinity (Gartzke and Jo, 2002). For each donor/recipient combination we calculate the average value of the index over the available years and use this average for every year.[4] For geographical distance, we use the inverse of the distance in kilometers between the recipient countries' capitals and the donor countries' capitals.[5] Cultural distance is measured by 2 dummies. The first dummy takes a value of unity if the donor and recipient share a common language (CIA Factbook 2003). The other dummy takes a value of unity if the same religious group dominates in both the donor and the recipient country.[6] All distance indicators are invariant over time but vary across recipient countries while the aid outflows vary over time but not across recipient countries. We construct 20 instruments by interacting each of the indicators with each of the aid outflows. These variables will be used as instruments for *the level of aid*. We first-difference the 20 instruments to create an additional 20 instruments for *differenced aid*. Next to the level and difference of aid we include several interactions of the aid variables with the shock variables. We create instruments for these interactions by regressing the aid variables on all aid instruments and other regressors and interacting the predicted values with the shock variables to construct additional instruments (following Goderis and Ioannidou, 2008). We use all instruments and perform two-stage least-squares estimation.

15.3 Estimation results

Table 15.3 reports estimation results for the model in equation (1) but without the vector of variables that potentially mitigate the effect of adverse shocks and its interactions with shocks and uncertainty. This allows us to test the effects of negative commodity export price shocks and commodity price uncertainty on GDP.

The contemporaneous and lagged negative export price shocks enter negative but only the lagged shock is significant (at 5 per cent). The coefficient is also much larger for the lagged shock, suggesting that, if there is an effect of negative export price shocks on growth, it occurs in the year after the shock.[7] The coefficient is –0.017 which suggests that for a country with sample average commodity exports to GDP (9.42 per cent), a sample average negative export price shock (30 per cent) lowers next year's growth by $0.017*\log(9.42)*0.30 = 1.14$ percentage points.

While negative commodity export price shocks significantly lower growth, we do not find evidence of a long-run negative effect of commodity export price uncertainty on GDP. Although the indicator of uncertainty enters with the expected negative sign, it is far from significant.

The other long-run coefficients all have the expected signs. Trade to GDP enters positive and is significant at 1 per cent, indicating that more open countries tend to have higher long-run GDP levels. External debt and the consumer price index enter negative, suggesting that countries with fiscal imprudence or historically high inflation rates have lower long-run GDP. However, the coefficients are insignificant, so should be viewed with caution. The same goes for M2 to GDP, which enters with a positive sign, indicating

Table 15.3 Estimation results cointegration model

Long-run coefficients		Short-run coefficients (cont'd)	
Trade to GDP (log)	0.456***	Δ CPI(log)$_{t-1}$	−0.009***
	(0.122)		(0.003)
External debt to GNI (log)	−0.071	Positive price shock$_t$	0.010**
	(0.048)		(0.005)
CPI (log)	−0.004	Positive price shock$_{t-1}$	0.011**
	(0.007)		(0.005)
M2 to GDP (log)	0.056	Negative price shock$_t$	−0.001
	(0.095)		(0.006)
Commodity export price index (log)	−0.014**	Negative price shock$_{t-1}$	−0.17**
	(0.006)		(0.008)
Export price uncertainty (log)	−0.076	Coup$_t$	−0.27***
	(0.154)		(0.009)
Oil import price index (log)	−0.106	War$_t$−0.019***	
	(0.118)		(0.006)
Short-run adjustment coefficient		Geological shock$_t$	−0.011
GDP per capita (log)$_{t-1}$	−0.058***		(0.005)
	(0.009)	Geological shock$_{t-1}$	−0.001
Short-run coefficients			(0.004)
Δ (GDP per capita (log))$_{t-1}$	0.138***	Geological shock$_{t-2}$	−0.008**
	(0.034)		(0.003)
Δ (GDP per capita (log))$_{t-2}$	−0.039	Climatic shock$_t$	−0.001
	(0.027)		(0.002)
Δ (GDP per capita (log))$_{t-3}$	0.043	Climatic shock$_{t-1}$	0.005**
	(0.033)		(0.002)
Δ (GDP per capita (log))$_{t-1}$	−0.072***	Climatic shock$_{t-2}$	0.005**
	(0.025)		(0.002)
Δ (Trade to GDP (log))$_{t-1}$	0.018*	Climatic shock$_{t-3}$	0.006***
	(0.010)		(0.002)
Δ (Trade to GDP (log))$_{t-2}$	0.019**	Humanitarian shock$_t$	−0.004
	(0.09)		(0.009)
Number of observations	2319	R-squared within	0.17
Number of countries	100		

Notes: The dependent variable is the first-differenced log of real GDP per capita in year t. All regressions include country-specific and time-specific fixed effects. Robust standard errors are clustered by country andare reported in parentheses, ***, **, and * denote sifnificance at the 1%, 5%, and 10% levels, respectively.

that financial development boosts long-run GDP. The commodity export price index enters negative and is significant at 5 per cent, consistent with Collier and Goderis (2007), who find that, while higher commodity prices boost growth in the short run, their long-run effect on GDP is negative. Higher oil import prices also negatively affect GDP, although this effect is insignificant. The coefficient of the lagged level of GDP per capita is negative and significant at 1 per cent. The size suggests a speed of adjustment of 6 per cent per year.

Most of the short-run coefficients also have the expected signs. The first lag of the dependent variable enters positive and is highly significant, while the fourth lag has a significant negative effect, suggesting some mean reversion. Contemporaneous and lagged increases in trade openness and inflation are also important for growth. As expected, positive export price shocks have a positive effect on growth, both in the same year as in the next, while coups and wars have large adverse effects. A coup appears to cut growth by around 2.7 percentage points in the same year, while for wars this effect is 1.9 per cent, roughly consistent with Collier (1999) who documents a growth loss during war of 2.2 per cent points. Geological shocks significantly reduce growth by 1.1 per cent in the same year and by another 0.8 per cent in year $t+2$. Climatic shocks have no significant effect in the same year but actually augment growth in the next three years by around 0.5 per cent, which may be due to external assistance. Humanitarian shocks do not appear to have significant growth effects.

15.3.1 The effect of negative commodity export price shocks

Having established that commodity export price shocks significantly harm growth in the next year, we now investigate whether aid mitigates this effect.[8] To save space, Table 15.4 only reports results for the variables of interest. Column (1) shows the coefficient of the lagged negative export price shock variable. We choose the lag of the shock rather than its contemporaneous value as, according to our preferred specification in Table 15.3 (which excludes the insignificant export price uncertainty variable), this is the most important for contemporaneous growth. The coefficient on the lagged shock is –0.018, which is similar to its previous value, and is again significant at 5 per cent. It indicates that for the average commodity-dependent country the effect of a negative shock of 30 per cent on next year's growth is a –1.21 percentage point reduction in the growth rate of GDP. But for a more commodity-dependent country like Cameroon, which has commodity exports of 15.2 per cent of GDP (around the 75th percentile of the distribution in our sample), this effect is higher: a –1.47 percentage point reduction. A highly commodity-dependent country like Zambia with commodity exports of 34.9 per cent of GDP, suffers even more severe: –1.92 per cent points.

We next add instrumented aid to test whether the effect of adverse shocks is less severe in countries that receive more aid. Because in principle both the level of aid and the change in aid could be important, we add nine additional regressors to the specification in column (1): the lagged level of aid, the contemporaneous and lagged first difference of aid, and interactions of each of these three variables with both the lagged positive and the lagged negative export price shock variables. Table 15.4, column (2), reports the results for the lagged negative export price shock and its interactions with the three aid

Table 15.4 The effect of negative commodity export price shocks – cointegration commodity model with instrumented aid

	Full sample (1)	Full sample (2)	Full sample (3)	Full sample (4)	Pegs (5)	Floats (6)
Negative export price shock$_{t-1}$	−0.018** (0.008)	−0.056*** (0.014)	−0.047*** (0.012)	−0.060*** (0.015)	−0.092*** (0.036)	−0.027** (0.011)
Aid$_{t-1}$ * Negative export price shock$_{t-}$		0.025*** (0.008)	0.023*** (0.007)	0.014** (0.007)	0.045** (0.021)	0.016** (0.007)
ΔAid$_{t-1}$ * Negative export price shock$_{t-1}$		0.063 (0.056)				
ΔAid$_t$ * Negative export price shock$_{t-1}$		0.017 (0.075)				
Flexible exchange rate$_{t-1}$ * Negative export price shock$_{t-1}$				0.38*** (0.011)		
Number of observations	2319	1513	1514	1170	405	765
Number of countries	100	88	88	70	45	54
R-Squared within	0.17	0.13	0.17	0.23	0.29	0.26

Notes: Table 15.4 only reports coefficients and standard errors of the variables of interest. The dependent variable is the first-differenced log of real GDP per capita in year t. All regressions include country-specific and time-specific fixed effects. Robust standard errors are clustered by country and are reported in parentheses. ***, **, and * denote significance at the 1%, 5%, and 10% levels, respectively. The six columns correspond to the following specifications: Column (1) – specification in Table 15.3 but without export price uncertainty; column (2) – previous column with nine additional regressors: lagged level of aid, contemporaneous and lagged differenced aid, and interactions of each of these three variables with both lagged export price shock variables; column (3) – specification in column (1) with four additional regressors: lagged level of aid, differenced aid, and the interaction of the lagged level of aid with both lagged export price variables; column (4) – previous column with six additional regressors: contemporaneous and lagged floating exchange rate indicator and interactions of these indicators with the contemporaneous and lagged two export price shock variables, respectively; column (5) – specification of column (3) but applied to subsample of countries and episodes with a pegged exchange rate: column (5) specification of column (3) but applied to subsample of countries and episodes with a flexible exchange rate.

variables. The lagged shock again enters negative, has gained in size and is now significant at 1 per cent. The interaction of the shock with the lagged level of aid enters positive and is also significant at 1 per cent. This indicates that the growth loss from shocks is smaller for countries with higher levels of aid. In other words, aid mitigates shocks. The interactions of the lagged negative shock with both contemporaneous and lagged first differenced aid enter positive as well, but are not significant. Hence, aid is effective in mitigating shocks but only through the *level* of aid in the year of the shock and not by any *increases* in aid, either in the year of the shock or the next year. In Table 15.4, column (3), we drop lagged differenced aid and the interactions of differenced and lagged differenced aid. The interaction of the level of aid with the shock again enters positive and remains significant at 1 per cent, while the size of the coefficient is similar to its previous value. Recall that for the average commodity-dependent country, the effect of a negative export price shock of 30 per cent on next year's growth is –1.21 percentage points. Although the results in Table 15.4, column (3) are best interpreted as linear approximations that apply within the core range of the observed variables, taken literally they imply that a country that received no aid would lose 3.16 percentage points,[9] while the adverse growth effects would be fully offset for a country that received aid of 6.72 per cent of GNI.

We next investigate whether a country's exchange rate regime also matters for shock mitigation. When an economy is hit by a real shock and prices are sticky, a flexible nominal exchange rate allows for a quicker adjustment of relative prices and limits the output loss. Broda (2004) has found that developing countries with more flexible exchange rates suffer lower growth losses from adverse terms-of-trade shocks. We test whether his finding is robust to adverse commodity export price shocks using the Reinhart and Rogoff (2004) classification of *de facto* exchange rate flexibility. Hence, we add six additional regressors to the specification in Table 15.4, column (3): a contemporaneous and a lagged indicator of exchange rate flexibility, and interactions of these two indicators with the contemporaneous and lagged export price shock variables, respectively. The results are reported in Table 15.4, column (4). The interaction of lagged exchange rate flexibility with the lagged export price shock enters positive and is significant at 1 per cent. This indicates that, consistent with Broda (2004), countries with flexible exchange rates suffer less from a negative shock. However, the mitigating effect of the level of aid is robust to adding exchange rate flexibility as an additional mitigation instrument. The interaction of aid with the shock again enters positive, although the coefficient is smaller, and is significant at 5 per cent. The shock itself again enters negative, is slightly bigger, and remains significant at 1 per cent.

Having established that both aid and exchange rate flexibility are important for the mitigation of adverse shocks, we again consider the effect of a negative export price shock of 30 per cent. Figure 15.1 illustrates the mitigating roles of both instruments by showing next year's growth loss for different levels of exports and different levels of aid and exchange rate flexibility. The

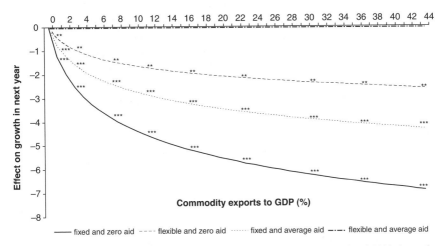

Figure 15.1 The effect of a negative commodity export price shock of 30% (sample mean) for different levels of exchange rate flexibility and aid.

Notes: This figure is based on the estimation results in Table 15.4, column (4). A value of −2 on the vertical axis corresponds to a growth loss of 2% points, *, **, and *** denote significance at the 10%, 5% and 1% levels, respectively.

'fixed and zero aid' line corresponds to the growth effect of a negative shock in countries that run a fixed exchange rate and do not receive aid. The effect is (log linearly) proportional to a country's exposure and for commodity exports to GDP ratios above 1 per cent, is always significant at 1 per cent. It is also economically relevant: a country with 20 per cent exports to GDP suffers a 5.5 per cent growth loss in the year after the shock. The 'flexible and zero aid' line shows the growth effect in countries that have a flexible exchange rate and do not receive aid. The location of the line above the 'flexible and zero aid' line indicates that a flexible exchange rate mitigates the effect of shocks, although not fully offsetting it. The country with 20 per cent exports to GDP that suffered a growth loss of 5.5 per cent points under a peg, suffers 'only' 2.1 per cent points of growth loss under a flexible exchange rate.

The 'fixed and average aid' line illustrates the growth effect in countries with a peg that receive a sample average of aid of 3.8 per cent of GNI. Average aid also mitigates the negative effect of shocks, although to a smaller extent than exchange rate flexibility. The country with exports to GDP of 20 per cent that suffered a growth loss of 5.5 percentage points under a peg with no aid, suffers 'only' 3.5 per cent points of growth loss with average aid. Finally, the 'flexible and average aid' line shows the growth effect in countries that have a flexible exchange rate and receive average aid of 3.8 per cent of GNI. The line is almost horizontal and lies just below the horizontal axis. The very small negative effects are never significant. This suggests that the combination of exchange rate flexibility and average aid fully offsets the negative effect of commodity export price shocks.

The results in Table 15.4, column (4), and Figure 15.1 assume that aid and exchange rate flexibility are *complements*. The mitigating effect of either one of them does not depend on whether the other instrument is also at work. We next investigate whether the two instruments are to some extent *substitutes*. It could be that there is less of a role to play for aid in countries that already have a mitigating instrument through their flexible exchange rate. Aid would then be most effective in countries with pegged exchange rates, as they are most in need of a shock cushioning instrument. However, if aid and exchange rate flexibility are complements, then aid can contribute to the mitigation of shocks in all countries, regardless of their exchange rate regime.

To test the potentially different effects of aid in countries with fixed and flexible exchange rates, we re-estimate the specification in Table 15.4, column (3), for sub-samples of countries and years with a pegged exchange rate in the year of the shock, and countries and years with a flexible exchange rate in the year of the shock. The results are reported in Table 15.4, column (5) and (6). In both columns, the interaction of aid and the shock enters negative and is statistically significant at 5 per cent. This provides evidence that aid and exchange rate flexibility are not full substitutes. Even in countries with flexible exchange rates aid can be used to further mitigate the negative effects of shocks. The smaller coefficient of the shock itself in column (6) is consistent with the earlier finding that countries with flexible exchange rates suffer less from adverse export price shocks. However, although the interaction of aid with the export price shock is significant in both columns, the coefficient is much smaller in column (6). This points at the possibility that, although aid always cushions shocks, it does so more strongly in countries with fixed exchange rates.[10]

This result is pertinent for the debate on whether aid is more effective in the context of good policies, a proposition initiated by Burnside and Dollar (2000). Our results imply that some 'good' policies, notably exchange rate flexibility, are substitutes for aid, suggesting that policies need to be decomposed before a clear relationship can be established. For example, aid effectiveness might plausibly be complemented by good processes for public spending. If aid and exchange rate flexibility are substitutes, what might this imply for aid allocation? Donors would presumably be reluctant to 'reward' poor choice of exchange rate policy with additional aid. However, there might be a case for reallocating aid *within* exchange rate regimes, so that among those countries with fixed exchange rates greater weight was given to the proneness of a country to shocks. This may be particularly pertinent to French aid to Franc Zone countries. Since the French government is committed to the maintenance of the fixed exchange rate regime for these countries, the issue of rewarding poor policy choices does not arise. But within the zone aid will be differentially effective in those countries most exposed to adverse shocks.

Table 15.5 The effect of negative commodity export price shocks – ARDL in differences with instrumented aid

	Full sample (1)	Full sample (2)	Full sample (3)	Pegs (4)	Floats (5)
Δ (GDP per capita (log))$_{t-1}$	0.173*** (0.032)	0.077*** (0.026)	0.073** (0.029)	–0.042 (0.061)	0.074** (0.035)
Negative export price shock$_{t-1}$	–0.018*** (0.007)	–0.036*** (0.012)	–0.062*** (0.015)	–0.100*** (0.035)	–0.035*** (0.011)
Aid$_{t-1}$* Negative export price shock$_{t-1}$		0.014** (0.007)	0.015** (0.007)	0.047** (0.021)	0.017*** (0.007)
Flexible exchange rate $_{t-1}$* Negative export price shock$_{t-1}$			0.031*** (0.012)		
Number of observations	3805	1620	1257	419	838
Number of countries	147	97	79	49	64
R-squared within	0.14	0.14	0.17	0.23	0.22

Notes: This table only reports coefficients and standard errors of the variables of interest. The dependent variable is the first-differenced log of real GDP per capita in year t. All regressions include country-specific and time-specific fixed effects. Robust standard errors are clustered by country and are reported in parentheses. ***, **, and * denote significance at the 1%, 5%, and 10% levels, respectively. The five columns correspond to the specifications in column (1) and (3) to (6) of Table 15.4 but excluding the long-run level variables as regressors.

15.4 Sensitivity analysis

The model in equation (1) assumes that the level variables are cointegrated. Collier and Goderis (2007) perform tests to establish whether this assumption is valid and find that this is the case. However, for sensitivity we also experiment with a model in which we strip the specification in (1) by removing the vector of long-run GDP determinants, $x_{i,t-1}$, and the lagged level of GDP per capita, $y_{i,t-1}$. We rerun the specifications in Table 15.4, columns (1) and (3) to (6) without these variables. The results are reported in Table 15.5.[11] Our findings prove robust to these alternative specifications. All our results on the effect of the shock, the cushioning effects of aid and exchange rate flexibility, and the difference in the effects of aid in countries with pegs and countries with flexible exchange rates, go through.

The model without the vector of long-run variables runs into a possible endogeneity problem. As the model is no longer a reparameterization of the autoregressive distributed lag model in levels, but a differenced model, the error terms are also first differenced. As a result, the error terms are first-order serially correlated by construction and the first lagged dependent variable is correlated with the contemporaneous error term, causing a biased coefficient. A second source of possible bias is the inclusion of fixed effects in our model, as the within group estimator is inconsistent for panels with relatively small T. This bias is likely to be small, given that for most countries T is relatively large. In the absence of other instruments for the lagged dependent variable in Table 15.5, we use an alternative instrumental variables technique first suggested by Anderson and Hsiao (1981). This technique proposes to first transform the model by first-differencing to eliminate possible individual effects and then instrument the lagged dependent variable with suitable lags of its own levels and first differences. Although consistent, the estimator is not efficient for panels with more than three periods, as for the later periods in the sample additional instruments are available. Arellano and Bond (1991) applied the generalized method of moments (GMM) approach to use all available instruments. Arellano and Bover (1995) extended this difference-GMM estimator by adding the equations in levels to the system, creating what is often called the system-GMM estimator. This addition increases the number of moment conditions, thereby increasing the efficiency of the estimator. Blundell and Bond (1998) showed that exploiting these additional moment conditions provides dramatic efficiency gains.

We use the system-GMM estimator to deal with the endogeneity of the lagged dependent variable.[12] In the differenced equation, which corresponds to the differenced version of the specification in Table 15.5, we instrument the lagged dependent variable with the third lag of its own level. This ensures that even if there is first-and second-order serial correlation in the error term of the differenced model, the instrument for the dependent variable is not correlated with the contemporaneous error term. In the levels equation, which corresponds to the specification in Table 15.5, we instrument the lagged dependent variable with the second lag of its own difference. This ensures that in the presence of first-order serial correlation in the errors, the instrument for the lagged dependent variable is not correlated with the contemporaneous error term.

The number of instruments in a system GMM can potentially grow very large, which causes problems of overfitting in finite samples and weakens the Sargan test of instrument validity up to the point where it generates implausibly good p values of 1.00. To minimize this problem, we take two steps to limit the instrument count (Roodman, 2006). First, we only use instruments at $t - 3$ and $t - 2$ in the differenced and levels equations, respectively, and thus leave out all instruments beyond $t - 2$ and $t - 3$. Second, we 'collapse' the instrument set, which means creating one instrument for each variable and lag distance, rather than one for each period, variable, and lag distance.

The system-GMM estimation results are reported in Table 15.6, columns (1) to (3). For the specifications in columns (4) and (5), the number of GMM instruments was very large compared to the number of countries. Therefore, we replaced the GMM estimator in these columns by a 2SLS fixed effects estimator in which we not only instrument for aid but also for the first lagged dependent variable. As an additional instrument, we use the second lag of the

Table 15.6 The effect of negative commodity export price shocks – System GMM and IV with instrumented aid

	Full sample (1)	Full sample (2)	Full sample (3)	Pegs (4)	Floats (5)
Δ (GDP per capita (log))$_{t-1}$	0.194*** (0.075)	0.304** (0.136)	0.266* (0.136)	0.311** (0.160)	0.379*** (0.139)
Negative export price shock$_{t-1}$	–0.017*** (0.006)	–0.081*** (0.029)	–0.079*** (0.025)	–0.073* (0.040)	–0.030** (0.012)
Aidt_1* Negative export price shock$_{t-1}$		0.039** (0.016)	0.020* (0.012)	0.026 (0.024)	0.016** (0.007)
Flexible exchange rate$_{t-1}$* Negative export price shockt$_{t-1}$			0.038** (0.019)		
Number of observations	3912	1634	1265	419	846
Number of countries	147	97	79	49	64
Number of instruments	136	90	94	39	39
P-value Sargan test	0.56	0.40	0.88	–	–
P-value Difference Sargan test	0.37	0.30	1.00	–	–
Arellano and Bond AR(1) test	–4.96***	–3.67***	–3.26***	–	–
Arellano and Bond AR(2) test	–1.34	0.79	0.70	–	–

Notes: The five columns correspond to the five columns in Table 15.5. In columns (1) to (3), instead of 2SLS fixed effects we apply the Arellano-Bover (1995)/Blundell-Bond (1998) two-step system GMM estimator with Windmeijer's finite-sample correction and drop the second, third, and fourth lagged dependent variable. We use the third lagged dependent variable (only) as an instrument for the lagged dependent variable in the differenced equation, and the second lagged differenced dependent variable (only) for the first lagged dependent variable in the levels equation. To limit the instrument count, we 'collapse' the instrument set. For the specifications in columns (4) and (5), the number of GMM instruments was very large compared to the number of countries. In fact, the Sargan/Hansen test of overidentifying restrictions generated implausibly good p values of 1.00 (see Roodman, 2006). Therefore, we replaced the GMM estimator in columns (4) and (5) by a 2SLS fixed effects estimator in which we not only instrument for aid but also for the first lagged dependent variable. As an additional instrument, we use the second lag of the level of log GDP per capita.

level of log GDP per capita. The results in Table 15.6 lend further support to the idea that negative export price shocks harm growth in the next year and that both aid and exchange rate flexibility mitigate this growth effect. In particular, the shock enters negative and is significant at 1 per cent in the preferred specifications of columns (1) to (3). The interaction of aid with the shock again enters positive and is significant at 5 per cent in column (2) and at 10 per cent in column (3). The coefficient on the interaction of exchange rate flexibility with the shock is also positive and is significant at 5%. The Sargan tests and Difference Sargan tests do not reject the null of exogenous instruments, while the Arellano and Bond $AR(1)$ and $AR(2)$ tests show negative first-order serial correlation and no second-order serial correlation in the error terms. The latter suggests that the error terms in the original model of Table 15.5 are not serially correlated, which together with the relatively large T in our panel casts doubts on whether the lagged dependent variable is in effect suffering from endogeneity. The results in column (1) of Table 15.6 are consistent with these doubts as the coefficient on the lagged dependent variable is very similar to the corresponding coefficient in Table 15.5, column (1). However, for the other four columns the coefficients are quite different and suggest that the coefficients on the lagged dependent variable in Table 15.5 were downward biased.

Finally, the specifications in Table 15.6, columns (4) and (5), should be viewed with caution as they do not use GMM but an instrumental variables technique which is known to be less efficient. In column (4), the shock enters with a negative sign and remains significant, although only at 10 per cent, while the interaction of the shock with aid is positive but no longer significant. While the coefficients of the shock and the interaction of the shock with aid are again smaller in countries with flexible exchange rates (column (5)), both coefficients are now significant at 5 per cent.

We next perform two more robustness checks. First, we experiment with an alternative shock definition by defining positive and negative shocks as the observations with equation (2) residuals above the 95th percentile or below the 5th percentile, respectively, instead of the 90th or 10th percentile. All our results are highly robust to this more restrictive shock definition. In particular, our results on the effect of the shock, the cushioning effects of aid and exchange rate flexibility, and the difference in the effects of aid in countries with fixed exchange rates and countries with flexible exchange rates, go through. Secondly, we check the robustness of our results when dropping all interaction terms except for the ones with the lagged negative export price shock. Again, all our results go through. To save on space, we do not report these results.

We next construct three sub-indices to investigate which commodities drive our results: one for oil only, one for agricultural commodities only, and one for non-oil, non-agricultural commodities only. For each of the three types, we construct a positive shock variable, which equals the first log difference of the index for the shock episodes identified using the methodology of Section 15.2.1, and zero for all other observations, and a negative shock variable, which equals minus the first log difference of the index for the shock episodes and zero for all other observations. To test the importance of each commodity type in explaining our findings, we rerun the specification in Table 15.4, column (4), but with the decomposed shock variables instead of the general shock variables. The results are reported in Table 15.7 and indicate that our results are primarily driven by non-agricultural commodity export

Table 15.7 Which commodities drive the effect of negative commodity export price shocks?

(a) estimation results	
(1) Negative oil price shock$_{t-1}$	−0.101***
	(0.023)
(2) Negative non-oil, non-agricultural price shock$_{t-1}$	−0.050
	(0.041)
(3) Negative agricultural price shock$_{t-1}$	0.020
	(0.029)
(4) Aid$_{t-1}$ * Negative oil price shock$_{t-1}$	0.033**
	(0.015)
(5) Aid$_{t-1}$ * Negative non-oil, non-agricultural price shock$_{t-1}$	0.030*
	(0.017)
(6) Aid$_{t-1}$ * Negative agricultural price shock$_{t-1}$	−0.009
	(0.011)
(7) Flexible exchange rate$_{t-1}$ * Negative oil price shock$_{t-1}$	0.059***
	0.016)
(8) Flexible exchange rate$_{t-1}$ * Negative non-oil, non-agricultural price shock$_{t-1}$	0.009
	(0.035)
(9) Flexible exchange rate$_{t-1}$ * Negative agricultural price shock$_{t-1}$	0.003
	(0.019)
Number of observations	1170
Number of countries	70
R-squared within	0.25

(b) Wald tests of coefficient equality

hypothesis	p-value	hypothesis	p-value	hypothesis	p-value
(1) = (2)	0.29	(4) = (5)	0.87	(7) = (8)	0.19
(2) = (3)	0.18	(5) = (6)	0.07*	(8) = (9)	0.89
(1) = (3)	0.00***	(4) = (6)	0.02**	(7) = (9)	0.02**

Notes: Panel (a) reports estimation results of the specification in Table 15.4, column (4), but with shock variables that are decomposed into oil price shocks, non-oil, non-agricultural commodity price shocks, and agricultural commodity price shocks. We only report coefficients and standard errors of the variables of interest. Robust standard errors are clustered by country and are reported in parentheses. Panel (b) reports Wald tests of coefficient equality for the estimated coefficients in panel (a). ***, **, and * denote significance at the 1%, 5%, and 10% levels, respectively.

price shocks. The coefficients of the oil price shock and its interactions with aid and exchange rate flexibility ((1), (4), and (7)) are fully consistent with the results in Table 15.4, column (4), and have the same levels of statistical significance. The coefficients for the other non-agricultural commodities ((2), (5), and (8)), although less significant, have the same signs as the coefficients for oil. Wald tests of coefficient equality, reported in Table 15.7, panel (b), do not reject the null of equal coefficients for oil and non-oil non-agriculture (tests (1)=(2), (4)=(5), and (7)=(8)). This indicates that there is no statistically significant difference between the effects of oil and other non-agricultural commodities. By contrast, the results for agriculture are not consistent with

Table 15.4, column (4). In particular, the coefficients of the agricultural price shock and its interaction with aid have the opposite sign, while all three agricultural price shock variables are insignificant. The Wald tests indicate that the coefficients of the agricultural shock are always significantly different from the coefficients of the oil shocks (tests (1)=(3), (4)=(6), and (7)=(9)). This clearly suggests that the results in Table 15.4, column (4), are not driven by agricultural price shocks but instead can be explained by non-agricultural price shocks. This does not imply that aid does not mitigate adverse agricultural shocks. It merely means that the results of our analysis should be interpreted as strong evidence that aid mitigates the adverse effects of non-agricultural commodity export price shocks.[13]

15.5 Does aid go to shock-prone countries?

Our results suggest that the level of aid can be used to mitigate commodity export price shocks. A natural question is whether historically aid has been targeted at shock-prone countries. If not, donors might want to consider a re-allocation of their aid to make it more effective. We next investigate whether past aid has been targeted at shock-prone countries. In particular, we regress the country average level of aid over the sample years on 3 indicators of vulnerability to shocks and several controls. All variables, except for the 1960 (initial) level of GDP per capita, are expressed as country averages over the sample years. Hence, our units of observation are countries and we estimate by OLS. The results are reported in Table 15.8. Our three measures of proneness to shocks are the average number of shocks per year, using both our shock definitions, and the standard deviation of changes in the commodity export price index. The results in Table 15.8 show a lack of any robust evidence that aid is targeted towards shock-prone countries. The coefficients of the indicators of shock proneness are almost always insignificant. This finding is robust to the inclusion of colonial dummies, and the use of initial GDP per capita instead of average GDP per capita (as the latter might be endogenous) as a control variable. As a result, a re-allocation of aid towards shock-prone countries might be beneficial as a means to improve aid effectiveness and assist commodity-dependent countries in coping with export price shocks.

15.6 Conclusions

We have found that large adverse commodity export price shocks reduce constant price GDP. The costs arise from realized shocks rather than the *ex ante* risk of shocks. This is a problem that continues to be faced by a relatively small group of low-income countries that have failed to diversify their exports. The decline in constant price GDP compounds the decline in income that is an inevitable consequence of terms of trade deterioration, and so subjects already fragile societies to episodes of economic crisis. It is now known

Table 15.8 Does aid go to shock-prone countries?

	(1)	(2)	(3)	(4)	(5)	(6)	(7)	(8)	(9)	(10)	(11)	(12)
Number of shocks per year (10)	0.19 (0.88)						-0.53 (1.05)			-0.25 (1.00)		
Number of shocks per year (5)		2.63* (1.43)			2.59*			0.06 (1.66)			0.37 (1.47)	
Standard deviation of change in commodity export price index (log)			0.41 (0.85)			0.49 (0.85)			-0.55 (0.97)			-0.31 (0.89)
GDP per capita, PPP (log)	-0.82*** (0.06)	-0.82*** (0.05)	-0.81*** (0.06)	-0.80*** (0.05)	-0.80*** (0.05)	-0.78*** (0.05)						
1960 GDP per capita, PPP (log)							-0.62*** (0.06)	-0.61*** (0.06)	-0.61*** (0.06)	-0.62*** (0.05)	-0.62*** (0.05)	-0.62*** (0.05)
Population (log)	-0.29*** (0.03)	-0.28*** (0.03)	-0.32*** (0.03)	-0.28*** (0.02)	-0.27*** (0.02)	-0.29*** (0.02)	-0.27*** (0.03)	-0.27*** (0.03)	-0.27*** (0.03)	-0.27*** (0.03)	-0.27*** (0.03)	-0.27*** (0.03)
German colony	-0.05 (0.09)	-0.04 (0.11)	-0.06 (0.09)				-0.21 (0.14)	-0.19 (0.13)	-0.19 (0.14)			
US colony	0.11 (0.07)	0.04 (0.08)	0.11 (0.07)				-0.02 (0.10)	-0.02 (0.10)	-0.02 (0.10)			
French colony	-0.03 (0.11)	-0.07 (0.11)	-0.10 (0.11)				0.21 (0.13)	0.21 (0.14)	0.22 (0.13)			
UK colony	-0.13 (0.12)	-0.12 (0.12)	-0.19 (0.12)				-0.08 (0.16)	-0.06 (0.15)	-0.07 (0.15)			
Japanese colony	0.58*** (0.08)	0.62*** (0.08)	0.58*** (0.10)				0.10 (0.11)	0.12 (0.10)	0.09 (0.11)			
Number of observations	147	147	78	147	147	124	78	78	78	78	78	78
R-squared	0.71	0.72	0.72	0.70	0.71	0.73	0.72	0.71	0.72	0.70	0.70	0.70

Notes: All columns report cross-sectional OLS results. The dependent variable is the country average level of aid for all available years in our sample. The number of shocks per year (10) and the number of shocks per year (5) denote the country average numbers of (10% and 5% threshold) shocks per year for the years in our sample. The standard deviation of the change in the export price index is calculated per country for all the available years. GDP per capita, PPP, and population, are expressed as country averages for the years in our sample. The colonial dummies are time invariant. Robust standard errors are reported in parentheses. ***, **, and * denote significance at the 1%, 5%, and 10% levels, respectively.

that even temporary periods of intensified poverty can have long-lasting effects. At the household level temporary poverty can lead to permanent deterioration in human capital. At the societal level, growth collapses increase the risk of civil war (Miguel *et al.*, 2004). Hence, it is pertinent to determine whether aid can mitigate such episodes. We find that shock-contingent aid does not appear to be effective but that a sustained higher level of aid does significantly mitigate shocks. *De facto* exchange rate flexibility also mitigates shocks and is, to an extent, a substitute for aid. However, even with a flexible exchange rate, aid significantly reduces the cost of adverse shocks.

Appendix 15A: Data sources

This appendix provides the data sources for the variables used in estimation.

Real GDP per capita   In constant 2000 US dollars (World Development Indicators, WDI).

Trade openness   Trade as a percentage of GDP (WDI).

External debt   To gross national product (Global Development Finance).

Inflation   Consumer price index (2000=100) (WDI).

Financial development   Money and quasi money (M2) as percentage of GDP (WDI).

Commodity export price index   1990 commodity export values from UNCTAD Commodity Yearbook 2000 and United Nations International Trade Statistics 1993/1994; quarterly world commodity price indices from International Financial Statistics (IFS, series 76, except for butter and coal where we use series 74). Coal, plywood, silver, and sorghum price series had several short gaps in the early sample periods. Following Dehn (2000), we filled these gaps by holding the price constant at the value of the first available observation. Palmkerneloil, bananas, tobacco, and silver price series had 1, 2, or 3 missing quarterly values in the middle. These gaps were filled by linear interpolation. Price series with larger gaps were not adjusted. However, where gaps would cause missing export price index observations in countries for which this commodity was relatively unimportant (share of commodity's exports in total < 10 per cent), these price series were left out. The geometrically weighted commodity export price index was first calculated on a quarterly basis and deflated by the export unit value (IFS, series 74. .DZF). We then calculated the annual averages and took the log, which gave us the unweighted commodity export price index. This index was used to construct the indicators of commodity export price shocks and uncertainty. In our estimation, we use the commodity export price index, weighted by the ratio of commodity exports to GDP (percentage).

Commodity exports to GDP (per cent)   1990 commodity export values, see commodity export price index. GDP is in current US dollars for 1990 (WDI).

Commodity export price shocks and export price uncertainty See Section 15.2.1.

Oil import price index world oil price index from IFS (series 00176AADZF); dummy variable for net oil importing countries based on 2001 net oil imports; net oil imports are crude oil imports plus total imports of refined petroleum products minus crude oil exports minus total exports of refined petroleum products, all from Energy Information Administration's (EIA) International Energy Annual 2002. Since these components are expressed in thousands of barrels per day, we multiplied them by 365 times the 2001 average weekly world oil price per barrel, also from EIA. If oil imports > 0, dummy=1, 0 otherwise.

Geological, climatic, and human disasters Geological disasters: earthquakes, landslides, volcano eruptions, tidal waves; climatic disasters: floods, droughts, extreme temperatures, wind storms; human disasters: famines, epidemics. Each variable is constructed as the annual number of episodes that qualify as large disasters according to the criteria of the IMF (2003): ≥ 0.5 per cent of population affected, or damage ≥ 0.5 per cent of GDP, or ≥ 1 death per 10,000 people. Data from WHO Collaborating Centre for Research on the Epidemiology of Disasters.

Civil war Dummy variable: 1 for civil war, 0 otherwise (Gleditsch, 2004).

Coup d'etat Number of extra constitutional or forced changes in the top government elite and/or its effective control of the nation's power structure in a given year (Banks' Cross-National Time-Series Data Archive). Unsuccessful coups are not counted.

Exchange rate flexibility Dummy variable based on the course classification of exchange rate regimes in Reinhart and Rogoff (2004); dummy=0 for episodes with no separate legal tender, a pre-announced peg, a currency board, a pre-announced horizontal band that is narrower than or equal to $+/-2$ per cent, or a de facto peg, 1 for all other episodes.

Foreign aid as a percentage of GNI Official development assistance from all donors as a percentage of GNI (OECD International Development Statistics, variable 286).

Notes

1 This model is based on the model in Collier and Goderis (2007). For sensitivity, we also run the model without the long-run cointegrating vector of level variables (see Section 15.4). Results are robust.
2 In order to use the log linear form, we use 1 + foreign aid.
3 These cut-off points are admittedly arbitrary. For sensitivity, we also run our specifications when using the 5th and 95th percentile as cut-off points. The results are robust to this alternative definition of shocks.
4 Due to the fact that data are only available until 1996 and for Germany only start in 1974 (UN admittance).

5 For the three European donor countries we use the distance to Brussels. Data are from the World Bank.
6 Source: Barrett (1982). The dummy takes a value of 1 if 30 per cent or more of the population belongs to one religious group in both the donor and recipient country.
7 We tried adding further lags but they proved unimportant.
8 Since it is insignificant, we drop commodity export price uncertainty in all subsequent specifications.
9 Hence the log of (1 + foreign aid) equals zero.
10 We tested this hypothesis by re-estimating the specification in Table 15.4, column (4), but adding an interaction between the exchange rate dummy and the aid-shock interaction. We also experimented with interactions between the exchange rate dummy and all other regressors. In both cases, the interaction between exchange rate flexibility and the aid-shock interaction entered with the expected negative sign but was insignificant.
11 Below we apply system GMM to deal with the endogeneity of the lagged dependent variable. We report the coefficient and standard error of the lagged dependent variable in Table 15.5 for comparison with Table 15.6.
12 We use the xtabond2 procedure in Stata (Roodman, 2005).
13 As a final sensitivity test, we reran all specifications in Tables 15.3 and 15.4 for a subsample of Sub-Saharan Africa. All results were highly similar.

References

Anderson, T. W. and Cheng Hsiao (1981) 'Estimation of Dynamic Models with Error Components,' *Journal of the American Statistical Association* 76:598–606.

Arellano, Manuel and Stephen Bond (1991) 'Some Tests of Specification for Panel Data: Monte Carlo Evidence and an Application to Employment Equations,' *Review of Economic Studies* 58:277–97.

Arellano, Manuel and Olympia Bover (1995) 'Another Look at the Instrumental-Variable Estimation of Error-Components Models,' *Journal of Econometrics* 68:29–52.

Barrett, David (1982) *World Christian Encyclopedia*, Oxford: Oxford University Press.

Blundell, Richard, and Stephen Bond (1998) 'Initial Conditions and Moment Restrictions in Dynamic Panel Data Models,' *Journal of Econometrics* 87:115–43.

Broda, Christian (2004) 'Terms-of-trade and Exchange Rate Regimes in Developing Countries,' *Journal of International Economics* 63:31–58.

Burnside, Craig and David Dollar (2000) 'Aid, Policies and Growth,' *American Economic Review* 90:847–68.

Collier, Paul (1999) 'On the Economic Consequences of Civil War,' *Oxford Economic Papers* 51:68–83.

Collier, Paul and Jan Dehn (2001) 'Aid, Shocks, and Growth,' Policy Research Working Paper 2688, World Bank, Washington DC.

Collier, Paul and Benedikt Goderis (2007) 'Commodity Prices, Growth, and the Natural Resource Curse: Reconciling a Conundrum,' CSAE Working Paper 2007–15, University of Oxford.

Deaton, Angus and Ron Miller (1996) 'International Commodity Prices, Macro economic Performance and Politics in Sub-Saharan Africa,' *Journal of African Economies* 5:99–191.

Dehn, Jan (2000) 'Commodity Price Uncertainty in Developing Countries,' CSAE Working Paper 2000–12, University of Oxford.

Gartzke, Erik, and Dong-Joon Jo (2002) 'The Affinity of Nations Index, 1946–1996'.

Goderis, Benedikt and Vasso P. Ioannidou (2008) 'Do High Interest Rates Defend Currencies During Speculative Attacks? New Evidence,' *Journal of International Economics* 74: 158–169.

Guillaumont, Patrick and Lisa Chauvet (2001) 'Aid and Performance: a Reassessment,' *Journal of Development Studies* 37:66–87.

Miguel, Edward, Shanker Satyanath and Ernest Sergenti (2004) 'Economic Shocks and Civil Conflict: An Instrumental Variables Approach,' *Journal of Political Economy* 112:725–53.

Raddatz, Claudio (2007) 'Are External Shocks Responsible for the Instability of Output in Low-Income Countries?,' *Journal of Development Economics* 84: 155–87.

Reinhart, Carmen M. and Kenneth S. Rogoff (2004) 'The Modern History of Exchange Rate Arrangements: A Reinterpretation,' *Quarterly Journal of Economics* CXIX:1–48.

Roodman, David M. (2005) 'XTABOND2: Stata Module to Extend XTABOND Dynamic Panel Data Estimator,' Center for Global Development, Washington.

Roodman, David M. (2006) 'How to Do xtabond2: An Introduction to "Difference" and "System" GMM in Stata,' Center for Global Development Working Paper 103.

Tavares, Jose (2003) 'Does Foreign Aid Corrupt?,' *Economics Letters* 79:99–106.

16 Rethinking trade preferences

How Africa can diversify its exports

With Anthony J. Venables

16.1 Introduction

Trade preferences for developing countries continue to be a major part of the world trading system. Under the Generalized System of Preferences (GSP) developing countries have access to most OECD markets, and historical ties have been recognized in schemes such as the EU's Lomé and Cotonou agreements. Recent years have seen several major extensions of preference schemes. The EU's Everything But Arms (EBA) scheme, initiated in 2001, gave duty-free access to least developed countries (LDCs) in (almost) all products. The US introduced the African Growth and Opportunities Act (AGOA) in 2000, improving market access for eligible Sub-Saharan African (SSA) countries. The US also operates the Caribbean Basin Initiative and the Andean Trade Promotion Act.[1]

These schemes have two main elements. One is the trade preference – the granting of market access at reduced tariff rates and with less restrictive quotas, possibly going all the way to duty- and quota-free market access. The other is the constraints on participation. These define eligible countries and products, and also impose rules of origin (ROOs). There has frequently been a tension between these elements, with the constraints severely reducing the effectiveness of preferences as an instrument of economic development. These constraints are likely to be particularly important for manufactured products, and redesign of preferences is needed if they are to facilitate developing country participation in a globalized world trading system.

The benefits of trade preferences accrue through two mechanisms. The one usually emphasized is a transfer of rent to recipient (developing) countries. Instead of being received by the developed country importer as tariff revenue or quota rent, the preference margin is instead transferred to producers in exporting countries. The magnitude of the rent transfer has been calculated by various researchers. A recent study estimates an upper bound (preference margins times the value of trade) of around \$11 bn p.a., of which around \$500 m goes to least developed countries.[2]

However, preferences can also generate benefits through a second mechanism: there may be a significant export supply response, creating employment in developing countries. This is the focus of the present paper. While the rent-transfer mechanism depends upon the existing quantity of exports, the supply response mechanism depends upon the potential of unrealized opportunities. For Africa, which is our geographic focus, this distinction between actual and potential exports approximates to that between agriculture and manufactures. Africa's rents from trade preferences depend upon market access for its existing agricultural exports, whereas preferences in manufactures might enable the region to break into markets that it has scarcely entered. Of course, rents for agricultural exports will also generate some quantity effect. However, the potential magnitude of the quantity effect is far greater in manufacturing exports. One reason for the greater potential is liberation from diminishing returns to scale. Production of manufactures for the domestic market encounters diminishing returns due to the constraint of small market size. Traditional agricultural and resource-based exports encounter diminishing returns because of limited endowments of suitable land and hence declining resource base per worker. By contrast, employment in manufacturing exports can be expanded without running into diminishing returns to scale due to markets or endowments. The other reason for the greater potential is that manufacturing exports are subject to scale thresholds which can generate multiple stable equilibria. The scale thresholds arise because of well-documented external economies that advantage those firms that are located within a cluster of similar firms. Potentially viable export locations may be uncompetitive relative to established clusters and so never develop unless induced. Hence, not only may trade preferences in manufactures generate a large supply response, they may switch a location to a new equilibrium and so have permanent effects even if only implemented temporarily.[3]

The importance of manufacturing and other modern sector exports to the wider process of economic growth is now supported by a good deal of evidence. The Asian experience is well documented, and a number of recent studies point to the role of exports in growth accelerations (Hausmann *et al.*, 2005). Jones and Olken (2006) identify growth accelerations, and show that these are associated with an average 13 percentage point increase in the share of trade in income (over a five-year period) as well as an acceleration of the rate of transfer of labour into manufacturing. Pattillo *et al.* (2005) point to the association between growth accelerations and trade growth in Sub-Saharan Africa.

How can trade preferences be designed to maximize their effectiveness in stimulating a manufacturing supply response? The argument developed in this paper is that manufacturing supply response is not a simple matter of moving up a supply curve, but depends on a wide range of complementary inputs, some of which can be imported and some of which have to be developed domestically, often involving increasing returns to scale. Trade preferences can have a catalytic role, but will only perform this role if they are designed to allow import of complementary inputs, and to operate in countries with the skills and infrastructure to be near the threshold of global manufacturing competitiveness.

Our argument is based on several analytical strands of work and on empirical evidence from recent preference schemes. The analytical strands argue that modern sector export growth is characterized by 'fragmentation' of production and by increasing returns to scale, typically external to the firm. These ideas are developed in Section 16.2. Section 16.3 presents empirical work based largely on the experience of AGOA which, with relatively liberal ROOs in apparel, has seen rapid growth in exports of some participating countries. Section 16.4 draws conclusions, arguing that appropriately designed trade preferences can make a much more significant contribution to development than is suggested by existing literature.

16.2 Modern sector trade and growth

Modern sector production is not simply a matter of transforming primary factors into final output. It requires primary factors and many other complementary inputs, ranging from specialist skills and knowledge to component parts. These are frequently supplied by many different countries, with design, engineering, marketing and component production occurring in different places – a process known as fragmentation of production. Furthermore, productivity levels in these different activities are not exogenously fixed. They are shaped by learning and by complementarities with other activities. These processes often give rise to increasing returns to scale, and imply that clusters are more productive than is dispersed activity. We briefly review existing literature on both these aspects of modern sector production.

a. Fragmentation

Fragmentation – otherwise known as unbundling or splitting the value chain – refers to the fact that the different stages involved in producing a particular final good are now often performed in many different countries. Particular 'tasks' may be outsourced (or offshored) and can be undertaken in different places. This occurs in response to productivity or factor price differences, and may take place within a single multinational firm or through production networks of supplier firms.[4] Although widely reported, solid evidence on the extent of fragmentation is quite hard to obtain. A good survey is contained in Grossman and Rossi-Hansberg (2006), whose discussion includes the fact that the share of imports in inputs to US goods manufacturing has doubled to 18 per cent over a 20-year period. To put this number in perspective, the US is by far the world's largest economy so that opportunities for competitive domestic sourcing of inputs are evidently radically superior to those in the typical African economy.

Fragmentation means that comparative advantage now resides in quite narrowly defined tasks. For some products tasks may be undertaken in parallel and then 'assembled' in a single place. For others a sequential production process still applies, under which each task adds value to a product that crosses borders at each stage. In this case the partially complete product is an essential input to the task to be performed at the next stage. The effect of tightly restrictive ROOs is to prohibit participation in production processes of this type. Countries are unable to use preferences to exploit a comparative advantage in a narrowly defined task, instead having to undertake a wide range of tasks domestically to meet ROO requirements.

b. Increasing returns to scale and market failure

Analyses of market failures in manufacturing development have a long history. They underpinned much of the theory of shadow pricing developed in the 1960s and 1970s. More recently they have re-entered mainstream literatures on trade theory and industrial organization with the development of models of trade with increasing returns to scale and models of complementarity and coordination failure.

Increasing returns to scale may be internal to the firm as costs fall with longer production runs and learning by doing. They are often external, meaning that firms in a particular location gain from the presence of other firms in related activities. One set of mechanisms creating these external returns to scale is technological externalities arising as firms learn from other firms, observing and borrowing best-practice technique. These technological spillovers have been extensively researched in the industrial organization and spatial economics literatures, and they are typically found to be important, particularly in high-tech industries, and to be spatially concentrated. Notice that the knowledge discovered need not be sophisticated technology – it might simply be discovery of the fact that it is possible to undertake a particular type of business profitably in a particular location. This has a demonstration effect which underlies theories of social learning and which Hausmann and Rodrik (2003) have termed 'economic development as self-discovery'.

In addition to technological externalities there are a number of pecuniary externalities associated with provision of complementary inputs. As a cluster of firms grows so specialist input suppliers develop, markets for intermediate goods become thicker, transport and infrastructure support improves, and workers have a greater incentive to acquire skills.[5] For example, consider a downstream industry that requires specialist inputs from upstream firms, or specialist skills from its workers. If there is a single firm in the downstream industry there will be no incentive for upstream suppliers or workers to invest in improving quality or acquiring skills, since they will be 'held up' by the monopsony power of the downstream firm. The complementarity is evident; it is only once the downstream industry is large enough that there is an incentive for its suppliers to upgrade and thereby raise the productivity of the combined operation.

There is a good deal of empirical work establishing the importance of thick market effects. Productivity is higher in areas of dense economic activity, and work on cities suggests that, over a wide range of city sizes, each doubling of size raises productivity by 3–8 per cent (see the survey by Rosenthal and Strange, 2005). The effects often operate over quite a small spatial range – within a city or travel-to-work area. The benefits may be shared among a number of sectors (as with improved transport or more regular shipping services) but are often quite sector or task specific, as in sectoral clusters in financial services, film production or electronics.

An important consequence of spatially concentrated increasing returns is that comparative advantage is, in part, *acquired* rather than fundamental. A particular location may have no inherent advantage in a sector or task, but as a cluster starts to develop so costs fall, creating the comparative advantage.

c. Implications – lumpy development

The facts of fragmentation and of increasing returns to scale imply that modern sector export growth is likely to be uneven or 'lumpy' in three senses; in product space, in geographical space and in time. Lumpiness in product space arises as the acquired comparative advantages of learning and clustering may be narrowly concentrated in a few tasks, implying that countries may come to specialize in a very narrow range of activities. Lumpiness in geographical space means that activity may be concentrated in small spatial areas – cities will acquire particular specializations. And lumpiness in time means that there are threshold effects; establishing a new activity in the face of existing competition may be quite difficult, but once it gets established costs start to fall and growth can become extremely rapid.[6]

All three of these aspects of 'lumpiness' are illustrated by recent experience. Hausmann and Rodrik (2003) draw attention to the very narrow specialization of many countries; both Pakistan and Bangladesh have more than one-quarter of their total exports concentrated in just three (different) six-digit product lines.[7] Spatial concentration is apparent from the rapid growth of urban areas and of clusters of activity (e.g. Henderson, 2002). An extreme example of product and spatial concentration is the city of Qiaotou, producing 60 per cent of the world's buttons. As for rapid growth, Bangladesh shipped its first consignment of garments to the US in 1978, had exports of $600 m by 1990 and more than $6 bn by 2005, employing 2.5 million people.

What are the implications of these facts for a region with abundant skilled labour and low levels of both hard and soft infrastructure, such as Sub-Saharan Africa? Successful participation in production networks and fragmented production processes requires a business environment that delivers security, contract enforcement and protection from predation. It also requires a level of infrastructure that can support continuous production and reliable delivery. However, the fact of spatial concentration means that it is not necessary that high quality infrastructure be provided everywhere – it can be provided in selected areas or in special economic zones. This is positive for Africa since it economizes on these scarce inputs. Infrastructure (and institutions) can be targeted so that some areas work well, and this is more efficient than spreading infrastructure at a uniformly low level.

The fact that globalization enables countries to specialize on a narrow product or task range is also positive for Africa. Instead of having to learn and acquire comparative advantage in all stages of a product's production, fragmentation makes it possible to progress incrementally, first learning narrow tasks – such as production of a particular type of garment using imported textiles and yarn. However, barriers to trade in intermediate goods are a critical obstacle to this. The barriers may arise because of domestic import restrictions, because of high trade costs due to geography and infrastructure, or because of rules of origin. They all have the effect of inhibiting participation in global production networks.

The temporal lumpiness of modern sector growth is also problematic. Coordination failures mean that getting started is hard, and it is only once a threshold has been passed that increasing returns start to reduce costs. This calls for some sort of catalytic action to overcome initial obstacles and get to the threshold level.

d. Trade and industrial policy

What implications follow for trade and industrial policy in general, and trade preferences in particular?

Past African discussion of industrialization strategies has generally focused upon the trade policies of African governments. Changes in African trade policy would indeed be a necessary part of catalytic action, but not in the form most commonly envisaged. For an African-based firm to succeed in exporting a manufacturing 'task' it would need to be able to import without restriction all the complementary upstream tasks. Hence, the catalytic trade policy for African governments is to remove their current tariffs on manufactured inputs. For example, in West Africa, ECOWAS imposes a uniform 10 per cent tariff on all such inputs. While 10 per cent may appear modest, suppose that in the absence of trade impediments an Africa-based firm would choose to import inputs constituting half of the value of its output, so that the tariff raises its total costs by five per cent. Now consider what this implies for what the firm can afford to pay as labour costs. Even in labour-intensive manufacturing, labour costs typically only constitute around 16 per cent of total cost. Hence, to keep its total costs constant in the face of the tariff on inputs, the firm would need an offsetting reduction in its labour costs to 11 per cent. Thus, to compete with firms based in a location that was identical other than that it did not impose tariffs on inputs the firm would need to pay wages that were around one-third lower. Of course, Africa's problem arises precisely because its locations are *not* currently identical to those of Asia – they have higher costs due to the lack of clusters. Tariffs on inputs intensify the problem rather than resolve it.

Should an astute government adopt a tariff structure with zero tariffs on inputs but positive tariffs on final goods? There are several reasons why such a strategy would also fail. First, the country's niche in the long chain of manufacturing 'tasks' that eventually generate a final product is unlikely to be precisely the final 'task'. For any task prior the protection would be useless. And products which are 'final' to one industry are 'inputs' to another industry. As the above examples demonstrate, modern manufacturing niches are so specialized that the domestic market for them in the typical African country is too small to be a significant inducement to relocation. How important is the prospect of a price premium in the Senegalese market for buttons in determining whether firms selling on the global market should relocate their production from Qiaotou? Even in the unlikely event that such protection would be significant, the political difficulties for the Senegalese government of imposing high tariffs on buttons alongside free trade in all the myriad inputs that button producers want to use would surely be overwhelming.

An alternative style of industrial policy for an African government would be to subsidize the costs of production rather than protect the domestic market. But such policies have a poor track record. As a claim on government expenditure it would have to compete with manifestly pressing social needs. Further, the most conventional form of subsidy, tax incentives for investment, subsidizes capital and this can be at the expense of employment. Untargeted production subsidies would be expensive because existing production for the domestic market would qualify, but targeting requires information that is typically not available to government, and a degree of discretion that risks eliding into corruption.[8] Perhaps the most effective way of targeting a subsidy towards exporting firms is to provide good quality infrastructure for geographically-defined export zones, but since Asian governments already do this, it may be merely a necessary but not a sufficient condition for inducing relocation.

Unlike these forms of industrial policy, trade preferences in OECD markets are not under the control of African governments; like aid, they are an instrument of development policies under the control of OECD governments. However, they have some major advantages over the policies that are available to African governments to provide the (temporary) advantage needed to get cluster formation. First, they are relatively immune from recipient country political economy problems, since they are set by foreign, not domestic government. Thus, there is no way in which their level can be escalated in support of failing firms. Second, since trade preferences support exports, they offer a performance-based incentive – firms benefit only if they export. Firms therefore face the discipline – on quality as well as on price – imposed by international competition. Rodrik (2004) argues that this discipline was an important positive factor underlying the success of export-oriented strategies, as compared to import substitution. Finally, they are fiscally costless to African governments and virtually costless to OECD governments and so compete with neither government spending on social needs nor aid.

Is there any evidence that trade preferences have had a positive effect on modern sector production? Before answering this question we need to be clear about what effects we expect. Preferences will be valuable if countries are able to participate in fragmentation and production networks. This is facilitated by liberal ROOs and by geographical proximity, as well as by standard determinants of comparative advantage. Even if these circumstances are met, their effects might be 'lumpy' – concentrated in a few sectors, regions or countries, and only setting in above some threshold.

In the next section we present analysis of the effects of AGOA and EBA on exports, but before doing this it is worth reviewing experience under other preferential trade schemes. The most successful such scheme has been the EU itself, where newly joining countries have generally experienced rapid growth of exports and of income as a whole. However, the EU extends far beyond trade preferences and so schemes that are purely concerned with trade and apply to developing countries are more pertinent.

NAFTA has had a strong effect on Mexican exports to the US, with exports growing five-fold in 12 years. This has led to increased employment in the border region, although the controversial issue is whether it has had significant repercussions for the rest of the Mexican economy (Hanson, 2004). The ASEAN Free Trade Area has been relatively successful in enabling low-income members (Cambodia and Laos) to participate in production networks with the middle-and high-income members (Indonesia, Philippines, Malaysia, Thailand and Singapore). It is notable that the ROOs are relatively straightforward and allow for cumulation across a wide range of member countries (see Cadot and de Melo, 2007).

Mauritius is the only African country to have decisively penetrated global markets in manufacturing, in the process transforming itself from an impoverished sugar island to Africa's highest-income economy. Famously, this performance defied the forecast of Nobel Laureate James Meade that the country was condemned to poverty. Subramanian and Roy (2003) investigate the reasons for the take-off. They find that export manufacturing success was the foremost proximate reason for economic success. In turn, the success in manufacturing was triggered by two coincident strategies. The Mauritian government granted duty-free inputs for manufactured exports and Subramanian and Roy find this to have been quantitatively important. However, they find that the OECD decision to grant Mauritius trade preferences in garments through the Multi-Fibre Agreement (MFA) was even more important. Crucially, the MFA gave Mauritius privileged access to OECD markets relative to established Asian producers. The MFA ended in 2004 but Mauritius is now well-established in OECD markets and has gradually shifted to more complex manufacturing 'tasks'. The temporary preference scheme was thus critical in permanently transforming the Mauritian economy.

16.3 Empirics: AGOA – a natural experiment

The cleanest 'natural experiment' which enables study of the effects of trade preferences – and in particular of ROOs – is the African Growth and

Opportunities Act (AGOA) which gives trade preferences to African countries in the US market.[9,10,11] This offers duty-free access for a wide range of products. Importantly, AGOA is not restricted to LDCs, and is currently available to 38 African countries, including Kenya, Nigeria and South Africa.[12] AGOA ROOs are strict (varying across products, but generally with inputs having to come from the US or other AGOA countries). However, they were relaxed for apparel under the 'special rule' clause. This allows eligible countries to use fabric imported from third countries in their apparel exports to the US so that the ROO is just a 'single transformation requirement' (i.e. that the transformation from fabric to garment is undertaken in the eligible country). This special rule is temporary and has been renewed under a series of waivers, most recently in December 2006 when the expiry date of end 2007 was pushed back to 2012. The special rule now applies to 25 African countries (including Kenya and Nigeria, but not South Africa).

Study of the effects of AGOA is particularly informative, as it can be compared with the EU's trade preferences under the Cotonou agreement and EBA. These are in many respects similar, but (a) have more restrictive ROOs for apparel, and (b) a somewhat different country coverage, only Least Developed Countries being eligible. The rationale for this restricted eligibility is that they are the countries that need it most. However, being the most lacking in skills and infrastructure, they are also the African countries least likely to be near the threshold of global manufacturing competitiveness.

a. Descriptive evidence

We focus attention on the apparel sector, Sub-Saharan African exports of which are illustrated in Figure 16.1. The solid lines give exports of apparel from the region, excluding Mauritius. Exports to the US and the EU (defined throughout as the EU15, see the Appendix) were of similar values during the 1990s, but since then exports to the US have quadrupled from $400 m to $1.6 bn, while exports to the EU, including those under EBA have stagnated. The dashed lines give exports from Mauritius. Exports from Mauritius to the US have stagnated throughout the period while EU imports soared in the first half of the 1990s for reasons discussed above, and have been constant since.

The growth of exports to the US has been concentrated in a few countries, as illustrated in Figure 16.2. The bottom line is exports from Kenya, now amounting to some $270 m p.a., and the difference between this and the line above is Madagascar, with exports to the US of around $300 m p.a. SACU exports have reached $700 m p.a. and Mauritius's exports have held around the $250 m p.a. level. The combined apparel exports to the US of all other SSA countries is only some $50 m p.a., although within this there are some very fast-growing totals, such as Malawi.

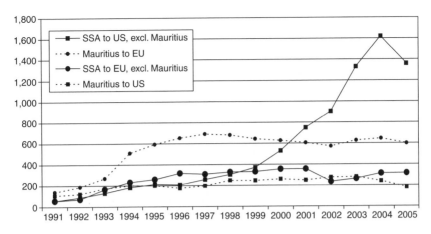

Figure 16.1 Apparel exports from SSA, $M.

Source: UN Comtrade.

b. Country Narratives

Kenya: Kenyan apparel exports to the US went from $40 m in 1999 to $270 m in 2005, this comparing to total goods exports of $2.8 bn. Apparel exports to the US employs over 30,000 workers accounting for 15 per cent of formal sector manufacturing employment. Apparel production is largely

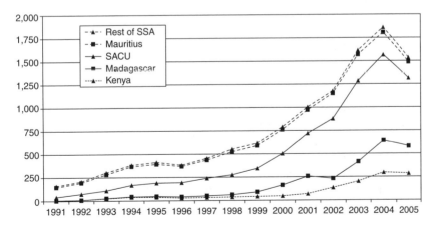

Figure 16.2 Apparel exports to the US from SSA, $M.

Source: UN Comtrade.

based in a number of special economic zones, within which it makes up 90 per cent of employment.

Madagascar: For eight months during 2002 political disturbance closed the port used by the Export Processing Zone and consequently drastically reduced its activity. The Zone thus has two phases, the expansion of the 1990s, and the recovery of the present decade. Launched at the beginning of the 1990s to take advantage of the MFA, the zone expanded to generate 300,000 jobs by the time of the political interruption. Given that the entire population of the country was only 15 million, this was a considerable addition to formal employment. Following the collapse of activity during the export blockade and the prospective phase-out of the MFA there was a prospect that firms would not return to the zone. Indeed, just as the MFA had produced a coordinated development of the cluster, the blockade produced a coordinated exit. However, AGOA was sufficient to trigger a strong recovery. Total exports of goods under AGOA are now $740 m (of which apparel is $300 m).

SACU: The position with SACU is given in Figure 16.3. Data for separate countries becomes available from 2000 (they are not all zero in 1999). Lesotho has been the largest beneficiary, with exports increasing from $140 m in 2000 to $400 m in 2005. Swaziland, Botswana and Namibia have all seen rapid growth from a smaller base. The remaining element is exports from South Africa which are not eligible for the ROO waiver. These stagnated before turning down sharply in 2005.

The 2005 downturn is apparent in Figures 16.1–16.3 and is largely due to the end of the Multi-Fibre Agreement. Some 70 per cent of the total decline in SSA apparel exports to the US is attributable to South Africa, outside the AGOA ROO waiver. For other countries, an additional factor behind the decline may have been uncertainty about expiry of this waiver at end 2007; as we have seen, this uncertainty was removed only at end 2006. Notice that the figures above run to 2005, since they are based on UN Comtrade data. More up-to-date data is available from USITC and indicates some continuing decline in exports in the earlier part of 2006 although the rate of decline is slowing.[13]

c. Econometrics

Although the raw data presented in the figures above is persuasive, we also present some econometric analysis. The simplest model expresses imports from country i to market j, x_{ij}, as a function of some supplier country characteristics, S_i, some importer country characteristics, M_j, and some between-country characteristics, d_{ij}. All of these may be time-varying so writing the relationship for the two importer markets that we study, the USA and the EU,

$$x_{iUS}(t) = S_i(t)M_{US}(t)d_{iUS}(t)u_{iUS}(t)$$

$$x_{iEU}(t) = S_i(tM_{EU}(t)d_{iEU}(t)u_{iEU}(t),$$

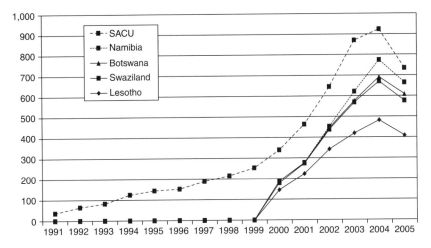

Fgure 16.3 Apparel exports to the US from SACU, $M.

Source: UN Comtrade.

where $u_{ij}(t)$ is an error term. By focusing on performance in one export market relative to the other, supplier country characteristics can be substituted out, giving

$$x_{iUS}(t)/x_{iEU}(t) = [M_{US}(t)/M_{EU}(t)][d_{iUS}(t)/d_{iEU}(t)][u_{iUS}(t)/u_{iEU}(t)],$$

and this provides the relationship that we will estimate.

The dependent variable, $x_{iUS}(t)/x_{iEU}(t)$, is the value of apparel exports from country i to the US relative to this country's apparel exports to the EU. The relative market size element, $M_{US}(t)/M_{EU}(t)$, we capture by total imports of apparel to the US and the EU from all countries other than country i. We also run specifications where this variable is replaced by a year fixed effect. The relative between-country component, $d_{iUS}(t)/d_{iEU}(t)$, contains some fixed parts – such as distance and invarying trade preferences – and also the time-varying and country-pair specific trade preferences in which we are interested. We capture the constant parts by exporter fixed effects, and the time-varying parts by dummy variables which are switched on at the date when the exporter receives preferential trade benefits. For imports to the US, we set the variable *AGOAA* equal to unity for complete years in which the exporter country has been eligible for the AGOA apparel waiver. For the EU we set the dummy variable *EBANC* equal to unity for years in which a country not eligible for EU trade preference under Cotonou received preferences under EBA. We use this specification because Cotonou (and preceding Lomé) were in place throughout the period, and are similar to EBA preferences. We also look at a specification in which the *EBANC* variable is replaced by a simple EBA dummy.

This specification is equivalent to a triple difference-in-differences approach. Exporter supply shocks are controlled for by looking at sales in the USA relative to the EU. Market demand shocks are controlled for by total imports of apparel in the US relative to the EU, or by time effects. Time-invariant differences in exporters' sales in the US relative to the EU are controlled for by exporter fixed effects. The effects of trade preferences are identified from time-series variation in exporters' sales to the USA relative to the EU.

Results are given in Table 16.1. Columns 1–3 work with the sample of 86 developing and middle-income countries (see Appendix 16A), excluding those where apparel exports to the USA and EU combined averaged less than $1 m p.a. over the period. We see that the AGOA apparel (*AGOAA*) provision has a positive and significant effect. A coefficient of 2 corresponds to an increase by a multiplicative factor of 7.4 (= exp(2)). In contrast, the EBA variables, both *EBANC* and simple *EBA* do not have a significant effect (and have the wrong sign).

Columns 4–6 have a sample of 110 countries, adding in countries with mean apparel exports between $100,000 and $1 m. Including these smaller countries causes a small increase in the AGOA coefficient. EBA effects now have the correct sign,[14] but it is only in the case where EBA is treated as an innovation with respect to Cotonou (column 6) that the effect is significant, indicating that it increases exports to the EU (relative to the US), by a factor of around 2.6 (= exp(0.97)).

Table 16.1 Apparel exports to the US relative to the EU, 1991–2005
Dependent variable: apparel exports to the US relative to exports to the EU, $\ln(x_{iUS}/x_{iEU})$

$\ln(x_{iUS}/x_{iEU})$	1	2	3	4	5	6
AGOAA	2.21	2.06	2.00	2.28	2.22	2.47
	(5.19)	(4.49)	(4.22)	(4.41)	(4.06)	(4.49)
EBANC	0.295	0.21		−0.58	−0.24	
	(0.52)	(0.36)		(−0.83)	(−0.33)	
EBA			0.14			−0.96
			(0.37)			(−2.52)
$\ln(M_{US}/M_{EU})$	1.14			2.15		
	(2.56)			(4.22)		
Year fixed effects	No	Yes	Yes	No	Yes	Yes
Exporter fixed effects	Yes	Yes	Yes	Yes	Yes	Yes
No. of observations	1,239	1,239	1,239	1,599	1,599	1,599
Countries	86	86	86	110	110	110

Notes:
Cols 1–3, exclude countries with mean apparel exports < $1 m.
Cols 4–6, exclude countries with mean apparel exports < $100,000.

Table 16.2 Textile and apparel exports to the US relative to the EU, 1991–2005

Dependent variable: apparel exports to the US relative to apparel exports to the EU, *relative* to, textile exports to the US relative to textile exports to the EU

$ln(x_{iUS}/X_{iEU}) - ln(y_{iUS}/y_{iEU}$	1	2
AGOAA	2.65	1.98
	(4.47)	(2.47)
AGOA	0.90	
		(1.28)
EBANC		0.48
		(0.46)
Year fixed effects	Yes	Yes
Exporter fixed effects	Yes	Yes
No. of observations	1,024	1,024
Countries	71	71

Note: Excludes countries with mean apparel or textile exports < $1 m.

Table 16.2 extends the analysis to a quadruple difference-in-differences. Suppose that the relative between-country component, $d_{iUS}(t)/d_{iEU}(t)$, varies over time because of factors other than trade preferences – for example, improving economic relations between the US and a particular country. If this effect is the same across commodity groups, then the AGOA apparel effect can be identified by looking at apparel trade relative to trade in some other commodity – we use textiles. AGOA affects both apparel and textile trade, but the AGOA apparel waiver operates for a smaller set of countries and (somewhat) shorter time period. In principle we can therefore separate out the effect of the AGOA apparel waiver from that of AGOA as a whole, while conditioning out shocks that affect both product classes.

Results are given in Table 16.2. The first column omits the simple AGOA and EBA (non-Cotonou) effects, since these should affect apparel and textiles in a similar way. The estimated AGOAA apparel effect is then highly significant, and of somewhat greater magnitude than we found in Table 16.1. Column 2 allows AGOA and EBA to affect apparel and textiles in different ways. We find that effects are insignificant, although the AGOAA apparel effect is brought back to a coefficient of 1.98, consistent with those in Table 16.1. This additional control therefore confirms the finding that the AGOA apparel treatment had a significant and large impact on apparel exports.

How do these results compare with others in the literature? Frazer and van Biesebroeck (2005) conduct an econometric study of US imports, working with a highly disaggregate commodity specification (at the six-digit level), but looking only at exports to the US market, and not therefore having the comparator of exports to the EU or any other market. They estimate a single equation across time, exporters and products, and use fixed effects to control for time-varying exporter and product effects, and (time-invariant) exporter-product effects. This involves 5.1 million observations and 850,000 fixed effects. The AGOA apparel effect is estimated to be highly significant, and accounts for a 51 per cent increase in trade. The likely reason that this number is so much smaller than our estimated effect is that we have the additional control provided by a comparison of exports to two markets. This enables us to have a time-varying fixed effect for each exporter which is specific to the commodity under study, apparel. This option is not possible for Biesebroeck and Frazer, lacking the control provided by a second import market.

16.4. Conclusions

For Africa to diversify its exports into manufacturing may require a catalyst to create clusters of activity and lift them to threshold productivity levels. Forty years of African domestic protectionism has failed to induce such clusters. However, the evidence suggests that – given the right conditions – it is possible for African countries to accelerate their modern sector export growth. Designing policy to promote such growth requires recognition of a number of features of modern global trade; fragmentation, increasing returns and the consequent lumpiness of development. Domestic policy and international policy are complements. Domestic policy needs to ensure a good business environment and infrastructure, but this can be spatially concentrated. International policy needs to redesign trading arrangements with rules of origin that do not penalize narrow specialization. Two of the past initiatives in trade preferences for African manufactures, the MFA and AGOA, have both demonstrated their effectiveness. However, at the time when the MFA was launched few African governments had adopted the complementary policies needed for success, and the MFA has now ended. The key feature that made AGOA effective, the apparel special waiver, has now been renewed through to 2012, but AGOA applies only to the US market. The natural large market for Africa is the EU. At the minimum there is thus an opportunity for the EU to redesign its trade preferences to promote African economic development, aligning its trade instrument with its aid instrument. However, the goal should be an integrated scheme across the OECD that subsumes both EBA and AGOA and thereby minimizes the information costs to exporting firms.

Country	Table 1 Cols 1–3	Table 1 Cols 4–6	Table 2
Afghanistan	x	x	
Albania	x	x	
Algeria	x	x	x
Argentina	x	x	x
Armenia	x	x	
Bangladesh	x	x	x
Benin		x	
Bhutan	x	x	
Bolivia	x	x	
Botswana	x	x	x
Brazil	x	x	x
Bulgaria	x	x	x
Burkina Faso		x	
Cambodia	x	x	x
Cameroon	x	x	x
Cape Verde	x	x	
Central African Republic		x	
Chad		x	
Chile	x	x	x
China	x	x	x
Colombia	x	x	x
Costa Rica	x	x	x
Croatia	x	x	x
Côte d'Ivoire	x	x	x
DR Congo		x	
Djibouti	x	x	
Dominican Republic	x	x	x
Ecuador	x	x	x
Egypt	x	x	x
El Salvador	x	x	x
Equatorial Guinea		x	
Eritrea		x	
Ethiopia	x	x	x
Gabon		x	
Gambia		x	
Ghana	x	x	x
Guatemala	x	x	x
Guinea		x	
Haiti	x	x	x
Honduras	x	x	x
India	x	x	x
Indonesia	x	x	x
Iran, Islamic Republic of	x	x	x
Jamaica	x	x	x
Jordan	x	x	x
Kazakhstan	x	x	x
Kenya	x	x	x
Kiribati		x	
Kyrgyzstan	x	x	x
Laos PDR	x	x	
Lebanon	x	x	x
Lesotho	x	x	
Liberia		x	
Moldova	x	x	x
Mongolia	x	x	x
Morocco	x	x	x

(continued overleaf)

Appendix 16A.1: continued

	Table 1 Cols 1–3	Table 1 Cols 4–6	Table 2
Mozambique	x	x	x
Namibia	x	x	x
Nepal	x	x	x
Nicaragua	x	x	x
Niger		x	
Nigeria	x	x	x
Oman	x	x	x
Pakistan	x	x	x
Panama	x	x	x
Papua New Guinea	x	x	
Paraguay	x	x	x
Peru	x	x	x
Philippines	x	x	x
Russian Fed.	x	x	x
Rwanda		x	
Samoa	x	x	
São Tomé and Principe		x	
Saudi Arabia	x	x	x
Senegal		x	
Seychelles	x	x	
Sierra Leone	x	x	x
Solomon Isles	x	x	

	Table 1 Cols 1–3	Table 1 Cols 4–6	Table 2
Somalia	x	x	
South Africa	x	x	x
Sri Lanka	x	x	x
Sudan	x	x	
Swaziland	x	x	x
Syrian Arab Republic	x	x	x
Tanzania	x	x	x
TFYR Macedonia	x	x	x
Thailand	x	x	x
Togo	x	x	
Trinidad and Tobago	x	x	x
Tunisia	x	x	x
Turkey	x	x	x
Tuvalu	x	x	x
Uganda	x	x	
United Arab Emirates	x	x	x
Uruguay	x	x	x
Vanuatu		x	
Venezuela	x	x	x
Yemen		x	
Zambia	x	x	x
Zimbabwe	x	x	x

Notes:

Importer countries:

USA.

EU15: Austria, Belgium-Luxembourg, Denmark, Finland, France, Fmr Dem. Rep. of Germany, Fmr Dem. Rep. of Germany/Germany & Former Fed. Rep. of Germany/Germany, Greece, Ireland, Italy, Netherlands, Portugal, Spain, Sweden, United Kingdom.

Notes

1 Both the EU and the US also have regional integration agreements extending preferences on a reciprocal basis, and the EU is moving towards replacing its Cotonou agreements with such Economic Partnership Agreements. Our focus is on unilateral rather than reciprocal preferences, although some of our policy messages will apply to both.
2 Hoekman *et al.* (2006) drawing on Low *et al.* (2005). See also Olarreaga and Ozden (2005) for an application to preferences in the apparel sector.
3 Computable general equilibrium studies of trade preferences include both rent and supply effects, but typically ignore the potential of scale thresholds. See, for example, Karingi *et al.* (2007) for a recent example.
4 See Arndt and Kierzkowski (2001) for discussion of this, and for more recent treatments see Grossman and Rossi-Hansburg (2006) and Markusen and Venables (2007).
5 See Duranton and Puga (2005) for a survey of the microeconomic mechanisms underlying clustering.
6 For further development of these ideas see Burgess and Venables (2004) and Puga and Venables (1999).
7 The six-digit classification is highly disaggregated – e.g. one of Bangladesh's three categories is 'hats and other headgear – knitted or from textile material not in strips'.
8 See Rodrik (2004) for discussion of these issues.
9 See http://www.agoa.gov/ for details.
10 Several other studies look at the effects of AGOA, notably Matto *et al.* (2003), Brenton and Ikezuki (2005), Frazer and van Biesebroeck (2005), Olarreaga and Ozden (2005) and Brenton and Ozden (2006), discussed more fully below.
11 For comprehensive analysis of the operation of ROOs see Cadot *et al.* (2006) and Cadot and de Melo (2007).
12 For details of eligibility see http://www.agoa.gov/eligibility/country_eligibility.html.
13 http://www.agoa.info/index.php?view=trade_stats&story=apparel_trade.
14 A negative sign corresponds to an increase, since exports to the EU are in the denominator of the (logged) dependent variable.

References

Arndt, S. and H. Kierzkowski (eds.) (2001), *Fragmentation; New Production and Trade Patterns in the World Economy*, Oxford: Oxford University Press.
Brenton, P. and T. Ikezuki (2005), 'The Value of Trade Preferences for Africa', processed, World Bank.
Brenton, P. and C. Ozden (2006), 'Trade Preferences for Apparel and the Role of Rules of Origin – The Case of Africa', processed, World Bank.
Burgess, R. and A. J. Venables (2004), 'Towards a Micro-economics of Growth', in F. Bourguignon and B. Pleskovic (eds.), *Accelerating Development: Annual World Bank Conference on Development Economics*, New York: World Bank and Oxford University Press.
Cadot, O. and J. de Melo (2007), 'Why OECD Countries Should Reform Rules of Origin', CEPR Discussion Paper No. 6172.
Cadot, O., A. Estevadeordal, A. Suwa-Eisenmann and T. Verdier (2006), *The Origin of Goods: Rules of Origin in Regional Trade Agreements*, Oxford: Oxford University Press.

Duranton, G. and D. Puga (2005), 'Micro-foundations of Urban Agglomeration Economies', in V. Henderson and J. Thisse (eds.), *Handbook of Urban and Regional Economics*, Vol. 4, North Holland, Amsterdam.

Frazer, G. and J. van Biesebroeck (2005), 'Trade Growth following AGOA', processed, University of Toronto.

Grossman, G. M. and E. Rossi-Hansberg (2006), 'The Rise of Offshoring: Its Not Cloth for Wine Any More' processed, Princeton.

Hanson, G. (2004), 'What Has Happened to Wages in Mexico since NAFTA?', in T. Estevadeordal, D. Rodrik, A. Taylor and A. Velasco (eds.), *FTAA and Beyond: Prospects for Integration in the Americas*, Cambridge, MA: Harvard University Press.

Hausmann, R. and D. Rodrik (2003), 'Economic Development as Self-discovery', *Journal of Development Economics*, 72, 2, 603–683.

Hausmann, R., L. Pritchett and D. Rodrik (2005), 'Growth Accelerations', *Journal of Economic Growth*, 10, 4, 303–29.

Henderson, J. V. (2002), 'Urbanization in Developing Countries', *World Bank Research Observer*, 17, 1, 89 –11.

Hoekman, B., W. Martin and C. A. Primo Braga (2006), *Preference Erosion: The Terms of the Debate*, Washington, DC: World Bank.

Jones, B. and B. Olken (2006), 'The Anatomy of Start-Stop Growth', NBER Working Paper No. 11528 (http://www.econ.brown.edu/econ/events/startstop.pdf).

Karingi, S. N., R. Perez and H. B. Hammoudah (2007), 'Could Extended Preferences Reward Sub-Saharan Africa's Participation in the Doha Round Negotiations?', *The World Economy*, 30, 3, 383–404.

Low, P., R. Piermartini and J. Richtering (2005), 'Multilateral Solutions to the Erosion of Nonreciprocal Preferences in NAMA', WTO, Geneva.

Markusen, J. R. and A. J. Venables (2007), 'Interacting Factor Endowments and Trade Costs: A Multi-country Multi-good Approach to Trade Theory', *Journal of International Economics* (forthcoming).

Mattoo, A., R. Devesh and A. Subramanian (2003), 'The Africa Growth and Opportunity Act and its Rules of Origin: Generosity Undermined?', *The World Economy*, 26, 6, 829 –51.

Olarreaga, M. and C. Ozden (2005), 'AGOA and Apparel: Who Captures the Tariff Rent in the Presence of Preferential Market Access?', *The World Economy*, 28, 1, 63 –77.

Pattillo, C., S. Gupta and K. Carey (2005), 'Sustaining Growth Accelerations and Pro-poor Growth in Africa', IMF Working Paper No. 05/195.

Puga, D. and A. J. Venables (1999), 'Agglomeration and Economic Development: Import Substitution vs. Trade Liberalisation', *Economic Journal*, 109, 455, 292–311.

Rodrik, D. (2004), 'Industrial Policy for the 21st Century' (processed, Harvard, http://ksghome.harvard.edu/~drodrik/UNIDOSep.pdf).

Rosenthal, S. S. and W. C. Strange (2005), 'Evidence on the Nature and Sources of Agglomeration Economies', in V. Henderson and J. Thisse (eds.), *Handbook of Urban and Regional Economics*, Vol. 4, North Holland, Amsterdam.

Subramanian, A. and D. Roy (2003), 'Who Can Explain the Mauritian Miracle?', in D. Rodrik (ed.), *In Search of Prosperity*, Princeton, NJ: Princeton University Press.

Index

Page numbers in *italics* refer to tables and figures.